EXAMPLES & EXPLANATIONS

Federal Income Tax

Federal Income Tax

Seventh Edition

Katherine Pratt
Professor of Law
Loyola Law School, Los Angeles

Thomas D. Griffith
Professor of Law
John B. Milliken Professor of Taxation
USC Gould School of Law

Joseph Bankman
Professor of Law
Ralph M. Parsons Professor of Law and Business
Stanford Law School

Wolters Kluwer
Law & Business

EXAMPLES & EXPLANATIONS

To contact Customer Service, e-mail customer.service@wolterskluwer.com, call 800-234-1660, fax 800-901-9075, or mail correspondence to:

> Wolters Kluwer Law & Business
> Attn: Order Department
> PO Box 990
> Frederick, MD 21705

Printed in the United States of America.

2 3 4 5 6 7 8 9 0

ISBN 978-1-4548-3390-1

Library of Congress Cataloging-in-Publication Data

Pratt, Katherine, 1955- author.
    Federal income tax : examples and explanations / Katherine Pratt, Professor of Law, Loyola Law School, Los Angeles, Thomas D. Griffith, Professor of Law, John B. Milliken Professor of Taxation, University of Southern California, Joseph Bankman, Professor of Law, Ralph M. Parsons Professor of Law and Business, Stanford University. — Seventh edition.
        p. cm.
    Includes bibliographical references and index.
        ISBN 978-1-4548-3390-1 (alk. paper)
1. Income tax — Law and legislation — United States. I. Griffith, Thomas D. author. II. Bankman, Joseph, 1955- author. III. Title.
    KF6369.B26 2014
    343.7305'2 — dc23
                            2014017786

About Wolters Kluwer Law & Business

Wolters Kluwer Law & Business is a leading global provider of intelligent information and digital solutions for legal and business professionals in key specialty areas, and respected educational resources for professors and law students. Wolters Kluwer Law & Business connects legal and business professionals as well as those in the education market with timely, specialized authoritative content and information-enabled solutions to support success through productivity, accuracy, and mobility.

Serving customers worldwide, Wolters Kluwer Law & Business products include those under the Aspen Publishers, CCH, Kluwer Law International, Loislaw, ftwilliam.com, and MediRegs family of products.

CCH products have been a trusted resource since 1913, and they are highly regarded resources for legal, securities, antitrust and trade regulation, government contracting, banking, pension, payroll, employment and labor, and healthcare reimbursement and compliance professionals.

Aspen Publishers products provide essential information to attorneys, business professionals, and law students. Written by preeminent authorities, the product line offers analytical and practical information in a range of specialty practice areas from securities law and intellectual property to mergers and acquisitions and pension/benefits. Aspen's trusted legal education resources provide professors and students with high-quality, up-to-date, and effective resources for successful instruction and study in all areas of the law.

Kluwer Law International products provide the global business community with reliable international legal information in English. Legal practitioners, corporate counsel, and business executives around the world rely on Kluwer Law journals, looseleafs, books, and electronic products for comprehensive information in many areas of international legal practice.

Loislaw is a comprehensive online legal research product providing legal content to law firm practitioners of various specializations. Loislaw provides attorneys with the ability to quickly and efficiently find the necessary legal information they need, when and where they need it, by facilitating access to primary law as well as state-specific law, records, forms, and treatises.

ftwilliam.com offers employee benefits professionals the highest-quality plan documents (retirement, welfare, and non-qualified) and government forms (5500/PBGC, 1099, and IRS) software at highly competitive prices.

MediRegs products provide integrated health care compliance content and software solutions for professionals in healthcare, higher education, and life sciences, including professionals in accounting, law, and consulting.

Wolters Kluwer Law & Business, a division of Wolters Kluwer, is headquartered in New York. Wolters Kluwer is a market-leading global information services company focused on professionals.

Summary of Contents

Contents

Contents

An Introductory Note to Students

If you're considering buying this book, you've probably already purchased a casebook. Most casebooks contain some explanatory text, as well as cases, and those explanations are usually pretty good. (Of course, at least one of us thinks the best explanations are found in the Bankman, Shaviro, and Stark casebook.) There are also a number of excellent treatises and student aids on the market.

What this book does — and other books generally do not do — is teach the subject through a question-and-answer approach. For each topic, we provide a summary of most of what you will cover in class. You should integrate these summaries with classroom discussion and the reading assigned in your tax course. We then ask a series of questions (called "examples") on each topic and provide you with answers to the questions (called "explanations").

The question-and-answer format is the heart of the book. Although, in practice, many questions do not have clear or simple answers, we have tried to draft discrete questions for which there are clear answers so that you can actively test your grasp of each specific rule or concept. If you can answer the questions correctly, you can be confident that you have mastered the basic rules and concepts covered in the introductory tax course. (Think of it as a "programmed learning" guide to tax rules and concepts.) This seventh edition incorporates changes made by various recent federal statutes, cases, and administrative pronouncements.

The book is designed to supplement, rather than supplant, the class and class reading. Although some of the answers to the questions in this book can be gleaned from the topic summaries, other questions can be answered correctly only after you carefully read the Internal Revenue Code and Treasury Regulation sections assigned for the topic. Note that, by deliberately breaking a complex subject into discrete questions, we unavoidably underplay the importance of issue spotting. You must develop issue-spotting skills by studying cases, participating in class discussion, and trying to answer more complex "real-world" questions. In order to give you an opportunity to answer some complex questions, we have included a diverse sample of actual law school exams, with suggested answers, at the end of the book.

An Introductory Note to Students

We have tried to include material on just about any topic that might be covered in your tax course. Most tax courses do not cover every topic in this book. For each topic assigned in your course, you can locate the corresponding material in this book by looking at the Table of Contents in the front or the Table of Code Sections, Table of Cases, and Topical Index in the back.

The first six editions of this book have received rave reviews from students. In this new edition, we have further refined the examples and explanations and added new material to address recent changes in the tax law. We hope this seventh edition will help you become proficient in your tax course. (And who knows? You, like many of our students, may be shocked to discover that you actually *like* tax.)

Katherine Pratt
Thomas D. Griffith
Joseph Bankman

July 2014

Acknowledgments

Thanks to all of our students, whose enthusiastic questions prompted us to write these examples and explanations; to Michelle Jones and Liz Luk for administrative assistance; and to research assistants Richard Bohm, Morgan Davis, Breanne Denning, Sarah Garrett, Jilda Kouroumlian, Rima Kundnani, Rebecca Layne, Anthony Ngo, Colin Shaff, and Armita Sobhi, as well as the scores of other research assistants who worked on the first six editions of this book. Thanks also to Professor Ed Kleinbard for helpful comments and suggestions, and to Professors William Blatt, (the late, great) Maureen Cavanaugh, Barbara Fried, and Nancy Kaufman for contributing to the sample exam appendix.

Federal Income Tax

Introduction

The income tax is the largest source of revenue for the federal government. In recent years, total income tax revenue has varied from around $1.5 to $1.7 trillion, about $1.2 to 1.4 trillion of which has been collected from individuals. Around $300 billion a year has been collected from corporations, which are generally separate taxpaying entities. The determination of taxable income is similar for individuals and corporations; however, some provisions apply specifically to either individuals or corporations. A much smaller amount of income tax is raised from estates and trusts.

Vying with the income tax for the dubious honor of being the greatest federal government revenue-raiser is what is commonly referred to as the payroll tax. (Although most of this tax revenue is used to fund Social Security benefits, a portion of it is used to fund Medicare health benefits.) The Social Security tax is levied on both employees and employers and is calculated as a percentage of salary income. Other sources of revenue for the federal government include excise taxes on fuel, alcohol, tobacco, firearms, and certain imports, and estate and gift taxes levied on the transferor (or the estate of the transferor) of significant wealth.

The income tax is also an important source of revenue for state and local governments. The determination of taxable income for the purpose of state and local income taxes is for the most part identical to the determination of taxable income under the federal income tax. Knowledge of the federal income tax therefore translates into knowledge of state and local income taxes. Sales and property taxes account for most of the revenue of state and local governments. The precise mix of income, sales, and property taxes varies from state to state. Some states, for example, have no income tax; other states tax individual or corporate income but not both.

A. INTRODUCTION TO TERMINOLOGY AND STRUCTURE

The starting point in computing a taxpayer's tax liability for the year is the taxpayer's *gross income*. In Chapter 2 we will discuss the concept of gross income at length; for now, note the items expressly included in or excluded from gross income in Internal Revenue Code §61 and §§71 — 140. (If you look at the table of contents at the front of your Code, you will see a list of the items covered in §§71 — 140.) Many of the items included in gross income are straightforward; for example, salary from a job is included in gross income. However, a couple of the §61 gross income items are not really "gross" income items.

For example, §61(a)(2) provides that gross income includes "[g]ross income derived from business." However, in this context, "gross" does not really mean "gross" because a taxpayer's gross income from business means the gross receipts from the business less the cost of the taxpayer's inventory sold. In Chapter 5 we will explore the rules for determining a taxpayer's inventory costs.

Also look at §61(a)(3), which states that gross income includes "[g]ains derived from dealings in property." Appreciation in the value of property is taxed when the gain is *realized*, for example when the property is sold or exchanged. When a taxpayer sells or exchanges property, the taxpayer must compute the gain or loss she realizes on the disposition of the property. The taxpayer realizes a gain if the taxpayer receives for the property more than the taxpayer's unrecovered investment in the property (in the simplest case, what the taxpayer paid for the property); the taxpayer realizes a loss if the taxpayer receives for the property less than the taxpayer's unrecovered investment in the property. The Code calls the amount the taxpayer receives on the sale or exchange the *amount realized*. §1001(a). The Code calls the taxpayer's unrecovered investment in the property *adjusted basis*. §§1011 — 1016. So, technically, a taxpayer's realized gain equals the amount realized less the taxpayer's adjusted basis in the property sold, and a taxpayer's realized loss equals the taxpayer's adjusted basis less the taxpayer's amount realized. In other words, a taxpayer's gross income from "dealings in property" is net of the taxpayer's unrecovered investment in the property.

For example, assume that in year 1 Betsy buys raw land as an investment for $400,000. In year 10, Betsy sells the land for $2 million. Betsy's amount realized is $2 million and her adjusted basis is $400,000, so her realized gain from the sale is $1.6 million. She will include $1.6 million in gross income under §61(a)(3). If Betsy had instead bought property with a limited useful life, such as an apartment building, she would be allowed to depreciate the property, meaning that she would be allowed to deduct, for purposes of computing the tax she owes, part of the cost of the property each year during the time she owned it. If, for example, Betsy were allowed to take $100,000 of depreciation deductions, her unrecovered investment in the property is no longer $400,000; since she recovered, for tax purposes, $100,000 of her investment through depreciation deductions, her unrecovered investment is $300,000. In this variation, her original basis is $400,000, but her adjusted basis is $300,000. §1016. If she sold the apartment building for $2 million, her realized gain on the sale would be $1.7 million.

Not all realized gains from dealings in property are included in gross income. A realized gain is included in gross income only if the gain is also *recognized*. The general rule is that a realized gain is recognized and included in income. §1001(c). However, a realized gain is not recognized if a specific *nonrecognition* rule in the Code applies to the sale or exchange. There are a number of such nonrecognition rules in the Code. They generally apply to transactions in which the taxpayer has exchanged property but has continued her investment in another form. If one of the specific nonrecognition rules applies to a transaction, the tax on the gain realized in the transaction is deferred until the taxpayer sells the property received in the nonrecognition transaction.

Suppose that Teresa owns land in Hilton Head. The land is worth $1 million and is held for investment. Teresa's unrecovered investment in the land, or adjusted basis, is $300,000. Teresa exchanges this land for land in Tampa, worth $1 million, that she also will hold for investment. Her realized gain on the exchange of the Hilton Head property is $700,000, the $1 million amount realized less her $300,000 adjusted basis in the property. However, that gain will not be recognized because the exchange was of like-kind property held for investment so the "like-kind exchange" non-recognition rule of §1031 applies. (We will consider §1031 in some detail in Chapter 3.) The realized gain will be deferred until Teresa sells the Tampa property. Teresa's basis in the Tampa land will be $300,000, the basis of the property exchanged for the Tampa property. For now, note that, although Teresa realized a gain on the exchange, the gain is not included in her gross income because it is not recognized.

After computing the taxpayer's gross income, the next step is to compute the taxpayer's adjusted gross income. Section 62 defines *adjusted gross income* as gross income less certain costs of earning income and a hodgepodge of other items, such as alimony paid by the taxpayer.

The next step is to compute the taxpayer's taxable income. Section 63 defines *taxable income* as the taxpayer's adjusted gross income less the sum of (i) the taxpayer's *personal exemptions* plus (ii) the greater of (a) the taxpayer's *standard deduction* or (b) the taxpayer's *itemized deductions*. The personal exemption amount is adjusted for inflation and was $3,950 in 2014. A taxpayer is allowed one personal exemption deduction for each of the following: (i) the taxpayer; (ii) the taxpayer's spouse; and (iii) each of the taxpayer's dependents. §151. The standard deduction amount is also adjusted for inflation; in 2014 it was $12,400 for married taxpayers filing a joint return, $9,100 for heads of households, and $6,200 for unmarried individuals. The standard deduction ensures that lower-income taxpayers do not have to pay tax and frees many taxpayers from having to keep records of their itemized deductions. Itemized deductions include all deductions other than the personal exemption deduction and the deductions allowable in computing adjusted gross income under §62. §63(d), Rev. Proc. 2013-35. For example, itemized deductions include the deductions for state and local property taxes and income or sales taxes, charitable contributions, and home mortgage interest.

Many types of expenses incurred in business or in the production of income (for example, rent and utility bills paid by a business) are deducted in full in the year in which they are incurred. However, if an expense creates an asset that will last beyond the year in which the expense is incurred, the expense cannot be deducted in full in the year in which it is incurred; this type of expense must instead be *capitalized*. If the expense is incurred to purchase an income-producing asset that will be used in the business and has a limited useful life, the taxpayer's expense for the asset is allocated across the years in which the asset is expected to produce income. Each year during the useful life of the asset, the taxpayer will deduct a portion of the cost of the asset, in the form of *depreciation* deductions. If the asset purchased by the taxpayer does not have a limited useful life (for example, raw land), the taxpayer is not permitted to recover her investment in the asset until she sells or exchanges it, at which time the taxpayer's amount realized for the asset is reduced by her adjusted basis in the asset.

After computing the taxpayer's taxable income, the next step is to compute the amount of tax due on the taxpayer's taxable income. Taxable income of individuals is taxed at rates specified in §1(a) — (d) of the Code. The §1 rates are *progressive*, meaning that as the taxpayer's income increases, the rate of tax increases. The rate applicable to the last dollar of income earned by the taxpayer is the taxpayer's *marginal rate*. The taxpayer's *effective rate* is his tax liability for the year divided by his taxable income for the year; it is the same as the taxpayer's average rate. A rate schedule exists for each of four possible filing statuses: married filing a joint return; head of household; individual; and married filing separately. There is also an implicit zero rate since a taxpayer does not owe tax if her taxable income does not exceed the sum of her personal exemptions and standard or itemized deductions. The top nominal rate in §1 is 39.6 percent. (The top rate actually is higher because personal exemptions and certain itemized deductions are subject to a phase-out as a taxpayer's income increases beyond certain threshold amounts.) The dollar amounts for the brackets in the §1 rate schedule are indexed for inflation. §1(f).

Individuals, estates, and trusts pay lower tax rates on capital gain other than short-term capital gain. *Capital gain* is gain from the sale of a capital asset. Capital gain is short-term if the capital asset sold was held by the taxpayer for a year or less before the sale. The precise rate that applies to capital gain other than short-term gain depends on the type of capital asset sold. §§1(h), 1222. The maximum capital gain rate is generally 20 percent. (The preferential capital gain rate also generally applies to dividend income.) A capital asset is, loosely speaking, an investment asset as opposed to an asset used in an operating business. For example, §1221 provides that inventory and depreciable property used in a business are not capital assets. The characterization of assets as capital or ordinary will be discussed further in Chapter 8 where we will see that this characterization is sometimes difficult to determine. For now, note that high bracket taxpayers pay less tax on capital gain than on ordinary gain, so they prefer to characterize gain as capital. For example, a taxpayer whose marginal tax rate is 39.6 percent owes $396,000 of tax on $1 million of gain if the gain is ordinary. If the gain is instead capital and is taxed at a 20 percent rate, the taxpayer will owe $200,000 of tax on the gain, thus saving $196,000 of tax. You can see why the taxpayer would prefer to characterize the gain as capital.

In addition, the progressivity of the income tax encourages high-bracket taxpayers to attempt to shift income to family members in lower rate brackets. In Chapter 7 we will consider the congressional and judicial responses to various income shifting techniques employed by taxpayers. For now, note that unearned income (that is, income not from personal services) of a child under age 19 (or a child between the ages of 19 and 23 who is a full-time student) is taxed at the parent's higher tax rate under §1(g), the so-called "kiddie tax." (The kiddie tax does not apply to a child who is age 18 or older and has annual earned income, i.e., wage income, in an amount that is greater than half of his support.) Also note that the income of spouses filing a joint return is aggregated so that attribution of income between the spouses is irrelevant.

Most married couples file jointly because doing so saves them tax. The tax rates for spouses filing a joint return are the lowest in §1. Married couples with only one income earner pay *less* tax than they would have if they were not married and each spouse were taxed individually. However, married couples with two income earners pay *more* tax than they would have if they were not married and each spouse were taxed individually. Why? Because each of the two earners would have benefited from the progressivity of the rates. The added tax owed by two income earners who marry is referred to as the *marriage penalty*. Recent tax statutes have reduced the effect of the marriage penalty temporarily for low-income and middle-income married couples (by making the 10 percent and 15 percent rate bracket amounts for married taxpayers filing jointly two times the 10 percent and 15 percent rate bracket amounts for single taxpayers).

In a recent change from previous law, federal tax law now recognizes the marriage of same-sex couples that were married in a state (or country) that recognizes same-sex marriage (even where couples currently reside in a state that does not recognize same-sex marriage). Rev. Rul. 2013-17. If a same-sex marriage is recognized under this "state of celebration" rule, each individual in the marriage is treated as a "spouse" for all federal tax purposes. Id. On the other hand, the Internal Revenue Service has asserted that unmarried Registered Domestic Partners (RDPs) and Civil Union Partners (CUPs) are not married for purposes of federal tax law. Id. Each partner in a Registered Domestic Partnership or Civil Union is not treated as the "spouse" of their partner for federal tax purposes. Note, however, that at the time this book went to press in June 2014, lawsuits were pending in which RDPs had challenged the constitutionality of the position asserted by the Internal Revenue Service. Note also that, if one of the partners earns little or no income and is supported by the other partner, the supported partner may qualify as the "dependent" of the income-earning partner, for purposes of some but not all federal tax rules. (In Chapter 7, we discuss various recent developments regarding the federal taxation of same-sex couples.)

C corporations are treated as separate taxpaying entities and are taxed at progressive rates specified in §11 of the Code. A C corporation is any corporation that is not an S corporation. A corporation is an S corporation only if it meets certain eligibility requirements and elects to be an S corporation. §§1361, 1362. (The names are derived from subchapter designations in the Code: S corporations are subject to the provisions of subchapter S of Chapter 1 of the Code and C corporations are generally subject to the provisions of subchapter C of Chapter 1 of the Code.) The special §1(h) capital gain rates do not apply to corporate taxpayers. §1201.

After applying the appropriate tax rates to the taxpayer's taxable income, the next step is to reduce the tax due by the credits for which the taxpayer is eligible. A credit is a direct reduction in tax. A deduction or exclusion, on the other hand, reduces the taxpayer's taxable income; it reduces the tax due from the taxpayer by an amount equal to the product of multiplying the deduction or exclusion by the taxpayer's tax rate. For example, a $1,000 deduction saves a taxpayer in the 39.6 percent tax bracket $396 of tax; a $1,000 credit, on the other hand, saves the same taxpayer $1,000 of tax. There are a number of credit provisions in the Code. The most generally applicable is the credit for taxes withheld from the taxpayer's wages by the taxpayer's employer. §31. If the taxpayer's refundable credits exceed the taxpayer's tax due, the taxpayer receives a tax refund. If the taxpayer's tax due exceeds the taxpayer's credits, the taxpayer owes tax.

Our tax system has adopted an annual accounting period, so taxpayers must compute the tax they owe each year. The annual accounting period is considered to be an administrative necessity but can create unfairness where transactions occur over a period of years. Congress and the courts have fashioned a number of special rules that ameliorate some of the potentially harsh effects of the annual accounting period. For example, §172 provides that a taxpayer with a net operating loss (deductions in excess of gross income) in a given year may use that loss to reduce its taxable income for other years.

I. Introduction

For purposes of computing their tax liability, taxpayers use either the *cash method of accounting* or the *accrual method of accounting*. A taxpayer must use the same method of accounting for both tax accounting and financial accounting. §446(a).

Under the cash method of accounting, a taxpayer includes an item of income in the year in which the item is actually or constructively received. Income is *constructively received* if it is made available to the taxpayer but the taxpayer decides to defer actual receipt of it. For example, suppose that on December 31 of year one a client hands her attorney a check for services already performed. The attorney refuses to accept the check, however, stating that she prefers to be paid in year two. The attorney will be said to have constructively received the check in year one. A cash method taxpayer generally deducts an expense in the year in which it is paid, but must capitalize an expense that creates an asset that lasts longer than the year in which the expense is incurred. (Capitalization is discussed in more detail in Chapter 5.)

The accrual method of accounting is more complex. In general, a taxpayer using this method includes an item of income in the year in which (i) all of the events have occurred that fix the right to receive the income and (ii) the amount of the income can be determined with reasonable accuracy. An accrual method taxpayer deducts an expense when (i) all the events have occurred that establish the fact of the liability, (ii) the amount of the liability can be determined with reasonable accuracy, and (iii) the "economic performance" requirement of §461(h) (which often requires payment before a deduction is allowed) is met.

The following example illustrates the operation of the accrual and cash methods of accounting. Suppose that in December of year one an accrual method taxpayer repairs a computer used by an attorney who is on the cash method of accounting. The cost of the repair is $1,000. The attorney pays for the repair in January of year two. The $1,000 is taken into income by the accrual method taxpayer in year one, the time at which the right to receive the income is fixed and the amount of income can be determined with reasonable accuracy. The repair is deducted as a business expense by the cash method taxpayer in the year of payment — year two.

In many cases, the operation of the cash and (especially) accrual methods of accounting is quite complicated. (Accounting methods are discussed in greater detail in Chapter 3.)

The cash method permits some manipulation of the timing of inclusions and deductions. However, not all taxpayers may use the cash method. Businesses that keep inventories, including wholesalers, retailers, and manufacturers, must use the accrual method. In addition, §448 places limitations on the use of the cash method of accounting. Section 446(b) also provides that if, in the Commissioner's view, the method of accounting used by the taxpayer does not clearly reflect income, the taxpayer's taxable income is recomputed using the method that the Commissioner thinks more clearly reflects income. Courts give the Commissioner's determination on this issue great deference.

Examples

1. a. In year 1, Tad bought a piece of raw land for $75,000. In year 10 Tad sells the land for $300,000. What amount does Tad include in his gross income in year 10?

   b. Suppose that, in year 10, instead of selling the land for $300,000, Tad exchanges the land for Greenacre, a parcel of land in another state. The exchange of like-kind property qualifies for the nonrecognition rule of §1031. At the time of the exchange, Greenacre is worth $300,000. In year 15 Tad sells Greenacre for $500,000. What amount does Tad include in gross income in year 10 and year 15?

   c. Now suppose instead that Tad sells the land in year 10 for $75,000. What amount does Tad include in gross income in year 10?

2. a. In year one, Tina, an unmarried individual with no dependents, has $100,000 of gross income, $15,000 of the types of deductions specified in §62, and $7,000 of itemized deductions. Assume that the standard deduction for year one is $6,000 and the personal exemption amount for year one is $4,000. What is Tina's year one adjusted gross income? What is her year one taxable income?

   b. Assume now that Tina's taxable income is $74,000 and that the following rate schedule (which is a fictitious, simplified version of the real §1 rate schedule) applies to unmarried individuals.

If taxable income is:	The tax is:
Not over $10,000	10 percent of taxable income
Over $10,000	$1,000 (10 percent of $10,000) plus 15 percent of the excess over $10,000
Over $50,000	$7,000 ($1,000 plus $6,000, which is 15 percent of the $40,000 of taxable income between $10,000 and $50,000) plus 30 percent of the excess over $50,000
Over $400,000	$112,000 ($7,000 plus $105,000, which is 30 percent of the $350,000 of taxable income between $50,000 and $400,000) plus 40 percent of the excess over $400,000

   Compute the tax due on Tina's $74,000 of taxable income.

   c. How would your answer in part (b) change if Tina's taxable income were instead $410,000?

   d. How, if at all, would your answers in part (a) change if Tina instead had $3,000 of itemized deductions in year one?

3. Is each of the following statements true or false?
   a. Business expenses are always deducted in the year in which they are incurred.
   b. The §1 tax rates are progressive.
   c. A taxpayer's marginal rate is the taxpayer's average rate of tax.
   d. All married and unmarried taxpayers are subject to the same rate schedule in §1.
   e. Individuals, trusts, estates, and corporations pay a reduced rate of tax on capital gain other than short-term capital gain.
   f. Our tax system utilizes an annual accounting period.
   g. Taxpayers are free to choose whether to adopt the cash method of accounting or the accrual method of accounting.
   h. A taxpayer using the cash method of accounting includes an item of income only when it is actually received by the taxpayer.
   i. A taxpayer using the accrual method of accounting generally includes an item of income in the year in which all of the events have occurred that fix the right to receive the income, and the amount of the income can be determined with reasonable accuracy.

Explanations

1. a. Tad includes $225,000, which is the realized and recognized gain on the sale. The realized gain equals the $300,000 amount realized on the sale less the $75,000 adjusted basis of the land. §§1001, 1011, 1012. Realized gain is recognized unless otherwise provided in the Code. §1001(c). Gross income includes gains from dealings in property. §61(a)(3).

   b. The realized gain on the year 10 exchange is still $225,000, the $300,000 amount realized less Tad's $75,000 adjusted basis in the land given up in the exchange. §§1001, 1011, 1012. Realized gain is recognized unless a specific nonrecognition rule applies. §1001(c). Here, the §1031 like-kind exchange nonrecognition rule applies, so Tad does not include any of the realized gain in his year 10 gross income. In year 15 Tad's realized gain on the sale of Greenacre is $425,000, the $500,000 amount realized less Tad's $75,000 basis in Greenacre. (Tad's basis in Greenacre, the property received in the year 10 exchange, is the same as the basis of the property Tad gave up in the year 10 exchange, $75,000.) Tad includes that $425,000 of gain in his year 15 gross income. §1001(c). Note that $200,000 of that gain is attributable to appreciation in the value of Greenacre between year 10 and year 15, and the remaining $225,000 of gain is the gain Tad realized in the exchange in year 10 but deferred under §1031.

c. Zero. Although Tad receives $75,000 in year 10, he has realized no gain on the land since the amount realized is $75,000 and his basis for the property is $75,000.

2. a. Tina's year one adjusted gross income is $85,000 ($100,000 gross income less $15,000 of §62 deductions). §62. Her taxable income is $74,000 — $85,000 adjusted gross income less $11,000, which is the sum of (i) her $7,000 of itemized deductions (which exceed the $6,000 standard deduction) and (ii) her $4,000 personal exemption. §63.

b. The tax due on $74,000 of taxable income is $14,200, which is $7,000 ($1,000, which is 10 percent of the first $10,000 of taxable income, plus $6,000, which is 15 percent of the $40,000 of taxable income between $10,000 and $50,000) plus $7,200 (30 percent of the $24,000 of taxable income in excess of $50,000).

c. The tax due on $410,000 of taxable income is $116,000, which is $112,000 ($1,000, which is 10 percent of the first $10,000 of taxable income, plus $6,000, which is 15 percent of the $40,000 of taxable income between $10,000 and $50,000, plus $105,000, which is 30 percent of the $350,000 of taxable income between $50,000 and $400,000) plus $4,000 (40 percent of the $10,000 between $400,000 and $410,000).

d. Her taxable income would instead be $75,000 — $85,000 adjusted gross income less $10,000, which is the sum of (i) the $6,000 standard deduction (which exceeds her $3,000 of itemized deductions) and (ii) her $4,000 personal exemption. §63.

3. a. The statement is false. Taxpayers generally deduct business expenses in the year in which the expense is incurred. (The exact timing standard depends on whether the taxpayer uses the cash or accrual method of accounting.) However, if an expense results in the creation of an asset with a useful life that extends substantially beyond the close of the year in which the expense is incurred, the expense must be capitalized, in which case the expense cannot be deducted in full in the year in which the expense is incurred. For example, if the expense is incurred to purchase an asset with a limited useful life, the taxpayer's cost for the property will be deducted over the period of time that the property is expected to be used, in the form of annual depreciation deductions. If the expense is incurred to purchase an asset with an unlimited useful life, such as raw land, the taxpayer recovers her cost for the property only when the property is later sold or exchanged.

b. The statement is true because under §1 a taxpayer's tax *rate* (not just the absolute amount of tax) increases as his taxable income increases.

c. The statement is false. A taxpayer's marginal rate is the tax rate applicable to the last dollar of income earned by the taxpayer. The taxpayer's average tax rate is sometimes referred to as the taxpayer's effective rate. The effective rate equals the tax due from the taxpayer divided by the taxpayer's taxable income.

d. The statement is false. Married taxpayers have two rate schedules, depending on whether they file a joint return or separate returns. There are separate rate schedules for heads of households and unmarried individuals without children. §1(a) — (d).

e. The statement is false. The preferential capital gain rates apply to individuals, trusts, and estates, but not to corporations. §§1(h), 1201, 11.

f. The statement is true. However, Congress and courts have created a number of special rules that are designed to ameliorate some of the potentially harsh effects of the annual accounting period.

g. The statement is false. Businesses that maintain inventories (manufacturers, wholesalers, and retailers) must use the accrual method of accounting. Section 448 also restricts use of the cash method of accounting. In addition, a taxpayer must use the same method of accounting for both financial and tax purposes. §446(a).

h. The statement is false. A cash method taxpayer includes either on actual receipt or constructive receipt. A taxpayer constructively receives an item of income if the item is made available to the taxpayer but the taxpayer chooses to defer receipt of the item.

i. The statement is true.

B. TIME VALUE OF MONEY AND THE VALUE OF DEFERRING TAX

A dollar received today is worth more than a dollar received in the future and a dollar paid today costs more than a dollar paid in the future. The longer the period of deferral, the greater the difference between the present value of an amount and the future value of the amount. The concept that the value of money depends on when it is paid or received is sometimes referred to as the *time value of money*.

You need to understand the concept of time value of money because (i) it is a basic financial concept that your business clients will understand thoroughly and will expect you to understand; (ii) it is essential in determining the benefit of tax deferral; and (iii) it is used in a number of specific Code sections. (For example, one Code provision imputes the amount borrowed in certain loan transactions by discounting the amounts to be paid on the loan to present value.)

1. Introduction

Tax lawyers spend much of their time counseling clients on how they can defer the payment of taxes. Deferral of tax is advantageous to a taxpayer because he can invest the deferred tax and earn income on it until it is paid to the government. We can quantify the savings from deferral by determining the amount that would have to be set aside in year one so that the sum of the amount set aside and the earnings on that amount would fund the future tax liability. We would calculate the amount to be set aside by computing the *present value* of the future tax liability. Students (and practicing lawyers) generally use tables or computers to determine present values or, depending on the nature of the work and size of the client, accept the present value calculations done by the client's accounting staff. For the record, however, the formula for determining present value is as follows:

$$\text{Present Value} = \frac{\text{Future Value}}{(1+r)^n}$$

(r is the interest rate, which also is sometimes called the discount rate, and n is the number of periods of deferral.)

For example, assume that a taxpayer defers a $10,000 tax payment for five years and that the appropriate annual interest rate is 8 percent. The amount that would have to be set aside in year one in order to fund that future payment is $6,806:

$$\text{Present Value} = \frac{\$10,000}{(1+.08)^5}$$

$$= \frac{\$10,000}{(1.08)(1.08)(1.08)(1.08)(1.08)}$$

$$= \frac{\$10,000}{1.46933}$$

$$= \$6,806$$

The value of deferral can be expressed in another way; it is the equivalent of a reduction in rates. If a taxpayer in the 40 percent bracket owes $10,000 of tax on $25,000 of taxable income, a reduction in the present value of the tax owed to $6,806 is the equivalent of reducing the taxpayer's tax rate to 27.22 percent (since $6,806 is 27.22 percent of $25,000).

The formula for computing the future value of an amount is:

$$\text{Future Value} = \text{Present Value}\,(1+r)^n$$

For example, assume a present value of $6,806. That amount will yield a return of 8 percent a year, payable in five years. (No interest will be paid during the five years.) What is the future value, in year five, of the $6,806 present value? It is $10,000:

$$\text{Future Value} = \$6,806(1.08)^5$$
$$= \$6,806(1.46933)$$
$$= \$10,000$$

Tables 1-1 and 1-2 show the present and future values of $1 at various interest rates and over various periods of time.

Using Table 1-1, we can determine the present value of an amount to be paid in the future if we know the period over which the amount will be discounted and the appropriate interest rate. For example, this table indicates that the present value of $1 to be paid in 40 years, assuming a 5 percent interest rate, is 14.2 cents.

Using Table 1-2, we can determine the future value of $1 if we know the period over which interest will compound and the appropriate interest rate. For example, the table indicates that the future value of $1 invested for 40 years, assuming a 5 percent interest rate, is $7.04.

Examples

4. Through careful tax planning, Tom, who is in the 40 percent tax bracket, is able to defer a $20,000 tax liability for five years. Assume an annual interest rate of 10 percent a year during that five-year period. Explain the way in which Tom benefits from the deferral of tax, incorporating the concept of present value. (You may use the table in the text below to compute the present value.)

5. Assume a present value of $10,000 and an interest rate of 10 percent a year. What is the future value in five years? (You may use the table in the text below to compute the future value.)

Explanations

4. Table 1-1 indicates that the present value of $1 to be paid in five years, assuming a 10 percent interest rate, is 62 cents. The present value of $20,000 to be paid in five years, assuming a 10 percent interest rate, is $12,400 ($.62 multiplied by $20,000). By deferring the $20,000 tax payment for five years, Tom saves $7,600 ($20,000 less $12,400).

How would we compute the present value using the formula? The future value is $20,000; the interest rate is 10 percent; the number of periods of deferral is five. Therefore, the present value of the $20,000 tax payment to be made in five years is $12,418, computed as follows:

13

1-1 Present Value of $1: What a Dollar at the End of a Specified Future Year Is Worth Today

Year	3 percent	4 percent	5 percent	6 percent	7 percent	8 percent	10 percent	12 percent	15 percent	20 percent	Year
1	.971	.962	.952	.943	.935	.926	.909	.893	.870	.833	1
2	.943	.925	.907	.890	.873	.857	.826	.797	.756	.694	2
3	.915	.889	.864	.840	.816	.794	.751	.712	.658	.579	3
4	.889	.855	.823	.792	.763	.735	.683	.636	.572	.482	4
5	.863	.823	.784	.747	.713	.681	.620	.567	.497	.402	5
6	.837	.790	.746	.705	.666	.630	.564	.507	.432	.335	6
7	.813	.760	.711	.665	.623	.583	.513	.452	.376	.279	7
8	.789	.731	.677	.627	.582	.540	.467	.404	.327	.233	8
9	.766	.703	.645	.592	.544	.500	.424	.361	.284	.194	9
10	.744	.676	.614	.558	.508	.463	.386	.322	.247	.162	10
11	.722	.650	.585	.527	.475	.429	.350	.287	.215	.135	11
12	.701	.625	.557	.497	.444	.397	.319	.257	.187	.112	12
13	.681	.601	.530	.469	.415	.368	.290	.229	.163	.0935	13
14	.661	.577	.505	.442	.388	.340	.263	.205	.141	.0779	14

	15	16	17	18	19	20	25	30	40	50
15	.0649	.123	.183	.239	.315	.362	.417	.481	.555	.642
16	.0541	.107	.163	.218	.292	.339	.394	.458	.534	.623
17	.0451	.093	.146	.198	.270	.317	.371	.436	.513	.605
18	.0376	.0808	.130	.180	.250	.296	.350	.416	.494	.587
19	.0313	.0703	.116	.164	.232	.277	.331	.396	.475	.570
20	.0261	.0611	.104	.149	.215	.258	.312	.377	.456	.554
25	.0105	.0304	.0588	.0923	.146	.184	.233	.295	.375	.478
30	.00421	.0151	.0334	.0573	.0994	.131	.174	.231	.308	.412
40	.000680	.00373	.0107	.0221	.046	.067	.0972	.142	.208	.307
50	.000109	.000922	.00346	.00852	.0213	.034	.0543	.087	.141	.228

1-2 Future Value of $1: What a Dollar Invested Today Is Worth at the End of a Specified Future Year

Year	3 percent	4 percent	5 percent	6 percent	7 percent	8 percent	10 percent	12 percent	15 percent	20 percent	Year
1	1.03	1.04	1.05	1.06	1.07	1.08	1.10	1.12	1.15	1.20	1
2	1.06	1.08	1.10	1.12	1.14	1.17	1.21	1.25	1.32	1.44	2
3	1.09	1.12	1.16	1.19	1.23	1.26	1.33	1.40	1.52	1.73	3
4	1.13	1.17	1.22	1.26	1.31	1.36	1.46	1.57	1.74	2.07	4
5	1.16	1.22	1.28	1.34	1.40	1.47	1.61	1.76	2.01	2.49	5
6	1.19	1.27	1.34	1.41	1.50	1.59	1.77	1.97	2.31	2.99	6
7	1.23	1.32	1.41	1.50	1.61	1.71	1.94	2.21	2.66	3.58	7
8	1.27	1.37	1.48	1.59	1.72	1.85	2.14	2.48	3.05	4.30	8
9	1.30	1.42	1.55	1.68	1.84	2.00	2.35	2.77	3.52	5.16	9
10	1.34	1.48	1.63	1.79	1.97	2.16	2.59	3.11	4.05	6.19	10
11	1.38	1.54	1.71	1.89	2.10	2.33	2.85	3.48	4.66	7.43	11
12	1.43	1.60	1.80	2.01	2.25	2.52	3.13	3.90	5.30	8.92	12
13	1.47	1.67	1.89	2.13	2.41	2.72	3.45	4.36	6.10	10.70	13
14	1.51	1.73	1.98	2.26	2.58	2.94	3.79	4.89	7.00	12.80	14

15	1.56	1.80	2.08	2.39	2.76	3.17	4.17	5.47	8.13	15.40	15
16	1.60	1.87	2.18	2.54	2.95	3.43	4.59	6.13	9.40	18.50	16
17	1.65	1.95	2.29	2.69	3.16	3.70	5.05	6.87	10.60	22.20	17
18	1.70	2.03	2.41	2.85	3.38	4.00	5.55	7.70	12.50	26.60	18
19	1.75	2.11	2.53	3.02	3.62	4.32	6.11	8.61	14.00	31.90	19
20	1.81	2.19	2.65	3.20	3.87	4.66	6.72	9.65	16.10	38.30	20
25	2.09	2.67	3.39	4.29	5.43	6.85	10.80	17.00	32.90	95.40	25
30	2.43	3.24	4.32	5.74	7.61	10.00	17.40	30.00	66.20	237.00	30
40	3.26	4.80	7.04	10.30	15.00	21.70	45.30	93.10	267.00	1,470.00	40
50	4.38	7.11	11.50	18.40	29.50	46.90	117.00	289.00	1,080.00	9,100.00	50

$$\begin{aligned}
\text{Present Value} &= \frac{\$20{,}000}{(1+.1)^5} \\[4pt]
&= \frac{\$20{,}000}{(1.1)(1.1)(1.1)(1.1)(1.1)} \\[4pt]
&= \frac{\$20{,}000}{1.61051} \\[4pt]
&= \$12{,}418
\end{aligned}$$

(Note that the present value calculated using the table is a little less due to rounding.)

The value of deferral can be expressed in another way; it is the equivalent of a reduction in rates. Tom, who is in the 40 percent bracket, owes $20,000 of tax (presumably on $50,000 of taxable income). Deferring the tax reduces the present value of the tax owed to $12,418, which is the equivalent of reducing Tom's tax rate to 24.83 percent (since $12,418 is 24.83 percent of $50,000).

5. Table 1-2 indicates that the value in five years of $1 invested today is $1.61, assuming a 10 percent interest rate. The value in five years of $10,000 invested today is $16,100, assuming a 10 percent interest rate.

How would we compute the future value using the formula? The formula for computing the future value of an amount is:

$$\text{Future Value} = \text{Present Value}(1+r)^n$$

Here the present value is $10,000, r equals 10 percent, and n equals 5, so the future value is $16,105.

$$\begin{aligned}
\text{Future Value} &= \$10{,}000(1.1)^5 \\[4pt]
&= \$10{,}000(1.1)(1.1)(1.1)(1.1)(1.1) \\[4pt]
&= \$10{,}000(1.61051) \\[4pt]
&= \$16{,}105.10
\end{aligned}$$

(Note that the future value calculated using the table is a little less due to rounding.)

C. ALTERNATIVE TAX BASES: CONSUMPTION TAX AND VALUE ADDED TAX

Most tax policy theorists advocate an ideal, comprehensive definition of income known as the *Haig-Simons* definition of income. Haig-Simons income equals the sum of (i) the taxpayer's personal expenditures for the period plus (or minus) (ii) the taxpayer's increase (or decrease) in wealth for the period. Under a Haig-Simons based income tax, a person is subject to an annual tax on net accretion to wealth — whether spent or saved. As we have seen earlier in this chapter, our tax system does not tax appreciation in assets until gain is realized on the sale or other disposition of the assets. The realization requirement represents a departure from the Haig-Simons ideal, but facilitates administration of the income tax. The tax treatment of other forms of saving also deviates from the Haig-Simons ideal. For example, savings held in qualified retirement plans are not taxed until they are withdrawn by the taxpayer.

Our tax system's various departures from the Haig-Simons ideal have led some commentators to suggest that we repeal the income tax and replace it with a consumption tax. The tax base is computed differently under an income tax than under a consumption tax. A pure Haig-Simons based income tax would require a taxpayer to pay tax each year on her net accretion to wealth, whether she spent it or saved it. (Said another way, the base is the taxpayer's change in wealth plus personal consumption.) In contrast, under a consumption tax, an individual is taxed only on her personal consumption. For these purposes, the term *personal consumption* refers to expenditures for non-business-related necessities such as food, clothing, and lodging, and for non-business-related luxuries such as entertainment and travel.

The most direct way to implement a consumption tax would be to tax an individual on gross income but allow a deduction for income that is invested. The net income will be the amount spent for personal consumption. This form of consumption tax is sometimes referred to as a *cash flow consumption tax*. Under a cash flow consumption tax, an individual who earns $200,000, puts $30,000 of that amount in the bank, and uses the remainder for consumption would pay tax on a base of $170,000. (If we adopted a cash flow consumption tax, the tax rates would likely continue to be progressive.) The taxpayer's tax liability would be the same if, instead of saving $30,000 in the bank, she used that sum to purchase stock. For consumption tax purposes, savings and investments are treated the same. Indeed, under a consumption tax, the term *savings* is a synonym for investment.

Suppose in the above example the individual sold her $30,000 investment or withdrew her savings and spent the proceeds on personal consumption. Under a cash flow consumption tax, the individual would be taxed on the proceeds in the year the funds were consumed. (This result can also be reached by applying the concepts of basis and realization. Since the individual will have already deducted the cost of her investment, her adjusted basis is zero. The entire sale proceeds are therefore taxable.)

Somewhat complex issues can arise under a cash flow consumption tax with respect to purchases of consumer durables. For example, if an individual buys an automobile for $20,000, it would be wrong to treat the transaction as $20,000 of consumption in the year of purchase because the automobile has a useful life of several years. The correct approach is to treat the rental value of the automobile as consumption. The proper treatment under a consumption tax, then, is to treat amounts used to purchase an automobile as an investment (not included in income) and then tax the purchaser on the rental value each year. The problem with such a scheme is its complexity. A similar problem arises with housing.

A roundabout way of achieving something very similar to a consumption tax would be to levy a tax on the entire Haig-Simons income but then to exempt the yield from any property purchased with that income. This type of tax system is often referred to as a *yield exemption consumption tax*. Suppose, for example, an individual received $100,000 in wages in year one and invested $50,000 in stocks, which she sold in year two for $60,000. Under a yield exemption consumption tax, the individual would receive no deduction in year one but instead would pay tax on her full Haig-Simons income of $100,000. In year two, however, the entire return from the sale of stock would be tax-free. Similarly, had the individual left $50,000 in a bank account in year one, the deposit would have yielded no current deduction but the interest earned on the account would be tax-free. The yield exemption form of consumption tax is less advantageous than the cash flow form of consumption tax when the investment is made, but more advantageous when the investment is sold. Under plausible assumptions, the advantages and disadvantages offset each other.

As may be obvious from the above descriptions, the treatment of savings and investments under a consumption tax is extremely favorable. Under a cash flow consumption tax, the full amount of the investment or saving is currently deductible. Under a yield exemption consumption tax, no tax is ever levied on the return of savings or investment. A consumption tax is often supported on the rationale that it would encourage saving and investment. A consumption tax is often opposed on the rationale that it would benefit the wealthy, who account for a disproportionate amount of the nation's savings and investment.

As an alternative to the consumption taxes described above, some people have suggested replacing or supplementing the federal income tax with a *value added tax*, often referred to by its acronym, VAT. As its name implies, a VAT is levied on the value added to goods and services by those who manufacture, distribute, and sell those goods or services. Each link in the chain of production pays a tax equal to the difference between its costs of materials and its sales proceeds. The following example may help illustrate the operation of a VAT. Suppose that a mining company sells $100,000 of processed iron ore to a widget manufacturer. The manufacturer processes the ore into widgets and sells the widgets to retailers for $250,000.

The retailers sell the widgets for $300,000. Assume the rate of the VAT is 10 percent. Here, the mining company has added $100,000 in value — the difference between its cost of goods ($0) and its sales ($100,000). The mining company would owe $10,000 of VAT (10 percent of $100,000 value added) on the sale of the ore to the manufacturer. The manufacturer has added $150,000 in value — the difference between its cost of goods ($100,000) and sales ($250,000). It would owe $15,000 of VAT (10 percent of $150,000) on the sale of the widgets to the retailers. The retailers have added $50,000 in value — the difference between their cost of goods ($250,000) and sales ($300,000). They would owe $5,000 of VAT (10 percent of $50,000 value added) on the sales to customers.

A VAT is a form of a sales tax; the effect of a VAT is virtually identical to the state and local sales taxes with which most of us are familiar — a tax collected by the retailer on the sales price of goods. The only real difference is that a VAT is collected piecemeal from the links of the chain of production, while a sales tax is collected solely from the retailer. The similarity of these two forms of sales taxes is evident from the above example. The total amount subject to the VAT is $300,000. That amount is also the retail price of the goods and the amount that would be subject to tax under the form of sales tax with which those of us in this country are more familiar. Ultimately, both a VAT and a retail sales tax increase the cost of goods to consumers, as those in the chain of production pass some of the tax on in the form of higher prices.

The consumption tax described above can also be thought of as a form of sales tax since it applies only to the extent an individual purchases goods and services. One significant difference between a consumption tax and a retail sales tax or a VAT is that a consumption tax can be levied at different rates for taxpayers with differing amounts of consumption. For example, someone who spends $20,000 a year might pay a tax of 10 percent on consumption while someone who spends $200,000 a year might pay a tax of 40 percent on consumption.

It is interesting to compare, in a necessarily summary fashion, the relative strengths of an income tax and the other above-mentioned taxes. As noted above, the retail sales tax, VAT, and consumption tax all tax purchases of goods rather than savings and investment. For this reason, most commentators believe a shift away from an income tax and toward these taxes would increase savings, though the amount of increase is hotly debated. The anticipated increase in savings leads many to favor such consumption-based taxes. For different reasons, the exemption of savings is also seen as the biggest disadvantage of these taxes. In any given year, those with high incomes account for nearly all savings; those with low incomes often "dissave," dipping into savings to pay the expenses of ordinary life. In the short run, at least, the exemption of savings from taxation benefits only high income taxpayers. As compared to an income tax, a retail sales tax, VAT, or consumption tax is regressive, raising a greater proportion of revenue from those who, it is argued, can least afford it.

Examples

6. Barbara is a junior partner at a large San Francisco law firm. Her year one taxable income is $200,000. She spends three-quarters of her earnings; the other quarter is placed in various stocks and money market accounts. What is her year one Haig-Simons taxable income? Her year one taxable income under a cash flow consumption tax? Her year one taxable income under a yield exemption consumption tax?

7. State whether the current tax treatment of each of the following items is more consistent with an income tax defined under the Haig-Simons definition of income or a consumption tax.
   a. Money market interest, which is included in income as it is earned.
   b. Individual retirement accounts. Taxpayers generally deduct their IRA contributions when they are made and are taxed on the proceeds in the account when the funds are withdrawn (usually at retirement).
   c. Appreciation in property.
   d. A whole life insurance policy that costs $10,000 and pays out $50,000. Taxpayers do not deduct their investment in an insurance policy, but are not taxed on the return on the policy.

8. At the beginning of year one, Alice has $10,000 of savings. During year one, Alice earns $30,000 in wages and $1,000 in interest, which she spends on her daily expenses. At the end of the year she takes an around-the-world vacation that costs an additional $13,000. To finance the vacation, she withdraws $5,000 from her savings account and borrows an additional $8,000. Calculate Alice's year one tax base under a Haig-Simons income tax and under a consumption tax.

9. Bob earns $50,000 in wages in year one. He saves $10,000 of his year one wages and spends the other $40,000. In year two he also earns $50,000 in wages and earns $1,000 on his $10,000 of savings. During year two Bob consumes all of his year two income and all of his savings from year one. Calculate Bob's tax base, in years one and two, under a Haig-Simons income tax and under a consumption tax.

10. Briefly compare a VAT and an income tax.

Explanations

6. Under the Haig-Simons definition, income equals accretions to wealth, whether spent or saved (or, said another way, income is the accretion to wealth left at the end of the year plus the amounts consumed during the year). Here, during year one, wealth increases by $200,000 of wages. Total year one Haig-Simons income, therefore, equals $200,000. (Under the alternate definition given above, net accretion to wealth left at the end of the year is $50,000 and personal consumption is $150,000, so income is $200,000.) Under a cash flow consumption tax, year one income equals personal consumption. Here $150,000 is consumed, so Barbara would have to pay tax on a base of $150,000. A yield exemption consumption tax uses the same definition of income as a Haig-Simons income tax, so Barbara would have to pay tax on $200,000. However, under a yield exemption tax, the proceeds on Barbara's $50,000 of investments would be tax-free.

7. a. Under current law, a taxpayer receives no deduction when amounts are placed in a money market account and is taxed on the annual accretion to wealth attributable to such amounts. This is consistent with an income tax under the Haig-Simons definition of income.
   b. Under a consumption tax, all savings are deductible from gross income, and the amounts saved are taxed when withdrawn and used for personal consumption. Thus, the treatment of IRAs is consistent with a consumption tax.
   c. The current treatment of property appreciation is not equivalent to either the Haig-Simons income tax or a consumption tax. It is not equivalent to a pure income tax because annual accretion to wealth accrued on property is not taxed until the property is sold. It is not equivalent to a cash flow consumption tax because the investment is not deductible. It is not equivalent to a yield exemption consumption tax because the proceeds are taxable. In fact, the current treatment of appreciation in property falls somewhere between the income and consumption tax bases. Property appreciation is treated more favorably than it would be under a pure income tax because taxation of annual accretion to wealth is deferred until realization (the timing of which is usually within the taxpayer's control). On the other hand, property appreciation is treated less favorably than it would be under a yield exemption consumption tax because the annual accretion to wealth is eventually taxed. It is also treated less favorably than it would be under a cash flow consumption tax because a taxpayer cannot deduct the amount she invests in the property.

    d. The treatment of the insurance is consistent with a yield exemption consumption tax.

8. Alice's consumption can be calculated as follows: $31,000 consumed in daily living and $13,000 consumed on the vacation. Thus, her year one tax base under a consumption tax is $44,000.

    Alice's change in wealth is negative $13,000 because she has $5,000 less savings and has incurred an $8,000 debt. The sum of her negative $13,000 change in wealth and $44,000 of consumption is $31,000. Thus, Alice's year one tax base under a Haig-Simons income tax is $31,000.

9. Under a Haig-Simons income tax, Bob has a tax base of $50,000 ($10,000 increase in wealth plus $40,000 consumption) in year one and $51,000 ($61,000 personal consumption plus negative $10,000 change in wealth) in year two. Under a consumption tax, Bob has a base of $40,000 in year one and $61,000 in year two.

10. Under an income tax, an individual is taxed both on the portion of income she spends and the portion of income she saves or invests. A VAT applies only to sales of goods or services so that no tax is collected on that portion of income that is saved. As a result, many feel that the shift from an income tax toward a VAT would increase savings. One perceived downside of a shift toward a VAT is that a VAT is more regressive than an income tax since it does not cover savings and in any given year high-income individuals account for virtually all savings.

D. TAX ADMINISTRATION AND LITIGATION

The main sources of the tax law are the Internal Revenue Code (the Code) (title 26 of the United States Code) and case law. The tax law is administered by the Treasury Department (headed by the Secretary of the Treasury), which in turn delegates most administrative responsibility to an agency under its authority, the Internal Revenue Service (the Service or the IRS). The person who is the head of the Service is known as the Commissioner. One important responsibility of the Treasury and the Service is to provide guidance to taxpayers as to interpretation of the law. This guidance generally is provided in the form of treasury regulations,[1] revenue rulings, and revenue procedures; however, the Service sometimes provides guidance in various other forms (for example, announcements and notices).

    Treasury regulations are generally interpretive regulations, meaning that they are promulgated under Code §7805, which grants to the Secretary of the Treasury

---

1. Any citation in this book to regulations refers to treasury regulations.

the authority to enforce the provisions of the Code. However, some regulations are instead *legislative regulations*, meaning that the regulations are promulgated pursuant to a specific grant of authority in a particular Code section. See, e.g., §108(c)(5) (providing that the Secretary of the Treasury "shall issue such regulations as are necessary to carry out this subsection, including regulations preventing the abuse of this subsection"). Congress typically grants authority to issue legislative regulations when a Code provision is incomplete and requires filling in. Regulations are, strictly speaking, not the "law." Instead, they represent the view of the Service as to the meaning of a Code section so a taxpayer may argue that a regulation is invalid. However, courts give regulations great deference and invalidate them only in unusual circumstances.

A regulation is usually first issued as a *proposed regulation* so that taxpayers and their counsel may formally comment on the regulation before it is finalized. Proposed regulations are published in the Federal Register. A final regulation is promulgated in the form of a Treasury Decision. The Treasury Decision includes the text of the regulation and a preamble that gives the name and telephone number of the principal drafter of the regulation.

A *revenue ruling* is the Service's view on a particular issue. The rulings, which are generally short, describe a hypothetical fact pattern, frame an issue, and give the Service's view as to the correct outcome of the case. *Revenue procedures* generally describe the internal practices and procedures of the Service, but occasionally also address issues that might be characterized as substantive. Both revenue rulings and revenue procedures are officially published in the weekly Internal Revenue Bulletin (IRB); at the end of the year, the IRBs for the year are compiled in the Cumulative Bulletin.

The Service is also frequently willing to rule on the tax consequences of a particular taxpayer's prospective transaction. Such a ruling, referred to as a *private letter ruling*, is not officially published and applies only to the taxpayer who requested the ruling. Private letter rulings are, however, published (in a redacted form, so that the taxpayer's identity is concealed) by commercial publishers. Code §6110(k)(3) provides that private letter rulings may not generally be cited as authority but they can be helpful in practice nonetheless; sometimes they provide the only indication of the Service's position on a particular issue. (At the beginning of each year, the Service issues a revenue procedure in which it states the specific tax issues on which it will not issue a private letter ruling.) A *technical advice memorandum* is similar to a private letter ruling except that the advice is requested after the transaction with uncertain tax consequences has occurred and the taxpayer has been audited.

To many taxpayers the Service is nothing more than the issuer and collector of tax returns (and payments). Our tax system is a *self-assessment* system, meaning that taxpayers compute their own tax liability. However, sometimes the Service audits a taxpayer and determines that the taxpayer owes additional tax (to the taxpayer's horror). For the most part, the Service selects for audit those returns that it believes are most likely to understate tax liability. (The formula under which returns are selected for audit is not public knowledge.) Only 1 or 2 percent of returns are audited, so the number of taxpayers who have to suffer through an audit is relatively small. If, at the conclusion of the audit, the revenue agent determines that the taxpayer owes additional tax for the year, the agent issues a *Revenue Agent's Report* (RAR) and a *30-day letter* in which the agent indicates the amount of the asserted tax deficiency and notifies the taxpayer that she has 30 days to file an administrative appeal of the agent's determination. The taxpayer also can agree that the asserted deficiency is owed and pay that amount. Once a taxpayer agrees that the asserted deficiency is owed, the taxpayer generally will pay the deficiency as soon as possible because interest runs on the deficiency from the original due date for the return for the tax year audited.

The Appeals Office of the Service hears the taxpayer's appeal of the revenue agent's determination; although a taxpayer might fear that an office that is part of the Service will just rubber stamp the agent's determination, that is not the case. Appeals officers are (at least in our experience) generally quite reasonable, and, in fact, many cases heard by appeals officers are settled for less than the deficiency asserted by the revenue agent.

If a taxpayer does not resolve a tax controversy in the appeals process or if the taxpayer fails to respond to the 30-day letter, the Service will issue the taxpayer a *statutory notice of deficiency* (also known as a *90-day letter*). The Service must issue the 90-day letter before it can begin collection of the asserted deficiency. The 90-day letter gives the taxpayer 90 days to file a petition in the United States Tax Court and litigate the issue. (The Tax Court is based in Washington, D.C., but Tax Court judges travel around the country hearing cases.) A taxpayer does not have to pay the asserted income tax deficiency to litigate in the Tax Court. If the taxpayer does not file a Tax Court petition during the 90-day period, the Service may begin collection of the asserted deficiency. Tax Court decisions are appealable to the court of appeals for the circuit where the taxpayer resides.

Instead of litigating in the Tax Court, the taxpayer can pay the asserted deficiency and sue for a refund of tax either in the federal district court where the taxpayer resides or in the United States Court of Federal Claims, which sits in Washington, D.C. In other words, the taxpayer has a choice of forum. Typically, taxpayers litigate in the Tax Court so they do not have to pay the asserted deficiency while the litigation is pending. However, there are a number of reasons why certain taxpayers might prefer to litigate in a court other than the Tax Court. Taxpayers may choose to litigate in district court because jury trials are available only in that forum. Taxpayers may choose to litigate in the claims court because that court follows the precedent of the Court of Appeals for the Federal Circuit, which may be more favorable to the taxpayer than the precedent of the court of appeals for the circuit where the taxpayer resides, which the Tax Court or district court would follow. The rule that the Tax Court follows the precedent of the court of appeals for the circuit where the taxpayer resides is sometimes called the *Golsen rule* because the rule was articulated in Golsen v. Commissioner, 54 T.C. 742 (1970).

The statute of limitations in tax cases is generally three years from the date the return for the year was filed or, if later, the due date for the return. §6501. If the taxpayer omits a substantial amount of income from his return, the statute of limitations is six years. §6501(e). If the taxpayer files a fraudulent return or fails to file a return, there is an open statute of limitations. §6501(c).

If a taxpayer underpays her tax due for a given year, she must pay interest on the tax deficiency from the due date for the return at a statutorily prescribed rate that approximates a market rate of interest. §§6201, 6621. For this reason, taxpayers generally pay any deficiency as soon as they settle a tax controversy. On the other hand, if a taxpayer overpays tax for a given year, the government pays interest on the amount of the overpayment. §§6611, 6621.

Taxpayers with a tax deficiency also may be subject to a variety of penalties, both civil and criminal. For example, they may be subject to the §6662 accuracy-related penalty if their underpayment of tax is attributable to negligence or one of the other reasons specified in the section. Taxpayers also are subject to §6662 if the understatement of tax is substantial, meaning that it exceeds the greater of (i) 10 percent of the tax actually owed for the year or (ii) $5,000. The §6662 penalty is 20 percent of the portion of the underpayment subject to §6662. Section 6663 also imposes a penalty for fraud equal to 75 percent of the portion of the underpayment attributable to fraud.

Additional civil and criminal penalties can apply to taxpayers who take "frivolous" positions, on tax returns or in other tax submissions to courts or the IRS, in a futile attempt to deny their legal obligation to file tax returns and pay tax, or to protest the existence of the income tax. (In common parlance, taxpayers who take such positions often are referred to as "tax protestors" or "tax deniers." The IRS is prohibited, by federal law, from using the term "illegal tax protestor" or similar designations in taxpayers' files, however. This rule was prompted by congressional concern that taxpayers might be stigmatized by such a designation.) The additional civil penalties include: (i) a penalty, under §6651(f), of up to 75 percent of the tax due, for a fraudulent failure to timely file a tax return; (ii) a $5,000 penalty, under §6702, for frivolous positions taken on tax returns or in other submission to courts or the IRS; and (iii) a $25,000 penalty, under §6673, if the Tax Court concludes that (A) a taxpayer instituted or maintained a Tax Court proceeding primarily for delay, (B) a taxpayer's position in a proceeding is frivolous or groundless, or (C) a taxpayer unreasonably failed to pursue administrative remedies.

Tax crimes include: (i) under §7201, the willful attempt to evade or defeat any tax, a felony punishable by a fine and up to five years in prison; (ii) under §7203, the willful failure to file a return or pay tax, a misdemeanor punishable by a fine and up to one year in prison; and (iii) under §7206, willful fraud or willfully making a false statement, a felony punishable by a fine and up to three years in prison. In criminal tax litigation, tax protestors often argue that they misunderstood the tax law (e.g., based on materials prepared by tax protestor promoters or their accountants) but did not willfully evade tax — even if their frivolous positions are unreasonable. See, for example, United States v. Cheek, 498 U.S. 192 (1991).

The Treasury and IRS publish lists of "frivolous" tax positions. §6702(c), Notice 2010-33. On the IRS website, www.irs.gov, the IRS lists dozens of frivolous positions and refutes each with multiple citations to relevant caselaw, indicating that the frivolous arguments are not only wrong, but preposterous. See "The Truth about Frivolous Tax Arguments," (2013), http://www.irs.gov/pub/irs-utl/friv_tax.pdf. These frivolous positions include the following bogus arguments: (i) filing tax returns and paying taxes are voluntary; (ii) wages cannot be taxed; (iii) taxpayers do not have to file tax returns because of the Fifth Amendment right against self-incrimination; (iv) the income tax is unconstitutional because of defects in the Sixteenth Amendment; (v) the income tax is unconstitutional because it violates tax protestors' beliefs, protected by the First Amendment, that they do not have to pay tax; and (vi) the income tax applies only to nonresident aliens.

Tax protestors' frivolous arguments unduly burden the IRS and courts. Crain v. Commissioner, 737 F.2d 1417 (5th Cir. 1984) provides an example of the judicial response to frivolous tax positions. The judge in the Crain case distinguished between a claim that simply lacks merit and one that is frivolous: "we are not obliged to suffer in silence the filing of baseless, insupportable appeals presenting no colorable claims of error and designed only to delay, obstruct, or incapacitate the operations of the courts or any other governmental authority. Crain's present appeal is of this sort. It is a hodgepodge of unsupported assertions, irrelevant platitudes, and legalistic gibberish. The government should not have been put to the trouble of responding to such spurious arguments, nor this court to the trouble of 'adjudicating' this meritless appeal." Id. at 1418. Another court has observed that, although tax protestors are free to hold absurd beliefs about the income tax, "the government . . . may penalize people who act on them." Coleman v. Commisioner, 791 F.2d 68 (7th Cir. 1986).

Examples

11. The Internal Revenue Service is part of what cabinet-level department?

12. Is each of the following statements true or false?
    a. Since private letter rulings may not be cited as authority, you should disregard them in doing tax research.
    b. If it is not clear how a recently issued set of regulations applies to a problem that you are researching, you can phone the drafter of the regulations and discuss the issue.

    c. Only around 1 or 2 percent of tax returns are audited.

    d. The Appeals Office of the Service rarely settles cases for less than the deficiency asserted by the revenue agent.

13. What happens at the conclusion of an audit in which the agent determines that additional tax is owed by the taxpayer, and what are the taxpayer's options at that point?

14. What must happen before a taxpayer can file a petition in the Tax Court?

15. Under what circumstances must the Service send the taxpayer a 90-day letter?

16. Compare the three courts in which one can litigate a tax controversy.

17. Ted lives in San Francisco, which is in the Ninth Circuit. He is litigating a case in the Tax Court that involves the issue of whether a particular item can be excluded from his income for tax purposes. In several earlier Tax Court cases the court ruled that this type of item is not excludable. Two taxpayers appealed the decision of the Tax Court. On appeal the Seventh Circuit affirmed the Tax Court decision in one of the cases, but in the other case the Ninth Circuit reversed and held that the item is excluded from gross income. In Ted's case will the Tax Court apply the prior Tax Court precedent or the Ninth Circuit precedent?

Explanations

11. The Treasury Department.

12. a. The statement is false. Although private letter rulings may not be cited, they are still helpful because they can give an indication of the Service's position on the issue discussed in the ruling. In fact, in practice they are sometimes the only source that you can find on an issue.

    b. The statement is true. The name and telephone number of the principal drafter of the regulations is published when the regulations are promulgated. The drafter of the regulations will often be quite helpful in interpreting any aspects of the regulations that are ambiguous.

    c. The statement is true.

    d. The statement is false. Many tax controversies are settled in the appeals process for less than the deficiency asserted by the revenue agent.

13. The agent will send the taxpayer the Revenue Agent's Report and a 30-day letter. The taxpayer can agree with the asserted tax deficiency

and pay it. If the taxpayer disagrees, the taxpayer can either file a protest with the Appeals Office or do nothing. If the taxpayer files a protest, the case will be heard by an appeals officer. If the taxpayer does nothing, the Service will then send the taxpayer a 90-day letter.

14. The taxpayer must receive a 90-day letter before filing a petition in the Tax Court.

15. The Service cannot begin collection of the asserted deficiency until it has first given the taxpayer an opportunity to litigate in the Tax Court by sending the taxpayer a 90-day letter. However, if a tax controversy is settled during the audit or appeals process, the Service does not have to send the taxpayer a 90-day letter.

16. A taxpayer can litigate a tax controversy in the Tax Court, the claims court, or the federal district court for the district in which the taxpayer resides. Taxpayers generally litigate in the Tax Court because a taxpayer does not have to pay the asserted deficiency to litigate there. A taxpayer must pay an asserted deficiency and then sue for a refund in order to be able to litigate in the district court or the claims court. A taxpayer who wants a jury trial must litigate in the district court. Sometimes there is favorable precedent in one court or another, which may affect the decision of where to litigate. The claims court follows the precedent of the Court of Appeals for the Federal Circuit, but the Tax Court and district court follow the precedent of the court of appeals for the circuit in which the taxpayer resides. Tax Court cases and district court cases are heard locally, whereas claims court cases are heard in Washington, D.C.

17. The Tax Court will follow the Ninth Circuit precedent because Ted resides in the Ninth Circuit. Golsen v. Commissioner, 54 T.C. 742 (1970).

E. TAX LEGISLATION

Under Article I of the Constitution, tax legislation originates in the House of Representatives (at least formally). The legislation begins in the House Ways and Means Committee, the committee that has jurisdiction over revenue, debt, customs, trade, health, welfare, and Social Security issues. The committee first conducts hearings at which various witnesses testify. After hearings are concluded, there are "mark-up" sessions during which the tax bill is drafted. Various parties, including the House Legislative Council, the staff of the Joint Committee on Taxation (described below), the Treasury Department, and the staff of the Ways and Means Committee, are involved in drafting the bill. When the Ways and Means Committee has completed the bill, it is sent to the floor of the House with the *House Report*. The House Report explains the existing law and the reasons for making the changes included in the bill. The bill is then debated on the floor of the House under procedural rules that limit amendment of the bill. The House then votes on the bill and, if it is approved, the Senate considers the bill.

In the Senate, the bill begins in the Senate Finance Committee, the committee that has jurisdiction over taxation, foreign trade, health, Social Security, and other financial matters. The Senate Finance Committee then holds hearings and prepares its version of the bill and the *Senate Report*. The bill then goes to the floor of the Senate for debate and a vote. The procedural rules in the Senate permit numerous amendments to the bill during the floor debate.

If the Senate approves its bill, the House and Senate bills usually go to the Conference Committee, which is made up of a small number of members of the House Ways and Means and Senate Finance Committees. The Conference Committee reaches compromises on the provisions that vary in the House and Senate versions of the bill and sometimes even adds new provisions. The Conference Committee also prepares the *Conference Committee Report* (which is designated by a House Report number).

Both chambers then vote on the conference bill. If both the House and Senate approve the bill, it goes to the President, who either signs or vetoes the bill. The date that the President signs the bill is the *enactment date*. The *effective date* of the various provisions of the bill may be an earlier or later date. The provisions of the new law are then incorporated into the Internal Revenue Code. Some provisions are phased in gradually over a number of years, and some provisions are scheduled to *sunset* (automatically expire) in a future year. In recent years, various tax cuts have included sunsets as a way of reducing the apparent revenue cost of the tax cuts. If a tax cut is subject to a sunset, the effect of the tax cut on the federal budget is determined as if the sunset will occur as scheduled. Congress often extends expiring tax cuts, however, because many voters think that an expiring tax cut is the same as a tax increase. The recent proliferation of gradual phase-ins and sunsets has added to the complexity of the Code.

After a major tax act is passed, the staff of the Joint Committee on Taxation (JCT) prepares an explanation of the new law. The JCT, which is made up of a small number of members of the House Ways and Means and Senate Finance Committees, has two main functions: First, it must review and approve or disapprove any large tax refunds; second, the JCT staff assist in drafting tax legislation and prepare the post-enactment explanation of the new tax act, referred to as "The General Explanation of the Revenue Provisions of [the name of the act]." Instead of using this cumbersome title, tax lawyers refer to this book as the "Blue Book" because the cover of the book is blue. (If a tax lawyer tells you to check the Blue Book, she may be telling you to look in this book, not in the Uniform System of Citation — the book you probably know as the Blue Book.) The Blue Book does not reprint the new law; instead, it explains the new law. It is not, strictly speaking, legislative history, although many courts treat it like legislative history.

Examples

18. What is the name of the House of Representatives committee responsible for tax legislation? The Senate committee?

19. Is each of the following statements true or false?
    a. The legislative history of a tax act includes the House Report, the Senate Report, and the Conference Committee Report.
    b. The effective date of a tax act is the date on which the President signs the bill.
    c. After enactment of a tax act, the text of the act is printed in the Blue Book prepared by the Joint Committee on Taxation.

Explanations

18. The House of Representatives committee responsible for tax legislation is the Ways and Means Committee. The Senate committee responsible for tax legislation is the Finance Committee.

19. a. The statement is true.
    b. The statement is false. The enactment date is the date on which the President signs the bill. The effective date of the provisions in the bill may be an earlier or later date than the enactment date.
    c. The statement is false. The Blue Book explains the new law but does not reprint it.

F. TAX RESEARCH

Suppose you are confronted with a client's real life tax issue as a law clerk or beginning lawyer, or a friend or relative has a tax problem. The issue may be too specialized or complicated to answer out of your casebook or notes, so you'll have no choice but to research the issue. But how do you proceed? If you're no better prepared than we were as young lawyers, you'll end up wandering around a law library (which, in your case, might be either a physical law library or a virtual law library), trying to find the tax materials and then looking, more or less at random, through the indexes of the most authoritative-looking volumes. This brief introduction to tax research is designed to give you some idea of how to start your research. We can't give you too much of a head start; every question is different, and the only way to become adept at tax research is to do it. But if you're as at sea as we were as beginning lawyers, you'll be grateful for any help you can get. If you would like more detailed information about how to do federal tax research, we suggest that you consult Federal Tax Research (8th ed.) by Gail Richmond.

The starting place in tax research is the Code, followed closely by case law and administrative pronouncements. How do you locate the relevant sources? There are several ways. First, you can search for relevant sources by looking in the topical index in the front of one of the federal tax loose-leaf services published by RIA and CCH. Each service consists of a dozen or so hardcovered three-ring binders that are continuously updated. The index in the front of the service will refer you to particular numbered paragraphs in the main volumes of the service (referred to as "compilation volumes"). The compilation volumes are organized by Code section in numerical order. For each Code section, the services contain the text of the Code section and regulations, an explanation of the law, and annotations of relevant cases, revenue rulings, and other administrative pronouncements.

Another way to locate the relevant sources is to read about your issue in a secondary source that explains the law, such as a treatise or journal article. There are many tax treatises, some of which are quite good, and two of which deserve special mention. Federal Taxation of Income, Estates and Gifts, the five-volume treatise by Professors Boris Bittker and Lawrence Lokken, is superb. It offers the most sophisticated treatment anywhere on some subjects but is well written enough to be intelligible to the novice. Federal Income Taxation of Corporations and Shareholders, by Professors Boris Bittker and James Eustice, is equally impressive. For many years it has been the "bible" of corporate tax lawyers.

The tax portfolios published by Bloomberg BNA (Bureau of National Affairs) are also frequently quite helpful. The BNA portfolio system consists of a few hundred gray, softcovered, spiral-bound portfolios on the most common tax issues. For example, there is a separate portfolio on §1031 that covers exchanges of like-kind property. Each portfolio is a hundred or so pages long and contains textual explanation with citations to relevant authority. At the end of the textual explanation there are sometimes appendixes with relevant statutes, regulations, rulings, and worksheets to aid in tax planning. The portfolios are kept up to date, though not quite as often as the tax services, and are organized according to a largely arbitrary numeric system. The subject matter of each portfolio is listed on its spine, however, and you can look up the topic (or Code section if you know what it is) in the index for the portfolios, which is usually shelved immediately after the portfolio binders.

There are also a number of journals that specialize in tax. Tax Notes, a weekly magazine, is a particularly useful starting place for researching recent or proposed legislation or administrative pronouncements, or for finding the "skinny" on important cases. Tax Notes also contains more wide-ranging "thought" pieces (called Special Reports) by leading tax authorities. Other tax journals include The Tax Lawyer, the Journal of Taxation, Corporate Taxation, Taxes — The Tax Magazine, the Tax Law Review, the Florida Tax Review, the Virginia Tax Review, and the Columbia Journal of Tax Law. Tax articles also appear in general law reviews. In addition, tax articles, including new draft articles on current developments topics, are available on two scholarship websites, the Social Science Research Network (SSRN), http://www.ssrn.com, and the Berkeley Electronic Press (Bepress), http://www.bepress.com. After registering on each of the websites (at no charge), a researcher can find published papers and works in progress using keyword or author searches. (To access a full-text article on SSRN, the researcher clicks on the download link on the page on which the article abstract appears. Bepress also allows a researcher to download a full-text document.)

Note that, even if you begin your research by looking in secondary sources that explain the law, you should always read any primary sources (for example, Code sections and cases) cited in the secondary sources. In your memoranda and briefs, cite directly to primary authority for a proposition if there is primary authority to support it; do not cite only a secondary source that describes a primary source. (Citing secondary authority when primary authority is available is one of the most common mistakes made by novice tax researchers.)

There are two types of Tax Court opinions, regular and memorandum. Regular decisions are officially published in the United States Tax Court Reporter (cited as T.C.). Memorandum decisions are not officially published, but are published by commercial publishers. The Chief Judge of the Tax Court decides which opinions are regular opinions and which are memorandum opinions. Memorandum opinions do not have the precedential force of regular opinions although the Tax Court occasionally cites memorandum opinions. Usually one Tax Court judge decides a Tax Court case. However, the Chief Judge of the Tax Court sometimes subsequently decides to have the case decided by the full Tax Court, in which case the decision is designated as "reviewed by the court." (CCH also publishes United States Tax Cases, sometimes cited as "U.S.T.C.," which are unofficial reprints of federal district court and court of appeals tax cases. We mention this item because if you were not aware of it, it would be easy to mistake a U.S.T.C. cite for an official cite to a regular decision of the Tax Court.) After losing a Tax Court case, the Service often indicates in the Internal Revenue Bulletin whether it *acquiesces* in the decision or not. The acquiescence or nonacquiescence lets the staff of the Service know whether to apply the case or not.

You can do tax research on various electronic tax research platforms, including the platforms offered by LexisNexis, Westlaw, RIA, CCH, and

Bloomberg BNA. The databases on these platforms include essential primary tax sources such as the Code, legislative history, tax cases, regulations, revenue rulings, revenue procedures, private letter rulings, and technical advice memoranda. Before relying on a revenue ruling or revenue procedure, check to see whether it has been *amplified, superseded,* or *revoked.* You also can check the subsequent history of cases and administrative pronouncements on the electronic platforms.

The secondary source content offered on each of the five platforms varies significantly, but may include numerous helpful sources such as authoritative treatises, practice-oriented journal articles, law review articles, Tax Notes magazine, daily tax newsletters (Tax Notes Today and The Daily Tax Report), and Tax Management Portfolios. You can search the databases by using keyword searches or browsing the contents as you would read a book. For electronic tax research tips and a detailed comparison of the content and functionality features of these five platforms, see The Virtual Tax Library: A Comparison of Five Electronic Tax Research Platforms, by Katherine Pratt, Jennifer Kowal, and Daniel Martin, http://papers.ssrn.com/sol3/papers.cfm?abstract_id=1017925.

You can obtain tax forms and explanatory taxpayer publications from the IRS website at http://www.irs.gov/Forms-&-Pubs. If you have a tax question, you can phone 1-800-829-1040 and chat with an IRS representative. Although IRS representatives often can help you with simple tax questions, they typically cannot answer the difficult tax research questions a lawyer encounters in a sophisticated tax practice. In one situation, however, you may be able to talk with an IRS expert about your tax research project. If the answer to the question you are researching turns on language in a recently issued regulation, you can call the drafter of the regulation (whose name and contact information are published when the regulations are issued). The drafter of the regulation often will be willing to explain, in an off-the-record manner, what he or she meant by a certain phrase or example.

Examples

20. You have been asked to research a question concerning the deductibility of an educational expense as an ordinary and necessary business expense. Explain how you might use the loose-leaf services to begin your research.

21. You have been asked to research the question of whether a plaintiff may exclude from income damages received in a personal injury suit. You have found concise and readable general discussions of the taxation of personal injury recoveries in a Bloomberg BNA Tax Management Portfolio and in the outstanding Bittker and Lokken treatise. You think that

you can extrapolate from these general discussions to answer your question. Have you finished your research?

22. Before relying on a revenue ruling you found in your research, what additional step should you take?

Explanations

20. If you did not know the Code section under which the issue arises, you would begin by looking it up in the topical index for the loose-leaf service. The topical index would indicate the compilation volume paragraph numbers covering your issue. An experienced tax lawyer would know that the issue arises under §162 and go directly to the compilation volume paragraphs that correspond to that section. The compilation volume paragraphs on the issue include the text of the Code section and regulations promulgated under the section, explanatory text, and annotations.

21. No! As good as the Bittker and Lokken treatise and BNA portfolios are, there is no substitute for reading the statute, cases, regulations, and other administrative pronouncements on an issue. Suppose you rely on general language in a treatise or portfolio, but your specific question is directly answered by the statute, regulations, or cases in a way that is either too remote to merit discussion in a secondary source or too recent to have been incorporated into the material updating the secondary service — and in a way that is contrary to the general statements made in the treatise. You have committed M-A-L-P-R-A-C-T-I-C-E. You must always read the applicable statute, cases, regulations, and other administrative pronouncements.

22. Before relying on a revenue ruling, you should always check to see whether the ruling has been amplified, revoked, or superseded. You check the subsequent history of a revenue ruling in a manner similar to "Shepardizing" a case — by looking for citations to the ruling in the electronic tax research databases.

Some Characteristics of Gross Income

As we saw in Chapter 1, in order to compute a taxpayer's tax liability, we must first determine the taxpayer's *gross income*. How does the Code define gross income? Section 61 provides that gross income includes "all income from whatever source derived." Although this circular definition, standing alone, would not help us much, case law and other specific Code provisions have embellished the statutory definition. Early this century, in Eisner v. Macomber, 252 U.S. 189, 207 (1920), income was narrowly defined as "gain derived from capital, from labor, or from both combined." However, in a later case, Commissioner v. Glenshaw Glass, 348 U.S. 426 (1955), income was defined much more broadly to include all "accessions to wealth, clearly realized, and over which the taxpayers have complete dominion." The Code also explicitly provides, in §61 and §§71 — 140, that certain items are to be included in or excluded from gross income. For example, §61 provides that gross income includes wages, interest, dividends, rents, and gains from dealings in property. In this chapter, we will consider whether various specific items are included or excluded for purposes of computing gross income. As we will see, the current law is not entirely coherent.

A. THE HAIG-SIMONS DEFINITION OF INCOME

The definition of income adopted in the *Glenshaw Glass* case approximates the Haig-Simons definition of income, which is the ideal definition of income that most tax theorists advocate. Recall that Haig-Simons income equals the sum of (i) the taxpayer's personal expenditures plus (or minus) (ii) the increase (or decrease) in the taxpayer's wealth. Not everyone agrees that the Haig-Simons definition of income is correct and even supporters admit that full implementation of the definition is impossible. Nonetheless, the Haig-Simons definition of income provides a widely accepted theoretical benchmark against which we can compare the current tax treatment of specific items.

Examples

1. Larry's total wealth at the beginning of year one is $10,000. During the next 12 months, Larry earns $35,000 in wages. He spends $20,000 on rent, food, and other consumption items. He deposits $15,000 in a savings account and earns $1,000 in interest on the deposit. At the end of year one, Larry's total wealth is $26,000 ($10,000 wealth at the beginning of the period, $15,000 savings and $1,000 interest). What is Larry's Haig-Simons income for year one?

2. Carolyn's total wealth at the beginning of year one is an acre of land with a fair market value of $15,000. During the year, Carolyn earns $40,000 in salary and spends the entire amount on rent, food, and other consumption items. By the end of year one, the fair market value of Carolyn's land has increased to $25,000.
   a. What is Carolyn's Haig-Simons income for year one?
   b. Which part of Carolyn's Haig-Simons income might not be subject to tax under current law? Why?

Explanations

1. Haig-Simons income is defined as personal consumption plus any change in year-end wealth. Here, Larry consumes $20,000 and increases his year-end wealth by $16,000 ($15,000 savings plus $1,000 interest income), so his Haig-Simons income in year one is $36,000.

2. a. Carolyn's Haig-Simons income in year one is $50,000 ($40,000 personal consumption plus a $10,000 increase in year-end wealth).
   b. The portion of Haig-Simons income that might not be subject to tax under current law is the $10,000 attributable to unrealized property appreciation. In general, gains and losses on property are not taxed until the property is sold or exchanged.

B. NONCASH COMPENSATION: FRINGE BENEFITS

Most people equate income with cash salary. However, noncash ("in-kind") employer-provided benefits such as medical care and life insurance may constitute a significant part of employee earnings. As we will see, the law adopts a neither-here-nor-there approach to fringe benefits. Some forms of fringe benefits are included in gross income in full, some are excluded entirely from gross income, and others are excluded subject to certain requirements and limitations.

Section 61(a)(1) provides that gross income includes "compensation for services," including "fringe benefits." Regulation §1.61-1(a) provides that "[g]ross income includes income realized in any form, whether in money, property, or services." Regulation §1.61-2(d)(1) adds: "[I]f services are paid for in property, the fair market value of the property taken in payment must be included in income as compensation." However, the Code contains various provisions that exclude from gross income specific noncash fringe benefits, several of which we will consider here.

As we consider each Code section, ask yourself the following questions: (i) Under what circumstances does the Code section apply? (ii) How does the section operate if it applies? (iii) Is the Code section consistent with the Haig-Simons definition of income? (iv) What policy goals are served or disserved by the provision?

I. Employer-Provided Meals and Lodging

Reading: §§61(a)(1), 107, 119; Reg. §1.61-1(a), -2(d)(1).
We begin our discussion of noncash compensation with an examination of §119, which under certain circumstances allows employees to exclude from income the value of employer-provided meals and lodging. Section 119 is not a terribly significant code provision — it does not affect many taxpayers and the amounts at stake are (relatively) small. Section 119 does, however, offer a useful starting point at which to begin thinking about statutory construction. Section 119 can also be used to explore how the tax law affects economic behavior.

Let's begin by examining the statute. Section 119(a) excludes from income the value of meals if (i) the employer furnishes meals to an employee, her spouse, or her dependents; (ii) the meals are provided for the convenience of the employer; and (iii) the meals are provided on the business premises of the employer. The same section excludes the value of lodging if (i) it is furnished on the business premises by the employer to an employee, her spouse, or her dependents; (ii) it is provided for the convenience of the employer; and (iii) the employee is required to accept the lodging as a condition of her employment.

Section 152 defines the term *dependent*. We will defer discussion of the technical definition of the term until Chapter 4. For now (simplifying somewhat), note that a member of the taxpayer's family (including a child, grandchild, parent, sibling, aunt, uncle, niece, or nephew) or household can qualify as the taxpayer's dependent if he or she: (i) has little income and is supported by the taxpayer; or (ii) is young, lives with the taxpayer more than half of the year, and does not support himself.

If a same-sex marriage is recognized under the "state of celebration" rule (discussed in Chapter 1), each individual in the marriage is treated as a "spouse" for all federal tax purposes. Rev. Rul. 2013-17. Federal tax law currently (as of March 2014) does not treat Registered Domestic Partners (RDPs) or Civil Union Partners (CUPs) as "spouses" of their partners. A taxpayer's same-sex partner may qualify as the taxpayer's "dependent," however. The term "dependent" is defined to include the taxpayer's "qualifying relative." §152(a). A same-sex partner is the taxpayer's qualifying relative if: (i) the partner's gross income for the year is less than the dependent exemption amount (e.g., $3,950 in 2014); (ii) the taxpayer provides more than half of the partner's support for the year; and (iii) the partner has the same principal place of abode as the taxpayer and is a member of the taxpayer's household during the year. §152(d)(1), (2)(H). If these requirements are met, meals and lodging provided by the taxpayer's employer to the taxpayer's partner may be excluded from the taxpayer's gross income if the requirements of §119 otherwise are satisfied.

Courts have had to clarify some of the other requirements under §119. For example, §119(a) covers meals "furnished" by the employer. Suppose the employer does not itself provide food but instead gives the employee a cash meal allowance. The Supreme Court considered whether such a cash allowance may be excluded, under §119, in Commissioner v. Kowalski, 434 U.S. 77 (1977). Robert Kowalski was a New Jersey state trooper who, while on call, was required to eat his meals at a public eating place within his assigned patrol area. Kowalski received meal allowances in an amount equal to approximately 19 percent of his cash wages. The Supreme Court held that §119 does not cover amounts reimbursed for meals and that Mr. Kowalski had to include the meal allowance in income.

The decision in *Kowalski* is almost certainly correct. Section 119 was intended to cover situations in which the employee is constrained in his or her choice of food or eating places. Kowalski was not so constrained: The system of reimbursement made it possible for him to choose from a wide range of restaurants. Still, the Court might have more plausibly based its decision on two other grounds: Kowalski was not on the business premises of the employer (he had argued that, for a state trooper, the entire state constituted the employer's business premises) and the reimbursement system did not appear to be instituted for the convenience of the employer.

In other cases, courts have focused more closely on the "business premises" requirement. In some of these cases, courts have held that the employer's business premises include homes that were located near the property where the employer conducted most of its business. For example, in Lindeman v. Commissioner, 60 T.C. 609 (1973), the Tax Court held that a house across the street from the employer's principal place of business was "on" the employer's business premises because the employee who lived in the house performed some of his duties in the house. However, in other cases, courts have held the employer's business premises did not include homes near the employer's principal place of business. For example, in Commissioner v. Anderson, 371 F.2d 59 (6th Cir. 1966), the court held that the business premises of a motel did not include a home for the motel manager, which was located two blocks from the motel, because the employee did not perform a significant portion of his duties there.

Other cases have revolved around the "convenience of the employer" requirement. Generally, a taxpayer can establish that the meals and lodging were provided for the convenience of the employer by showing that the employee is required to be on-call even when the employee is not working. For example, in Benaglia v. Commissioner, 36 B.T.A. 838 (1937), the manager of a luxury hotel in Hawaii was permitted to exclude the value of meals and lodging provided at the hotel because the manager was required to be on duty continuously. Although the meals and lodging provided were quite valuable, the court concluded that the meals and lodging were provided so that the manager could perform his duties, not as additional compensation.

Who benefits from §119? At first glance, it might appear that favored employees are the sole beneficiaries. Employers, however, who are able to offer tax-free benefits may be able to attract employees at lower salaries. If that is the case, some of the benefit of the statute might be captured by employers. A reduction in labor costs may lead to new entrants and price-cutting in the affected industry. If this occurs, consumers will benefit. Depending upon the economics of the particular industry, §119 may benefit employees, employers, consumers, or, most likely, some combination of the three groups. The losers in all of this are the taxpayers who must pay higher taxes to make up for the revenue lost by the §119 exclusion.

It is easy to criticize a provision that benefits an arbitrary class of employees, employers, and consumers. It is difficult, however, to implement a better method of taxing these sorts of in-kind benefits. One possibility would be to tax the employee on the retail value of the benefits so that a manager of a resort who was required to live on the premises for business reasons would be taxed on the retail cost of his room and board. This approach ignores the limitation on the manager's choice of where to eat and sleep. Another possibility would be to tax the manager on the cost of alternative arrangements. This approach requires speculation as to what arrangements the manager would have made and, in any event, ignores the fact that the provided room and board may be more or less desirable than those alternative arrangements. It would be best, perhaps, to tax the employee on his or her subjective valuation of the room and board. As a practical matter, however, that value is impossible to determine.

Section 107 sets forth another specific exclusion for employer-provided lodging. That section states that "ministers of the gospel" may exclude from gross income the value of lodging provided to the minister or the portion of a cash lodging allowance used by the minister to rent a home.

Examples

3. Donald earns $40,000 a year as the manager of the Sea Air Hotel. Donald also receives free meals and lodging at the hotel. A year-round guest would pay $50,000 for such lodging and food. In order for Donald to effectively perform his duties as hotel manager, it is necessary for him to live at the hotel. Also, Donald's employment contract requires him to reside at the hotel.
   a. Is Donald taxed on the free lodging and meals he receives as hotel manager?
   b. Is Donald taxed if his employer also provides free lodging and meals to Donald's spouse and dependent children?
   c. Suppose that Donald's employment contract provides that he may accept either lodging at the hotel or a salary increase of $5,000. Donald chooses to accept the free lodging. Is Donald taxed on the employer-provided lodging?
   d. Is each of the following statements true or false?
      i. Free food and lodging leaves Donald wealthier than similarly situated persons earning $40,000 a year.
      ii. Nontaxation of food and lodging may lead to compensation arrangements that otherwise would be inefficient.
      iii. Fairness and efficiency require that Donald be taxed on the fair market value of his bed and board, $50,000 per year.
      iv. If we could determine the amount that Donald otherwise would have spent on board and lodging, then it would be fair and efficient to tax Donald on that sum since that is the amount Donald saves each year by virtue of his compensation arrangement.
   e. How *should* Donald be taxed on the benefit?

4. Alice is the manager of the Traveltime Motel. As a condition of her employment, the motel requires her to live in a home, owned by the

motel, which is located one-half mile from the motel so that she will be close enough to arrive quickly in an emergency. Alice is on-call 24 hours a day. The motel can contact her at any time by calling her cell phone. The value of the lodging is $10,000 per year. Is Alice entitled to exclude the value of the lodging under §119?

5. Sally, a police officer, is on duty from 8 A.M. to 4 P.M. each day. Her employment contract requires her to remain on duty during her lunch hour. The police department reimburses Sally for lunch expenses up to a maximum of $5.00 per day. A state statute setting out the terms for employment for police officers provides that the meals are a working condition and not a part of Sally's compensation. Is Sally taxed on the reimbursement?

6. Jack is the president and sole shareholder of the Rustic Inn, Inc., a motel located alongside Interstate 80. The Rustic Inn consists of 80 motel rooms and an adjoining house where Jack and his wife and young children live. The phone line and door bell to the motel ring in Jack's house so that he can answer calls and welcome guests 24 hours a day. Most other motels the size of the Rustic Inn have full-time managers who are required to live on the premises. However, most managers of comparable motels are not given accommodations as nice as the house in which Jack and his family live. The motel deducts all expenses associated with the adjoining house, including those (such as utilities) that clearly would be nondeductible for ordinary homeowners. Is Jack entitled to exclude the value of the lodging from his gross income under §119?

Explanations

3. a. No. Under §119 the value of any meals or lodging furnished by an employer to an employee is excluded from gross income if (i) such meals and lodging are provided for the convenience of the employer; (ii) the meals are furnished on the business premises of the employer; and (iii) the employee is required to accept such lodging on the business premises as a condition of his employment. These requirements are met here. The convenience of the employer requirement is met, as in *Benaglia*, because Donald must reside at the hotel to perform his duties as the hotel manager.

   b. No. The exclusion under §119 extends to meals and lodging provided to an employee's spouse and dependents. §119(a).

   c. Yes. Since Donald is no longer required to accept the lodging as a condition of his employment, the exclusion from gross income is not available. §119(a)(2).

   d. i. True. Nontaxation of food and lodging leaves Donald wealthier than other individuals with the same monetary income.

ii. True. Suppose the meals and lodging cost the hotel $18,000 per year but are worth only $15,000 to Donald. In the absence of taxes, the hotel obviously would not provide meals and lodging because both parties would be better off if Donald were given an additional $16,000 in cash. But if Donald is in the 25 percent tax bracket and meals and lodging are tax-free, the incentives change. The tax-free meals and lodging worth $15,000 to Donald provide the same benefit as $20,000 in taxable salary. (If Donald's marginal tax rate is 25 percent, the tax on $20,000 is $5,000, leaving Donald with $15,000 of after-tax income.) It costs the hotel $18,000 to provide meals and lodging with a value equal to $20,000 of cash compensation. Thus, the hotel will provide the meals and lodging.

iii. False. Taxation of the lodging at fair market value would give Donald an income of $90,000 per year. However, Donald is not as well off as most persons who earn that sum because he is forced to spend $50,000 per year on hotel food and lodging. It would not be equitable to treat Donald the same as other individuals earning $90,000. Said another way, the food and lodging are obviously not worth $50,000 to Donald and it seems unfair to tax him on that sum.

It also may be economically inefficient to tax Donald on the retail value of his meals and lodging. One way to determine whether a tax is inefficient is to ask whether it prevents (or induces) transactions that would be attractive (or unattractive) in a no-tax world. We saw above that the nontaxation of meals and lodging under current law might well be inefficient because it encourages otherwise uneconomical compensation arrangements. Taxation at full retail value would be inefficient for the opposite reason — in some cases it would discourage the parties from sensible compensation arrangements that included meals and lodging.

The provision of meals and lodging might be attractive to both Donald and the hotel in a no-tax world. First, the meals and lodging might cost the hotel a modest amount, say $8,000 per year, but might be worth $10,000 a year to Donald. Second, the hotel might benefit from having Donald easily available during nonworking hours. If the meals and lodging are taxed at the retail value of $50,000, it will no longer make sense for the parties to reach agreements that include this benefit. The tax alone ($12,500, assuming a 25 percent rate) will be greater than its benefit.

iv. Probably false. The meals and lodging may be more or less valuable to Donald than the cost of the alternative arrangements. Donald may not be willing to pay the retail price to live in the hotel, but may still prefer the hotel food and lodging to the food and lodging he would otherwise purchase. Or suppose this issue comes up in the context of someone who pilots a freighter. The employee may find ship's quarters and food much less desirable than the food and lodging he or she would otherwise purchase.

e. The ideal solution would be to tax the meals and lodging at their value to Donald. Taxation at that value, often referred to as the good's *shadow price*, would be efficient because a benefit that is attractive in a no-tax world will be equally attractive if taxed at each individual's shadow price. Taxing Donald on the shadow price of the benefit also seems fair since that price represents the amount of cash income Donald would pay for the benefit. The obvious difficulty with this approach is that it is impossible to know the value that Donald puts on the meals and lodging.

Students should note that the subject of efficiency can get quite complicated very quickly. For example, virtually all taxes cause some distortion; the amount of distortion depends not only on the tax itself, but on the interaction among the tax, other taxes, and non-tax economic forces. Moreover, some tax-induced changes in behavior, such as reduced smoking due to an excise tax on tobacco, may be desirable and efficient. Nonetheless, when evaluating particular provisions of the tax law, it is useful to ask yourself whether such provisions distort decisionmaking. In many cases this question can be answered without elaborate analysis and it will be obvious that the change is not justified by any compelling social policy. For example, a law that taxes employer-provided bus passes but does not tax employer-provided parking will distort the decision between use of private automobiles and reliance on mass transit. The result will be that more employees will drive to work than is economically efficient.

4. Probably not. An employee can exclude the value of lodging under §119 only if the employee is required to accept such lodging on the "business premises" of her employer. §119(a)(2). It is unlikely that a home one-half mile from the motel would be considered on the business premises of the motel. See Commissioner v. Anderson, 371 F.2d 59 (6th Cir. 1966).

5. Yes. In a number of cases decided in the 1960s, courts held that the business premises of the state police included the entire area under police jurisdiction and thus state police could exclude meal money under §119. However, the Supreme Court later put an end to this exclusion, but not by limiting the definition of business premises. Instead, the Supreme Court held that meals purchased with money provided by the state are not

"furnished" by the employer, and so do not qualify for the exclusion. Commissioner v. Kowalski, 434 U.S. 77 (1977). The state statute does not determine whether the meals are intended for compensation. §119(b)(1).

6. Here Jack is both an employee of the corporation and its owner. Does that dual role prevent him from qualifying for the §119 exclusion? Probably not. Jack can establish that his residence on the business premises is for the convenience of the employer because he is on-call 24 hours a day and comparable motels require that their managers live on the motel premises. However, the potential for abuse of §119 is great here because Jack can set the conditions of his own employment, as owner of the corporation, and his accommodations are nicer than the accommodations motels generally give their managers. Courts and the Service may carefully scrutinize such potentially abusive arrangements. See Hatt v. Commissioner, 28 T.C.M. 1194 (1969). On these facts, however, Jack can probably qualify for the §119 exclusion.

2. Employer-Provided Insurance and Health, Accident, and Death Benefits

Reading: §§36B, 79, 101(a), 105, 106, 125, 213, 223, 1411, 4980H, 4980I, 5000A.

If an employer buys life insurance for an individual employee and the employee designates the policy beneficiary, the value of the life insurance is income to the employee. Reg. §1.61-2(d)(2)(ii)(a). Under §79, however, if the employer buys group term life insurance for its employees, the employees can exclude the value of the insurance from gross income to the extent that the insurance provides death benefits not greater than $50,000. Section 79 requires that the employer not discriminate in favor of highly compensated employees.

Section 101(a) provides an exclusion from gross income for life insurance proceeds received by a beneficiary.

Section 105 excludes from gross income amounts employees receive from their employers as reimbursement for medical expenses and the value of services employees receive under an employer-provided health care plan. The benefits of §105 are conditioned upon the requirement that the employer health care plan not discriminate in favor of highly compensated employees. In general, a health plan will meet the nondiscrimination requirement if the benefits provided to highly compensated employees are also provided to rank and file employees. Section 106 complements §105 by excluding from gross income the value of health and accident insurance premiums paid by the employer to cover employees.

The exclusion for employer-provided health care benefits has the same effect as requiring employees to include in income the value of employer-provided medical care and allowing the employees to take a corresponding deduction for those expenses. In either event, medical costs would be paid out of before-tax dollars. Section 213 (discussed in Chapter 4) allows a deduction for unreimbursed medical expenses, although the §213 medical expense deduction is subject to significant limitations, including a floor of 10 percent of adjusted gross income. In addition, §223 (also discussed in Chapter 4) provides that taxpayers can deduct their contributions to a Health Savings Account (HSA) and exclude employer contributions to HSAs. §223(a). Also, distributions from HSAs are not taxed if the distributions are used to pay unreimbursed medical expenses. §223(f). Taken together, §§105, 106, 213, and 223 represent a significant, albeit indirect, form of government support for medical expenses.

The Patient Protection and Affordable Care Act (PPACA) (as amended), provides additional forms of government support for health care, along with new health insurance coverage mandates and excise taxes on high-cost health insurance plans. We briefly discuss only a few of the provisions of PPACA here. In addition to the tax provisions discussed here, the legislation includes various revenue-raising provisions, such as a new 3.8 percent "Medicare" tax on the investment income of individuals. §1411. Also, PPACA includes numerous new information reporting requirements. For example, PPACA amended §6051 to require employers to inform their employees (on employees' W-2 forms) of the value of employer-provided health care. PPACA generally takes effect in 2014 and later years.

Two of the goals of health care reform are (1) to increase access to health care, especially for the poor, and (2) to contain the rate of growth of health care spending. Various provisions of PPACA, including an "individual mandate," an "employer mandate," and "premium assistance credits," are designed to increase access to health care.

The individual mandate is a requirement that individuals obtain health insurance, for example, from an employer or state-run health insurance exchange or through government-maintained insurance, such as Medicaid or Medicare. Section 5000A imposes a "shared responsibility" penalty on individuals who fail to purchase basic health insurance, but there is an exception for individuals for whom insurance is not affordable. The federal government also will provide subsidies for the purchase of health insurance in the form of new refundable "premium assistance credits" for low-income individuals and families. §36B. These credits can be paid directly to health insurers for health insurance premium costs.

The employer mandate is a requirement that large employers offer health insurance coverage to employees. Employers that do not provide coverage to employees must pay a penalty, but small businesses (employers with fewer than 50 employees) are exempt. §4980H.

Certain small employers (for example, in 2014, employers with 25 or fewer full-time equivalent employees and average annual wages of $50,800 or less) can qualify for a health insurance tax credit if they make certain contributions toward their employees' health insurance premiums. §45R, Rev. Proc. 2013-35 §§2.01, 3.09. This credit is temporary; qualifying small employers can take this credit in just two years after 2013.

PPACA also includes various provisions to contain the growth of health care spending, but it does not cap or repeal the §105 and §106 exclusions. For many years, health care economists of all political stripes have criticized the unlimited income tax exclusions for employer-provided health care, arguing that the exclusions provide an inefficient incentive to convert taxable cash wages into nontaxable health care benefits, such as lower copayments or deductibles, which drive up the cost of health care. Proposals to cap the §105 and §106 exclusions or to replace the exclusions with a limited credit or deduction have been a conspicuous part of the national debate regarding health care reform. Although capping or replacing the §105 and §106 exclusions has proved to be politically unpalatable, a new excise tax provision in PPACA likely will have an effect that will be similar to a cap on the income tax exclusions. The PPACA excise tax, a 40 percent tax that will be imposed on high-cost employer-provided plans, beginning in 2018, will encourage employers to reduce "Cadillac" health insurance coverage benefits and instead pay increased cash wages. §4980I.

PPACA continues the historic connections between employment and health insurance and between health care and the federal tax system. The United States is the only country in which health insurance generally is provided by employers rather than purchased on an open market or provided by the government in the form of national health insurance. This structural anomaly was created by accident, during World War I, when the federal government determined that employer-provided health insurance would not be treated as wages, for the purpose of wartime wage and price controls. In response, employers provided health care benefits in lieu of prohibited wage increases. The IRS subsequently ruled that taxpayers could exclude employer-provided health benefits from income — which ultimately led to where we are today. During the recent health care reform debates, some constituencies favored a rejection of employer-provided health care in favor of a single-payer, government-run system, and other constituencies favored greater reliance on private insurance markets. PPACA is a mammoth compromise, retaining and increasing tax incentives (both carrots and sticks) for employers to provide health insurance to employees and their families, yet also attempting to expand opportunities for increased access to health care through new tax subsidies and state-run insurance exchanges.

Examples

7. David receives $50,000 of group term life insurance from his employer. He names his long-time companion Fred as beneficiary. Is David subject to tax on the value of the life insurance? If David dies, is Fred taxed on the $50,000 death benefit?

8. a. Larry is paid a cash salary of $25,000 and his employer provides him with health insurance valued at $4,000 per year. The health insurance covers all of Larry's health care costs. How much, if any, of the value of the employer-provided health insurance must Larry include in gross income?

   b. Leslie is paid a cash salary of $29,000 and spends $4,000 on health care. How much, if any, of her health care costs may Leslie deduct?

   c. What is the likely impact of the differential tax treatment of employer-paid and employee-paid medical expenses?

9. Management offers the union representing employees of Xenon Corporation a choice of new salary packages. The first package offers employees additional medical insurance at a cost of $1,000 per employee per year. The second package does not offer additional insurance but provides for a salary bonus of $1,000 per employee. The union polls its employees and discovers that, on the average, $1,000 of insurance is valued by employees at $900; that is, the average employee would be indifferent between receiving $900 in cash and $1,000 of medical insurance.

   a. Assume the employees were not subject to income tax. Will the union accept the package with the insurance or the package with the $1,000 salary bonus?

   b. Assume that both the insurance and the salary increase are subject to income tax and that all employees are in the 25 percent bracket. Will the union accept the package with the insurance or with the $1,000 salary bonus? What will be the after-tax value of the chosen benefit to each employee? How much tax will the government collect? What is the sum of the cash value of the benefit to the employee and the cash value of the taxes raised to the government?

   c. Assume that the salary bonus is subject to income tax but the medical insurance is tax-free, and that all employees are subject to a marginal tax rate of 25 percent. Will the union accept the package with the insurance or the package with the $1,000 bonus? What will the after-tax value of the chosen benefit be to each employee? How much tax will the government collect from each employee? What is the sum of the cash value of the benefit to the employee and the cash value of the taxes raised by the government?

Explanations

7. David is not taxed on the value of the term life insurance, and Fred is not taxed on the value of the death benefit if David dies. Section 79 excludes from income the premiums that finance the first $50,000 of group term life insurance coverage. If David dies, Fred will exclude the $50,000 proceeds of the life insurance. §101(a).

8. a. Larry excludes the entire $4,000 of health insurance costs, under §106.
   b. Leslie will be able to deduct her health care costs under §213 (a) only to the extent such costs exceed a floor of 10 percent of adjusted gross income, here $2,900 if her adjusted gross income is $29,000. She may deduct only $1,100 ($4,000 less $2,900) of her costs.
   c. The fact that individuals who receive employer-provided medical benefits pay less tax than individuals who pay for their own medical care encourages employees to take a portion of their salary in the form of in-kind medical benefits. Employees who must purchase medical insurance with after-tax dollars will pay higher taxes than employees with identical economic incomes who are able to secure tax-free employer-provided medical care.

9. a. The union will prefer the salary bonus.
   b. The union will still prefer the salary bonus. The salary is worth $1,000 before-tax and $750 after-tax; the benefit package is worth only $900 before-tax and $675 after-tax. The government will collect $250 per employee. The cash value of the benefit to the employee is $750 and the government raises taxes of $250 for a total benefit of $1,000.
   c. The union will now prefer the insurance. The insurance will return a before-tax and after-tax benefit to each employee of $900; the salary bonus will return an after-tax benefit to each employee of only $750. The government will not collect any tax so the total benefit will be the $900 benefit to the employee. The tax-induced reduction in value of the total amount of goods and services is called the *deadweight loss* of the tax. Here the deadweight loss associated with the differential tax treatment of a salary bonus and of medical insurance is $100 (the $1,000 value of the bonus as compared to the $900 value of the medical insurance).

3. The Section 132 Exclusion for Miscellaneous Fringe Benefits

Reading: §132; Reg. §§1.132-1, -2, -6, -8; 1.61-21(g)(12).

Thus far we have considered a number of specific exclusion sections, including the exclusions for employer-provided food, lodging, insurance, and health care. What is the tax treatment of other types of fringe benefits? Section 132 covers miscellaneous fringe benefits that are not covered by other specific exclusion sections. Section 132 excludes from income the following eight categories of benefits: (i) no-additional-cost services; (ii) qualified employee discounts; (iii) working condition fringe benefits; (iv) de minimis fringe benefits; (v) qualified transportation fringe benefits; (vi) qualified moving expense reimbursements; (vii) qualified retirement planning services; and (viii) qualified military base realignment and closure fringe benefits.

To be excluded under §132, the fringe benefits generally must be provided to the taxpayer-employee. No-additional-cost services and qualified employee discounts provided to retired employees, disabled employees, surviving spouses of employees, spouse of employees, and "dependent children" of employees also may be excluded, however, because such fringe benefits are treated as though they are provided to employees. §132(h)(1), (2). In addition, air transportation provided to the parents of an employee is treated as though it is provided to the employee. §132(h)(3). No-additional-cost services and qualified employee discounts provided to a taxpayer's same-sex spouse can be excluded pursuant to §132, if the employee's marriage is recognized under the "state of celebration" rule, discussed in Chapter 1. Rev. Rul. 2013-17. A taxpayer cannot exclude such employee fringe benefits that are provided to the taxpayer's partner however, because the same-sex partner is not treated as a "spouse," for federal tax purposes, and is not the taxpayer's dependent "child." §§132(h)(2), 152(f)(1), Rev. Rul. 2013-17.

Two principal requirements must be met before a benefit qualifies as an excludable *no-additional-cost service*. Not surprisingly, the first requirement is that the benefit constitutes a service that imposes no substantial additional cost on the employer. §132(b)(2). The second requirement is that the service is offered for sale in the ordinary course of the line of business of the employer in which the employee is performing services. §132(b)(1). Thus, a hotel might allow employees free use of otherwise unused hotel rooms. However, due to the line of business limitation, a manufacturer could not offer its employees, as a tax-free benefit, hotel rooms it was not using but for which it had paid. The line of business limitation is designed to limit the loss of tax revenue from the exclusion and to prevent conglomerates from receiving an unfair advantage over other firms.

Services provided pursuant to reciprocal written agreements among employers operating similar businesses can qualify for the §132 no-additional-cost service exclusion so long as no employer incurs any substantial additional cost in providing the service. §132(i). Such reciprocal agreements, for example, might permit an employee of one airline to fly (on a stand-by basis) on another airline at no charge.

The §132(c) test for excluding an *employee discount* varies depending on whether the employee is purchasing goods or services at a discount. An employee purchasing goods can exclude a discount up to the employer's *gross profit percentage.* §132(c)(1)(A). If, for example, an employer sold goods for an aggregate sale price of $100,000 and the employer's aggregate cost of the goods is $60,000, the employer's gross profit percentage is 40 percent, which is $40,000 (the $100,000 aggregate sale price less the $60,000 aggregate cost) divided by the $100,000 aggregate sale price. The employer could offer its employees tax-free discounts of up to 40 percent. An employee purchasing services may exclude a discount of up to 20 percent. §132(c)(1)(B). The exclusion for qualified employee discounts is limited to goods or services sold in the line of business in which the employee is providing services. §132(c)(4).

Both the qualified employee discount exclusion and the no-additional-cost service exclusion are conditioned upon compliance with a nondiscrimination provision. §132(j)(1). This provision, like the non-discrimination provision governing employer health care plans, generally requires that the benefit be made available to a wide cross section of employees, including non-highly compensated employees. Section 132(j)(6) and Regulation §1.132-8(f)(1) provide that the term *highly compensated employee* is defined by reference to §414(q). (Although the regulation provides a formula for determining whether an employee is a "highly compensated employee," the formula in the regulation is outdated because it has not been amended to reflect changes in §414(q).) As amended, §414(q) defines "highly compensated employee" as any employee who (i) was a 5 percent owner during the year, or the preceding year, or (ii) for the preceding year (A) was paid more than $115,000, and (B) was in the top-paid (top 20 percent) group of employees. §414(q)(1), Notice 2013-73.

A *working condition fringe benefit* is defined, generally, as an item that could be deducted as a business expense under §162 or §167 if paid directly by the employee. §132(d). Section 162 allows taxpayers to deduct all the "ordinary and necessary" expenses paid or incurred during the taxable year in carrying on any trade or business. Thus, an employee who would be able to deduct the costs of a subscription to a professional journal if she bore those costs herself is not taxed if her employer supplies the journal free of charge. (We defer detailed discussion of what constitutes a deductible business expense until later.) Section 167 allows taxpayers to take depreciation deductions on property used in a trade or business or held for the production of income.

A *de minimis fringe benefit* is defined as any property or service the value of which is so small as to make accounting for it unreasonable or administratively impracticable. §132(e)(1). Regulation §1.132-6(e) lists the following items as examples of de minimis fringe benefits: occasional parties, occasional theater or sporting event tickets, coffee, doughnuts, soft drinks, and local telephone calls. In addition, §132(e)(2) provides a special rule for eating facilities operated by employers for their employees: The eating facility will be treated as a de minimis fringe if (i) it is on or near the employer's business premises and (ii) the revenue from the facility generally equals or exceeds the employer's cost of operating the facility.

Qualified transportation fringe benefits include "qualified parking," transit passes (such as bus passes), "qualified bicycle commuting reimbursement," and transportation provided in a "commuter highway vehicle" that is used principally to drive employees to and from work. §132(f)(1). *Qualified parking* is defined as parking provided to an employee on or near the business premises of the employer. §132(f)(5)(C). A *commuter highway vehicle* must have a seating capacity of at least six adult passengers (not including the driver) and at least 80 percent of the expected mileage of the vehicle must be incurred in transporting employees (at half-capacity or greater) to and from work. §132(f)(5)(B). A taxi or limousine with a driver thus is not a commuter highway vehicle. *Qualified bicycle commuting reimbursement* means reimbursement of an employee's reasonable annual expenses to purchase, maintain, or store a bicycle that the employee regularly uses to commute from home to work. §132(f)(5)(F)(i).

Section 132 caps the exclusion for qualified transportation fringe benefits. §132(f)(2), (f)(5)(F)(ii). If the transportation benefit received by the employee exceeds the exclusion limits, the employee is taxed on the excess. The exclusion limits generally are indexed for inflation. §132(f)(6); but see §132(f)(5)(F)(ii). For example, in tax year 2014, an employee could exclude (1) up to $250 per month of qualified parking cost, and (2) up to $130 per month of qualified highway vehicle cost or transit pass cost. §132(f)(2), (f)(6), Rev. Proc. 2013-35. (A temporary increase in the exclusion caps for qualified highway vehicle costs and transit pass costs, to equal the exclusion cap for qualified parking costs, expired on December 31, 2013. Congress may extend this provision again however.) The exclusion for qualified bicycle commuting reimbursement is limited to $20 per month of qualifying months during the year. §132(f)(5)(F)(ii).

Qualified moving expense reimbursements are amounts received by an individual from an employer as payment for expenses that would be deductible by the employee as moving expenses under §217 if paid by the employee. §132(g).

Qualified retirement planning services include retirement planning advice or information provided to an employee and her spouse by an employer maintaining a retirement plan. §132(m)(1). The legislative history of §132(m) indicates that this exclusion applies to advice about retirement income planning, but does not apply to tax preparation, accounting, legal or brokerage services related to retirement planning. A separate nondiscrimination rule applies to the qualified retirement planning services exclusion. §132(m)(2).

2. Some Characteristics of Gross Income

A special rule provides that gross income does not include the value of any *on-premises athletic facility* provided by an employer to employees. §132(j)(4)(A). An on-premises athletic facility must be located on the premises of the employer and operated by the employer. In addition, substantially all the use of the facility must be by employees, their spouses, and their dependent children. §132(j)(4)(B)(iii).

The following examples review the rules described above and test your knowledge of other aspects of §132 that should be apparent from a careful reading of the statute.

Examples

10. Dean, an airline reservation clerk for Friendly Airlines, is allowed to fly free of charge on Friendly Airlines flights. Dean is required to fly on a stand-by basis and is permitted to board only when there otherwise would be unoccupied seats. Is the flight taxable to Dean?

11. Donald works as a salesman for a retailer that sells tools. Donald's employer gives him an airline voucher, good for a round-trip ticket to Hawaii. Donald's employer received the voucher at no cost as part of a promotional effort of the airline. The voucher is subject to seat availability and may be used only when there are otherwise unoccupied seats. Is the flight taxable to Donald?

12. Sarah works as a proofreader for Jones Books, Inc., a successful publishing company. Jones Books owns a jet that can carry 20 passengers. When the jet makes a business trip, there is often additional space on board. The company usually permits employees who are on vacation to "hitch a ride" on the jet if there is extra space available. Jones Books, Inc. flies several of its employees to New York for a business convention and Sarah "hitches a ride" on the flight in order to visit friends. What amount, if any, does Sarah have to include in income as a result of the flight to New York?

13. a. Allison works at the candy counter of the Imperial Theater, a movie theater owned by Globe, Inc. Allison is allowed free midweek admission to films showing at any of the eight Globe theaters in the city if the show is not sold out prior to the time the feature movie begins. Is Allison taxed on the value of the free movie admissions?
    b. How, if at all, would your answer in part (a) change if Allison's spouse and dependent children were also allowed free admission to the films?
    c. How, if at all, would your answer in part (a) change if Allison were a retired former employee of the Imperial Theater rather than a current employee?

d. How, if at all, would your answer in part (a) change if Allison were a veterinarian working for Hollywood Milk, a dairy owned by Globe, Inc., the owner of the theaters?

e. Globe, Inc. signs an agreement with a rival theater owner, Johnson Film Exhibitors, Inc. (JFE), under which the movie house employees of either corporation are permitted free midweek admission to films showing at any Globe- or JFE-owned theater if the film is not sold out. Is Allison taxed on her free admissions to JFE theaters?

14. Betty is the highly compensated vice president of Malibu Tanning Centers, Inc., a chain of tanning salons. Officers of the corporation (but not other employees) are permitted to use the facilities at no cost when they are not being used by paying customers. Betty takes advantage of this program by visiting the salon three times a week. Is this fringe benefit taxable to Betty?

15. Albert is a sales clerk at City Sporting Goods. The store's total sales for the prior year were $600,000 and its cost of goods sold was $400,000. Albert wishes to purchase a ski outfit that the store sells to ordinary customers for $240. The store's cost for the ski outfit is $180.

a. City Sporting Goods permits its employees to purchase goods for their personal use at one-third off the retail price so Albert will be able to purchase the ski outfit for $160. Is the discount taxable income to Albert? If so, what amount is included in his gross income?

b. Suppose City Sporting Goods permits its employees to purchase goods at one-half off the retail price so that Albert will be able to purchase the ski outfit for $120. Is the discount taxable income to Albert? If so, what amount is included in his gross income?

16. Mary is an accountant for the Eastside Cleaning Service. The business pays housecleaners $10 an hour to clean customers' homes. The gross receipts of the business for the year were $500,000 and its total expenses were $450,000. Employees of Eastside are permitted to purchase cleaning services at a 20 percent discount. Mary hires the service to clean her apartment once a week for $40, which is 20 percent less than the ordinary price of $50. Is Mary subject to tax on the $10 discount?

17. Carol is an attorney employed by Bears Investments. Bears is in the business of purchasing and selling stock, bonds, and limited partnership interests in various new businesses. Bears' gross profit percentage is 10 percent. Bears permits its employees to purchase investments at a 5 percent discount. Carol purchases $20,000 of such investments for $19,000. What are the tax consequences to Carol?

18. Jack is the sales manager of Elegant Clothing, Inc., a corporation that runs a chain of men's clothing stores. The corporation permits senior sales managers, the vice president, and the president of the corporation to purchase clothing at a 25 percent discount. In the prior year, the corporation had sales of $5 million and its cost of goods sold was $3 million. Jack purchases $1,000 of clothing for $750. What are the tax consequences to Jack?

19. Joan is an associate for a large law firm. State whether each of the following benefits is excludable as a §132(d) working condition fringe.
    a. Joan travels to New York to take a deposition. The firm pays for her travel, meals, and lodging.
    b. Each day the firm hires a caterer to provide sandwiches and soft drinks for all employees who wish to eat in their offices. Joan takes advantage of this free lunch two or three times a week.
    c. The firm provides Joan with free parking in the office building housing the law firm. It would cost Joan $100 per month to purchase such parking herself.
    d. At Joan's request, the firm buys her a subscription to The Litigation News, a weekly legal magazine. She is the only member of the firm who reads the magazine and, with the firm's permission, she discards the periodical after reading it.

20. Albert says, "In general, the Treasury does not lose revenue by the exclusion of working condition fringe benefits from an individual's gross income. If working condition fringe benefits were included in the individual's gross income, the taxpayer would be able to deduct the same amount as a business expense." Is Albert correct? (Before answering, take a look at §§63 and 67.)

21. a. Ellen works at a small rural law firm. Her employer pays for her dinners, which are delivered to the firm on those occasional evenings when she has to work late. Is Ellen taxed on the value of the dinners?
    b. Instead of paying for dinners delivered to the firm, the firm gives Ellen a cash meal allowance for her dinners when she works late. Is Ellen taxed on the meal allowance?

22. a. Andy works at a large urban law firm. His employer pays for his dinners, which are delivered to the firm on the five to ten days a month when he works late. Is Andy taxed on the value of the dinners?
    b. Instead of paying for dinners delivered to the firm, the firm gives Andy a cash meal allowance for his dinners when he works late. Is Andy taxed on the meal allowance?

23. Debby works for Ace Accountants. Ace provides free coffee, soda, and donuts to its employees. Is Debby taxed on the value of the refreshments?

24. a. Susan works for Able, Baker & Gonzalez, a large downtown law firm. In order to encourage their attorneys and staff to keep fit, the firm will pay 50 percent of the cost of any health club membership that an employee purchases. The firm reimburses Susan for $500 of a $1,000 fee that she paid for membership in the Downtown Squash and Tennis Club. Can Susan exclude the $500 reimbursement from her income?
    b. What if the law firm instead built exercise facilities on the firm premises for its employees and allowed Susan to use it at no charge?

25. Urban Hospital sets the meal prices at its cafeteria at a level just high enough to cover its operating costs, so the cafeteria meals are considerably less expensive than comparable meals at off-site restaurants. Jane, a doctor at the hospital, saves approximately $20 per week by eating at the cafeteria. Is Jane taxed on the savings?

26. Sam is the general manager of the Mountainview Country Club restaurant. The Club charges an annual membership fee of $1,000. In addition, the Club charges members $80 per round of golf and $20 per hour of tennis court time. However, employees and their dependents are allowed to use the facilities free of charge. Sam and his wife play tennis at the club two to three times a week. Is Sam taxed on the value of the free court time?

27. Mark is a professional hockey player for the Boston Brawlers. During the off-season Mark lives in Mystic, Connecticut. The Brawlers purchase a membership for Mark in a Mystic health club at a cost of $2,000 and hire a private trainer at a cost of $3,000 to supervise Mark's workouts. Is Mark taxed on the cost of the club membership and trainer?

28. In each circumstance described below, state whether the value of the transportation-related fringe benefit is taxable to employees receiving the benefit, and, if so, the amount that would be included. Assume the employees received the benefit in 2014.
    a. The Arnold Manufacturing Company provides free parking for employees who drive to work. The value of the parking is $250 per month.
    b. Betty's Furniture World provides free parking only to its highly compensated employees. The value of the parking is $250 per month.

    c. Carol's Cakes reimburses its employees for their monthly job-related parking costs, up to a maximum of $250 per month.

    d. Dan's Drapes provides its employees with monthly mass transit passes. The value of the monthly passes is $125 per month.

    e. Earl's Enterprises hires a taxi (with a driver) to pick up its top executives and drive them to work. Typically, two or three executives are driven to work in each cab. The value of the cab rides to each executive is $125 per month.

    f. Fabian's Flip-Flops reimburses its employees for the cost of purchasing and maintaining high-end road bicycles that the employees regularly use to commute from their homes to the Flip-Flop store and headquarters on Miami Beach. The value of the bicycle reimbursement is $125 per month.

Explanations

10. The flight is not taxable to Dean. Under §132(a)(1), an employee may exclude from gross income a fringe benefit that qualifies as a no-additional-cost service. Section 132(b) defines a *no-additional-cost service* as a service provided by an employer to an employee if such service is offered for sale to customers "in the ordinary course of the line of business of the employer in which the employee is performing services" and if the employer incurs no substantial additional cost (including forgone revenue) in providing such services to the employee.

    Dean meets all of these tests. His employer, the airline, is providing the service, is in the business of selling flights to the public, and will incur no substantial additional costs in providing Dean with the seat on the plane since the seat would not otherwise be occupied by a paying customer. If, on the other hand, Dean were permitted to reserve a seat on the flight, he would be taxed on its value because he might displace a paying customer. Reg. §1.132-2(c).

11. The flight is taxable to Donald. A taxpayer may exclude a no-additional-cost service from income only if the taxpayer's employer offers the service to customers. §132(b)(1). Here Donald's employer is a retailer of tools and, quite obviously, does not sell airplane flights to its customers.

12. The flight does not qualify for the §132 no-additional-cost service exclusion. Although the company will not incur an additional expense by allowing Sarah to "hitch a ride," the flight is not a §132 no-additional-cost service because Jones Books, Inc. does not offer airline service for sale to customers in the ordinary course of its business. §132(b)(1). How much does Sarah have to include in income?

Regulation §1.61-21(g)(12) provides a special valuation rule where most of the passengers on a company airplane are traveling for business and an employee "hitches a ride" on the plane. This special (and admittedly obscure) valuation rule may permit Sarah to exclude the value of the flight. The regulation provides that if at least half of the seats on the employer's airplane are occupied by employees traveling primarily for the employer's business, the value of the flight to the employee traveling for personal reasons will be deemed to be zero.

13. a. The free passes do not deprive the theater of substantial revenue it would otherwise earn and the theater is in the business of selling seats to movies, so the benefit would qualify as a no-additional-cost service. §132(b)(2).
   b. The tax treatment of the benefit does not change. Under §132(h)(2)(A), the spouse and dependent children of an employee are treated as employees for purposes of both §132(a)(1) (no-additional-cost service) and §132(a)(2) (qualified employee discount).
   c. The tax treatment of the benefit does not change. Under §132(h)(1), an employee who is retired or disabled or a surviving spouse of an employee is treated as an employee for purposes of §132(a)(1), (2).
   d. Here the free tickets would be taxable to Allison. To qualify for exclusion under §132, the free service must be provided by the line of business in which the employee is performing services. §132(b)(1). This rule is designed to prevent employees of corporations that operate a number of different types of businesses from receiving a wide variety of services on a tax-free basis.
   e. Allison is not taxed on her free admissions to the movie theaters owned by the rival company. Under §132(i), two or more employers are permitted to make a reciprocal agreement for the provision of tax-free no-additional-cost services to their employees. Such agreements must be in writing and neither employer may incur any substantial additional cost (including forgone revenue) in providing such service pursuant to the agreement. If these conditions are met, as they are here, services provided to an employee by any party to such a reciprocal agreement will be treated as though they were provided by the employee's actual employer.

14. Betty is taxed on the use of the tanning salon. The §132 exclusions for no-additional-cost services and qualified employee discounts are available to highly compensated employees only if the nondiscrimination requirement of §132(j)(1) is met. That requirement is not met here because the fringe benefit is not available on substantially the same terms to both highly compensated and non-highly compensated employees.

15. a. None of the discount is taxable. Section 132(a)(2) excludes from income the amount of any "qualified employee discount." In the case of a discount on goods, the discount may be excluded from income only to the extent it does not exceed the gross profit percentage of the price at which property is being offered by the employer to customers. §132(c)(1)(A). *Gross profit percentage* equals:

$$\frac{\text{aggregate sale price} - \text{aggregate cost of}}{\text{of goods sold} \qquad \text{goods sold}}$$
$$\text{aggregate sale price of goods sold}$$

Said another way, the gross profit percentage is equal to the gross profit on goods sold divided by the aggregate sale price of goods. The calculation must be based on the employer's sales during a representative period. §132(c)(2)(B)(ii).

In this problem, the aggregate sale price of goods sold is $600,000 and the aggregate cost of goods is $400,000. City Sporting Goods' gross profit percentage is 33.33 percent, which is:

$$\frac{\$600,000 - \$400,000}{\$600,000}$$

Albert is given a discount of one-third or 33.33 percent. This discount equals, but does not exceed, the gross profit percentage and otherwise meets the requirements of §132 so the discount will not be taxable to Albert. The amount that the employer paid for the particular item sold to the employee at a discount is irrelevant for purposes of §132.

b. In this case, Albert's employee discount of 50 percent exceeds the gross profit percentage of 33.33 percent, so Albert is taxed on the excess discount. The maximum permissible discount of 33.33 percent would reduce the price of the ski outfit to $160. Albert paid $120 for the outfit, so he must include the $40 difference in his gross income.

16. No. Section 132(c)(1)(B) defines a qualified employee discount on services as a discount that does not exceed 20 percent of the price at which the service is offered to customers. The employer's profit percentage and cost of providing the service are irrelevant. Here the discount provided to Eastside employees equals but does not exceed 20 percent, so Mary may exclude the value of the discount from her gross income.

17. Carol must include the $1,000 in her gross income. Discounts on property held for investment (as well as discounts on real property) are not excludable from income. §132(c)(4).

18. Jack must include the $250 discount in his gross income because the discount does not meet the requirements of §132. As in the case of no-additional-cost services, employee discounts provided to highly compensated employees are excluded from gross income only if the discount is provided on substantially the same terms to both highly compensated and non-highly compensated employees. §132(j)(1). The discount offered by Elegant Clothing, Inc. is only available to employees who are probably highly compensated employees within the definition of §132(j)(6), so the discount fails the nondiscrimination requirement.

19. a. The payment of the expenses of the New York trip is excludable as a working condition fringe under §132(a)(3). Working condition fringes are defined in §132(d) as property or services provided to an employee to the extent that the employee would have been able to take a §162 trade or business deduction or §167 depreciation deduction had the employee paid for the services or property. If Joan had paid these travel expenses herself, she would have been able to deduct the expenses under §162, as ordinary and necessary business expenses, so the payment of the items by her employer will be considered a working condition fringe. Trade or business expenses and depreciation are considered in more detail in later sections of this book. It is worth noting here, however, that Joan's employer would be permitted to deduct only 50 percent of the cost of Joan's meals. See §274(n).

    b. The free meals do not qualify as a §132(d) working condition fringe because an employee buying her own lunches would not be able to deduct the cost of lunches under these circumstances. However, if the law firm provides the free meals so that the lawyers in the firm work through lunch and bill more hours, the meals may be provided "for the convenience of the employer" so Joan may be able to exclude the value of the meals under §119.

    c. Joan would not be able to deduct the cost of parking if she purchased it herself, so the payment would not be excludable as a working condition fringe. The value of the free parking would be excludable, however, as a qualified transportation fringe under §132(f)(1)(C).

    d. Joan would be able to deduct the cost of the subscription as a business expense under §162 if she had purchased it herself, so the cost is excludable as a working condition fringe under §132.

20. No. The exclusion is more valuable than the corresponding business expense deduction for most taxpayers. First, certain employee business expenses are deductible only if a taxpayer itemizes deductions. §63. Second, employee business expenses generally are deductible only to the extent they exceed 2 percent of the taxpayer's adjusted gross income. §67.

21. a. Ellen is not taxed on the value of the dinners. If the meals furnished to Ellen at the law firm are provided for the convenience of the employer (so that Ellen will work late), the meals qualify for the §119 exclusion. In the alternative, Ellen can exclude the meals as a §132(e) de minimis fringe because the meals are provided only occasionally and to allow her to extend her normal work hours. Reg. §1.132-6(d)(2).

    b. Ellen can exclude the meal money, which qualifies as a de minimis fringe because the meals are provided only occasionally and so that she can extend her normal work hours. §132(e), Reg. §1.132-6(d)(2).

22. a. Andy is probably not taxed on the value of the dinners. It is not totally clear whether the meals would qualify as a de minimis fringe, under §132(e), because the meals have probably been provided more than occasionally. However, even if the meals are not within §132(e), Andy can exclude the value of the meals under §119 if the meals are furnished "for the convenience of the employer" (for example, so that Andy will work late).

    b. It is uncertain whether Andy will be permitted to exclude the value of the dinners from his gross income. Cash meal allowances do not qualify for the §119 exclusion. Commissioner v. Kowalski, 434 U.S. 77 (1977). However, the meals may qualify for exclusion as a §132(e) de minimis fringe. Section 132(e) defines a de minimis fringe as a property or service the value of which is so small (taking into account the frequency with which similar fringes are provided to the employer's employees) as to make accounting for it unreasonable or administratively impracticable.

       Regulation §1.132-6(d)(2) states that meal money qualifies as a de minimis fringe benefit if it is reasonable and satisfies three conditions. First, the meal money must be provided only on an occasional basis. Second, it must be provided because overtime work necessitates an extension of the employee's normal work schedule. Third (and somewhat repetitively), the meal money must be provided to enable the employee to work overtime.

       The application of these provisions to these facts raises more questions than answers. Is the providing of one or two meals per week "occasional"? What is Andy's "normal workday"? If Andy works late once per week and spends $20 per meal, the annual amount of employer-provided meal money will be approximately $1,000. Is $1,000 a small amount? Would it be unreasonable or administratively impracticable to record each meal payment? Would it be relevant whether the firm keeps such records for purposes of billing clients?

Regulation §1.132-6(b)(1) provides that if an employer provides a free meal to one employee on a daily basis, the value of the meals is not de minimis even though with respect to the entire workforce the meals are provided infrequently. On the other hand, the regulation states that where it would be "administratively difficult" to determine frequency with respect to individual employees, the frequency with which the fringes are provided to employees in general is considered rather than the frequency with which the individual employees receive them. Reg. §1.132-6(b)(2). The special rule of Regulation §1.132-6(b)(2) does not apply, however, for purposes of applying Regulation §1.132-6(d)(2).

As a practical matter, Andy may be able to justify taking a "reporting position" on his return that excludes the meal money from income. However, the Service and some courts might take the position that Andy receives meals more than "occasionally" and that the meals cannot be excluded as a §132(e) de minimis fringe.

23. No. The value of the refreshments is small and it would be administratively difficult to keep track of each individual's consumption, so the refreshments qualify for exclusion as a §132(e) de minimis fringe. Reg. §1.132-6(e)(1).

24. a. The $500 payment is taxable to Susan. Regulation §1.132-6(e)(2) states that membership in a private country club or athletic facility will not qualify as a de minimis fringe.
   b. If the law firm built exercise facilities on the firm's premises for its employees, Susan would not have to include in her income the value of the use of those facilities. §132(j)(4).

25. No. Section 132(e)(2). Note that, even if the hospital gave Jane free meals in the hospital cafeteria, she would probably still be able to exclude the value of the meals under §119.

26. Sam will be taxed on the fringe benefit if his use of the court deprives the club of revenue it might have obtained from members. Thus, Sam's use is likely to be tax-free only if he uses the court on a stand-by (rather than on a reservation) basis, so that his use can qualify as a no-additional-cost fringe benefit. §132(a)(1), §132(b).

Use of the tennis courts is not tax-free as an on-premises athletic facility under §132(j)(4) because that exclusion only applies where substantially all the use of the facility is by employees of the employer, their spouses, and their dependent children. §132(j)(4)(B)(iii).

27. No. These costs would be excluded as a working condition fringe since training costs are ordinary and necessary business expenses of a professional athlete. If training were not an ordinary and necessary expense in his profession, Mark would be taxed on these fringe benefits.

28. a. The free parking is nontaxable as a qualified transportation fringe under §132(a)(5) and (f)(1)(C). Note that §132(f)(2)(B) limits the value of free parking to $175 per month but, for tax year 2014, that figure was inflation adjusted upward to $250. Rev. Proc. 2013-35.

   b. The free parking still is nontaxable as a qualified transportation fringe under §132(a)(5) and (f)(1)(C). The nondiscrimination requirement does not apply to qualified transportation fringe benefits.

   c. The free parking again is nontaxable as a qualified transportation fringe under §132(a)(5) and (f)(1)(C). Section 132(f)(3) provides that free parking may be provided directly or through cash reimbursement.

   d. The transit passes are nontaxable as a qualified transportation fringe under §132(a)(5) and (f)(1)(B). Although §132(f)(2)(A) limits the excludable value of transit passes to $100 per month, the inflation adjusted limit for transit passes is $130 per month in 2014. §132(f)(6), Rev. Proc. 2013-35.

   e. The top executives are taxed on the full value of the cab ride. In order to qualify as a commuter highway vehicle (i) the vehicle must have a seating capacity of at least six adults (not including the driver) and (ii) at least 80 percent of the mileage must be incurred in transporting employees to and from work and on trips during which at least one-half the seats are filled with employees. §132(f)(5)(B). Neither condition is met here.

   f. Section 132(f)(5)(F)(ii) limits the excludable amount of bicycle reimbursements to $20 per month. Employees who receive bicycle reimbursements in excess of the exclusion limit must include the reimbursement in excess of the limit. Employees receiving $125 per month of reimbursement for bicycle commuting expenses must include $105 per month in income. Note that the amount of tax-free benefit available for bicycle commuting is much less than the amount of tax-free benefit available through employer-provided parking, transit passes, or transportation in a commuter highway vehicle.

C. IMPUTED INCOME

Almost everyone agrees that persons ought to be taxed on increases in wealth realized through wages. But what about increases in wealth realized through non-market transactions? If the individual who spends his salary on food and lodging is subject to tax, should the individual who grows his own food and builds his own home be subject to tax as well? As a practical matter, the answer to the latter question is "No." Taxation of imputed income raises seemingly insurmountable problems of valuation and liquidity and may be objectionable for other reasons. Do we really want a system that monitors whether we clean our home ourselves (rather than employ a maid or cleaning service) and then taxes us on the value of our housekeeping efforts?

Nonetheless, nontaxation of imputed income raises equity and efficiency problems. As noted in the questions below, one effect is to encourage persons to provide services in the home rather than accept "formal" jobs outside the home.

Examples

29. Xavier receives $12 per hour working as an accountant. A cleaning service would charge him $10 an hour to clean his home. He can save the $10 an hour fee by cleaning his own home rather than hiring the cleaning service. Xavier likes (or dislikes) cleaning as much as accounting.

    a. In a tax-free world, will Xavier clean his own house or will he work as an accountant?

    b. If Xavier is taxed on the value of both his accounting and his cleaning at a 25 percent rate, will he clean his own house or will he work as an accountant?

    c. If Xavier's accounting income is taxed at a 25 percent rate but his imputed income from cleaning his own home is not subject to tax, will he clean his own house or will he work as an accountant?

30. Larry has $400,000. He can use the money to purchase a home and an automobile. Alternatively, Larry can invest the money at 8 percent interest and use the interest income ($32,000 per year) to rent an equivalent home and automobile. Assume Larry is taxed at a 35 percent rate. What should he do?

31. Denise, who is taxed at a 25 percent rate, is offered $12 per hour to work on Saturday. Denise values her weekend leisure at $10 per hour. Will she work on Saturday?

32. Which, if any, of the following provide untaxed imputed income?
    a. ownership of a home;
    b. ownership of a pound of flour;
    c. ownership of a tuxedo;
    d. ownership of an automobile;
    e. driving oneself to work;
    f. filling out a tax return without the aid of an accountant.

33. Sheila, who has worked for Xenon Corporation for 10 years, accepts a new job with Yaba Corporation. The jobs differ in only one significant respect: Xenon is located in an industrial area and the office in which Sheila worked has poor lighting and ventilation. Yaba offered Sheila an attractive, comfortable office with a beautiful view. Sheila regards her new office as a valuable benefit of her new job. Indeed, Sheila regards her new environment as equal to a $5,000 per year pay increase. Is Sheila taxed on the improvement in her working environment?

34. Reconsider the forms of imputed income discussed in examples 29-33 above. Can you think of any ways to directly or indirectly tax such income? Are there any other measures that might offset the distortion and unfairness caused by nontaxation of such income?

Explanations

29. a. Xavier will work as an accountant and earn an extra $2 per hour.
    b. Xavier would still choose to work as an accountant. The $12 per hour he earns, less the tax of 25 percent, yields $9 per hour after-tax. The $10 per hour he earns cleaning his own home yields only $7.50 per hour after-tax.
    c. Xavier will clean his own home and earn $10 an hour tax-free. Work as an accountant will pay Xavier only $9 per hour ($12 less 25 percent tax) after-tax.

30. Larry should purchase the home and car. Unlike interest income, the imputed rental value of the home and car are not taxed. If Larry earns $32,000 per year of taxable interest and uses that amount to rent an equivalent home and car, he'll find himself with an additional tax burden of $11,200 per year.

31. No. If she works on Saturday, she will earn only $9 an hour ($12 less 25 percent tax), $1 less per hour than the imputed value of her leisure. Note that Denise would choose to work on Saturday if both income and leisure were taxed or if neither income nor leisure were taxed.

32. All choices except (b) involve untaxed imputed income. The rental value of an owner-occupied home is not taxed. Similarly, an individual who

owns a tuxedo or an automobile is not taxed on its rental value. Flour, on the other hand, does not produce imputed rent. Unlike a home or a tuxedo, flour is consumed when it is used. Driving oneself to work and doing one's own tax return produce untaxed imputed income from services.

33. No. The move to a more attractive office clearly enriches Sheila. As stated in the example, Sheila's welfare is improved as much as it would be by a $5,000 raise. However, this kind of employer-provided fringe benefit is treated as a form of imputed income and it is not subject to tax because of valuation, reporting, and other problems. The nontaxation of imputed income does not depend on the existence of a statutory exclusion.

34. We could directly tax imputed income from home ownership by determining the rental value of the home and taxing the homeowner on that amount. (In fact, that approach was taken as recently as the Civil War!) We could do the same for automobile ownership. On the zanier side, we might indirectly tax the imputed income one receives from leisure by levying excise (or sales) taxes on leisure-related goods and services (for example, television sets, tennis balls, ski lift tickets), or by subjecting leisure-related businesses to an additional layer of income tax. That way, to return to example 31, Denise might end up (indirectly) paying a tax whether she works or not. (But what could we do about Sheila or those persons who obtain imputed income from a walk in the park?)

    Somewhat more realistically, we could remove the distortion and inefficiency caused by the nontaxation of household services by allowing individuals who accept jobs paying taxable wages to deduct the cost of obtaining household services. In example 29, we could allow Xavier to deduct the cost of hiring a cleaning service or a child care provider. That would allow Xavier to earn tax-free income equal to the cost of the provided household services. If Xavier provided the services himself, he would have tax-free imputed income. Alternatively, Xavier could accept a formal job and the taxable income he receives that is used to pay for the household services would be offset by the deduction for those services. If Xavier earns $12 per hour, $10 of which goes to pay for child care and cleaning services, then Xavier would have gross income of $12, offset by a $10 deduction, for a taxable income of $2. In effect, the money used to pay household services would be tax-free.

    We could remove the distortion illustrated by example 30 by allowing individuals who rent to deduct their rental payments. That way, Larry ends up with no taxable income from his $400,000 investment whether he purchases the car and home or invests his funds and uses the taxable interest from the investment to rent the car and home.

    There is no practical way to eliminate the distortion illustrated in example 31. Although, as noted above, we can attempt to tax leisure indirectly by taxing leisure-related goods and services, it is impossible to remove the distortion completely. We can't very well allow individuals to deduct from wages the value of the leisure they could have received tax-free.

D. WINDFALLS, GIFTS, SCHOLARSHIPS, PRIZES, AND TRANSFER PAYMENTS

I. Windfalls

Early in the last century, the term "income" was narrowly defined in cases as the gain from capital, from labor, or from both combined. See, e.g., Eisner v. Macomber, 252 U.S. 189 (1920). However, in a later case, Commissioner v. Glenshaw Glass, 348 U.S. 426 (1955), the Supreme Court expanded the definition of income to include any "undeniable accessions to wealth, clearly realized, and over which the taxpayers have complete dominion." Applying this definition of income, the Supreme Court held that Glenshaw Glass had to include in its gross income punitive damages it received in settlement of an antitrust lawsuit.

The *Glenshaw Glass* case is cited narrowly for the proposition that taxpayers must include in income any windfalls they receive, and broadly for its expansive definition of income. The *Glenshaw Glass* definition of income is consistent with the Haig-Simons definition of income. Under this definition it is irrelevant whether the taxpayer, through the provision of her labor or capital, "earned" the income; instead, what matters is whether receipt of the item increased the taxpayer's wealth.

Cesarini v. United States, 296 F. Supp. 3 (N.D. Ohio 1969), is another famous case involving the receipt of a windfall by a taxpayer. The lucky taxpayer in *Cesarini* bought an old piano for $15 at an auction and later discovered almost $4,500 in cash hidden in the piano. The court held that the cash was income to the taxpayers in the year in which they found it, citing *Glenshaw Glass*, as well as a revenue ruling and treasury regulation, both of which provided that a taxpayer must include the value of "treasure trove" in income in the year in which the taxpayer discovers it and reduces it to possession. Note, however, that the circumstances in *Cesarini* should be distinguished from situations in which a taxpayer discovers that something that he had bought was worth more than he originally paid for it. In the latter situation the taxpayer would not have an income inclusion until the property was sold or exchanged — in other words, until the gain was "realized." (For more on the realization requirement, see Chapter 3 of this book.)

Examples

35. a. In year one, Ellie pays $300 for an antique dresser at an estate sale. In year three, as Ellie is refinishing the dresser, she finds that one of the dresser drawers has a false back. When she removes the false back, she discovers $10,000. Does Ellie have to include the value of the money in income, and, if so, in which year?

    b. Assume that, in year three, instead of finding the money, Ellie discovers that the dresser is a rare antique, worth $10,000. Later, in year five, Ellie sells the dresser for $12,000. What amounts, if any, does Ellie have to include in income, with respect to the dresser, in years three and five?

Explanations

35. a. Ellie must include $10,000 in income in year three, the year in which she discovers the money and reduces it to possession. Cesarini v. United States, 296 F. Supp. 3 (N.D. Ohio 1969) and Reg. §1.61-14.

    b. Ellie does not have an income inclusion in year three, the year in which she discovers that the dresser is worth $10,000, because the gain has not yet been realized. In year five, in which Ellie sells the dresser for $12,000, she realizes and recognizes $11,700 of gain because the $12,000 amount realized exceeds her $300 basis in the dresser by that amount. §§1001(a), (b), (c), and 1012. Under §61(a)(3), Ellie must include in gross income the $11,700 of gain from dealings in property.

2. Gifts and Bequests

Reading: §§102, 1014, 1015.

If we applied *Glenshaw Glass* and the Haig-Simons definition of income to gifts, what would be the tax consequence to the donee of a gift? The gift would increase the donee's wealth, so the donee would have to include the gift in income (and the donor might be allowed a corresponding deduction for the gift). However, we have not adopted this approach: Instead, §102 provides that a donee excludes gifts from income.

Gifts are generally included in the donor's tax base (that is, the donor generally cannot deduct the gift) and excluded from the donee's base instead of being excluded (that is, deducted) from the donor's tax base and included by the donee. This tax treatment is best justified, perhaps, on the grounds that most gifts are made to family members. It makes sense in such circumstances to treat the family as a single taxable unit and ignore both the nominal decline in the donor's wealth and the corresponding increase in the donee's wealth.

Even if gifts are made to donees outside the family, the rule requiring inclusion of the gift in the donor's base is generally easier to administer than requiring inclusion in the donee's base. Consider, for example, the tax treatment of 10,000 commuters each giving a subway panhandler a dollar. It is much easier to collect tax on the $10,000 from the donors, by leaving that amount in their tax base, than it would be to collect it from the donee panhandler. Note, however, that, if the donor is in a higher tax bracket than the donee (which is often the case), more tax is owed under the current approach than would be owed if the donee were taxed on the gift.

What about gifts of appreciated or depreciated property? If, at the time of transfer, the fair market value of the property is equal to or greater than the basis of the property in the hands of the donor, the rule is simple: The donee takes the donor's basis. Suppose, for example, that Mother owns a piece of property. She paid $20 for the property so that is her basis in the property under §1012. Mother gives Daughter the property after it has appreciated in value to $50. At the time of the gift, the property has "built-in gain" of $30 (because the $50 value of the property exceeds Mother's $20 basis by $30). Instead of taxing Mother on the $30 pre-gift appreciation in the property, that gain is deferred until Daughter sells the property. This is accomplished by assigning Daughter a basis in the property equal to Mother's basis of $20. If Daughter then sells the property for $50, she will realize the $30 of gain that was inherent in the property at the time of the gift. §§1001(a), 1015(a).

If the property has declined in value in the hands of the donor so that the fair market value of the property at the time of transfer is less than the donor's basis in the property, the rule is more complicated. For the purpose of determining *gain* on a subsequent disposition of the property by the donee, the donee again takes the donor's basis. However, for the purpose of determining *loss* on a subsequent disposition of the property by the donee, the donee takes a basis equal to the fair market value of the property at the time of transfer. §1015(a). To illustrate the operation of this rule, suppose Mother gives property worth $10, with a $20 basis, to Daughter. If Daughter sells the property for $10, she realizes no loss because, for the purpose of determining loss, the property has a basis equal to its $10 fair market value at the time of transfer. Now suppose that Daughter sells the property for $15. For the purpose of determining loss, Daughter has a basis of $10 and so realizes no loss. For the purpose of determining gain, Daughter inherits a basis of $20 and so realizes no gain. Thus, Daughter realizes neither gain nor loss on the sale.

In other words, if a taxpayer sells property that she received as an inter vivos gift (that is, not as a bequest), compute her gain or loss from the sale of the property as follows: First, if at the time she received the gift, the fair market value of the property transferred was greater or equal to the donor's basis, the donee takes the donor's basis. On a subsequent disposition of the property by the donee, she has gain to the extent that her amount realized on the sale exceeds her basis.

Suppose, on the other hand, the property declined in value in the donor's hands so that the property had a basis greater than its fair market value at the time the donee received the gift (that is, the property had "built-in loss"). On a subsequent disposition of the property by the donee, first apply the "gain rule" and give the donee the same basis as the donor. If that produces a gain to the donee, you have finished your calculations. If that calculation does not produce a gain, apply the "loss rule" and give the donee a basis in the property equal to its fair market value at the time of transfer. The donee realizes the amount of loss that results from that calculation. If, as was the case in the preceding example, the gain rule does not produce a gain and the loss rule does not produce a loss, the donee realizes neither gain nor loss on the sale.

If a beneficiary receives a gift as a bequest upon the death of the donor, the beneficiary excludes the gift from income, again under §102. However, under these circumstances the beneficiary's basis will not be determined under §1015. The special basis rule of §1014 will instead apply. Property acquired by reason of death takes a basis in the hands of the beneficiary equal to its fair market value on the date of the decedent's death (or, as provided in §2032(a), six months after the decedent's death). §1014(a)(1). The date-of-death basis rule means that the appreciation of the property during the decedent's lifetime will *never* be taxed. The date-of-death rule thus encourages individuals to retain appreciated property until their death, but to sell before death any property that has declined in value. (Some commentators have described the tax-free step-up in basis of appreciated property at death as the single largest loophole in the income tax.)

Neither §102 nor any other Code section defines the term *gift*. The Supreme Court, however, has defined a gift as a transfer that stems from the "detached and disinterested" generosity of the donor. Commissioner v. Duberstein, 363 U.S. 278 (1960). The *Duberstein* test, which focuses on the donor's state of mind, is subject to a number of exceptions.

For example, §102(c) explicitly provides that a transfer from an employer to an employee cannot be a gift. Thus, unless some other Code exclusion (for example, §132(e) or §74(c)) applies, even the rare transfer to an employee that arises from an employer's "detached and disinterested" generosity is taxable compensation to the employee. (If an employer occasionally gives employees inexpensive gifts, such as Christmas turkeys, the employees may still be able to exclude the value of the gifts as a §132 de minimis fringe. Employees can also exclude the value of certain achievement awards from their employers, under §74(c).)

What if a taxpayer receives tips from customers? Can the tips be characterized as gifts for purposes of §102? Regulation §1.61-2(a)(1) specifically provides that tips that constitute compensation for services must be included in gross income. What if it is not clear that the tips were compensation for services? In Olk v. United States, 536 F.2d 876 (9th Cir. 1976), the issue was whether a craps dealer at a casino could exclude the tips (in the form of "tokes") he received from gamblers. The district court in the case found that the tokes were not given as compensation for services, but were instead given by gamblers as a result of "impulsive generosity" or "superstition." Applying the *Duberstein* test, the court concluded that the dealer could exclude the tokes as gifts. However, the court of appeals reversed the district court, concluding that the gamblers' generosity was not "detached and disinterested" and that tokes were not gifts within §102. (The court also was not convinced that the transfers were noncompensatory since the tokes were received by the taxpayer as a result of being employed as a dealer.)

Examples

36. On his 39th birthday Steven receives a $10,000 gift from his mother, and (as luck would have it) a $15,000 bequest distributed from his late aunt's estate. Is Steven required to include the gift and/or the bequest in income?

37. Carol gives Doug a parcel of land. The parcel has a basis in Carol's hands of $50,000; however, the fair market value of the parcel is only $40,000.
    a. Doug sells the parcel the next year for $60,000. Determine Doug's realized and recognized gain or loss on the sale.
    b. Doug sells the parcel the next year for $35,000. Determine Doug's realized and recognized gain or loss on the sale.
    c. Doug sells the parcel the next year for $45,000. Determine Doug's realized and recognized gain or loss on the sale.

38. Ms. Moneybags gives her daughter 1,000 shares of Xenon stock. Ms. Moneybags paid $10,000 for the stock, which is worth $100,000 at the time of the transfer.
    a. Assume the gift is made while Ms. Moneybags is still alive. What is her daughter's basis in the stock?
    b. Assume the stock is transferred upon Ms. Moneybags's death in 2014. What is her daughter's basis in the stock?

39. a. Ski resort owner Max Mogul contracts with Home Builders, to plan and complete a new lodge for his resort. The owners and principal employees of Home Builders, Inc. are architect Amy and contractor Ken. The lodge is completed on schedule. Max Mogul pays Home Builders, Inc. the agreed price for the work and gives both Amy and Ken nontransferable gift certificates for $1,000 ski outfits from the shop at his ski resort. As Mr. Mogul hands them the gift certificates, he tells them that the certificates are in appreciation for the excellent

quality of their work. Are Amy and Ken taxed on the value of the gift certificates? Is it relevant to inquire whether Max Mogul deducted the cost of the certificates as a business expense?

b. Assume instead that Amy and Ken are Max Mogul's employees. In addition to paying them their normal salaries for the work that they did on the lodge, he gives them the gift certificates. Are Amy and Ken taxed on the value of the gift certificates?

40. New York City taxi driver Tom takes Fred to the airport. Fares are set by city ordinance and cannot be raised by agreement of the parties. However, taxi drivers are allowed to accept unsolicited tips. Fred pays the fare and gives Tom a $20 tip. Is Tom taxed on the tip?

41. Lawyer Leslie sends each of her clients a $40 bottle of wine each Christmas. Are the clients taxed on the value of the wine? Is the cost of the wine deductible to Leslie?

42. Under current law, donees exclude gifts received from income and donors cannot generally deduct the gifts they make. Assume that §102 is amended to provide that donees have to include gifts in income.
a. Why might such a change be justified?
b. What practical problems might be posed by a law that taxed all gifts as income?

Explanations

36. No. Gifts and bequests are excluded from the recipient's gross income. §102(a).

37. a. This example illustrates the special §1015 basis rule and the calculation of gain or loss on the sale of property that was received as a gift by donee Doug. For the purpose of determining *gain*, Doug inherits Carol's basis of $50,000. The property is sold for $60,000, so Doug realizes and recognizes $10,000 of gain. §§1001, 1015(a).
b. Doug's $35,000 amount realized is less than Doug's $50,000 basis in the property, so there is no gain. Is there a loss? The $40,000 value of the property was less than its $50,000 basis at the time of transfer, so, for the purpose of determining loss, the donee has a basis equal to the value of the property at the time of transfer, in this case $40,000. The property is sold for $35,000, so the donee, Doug, realizes and recognizes a $5,000 loss ($40,000 basis less the $35,000 amount realized). §§1001, 1015(a).
c. Doug's $45,000 amount realized is less than his $50,000 basis in the property, so there is no gain on the sale. The $40,000 value of

the property was less than its $50,000 basis at the time of transfer, so, for the purpose of determining loss, the donee has a basis equal to the value of the property at the time of transfer, in this case $40,000. The property is sold for $45,000, so there is no loss on the sale. Doug does not realize gain or loss on the sale.

38. a. The daughter will receive a carryover basis of $10,000 in the §1015(a). (Note that since the value of the property exceeds the donor's basis in the property at the time of the transfer, we do not have to worry about the special rule under which a different basis is used for calculating gain and loss.)

b. The daughter's stock basis will be stepped up to the $100,000 value at the date of the decedent's death. §1014(a).

39. a. The issue presented here is whether the gift certificates are gifts for tax purposes. In Commissioner v. Duberstein, 363 U.S. 278 (1960), the Supreme Court defined a gift for income tax purposes as a transfer made out of "detached and disinterested generosity." The taxpayer in that case regularly provided a list of potential customers to a metal manufacturer. The manufacturer provided the taxpayer with a new Cadillac. The Cadillac was unsolicited and, apparently, unexpected. The Court held that the transfer was intended as compensation for past service or an inducement for future service and, therefore, was taxable to the transferee.

The transfer here is also business-related and might be regarded as compensation for past services. Amy and Ken's argument for gift characterization will be helped if there is no prospect of ongoing work for the ski resort. And while the treatment of the transaction by the payor is not dispositive, Amy and Ken's argument for gift characterization will also be helped if the gift certificates are not deducted by Max Mogul as a business expense.

If the certificates are not treated as a gift, the receipt of the certificates will constitute income to Ken and Amy. But how much income should the two recognize? The certificates are not transferable. It may be that neither Ken nor Amy skis or wants to purchase ski outfits. In somewhat analogous circumstances, courts have taxed recipients of nontransferable property on amounts substantially less than the retail value of the property. See, e.g., United States v. Drescher, 179 F.2d 863 (2d Cir. 1950); Turner v. Commissioner, 11 T.C.M. 604 (1952).

If the certificates were transferable, Ken and Amy would recognize income equal to the lesser of the retail price of the certificates or, if the certificates were sold, the amount realized upon sale. See McCoy v. Commissioner, 38 T.C. 841 (1962) (where a game show contestant won a car and immediately sold it to a dealer at wholesale, the contestant was required to include in income the wholesale, not retail, value of the car). The obvious difficulty in determining how much income is recognized upon the receipt of the certificates might well lead a court to give Amy and Ken the benefit of the doubt and treat the receipt of the certificates as a gift.

b. Since Amy and Ken are Max Mogul's employees, the transfers cannot be excluded as gifts. §102(c). (However, Amy and Ken might be able to exclude all or a part of the value of the gift certificates under §132 or §74.)

40. Tom might argue that the tip constitutes a nontaxable gift under the *Duberstein* standard because it is made out of Fred's detached and disinterested generosity. Tom would point out that no tip is required and that Fred has nothing to "gain" by the tip since it is unlikely that Fred will ever again choose Tom's taxi.

   Not surprisingly, the government has always regarded tips as taxable compensation. Reg. §1.61-2(a)(1). The government's position has been upheld by the courts. Courts have held that there is an "element of compulsion" in tipping and that tips are intended as recompense for past services. See Killoran v. Commissioner, 709 F.2d 31 (9th Cir. 1983); Roberts v. Commissioner, 176 F.2d 221 (9th Cir. 1949) (both cases holding that taxi drivers must include tips in gross income). The fact that tips are regarded as compensation by the recipient, though irrelevant under the *Duberstein* test (which looks to the state of mind of the donor), forms an implicit basis for taxation in many of the cases. See, e.g., Olk v. United States, 536 F.2d 876 (9th Cir. 1976).

41. Section 274(b)(1) allows Leslie a business deduction for the first $25 per year of untaxed gifts made to each client. How does one determine the scope of the §274(b)(1) business gift exception? In practice, the exception appears to apply only to small gifts given to customers in an effort to bolster goodwill. Leslie's purchase appears to fit within the scope of the §274(b) business gift exception; the first $25 of the $40 cost of each bottle of wine would be deductible and the customers would not be taxed on the value of the wine.

42. a. The justification for including the value of gifts in income is that recipients are enriched by gifts. We tax individuals on other forms of enrichment, such as salary or investment return, so why not levy a tax on enrichment realized through gifts? Indeed, it seems odd to tax increases in wealth that require effort (such as wages) but to exclude an increase in wealth that for the most part is "unearned" and determined largely by relationship to those who are financially successful.

If we taxed recipients on the value of gifts, would we have to give donors a deduction? If so, the result would be a net loss for the Treasury since donors are generally in higher tax brackets than recipients. Henry Simons, the economist who, along with Robert Haig, is credited with the Haig-Simons definition of income, didn't think taxing the donee required giving the donor a deduction. Simons argued that for donors giving was a form of consumption and should be no more deductible than the cost of an expensive meal.

b. Most gifts are between family members, and a law that taxed donees on all gifts would be impossible to administer. Would we tax a child on the value of food and lodging provided by his parents? A teenager on her allowance? A 20-year-old on the value of a used car received as a gift? Would the exchange of Christmas presents generate tax liability all around?

We could get around some of these problems, at least, by requiring taxation only on gifts above a certain threshold amount. We could adopt, for example, a system similar to that used for estate and gift tax purposes and treat gifts as a taxable event only to the extent that the value of the gifts exceeded a certain floor. (The federal estate and gift tax system, which taxes transfers of property, is separate from the federal income tax. The estate and gift tax system applies to donors. Under that transfer tax system, a donor incurs no liability on the first $10,000, increased by an annual inflation adjustment, transferred each year to each donee. §2503(b). For 2014, the inflation adjusted amount was $14,000. Rev. Proc. 2013-35.)

On a more theoretical level, a system that treated the transfer of funds between family members as a taxable event seems somewhat odd, perhaps because in many ways we regard the family as a single unit for tax purposes.

3. Scholarships, Prizes, and Awards

Reading: §§74, 117.

Until 1954, courts cited the forerunner of §102 for the proposition that scholarships and some prizes and awards could be excluded from income. Since 1954 the Code has contained specific provisions governing the tax treatment of these items. In 1986, the exclusions for these items were substantially curtailed. Section 117 now excludes only "qualified scholarships" received by "degree candidates." A student is a *degree candidate* if she is a primary, secondary, undergraduate, or graduate student. Prop. Reg. §1.117-6(c)(4). A scholarship is *qualified* to the extent that it covers the student's tuition and required fees, books, and supplies. §117(b). Students must include in income scholarships that cover other incidental expenses such as room and board. Prop. Reg. §1.117-6(c)(2). The term *scholarship* includes both cash scholarships and tuition reductions (for example, tuition reductions for in-state students at state universities).

The exclusion for qualified scholarships does not apply to the extent that the scholarship is compensation for services, including teaching and research. §117(c). Does this exception to the exclusion apply to athletic scholarships? The answer may depend on the terms of the scholarship. If continued participation in the sport is required as a condition of retaining the scholarship, §117(c) would appear to apply. On the other hand, if the scholarship is not conditioned on the student continuing to play the sport, §117(c) would not apply. On a more practical level, the Service has, to date, not taken the position that athletic scholarships are within the §117(c) exception to the exclusion for qualified scholarships.

Section 74(a) provides that gross income includes amounts received as prizes or awards. There are limited exceptions, in §74(b) and (c), for prizes transferred directly to charities and for certain employee achievement awards.

Examples

43. Donna attends Private University. During the year, Donna spends (i) $28,000 on tuition, (ii) $2,000 on books and supplies, and (iii) $12,000 on room and board. Donna, a National Merit Scholar, receives a $42,000 scholarship designed to cover all of the above expenses. What portion, if any, of the scholarship is taxable to Donna?

44. Eastern Law School uses second- and third-year law students as teaching assistants in its first-year legal writing program. Many of the students hired as teaching assistants already are receiving scholarships from the law school for part of their tuition. The law school is considering giving all students selected as teaching assistants full tuition scholarships. Student teaching assistants who had previously received partial tuition scholarships would instead receive a full tuition scholarship. Discuss the tax consequences of this plan.

Explanations

43. Section 117 excludes from gross income scholarships covering tuition and required fees, books, supplies, and equipment at nonprofit schools. Thus, Donna excludes from gross income the portion of the scholarship that she spent on tuition and required books and supplies, $30,000. However, Donna must include in gross income the portion of the scholarship that she spent on room and board, $12,000.

44. As noted in the explanation for example 43 above, students exclude from gross income tuition scholarships. However, the exclusion does not apply to scholarships conditioned upon the performance of teaching, research, or other services, which students must include in gross income. §117(c). If the school replaces the old partial scholarships with full tuition teaching stipend scholarships, the students will have to pay more tax than they would have to pay if the school instead gives them (i) partial scholarships that are not conditioned on performing services and (ii) taxable teaching stipend scholarships only to cover the tuition not covered by the nontaxable partial scholarship.

4. Transfer Payments

Reading: §§85, 86.

Federal tax payments reduce an individual's wealth, but such payments are not deductible, of course, in determining federal tax liability (think about it). Government expenditures for items that benefit the public, on the other hand, may increase an individual's wealth. Is an individual's increased wealth due to such expenditures taxable? Generally speaking, the answer is no. Individuals are not taxed on the indirect increase in wealth due to government-supplied highways, education, and the like. (But if such expenditures increase the value of a taxpayer's assets, then the individual will be taxed on the increase when the assets are sold.)

The tax treatment of direct transfers from government is more complicated and varies from program to program. For example, Temporary Assistance to Needy Families (TANF) (formerly referred to as "welfare") payments are nontaxable. Rev. Rul. 73-87. On the other hand, unemployment compensation is taxable. §85. Why are these transfers treated differently? The legislative history of §85 and other Congressional and Treasury reports draw a distinction between (i) payments that provide subsistence benefits to families living in poverty and (ii) payments that are the equivalent of wages: The former are generally excluded from gross income, but the latter are generally included in gross income.

The tax treatment of Social Security payments is annoyingly complex. §86. Section 86 provides for inclusion of a percentage — from zero percent to 85 percent — of Social Security benefits, depending on how much additional income the taxpayers have. Simplifying somewhat, lower-income taxpayers, whose adjusted gross income plus half of their Social Security benefits do not exceed the "base amount" ($34,000 for married couples or $25,000 for individuals) are not taxed on their Social Security benefits. Taxpayers with more income, whose adjusted gross income plus half of their Social Security benefits exceed the base amount, but do not exceed the "adjusted base amount" ($44,000 for married couples or $34,000 for individuals), include 50 percent of their Social Security benefits. Taxpayers with even more income, whose adjusted gross income plus half of their Social Security benefits exceed the adjusted base amount, include 85 percent of their Social Security benefits. Phase-ins of the 50 percent and 85 percent inclusion percentages (which are too byzantine to warrant a detailed explanation here) prevent a sudden increase in tax liability when the threshold amounts are reached. (The rationale for the 85 percent inclusion percentage is that only around 15 percent of the benefits payable to Social Security recipients are attributable to nondeductible employee contributions to Social Security.)

Examples

45. Jill, a single taxpayer, is a retired bank executive with an adjusted gross income of $80,000 per year from investments. She also receives $10,000 per year in Social Security payments. What portion, if any, of the Social Security payments is subject to tax?

46. Shannon receives TANF payments of $6,000. Shannon's adjusted gross income for the year is $10,000. What portion, if any, of the welfare payments is subject to tax?

Explanations

45. Jill is well above the $34,000 adjusted base amount for an individual return, so she has to include in gross income $8,500 (85 percent) of the $10,000 Social Security benefits she receives. §86(a)(2), (c).

46. Shannon will not have to include any of the $6,000 TANF payments in gross income. Rev. Rul. 73-87.

E. SELECTED RECOVERY OF CAPITAL ISSUES: PARTIAL SALES, ANNUITIES, INSURANCE POLICIES, LIFE ESTATES, AND REMAINDER INTERESTS

A person who buys property for $100 and sells the same property for $120 is taxed on a profit of $20 — the remaining $100 of sales proceeds is excluded from taxable income as recovery of the taxpayer's invested capital. The recovery of capital rule that applies to the above situation is intuitively obvious. In other cases, however, the recovery of capital rules can be quite complex. Here we cover four recovery of capital rules — partial sales, annuities, insurance policies, and life interests. Other recovery of capital rules are covered elsewhere in this book. (For example, the rules governing depreciation are discussed in Chapter 5, and the installment sale rules are discussed in Chapter 3.)

1. Partial Sales

Reading: §§61, 1001; Reg. §1.61-6.

The term *partial sale* is defined, for our purposes, as a sale of a portion of property currently held by a taxpayer. For example, a person may purchase 10 acres of land for $100,000 and sell one of those acres the next year for $20,000. The applicable recovery of capital rule requires the taxpayer to allocate basis to the acre sold, based on the relative value of the sold and unsold portions of the property at the time of purchase. Reg. §1.61-6(a). Thus, if all acres were equally valuable at the time of purchase, each acre would receive one-tenth of the total basis, or $10,000. If, at the time of purchase, the acre sold was worth 20 percent of the amount paid for the property, it would receive a basis of 20 percent of the aggregate basis, or $20,000. The rule can be expressed as a formula:

$$\text{The basis of the parcel sold} = \text{the total basis of all of the parcels} \times \frac{\text{the value of the parcel sold}}{\text{the total value of all of the parcels}}$$

(Note that this simplified formula assumes that there are no upward adjustments to basis for improvements to the property or downward adjustments to basis for depreciation taken with respect to the property. If there were such adjustments, they would have to be taken into account.)

In certain rare circumstances, taxpayers have been allowed to ignore the allocation rule stated above and treat the entire proceeds of a partial sale as tax-free recovery of capital. For example, in Inaja Land Co. v. Commissioner, 9 T.C. 727 (1947), the taxpayer owned riverfront property that was damaged by the actions of an upstream user. The taxpayer threatened legal action and ultimately reached a settlement with the tortfeasor. Under that settlement the taxpayer received approximately $50,000 and, in exchange, gave the upstream user certain rights with respect to the land. The Tax Court allowed the taxpayer to treat the proceeds from the sale of those rights as tax-free recovery of capital. In effect, the taxpayer was allowed to allocate basis first to the rights sold, up to the sale proceeds. In so ruling, the Tax Court was no doubt influenced by two facts: First, basis allocation in the case would have been difficult, and, second, the sale was involuntary.

Examples

47. Sally purchases four acres of land for $40,000. She later sells the north acre for $30,000. How much gain or loss does Sally realize on the sale of the land?

48. David pays $250,000 for a 10-acre parcel of land. A few years later, the government condemns a tiny strip of David's parcel, upon which it places power lines. The government agrees that it will remove the power lines when they are replaced by underground power lines. It is unclear when the power lines will be removed from his property. David receives $20,000 of compensation for the condemned strip of property. Discuss the proper tax treatment of the proceeds.

Explanations

47. Regulation §1.61-6(a) requires Sally to allocate her $40,000 purchase price among the four acres based on the relative value of each acre. If the acres were equally valuable, each acre would receive a $10,000 basis and Sally's gain would be $20,000. If the north acre were as valuable as the other three acres combined, the north acre would receive a $20,000 basis and Sally's gain would be $10,000. In other words, Sally's gain or loss would depend upon the extent to which her $40,000 basis was allocable to the land sold. Sally cannot allocate the entire $40,000 basis to the portion of the land sold because these facts are distinguishable from the facts of Inaja Land Co. v. Commissioner, 9 T.C. 727 (1947), (where allocation of the basis according to the value of the sold and unsold interests was particularly problematic).

48. As noted in the explanation for Example 47 above, the basis of property sold in a partial sale generally is determined by allocating some portion of the basis to the portion of property sold. That allocation is based on the value of the land at the time of purchase. If, for example, at the time of purchase, the parcel sold represented one-fiftieth of the total value of the property, then one-fiftieth of the total basis of the land will be allocated to the parcel sold. Where the parcel is involuntarily "sold" through government action, however, and the parcel sold is not susceptible to easy valuation, at least one court has treated the entire sale proceeds as tax-free recovery of basis. See Inaja Land Co. v. Commissioner, 9 T.C. 727 (1947).

2. Annuities

Reading: §72.

An *annuity* is a contract that provides for a series of payments in return for a fixed sum. Annuities are often purchased to ensure sufficient funds for a financially stable retirement. For example, an individual may pay an insurance company (the usual purveyor of annuities) $100,000 in return for annual payments of $10,000, ending upon the death of the purchaser/annuitant. Assume that, at the time of purchase, the annuitant is expected to live 15 years and that the payments begin immediately after purchase, so that the annuitant is expected to receive $150,000. The difference between the cost and the expected return represents interest. The insurance company will have the use of the $100,000 for many years. It will earn interest on that sum, and some or all of that interest will be passed on to the annuitant in the form of annual payments. Assume also that the annuitant is still alive at the end of the first year, at which time she receives the $10,000. How should that sum be taxed?

There are several possible basis recovery methods. One approach, the *basis first* method, would treat each payment as a tax-free recovery of capital until the entire $100,000 investment in the annuity is recovered. (You will recognize this method as the allocation method used in Inaja Land Co. v. Commissioner, 9 T.C. 727 (1947), discussed in the unit on partial sales.) The rationale for the basis first rule would be that the annuitant may die before year 10 and therefore never show a profit on the contract. Under this approach, the first $10,000 payment would be tax-free. After the annuitant recovered her $100,000 investment in the annuity, all remaining payments would be fully taxed.

Another approach, the *income first* method, would treat all payments as income to the extent of any income set aside for the policyholder in the insurance company's policyholder reserves. The insurance company will invest the annuitant's $100,000 and earn a return on it. Assume that the insurance company loans the $100,000 to a borrower who will pay the insurance company 15 $10,000 payments. The investment will fund the 15 $10,000 annuity payments to be made by the insurance company to the annuitant. Each of the 15 level $10,000 payments has two components: first, interest on the outstanding balance of the loan, and, second, a partial payment of the principal on the loan. (In other words, the principal would be "amortized," so that the 15 $10,000 payments would repay the $100,000 of principal on the loan, as well as interest on the loan.) Most of the early $10,000 payments would be interest, but over time the interest component of the $10,000 payment would decrease and the principal repayment component would increase. Under this approach, the interest would start out high, then decrease over time, and the principal repayment would start out low and increase over time. In other words, in the annuity context, most of the early payments to the annuitant would be income and most of the later payments to the annuitant would be received tax-free as basis recovery.

A third approach, the *pro rata* method, would allocate a pro rata portion of the taxpayer's $100,000 investment to each of the 15 payments. Under this approach, the income and basis-recovery portions of each $10,000 payment would be constant.

The basis first method would be the most favorable to an annuitant because it provides the maximum possible deferral of the income from the annuity. The income first approach would be the least favorable to an annuitant because it defers basis recovery and accelerates the income from the annuity. The pro rata approach is less favorable than the basis first approach but more favorable than the income first approach.

The Code adopts the pro rata method for annuities. Section 72(a) provides that gross income includes annuity payments. However, §72(b) provides that the taxpayer may exclude from each annuity payment the product of the payment multiplied by the *exclusion ratio*, which, in turn, equals the cost of the annuity contract divided by the expected return on the annuity contract. In our example, the exclusion ratio would be 2/3 ($100,000 cost/ $150,000 expected return). Two-thirds of each $10,000 payment, or $6,666.67, which is treated as recovery of capital, is excluded from income under §72(b). The remaining one-third of each payment, $3,333.33, which is treated as gain, is included in income under §72(a).

If the taxpayer lives for exactly her life expectancy of 15 years, she will recover tax-free $6,666.67 in each of the 15 years, for a total recovery of $100,000 — which is exactly what she invested in the contract. If the taxpayer outlives her life expectancy, all of each subsequent annuity payment must be included in income. If the taxpayer dies "early," her estate will be able to deduct the difference between the aggregate amount excluded from income under §72(b) and the cost of the contract. Put differently, the estate will be able to deduct her "unrecovered" basis.

Individuals often purchase annuities that do not provide for any payments for many years. For example, payments may begin at retirement. The tax treatment of such "deferred annuities" is the same as outlined above: An exclusion ratio is determined by dividing the cost of the contract by the expected return; a portion of each payment, equal to the exclusion ratio multiplied by the payment, is treated as recovery of capital.

The tax treatment of deferred annuities is quite favorable. If an annuitant lives to life expectancy, the annuity payments will exceed the annuity cost. The difference represents interest. The longer the period of deferral, the greater the interest return on the taxpayer's annuity investment. The beneficiary of a deferred annuity pays no tax on this interest until the receipt of the annuity payments. In contrast, an individual who decides to save for retirement by earning interest on amounts invested in a savings account or other interest-bearing investment must pay an annual tax on any interest earned, even if the taxpayer does not withdraw the interest.

The favorable treatment of deferred annuities has given rise to several tax avoidance schemes. For example, at one time, individuals could use annuities to build up interest income tax-free and borrow the increase in value in the policy. Typically, the loan was made by the annuity company and secured by the annuity. Under the general rules applicable to loans, no tax would be paid on receipt of the loan proceeds. (Loans are discussed in more detail later in this chapter.) This tax avoidance scheme is no longer available. Under current law, amounts borrowed on a loan secured by an annuity policy are treated as taxable income to the extent that (due to the build-up of interest) the value of the policy has risen as the payout date approaches. §72(e). In addition, unless the recipient is age 59½ or older, a 10 percent tax penalty (10 percent of the amount included in income) applies to such amounts. §72(q). Thus, as a practical matter, deferred annuities are desirable only for those individuals who are willing to "lock up" their money until retirement.

Examples

49. Barbara, who is 88 years old, pays $4,000 for an annuity that, should Barbara live to her five-year life expectancy, will pay her $5,000 ($1,000 per year for five years). Assume this sum reflects a return on Barbara's investment of 8 percent. (The actual return is a bit less — 7.93 percent.) How much of the first $1,000 payment does Barbara include in income?

50. Tom agrees to loan Peter $4,000 for five years. The loan will be amortized with five $1,000 payments. (In other words, a portion of each payment constitutes repayment of part of the principal so that, after five years, the principal has been fully repaid. Each payment also includes interest on the principal still outstanding.) Assume that the loan bears interest at 8 percent. (The actual interest rate is slightly lower — 7.93 percent.)
    a. How much of the first $1,000 payment does Tom include in income?
    b. Compare the tax treatment of the annuity and the loan in this example and in example 49. Which is more favorable to the annuitant/lender?

51. Dan paid $4,000 for an annuity that pays $1,000 per year for life. At the time of the purchase, Dan has a life expectancy of five years. Dan actually lives to collect on the annuity for 10 years. How much of the $1,000 payment in year six is treated as recovery of capital?

52. In year one, Steven, who is 70 years old and has a life expectancy of 10 years, purchases a deferred annuity for $2,000. Under the annuity contract, Steven receives nothing during years one through five, but will be paid $1,000 a year, beginning in year six, until he dies.

    a. Steven receives five $1,000 payments on the annuity, then dies, as expected, at age 80. How much of the first payment constitutes income to Steven?

    b. Steven dies at age 78 and therefore receives only three $1,000 payments. Discuss the tax treatment of the payments.

53. Tracy, who is 45 years old, is interested in assuring herself of retirement income. Stan is an agent for a company that sells deferred annuities. Stan tells Tracy that for $100,000 his company will provide her with an annuity contract that pays $50,000 a year for life, beginning at age 65. Tracy is expected to live until age 83, so that if she lives to life expectancy, she will receive total payments of $900,000. Stan informs her that that number represents an annual return of 8 percent. "Big deal," replies Tracy. "I can earn 8 percent on long-term government bonds and I can probably average about that on deposits with my local bank. Why should I buy the deferred annuity?" What is the best answer to Tracy's question?

54. At age 39, rock star Roger records a hit record that generates large royalties and leads to a lucrative concert schedule. A few months shy of his 40th birthday, Roger pays $100,000 for a deferred annuity that will pay him (i) nothing for slightly over 20 years, and (ii) beginning when Roger is 60 years old, $50,000 a year for the rest of his life. Roger is expected to live until age 78, so the annuity is expected to provide Roger with 18 annual payments of $50,000 each, for a total return of $900,000. The expected return of $900,000 represents an 8 percent annual before-tax return on Roger's initial $100,000 investment. Under §72(b)(1), Roger's exclusion ratio will be $100,000/$900,000, or 1/9 (11.11 percent). Thus, he will exclude $5,556 (rounding a little) of each $50,000 payment and include the rest of each payment. (Said another way, he will recover 1/18 of his $100,000 investment, or $5,556, from each of the 18 expected $50,000 payments.) Suppose, however, that when Roger is 58 years old, the annuity company loans him $50,000. Assume that the loan is non-recourse and is secured only by Roger's right to future payments on the annuity. What is the tax treatment of the loan proceeds?

Explanations

49. Section 72 allows Barbara to recover a percentage of each payment equal to her exclusion ratio as tax-free recovery of capital. A taxpayer's exclusion ratio is defined as the total cost of the contract divided by the expected return. Here the cost of the contract is $4,000 and the expected return is $5,000, so Barbara's exclusion ratio is $4,000/$5,000 or 80 percent. Thus, 80 percent of each $1,000 payment, or $800, will be treated as recovery of capital. §72(b). Only the remaining $200 of each of those installments will be treated as income.

§72(a). Note that, for an annuity with level payments, the effect of §72 will be to allow the taxpayer to recover her cost in equal increments over the expected number of payments.

50. a. $320. This is an example of a common self-amortizing level payment loan — the kind of loan you may enter into when you buy a car or home. Each $1,000 payment has two components: (i) interest on the outstanding balance and (ii) repayment of part of the loan principal. Over time the portion of the payment that represents interest will decrease and the portion of the payment that represents principal repayment will increase. Here, the first year's interest would be $320 (8 percent of $4,000). The last year's interest would be only $75. (The actual return is 7.93 percent. However, we have assumed that the return is 8 percent, to simplify the explanation, so an adjustment to correct the numbers is required in the last year.)

Beginning balance, year one	$4,000
Interest at 8 percent	320
Reduction of principal/Recovery of capital	680
Beginning balance, year two	3,320 (4,000−680)
Interest at 8 percent	266
Reduction of principal/Recovery of capital	734
Beginning balance, year three	2,586 (3,320−734)
Interest at 8 percent	207
Reduction of principal/Recovery of capital	793
Beginning balance, year four	1,793 (2,586−793)
Interest at 8 percent	143
Reduction of principal/Recovery of capital	857
Beginning balance, year five	936 (1,793−857)
Interest at 8 percent	75
Reduction of principal/Recovery of capital ($925 + $11 adjustment required by 8 percent interest assumption)	936

b. The annuity is more favorable to the annuitant/lender. Income from an annuity is determined as a constant portion of each payment.

Under a level-payment loan, early payments contain a relatively large portion of interest; later payments contain relatively little interest. In example 49 above, the first $1,000 annuity payment received by Barbara is characterized as $800 of capital recovery and $200 of income, whereas in this example the first $1,000 loan payment received by Tom is characterized as $680 of capital recovery and $320 of income. Taxpayers, of course, generally prefer to defer recognition of income as long as possible, so they would consider the annuity tax treatment to be more favorable than the loan tax treatment.

51. None of the payment in year six is treated as recovery of capital. The cost of the annuity is $4,000 and the annuity is expected to return five payments of $1,000 for a total of $5,000. Under §72, the $4,000 cost is recovered on a pro rata basis during the expected payout period. Here, the expected payout period is five years, so one-fifth of the capital, or $800, is treated as recovery of capital during the first five payments. (The exclusion ratio is 80 percent, which represents the $4,000 investment in the contract divided by the $5,000 expected return. §72(b)(1).) After the fifth payment, all of the subsequent payments are income because the taxpayer has already recovered his $4,000 investment in the annuity. §72(b)(2). Here, Dan must include in income the entire $1,000 year six payment. (If the annuitant dies before his capital is recovered, the annuitant's estate deducts the amount of unrecovered capital. §72(b)(3).)

52. a. An annuity that provides the beneficiary with no payments for a period of time following purchase is called a deferred annuity. A deferred annuity is taxed in the same manner as any other annuity: Cost is recovered pro rata from each expected 1,000 payment; the portion of each payment that is not allocated to cost is income. Here, the cost of the annuity is $2,000 and there are five expected $1,000 payments. Thus, one-fifth of the cost, or $400, is recovered tax-free in each payment. (The exclusion ratio is 40 percent, which represents the $2,000 investment in the contract divided by the $5,000 expected return. §72(b)(1).) Each payment consists of $400 of capital recovery ($1,000 payment multiplied by the 40 percent exclusion ratio) and $600 of income.

b. The first three payments are treated under the rule described immediately above. There are five expected payments, so one-fifth of the total cost is recovered from each payment. At the end of the third payment, Steven will have recovered $1,200 of his total $2,000 cost. If Steven had lived to life expectancy, he would have recovered the remaining $800 as part of the fourth and fifth $1,000 payments. Steven does not live to life expectancy, so his estate will deduct the $800 of unrecovered basis on his final tax return. §72(b)(3). Ultimately, then, net income of $1,000 is recognized on Steven's investment: $1,800 of income ($600 per year for three years) less a deduction of $800 when Steven dies. This is as it should be since the difference between the amount Steven received from the annuity, $3,000, and the amount Steven paid for the investment, $2,000, is $1,000.

53. The tax treatment of the deferred annuity will be much more favorable than the tax treatment of the other investments Tracy is considering. Suppose that Tracy can earn 8 percent simply by leaving her money in a savings account and that she lives to life expectancy. Suppose, further, that if Tracy leaves her money in a savings account, she will want to withdraw $50,000 per year, starting at age 65. (In other words, assume that she withdraws the same amounts that the annuity contract would have paid, at the same times that the annuity contract would have paid those amounts.) In that case, both the savings account and the deferred annuity will offer identical before-tax returns, and the total income recognized on each investment will be $800,000.

   If Tracy invests in the savings account, she will be taxed on the growth in the account. If, in the year in which she deposits her $100,000 into the savings account, she earns $8,000 of interest, she will have to include that interest in income. If Tracy invests in the deferred annuity, the value of her investment will also increase by $8,000 during the first year of the investment. However, Tracy will not have to include any income (or pay any tax) on that increase until payments begin. Even after payments begin, the annuity recovery of capital rules will defer recognition of income. Thus, the annuity provides Tracy with a substantial deferral of the tax liability on her investment. There may be nontax reasons, however, why Tracy does not want to tie up her money in a deferred annuity.

54. This example is most easily understood if the deferred annuity is seen as a type of savings account: an investment of $100,000 that earns 8 percent a year. Obviously, the value of the investment increases each year; after 20 years, the value of the account is sufficient to pay out $50,000 a year for 18 years. As noted in example 53, the deferred annuity is taxed more favorably than a savings account because the annual increase in value of the annuity is not taxed until the proceeds are withdrawn.

   At one time, taxpayers could combine the favorable treatment of a deferred annuity with the liquidity of a savings account by borrowing against the annuity. So long as the amount borrowed did not exceed the investment in the annuity, the loan proceeds were tax-free. Today, the tax treatment of such loans is far less favorable. First, such loans are taxable to the extent of the increase in the value of the policy. Thus, if the $100,000 invested by Roger in the contract has increased by more than $50,000 in the intervening 20 years, the entire loan will be treated as taxable income. §72(e). (In this case, if the annuity provides a return of 8 percent per year, the value of the contract after 20 years will be almost $400,000, so the entire loan will be treated as taxable income.) In addition, there is a special 10 percent penalty on "premature distributions" from annuity contracts. §72(q). Generally speaking, a premature distribution is any non-periodic payment made to a recipient who is not at least age 59½. So Roger will pay tax on the $50,000 and will also pay a penalty tax of $5,000. The unfavorable treatment of such loans is designed to ensure that annuities are used for retirement security rather than simply as a tax-favored means of investment.

3. Life Insurance

Reading: §101.

Life insurance policies may be divided into two broad categories: term and whole life. As the name implies, *term insurance* provides protection for a specific term, almost always a single year. If the insured dies within the year, the policy pays a specified amount to the designated beneficiary. If the insured does not die during the year, the insurer retains the premium, or policy cost. Quite obviously, then, a term insurance policy represents a gamble, which is "won" by the purchaser only if the insured dies. The cost of the gamble depends on the age and health of the insured. A 25-year-old male, for example, may be able to purchase $250,000 of term insurance for only a few hundred dollars a year. The same policy purchased by a 65-year-old male will cost many times more.

One might expect that the purchase of an insurance policy would be treated like an equally risky investment in the stock market: In the event of death, a tax would be levied (presumably on the estate of the insured-purchaser) on the difference between the cost of the policy and the amount paid out. If the insured does not die, a loss would be allowed equal to the cost of the policy. In fact, an individual who purchases a policy on her own life and lives out the term of the policy is not allowed to deduct the cost of the policy as a loss. On the other hand, no tax is levied on the "profit" from a policy. Instead, under §101, the beneficiary receives the insurance proceeds tax-free.

A *whole life insurance* policy provides protection for the entire life of the insured. Generally, a whole life policy requires annual premiums. However, the amount of the annual premium in a whole life policy does not increase with the age of the insured. Thus, a 25-year-old might purchase a policy that provides $250,000 of coverage in return for an annual premium of $2,000 a year.

The purchase of a whole life insurance policy also represents a gamble of sorts. If the 25-year-old who purchases the policy described above dies after a single year, the policy will represent a profitable gamble. The purchase of a whole life policy represents a form of savings as well. The amounts paid to beneficiaries under a whole life policy always exceed the expected premiums received by the insurance company. That is because, if the insured lives to life expectancy, the insurance company will be able to invest the premiums paid in early years and earn interest from the investment.

Assume, in the example above, that the 25-year-old insured lives to be 80. The insurance company will keep the first $2,000 premium paid by the 25-year-old for 55 years. At an interest rate of 5 percent, the insurance company will be able to earn over $27,000 of income on that first $2,000 premium alone. Some portion of the income is returned to the beneficiary in the form of payments that exceed the premiums paid. In cases in which the insured lives exactly to life expectancy, there is no mortality gain or loss, so the excess of the amounts paid to beneficiaries over the premiums paid by the insured represents interest income.

Even though its savings component distinguishes a whole life policy from a term policy, the proceeds of a whole life policy qualify for the same exclusion under §101 as the proceeds of a term policy. This makes a whole life policy a tax-favored form of investment. An individual who places $2,000 per year in a savings account and gives that sum, together with interest, to her children upon her death will pay tax on the annual interest income. The same individual who purchases a whole life policy and lives to life expectancy earns, in effect, the same interest, but is not taxed.

An individual may assign the benefits of her life insurance, during her life, in order to raise money for living or medical expenses. Section 101(g) permits a terminally ill or chronically ill taxpayer to exclude amounts paid to her, during her life, pursuant to a life insurance contract. An individual is considered "terminally ill" if a physician certifies that the individual is not expected to live longer than 24 months. §101(g)(4)(A). An individual is considered "chronically ill" if medical personnel certify that (i) the individual is unable to perform at least two activities of daily living, such as eating and dressing, (ii) the individual is disabled, or (iii) the individual's cognitive functioning is so impaired that he requires supervision in order to avoid harming himself. §§101(g)(4)(B), 7702B(c)(2). The §101(g) exclusion applies regardless of whether the payment is made by the insurer or is made by a "viatical settlement provider." A viatical settlement provider is a party who regularly pays insured individuals to assign their life insurance benefits. §101(g)(2).

Examples

55. Assume you invest $100 in a one-year term life insurance policy. If you die within the year, how will the proceeds be taxed to your beneficiaries? If the policy does not pay off (because you do not die), can you take a loss on the $100 that you invested in the policy?

56. On what grounds might one criticize the present treatment of whole life insurance? Can you think of any way you might defend the current treatment?

Explanations

55. If you die, the proceeds will be tax-free to your beneficiaries under §101. You are not permitted to deduct the cost of the policy if you live.

56. Whole life insurance is, as the name implies, insurance that provides benefits regardless of when the insured dies — the coverage extends over the "whole life" of the insured. If the insured lives to life expectancy, the return on a whole life policy is considerably greater than its cost. For example, a 30-year-old might pay a single premium of $20,000 for a whole life policy that pays her beneficiaries $300,000 upon her death. The $300,000 represents about a 6 percent return on the original investment, a return that is perhaps most appropriately characterized as interest. In effect, the insurance company is borrowing money and repaying the loan, plus interest, at the time of the death of the insured. Neither the insured nor the insurance company is taxed on this interest as it accrues, and the proceeds are tax-free to the beneficiaries. In contrast, had the insured put $20,000 in the bank, allowed the interest to accumulate, and bequeathed the account to her beneficiary upon her death, she would have been subject to income tax on the annual interest as it was earned. Thus, as compared to the treatment of other investments, the annual returns on which are taxable, the purchase of a whole life insurance policy is tax-favored. One might argue that life insurance should not be tax-favored, relative to other forms of savings.

    One could defend the present treatment on the grounds that we ought to encourage wage earners to provide for dependents in the event of (timely or untimely) death. One might also argue that the treatment of life insurance is no more tax-favored than investments that appreciate in value but do not return annual interest or dividends and are given at death to one's beneficiaries. Under current law, such investments benefit from the step-up in basis at death rule of §1014 and can be sold by the beneficiary tax-free. To illustrate the similar tax treatment of life insurance and this latter sort of investment, imagine that, instead of purchasing a whole life insurance policy for $20,000, the taxpayer described above pays $20,000 for rare coins. If the rare coins appreciate by 6 percent per year, their value at the time of the taxpayer's death (assuming she lives to life expectancy) will be about $300,000 (the same amount as the death benefit of the insurance policy). Under current law, the property will have a fair market value basis in the hands of the taxpayer's beneficiaries and can be sold immediately after acquisition without recognizing any taxable gain. §1014. This produces precisely the same tax result as the purchase of the whole life insurance policy. Another possible justification for the favorable tax treatment of life insurance is that the life insurance companies make long-term investments with the premiums they are paid and that such investments provide a needed source of capital.

4. Gambling Winnings and Losses

Reading: §165(d).

A taxpayer must include annual gambling winnings (the *gross* amount of gambling winnings during the year less the cost of the specific wagers that generated the winnings) in gross income, but can deduct gambling losses from the same year, up to the amount of the taxpayer's gambling winnings. §165(d), Reg. §1.165-10. Section 165 thus allows taxpayers to offset gambling losses against gambling winnings, but not other types of income. The reason for this is that gambling losses are conceptualized, at least in part, as nondeductible costs of consumption (i.e., as the price paid for the fun of gambling).

Gambling raises significant substantiation issues and exposes taxpayers to the risk of a tax "whipsaw": inclusion of potentially large gambling winnings, but disallowance of offsetting gambling losses for failure to substantiate the losses. Casinos and other payors of gambling winnings are required to report to the IRS (on Form W-2G) the payment of winnings above certain threshold amounts, generally $600. §6041(a). This information reporting requirement is triggered only if the winnings are at least 300 times the wager. 2013 Instructions for Forms W-2G, 5754. The information reporting threshold is higher for winnings from certain types of gambling. For example, the threshold is: (1) $1,200 for winnings from a bingo game or a slot machine; (2) $1,500 for winnings from a keno game; and (3) $5,000 for winnings from a poker tournament. Id.

Taxpayers who take a deduction for gambling losses must substantiate their claimed losses. Gamblers who do not keep track of their losses but later try to estimate them will be allowed to take the deduction only to the extent they can prove their estimated losses. Many gamblers are unaware of the need to keep records of their gambling for tax purposes. Taxpayers who gamble should keep a diary of gambling winnings and losses, in which they record: (1) the date and time of specific wagers and details regarding the wagers (such as the number of a slot machine played or number of a table at which table games are played); (2) the name and address of the gambling establishment; and (3) the amounts won or lost. Gamblers also should keep paper records such as tickets, bank statements, canceled checks, and credit card receipts.

The classification of a gambling loss deduction as an above-the-line or below-the-line deduction turns on whether the taxpayer's gambling activity is a trade or business. Unless a taxpayer is a professional gambler, the deduction is a below-the-line itemized deduction, although it is not subject to the 2 percent floor for itemized deductions, the overall limitation on miscellaneous itemized deductions, or disallowance under the AMT. §§67(b)(3), 68(c)(3), 56(b)(1)(A). (Note that all three of these limitations apply to a taxpayer's miscellaneous itemized deductions for a recreational activity or hobby, other than gambling, that is not a trade or business but is entered into for profit. In this respect, the tax treatment of gambling losses is more favorable than the tax treatment of other recreational activities.) If the taxpayer's total itemized deductions, including the allowable gambling loss, are less than the standard deduction amount, the taxpayer will not be able to take a gambling loss deduction, but must include the gambling winnings in income nonetheless.

If a taxpayer's gambling is a trade or business, the allowable gambling loss deduction is an above-the-line trade or business deduction. §62(a)(1). In other words, the AGI of a professional gambler includes only the net gambling winnings, not the gross winnings. (Taxpayers generally prefer to keep AGI as low as possible because a lower AGI increases the tax benefits of various other provisions in the Code, due to AGI floors and phase-outs.)

In Commissioner v. Groetzinger, the Supreme Court set forth a test for determining whether a gambler is in the trade or business of gambling: "to be engaged in a trade or business, the taxpayer must be involved in the activity with continuity and regularity [and] the taxpayer's primary purpose for engaging in the activity must be for income or profit. A sporadic activity, a hobby, or an amusement diversion does not qualify." 480 U.S. 23, 35 (1987). The Court held that the taxpayer was in the trade or business of gambling because he: (i) devoted 60–80 hours of study and gambling per week, over 48 weeks, to his gambling activity and thus satisfied the regularity and continuity requirements; and (ii) satisfied the primary profit purpose requirement because he (A) had no other employment or source of income for 11 months of the year, (B) gambled solely for his own account, and (C) maintained reliable, businesslike records of his gambling activity. Given the fact that regular and continuous gambling may be a sign of personal addiction to gambling, the primary profit purpose requirement may be particularly important. Courts have analyzed the primary profit purpose requirement by considering various factors, such as the businesslike or nonbusinesslike manner in which the taxpayer conducted the activity, that are relevant under the hobby loss rules of §183 (discussed in Chapter 6).

Example

57. Third-year law student Tim developed a passionate interest in gambling two years ago. He currently spends 16-20 hours a week gambling or reading books (gambling "classics" such as Ed Thorpe's *Beat the Dealer* and Doyle Brunson's *Super System*) about his two favorite games, Blackjack and Texas Hold 'Em. Tim, who majored in math as an undergraduate, thinks he has what it takes to make money playing these two games at local casinos and has developed various strategies for his gambling activities. For example, on any given day he stops gambling and leaves the casinos if he has won or lost more than specific predetermined amounts. He keeps track of each day's winnings and losses in his head, but does not keep paper records of his gambling. Tim estimates that he has $350,000 of gambling winnings and $375,000 of gambling losses in the current year. Although he has lost money gambling in the current year, he feels that he has learned a great deal from his gambling activities and is optimistic about his prospects for gambling profits in the future. During the summer of the current year, Tim took a three-month break from his gambling activities while he worked full-time at a large law firm. The firm paid him $30,000 for his summer associate work.

    Tim has asked you whether he can take a deduction for his $25,000 net gambling loss to reduce the income tax he will owe on his $30,000 of summer associate pay. He hopes to receive a refund of the income tax withheld from his summer associate pay. What advice do you give Tim?

Explanation

57. Tim cannot deduct his net gambling losses to offset his summer associate income. He must include in gross income all of his gambling winnings (the $350,000 *gross* amount of gambling winnings during the year less the cost of the specific wagers that generated the winnings) and can deduct his gambling losses, up to the amount of his winnings — but only if he can substantiate those losses. §165(d), Reg. §1.165-10. Tim has not kept records of his gambling winnings and losses. The casinos will have reported some of the $350,000 of winnings to the IRS, and Tim must do what he can to tally the rest of his winnings. Due to his inadequate record-keeping, he could wind up with a large income inclusion and relatively little in the way of an offsetting deduction.

    As a partial substitute for a record of all gambling winnings and losses, taxpayers can offer bank records and credit card records to prove as least some of their gambling losses. For example, in Lamb v. Commissioner, the Tax Court allowed the taxpayer a gambling loss deduction for $23,480 that the taxpayer withdrew from an ATM located at the Kickapoo Casino, one of the three casinos where the taxpayer gambled.

T.C. Memo 2013-155 (2013). The court disallowed the taxpayer's other claimed gambling losses, however, due to lack of substantiation. Tim should review all of his bank records and credit card records, to determine whether he can establish that he made cash withdrawals at casinos or paid casinos for gambling losses or debts with a check or credit card.

Where a taxpayer fails to maintain records of gambling winnings and losses, courts also may consider accounting records prepared by the casinos where the taxpayer gambled. Although a taxpayer might offer a casino-generated record of the taxpayer's "player card" activity at a particular casino to prove losses at the casino, some courts have noted that such records (1) reflect only the gambling transactions for which the player card was used, which may not be all of the transactions at that casino for the year and (2) do not reflect gambling winnings and losses at other casinos for which records are not offered. In addition, relying on a casino's records, instead of the taxpayer's own records of gambling winnings and losses, makes it more likely that a court will conclude that the taxpayer was not in the trade or business of gambling. See, e.g., Merkin v. Commissioner, T.C. Memo 2008-146 (2008). As a last resort, Tim can try to obtain "player card" records from the casinos where he gambled and offer those records as proof of his gambling losses. If Tim plans to continue his gambling activities, he should start keeping a detailed diary and paper records of his winnings and losses.

If Tim is a professional gambler, his gambling loss deduction is an above-the-line deduction, and Tim's AGI includes only the net gambling winnings, here zero; otherwise Tim's AGI includes all of the gambling winnings, and the gambling loss deduction is a below-the-line deduction. §62(a)(1). If his gambling losses are a below-the-line deduction, his $380,000 of adjusted gross income may result in the loss or reduction of various deductions or credits that are tied to AGI.

A court would apply the *Groetzinger* test to determine whether Tim is in the trade or business of gambling. 480 U.S. 23, 35 (1987). Tim can argue that his gambling activity is regular and continuous for most of the year, consuming 16–20 hours a week of his time for nine months of the year, but it is not as regular and continuous as the gambling activities in *Groetzinger*, where the taxpayer's gambling activities consumed 60–80 hours a week for 48 weeks of the year. Tim thinks he can make a profit and has developed some strategies to try to achieve that goal, but the question is whether profit-making is a primary purpose of his gambling activities. His "passionate" interest in gambling indicates that he also enjoys the activity as recreation. In addition, his failure to keep businesslike records indicates that he did not enter into his gambling activity with the requisite primary profit purpose. On balance, his gambling probably is not a trade or business and the gambling loss deduction is a below-the-line deduction.

5. Life Estates and Remainder Interests

Reading: §102.

Recovery of capital issues, no matter how complicated, usually involve only a single taxpayer. Occasionally, however, a question arises as to the allocation of capital and income between two (or more) persons. For example, suppose that Mother leaves $1 million in her will, with the interest earned on the $1 million to go to Daughter during Daughter's life, and the $1 million to go to Granddaughter upon Daughter's death. In the language of bequests, Daughter is said to have a life interest; Granddaughter is said to have a remainder interest.

Assume that, at the time of Mother's death, Daughter's life expectancy is 20 years and the prevailing interest rate is 8 percent. The total amount expected to be paid out under the will is then $2.6 million — Daughter will receive $80,000 a year ($1 million times 8 percent) for 20 years, or $1.6 million, and Granddaughter will receive $1 million. The basis of the bequest is $1 million and the income earned on the bequest is $1.6 million. Under §102(b), the entire basis goes to the person who is granted the remainder interest — in this example Granddaughter. Daughter has no basis in her annual payout, so she pays tax on the entire $80,000 a year.

The rule that all of the basis goes to the remainder interest is subject to one exception. If both the life and remainder interest are sold at the same time, then for purposes of determining gain on the sale, each interest receives a basis equal to its fair market value at the time of the bequest.

The treatment of interests that are split over time may seem intuitively obvious. After all, Daughter is simply getting the interest income on the original bequest — the $1 million is going to Granddaughter. Suppose, though, that Mother had left two separate bequests, one to Daughter in the form of an annuity that paid out $80,000 a year until Daughter's death, and one to Granddaughter in the form of an interest bearing account that was calculated to yield $1 million in principal and interest at the time of Daughter's death.

Under the interest and life expectancy assumptions stated above, the value of the annuity would be about $800,000; the value of the amount left to Granddaughter would be about $200,000. Had the bequests taken this explicitly separate form, Daughter would receive a separate basis in her annuity of $800,000 under the date-of-death basis rule of §1014. The difference between this basis and the $1.6 million received would be taxed as gain. Granddaughter, on the other hand, would receive a basis in her remainder interest equal to its value upon receipt of $200,000. The difference between the $200,000 and the $1 million in the account upon Daughter's death (assuming the sum were left to accumulate interest until Daughter's death) would be taxable as interest income.

To summarize: In situations where a bequest is split into life and remainder interests, the entire basis is allocated to the remainder interest and all of the income from the life interest is taxable. Basis is allocated between the two interests in accordance with their respective fair market values in only one situation: where both the remainder and life interest are sold concurrently.

Examples

58. Dr. Dean leaves $5 million in trust for her husband and her niece. The husband receives all of the income from the trust during his lifetime; thereafter, the property is distributed to the niece. At the time of the gift, the $5 million is expected to earn $2 million in interest before the husband's death. The present value of the husband's interest is $1 million. The present value of the niece's interest is $4 million.
    a. If the husband receives exactly $2 million from the trust, how much of that sum is excluded from income as recovery of capital?
    b. How much of the $5 million basis is allocated to the niece's remainder interest?

59. Dr. Dale dies. His will provides for a current distribution of $1 million to his wife, Willa, and $4 million to his daughter, Donna. Willa invests the $1 million in an annuity that is expected to return a total of $2 million over her life. Donna invests the $4 million in the bank where it is expected to earn $1 million of interest prior to Willa's death.
    a. How much basis is allocated to the bequest to Willa? To the bequest to Donna?
    b. Assume Willa receives exactly $2 million from the annuity. How much of that sum does Willa include in income?

Explanations

58. a. None of the sum is excluded from income as recovery of capital because the husband receives no basis in his life interest. §102(b).
    b. The niece receives the entire $5 million basis.

59. a. Willa receives a basis of $1 million; Donna receives the remaining $4 million basis.
    b. She includes in income $1 million—the difference between the proceeds of $2 million and her $1 million basis.

        Note that this transaction is economically equivalent to the transaction described in example 58. The tax consequences, however, are quite different.

F. ANNUAL ACCOUNTING

Reading: §§61, 111, 172, 441, 1341.

The income tax is based on annual accounting. §441. For nearly all individuals, the taxable year is the calendar year, beginning on January 1 and ending on December 31. On the other hand, corporations frequently have taxable years that begin and end on a different date. A corporation that runs a professional sports franchise, for example, may have a taxable year that ends just after the close of its season. Thus, a major league baseball team might adopt a taxable year that begins on November 1 and ends on October 31.

The convention of annual accounting is necessary for practical and administrative reasons. If unmodified, however, the convention could lead to unfair results. For example, a newly formed company might lose $100,000 in its first year of operation and earn $100,000 in the following year. Strictly applied, the annual accounting convention would require the company to pay tax on its second year income of $100,000 even though the company has broken even during its first two years. In fact, however, the company can take advantage of the net operating loss provisions of §172.

Under §172(a) and (b)(1), a net operating loss suffered in any year can be carried back to the previous two taxable years. The taxpayer files an amended return for the prior year, reducing its income for that year by the loss carryback. This amended return produces a refund for the taxpayer. Any loss not used up in offsetting income from prior years can be carried forward and applied against income from the next 20 years. If the company prefers, it can forgo the loss carryback and simply carry the loss forward. (A company might choose to forgo the carryback if tax rates were low in the past, but are expected to rise in the future.)

The mechanics of the net operating loss rules are quite complex. Basically, a loss carryback is applied first against income from the earliest eligible prior year; any loss left after reducing operating income to zero in that year is applied against income from the next earliest year, and so on. Loss carryforwards are applied first against income recognized during the first year following the loss; any loss left over is applied against income recognized during the following year, and so on. In the example above, the company has no prior income and so would apply its first year loss against its second year income. After application of the net operating loss carryforward, the company would have no second year income and thus would pay no tax in year two. The net operating loss rules apply to individuals as well as corporations, although salaried employees cannot have an operating loss and the interaction of the net operating loss rules with the regime of personal deductions can be quite complex.

The convention of annual accounting is subject to a number of other rules and exceptions. For example, imagine that two taxpayers claim ownership over the same stream of income. Under the so-called *claim of right doctrine*, the taxpayer who has possession of the income is taxed on the income despite the dispute. North American Oil Consolidated v. Burnet, 286 U.S. 417 (1932). If the taxpayer later is forced to give up this income, an adjustment in her tax liability will be needed. The adjustment is not made on the return for the year in which the amount was included. Instead, the adjustment takes the form of a deduction in the year in which the income is repaid. United States v. Lewis, 340 U.S. 590 (1951).

What happens if the taxpayer's tax bracket in the year in which the amount is repaid is lower than it was in the year in which the taxpayer included the amount? In these circumstances, allowing the taxpayer to take a deduction in the year of repayment will not make the taxpayer whole for the extra tax that the taxpayer paid in the year in which the amount was included. Section 1341 addresses this problem. If the requirements of that section are met (for example, if the amount of the deduction exceeds $3,000), the taxpayer will reduce her *tax liability* (not income) in the year of repayment by the reduction in tax that would have occurred in the year in which the income was included had the taxpayer not included that amount. This reduction in tax is taken in lieu of the deduction.

If, on the other hand, the taxpayer's tax bracket is lower in the year of inclusion than in the year of repayment, §1341 allows the taxpayer to deduct the amount repaid, in the year of repayment, despite the fact that the deduction saves the taxpayer more than she paid in tax when the item was included in the earlier year.

Suppose, for example, that under the claim of right doctrine, a taxpayer includes $20,000 in year one. The taxpayer, who is in the 35 percent bracket, pays $7,000 of tax on that amount. In year two, the taxpayer, who is now in the 25 percent bracket, is forced to return the disputed funds. The taxpayer is allowed a deduction in year two for the $20,000 repaid in that year. The deduction, which would save the taxpayer $5,000 in year two, would not make the taxpayer whole for the $7,000 of tax that the taxpayer paid in year one. However, §1341 allows the taxpayer to reduce her year two tax liability by $7,000, which is the reduction in tax that would have occurred in year one (the year in which the income was included) had the taxpayer not included that amount.

If the taxpayer had instead been in the 25 percent bracket in year one and the 35 percent bracket in year two, §1341 would allow the taxpayer to deduct the $20,000 in year two for a tax savings of $7,000, despite the fact that the taxpayer paid only $5,000 of tax on the $20,000 inclusion in year one.

The so-called *tax benefit rule* provides another exception to the annual accounting rule. The term *tax benefit rule* is used for two separate rules: one that requires the taxpayer to include an item in income (the *inclusionary tax benefit rule*), and the other that permits a taxpayer to exclude an item that would otherwise be included in income under the inclusionary tax benefit rule (the *exclusionary tax benefit rule*). Both branches of the tax benefit rule have their origins in case law, but the exclusionary tax benefit rule also has been codified in §111.

The inclusionary tax benefit rule triggers an inclusion whenever an event occurs that is fundamentally inconsistent with a tax benefit recognized in an earlier year. Hillsboro National Bank v. Commissioner, 460 U.S. 370 (1983). Suppose, for example, that a taxpayer with $200,000 of adjusted gross income donates $10,000 to a college in year one. As discussed later in this book, the taxpayer would be able to deduct the charitable contribution. Suppose that the college is forced to give up operations in year two and returns the money to the taxpayer at that time. The taxpayer's receipt of the $10,000 in year two is inconsistent with the charitable deduction taken by the taxpayer in year one. Thus, the taxpayer must "give back" the year one deduction by including $10,000 of income in year two.

However, the exclusionary tax benefit rule of §111(a) permits a taxpayer to exclude the recovered item in the later year to the extent that it did not reduce the taxpayer's tax liability in the earlier year. Continuing our example, if the charitable contribution did not reduce the taxpayer's tax liability in year one, she may exclude the $10,000 in year two. For example, a charitable contribution would not reduce an individual's tax liability if the taxpayer had no taxable income in the year in which the deduction would have been taken.

Both the §1341 and tax benefit rules apply where a return was correct at the time that it was filed, but a *subsequent* event renders it incorrect. Compare this situation with one in which a return is incorrect at the time it was filed, but the mistake is not discovered until after the return was filed. For example, a taxpayer might discover in year two that she had incorrectly added a column of figures in calculating her taxable income for year one. In that situation, the taxpayer would file an *amended return* for year one, which serves as a *claim for refund* for the tax she overpaid in that year. Most taxpayers supplement this claim for refund with a brief explanation of the grounds on which the refund is sought. If the Service denies the taxpayer's claim for refund, the taxpayer may file a suit for refund in either the district court or the United States Court of Federal Claims. A claim for refund must generally be filed within three years from the date the return was filed. §6511(a). (A return filed before the due date for the return is deemed filed on the due date. §6513(a).) However, if the taxpayer makes a payment of tax after filing a return (for example, as a result of the Service asserting that the taxpayer owes additional tax for that year), the period for filing the claim for refund may be longer. §6511(a).

Examples

60. In May of year one, college roommates Allison and Zelda devise a new computer word-processing program. The program is powerful but unwieldy and is rejected by software distributors. After graduation, Allison enters law school and loses interest in the program. Zelda continues to work on the project and eventually manages to make the program "user friendly." The program is successfully marketed; Zelda receives $20,000 per year in royalties during years three through five for a total of $60,000. Zelda is in the 35 percent bracket during those three years.

    In year six, Allison sues Zelda for 50 percent of all program royalties. In December of year seven, a jury finds for Allison and awards her a $30,000 payment, which represents a one-half interest in the royalties Zelda received for years three through five, plus a one-half interest in all future program royalties. Zelda, who is in the 25 percent bracket in year seven, pays Allison the $30,000 late in December of year seven. The deadline for filing an appeal in the case is February 28 of year eight, but Zelda does not file an appeal.

    a. Advise Allison on how the $30,000 she receives from Zelda should be treated for tax purposes.

    b. Advise Zelda on how the $30,000 payment to Allison should be treated for tax purposes. Should she file an amended return for years three through five?

61. Larry suffers an uninsured business theft loss of $20,000 in year one. He deducts the loss in year one, but recovers the stolen property in year two.

    a. Assume that Larry is in the 15 percent tax bracket in year one and the 35 percent tax bracket in year two. Must Larry report the $20,000 as income in year two?

    b. Assume that Larry is in the zero percent tax bracket in year one and the 35 percent tax bracket in year two. Must Larry report the $20,000 as income in year two?

62. In year one, David contributes $10,000 to charity. David neglects to list this contribution on his year one tax return, which he files on April 15 of year two. After filing the return for year one, David does not pay any additional tax for that year. David does not discover his $10,000 mistake on the year one return until February of year five. Is each of the following statements true or false?

    a. If the charitable contribution would reduce his year one tax payment, David may file an amended return for year one and claim a refund.

    b. David may not file an amended return for year one and claim a refund because the statute of limitations has run.

    c. Instead of filing an amended return for year one, David may report the charitable contribution on his year five return.

Explanations

60. a. Allison will include the $30,000 in year seven, the year in which she received the funds under a "claim of right," despite the fact that she might have to return the $30,000 to Zelda if the case were reversed on appeal. North American Oil Consolidated v. Burnet, 286 U.S. 417 (1932).

    b. If Zelda deducts the $30,000 in year seven, the deduction would reduce her taxes in year seven by $7,500 ($30,000 deduction multiplied by her 25 percent tax rate). Zelda paid $10,500 of tax ($30,000 multiplied by her 35 percent tax rate) on the royalties when they were included in years three through five. Said another way, if, in those three years, she had excluded the $30,000 from her gross income, she would have paid $10,500 less in taxes. This $10,500 reduction in her tax liability that would have occurred had she not included the items in years three through five exceeds the $7,500 that she would save in taxes in year seven if she deducted the $30,000. Therefore, Zelda will reduce her tax liability for year seven by $10,500 instead of deducting the $30,000 payment. §1341.

       Zelda cannot amend her returns for years three through five because the return was correct at the time it was filed, but was rendered incorrect by a subsequent event. United States v. Lewis, 340 U.S. 590 (1951). However, the effect of §1341, saving her $10,500 in tax in year seven, is almost the same as allowing her to amend the returns for years three through five and receive a $10,500 refund. (They are not exactly the same because the government has to pay interest on refunds owed to taxpayers, but does not have to pay interest on Zelda's $10,500 tax reduction under §1341.)

61. a. Yes. Recovery of the stolen item is inconsistent with the $20,000 theft deduction taken in year one. Under the inclusionary tax benefit rule, Larry must give the year one tax benefit back by including the $20,000 in income in year two. Hillsboro National Bank v. Commissioner, 460 U.S. 370 (1983). Note that, although Larry's tax benefit from the deduction was only $3,000 (15 percent of $20,000) in year one, he will be required to pay an additional $7,000 (35 percent of $20,000) in tax in year two; unlike §1341, the tax benefit rule does not generally take into account any changes in the taxpayer's bracket between the year in which the item is deducted and the year in which it is included. In other words, §1341 is a more precise error correction device than the tax benefit rule.

    b. No. Larry received no tax benefit from the $20,000 deduction in year one. Under the exclusionary tax benefit rule, he may exclude the $20,000 item recovered in year two. §111.

62. Statement (a) is correct and statements (b) and (c) are false. A taxpayer generally may file a claim for refund anytime within three years of the time of filing. §6511(a). (Since David did not pay any additional tax for year one after filing the return, the "two-years-from-payment" rule in §6511(a) does not apply.) February of year five is within three years of the date on which the year one return was filed, April 15 of year two, so David's claim for refund is not barred by the statute of limitations. Thus, statement (a) is correct and statement (b) is false.

David, an individual, is a cash method taxpayer. He must report the charitable contribution deduction on the return for the year in which the contribution was made, here, year one. The failure to take the deduction was a mistake at the time the return was filed, so David cannot take it on his year five return. Statement (c) is therefore false.

G. PERSONAL INJURY RECOVERIES

Reading: §104.

Section 104 excludes from gross income damages (other than punitive damages) received "on account of personal physical injuries or physical sickness." §104(a)(2). This exclusion applies to recoveries for medical expenses, lost wages, and pain and suffering.

The taxpayer excluding the recovery can be someone other than the person who suffered the physical personal injury or sickness. For example, a taxpayer can exclude damages received on account of a physical personal injury to his or her spouse. Similarly, recoveries for wrongful death are excludable under §104. (Although punitive damages are not generally excludable under §104, a taxpayer can exclude punitive damages if, under state law, punitive damages are the only remedy for wrongful death. §104(c).)

A taxpayer can exclude a recovery for emotional distress only if the emotional distress is the byproduct of other physical injury or sickness. If the emotional distress does not result from some other physical injury or sickness, the emotional distress and any physical symptoms resulting from the emotional distress (e.g., insomnia, headaches, and stomach disorders) are not considered a physical injury, so damages received in such a case do not qualify for the §104 exclusion. However, the taxpayer can, in such a case, exclude the portion of the recovery that is for the cost of medical care attributable to the emotional distress. §104(a) (flush language, last two sentences).

The personal injury exclusion does not apply to recoveries for medical expenses already deducted under §213, which permits a personal deduction for medical expenses in excess of 10 percent of a taxpayer's adjusted gross income. §§104(a), 213(a).

Interest earned on damages received is taxable under §61(a)(4), but if payments are received over a period of years, the entire recovery is excluded from income — even if the payments to be made in the future include implicit interest as compensation for the delay in payment. §104(a)(2). This disparity in tax treatment may create an incentive to pay the award over time (usually in a structured settlement) instead of in a lump sum.

The §104(a)(2) exclusion applies to amounts received pursuant to a judgment in a lawsuit or a settlement agreement.

Compensatory recoveries received under workers' compensation acts, for both physical and nonphysical personal injuries, are excludable under §104(a)(1).

Compare the tax treatment of damages received on account of personal physical injury to the treatment of recoveries for business injuries. Compensation received for a business injury is taxed according to the nature of the loss. If the compensation is received for lost profits, for example, the recovery will be taxed as ordinary income. If the compensation is received for the destruction of a capital asset, capital gain treatment will apply. Damages received on account of personal physical injury, on the other hand, may be excluded from income even if they are based on lost wages, which normally would be taxed.

Should personal injury recoveries be excluded from taxation? To answer this question, it is useful to consider separately four types of recoveries: (i) recoveries for medical expenses; (ii) recoveries for lost wages; (iii) recoveries for pain and suffering; and (iv) punitive damages.

Medical expense recoveries present the strongest case for tax-free treatment. The medical expense recovery places the injured person in the same financial position that she would have occupied had she not been injured. It seems fair, then, that she should pay the same amount of tax. This can be achieved by excluding the medical expense recovery from the tax base.

Recoveries for lost wages, on the other hand, replace funds that would have been taxed if the person had earned them by working. Taxing lost wage recoveries places the person in the same financial position that she would have occupied had she been able to work.

The proper taxation of recoveries for pain and suffering is controversial. Supporters of tax-free treatment argue that pain and suffering recoveries compensate the injured person for the loss of imputed income from good health. Since the imputed income from good health would not have been taxed, damages received for the loss of good health also should not be taxed. Advocates of taxing pain and suffering recoveries argue that an individual's tax burden should depend on her financial position, not on her psychic well-being. Pain and suffering damages compensate an injured person for a nonmonetary loss and place the recipient in a better financial position than she would have occupied had she not been injured. An individual who receives pain and suffering damages has a greater financial ability to pay and thus should bear a higher tax burden.

Punitive damages represent a windfall gain to the recipient and thus present a strong case for taxation. The best argument for tax-free treatment is that excluding punitive damages from taxation will encourage taxpayers to file suit.

Where a personal injury award is taxable (i.e., cannot be excluded under §104), the taxpayer must include in income the gross amount of the recovery, without reduction for large amounts the plaintiff may have paid her attorneys. Commissioner v. Banks (and the companion case, Commissioner v. Banaitis), 543 U.S. 426 (2005).

However, §62 provides an above-the-line deduction for attorneys' fees in cases involving a claim of "unlawful discrimination." §62(a)(20). Section 62(e) defines the term unlawful discrimination as an act that is unlawful under the statutes listed in §62(e). The listed statutes include various federal employment related antidiscrimination statutes, the False Claims Act, and "[a]ny provision of Federal, State, or local law, or common law claims permitted under Federal, State, or local law — (i) providing for the enforcement of civil rights, or (ii) regulating any aspect of the employment relationship, including claims for wages, compensation, or benefits, or prohibiting the discharge of an employee, the discrimination against an employee, or any other form of retaliation or reprisal against an employee for asserting rights or taking other actions permitted by law."

Below-the-line deductions for attorneys' fees may be limited (e.g., by the Alternative Minimum Tax, which is discussed in Chapter 5) with respect to claims that are not employment related, such as defamation claims and false imprisonment claims.

Examples

63. Lucy assaulted Dan. Dan sustained a broken arm and filed a civil suit against Lucy. After a trial, Dan is awarded $10,000 for pain and suffering, $10,000 for medical expenses, $12,000 for lost wages, and $25,000 for punitive damages. What are the tax consequences to Dan?

64. Martin, a longshoreman, injured his back while unloading a crate at the docks. He was on duty at the time, performing tasks pursuant to his employment contract. He was compensated $10,000 for his medical expenses and lost wages under the Longshoremen's and Harbor Workers' Compensation Act. What portion, if any, of his recovery is excludable?

65. Ken Kanter, a teacher, is fired for criticizing the school's staff and administration. He sues the school, claiming that his First Amendment rights were violated. He settles with the school for $50,000, an amount equal to his lost wages. What are the tax consequences to Mr. Kanter?

66. Todd suffered a surfing accident at Boogie Beach that left him paralyzed from the neck down. He filed a negligence suit against Boogie Beach for failure to give adequate warning with respect to the dangerous tides. After a trial, Boogie Beach was ordered to pay Todd $100,000 for pain and suffering, $75,000 for medical expenses, and $200,000 for lost wages. Todd's wife Rebecca was also awarded $50,000 due to loss of consortium resulting from her husband's injuries. What are the tax consequences to Todd and Rebecca?

67. Walker, a truck driver, suffered a severe ankle sprain when the ladder he was using to repair the roof of his home collapsed. His medical expenses were insignificant, but he was unable to work for 12 weeks. He also missed his opportunity to compete in the local marathon, an event for which he had been training for the past year. Walker filed suit against the ladder manufacturer. Two days before the trial was scheduled to begin, Walker agreed to settle his claim in exchange for $20,000. Of this award, $12,000 was compensation for lost wages, and $8,000 was compensation for pain and suffering.
    a. Is Walker taxed on the settlement?
    b. *Should* Walker be taxed on the settlement as a matter of tax policy?

68. a. Jennifer's husband Miguel was killed in a subway accident. She brought a civil suit for wrongful death against the transit authority and was awarded $500,000 for pain and suffering plus $1,000,000 in punitive damages. What are the tax consequences of this award to Jennifer?
    b. Assume the same facts as above, except that Jennifer's lawsuit is brought in a state that allows only punitive damages in wrongful death cases, and she receives a $1,500,000 award. What are the tax consequences of this award to Jennifer?

69. Jack is a teacher at Pleasantville High School. The terms of his contract provide that he will receive paid sick leave for up to 15 days per year and that unused days will carry over to future years. In his ninth year of teaching, Jack suffers a skiing accident and misses 12 weeks of work. Fortunately, he has accumulated substantial sick leave and thus he receives his full salary of $1,000 per week (for a total of $12,000) during his illness. Is Jack taxed on the $12,000 he received?

70. Joe was falsely imprisoned for two months by the police department. After his release, he won a civil suit against the police and was awarded $10,000 for lost wages, $40,000 for medical treatment, and $300,000 in punitive damages. What are the tax consequences of this award to Joe?

71. In year one, Marna receives a $10,000 settlement for a personal physical injury she suffered. She invests the $10,000 for 10 years, earning

$20,000 of interest on it. What are the tax consequences to Marna in years one through ten?

72. a. Pablo is injured by Mr. Negligent in an auto accident. Pablo's estimated damages are $10,000. Pablo accepts Mr. Negligent's offer to settle the suit with monthly payments totaling $30,000 over the next 10 years. In order to meet his legal obligation to provide Pablo with monthly payments for the next 10 years, Mr. Negligent purchases an annuity contract from Helping Hands Insurance Company for $10,000, naming Pablo as the beneficiary. Mr. Negligent retains rights of ownership of the annuity, including the right to change the beneficiary. What are the tax consequences to Pablo in years 1 through 10?

    b. Assume the same facts as above, except that Mr. Negligent buys an annuity from an insurance company that will make the required monthly payments. Mr. Negligent pays $10,000 for the annuity, but Pablo has all rights of ownership. What are the tax consequences to Pablo in years one through ten?

In each of the following examples, assume (i) that the taxpayers are subject to a fictitious flat 30 percent rate on their taxable income and (ii) that their taxable income equals their adjusted gross income.

73. Albert and Betty each earn $100,000 per year. Betty is negligently injured in an automobile accident, incurs $5,000 of medical expenses, and receives a $5,000 recovery for her medical expenses. Albert and Betty have no other medical expenses.

    a. How much does Albert have to live on after paying his taxes?

    b. How much does Betty have to live on after paying her taxes and medical expenses if her medical expense recovery is taxed?

    c. How much does Betty have to live on after paying her taxes and medical expenses if her medical expense recovery is not taxed?

    d. What do the answers to parts (a) through (c) suggest about the proper tax treatment of medical expense recoveries?

74. Carl and Debby each earn $5,000 per month. Carl works 12 months and earns $60,000. Debby is negligently injured in an automobile accident and cannot work for a month. She works for 11 months and earns $55,000. Debby receives a $5,000 recovery for her lost wages.

    a. How much does Carl have to live on after paying his taxes?

    b. How much does Debby have to live on after paying her taxes if her lost wage recovery is taxed?

    c. How much does Debby have to live on after paying her taxes if her lost wage recovery is not taxed?

    d. What do the answers to parts (a) through (c) suggest about the proper tax treatment of lost wage recoveries?

75. Ed earns $60,000 per year. Flora earns $50,000 per year. Flora is negligently injured in an automobile accident and receives a $10,000 recovery for her pain and suffering.
    a. How much does Ed have to live on after paying his taxes?
    b. How much does Flora have to live on after paying her taxes if her pain and suffering recovery is taxed?
    c. How much does Flora have to live on after paying her taxes if her pain and suffering recovery is not taxed?
    d. What do the answers to parts (a) through (c) suggest about the proper tax treatment of pain and suffering recoveries?

76. Greta earns $80,000 per year and Harry earns $60,000 per year. Harry receives $20,000 in punitive damages from an automobile accident.
    a. How much does Greta have to live on after paying her taxes?
    b. How much does Harry have to live on after paying his taxes if the punitive damages are taxed?
    c. How much does Harry have to live on after paying his taxes if the punitive damages are not taxed?
    d. What do the answers to parts (a) through (c) suggest about the proper tax treatment of punitive damages?

Explanations

63. Damages received for pain and suffering, lost wages, and medical expenses on account of personal physical injury or sickness are all excludable under §104. Thus, Dan can exclude the $10,000 award for pain and suffering, the $10,000 award for medical expenses, and the $12,000 award for lost wages. Punitive damages are not excludable under §104, so Dan will include the $25,000 in income.

64. The entire $10,000 will be excludable from Martin's gross income. Amounts that are received by an employee under a workers' compensation act or under a statute that provides compensation to employees for personal injuries or sickness sustained in the course of employment are excludable from gross income. The Longshoremen's and Harbor Workers' Compensation Act is a workers' compensation act. Reg. §1.104-1(b).

65. In order to qualify for the §104 exclusion, the damages must result from a personal physical injury or physical sickness. Here, the damages are for a nonphysical injury, so Kanter must include the entire $50,000 in income.

66. Damages received for pain and suffering, lost wages, and medical expenses on account of a personal physical injury or physical sickness are all excludable under §104. Thus, Todd and Rebecca can exclude Todd's $100,000 award for pain and suffering, the $75,000 award for

medical expenses, and the $200,000 award for lost wages. They can also exclude Rebecca's $50,000 loss of consortium award (even though she was not physically injured herself) since it stems from the physical injury to her husband.

67. a. Damages received for lost wages and pain and suffering on account of a personal physical injury or physical sickness are excludable under §104. Thus, Walker can exclude the $12,000 award for lost wages and the $8,000 award for pain and suffering.

   b. Walker would have been taxed on his earnings, so it seems reasonable to tax him on compensation for the loss of those earnings. Walker's "ability to pay" taxes seems to be the same whether he receives income from his own earnings or as compensation for lost earnings.

   With respect to compensation received for pain and suffering, some individuals might argue that Walker should not be taxed because he is only being placed in the same situation that he would have been in if he had not been injured. This position is similar to that taken in Solicitor's Opinion 132, 1-1 C.B. 92 (1922), which held that compensatory damages for certain personal injuries were not income because they did not represent gain or profit.

   Under general tax principles, however, gain is equal to the amount received less the taxpayer's basis. Calculating a sensible basis for human capital is extremely difficult; it is simply not possible to determine whether Walker has received an amount in excess of his basis. Perhaps we could arbitrarily give human capital a basis equal to its fair market value. Recovery of damages to human capital would therefore never exceed basis and never be taxed. Such a rule would be consistent with the view that someone who has suffered personal injury and who has (at best) simply been "made whole" by a damage award should not be taxed. On the other hand, a taxpayer who receives a damage award for nonpecuniary losses is better off financially than a similarly situated taxpayer who suffered no injury and receives no award. Since the injured taxpayer receiving the damage award has a greater financial ability-to-pay than the uninjured taxpayer, perhaps he should pay higher taxes.

   Aside from the conceptual "human capital" problems raised by personal injury awards, are there any other reasons to exclude the damages received? Although most property transactions are voluntary, in personal injury cases the taxpayer plaintiff has involuntarily entered into the transaction giving rise to the damage award. In addition, we might feel sorry for personal injury victims and want them to be able to keep all of their recovery. However, if that is the justification for the exclusion, is it fair to deny a deduction to the more unfortunate taxpayer who is injured but does not recover damages?

68. a. The $500,000 for pain and suffering is excludable under §104 as damages received on account of personal physical injury or physical sickness. The taxpayer seeking the exclusion need not be the person who suffered the physical injury. Punitive damages are not excludable under §104, so the $1,000,000 punitive damage award is taxed.
    b. In states in which punitive damages are the only damages available in wrongful death actions, punitive damages are excludable. Thus the entire $1,500,000 award is excludable. This is the only case in which punitive damages are not taxed under §104.

69. Although Jack suffered a physical injury, he is taxed on the full $12,000. The $12,000 is not a workers' compensation recovery because his injury did not arise out of his employment. The $12,000 payment does not qualify as "damages . . . received . . . on account of personal physical injuries" because the payment was made pursuant to his employment contract; it was not received "under a statute" or "through prosecution of a legal suit or action, or through a settlement agreement entered into in lieu of prosecution." Reg. §1.104-1(c). The $12,000 is therefore taxed as ordinary income.

70. Joe must include the punitive damages. The inclusion of the award for lost wages will depend on whether Joe suffered a "personal physical injury" or a "physical sickness" while wrongly incarcerated. Although some commentators have argued that recoveries for false imprisonment (which entail a physical loss of freedom and violation of personal rights) always should be excludable, the Tax Court has made exclusion turn on whether the particular taxpayer suffered a personal physical injury or illness while wrongfully incarcerated. See, for example, ILM 201045023 (taxpayer who suffered physical injuries while wrongfully incarcerated could exclude the damages received for the injuries); Stadnyk v. Commissioner, T.C. Memo. 2008-289 (2008) (taxpayer who was wrongly handcuffed, searched, and incarcerated for eight hours could not exclude her recovery because she did not suffer any physical injury while incarcerated). The fact that Joe recovered his medical expenses in the suit against the police indicates that he either suffered an injury or from an illness related to the wrongful incarceration, but the injury or illness may or may not have been "physical." Emotional distress and other psychological disorders are not considered physical injuries for purposes of §104 even if the disorders produce physical manifestations that require medical treatment. Even if Joe cannot establish that he suffered a physical injury, he can exclude the recovery for his medical expenses. Thus, Joe will be taxed on the punitive damages, can exclude the damages received for medical treatment, and may or may not be able to exclude the damages received for lost wages.

71. Marna excludes the $10,000 settlement in year one, but will pay tax on the $20,000 of interest earned on her investment in years one through ten. §§61(a)(4), 104(a)(2).

72. a. Section 104(a)(2) allows the taxpayer to exclude amounts received for personal physical injuries "whether as lump sums or as periodic payments." Pablo may exclude all of the monthly payments received in settlement of the suit despite the fact that $20,000 of the $30,000 payments represent interest on the original $10,000 settlement. Compare the tax treatment of Marna, in example 71 above, who had to include the $20,000 of interest on her invested damages. Rev. Rul. 79-220.

   b. In this case, Pablo is receiving, in effect, an annuity in year one as settlement for his damages. Since Pablo has full control over the annuity, he will be treated as if he received a $10,000 personal injury recovery, which is excludable under §104, and purchased the annuity himself. Pablo would then be taxed on the monthly payments received under the standard rules governing the taxation of annuities. Rev. Rul. 79-220.

73. a. Albert has taxable income of $100,000 and pays a 30 percent tax of $30,000. He has no medical expenses. Thus, Albert has $70,000 to live on after paying taxes and medical expenses.

   b. If Betty's $5,000 medical expense recovery is taxed, she will have taxable income of $105,000 and pay a 30 percent tax of $31,500. She has $5,000 in medical expenses. Thus, Betty will have $68,500 to live on after paying taxes and medical expenses.

   c. If Betty's $5,000 medical expense recovery is not taxed, she will have taxable income of $100,000 and pay a 30 percent tax of $30,000. She has $5,000 in medical expenses. Thus, Betty will have $70,000 to live on after paying taxes and medical expenses.

   d. Betty's income is $5,000 greater than Albert's, but she has $5,000 of additional medical expenses. Albert and Betty appear to have a similar ability to pay and should bear the same tax burden. This can be achieved by excluding the medical expense recovery from taxation.

74. a. Carl has taxable earnings of $60,000 and pays a 30 percent tax of $18,000. Thus, Carl has $42,000 to live on after paying taxes.

   b. If Debby's $5,000 lost wage recovery is taxed, she will have taxable income of $60,000 and pay a 30 percent tax of $18,000. Debby will have $42,000 to live on after paying taxes.

   c. If Debby's $5,000 lost wage recovery is not taxed, she will have taxable income of $55,000 and pay a 30 percent tax of $16,500. Debby will have $43,500 to live on after paying taxes.

   d. Carl and Debby each have $60,000 of income and there is no evidence that their needs are different. Carl and Debby appear to have a similar ability to pay and should bear the same tax burden. This can be achieved by taxing the lost wage recovery.

75. a. Ed has taxable earnings of $60,000 and pays a 30 percent tax of $18,000. Thus, Ed has $42,000 to live on after paying taxes.
    b. If Flora's $10,000 pain and suffering recovery is taxed, she will have taxable income of $60,000 and pay a 30 percent tax of $18,000. Flora will have $42,000 to live on after paying taxes.
    c. If Flora's $10,000 pain and suffering recovery is not taxed, she will have taxable income of $50,000 and pay a 30 percent tax of $15,000. Flora will have $45,000 to live on after paying taxes.
    d. The answer is not clear. Ed and Flora each have $60,000 of income and there is no evidence that their needs are different. Since Ed and Flora appear to have a similar ability to pay, they should bear the same tax burden. This can be achieved by taxing the recovery for pain and suffering. On the other hand, Flora is worse off than Ed because she has endured a lot of pain and suffering ($10,000 worth, according to the court). This nonfinancial loss doesn't affect Flora's financial ability to pay taxes, but it might justify subjecting her to a lower tax burden.

76. a. Greta has taxable earnings of $80,000 and pays a 30 percent tax of $24,000. Thus, Greta has $56,000 to live on after paying taxes.
    b. If Harry's $20,000 of punitive damages is taxed, he will have taxable income of $80,000 and pay a 30 percent tax of $24,000. Harry will have $56,000 to live on after paying taxes.
    c. If Harry's $20,000 of punitive damages is not taxed, he will have taxable income of $60,000 and pay a 30 percent tax of $18,000. Harry will have $62,000 to live on after paying taxes.
    d. Greta and Harry each have $80,000 of income and there is no evidence that their needs are different. Thus, Greta and Harry appear to have a similar ability to pay and should bear the same tax burden. This can be achieved by taxing the punitive damages.

H. TRANSACTIONS INVOLVING LOANS AND INCOME FROM DISCHARGE OF INDEBTEDNESS

Reading: §§61(a)(12), 108, 1001, 1011, 1012, 1016; Reg. §1.1001-2(a)(3). An individual is not taxed on amounts that he borrows on the theory that the obligation to repay the loan offsets the amount received. In other words, the loan does not increase the taxpayer's net worth. Similarly, an individual does not receive a deduction for amounts used to repay a loan.

Although the repayment of a loan generally has no tax consequences, if a loan is discharged for less than the amount owed, the borrower must include in income the amount of the discount (the amount owed less the amount paid to discharge the debt). §61(a)(12). There are two reasons why lenders might discharge debt for less than the amount owed. First, if the taxpayer is financially troubled and cannot repay the debt, the lender may discharge the debt for the amount that the borrower can pay. Second, if the interest rate on the debt is lower than the current market interest rate, the lender may make money by letting the borrower pay back less than the full amount owed, then relending the money at a higher interest rate.

For example, suppose an individual borrows $100,000 from a bank, at a 10 percent rate of interest, with an obligation to repay the loan over a 30-year period. If interest rates rise to 15 percent, the bank might be willing to discharge the debt for an immediate payment of less than $100,000 since the amount repaid could be reloaned at 15 percent. If the loan were discharged for a payment of $90,000, the borrower would recognize *discharge of indebtedness* income of $10,000. §61(a)(12).

What if, instead, interest rates stay at 10 percent and the lender discharges the $100,000 debt for $90,000 because the borrower is financially troubled and cannot repay the full $100,000? The taxpayer has $10,000 of debt discharge income, but may be able to exclude it under §108(a). A financially troubled taxpayer can exclude discharge of indebtedness income if the taxpayer has filed a bankruptcy petition. §108(a)(1)(A), (d)(2). If the taxpayer has not filed a bankruptcy petition, the taxpayer can exclude the discharge of indebtedness income only to the extent of the taxpayer's insolvency (the taxpayer's liabilities less the value of the taxpayer's assets) at the time of the debt discharge. §108(a)(1)(B), (a)(3), (d)(3). Continuing our example, if the taxpayer's liabilities exceed the value of her assets by $6,000 at the time of the discharge, she could exclude $6,000 of the $10,000 of debt discharge income, leaving her $4,000 to include under §61(a)(12).

Section 108 also provides several other specific rules that may permit a taxpayer to exclude discharge of indebtedness income, including the following: Section 108(e)(5) provides that if the seller of property takes back debt on the property sold (so-called *purchase money* debt) and later reduces the purchaser's debt, the reduction in the debt is treated as a purchase price adjustment; it does not create discharge of indebtedness income that has to be included under §61(a)(12). Section 108(e)(2) also provides that the discharge of a liability does not result in discharge of indebtedness income to the extent that the liability would have been deductible had it been paid. Thus, the discharge at a discount of a liability to pay compensation to an employee will not result in any discharge of indebtedness income to the employer since the compensation paid would have been deductible by the employer (under §162, as an ordinary and necessary business expense). The discharge of certain student loans also qualifies for an exclusion, under §108(f). For example, if a law school agrees to discharge a law student's loan and the discharge is contingent on the student working in public interest law, the student may be able to exclude the discharged debt from income.

Beyond §108, other exceptions to the debt discharge inclusion rule may permit the taxpayer to exclude the debt discount. For example, if a lender and borrower disagree about the amount owed and the borrower ultimately pays the lender less than the amount that the lender said was owed, the difference between the amount the lender said was owed and the amount the borrower pays does not have to be included in income. N. Sobel, Inc. v. Commissioner, 40 B.T.A. 1263 (1939). In addition, if a lender cancels the debt at a discount as a gift to the borrower, the borrower does not have to include the discount in income. §102(a).

If a taxpayer is relieved of a nonrecourse liability in connection with the disposition of encumbered property, the consequences are not determined under §§61(a)(12) and 108; instead, the debt relief is included in the taxpayer's amount realized for the purpose of computing her gain or loss realized in the property transaction. Realized gain equals the amount realized less the adjusted basis of the property (and loss equals the adjusted basis less the amount realized). §1001(a). Amount realized equals the cash received by the taxpayer plus the value of any other property received by the taxpayer. §1001(b).

In the case of nonrecourse debt incurred to acquire or improve the property, the rationale for this rule is as follows: The debt relief is included in the taxpayer's amount realized because the debt will have been included in the taxpayer's basis for the property when the taxpayer acquired the property. Crane v. Commissioner, 331 U.S. 1 (1947), Reg. §1.1001-2(a). The amount realized includes the debt relief even if the encumbered property is worth less than the amount of debt at the time the taxpayer disposes of the property. Commissioner v. Tufts, 461 U.S. 300 (1983).

Consider the following example, which illustrates the "symmetry" principle: In year one, an individual purchases depreciable real estate worth $200,000 with $50,000 of his own funds and $150,000 of proceeds from debt that is secured by the property. Under §1012 and the *Crane* case, the taxpayer's basis in the property is $200,000 (the sum of the cash plus the debt proceeds). Assume the taxpayer takes $70,000 of depreciation deductions on the property in years one through ten and, in year ten, sells the property for $10,000 in cash. The purchaser also assumes the $150,000 of debt on the property. The taxpayer's adjusted basis in the property equals $130,000 ($200,000 basis less $70,000 of depreciation deductions). §§1011, 1016. Under §1001 and the *Crane* case, the taxpayer's amount realized equals $160,000 ($10,000 of cash received by the taxpayer plus $150,000 of debt relief) and the taxpayer's gain realized thus equals $30,000 ($160,000 amount realized less $130,000 adjusted basis).

The value of the encumbered property at the time the taxpayer sells the property is irrelevant: Even if the property is worth only $140,000 at the time of the sale, the taxpayer will include the full $150,000 of debt relief in income. Commissioner v. Tufts, 461 U.S. 300 (1983).

The debt relief is included in amount realized based on the symmetry theory: The $150,000 of debt was included in the taxpayer's basis for the property, permitting the taxpayer to take depreciation deductions on the property in excess of the taxpayer's cash investment in the property, so the debt relief should be included in amount realized on the sale of the property. (If the debt were included in basis but not in amount realized, the taxpayer would realize a $120,000 loss on the sale, measured by the difference between the $130,000 adjusted basis and the $10,000 cash received on sale. This, together with the $70,000 depreciation deductions, would yield a taxable loss of $190,000. The taxpayer's actual economic loss, however, would only be $50,000, the cash invested in the property.) The upshot of *Crane* and *Tufts* is that taxpayers can trade current depreciation deductions on encumbered depreciable property, the basis of which has been increased to reflect debt used to purchase the property, for deferred gain on the later disposition of the property. This treatment benefits taxpayers because it permits them to defer taxes.

If the debt encumbering the taxpayer's depreciable property is a recourse liability, the tax consequences of a disposition of the property are determined using a "bifurcated" approach: (i) the debt discharge is included in amount realized, up to the fair market value of the property; and (ii) any additional debt discharge is treated as §61(a)(12) debt discharge income. Reg. §§1.1001-2(a), 1.1001-2(c) Example 8. To illustrate this approach, assume the same facts as in the previous example, except the debt is recourse and the property is worth $140,000 at the time of the property disposition. Also assume the buyer assumes the debt, but does not pay the seller $10,000. In this example, only $140,000 of the $150,000 of debt discharge is included in the taxpayer's amount realized. This reduces the property transaction gain to $10,000 (the $140,000 amount realized less the $130,000 adjusted basis), but the taxpayer would also have $10,000 of §61(a)(12) debt discharge income, which might be excludable under §108.

Applying the encumbered property debt relief approaches (the *Crane* and *Tufts* approach to nonrecourse debt discharge and the bifurcated approach to recourse debt discharge) to the disposition of a personal residence can produce a nondeductible personal loss where the residence has declined in value. Taxpayers are not allowed to depreciate their principal residence and their basis in the property will not have been reduced by depreciation deductions. If the debt encumbering the property is nonrecourse and, at the time of the disposition, the amount of the nonrecourse debt is more than the value of the residence but less than the taxpayer's basis in the residence, the taxpayer will realize a nondeductible personal loss, not a gain, on the disposition of the property, notwithstanding the *Crane* and *Tufts* inclusion of the full amount of the nonrecourse debt discharge in the amount realized. §165(c).

To illustrate the application of the *Crane* and *Tufts* approach in this residential mortgage context, assume the same facts as in our last example, except the debt is nonrecourse and the property is the taxpayer's personal residence. At the time of the disposition, the property is worth $140,000, the taxpayer's adjusted basis in the residence is $200,000 (the taxpayer's original basis with no reduction for depreciation), and the outstanding debt is $150,000. The taxpayer receives no cash on the disposition because the residence is worth only $140,000. The amount realized on the disposition is $150,000, under the *Crane* and *Tufts* approach, and the taxpayer realizes a nondeductible personal loss of $50,000 — $150,000 amount realized less $200,000 basis. §§1001(a), 165(c). The taxpayer has no §61(a)(12) debt discharge income.

If the debt encumbering the residence is instead recourse debt, the bifurcated approach produces different tax consequences. Applying this approach reduces the taxpayer's amount realized, increases the taxpayer's nondeductible personal loss, and generates §61(a)(12) debt discharge income (in an amount equal to the debt owed less the value of the property at the time of the property disposition), which will be taxed unless the taxpayer qualifies for one of the §108(a)(1) exclusions. To illustrate this approach, assume the same facts as in the previous example, except the debt is recourse. The debt discharge is bifurcated. The amount realized is $140,000 (the debt discharge up to the value of the residence at the time of the disposition), and the taxpayer realizes a nondeductible personal loss of $60,000 — $140,000 amount realized less $200,000 basis. The taxpayer also has §61(a)(12) debt discharge income of $10,000 — $150,000 of debt discharge less the $140,000 value of the property at the time of the disposition.

When variable rate mortgage payments and residential foreclosure rates began to increase in the second half of 2007, members of Congress became concerned that a wave of foreclosures and workouts might cause many homeowners to have taxable §61(a)(12) debt discharge income. A foreclosure is treated as a disposition of property and can produce §61(a)(12) debt discharge income if the discharged debt is recourse. Rev. Rul. 90-16. In addition, a debt workout, in which terms of the debt are modified but the property is not transferred to the lender, is not treated as a disposition of property, but can nonetheless generate §61(a)(12) debt discharge income, whether the debt is recourse or nonrecourse. Rev. Rul. 91-31.

Taxpayers with §61(a)(12) debt discharge income from a residential foreclosure or workout often would not qualify for the §108(a)(1) bankruptcy and insolvency exclusions. Taxpayers qualify for the §108(a)(1)(A) bankruptcy exclusion only if they have filed a bankruptcy petition. Many taxpayers would not meet the §108(a)(1)(B) insolvency test because insolvency is defined under §108(d)(3) as balance sheet insolvency (liabilities exceed assets), not equity insolvency (unable to pay debts as they come due), and many taxpayers who cannot pay their mortgages have significant (but illiquid) assets, such as assets held in qualified retirement plans.

In response to the concern about increasing residential mortgage defaults, Congress added a §108(a)(1) exclusion for income from the discharge of "qualified principal residence indebtedness." §108(a)(1)(E). (The §108(a)(1)(E) exclusion was temporary when enacted, but has been extended through 2013, as part of a package of individual income tax "extenders," and is likely to be extended again in the future.) The term "qualified principal residence indebtedness" is defined as indebtedness that is secured by the taxpayer's principal residence and was incurred in acquiring, constructing, or substantially improving that residence. The term also includes indebtedness, secured by the taxpayer's principal residence, from refinancing qualified acquisition indebtedness, but only up to the amount that was refinanced. §§108(h)(2), 163(h)(3)(B)(i). For purposes of the §108(a)(1)(E) exclusion, qualified principal residence indebtedness cannot exceed $2 million. §§108(h)(2), 163(h)(3)(B)(ii). The taxpayer reduces the basis of the residence by the amount of debt discharge income excluded. §108(h)(1). The exclusion applies to §61(a)(12) debt discharge income generated by a disposition (including a foreclosure) of property encumbered by a recourse debt, or workouts of recourse or nonrecourse debt.

The §108(a)(1)(E) exclusion does not apply to §61(a)(12) debt discharge income where the discharged debt is secured by the taxpayer's residence but was incurred to fund personal consumption, not to acquire, construct, or improve the residence. This type of debt is not "qualified personal residence indebtedness," as that term is defined in §108(a)(1)(E). If such a loan is discharged in a workout, the debt discharge is income under §61(a)(12) and the exclusion does not apply. If the debt discharge occurs in a foreclosure or sale, the consequences depend on whether the debt is nonrecourse or recourse. If the discharged debt is recourse debt, the resulting §61(a)(12) debt discharge cannot be excluded under §108(a)(1)(E). If the discharged debt is nonrecourse debt, the full amount of the discharged debt is included in the taxpayer's amount realized, under *Crane* and *Tufts*. In the context of home equity indebtedness that was incurred to fund personal consumption, the taxpayer's basis in the property does not reflect the debt, so the debt discharge could produce gain.

To illustrate these consequences, assume the same facts as in the previous example, except that years after the taxpayer purchased the residence, the taxpayer borrowed an additional $60,000, secured by the residence, to pay off consumer credit card debt: At the time of the disposition, the property is worth $140,000; the taxpayer's adjusted basis in the residence is $200,000 (the taxpayer's original basis with no reduction for depreciation and no increase for the home equity indebtedness); and the outstanding debt is $210,000 — the original $150,000 of debt plus the $60,000 of home equity indebtedness. The taxpayer receives no cash on the disposition because the residence is worth only $140,000. The amount realized on the disposition is $210,000, under the *Crane* and *Tufts* approach, and the taxpayer realizes $10,000 of gain — $210,000 amount realized less $200,000 basis — which the taxpayer may be able to exclude under §121. The taxpayer has no §61(a)(12) debt discharge income.

If the debt encumbering the residence is instead recourse debt, the debt discharge produces a $60,000 nondeductible personal loss (as in our earlier example) and $70,000 of §61(a)(12) debt discharge income. Section 108(a)(1)(E) allows the taxpayer to exclude $10,000 of the debt discharge (the debt discharge attributable to the discharge of the original debt, which is "qualified personal residence indebtedness"). The taxpayer has to include the remaining $60,000 of debt discharge income unless another §108(a)(1) exclusion applies.

Given the different tax consequences of nonrecourse debt discharge and recourse debt discharge, one might think that it always would be clear whether a residential mortgage is recourse or nonrecourse. However, it is often difficult to determine whether residential mortgage debt should be classified as nonrecourse or recourse. Although mortgage loan documents generally purport to create recourse indebtedness, lenders often look only to the property to satisfy the debt. In addition, the law of some states discourages lenders from proceeding personally against borrowers.

What if a family member transfers encumbered property to another family member as a gift and the donee assumes the donor's debt? Does *Crane* apply to the donor's debt relief? In Diedrich v. Commissioner, 457 U.S. 191 (1982), the donors gave family members "net" gifts, meaning that the donees agreed to pay the donors' gift tax liability that arose as a result of making the gifts. The court held that the transaction was partly a gift and partly a sale because the donees assumed the donors' gift tax liability, citing both *Crane* and Old Colony Trust Co. v. Commissioner, 279 U.S. 716 (1929) (where a taxpayer had to include in income a debt that his employer paid on his behalf). In *Diedrich*, the donors' gain from the sale portion of the transfer equaled their amount realized as a result of the debt relief less their entire basis in all of the assets transferred. (In other words, even though the transaction was treated as part gift and part sale, the donors were not required to allocate their basis between the sale and gift portions of the transfer.)

Examples

77. a. Bob borrows $10,000 in year one and uses the proceeds to finance a ski trip. Is Bob taxed on the $10,000 he receives from the lender?
    b. Bob earns $100,000 in year two and uses $10,000 of the money to repay the loan. What are the tax consequences to Bob of repayment of the loan in year two?

78. In year one, Linda borrows $200,000 from a bank. The term of the loan is 30 years; the interest rate on the loan is 11 percent. In year two, interest rates skyrocket to 15 percent. The bank decides it would rather have $150,000 to lend out at 15 percent than a $200,000 loan on which it earns only 11 percent. The bank tells Linda that if she will pay them $150,000 immediately, they will forgive the loan. Linda pays the bank $150,000 in year two. What are the tax consequences to Linda of repayment of the loan in year two?

79. a. In year one, Donald borrows $100,000 from a bank. The 10 percent interest on the loan is payable annually and the principal is to be repaid 10 years later. In year 10, Donald notifies the bank that he cannot repay the full $100,000 of principal. After some negotiations, the bank agrees to discharge the debt for $85,000. Immediately before the discharge, Donald has $300,000 of debt and $290,000 of assets; after the discharge, he has $200,000 of debt and $205,000 of assets. What are the tax consequences to Donald in year 10?
    b. How, if at all, would your answer in part (a) change if Donald filed a bankruptcy petition before discharging the bank debt?

80. Jill purchases a television from Nat's Department Store on an installment plan requiring her to pay Nat's $100 a month for 12 months (for a total of $1,200) plus interest. One week later, Jill sees an identical set for sale at another store for $1,000. Jill complains and Nat agrees to reduce the amount Jill owes to $1,000. What are the tax consequences to Jill of Nat reducing the debt by $200?

81. Ralph writes his neighbor, Sam, a check for $1,000. Sam builds a fence between their yards with the $1,000 Ralph gave him plus $1,000 of his own money. When Ralph later asks Sam to repay the $1,000, Sam refuses, claiming that Ralph had earlier promised to pay half of the cost of constructing the fence. Ralph denies making such a promise and insists on repayment, but ultimately agrees to discharge the debt for $600. What are the tax consequences to Sam of Ralph reducing the debt by $400?

82. In year one, Lawrence loans his sister, Shantelle, $5,000. In year two, Lawrence forgives the debt as a birthday present to Shantelle. What are the tax consequences to Shantelle in year two?

83. Ted owes $1,000 to Valerie. Valerie agrees to discharge the debt in exchange for Ted's baseball card collection. Although Ted originally bought the cards for $50, they are now worth $1,000. What are the tax consequences to Ted of this transaction?

84. Dan purchases Greenacre from Emily, giving her a 10-year $100,000 purchase money nonrecourse note bearing 12 percent interest, in exchange for the property. Dan's note requires him to pay Emily $12,000 interest per

year and to repay the principal of $100,000 in a balloon payment at the end of the 10th year. Four years later, Dan sells Greenacre to Frank for $20,000 cash and assumption of the $100,000 debt.

a. What are the tax consequences to Dan on the sale?

b. What is Frank's basis in Greenacre?

85. Harry owns Blackacre with an adjusted basis of $100,000 and a gross fair market value of $700,000. The property is subject to a mortgage of $500,000. (Harry's original basis in Blackacre included the entire $500,000 of debt.) Carol wishes to purchase the property subject to the mortgage. How much cash will she pay for the property? What will be her basis in the property? How much gain will Harry realize and recognize on the sale?

86. John purchases real property in year one for $100,000 cash and a $900,000 interest-only loan. The loan is secured by the property. At the end of year five, John still owes $900,000 on the loan, but the value of the property has declined to $850,000. Assume that year five is 2013.

a. The property is an apartment building and the loan is nonrecourse. In years one through five, John has taken depreciation deductions totaling $170,000 on the building. At the end of year five, John defaults on the loan. The lender forecloses and takes title to the property. What are the tax consequences to John?

b. The facts are the same as in part (a) except the property is John's principal residence and he has taken no depreciation deductions with respect to the property.

c. The facts are the same as in part (b) except the loan is recourse.

d. The facts are the same as in part (b) except that after negotiations between the lender and John, the lender discharges $50,000 of John's debt and does not foreclose.

e. The facts are the same as in part (d) except the loan is recourse.

Explanations

77. a. Bob is not taxed because his receipt of cash is balanced by an off-setting liability to repay the loan.

b. The repayment of loan principal is not deductible. The non-deductibility of loan repayment is a necessary corollary of the exclusion of loan proceeds.

78. Under §61(a)(12), Linda includes discharge of indebtedness income of $50,000 (the $200,000 owed less the $150,000 paid to discharge the debt). This makes sense because the discharge of the $200,000 liability for $150,000 increases her net worth by $50,000.

79. a. The discount on the debt is $15,000 ($100,000 owed less the $85,000 paid to discharge it). Donald can exclude $10,000 of the discount under §108, but must include the other $5,000 of discount under §61(a)(12). Since Donald has not filed a bankruptcy petition, he can exclude the $15,000 of discharge of indebtedness income only to the extent of his $10,000 insolvency immediately before the debt discharge ($300,000 liabilities less the $290,000 value of his assets). §108(a)(1)(B), (a)(3), (d)(3). The remaining $5,000 of debt discharge income must be included under §61(a)(12).

    b. Donald can exclude the entire $15,000 of debt discharge income because the discharge occurs in a bankruptcy proceeding. §108(a)(1)(A), (d)(2). The fact that debt discharge income is treated more favorably in bankruptcy cases than in out-of-court workouts creates an incentive to file a bankruptcy petition before discharging debt instead of restructuring the debt out-of-court.

80. The $200 reduction in Jill's purchase money liability by the seller, Nat, is treated as a nontaxable reduction in the purchase price of the television. §108(e)(5).

81. Sam will not have to include the $400 discount on the debt, because the original $1,000 liability was disputed. N. Sobel, Inc. v. Commissioner, 40 B.T.A. 1263 (1939).

82. Shantelle does not have to include the $5,000 discount on the debt. Lawrence forgave the debt out of "detached and disinterested generosity," so the debt forgiveness is an excludable §102 gift. Commissioner v. Duberstein, 363 U.S. 278 (1960).

83. Ted is giving Valerie property worth $1,000 to discharge his $1,000 debt, so the transaction does not result in any debt discharge income. However, when a taxpayer pays a debt with appreciated property, the taxpayer must realize and recognize the gain on the transferred property. Here, Ted will recognize $950 of gain ($1,000 amount realized less $50 basis) on the transfer of the cards.

84. a. Dan's basis includes the $100,000 he borrowed to purchase the property. §1012 and Crane v. Commissioner, 331 U.S. 1 (1947). Relief of the indebtedness is included in amount realized, so the amount realized is $120,000 ($20,000 cash received plus $100,000 of debt relief). Crane v. Commissioner, 331 U.S. 1 (1947), §1001(b), Reg. §1.1001-2(a). Dan's realized gain equals $20,000 ($120,000 amount realized less $100,000 basis). §1001(a). His $20,000 realized gain is recognized under §1001(c).

    b. The assumption of indebtedness is included in the basis of the property, under *Crane*, so Frank's basis is $120,000 ($20,000 cash plus $100,000 of debt assumed).

85. Carol will pay $200,000 in cash for the property subject to the $500,000 mortgage because the gross value of the property is $700,000. Her basis in the property will be $700,000 ($200,000 cash paid plus the $500,000 of debt). *Crane*, §1012. Harry's amount realized equals $700,000 ($200,000 of cash received plus $500,000 of debt relief) and his basis is $100,000, so he realizes and recognizes $600,000 of gain on the sale. *Crane*, §1001(a)-(c), Reg. §1.1001-2(a)(1).

86. a. The foreclosure is treated as a disposition of the property. Rev. Rul. 90-16. John realizes and recognizes $70,000 of gain ($900,000 amount realized less $830,000 adjusted basis) in year five. John's adjusted basis in the apartment building is $830,000 ($1 million basis less the $170,000 depreciation taken). John's amount realized includes the full $900,000 of debt discharged, despite the fact that the property is worth only $850,000 at the time of the foreclosure. Commissioner v. Tufts, 461 U.S. 300 (1983).

       John's out-of-pocket loss on the apartment building is the $100,000 of his own funds that he used to purchase the property. However, he was permitted to take $170,000 of depreciation deductions on the building. In other words, for tax purposes he was treated as having lost $170,000, when he really only lost $100,000. Thus, the $70,000 difference between his out-of-pocket loss and the tax losses that he took should be included in income, which it is.

    b. John realizes a $100,000 loss ($900,000 amount realized less $1 million adjusted basis). As in part (a), John's amount realized includes the full amount of the nonrecourse debt discharge, under the *Tufts* approach. The loss is a nondeductible personal loss because the residence is personal property. §165(c).

    c. John realizes a $150,000 loss ($850,000 amount realized less $1 million adjusted basis) and has $50,000 of §61(a)(12) debt discharge income. In this part, the transaction is bifurcated because the discharged debt is recourse. John's amount realized includes the discharged recourse debt, but only up to the value of the property at the time of the discharge, $850,000. As in part (b), the loss is a nondeductible personal loss, but here the loss is larger. The discharge of the $50,000 of debt in excess of the value of the property is income under §61(a)(12). Reg. §§1.1001-2(a), 1.1001-2(c) Example 8.

       John will be taxed on the $50,000 of debt discharge income unless one of the §108(a)(1) exclusions applies. If John has not filed a bankruptcy petition, the §108(a)(1)(A) bankruptcy exclusion does not apply. The §108(a)(1)(B) insolvency exclusion does not apply if John is solvent. If John has assets in a retirement plan, he probably will be considered solvent under the balance sheet insolvency test (liabilities less assets) of §108(d)(3), in spite of the fact that the assets in his retirement plan are illiquid. John can exclude the $50,000 of debt discharge income under the §108(a)(1)(E) exclusion because the debt discharge occurs before January 1, 2014. The discharged debt is "qualified principal residence indebtedness" because it is secured by John's principal residence and was incurred in acquiring that residence. §§108(h)(2), 163(h)(3)(B)(i). Section 108(h)(1) provides that the taxpayer reduces his basis in the principal residence by the amount of debt discharge income excluded under §108(a)(1)(E), but John no longer owns the property.

d. John has $50,000 of debt discharge income that is excluded under §108(a)(1)(E), as in part (c). In this part, however, John reduces his basis in the residence, which he still owns, by the $50,000 of excluded debt discharge income. §108(h)(1). John does not realize a loss in this part because a debt workout is not treated as a disposition of property. Rev. Rul. 91-31.

e. The answer is the same as in part (d).

I. TAX-EXEMPT BONDS

Section 103 provides that taxpayers may exclude the interest they receive on certain state, municipal, and other bonds. Tax-exempt bonds bear a lower rate of interest than taxable bonds; nonetheless, people invest in tax-exempt bonds because the interest on them is not taxed.

To illustrate, assume that the interest rate on taxable bonds is 10 percent and the rate on comparable tax-exempt bonds is 7 percent. The after-tax return on either type of bond would be equal for a taxpayer in the 30 percent tax bracket; if the taxpayer invests $1,000 in a taxable bond and earns annual interest of $100, the tax on that interest is $30 (30 percent of $100), leaving the taxpayer with $70, the same after-tax amount that the taxpayer could earn on a $1,000 investment in the tax-exempt bond. The $30 of pretax interest that the investor loses by investing in the tax-exempt bond is referred to as a *putative tax*.

If all taxpayers were in the 30 percent bracket, the exemption would simply shift the $30 of tax that the federal government would have collected to the state or local entity that issued the bonds. However, some taxpayers are taxed at higher rates. Consider, for example, a taxpayer in the 40 percent bracket who invests $1,000 in either a taxable or tax-exempt bond; if the taxpayer invests $1,000 in a taxable bond and earns annual interest of $100, the tax on that interest is $40 (40 percent of $100), leaving the taxpayer with $60, but if the taxpayer invests the $1,000 in a tax-exempt bond, the taxpayer earns $70 after-tax. If this taxpayer invests in the tax-exempt bond, the taxpayer pays a putative tax of $30 instead of an actual tax of $40. In other words, the federal government has given up $40 of tax to transfer $30 to the state or local entity; the extra $10 goes to the taxpayer. (Compare a taxpayer in the 40 percent bracket who earns $100 of wages and would have to pay $40 of tax on the wages.) Many individual investors are in the top tax brackets, so the exemption has been criticized as an inefficient form of federal subsidy to state and local governments.

J. GAIN FROM THE SALE OF A PERSONAL RESIDENCE

Reading: §121.

Section 121 allows qualifying taxpayers to permanently exclude from income up to $250,000 (or, for married taxpayers filing a joint return, up to $500,000) of gain from the sale or exchange of their personal residence. §121(a), (b). In order for the §121 exclusion to apply, the taxpayer must have owned and occupied the property as a principal residence for at least two of the last five years prior to the sale or exchange. §121(a). Taxpayers can qualify for the full exclusion only once every two years. §121(b)(3).

A taxpayer who has not occupied the residence for the requisite two years, or who has taken a §121 exclusion within the preceding two years, may qualify for a reduced exclusion, under §121(c). The reduced exclusion is available if the taxpayer has had to move because of a change of place of employment, health, or other unforeseen circumstances. If the taxpayer cannot satisfy the occupancy requirement, but qualifies for the reduced exclusion, the taxpayer can exclude $250,000 (or $500,000 for married taxpayers filing a joint return), multiplied by the following ratio: the period of time (in the five years before the sale or exchange) during which the taxpayer owned and used the residence as a principal residence divided by two years. If the taxpayer has excluded gain under §121 within the two preceding years, and §121(c) applies, the taxpayer can exclude $250,000 (or $500,000 for married taxpayers filing a joint return), multiplied by the following ratio: the period of time between the sale or exchange of the previous principal residence (for which the §121 exclusion was claimed) and the sale or exchange of the most recent principal residence divided by two years. §121(c).

In Gates v. Commissioner, a husband and wife excluded gain from the sale of a new home they constructed on the site of their former principal residence. The couple met the §121(a) two-year residency requirement with respect to the old home, which they demolished and replaced (instead of remodeling) on the advice of their architect. The question in the case was whether they could exclude gain from the sale of the new replacement home, in which they never had lived. In a reviewed decision (i.e., a decision in which all Tax Court judges participate), a majority of the court held that the couple could not exclude the gain from the sale of the replacement home because that home was not used as the couple's principal residence for the period required by §121(a). Gates v. Commissioner, 135 T.C. No.1 (2010).

Examples

87. Jim bought his first home for $100,000. He occupies the house as his principal residence until he sells it for $150,000 because he has to move to another city to take a new job. His gain from the sale is $50,000 ($150,000 selling price less the $100,000 he paid). What are the tax consequences to Jim of the sale of the residence in each of the following situations?

   a. Jim owned and occupied the home for three years.
   b. Jim owned the property for three years, but occupied the property for only three months.

Explanations

87. a. Since this is the first property Jim has ever owned, he has not used the §121 exclusion within the last two years. He satisfies the eligibility requirements for §121 because he has owned and occupied the property as his principal residence for at least two of the previous five years. He can therefore permanently exclude the entire $50,000 of gain.

   b. Jim moved because of a change in employment, so he is still eligible to exclude a portion of his gain even though he occupied the home for less than two of the previous five years. He can exclude $31,250 ($250,000 × 3 months/24 months). He will include in income $18,750 of gain ($50,000 gain realized on the sale less $31,250 excluded under §121).

Problems of Timing

Timing issues play a central role in tax planning. Taxpayers generally prefer to defer income and accelerate deductions because tax deferral is valuable to them. Even if the tax paid in a later year is, in absolute terms, the same amount that would have been paid in the earlier year, absent deferral, deferring the tax saves the taxpayer money. For example, assume that Yvette can structure a pending transaction in two ways. If she structures the transaction one way, she will have to include $80,000 of income in year one. If she structures the transaction the other way, she will have to include the $80,000 of income in year 10. Assume that Yvette is in the 25 percent tax bracket in years one and 10, so that she would owe $20,000 of tax on the income regardless of the year in which it is included.

If Yvette can defer the $20,000 of tax for 10 years, she can invest the $20,000 and earn income on it. If, for example, she invests it in bonds that earn 10 percent (after-tax) a year, she will earn $20,000 ($2,000 per year of interest for 10 years) on the invested amount. Permitting Yvette to defer the $20,000 of tax for 10 years is thus comparable to a 10-year, interest-free $20,000 loan to Yvette from the federal government. The tax deferral has the effect of reducing Yvette's tax rate on the $80,000 of income. With the deferral, Yvette pays $20,000 of tax in year 10. How much money would Yvette have to invest in year one if she wanted the investment to grow to $20,000 by year 10 — and fund the tax payment due in that year? Assume that Yvette could earn 10 percent (after-tax) on funds invested in years one through 10. If Yvette invests $7,711, and earns 10 percent a year on that investment for 10 years, the $7,711 investment grows to $20,000 by year 10. If Yvette pays the $20,000 tax in year one, her tax rate is 25 percent.

On the other hand, if Yvette pays the $20,000 tax in year 10, it costs her only $7,711 in year one; in other words, the deferral reduces Yvette's tax rate from 25 percent to 9.64 percent ($7,711/$80,000).

In this chapter we will examine various timing rules that determine when taxpayers include certain items of income and deduct certain expenses. First, we will consider several rules that determine when gains and losses from property transactions are taken into account by taxpayers. As we will see, appreciation or decline in the value of property is not taxed until it is "realized." In addition, taxpayers can, in some circumstances, temporarily defer their realized gains. However, subject to a very small number of exceptions (for example, the §1014 basis step-up rule, which permanently excludes pre-death appreciation in property), taxpayers cannot permanently defer their property gains. Second, we will examine the rules that apply to transfers incident to divorce, including a rule that defers gain realized on the transfer of appreciated property incident to divorce. We will also consider the tax treatment of alimony and child support. Third, we will consider the differences between the cash and accrual methods of accounting and discuss the tests for determining when taxpayers using each method include income and deduct expenses. We will also review the original issue discount rules, which require both cash and accrual taxpayers to use economic accrual concepts to determine when the interest on certain loans is included and deducted.

A. GAINS AND LOSSES FROM INVESTMENT IN PROPERTY

1. Realization of Gains and Losses

Reading: §1001; Reg. §1.1001-1(a).

If the tax law adopted and applied the Haig-Simons definition of income in its purest form, taxpayers would be taxable on their annual increase in wealth. For example, an individual holding appreciated property would be taxed in the year the appreciation occurred, rather than in the year the property is sold. A tax system based strictly on the Haig-Simons definition of income would have the virtue of treating all increases in wealth in a uniform manner. However, such a tax regimen would raise serious liquidity and valuation problems. In light of these problems, our tax system defers the tax on appreciation until it is "realized." Eisner v. Macomber, 252 U.S. 189 (1920).

Realization is a term of art that does not have a single, all-encompassing definition. Sometimes it will be obvious when realization has occurred. For example, a sale of property for cash is obviously a realization event. In other cases, the time of realization will be less clear. For example, suppose that in year one a taxpayer buys land and leases it to a tenant for 10 years. In year two, the tenant constructs a valuable new building on the property. In year 11, the taxpayer sells the land with the building. In which year does the taxpayer realize gain from the new building on the property? In Helvering v. Bruun, 309 U.S. 461 (1940), the Supreme Court held that a lessor realized gain from improvements made by the tenant upon termination of the lease. (However, Congress later enacted §§109 and 1019, which defer the gain from tenant improvements realized by a lessor on the termination of a lease, provided that the improvements were not a form of rent.)

Although the Code does not define the term *realization*, Regulation §1.1001-1(a) provides that gain or loss is realized when property is exchanged for cash or other property "differing materially either in kind or in extent." In Cottage Savings Association v. Commissioner, 499 U.S. 554 (1991), the Supreme Court held that exchanged properties are "materially different" if they "embody legally distinct entitlements." In *Cottage Savings*, a savings and loan association exchanged a group (or "pool") of residential mortgages that had declined in value for another pool of residential mortgages. For bank regulation purposes, Cottage Savings did not have to report the loss on the mortgage pool given up in the exchange because the mortgage pools were "substantially identical" (within the meaning of federal bank regulations). However, for tax purposes, Cottage Savings took the position that the loss was realized on the exchange of the mortgage pools. The Supreme Court concluded that the exchanged mortgage pools embodied legally distinct entitlements (since, for example, the obligors on the mortgages varied between the two pools) and that the exchange was thus a realization event for tax purposes.

2. Recognition of Gains and Losses

Realized gains and losses are taken into account, for purposes of computing the taxpayer's gross income, only to the extent that they are also "recognized." Section 1001(c) provides that realized gains and losses are recognized unless otherwise provided in the Code. A number of nonrecognition rules are scattered throughout the Code. If a nonrecognition rule applies to a transaction, the taxpayer's realized gain or loss from the transaction will be deferred in whole or in part. Nonrecognition rules apply to some but not all of the many situations in which a taxpayer shifts her investment from one piece of property to another piece of property of a similar character. For example, assume that a taxpayer exchanges land in Houston held for investment for land in Austin that she also will hold for investment. Although the exchange is a realization event, the taxpayer is simply continuing her investment, so it may make sense to defer her gain realized on the exchange of the Houston property until she sells the Austin property. Section 1031, the first nonrecognition rule that we will consider, does just that.

a. Like-Kind Exchanges

Reading: §§1001, 1031; Reg. §§1.1031(a)-1, 1.1031(a)-2, 1.1031(d)-2.
Section 1001(c) provides that realized gains and losses are recognized unless otherwise provided in the Code. Sections 1031 through 1045 provide a series of nonrecognition rules that apply in certain property transactions. A number of other nonrecognition rules are scattered throughout the rest of the Code. Section 1031 provides for nonrecognition of gain or loss realized on the exchange of trade or business or investment property for like-kind property that will also be used in the taxpayer's trade or business or held for investment. Section 1031 is not elective; if the requirements of the section are met, it applies.

In practice, the great majority of §1031 like-kind exchanges involve exchanges of real property for two reasons. First, §1031 does not apply to many other types of property exchanges, including exchanges of inventory, stocks, bonds, notes, other securities or evidences of indebtedness, partnership interests, beneficial interests in trusts, or contract rights. §1031(a)(2). Second, administrative rulings and regulations treat all real property — developed or undeveloped and commercial or residential — as like-kind, making it relatively easy to qualify real property exchanges for §1031. See, e.g., Reg. §1.1031(a) — 1(b) (which provides that the term *like-kind* refers to "the nature or character of the property and not to its grade or quality"). Even nonsimultaneous exchanges qualify for §1031, provided that the requirements of §1031(a)(3) and Regulation §1.1031(k)-1 are met. Thus, most real estate may be exchanged for other real property without recognition, provided, of course, that the real property is held for investment or for productive use in a trade or business. If real estate is held for sale to customers, however, an exchange of that property would not qualify for §1031 nonrecognition. §1031(a)(2)(A).)

Section 1031 does not eliminate the gain realized in the §1031 exchange; instead, it defers the gain by assigning the property received in the §1031 exchange a basis such that, if the property received were sold immediately after the exchange, the taxpayer would realize gain in an amount equal to the amount of gain realized in the §1031 exchange that went unrecognized under §1031. Section 1031(d) thus provides that a taxpayer's basis in the property received in the §1031 exchange equals the taxpayer's basis in the property given up in the exchange. §1031(d). For example, suppose Bill owns Blackacre, which has a basis of $80 and a fair market value (FMV) of $200, and Carla owns Greenacre, which has a basis of

$50 and a fair market value of $200. Bill and Carla exchange their properties, which are like-kind properties.

Bill		**Carla**
Blackacre	→ ←	Greenacre
200 FMV		200 FMV
80 Basis		50 Basis

Bill's realized gain in the exchange is $120 ($200 amount realized less $80 basis) and Carla's realized gain is $150 ($200 amount realized less $50 basis), but neither will recognize their realized gain. §1031(a). Bill's basis in the new property, Greenacre, is $80, Bill's basis in the property given up, Blackacre. §1031(d). If Bill sells Greenacre immediately after the exchange, he will realize and recognize $120 of gain ($200 amount realized less $80 basis), which makes sense since Bill's realized but unrecognized gain from the exchange of Blackacre was $120. Said another way, on the sale of Greenacre, the property received in the §1031 exchange, Bill will realize and recognize the $120 of deferred gain from the §1031 exchange. In similar fashion, Carla's basis in Blackacre is $50, her basis in the property given up, Greenacre. If Carla sold Blackacre right after she received it, she would realize and recognize the $150 of gain that she realized but did not recognize in the §1031 exchange of Greenacre.

The nonrecognition rule of §1031(a)(1) provides that no gain is recognized on qualifying like-kind exchanges provided the property is exchanged *solely* for other like-kind property. However (as is true under some other nonrecognition sections) "solely" does not really mean "solely." Section 1031 applies even if the taxpayer receives both like-kind property (called *permitted property* because the taxpayer is permitted to receive it without recognition) and other property or money (called *boot* or *nonpermitted property*). If a taxpayer *receives* boot in a §1031 exchange, any gain realized is recognized up to the value of boot received in the §1031 exchange. §1031(b). Said another way, gain recognized equals the lesser of (i) the gain realized in the exchange or (ii) the fair market value of the boot received. If the taxpayer realizes a loss in a §1031 exchange, the loss is not recognized even if the taxpayer receives boot in the exchange. §1031(c). If gain is recognized in a like-kind exchange, the basis of the like-kind property received in the exchange is equal to (i) the basis of the like-kind property given up, (ii) less the fair market value of the cash or other boot (for example, appreciated stock) received, (iii) plus the gain recognized in the exchange. §1031(d). A taxpayer's basis in noncash boot received is its fair market value. §1031(d). The party *paying* boot adds the boot to the basis of the like-kind property given up in the exchange, for purposes of computing (i) the gain realized in the exchange, and (ii) the basis of the like-kind property received in the exchange.

3. Problems of Timing

Suppose, for example, that Emma transfers Seaview, which has a basis of $80 and a fair market value of $100, to Jean in exchange for $5 in cash and Mountainview, like-kind property which has a basis of $60 and a fair market value of $95.

Emma		Jean
Seaview	→ ←	Mountainview
100 FMV		95 FMV
80 Basis		60 Basis
	←	5 cash

Emma's realized gain on the exchange is $20, which is the $100 amount realized ($95 of property plus $5 of cash) less the $80 basis of the property. Had Emma exchanged Seaview solely for like-kind property, she would not have recognized any of the realized gain. Here, under §1031(b), Emma recognizes gain of $5, the amount of the cash boot she received. Emma's basis in Mountainview is $80 ($80 basis less $5 boot received plus $5 of gain recognized). §1031(d). Mountainview has a value of $95. If Emma sells Mountainview immediately after the exchange, she will realize and recognize another $15 of gain. In the §1031 exchange, only $5 of the $20 of realized gain was recognized, so Emma should and will realize $15 of gain on the sale of Mountainview.

Jean's realized gain on the exchange is $35, which is the $100 amount realized (the value of Seaview) less $65 (the sum of Jean's $60 basis in Mountainview plus the $5 Jean pays Emma). Jean receives no boot in the exchange and recognizes no gain on the exchange. Jean's basis in Seaview is $65, which is the sum of Jean's $60 basis in Mountainview plus Jean's $5 payment to Emma. If Jean sells Seaview immediately after the exchange, she will realize and recognize $35 of gain ($100 value of Seaview less Jean's $65 basis in the property), which is the amount of gain that was realized but not recognized in the §1031 exchange. The consequences to Emma and Jean are summarized below.

Emma:
Realized Gain = 100 AR - 80 AB = 20
  AR = 95 FMV of Mountainview + 5 cash Emma received = 100
  AB = 80 basis in Seaview
Boot Received = 5 cash Emma received
Recognized Gain = 5
Basis in Mountainview = 80

$$
\begin{array}{l}
80 \text{ basis in Seaview}\\
-5 \text{ boot Emma received}\\
+5 \text{ gain recognized}\\
\hline
80
\end{array}
$$

Jean:
Realized Gain = 100 AR – 65 AB = 35
   AR = 100 FMV of Seaview
   AB = 60 basis in Mountainview + 5 Jean paid = 65
Boot Received = 0
Recognized Gain = 0
Basis in Seaview = 60 basis in Mountainview + 5 Jean paid = 65

Why, in this example, did we add and subtract the same amount, $5, from Emma's basis for Mountainview? Recall that §1031(d) provides that the basis of the like-kind property received in the exchange is equal to (i) the basis of the property given up, (ii) less the fair market value of the cash or other boot received, (iii) plus the gain recognized. Students often ask: Can we just forget about the second and third terms in this formula because they cancel each other? In our example, we subtracted the $5 of boot received and added the $5 of gain recognized as a result of receipt of that boot — so Emma's basis in Mountainview is ultimately the same as her $80 basis in the property given up, Seaview. The second and third terms in the basis formula cancel each other out if (i) the taxpayer realizes a gain in the §1031 exchange and (ii) the taxpayer's realized gain equals or exceeds the amount of boot received in the exchange; in these circumstances, the gain recognized will equal the amount of boot received. However, the second and third terms in the basis formula do not cancel each other if either (i) the realized gain is less than the amount of boot received or (ii) the taxpayer realizes a loss in the §1031 exchange; in these circumstances, the gain recognized will not equal the amount of boot received.

To illustrate, assume that Emma instead exchanges Seaview for $25 in cash and Lakeview, which is worth $75. Emma's realized gain is $20, the $100 amount realized ($75 of property plus $25 cash) less $80 basis, all of which is recognized because she receives $25 of boot. Her recognized gain is not $25; although she receives $25 of boot, the recognized gain is limited to the $20 of gain realized in the exchange. Emma's basis in Lakeview is $75 (Emma's $80 basis in Seaview less $25 boot received plus $20 gain recognized). (Note that the second and third terms do not cancel each other.) Lakeview has a value of $75. If Emma sells Lakeview immediately after the exchange, she will realize no gain or loss on the sale. This makes sense because Emma's $20 of gain realized in the §1031 exchange has already been fully recognized.

Like-kind exchanges sometimes involve properties subject to debt. If, in a §1031 exchange, a taxpayer is relieved of indebtedness on the transfer of encumbered like-kind property, the debt relief is (i) added to the amount realized (under *Crane* and *Tufts*, discussed earlier), for purposes of computing the gain realized in the exchange, and (ii) subtracted (as a form of boot received) from the basis of the like-kind property given up in the exchange, for purposes of computing the taxpayer's basis in the like-kind property received in the exchange. If a taxpayer incurs debt on the receipt of encumbered like-kind property, the debt incurred is added to the taxpayer's basis in the property given up in the exchange, for purposes of computing (i) the gain realized in the exchange, and (ii) the taxpayer's basis in the like-kind property received in the exchange.

If only one like-kind property is encumbered, the operation of these rules is straightforward. If both like-kind properties are encumbered (and the amounts of debt are unequal), one party to the exchange will have a net increase in indebtedness and the other party will have a net decrease in indebtedness. For purposes of determining the amount of gain recognized in the exchange, the party whose *net* indebtedness *increases* as a result of the exchange does not treat the relief of indebtedness on the property transferred as boot. The party whose *net* indebtedness *decreases* as a result of the exchange treats the *net* debt relief as boot. If one of the parties pays cash to the other party, the cash payment is added to the debt that party incurs in the exchange, for purposes of determining that party's boot from net debt relief. In other words, a taxpayer's boot from net debt relief equals (i) the liability that the taxpayer gave up in the exchange less (ii) the sum of (a) the liability that the taxpayer assumed in the exchange plus (b) the cash that the taxpayer *paid* in the exchange.

Suppose, for example, that Dolly owns Campusview, which is subject to $80 of indebtedness and has a basis of $100 and gross fair market value of $220. Ellen owns Sunview, which is subject to $150 of indebtedness and has a basis of $175 and gross fair market value of $250. The net value of Campusview is $140 (the $220 gross fair market value less the $80 debt) and the net value of Sunview is $100 ($250 gross fair market value less $150 debt). Dolly and Ellen exchange properties and Ellen pays Dolly $40 to equalize the value of the two sides of the exchange.

Dolly		Ellen
Campusview	→ ←	Sunview
220 Gross FMV		250 Gross FMV
80 Debt		150 Debt
140 Net FMV		100 Net FMV
100 Basis		175 Basis
	←	40 cash

As a result of the exchange, Ellen's indebtedness has decreased by $70, the amount by which the $150 debt on Sunview, the property she transfers in the exchange, exceeds the $80 debt on Campusview, the property she receives in the exchange. Dolly's indebtedness has increased by the same amount.

Dolly's realized gain is $120. The amount realized is $370, which is the sum of the $250 gross fair market value of Sunview, the property Dolly receives in the exchange, plus the $80 of debt relief from the transfer of the Campusview debt to Ellen, plus the $40 Dolly receives from Ellen.

For purposes of computing realized gain, Dolly's $100 basis in Campusview is increased by the $150 of debt on Sunview. Reg. §1.1031(d)-2. Dolly's realized gain thus is $120 — $370 amount realized minus $250 of basis plus adjustments. The $40 of cash Dolly receives from Ellen is boot. (Dolly does not have boot from net debt relief because her net indebtedness has increased in the exchange.) Dolly recognizes $40 of gain. Her basis in Sunview is $170; this is her $100 basis in Campusview, plus the $150 of debt on Sunview, less the $80 of debt on Campusview, less the $40 of cash she receives from Ellen, plus the $40 gain recognized. If Dolly sold Sunview for $250 immediately after the exchange, she would realize $80 of gain, which makes sense because she already recognized $40 of the $120 of gain realized in the §1031 exchange.

Ellen's realized gain is $75. The amount realized is $370, which is the sum of the $220 gross value of Campusview, the property Ellen receives in the exchange, plus the $150 of debt relief from the transfer of the Sunview debt to Dolly. For purposes of computing realized gain, Ellen's $175 basis in Sunview is increased by the $80 of debt on Campusview and the $40 she pays Dolly. Reg. §1.1031(d)-2. How much boot has Ellen received? Ellen's net indebtedness has increased by $70, but that amount is reduced by the $40 of cash Ellen pays Dolly. Id. Ellen thus has $30 of boot and recognizes $30 of gain. Her basis in Campusview is $175; this is her $175 basis in Sunview less $30 net debt relief boot plus $30 gain recognized (or if it helps you to break down all of the parts of this calculation, her basis is her $175 basis in Sunview, plus the $80 of debt on Campusview, plus the $40 of cash Ellen pays Dolly, less the $150 of debt on Sunview, plus the $30 gain recognized). If Ellen sold Campusview for $220 immediately after the exchange, she would realize $45 of gain, which makes sense because she already recognized $30 of the $75 gain realized in the §1031 exchange. The consequences of the exchange are summarized below:

Dolly:

Realized Gain = 370 AR − 250 AB = 120

  AR = 370

> 250 gross FMV of Sunview
> + 80 relief of debt on Campusview
> + 40 cash received from Ellen
> —————————————
> 370

  AB = 250

> 100 basis in Campusview
> +150 debt on Sunview
> —————————————
> 250

Boot Received = 40 cash boot Dolly received from Ellen (Dolly does not have net debt relief because 150 debt incurred > 80 debt relief)

Recognized Gain = 40

3. Problems of Timing

Basis in Sunview = 170

> 100 basis Campusview
> + 150 debt on Sunview
> − 40 cash Dolly received from Ellen
> − 80 relief of Campusview debt
> + 40 gain recognized
> —————————————————
> 170

Ellen:

Realized Gain = 370 AR − 295 AB = 75

AR = 370

> 220 Gross FMV of Campusview
> + 150 relief of debt on Sunview
> ——————————————
> 370

AB = 295

> 175 AB in Sunview
> + 80 debt on Campusview
> + 40 cash Ellen paid Dolly
> ——————————————
> 295

Boot Received = 30

> 150 relief of debt on Sunview
> − 120 (80 of debt on Campusview + 40 cash Ellen paid Dolly)
> ——————————————————————————
> 30 "money received" (i.e., boot)

Recognized Gain = 30

Basis in Campusview = 175 AB in Sunview−30 boot received + 30 gain recognized = 175

Or:

> 175 AB of Sunview
> + 80 debt on Campusview
> + 40 cash Ellen paid Dolly
> − 150 relief of Sunview debt
> + 30 gain recognized
> ——————————————
> 175

Examples

1. State whether the following exchanges would qualify as like-kind exchanges under §1031.
   a. Improved commercial rental real estate in New York City is exchanged for undeveloped investment real property in Vail, Colorado.
   b. Corporate stock in Xenon Corporation is exchanged for corporate stock in Yaba Corporation. Both corporations produce medical equipment.

    c. A real estate developer exchanges unimproved lots in Santa Barbara, which were held for development and sale to customers, for unimproved oceanfront property in Oregon, which will also be developed and sold to customers.

2. Alice owns Blackacre, investment property that has a fair market value of $100,000 and basis of $40,000. Bob owns Whiteacre, investment property that has a fair market value of $100,000 and a basis of $80,000. Alice and Bob exchange their properties and hold the property received for investment. What are the tax consequences of the exchange to Alice and Bob?

3. Carol owns a used Ford truck with a fair market value of $1,500 and a basis of $800. Doug owns a used GM truck with a fair market value of $1,000 and a basis of $400. Both Carol and Doug use their trucks exclusively in their businesses. Carol and Doug exchange their trucks and Doug pays Carol $500. The trucks still are used exclusively in their businesses. What are the tax consequences of the exchange to Carol and Doug?

4. a. Emily owns Greenacre, investment property with a fair market value of $200,000 and a basis of $120,000. Fred owns Whiteacre, investment property with a fair market value of $180,000 and a basis of $80,000. Emily and Fred exchange their properties and Fred pays Emily $20,000. What are the tax consequences of the exchange to Emily and Fred?
    b. How, if at all, would the consequences to Emily change in part (a) if her basis in Greenacre were $185,000 instead of $120,000?

5. George owns Gulfview, investment property with a fair market value of $100,000 and a basis of $150,000. Harriet owns Pineacre, investment property with a fair market value of $90,000 and basis of $50,000. George and Harriet exchange their properties and Harriet pays George $10,000 in cash. What are the tax consequences of the exchange to George and Harriet?

6. Juan borrows $60,000 and uses the proceeds, together with $40,000 of his own funds, to purchase investment property, Ranchview, for $100,000. Juan's debt is nonrecourse and is secured by Ranchview. Samantha owns Cityview, investment property that has a value of $240,000 and basis of $150,000 and is not subject to any debt. Juan and Samantha exchange their properties. At the time of the exchange, Ranchview is still subject to the $60,000 of debt. Absent that debt, Ranchview would have a fair market value of $300,000; the value net of the debt is $240,000. What are the consequences of the exchange to Juan and Samantha?

7. Alice acquired Blackacre, which she held for investment, in exchange for $20,000 of her own funds and $80,000 that she borrowed. The $80,000 of debt is nonrecourse and is secured by Blackacre. Bob owns Whiteacre, investment property with a $50,000 basis. Whiteacre is subject to

a $70,000 mortgage. Alice exchanges Blackacre for Whiteacre. At the time of the exchange (i) Whiteacre has a gross value (without taking into account the debt) of $95,000 and a net value (taking into account the debt) of $25,000; (ii) Blackacre has a gross value of $105,000 (without taking into account the debt) and has a net value (taking into account the debt) of $25,000; and (iii) all of the $80,000 debt on Blackacre and the $70,000 debt on Whiteacre is still outstanding. What are the tax consequences of the exchange to Alice and Bob?

8. Emily owns Riverview, investment property, with a gross value of $110,000 and basis of $100,000, which is subject to $20,000 of debt (so that the net value of the property is $90,000). Fred owns Mountain-view, investment property with a value of $60,000 and basis of $40,000. Emily and Fred exchange their properties and Fred pays Emily $30,000. What are the tax consequences of the exchange to Emily and Fred?

Explanations

1. a. Section 1031 applies to the exchange. Regulation §1.1031(a)-1(b) treats improved realty and unimproved realty as "like-kind." If both properties are held for productive use in a trade or business or for investment, §1031 applies to the exchange.

   b. Section 1031 does not apply to the exchange of stock. §1031(a)(2)(B). It is irrelevant that the two corporations manufacture the same products.

   c. Section 1031 does not apply to the exchange of the lots because they are "stock in trade or other property held primarily for sale." §1031(a)(2)(A).

2. Alice realizes gain of $60,000 ($100,000 amount realized less $40,000 basis) and Bob realizes gain of $20,000 ($100,000 amount realized less $80,000 basis). However, neither one recognizes any gain because the exchange is within §1031 and there is no boot involved in the exchange. §1031(a). Alice's basis in Whiteacre is her basis in the property given up in the exchange, $40,000. Bob's basis in Blackacre is his basis in the property given up, $80,000. §1031(d).

3. The exchange qualifies for §1031. The trucks are "like-kind" because they are in the same asset class for purposes of determining depreciation deductions. Reg. §1.1031(a)-2(b). Carol realizes gain of $700 and receives boot of $500. In a §1031 exchange, realized gain is recognized up to the amount of boot received, so Carol recognizes a gain of $500. §1031(b). Carol's basis in the GM truck received is $800 (her $800 basis in the property given up, plus $500 of gain recognized on the exchange, less $500 of boot received). Following the exchange, Carol owns a truck,

with a basis of $800 and value of $1,000, plus $500 of cash. If she sold the GM truck immediately after receiving it, she would realize $200 of gain ($1,000 amount realized less $800 basis) on the sale. She has already recognized $500 of the $700 of gain realized on the exchange of the Ford truck, so it is appropriate that she has $200 of potential gain in the GM truck she received in the exchange.

Doug realizes a gain of $600 on the exchange, but does not recognize any gain because he does not receive any boot. §1031(a). Doug's basis in the property received is $900 (his $400 basis in the GM truck he gave up plus the $500 of cash he paid). §§1012, 1031(d). Doug now owns a truck with a basis of $900 and a FMV of $1,500. If he sold the Ford truck immediately after receiving it, he would realize $600 of gain ($1,500 amount realized less $900 basis) on the sale. He has not recognized any of the $600 of gain realized on the exchange of the GM truck, so it is appropriate that he has $600 of potential gain in the Ford truck he received in the exchange.

4. a. Here is a diagram of the exchange:

Emily		**Fred**
Greenacre	→ ←	Whiteacre
200 FMV		180 FMV
120 Basis		80 Basis
	←	20 cash

Emily's realized gain in the exchange is $80,000 — $200,000 amount realized ($180,000 of property received plus $20,000 of cash received) less her $120,000 basis in Greenacre. That realized gain is recognized up to the amount of boot received, here $20,000, so Emily will recognize $20,000 of gain on the exchange. §1031(b). Emily's basis in Whiteacre is $120,000 (her $120,000 basis in Greenacre, plus the $20,000 of gain she recognizes on the exchange, less the $20,000 of boot she receives in the exchange). §1031(d). If Emily sold Whiteacre immediately after she received it in the exchange, she would realize $60,000 of gain ($180,000 amount realized less $120,000 basis). This is appropriate because she has already recognized $20,000 of the $80,000 of gain realized in the §1031 exchange.

Fred's realized gain in the exchange is $100,000 — $200,000 value of Greenacre less $100,000 (his $80,000 basis in Whiteacre plus $20,000 of cash Fred paid). Fred's recognized gain is zero because he receives no boot in the exchange. §1031(a)(1). Fred's basis in Greenacre is $100,000 — his $80,000 basis in Whiteacre plus the $20,000 of cash he paid. §1031(d), Reg. §1.1031(d)-1. If Fred sold Greenacre immediately after he received it in the exchange, he would realize $100,000 of gain ($200,000 amount realized less $100,000 basis). This is appropriate because he will not have recognized any of the $100,000 of gain realized on the §1031 exchange.

b. Emily's realized gain in the exchange is $15,000—$200,000 amount realized ($180,000 of property received plus $20,000 of cash received) less her $185,000 basis in Greenacre. Although Emily receives $20,000 of boot, the gain recognized is limited to her realized gain, so Emily's recognized gain is $15,000. §1031(b). Emily's basis in Whiteacre is $180,000 (her $185,000 basis in Greenacre, plus the $15,000 of gain she recognizes on the exchange, less the $20,000 of boot she receives in the exchange). §1031(d). If Emily sold Whiteacre immediately after she received it in the exchange, she would realize no gain or loss ($180,000 amount realized less $180,000 basis). This is appropriate because she has already recognized all of the $15,000 of gain realized in the §1031 exchange.

5. George realizes a loss of $50,000 ($100,000 amount realized less his $150,000 basis in Gulfview), but does not recognize that loss despite the fact that he received $10,000 of boot. §1031(a), (c). George's basis in Pineacre will be $140,000 (his $150,000 basis in Gulfacre, plus his gain recognized of $0, less the $10,000 of boot he received). §1031(d). Pineacre is worth $90,000. If George sold Pineacre immediately after the exchange, he would realize a $50,000 loss. This makes sense because he has not recognized any of the $50,000 loss that he realized in the exchange.

Harriet realizes a gain of $40,000, but recognizes no gain because she receives no boot. §1031(a), (b). Her basis in Gulfview is $60,000 (her $50,000 basis in Pineacre, plus $10,000 of cash she paid George). §1031(d). Gulfview has a value of $100,000; this $60,000 basis preserves the $40,000 of gain that Harriet realized but did not recognize in the §1031 exchange.

6. Here is a diagram of the exchange:

Juan		Samantha
Ranchview	→ ←	Cityview
300 Gross FMV		240 FMV
60 Debt		150 Basis
240 Net FMV		
100 Basis (40 cash + 60 debt)		

Juan's realized gain on the exchange is $200,000—$300,000 amount realized ($240,000 of property received plus $60,000 of debt relief) less $100,000 basis ($40,000 cash investment plus $60,000 of nonrecourse debt, under *Crane*). Reg. §1.1031(d)-2. Juan recognizes gain equal to the lesser of (i) the gain realized or (ii) the boot received. Net relief from indebtedness is treated as boot for purposes of §1031. Reg. §1.1031(d)-2. In this exchange Juan gave up a $60,000 liability and did not take on any liability, so his net debt relief, which is treated as boot, is $60,000. Thus, Juan recognizes gain of $60,000. Juan's basis in Cityview is $100,000 (his $100,000 basis in Ranchview, plus the $60,000 of gain recognized, less the $60,000 of boot received). Cityview is worth $240,000. If Juan sold it immediately after the exchange, he would realize $140,000 of gain ($240,000 amount realized less $100,000 basis), which makes sense since he will have already recognized $60,000 of the $200,000 of gain realized in the §1031 exchange.

In the exchange, Samantha realizes $90,000 of gain — $300,000 amount realized less $210,000 basis plus adjustments (her $150,000 basis in Cityview, plus $60,000 debt on Ranchview). She will not recognize any gain because she does not receive any boot in the exchange. §1031(a). Samantha's basis in Ranchview is $210,000 — her $150,000 basis in Cityview plus the $60,000 debt on Ranchview. Reg. §1.1031(d)-2. Ranchview is worth $300,000. If Samantha sold it immediately after the exchange, she would realize $90,000 of gain ($300,000 amount realized less $210,000 basis), which makes sense since she will not have recognized any of the $90,000 of gain realized in the §1031 exchange.

7. Here is a diagram of the exchange:

Alice		Bob
Blackacre	→ ←	Whiteacre
105 Gross FMV		95 Gross FMV
80 Debt		70 Debt
25 Net FMV		25 Net FMV
100 Basis (20 cash + 80 debt)		50 Basis

Alice's realized gain in the exchange is $5,000 — $175,000 amount realized ($95,000 of property received plus relief of the $80,000 of indebtedness on Blackacre) less $170,000 basis plus adjustments (her $100,000 basis in Blackacre, plus the $70,000 of debt on the new property, Whiteacre). Reg. §1.1031(d)-2. Alice receives net debt relief of $10,000 ($80,000 liability on Blackacre, the property she gave up, less $70,000 liability on Whiteacre, the property she received in the exchange). That $10,000 of net debt relief is boot and her recognized gain is $5,000. §1031(b). (Even though she receives $10,000 of boot, her recognized gain cannot exceed her realized gain, here $5,000.) Alice's basis in Whiteacre is $95,000 (her $100,000 basis in Blackacre, less the $10,000 of net debt relief, plus the $5,000 of gain recognized). Reg. §1.1031(d)-2. Whiteacre is worth $95,000. If Alice sold it immediately after receiving it, she would not realize any gain or loss, which makes sense since she will have already recognized all of the $5,000 of gain realized in the §1031 exchange.

Bob's realized gain in the exchange is $45,000 — $175,000 amount realized ($105,000 of property received, plus relief of the $70,000 of indebtedness on Whiteacre) less $130,000 basis plus adjustments (his $50,000 basis in Whiteacre, plus the $80,000 of debt on the new property, Blackacre). Bob does not have any net debt relief because he gave up a $70,000 liability and incurred an $80,000 liability. Since he receives no boot in the exchange, he does not recognize any of the realized gain. Bob's basis in Blackacre is $60,000 (his $50,000 basis in Whiteacre, plus the $80,000 liability on Blackacre, less the $70,000 liability on Whiteacre). Reg. §1.1031(d)-2. Blackacre is worth $105,000. If Bob sold it immediately after receiving it, he would realize $45,000 of gain, which makes sense since Bob will not have recognized any of the $45,000 of gain realized in the §1031 exchange.

The consequences to Alice and Bob are summarized below:

Alice:
Realized Gain = 175 AR − 170 AB = 5
  AR = 95 gross FMV of Whiteacre + 80 relief of debt on Blackacre = 175
  AB = 100 basis in Blackacre + 70 debt on Whiteacre = 170
Boot Received = 80 relief of Blackacre debt − 70 debt on Whiteacre = 10
Recognized Gain = 5
Basis in Whiteacre = 100 basis in Blackacre − 10 boot received + 5 gain recognized = 95
  Or:

$$\begin{array}{r}
100 \text{ Basis in Blackacre} \\
+\,70 \text{ debt on Whiteacre} \\
-\,80 \text{ relief on Blackacre debt} \\
\underline{+\ \ 5 \text{ gain recognized}} \\
95
\end{array}$$

Bob:
Realized Gain = 175 AR − 130 AB = 45
  AR = 105 gross FMV of Blackacre + 70 relief of debt on Whiteacre = 175
  AB = 50 basis in Whiteacre + 80 debt on Blackacre = 130
Boot Received = 0 (no net debt relief)
Recognized Gain = 0
Basis in Blackacre = 60

$$\begin{array}{r}
50 \text{ basis in Whiteacre} \\
+\,80 \text{ debt on Blackacre} \\
\underline{-\,70 \text{ relief of Whiteacre debt}} \\
60
\end{array}$$

8. Here is a diagram of the exchange:

Emily		**Fred**
Riverview	→ ←	Mountainview
110 Gross FMV		60 FMV
20 Debt		40 Basis
90 Net FMV		
100 Basis	←	30 cash

Emily's realized gain on the exchange is $10,000 — $110,000 amount realized ($60,000 of property received, plus $30,000 of cash, plus relief of $20,000 of debt on Riverview) less her $100,000 basis in Riverview. Emily receives $50,000 of boot — $30,000 of cash boot plus $20,000 of debt relief. Thus, she recognizes $10,000 of gain, which is the lesser of (i) the $10,000 realized gain and (ii) the $50,000 boot received. Her basis in Mountainview is $60,000 — her $100,000 basis in Riverview, plus $10,000 of gain recognized, less the $50,000 of boot she received. Mountainview is worth $60,000. If she sold it immediately after receiving it, she would not realize any gain or loss, which makes sense since she will have already recognized all of the $10,000 of gain realized in the §1031 exchange.

Fred's realized gain on the exchange is $20,000 — $110,000 amount realized (the value of Riverview) less $90,000 basis plus adjustments (his $40,000 basis in Mountainview, plus $20,000 of debt on Riverview, plus $30,000 of cash Fred paid). Reg. §1.1031-2(d). Fred will not recognize any gain on the exchange because he receives no boot. §1031(a), (b). His basis in Riverview is $90,000 — his $40,000 basis in Mountainview, plus $20,000 of debt on Riverview, plus $30,000 of cash Fred paid. Riverview is worth $110,000. If Fred sold it immediately after receiving it, he would realize $20,000 of gain, which makes sense since Fred will not have recognized any of the $20,000 of gain realized in the §1031 exchange.

The consequences to Emily and Fred are summarized below:

Emily:

Realized Gain = 110 AR - 100 AB = 10

    AR = 60 FMV of Mountainview + 30 cash received + 20 relief of debt on
        Riverview = 110

    AB = 100 basis in Riverview

Boot Received = 30 cash received + 20 relief of Riverview debt = 50

Recognized Gain = 10

Basis in Mountainview = 100 basis in Riverview − 50 boot received + 10 gain recognized = 60

Or:

> 100 basis in Riverview
> − 20 relief of Riverview debt
> − 30 cash received
> +10 gain recognized
> _____
> 60

Fred:

Realized Gain = 110 AR − 90 AB = 20

AR = 110 FMV of Riverview

AB = 40 basis in Mountainview + 20 Riverview debt + 30 cash Fred paid = 90

Boot Received = 0

Recognized Gain = 0

Basis in Riverview = 40 basis in Mountainview + 20 Riverview debt + 30 cash Fred paid = 90

b. Other Nonrecognition Rules

Reading: §1033; Reg. §1.1033(b)-1.

A number of other Code sections also provide for nonrecognition in certain types of property transactions. Section 1033 applies to involuntary conversions of property on which gain is realized. (The section does not apply to losses realized on involuntary conversions.) Section 1033(a) provides that a taxpayer may elect to not recognize gain realized on the involuntary conversion of property into cash due to the complete or partial destruction of the property (e.g., due to fire), theft, or condemnation, provided that the taxpayer reinvests the cash in property that is similar or related in use to the lost property. Thus, §1033 would permit a taxpayer to avoid recognition of gain realized where an appreciated building was lost due to an earthquake, the taxpayer received insurance proceeds on the destroyed building, and the insurance proceeds were used to construct a similar building. If some of the proceeds are not reinvested in similar use property, §1033 provides a rule that is similar to the boot gain recognition rule in §1031; realized gain is recognized to the extent that proceeds are not reinvested in similar use property. §1033(a)(2). The basis of the new similar use property is equal to the cost of the similar use property less any gain realized on the involuntarily converted property that was not recognized. §1033(b)(2). (This basis formula is the equivalent of the sum of the basis of the lost property, plus any additional cash or debt invested in the new property, plus any gain recognized on the involuntary conversion transaction, less any proceeds not reinvested in the similar use property. Reg. §1.1033(b)-1.)

Suppose, for example, that an apartment building with a fair market value of $750,000 and a basis of $500,000 is destroyed in a fire and that the building owner receives an insurance payment of $750,000. The building owner realizes a gain of $250,000 on the conversion. If he reinvests all of the $750,000 in similar use property and makes an election under §1033, he will not recognize any of the $250,000 of realized gain. However, if he does not reinvest the entire $750,000 in similar use property, he will recognize gain in an amount equal to the lesser of (i) the $250,000 of realized gain or (ii) the portion of the proceeds that were not reinvested in similar use property. §1033(a)(2). If the owner purchases a new apartment building for $650,000, for example, he will recognize gain of $100,000, the amount of the insurance proceeds he does not reinvest. His basis in the new building would in that case be $500,000—the $650,000 purchase price of the new building less the $150,000 of gain that was realized in the conversion but not recognized. (Equivalently, we could calculate the basis as the $500,000 basis in the destroyed building plus the $100,000 gain recognized less the $100,000 proceeds that were not reinvested in similar use property.)

Examples

9. Linda's warehouse burned down. It had a basis of $250,000 and an estimated fair market value of $400,000. Describe the tax consequences to Linda of the alternative transactions below. (Assume that each of the transactions qualifies as an involuntary conversion under §1033 and that Linda elects nonrecognition treatment.)
   a. She receives $400,000 from insurance and uses the proceeds to purchase a new warehouse for $400,000.
   b. She receives $400,000 from insurance and uses the proceeds to purchase (i) a new warehouse for $300,000 and (ii) a race horse for $100,000.
   c. She receives $300,000 from insurance, borrows an additional $100,000, and uses the $400,000 of insurance and debt proceeds to purchase a new warehouse.
   d. She receives nothing from insurance, borrows $400,000, and uses the debt proceeds to purchase a new warehouse for $400,000.
   e. She receives $400,000 from insurance, purchases a new warehouse for $220,000, and keeps the rest of the money.

Explanations

9. a. Linda's realized gain is $150,000 ($400,000 amount realized less $250,000 basis), but she does not recognize any of that gain. Her basis in the new warehouse is $250,000 (the $400,000 purchase price for the new warehouse less the $150,000 of gain realized but not recognized on the conversion). §1033(a)(2)(A), (b)(2).
   b. Linda's realized gain is $150,000 ($400,000 amount realized less $250,000 basis). The nonrecognition rule of §1033 applies only to the extent that the amount received from the involuntary conversion is used to purchase similar-use replacement property.

145

§1033(a)(2)(A). Here, Linda spends $100,000 of the proceeds on a race horse, which is not similar-use property, so she recognizes $100,000 of gain. §1033(a)(2). She will have a $100,000 basis in the race horse, under §1012. Her basis in the new warehouse is $250,000 — the $300,000 purchase price of the new warehouse less the $50,000 of gain that was realized but not recognized on the conversion. §1033(a)(2)(A), (b)(2).

c. Linda's realized gain is $50,000 ($300,000 amount realized less $250,000 basis). Linda uses all of the proceeds to acquire similar-use property, the new warehouse, so she does not recognize any gain on the conversion. Her basis in the new warehouse is $350,000 — the $400,000 purchase price of the new warehouse less the $50,000 of gain that was realized but not recognized. §1033(a)(2)(A), (b)(2).

d. Linda realizes a loss of $250,000 ($250,000 basis less zero amount realized). Section 1033 does not apply to realized losses. Her realized loss may or may not be deductible under §165 (discussed in Chapter 4). Linda's basis in the new warehouse is $400,000. §1012 and Crane v. Commissioner, 331 U.S. 1 (1947).

e. Linda's realized gain is $150,000 ($400,000 amount realized less $250,000 basis). The nonrecognition rule of §1033 applies only to the extent that the amount received from the involuntary conversion is used to purchase similar-use replacement property. §1033(a)(2)(A). Here, Linda does not spend $180,000 of the insurance proceeds on similar use property, so she recognizes all of the $150,000 realized gain. Her basis in the new warehouse is $220,000 (the $220,000 purchase price of the new warehouse less zero realized but unrecognized gain). §1033(a)(2)(A), (b)(2).

B. TRANSFERS INCIDENT TO MARRIAGE AND DIVORCE

Reading: §§62(a)(10), 71, 215, 1041.

Transfers made pursuant to marriage and (more commonly) divorce raise a number of interesting tax issues. For example, suppose pursuant to a divorce John gives Sarah property with a basis of $10,000 and a fair market value of $30,000. Should Sarah be taxed on the fair market value received? And what about John? Should John receive a deduction equal to the basis of the property? Or should John be treated as if the property were sold and the proceeds used to purchase freedom from a bad marriage? Should it matter whether the property was community property or John's separate property?

In United States v. Davis, 370 U.S. 65 (1962), the Supreme Court held that a transfer of appreciated property incident to a divorce was a realization event to the transferor. In effect, the Court held that the exchange of property for freedom from marriage was similar to the exchange of property for services or other non-like-kind property and so was taxable. The holding in *Davis* did not apply, however, to a transfer between divorcing spouses of property held as community property. The *Davis* decision was subject to a great deal of criticism, both for its view of divorce settlements and the distinction it set up between community property and non-community property states.

Eventually the holding in *Davis* was overturned by statute. Section 1041 now provides that no gain or loss is recognized by either party on the transfer of property to (i) a spouse or (ii) a former spouse, provided that the transfer is incident to divorce. Note that §1041 applies to transfers of property between divorcing same-sex spouses whose marriage is recognized under the "state of celebration" rule, discussed in Chapter 1. *Davis* may apply, however, to transfers of property between unmarried partners in a Registered Domestic Partnership or Civil Union, regardless of the fact that their relationship is legally recognized by state law, because the IRS has asserted that partners in such relationships are not married and thus are not "spouses" for purposes of federal tax law. Rev. Rul. 2013-17. In addition, the holding in *Davis* may apply to transfers of property in anticipation of marriage.

As is customary in nonrecognition provisions, §1041 provides that the transferee takes the transferor's basis in the property. Thus, in the above example neither party would recognize gain or loss, and Sarah would receive a $10,000 basis in the property received.

Transfers of cash made incident to divorce do not raise realization issues and might therefore be dealt with elsewhere in this book. However, in order to provide a more unified view of transfers incident to divorce, we will discuss these transfers here. Payments of cash made incident to divorce are treated as either *alimony* or *child support payments*. Alimony payments are included in the income of the payee and are deducted (as an above-the-line deduction) from the payor's gross income. On the other hand, child support payments are not deductible by the payor or includible by the payee. §§62(a)(10), 71(a), (c), 215.

In order to qualify as alimony, a payment must meet the following tests. First, as noted above, it must be made in cash. §71(b)(1). (As described above, §1041, not §71, applies to noncash transfers incident to divorce.) Second, the payment must be made pursuant to a written divorce or separate maintenance agreement or decree. §71(b)(1)(A), (2). Third, the payor and payee must live in separate households. §71(b)(1)(C). Presumably, this provision is intended to prevent couples from using divorce to obtain the benefits of income splitting, as described below in an example. Fourth, the payment must not be for child support. §71(c)(1). Any payments that end when a child dies or reaches a certain age (for example, age 18) will be characterized as child support payments. §71(c)(2). Fifth, the payment obligation must not continue after the death of the payee spouse. §71(b)(1)(D). Sixth, §71(f) provides, generally, that payments are treated as alimony only to the extent they are substantially equal in the first three years in which alimony payments are made.

Payments that are "front loaded" in this three-year period are recharacterized as property settlements. In effect, §71(f) requires recapture of any disproportionately high amounts of alimony (referred to in §71 as *excess alimony payments*) paid in the first two years. The excess alimony paid in years one and two is recaptured by requiring the payor spouse to include it in income in year three; the spouse who receives the alimony deducts the same amount from gross income in year three. In a tax practice you will not usually have to compute the amount of excess alimony payments under §71(f) because family lawyers typically structure alimony as level payments to avoid triggering §71(f). If you plan to practice family law, however, you may need to know more about how such excess alimony payments are calculated, to prevent application of the rules to the alimony that you negotiate for your clients.

How are excess alimony payments calculated under §71(f)? First, determine the excess payments for the *second* year in which alimony payments are made. §71(f)(4). The excess payments for this year equal (i) the alimony payments made in the second year less (ii) the sum of (a) the alimony payments made in the third year of payment plus (b) $15,000. Second, determine the excess payments for the *first* year in which payments are made. §71(f)(3). The excess payments for this year equal (i) the alimony payments made in the first year less (ii) the sum of (a) $15,000 plus (b) the average alimony payment made in the second and third years (which is computed after reducing the second year payment by any portion of that payment treated as an excess payment under §71(f)(4)).

For example, suppose an alimony schedule provides for the payment of $100,000 in the first and second years and $20,000 thereafter. In years one and two, the payor spouse deducts the $100,000 of alimony from gross income and the payee spouse includes it in income. In year three, the payor spouse deducts the $20,000 of alimony from gross income and the payee spouse includes it in income.

Is this payment schedule subject to §71(f)? In order to answer that question, we must determine whether there will be excess alimony payments in the first and second years of payment. First, we determine the excess payments for the *second* year in which payments are made. §71(f)(4). The excess payment for this year equals $65,000 (the $100,000 second year alimony payment less $35,000, which is the sum of the $20,000 year three alimony payment plus $15,000). Second, we determine the excess payments for the *first* year in which payments are made. §71(f)(3). The average alimony payment in years two and three is $27,500, which is the average of (i) the $20,000 year three payment and (ii) the $35,000 year two payment, net of excess payments (that is, the $100,000 second year payment less the $65,000 portion of that payment that is treated as an excess payment under §71(f)(4)). The excess payment for the first year thus equals $57,500 (the $100,000 first year alimony payment less $42,500, which is the sum of $15,000 plus the $27,500 average alimony payment made in the second and third years). In year three, the payor spouse includes and the payee spouse deducts $122,500 (the sum of the $65,000 year two excess payment plus the $57,500 year one excess payment). §71(f)(1). In other words, of the $200,000 of "alimony" paid in years one and two, (i) $77,500 is treated as alimony and (ii) the other $122,500 is recharacterized in year three and is not treated as alimony. If all this seems a bit much, keep in mind that in practice, family lawyers structure alimony payments so the payments do not trigger §71(f).

There are a number of exceptions to the recapture rules of §71(f). §71(f)(5). For example, §71(f) does not apply if the alimony payments cease because the payee spouse remarries or either spouse dies. §71(f)(5)(A). In addition, §71(f) does not apply if the alimony schedule provides that for at least three years the payee spouse is to receive a fixed percentage of (i) income from a business or property or (ii) compensation from employment or self-employment. §71(f)(5)(C).

The intuitive justification for the §71(c) child support exception and the §71(f) recapture provisions is that alimony is a periodic payment for the support of the recipient spouse. A payment that is received all up front or continues after the death of the recipient spouse (for example, through her estate) is thus more in the nature of a property settlement, which is not deductible by the payor or includible by the payee when paid.

If a payor spouse has much higher income than the payee spouse, §§71, 215 permit the divorcing spouses to shift income from the high-income payor spouse to the low-income payee spouse. Consider the following example. Assume that the following rate schedule (which is a fictitious, simplified version of the real §1 rate schedule) applies to all parties:

If taxable income is:	The tax is:
Not over $10,000	10 percent of taxable income
Over $10,000	$1,000 (10 percent of $10,000) plus 15 percent of the excess over $10,000
Over $50,000	$7,000 ($1,000 plus $6,000, which is 15 percent of the $40,000 of taxable income between $10,000 and $50,000) plus 30 percent of the excess over $50,000
Over $400,000	$112,000 ($7,000 plus $105,000, which is 30 percent of the $350,000 of taxable income between $50,000 and $400,000) plus 40 percent of the excess over $400,000

3. Problems of Timing

Assume that Charlie agrees to pay Shannon $15,000 a year pursuant to a divorce decree. The payment will constitute alimony under §71. Assume that, without taking the alimony into account, Charlie has taxable income of $70,000 a year and is in the 30 percent rate bracket, and Shannon has taxable income of $15,000 a year and is in the 15 percent rate bracket. Taking into account the alimony, Shannon has $30,000 of income, so she is still in the 15 percent rate bracket. §71(a). She will owe $2,250 of tax on the $15,000 of alimony she receives. Charlie deducts the $15,000 he pays Shannon, reducing his income to $55,000. §215(a). He is still in the 30 percent rate bracket. The $15,000 deduction reduces Charlie's taxes by $4,500 (30 percent of $15,000). The alimony increases Shannon's tax by $2,250 but decreases Charlie's tax by $4,500. Thus, the alimony saves Charlie more in tax than it costs Shannon. The net tax on the alimony payments is *negative* $2,250!

Section 71 also contains an elective provision that allows parties to treat what otherwise would be characterized as alimony as a property settlement. §71(b)(1)(B). Thus, in lieu of alimony, which is deductible to the payor and taxable to the payee, the parties can opt for the nonrecognition treatment of property settlements. The parties cannot, however, treat what otherwise would be characterized as a property settlement as alimony.

Examples

10. Carla gives Don stock with a basis of $5,000 and a fair market value of $50,000. State the tax consequences under the following assumptions.
    a. The stock was held by Carla and Don as community property and is given to Don incident to a divorce.
    b. The stock was held by Carla as separate property and is given to Don incident to divorce.
    c. The stock was held by Carla as separate property and is given to Don as part of an antenuptial agreement. In return, Don waives any right to alimony or property upon divorce.

11. Which of the following characteristics will prevent a series of payments from being characterized as alimony?
    a. The payments are equal but last only three years.
    b. The payments are made under a separate maintenance agreement prior to divorce.
    c. Upon the death of the payee spouse, the payments continue and so may be passed by will to the payee's beneficiaries.

12. a. Ed will pay Fiona $70,000 of alimony in years one and two, and $30,000 a year thereafter. What are the tax consequences to Ed and Fiona, in years one, two, and three, of the alimony payments?
    b. How, if at all, would the answer in part (a) change if the amounts Ed paid Fiona were calculated by applying a fixed percentage to Ed's employment compensation?

c. How, if at all, would the answer in part (a) change if Ed will pay Fiona $56,667 a year in years one through three?

In answering examples 13 through 15 assume that the following rate schedule (which is a fictitious, simplified version of the real §1 rate schedule) applies to all parties:

If taxable income is:	The tax is:
Not over $10,000	10 percent of taxable income
Over $10,000	$1,000 (10 percent of $10,000) plus 15 percent of the excess over $10,000
Over $50,000	$7,000 ($1,000 plus $6,000, which is 15 percent of the $40,000 of taxable income between $10,000 and $50,000) plus 30 percent of the excess over $50,000
Over $400,000	$112,000 ($7,000 plus $105,000, which is 30 percent of the $350,000 of taxable income between $50,000 and $400,000) plus 40 percent of the excess over $400,000

13. Xavier agrees to pay Yvonne $40,000 a year as alimony, pursuant to a divorce decree. Assume that, without taking the alimony into account, Xavier has taxable income of $100,000 a year and is in the 25 percent rate bracket, and Yvonne has taxable income of $20,000 a year and is in the 15 percent rate bracket.
    a. How much tax will Yvonne pay on the alimony payment?
    b. How much will Xavier save by making the alimony payment?

14. Eloise and Fabian hold as community property shares of stock in two corporations, Hibasis Inc. and Lobasis Inc. The Hibasis stock has a basis of $20,000 and a fair market value of $20,000. The Lobasis stock has a basis of $5,000 and a fair market value of $20,000. Eloise and Fabian plan to get divorced. After the divorce Eloise is expected to have annual taxable income, determined without regard to extraordinary income from property, of $135,000 a year; Fabian is expected to have annual taxable income of only $7,000 a year. Eloise and Fabian agree that Fabian should receive one of the two blocks of stock in addition to annual alimony. Advise Eloise and Fabian on how the divorce agreement should be structured.

15. George and Helen decide to divorce. In future years George expects to have taxable income, determined without regard to the treatment of alimony, of $60,000; Helen expects to have taxable income, determined without regard to the treatment of alimony, of $15,000. George

and Helen own undeveloped land that has a basis of $50,000 and a fair market value of $50,000. George and Helen have tentatively decided that Helen should receive either (i) the undeveloped land or (ii) alimony of $10,000 a year for six years, which has a present value of $50,000. Advise the parties on how they might structure the divorce settlement.

Explanations

10. a. Don does not recognize any gain on the receipt of the stock and Carla cannot deduct the stock transferred. Don's basis in the stock is the old $5,000 basis in the stock. §1041.

    b. Under the holding in *Davis*, Carla would have recognized gain on the transfer because the stock was held as separate property. Under current law, however, the result is the same as described in part (a); no gain is recognized on the receipt of stock and the basis remains unchanged. §1041.

    c. Section 1041 provides for the nonrecognition of gain upon transfer to either (i) a spouse or (ii) a former spouse, incident to divorce. If the property is transferred after marriage, §1041 applies. However, if the property is transferred prior to marriage, §1041 would not apply. The transaction would probably be treated as a sale in which appreciated property was used to acquire marital rights. The purchaser of the rights (here, Carla) would be treated as if the stock were sold and the sale proceeds used to acquire the marital rights Don gave up in the agreement. Don would then have a basis in the stock equal to its value on the date of the transfer, $50,000. See Farid-Es-Sultaneh v. Commissioner, 160 F.2d 812 (2d Cir. 1947) (where a transfer of appreciated property to a wife pursuant to an antenuptial agreement was treated as a sale of inchoate marital rights by the wife, who then received a fair market value basis in property).

11. Under §71(f), payments that would otherwise qualify as alimony but are too "front loaded" are recharacterized as property settlements. However, that section only applies to that portion of the payments that are "front loaded" in the first three years. A payment that is substantially equal during the first three years will not run afoul of §71(f). Thus, the condition described in part (a) will not prevent alimony treatment. The same is true of the condition described in part (b); parties need not be divorced so long as there is a written agreement as to separate maintenance and the other requirements of §71 are met. The condition described in part (c) will prevent alimony treatment. §71(b)(1)(D).

12. a. In years one and two, Ed deducts the $70,000 of alimony from gross income and Fiona includes it in income. In year three, Ed deducts the $30,000 of alimony from gross income and Fiona includes it in income. Do the year one or year two payments include "excess alimony payments" that are subject to the recapture rule of §71(f)? In order to determine the recapture amount under §71(f), we must calculate the excess alimony payments for years one and two.

    First, we calculate the excess payments for the *second* year in which payments are made. §71(f)(4). The excess payment for this year equals $25,000 — the $70,000 second year alimony payment less $45,000, which is the sum of the $30,000 year three alimony payment plus $15,000.

    Second, we determine the excess payments for the first year in which payments are made. §71(f)(3). The average alimony payment in years two and three is $37,500, which is the average of (i) the $30,000 year three payment and (ii) the $45,000 year two payment, net of excess payments (that is, the $70,000 second year payment less the $25,000 portion of that payment that is treated as an excess payment under §71(f)(4)). The excess payment for the first year thus equals $17,500 — the $70,000 first year alimony payment less $52,500, which is the sum of $15,000 plus the $37,500 average alimony payment made in the second and third years.

    In year three, Ed includes and Fiona deducts $42,500, which is the sum of the $25,000 year two excess payment plus the $17,500 year one excess payment. §71(f)(1). In other words, of the $140,000 of "alimony" paid in years one and two (i) $97,500 is treated as alimony and (ii) the other $42,500 is recharacterized in year three and is not treated as alimony.

    b. The answer is the same, except that the §71(f) recapture rule would not apply since the payments were computed by applying a fixed percentage to Ed's employment compensation. §71(f)(5)(C).

    c. The answer is the same except that the §71(f) recapture rule would not apply because the payments during years one through three are level. Divorce lawyers often use level payments in the first three years to avoid triggering §71(f).

13. a. Yvonne includes the alimony in income and pays $7,500 of tax on it. §71(a). Without the alimony she would have had $20,000 of taxable income and would have paid tax of $2,500, which is $1,000 (10 percent of $10,000) plus $1,500 (15 percent of the $10,000 taxable income in excess of $10,000). With the alimony she has $60,000 of taxable income and pays a tax of $10,000, which is the sum of $1,000 (10 percent of the first $10,000 of taxable income)

  plus $6,000 (15 percent of the $40,000 of taxable income between $10,000 and $50,000), plus $3,000 (30 percent of the $10,000 of taxable income between $50,000 and $60,000). (In other words, $30,000 of the alimony is taxed at the 15 percent rate, and the other $10,000 is taxed at the 30 percent rate). The tax on the $40,000 of alimony is $7,500.

 b. Xavier deducts the $40,000 of alimony. With or without the alimony payment, Xavier is in the 30 percent rate bracket. A $40,000 deduction will reduce Xavier's taxes by $12,000 (30 percent of $40,000). Thus, the alimony saves Xavier more in tax than it costs Yvonne. The net tax on the alimony payments is negative $4,500.

14. Fabian should receive the Lobasis stock. The blocks of Hibasis stock and Lobasis stock both have a fair market value of $20,000, but are not the same from a tax perspective. If, after the divorce, the Hibasis stock were sold, there would be no gain realized on the sale (because the value of the stock equals its basis), regardless of who owned it. If the Lobasis stock were sold after the divorce, there would be $15,000 of gain realized and recognized. The spouse in the lower tax rate bracket should receive this stock. Fabian is in a lower tax rate bracket than Eloise. Thus, the combined tax burden of the parties will be minimized if Fabian receives the Lobasis stock. Fabian can be compensated for the tax liability involved in accepting Lobasis stock through payment of additional alimony, if necessary.

15. In the divorce, the parties should provide for the payment of alimony. The transfer of land would have no immediate tax consequences. §1041. The $10,000 a year of alimony will be deductible to George and included in income by Helen. However, since George is in a higher tax bracket than Helen, George will save more from the deduction than Helen will pay in additional tax. George is in the 30 percent tax bracket so will save $18,000 (30 percent of $60,000) by deducting the alimony. Helen is in the 15 percent tax bracket so will pay only $9,000 (15 percent of the $60,000 she receives over the six years) upon receipt of the alimony. Structuring the payment as alimony will result in a net tax savings of $9,000. The savings could be left entirely to George or, more likely, split between the parties through an additional transfer. For example, suppose Helen agreed to accept taxable alimony on the condition that she receive an additional property worth $12,000. The $12,000 would more than offset the $9,000 of tax Helen must pay on the alimony, but would be only two-thirds of the $18,000 of tax George would save by deducting the alimony.

C. INSTALLMENT SALE AND OPEN TRANSACTION REPORTING

Reading: §§453, 453A, 453B; Reg. §15a.453-1.

There are several alternative approaches that could be used to determine the tax consequences to a seller on the sale of property in exchange for a series of payments to be made in the future. In order to illustrate these different approaches, consider the following hypothetical: Suppose Catherine owns property with a basis of $100,000 and a fair market value of $500,000. She sells the property to Bob for $500,000. Under the terms of the sales contract, Bob does not have to pay the full $500,000 immediately. Instead, he is required to pay $100,000 a year for five years. In addition, he must make annual payments, of interest, at a market rate, on the unpaid balance of the installments. In the first year, Catherine receives $100,000 of the $500,000 sales price owed her. (She also receives interest, which we will ignore for the remainder of this hypothetical.)

Catherine might argue that the first $100,000 payment of principal should be treated as tax-free recovery of her $100,000 basis. Under this "basis first" approach, Catherine would not recognize any gain until she recovers her basis; the remaining payments would be taxable in full. Another approach would tax Catherine on the full $400,000 of realized gain in the year of the sale — even though she receives only a quarter of that amount. A third approach would treat a pro rata share of each principal payment as recovery of capital and the remaining share of each principal payment as gain.

Congress has adopted the last approach. Section 446(c) provides that taxpayers may adopt the following accounting methods: (i) cash method, (ii) accrual method, or (iii) any other special accounting method permitted by the Code. (We will discuss the cash and accrual methods later in this chapter.) Section 453 provides a special accounting method for reporting gain from the sale of property in exchange for deferred payments. Under §453(c), a seller first determines the overall ratio of the gain to the sales price in order to determine what portion of each payment should be included as gain from the sale. Here Catherine has $400,000 of gain and a $500,000 sales price, so the ratio is 400,000/500,000 (or 4/5 or 80 percent). Next, the seller determines the annual inclusions of gain from the sale by multiplying any installment payment (other than interest) received during the year by the ratio determined under §453(c). Catherine receives $100,000 each year, so her annual gain inclusion is $80,000 (80 percent of the $100,000 payment she receives). Thus, she will include 80 percent (or 4/5) of each payment as gain from the sale.

Using the §453 terms of art, the *gross profit ratio* is the ratio of the *gross profit* to the *contract price*. §453(c). The gross profit is (i) the *selling price* (ii) less the seller's adjusted basis in the property sold. Reg. §15a.453-1(b)(2). The selling price is the amount to be paid by the buyer (other than interest). Id. If the property sold is subject to a liability that is assumed by the buyer, for the purpose of computing the §453(c) gross profit ratio, the selling price includes the amount of the debt. Id. The contract price is the selling price less the debt assumed by the buyer. Id. Even though it might make sense to treat the debt relief like a cash payment in year one, that approach is not generally used. Instead §453 generally spreads the gain from debt relief in the same way that the rest of the gain is spread. If, however, the debt assumed or taken subject to exceeds the seller's basis in the property sold, the liability in excess of the basis is treated as a cash payment in the year of the sale. Reg. §15a.453-1(b)(3)(i).

To illustrate the operation of §453 where the property sold is encumbered, consider the following example: Suppose Lee owns property with a basis of $300,000 and a gross fair market value of $700,000. The property is encumbered by a $200,000 mortgage, so the value of the property net of the liability is $500,000. She sells the property to George for $500,000 and assumption of the mortgage. George will pay Lee $100,000 a year for the next five years, but nothing in the year of the sale. (George will also pay interest, but disregard it in this example.) How much gain does Lee include when she receives each of the five $100,000 payments from George? Lee's gross profit is $400,000 — the $700,000 selling price (which includes both the $500,000 of installment payments to be made and the $200,000 of debt George assumed) less her $300,000 basis. The contract price is $500,000 ($700,000 selling price less $200,000 of debt assumed by George). The gross profit percentage is 80 percent ($400,000 gross profit/$500,000 contract price). Lee will include $80,000 of gain when she receives each $100,000 payment from George, for a total inclusion of $400,000 over the five installments. This makes sense since Lee's total gain realized on the sale is $400,000.

Under what circumstances does §453 apply? Section 453 applies automatically to a sale of property if the seller realizes a gain on the sale and at least one payment for the property will be received by the seller after the close of the taxable year of the sale. §453(a), (b). However, taxpayers can elect out of §453 and recognize the entire gain in the year of the sale. §453(d). (Presumably, taxpayers will so elect only when they face an unusually low tax bracket in the year of sale.) Section 453 does not apply to sales of personal property by taxpayers who regularly sell personal property on the installment plan, such as department stores, and sales of real property by taxpayers who hold real property for sale to customers in the ordinary course of business, such as real estate developers. §453(b)(2), (l)(1). Section 453 also does not apply to the sale of publicly traded stocks or securities. §453(k). (Taxpayers who do not qualify for §453 must include the full gain in the year of sale — even if the payments are to be made over a period of many years.) Finally, §453 does not apply if the seller realizes a loss on the sale.

What if the total amount of the deferred payment on the sale is uncertain at the time of the sale? Can the taxpayer then use the "basis first" approach instead of §453? In Burnet v. Logan, 283 U.S. 404 (1931), the Supreme

Court held that a taxpayer who sold stock in a mining company in exchange for cash and payments that were to be based on the amount mined in the future could adopt an open transaction (basis first) approach to report the gain from the sale. Since the amount to be received in the future was not ascertainable, Mrs. Logan was permitted to recover all of her basis first, then include all amounts received after she had recovered her basis. However, §453(j)(2), enacted in 1980, and various regulations promulgated after the Logan decision require sellers receiving contingent payments to apply §453 in the year of the sale and preclude open transaction reporting except in extraordinary cases. See, e.g., Reg. §§15a.453-1(c), 1.1001-1(a). Regulation §15a.453-1(c) provides three special rules for determining the timing of basis recovery and gain inclusion where the amount paid for property is contingent: First, if a maximum payment for the property can be determined, that amount is treated as the selling price for the purpose of computing the §453 inclusion ratio. Reg. §15a.453-1(c)(2). Second, if a maximum payment cannot be determined, but the number of years over which payments will be made can be determined, the taxpayer's basis is allocated equally over that period. Reg. §15a.453-1(c)(3). Third, if neither a maximum payment nor time period for payment can be determined, the taxpayer recovers basis equally over 15 years. Reg. §15a.453-1(c)(4).

Although §453 reporting is not as beneficial to taxpayers as the "basis first" approach, it is much more beneficial to taxpayers than the approach that would require taxpayers to include gain in the year of the sale even if no payments were to be received in the year of the sale. The deferral of tax under §453 is like an interest-free loan from the government to the taxpayer in an amount equal to the tax on the gain realized in the sale. The tax benefits of §453 are limited by several provisions, however. For example, if the installment payments exceed $5 million, the taxpayer will have to pay the government interest on the tax liability deferred under §453. §453A(a)(1), (b)(2). Section 453A(d) also provides that if an installment obligation is pledged as security for a loan, the proceeds of the loan will, in some circumstances, be treated as a payment on the installment obligation, triggering an inclusion under §453. If the taxpayer receives a bond or other evidence of indebtedness from the purchaser, the taxpayer's receipt of the debt is also treated as a payment if the debt received from the purchaser is payable on demand or is readily tradable. §453(f)(3), (4).

Examples

16. a. Barbara owns Blackacre, which has a value of $40,000 and basis of $10,000. On January 1 of year one, Barbara sells Blackacre to Susan for $40,000; Susan will pay Barbara $10,000 a year in years two through five (plus a market rate of interest on the unpaid balance). How much gain from the sale, if any, does Barbara include in years one and two?

b. How, if at all, would your answer in part (a) change if, instead of making the four $10,000 payments, Susan paid Barbara the entire $40,000 sale price at the end of the fifth year?

17. Alice owns Whiteacre, which has a gross value of $10,000 and basis of $7,000 and is subject to a $6,000 mortgage (so the value, net of the mortgage, is $4,000). Alice sells Whiteacre to Bob, who takes White-acre subject to the mortgage and agrees to pay Alice $1,000 immediately and an additional $1,000 per year for the next three years (plus interest). What are the tax consequences to Alice?

18. Carol sells her mineral rights in certain land to the Douglas Mining Corporation. Her basis in the mineral rights is $10,000. Douglas agrees to pay her $5,000 immediately plus an additional amount depending on how much ore is mined in the future. The parties estimate that payments are likely to vary in amount from $1,250 to $2,000 per year and that mining is likely to continue for eight to ten years. In year two Carol receives a payment of $1,500.

a. Under the open transaction approach adopted in Burnet v. Logan, how much of the payments received in years one and two would Carol have to include in income?

b. How much income would Carol report from the payments received in years one and two if the method of allocating basis stated in the §453 regulations were adopted?

c. What alternative method of allocation might be fairer than either of the two methods above?

Explanations

16. a. Section 453 applies because Barbara has sold property at a gain and will receive at least one payment after year one, the year of the sale. §453(a), (b)(1). Barbara's gross profit is $30,000 ($40,000 selling price less her $10,000 basis). The contract price is $40,000. The gross profit percentage is 75 percent ($30,000 gross profit/$40,000 contract price). Thus, Barbara must include 75 percent of each payment she receives. §453(c). In year one Barbara does not receive any payment, so she does not have to include any of the gain. In year two Barbara must include $7,500, which is 75 percent of the $10,000 payment she receives in that year. By the fourth payment, in year five, Barbara's four $7,500 inclusions will total $30,000, her total gain realized on the sale of Blackacre.

b. The gross profit percentage is the same as in part (a), 75 percent. As in part (a), Barbara does not have to include any of the $30,000 gain in year one because she receives no payment in that year. The answer changes for years two through five. Here, since Barbara does not receive any payments in years two through four, she will not include any gain in those years. In year five Barbara will include $30,000 of gain (75 percent of the $40,000 payment she receives in year five). Said another way, Barbara reports her entire gain in the year in which she receives the entire deferred payment for the property.

17. Alice's gross profit is $3,000 ($10,000 selling price, which includes the debt, less her $7,000 basis). §453(c), Reg. §15a.453-1(b)(2). The contract price is $4,000 ($10,000 selling price less the $6,000 debt Bob took the property subject to). Reg. §15a.453-1(b)(2). The gross profit percentage is 75 percent ($3,000 gross profit/$4,000 contract price). Alice will include $750 (75 percent of each $1,000 payment received) in each of years one through four. §453(c). (Even though it might make sense to treat the debt relief like a cash payment in year one, that approach is not adopted unless the mortgage assumed by the buyer exceeds the seller's basis in the property sold. Reg. §15a.453-1(b)(3)(i).)

18. a. Under the open transaction, or basis first, approach, Carol would not report any gain until the amounts received exceed her basis, $10,000. Carol receives total payments of $6,500 ($5,000 plus $1,500) in years one and two. Thus, she would not have to include any income in those years.

    b. Where payments are contingent, Regulation §15a.453-1(c) requires the taxpayer to calculate the inclusion amount, under §453(c), based on an assumption that the maximum possible payments will be received. In this case, that would require Carol to assume that $2,000 per year will be received for 10 years, for a total of $25,000 (including the $5,000 year one payment). Carol's gross profit is $15,000 ($25,000 selling price less $10,000 basis) and the contract price is $25,000, so the gross profit percentage is 60 percent ($15,000/$25,000 or 3/5). In year one Carol must include $3,000 (60 percent of the $5,000 payment she receives in that year). In year two Carol must include $900 (60 percent of the $1,500 payment she receives in that year).

    c. A fairer approach might be to attempt to estimate the most likely total payments rather than the maximum. In this case, total contingent payments are expected to fall between $10,000 (eight years at $1,250 per year) and $20,000 (10 years at $2,000 per year). You might choose a number somewhere in between, say $15,000. Then the total expected payment would be $20,000 for a gain of $10,000, so $10,000/$20,000 or 50 percent of each payment would be gain. Thus, $2,500 of gain would be reported in year one and $750 in year two. Although this approach seems more accurate and reasonable than the Treasury approach, it would make it easier for the taxpayer to underestimate total expected payments and thus underreport gain in the early years.

Note that if the Treasury's allocation method is adopted and the taxpayer receives less than the maximum expected amount, the taxpayer will have basis remaining after all payments have been received. At that point she will take a loss deduction for her unrecovered basis. Reg. §15a.453-1(c)(2)(iii). Similarly, if the taxpayer receives more than the expected amount, her basis will be used up before all installment payments have been made; the payments she receives after her basis has been fully recovered will be included in income (with no basis reduction).

D. ORIGINAL ISSUE DISCOUNT

Reading: §§1271–1278.

A borrower must pay a lender interest on principal borrowed in order to compensate the lender for the borrower's use of the lender's funds while the loan is outstanding. *Compound interest* is determined by applying the interest rate on the debt to the sum of (i) the amount originally loaned plus (ii) any interest on the debt that has already accrued but has not been paid. (In other words, the unpaid, accrued interest increases the principal owed.) *Simple interest* is interest paid on only the amount originally loaned. Interest can be either (i) stated explicitly or (ii) unstated and implicit. *Original issue discount* (OID) is the term for unstated interest on debt, determined at the time the debt is issued. To illustrate the concepts of stated interest and unstated interest, consider the following examples.

In year one Sherry places $377 in a bank savings account that pays interest every six months. (In other words, the interest is compounded semi-annually.) The annual interest rate is 10 percent, compounding semiannually. The interest in the first six months of year one is $18.85. This amount is the product of the 5 percent semiannual interest rate (the annual 10 percent rate/two compounding periods in each year) multiplied by the $377 of principal. If that interest is not withdrawn, the balance in the account after the first six months is increased to $395.85 ($377 original principal plus $18.85 of interest for the first six months). The interest in the second six months of year one is $19.79 (5 percent semiannual interest on $395.85 principal). This increases the balance to $415.64 ($395.85 plus $19.79 of interest for the second six months of year one). Sherry includes $38.64 ($18.85 plus $19.79) of interest in her gross income for year one even if she leaves it in the bank. §61(a)(4). In this example, the bank is paying Sherry 10 percent annual stated interest, compounding semiannually on the balance in her savings account. (This is the economic equivalent of paying Sherry 10.25 percent annual interest, compounding annually.) The semiannual interest calculations are carried out until the 10th year in the chart below.

3. Problems of Timing

Note that the dollar amount of interest grows every six months despite the fact that the 5 percent interest rate is constant because the constant interest rate is being applied to an ever-increasing principal balance.

	Beginning balance	Semiannual 5 percent interest	Ending balance
Year 1: 1st 6 months	$377.00	$18.85	$395.85
Year 1: 2d 6 months	395.85	19.79	415.64
Year 2: 1st 6 months	415.64	20.78	436.42
Year 2: 2d 6 months	436.42	21.82	458.24
Year 3: 1st 6 months	458.24	22.91	481.15
Year 3: 2d 6 months	481.15	24.06	505.21
Year 4: 1st 6 months	505.21	25.26	530.47
Year 4: 2d 6 months	530.47	26.52	556.99
Year 5: 1st 6 months	556.99	27.85	584.84
Year 5: 2d 6 months	584.84	29.24	614.08
Year 6: 1st 6 months	614.08	30.70	644.78
Year 6: 2d 6 months	644.78	32.24	677.02
Year 7: 1st 6 months	677.02	33.85	710.87
Year 7: 2d 6 months	710.87	35.54	746.41
Year 8: 1st 6 months	746.41	37.32	783.73
Year 8: 2d 6 months	783.73	39.19	822.92
Year 9: 1st 6 months	822.92	41.15	864.07
Year 9: 2d 6 months	864.07	43.20	907.27
Year 10: 1st 6 months	907.27	45.36	952.63
Year 10: 2d 6 months	952.63	47.63	1,000.00[*]

[*]Due to rounding amounts in the chart, the balance plus interest in the last year is a little over $1,000.

Now consider another example. Mary purchases a bond from BigCo for $377. The bond does not provide for annual cash payments of interest or principal, but is redeemable in 10 years for $1,000. (Such bonds are often referred to as *zero coupon bonds* because there is zero stated interest on the debt.) What is the tax treatment of the $623 difference between the amount Mary paid for the bond, $377, and the $1,000 amount that she will receive at maturity in 10 years? One approach would be to treat the $623 as property gain when the bond matures, just as if Mary had bought a parcel of land for $377 and sold it 10 years later for $1,000. Mary would not have to pay tax on such gain until year 10, and the gain probably would qualify as capital gain and be taxed at low rates. (For a discussion of capital gains, see Chapter 8.) The other approach would be to treat the $623 as interest income. Current law adopts the second approach; the $623 will be treated as interest income.

The $623 that Mary earns on the BigCo bond is governed by the OID rules in the Code. The total unstated interest, or OID, on a debt instrument equals (i) the *stated redemption price at maturity* of the debt instrument (the amount payable under the debt instrument less any stated interest that is paid at least annually) less (ii) the *issue price* of the debt instrument, which is generally the amount of cash the bondholder paid for the debt. §1273(a), (b). The stated redemption price at maturity of Mary's BigCo bond is $1,000, the amount payable at maturity. §1273(a)(2). The issue price of the bond is $377, the amount Mary paid for it. §1273(b). The OID on Mary's BigCo bond is thus $623 (the $1,000 stated redemption price at maturity less the $377 issue price).

The $623 of OID on the bond is then allocated over the 10-year period during which the bond is outstanding. Here again, there are two possible approaches. One approach would be to allocate the $623 of OID equally over the 10 years so that Mary would include $62.30 per year of interest for 10 years. The other approach (called either the *constant-yield-to-maturity* method or the *economic accrual* method) is to tax Mary in the same way that Sherry is taxed on her savings account, by requiring her to include amounts of interest that increase each year — because the interest inclusion is calculated by applying a constant rate of interest to a balance that keeps increasing to reflect prior accrued but unpaid interest. The implicit interest rate, referred to as the *yield-to-maturity*, on the bond is 10 percent, compounding semiannually — because $377 invested at 10 percent annual interest, compounding semiannually, would grow to $1,000 in 10 years. (The implicit interest rate for a given issue price and redemption amount can be determined by a formula that is "hard wired" into programmable calculators and comes with computer spreadsheet programs. Lawyers will seldom, if ever, be required to calculate the yield-to-maturity of a debt instrument.)

Mary must compute her OID inclusion for each six-month period during which she owns the bond. §1272(a)(1), (3), (5). Her OID inclusion for each semiannual period is the product of multiplying (i) the yield-to-maturity, which is 5 percent for each semiannual period, by (ii) the *adjusted issue price* of the bond. §1272(a)(1), (3). The adjusted issue price is (i) the issue price of the bond plus (ii) any unstated interest that has already accrued on the bond but not been paid to the bondholder. §1272(a)(4). In our example, the issue price of the bond is $377, the amount Mary paid for the bond. The OID for the first six-month period in year one equals $18.85 (5 percent semiannual interest on $377). The OID for the second six-month period in year one is $19.79 — 5 percent semiannual interest on the $395.85 adjusted issue price ($377 issue price plus the $18.85 of accrued but unpaid interest from the first six-month period). In year one Mary includes the total OID for year one, $38.64, as interest. §1272(a)(1). If you refer back to the chart from our first example, you will see that Mary's OID inclusions on the BigCo bond track the interest inclusions from Sherry's savings account. The OID that Mary must include each year is added to her basis for the bond so that when she receives the $1,000 at maturity she realizes no gain or loss on the redemption. Reg. §1.1272-1(g). If the issuer, BigCo, does not pay the full redemption amount due to bankruptcy or some other event, Mary will recognize a loss (probably a capital loss) equal to the difference between her basis at that time and the amount received. §§1221, 1271(a)(2).

Mary, an individual, is a cash method taxpayer. Cash method taxpayers include items of income in the year in which they receive the item of income. Reg. §1.451-1. (The cash method of accounting is discussed later in this chapter.) Why do the OID rules require Mary to include annual interest income if she is not going to receive any interest until year 10? To answer that question, we have to consider the treatment of the OID to BigCo, the issuer of the bond. BigCo, like all corporate bond issuers, is an accrual method taxpayer. If we did not have the OID rules, cash method individual bond-holders would not have to include unstated interest until the maturity date for the bond, but, under the accrual method, corporate issuers would deduct the unstated interest as it accrues economically (that is, as we just described in the above example with Mary) in each of the 10 years. In order to avoid this asymmetry in the timing of OID interest income and deductions, the OID rules put both issuers and bondholders on the same accounting method, the accrual method, for the purpose of determining OID interest deductions and inclusions. §§163(e)(1), (2), 1272(a)(1). (Of course, we could also avoid the asymmetry by allowing cash method bond purchasers to defer recognition of interest income until payment, and putting the accrual method issuers on the cash method so that interest could not be deducted until payment.)

The application of the original discount rules is not limited to the purchase or issuance of zero coupon bonds for cash—the rules also apply to certain property sales. Suppose, for example, that Xavier owns property with a basis of $100,000 and a fair market value of $377,000. If Xavier sells the property for cash and purchases 1,000 10-year zero coupon BigCo bonds that pay $1,000 each upon redemption, the tax treatment is obvious: Xavier will recognize $277,000 gain on the property sale, and then, under the OID provisions, will recognize interest income as described above. In other words, he will include $623,000 of interest over the 10 years and the interest will be allocated over each of the 10 years using the constant yield-to-maturity method described above. Would the result change if Xavier sold the property in exchange for a single $1 million payment in 10 years?

Xavier might hope that the entire $1 million payment would be characterized as proceeds from the sale of property. The gain in that case might be capital gain, which is taxed at a lower rate than other income. §1(a) — (d), (h). The transaction might also qualify for installment sales treatment, which, as we discussed in the previous section, would defer taxation until payment in year 10. Instead, under the OID rules the transaction will effectively be divided into two separate tax transactions: The first transaction, the property transaction, is Xavier's sale of his property for the 10-year zero coupon BigCo bonds. Xavier's gain from the sale may be capital gain and may qualify for the installment sale method, described in the preceding section, in which case the tax on the gain would be deferred until payment is made in year 10. The second transaction is the debt transaction. Xavier must include in income the interest that accrues on the bond in each of the 10 years the bond is outstanding.

How does the tax law determine the exact amount of interest income and property sale proceeds? If no interest is stated on the debt instrument issued in exchange for property, the payments to be made on the debt instrument are discounted to present value using the *applicable federal rate* (AFR). §1274(b). The AFR is set monthly by the Treasury, pursuant to §1274(d), to reflect prevailing interest rates on U.S. government bonds. (If the stated principal on debt issued in exchange for property does not exceed the amount specified in §1274A(b), adjusted for inflation—for example, $5,468,200 in 2013—the rate used in the OID calculations cannot exceed 9 percent. §1274A(a), (b), (d) Rev. Rul. 2012-33.) The unstated interest on the debt instrument equals the gross amount of payments to be made on the debt instrument less the present value of those payments. §§1273(a)(1), (b)(4), 1274(a), (b)(1). Assume that the AFR is 10 percent, compounding semiannually. (Disregard §1274A(a) to simplify the example and keep it comparable to our earlier two examples.) The present value of $1 million received in 10 years, discounted at 10 percent, compounding semiannually, turns out to be $377,000, so the $623,000 difference between the $1 million amount to be paid and the $377,000 present value of that payment is treated as OID interest. In other words, Xavier will include interest in each of the 10 years that the bond is outstanding based on the constant yield-to-maturity method described above. His OID interest inclusion in year one is $38,640 ($18,850 of OID for the first six months of year one plus $19,790 of OID for the second six months of year one). Note that, in this process, we have imputed the amount for which Xavier's property was exchanged in year one, $377,000. For the purpose of determining his gain from the property transaction, this $377,000 amount will be treated as the amount realized. Reg. §1.1001-1(g). Xavier's gain from the sale of the property is thus $277,000 ($377,000 amount realized less his $100,000 basis in the property).

Section 1274 does not apply to (i) sales of principal residences, (ii) sales in which payments are not deferred for more than six months, and (iii) certain sales of farmland. §1274(c). In addition, if debt issued in exchange for property is publicly traded, or the property for which the debt is exchanged is publicly traded (for example, traded stock), we do not use §1274 to impute an issue price for the debt, in order to calculate the OID on the debt. §1274(c)(3)(D). Instead, the issue price of the debt is the value of the property in exchange for which the debt is issued, so the OID on the debt equals the stated redemption price at maturity of the debt less the value of the property exchanged for the debt. §1273(a), (b)(3).

Moreover, the OID rules have no effect on property sales that require at least annual interest payments provided that the stated interest rate on the debt at least equals the AFR. §§1273(a)(2), (b)(4), 1274(c)(1), (2), Reg. §1.1274-1(b)(1). If, however, the debt bears stated interest at a rate that at least equals the AFR, but that interest is not payable until maturity, the debt will have OID in an amount equal to the stated interest payable at maturity. §§1273(a)(1), (2), (b)(4), 1274(a)(1), (c)(1), (2). The holder and issuer of the debt will thus have to include and deduct the interest each year using the constant yield-to-maturity method described above.

Section 1274 also does not apply to a sale if the total payments to be made on a debt instrument exchanged for property are no more than $250,000. §1274(c)(3)(C). However, §483 may still apply to such a debt instrument. Section 483, like §1274, determines the amount of unstated interest on a debt instrument issued for property by comparing the payments to be made on the debt and the present value of the payments to be made (again discounting the payments at the AFR). §483(b). Unlike the OID rules, however, §483 does not require accrual of the unstated interest, calculated using the constant yield-to-maturity method. Instead, the holder and issuer of the debt instrument report the unstated interest under their normal methods of accounting (despite the fact that this results in asymmetrical treatment of the interest where the holder is a cash method taxpayer and the issuer is an accrual method taxpayer). Reg. §1.483-1(a)(2)(ii).

Examples

19. At the beginning of year one, Abe pays $1,000 for a three-year zero-coupon BigCo bond, which will pay Abe $1,340 at maturity, in three years, and nothing before then. The constant interest rate necessary to produce $1,340 at the end of three years on a $1,000 investment is 10 percent, compounding semiannually, so the yield-to-maturity on the bond is 10 percent compounding semiannually. What are the tax consequences to Abe and BigCo in year one?

20. a. Bernice sells business property with a basis of $400,000 to Carl in exchange for one payment of $1,340,000 to be made in three years. The applicable federal rate is 10 percent, compounding semiannually. Applying this rate, the present value of the $1,340,000 payment due in three years is $1 million. What are the tax consequences to Bernice? (Disregard §1274A to simplify the example.)

   b. How, if at all, would your answer in part (a) change if Bernice had exchanged her property for $1 million payable in three years, and six semiannual interest payments of $50,000 each?

Explanations

19. The bond has $340 of OID ($1,340 stated redemption price at maturity less $1,000 issue price, which is the amount Abe paid for the bond). §1273(a)(1), (2), (b). The $340 of OID will be allocated over the three-year term of the debt using the constant yield-to-maturity method. §§163(e), 1272(a)(1). The OID for the first six months is $50 — 5 percent (the semiannual interest rate) of the issue price of the bond, $1,000. §1272(a)(1), (3), (4). The OID for the second six months is $52.50 — 5 percent of the $1,050 adjusted issue price of the bond (the issue price plus prior OID). §1272(a)(1), (3), (4). The OID for year one equals $102.50 ($50 plus $52.50). Abe will include and BigCo will deduct $102.50 of interest in year one. §§163(e), 1272(a)(1). The chart below shows the amount of OID allocated to each six-month period during the three-year term of the debt.

	Beginning balance	Semiannual 5 percent interest	Ending balance
Year 1: 1st 6 months	$1,000.00	$50.00	$1,050.00
Year 1: 2d 6 months	1,050.00	52.50	1,102.50
Year 2: 1st 6 months	1,102.50	55.13	1,157.63
Year 2: 2d 6 months	1,157.63	57.88	1,215.51
Year 3: 1st 6 months	1,215.51	60.78	1,276.29
Year 3: 2d 6 months	1,276.29	63.81	1,340.00*

*Due to rounding amounts in the chart, the sum of the beginning balance plus interest in the last year is a little over $1,340.

20. a. The transaction will be split into two transactions for tax purposes: (i) a property transaction and (ii) a debt transaction. First consider the tax consequences of the debt transaction. The debt does not bear any stated interest. However, it does have unstated interest. The stated redemption price at maturity is $1,340,000. §1273(a)(2). The issue price of the debt is the $1 million present value of the payment to be made in three years, discounting at the 10 percent AFR. §§1273(b)(4), 1274(a)(2), (b). There is $340,000 of OID on the debt ($1,340,000 stated redemption price at maturity less $1 million issue price). The $340,000 of OID will be allocated over the three-year term of the debt using the constant yield-to-maturity method. §§163(e), 1272(a)(1). The OID for the first six months is $50,000 — 5 percent (the semiannual interest rate) of the $1 million issue price of the debt. §1272(a)(1), (3), (4). The OID for the second six months is $52,500 — 5 percent of the $1,050,000 adjusted

issue price of the debt (the issue price plus prior OID). §1272(a)(1), (3), (4). The OID for year one thus equals $102,500 ($50,000 plus $52,500). Bernice will include $102,500 of interest in year one. §1272(a)(1). She will also include $113,000 of OID in year two and $124,500 of OID in year three. (See the chart above in the previous explanation for an illustration of the computations in years two and three.)

Now consider the tax consequences of the property transaction. Bernice's gain realized on the property transaction is $600,000 — $1 million amount realized (which is the present value of the payment to be made, discounting at the 10 percent AFR) less her $400,000 basis in the property. §1001; Reg. §1.1001-1(g). Bernice may qualify for installment reporting of the gain (discussed earlier in this chapter), in which case she would not be taxed on the $600,000 of gain until the year three payment is made. §453(c).

b. The OID rules do not apply to the debt transaction because the debt bears stated interest, payable at least annually, at the 10 percent annual rate. §§1273(a)(2), (b)(4), 1274(c)(1), (2); Reg. §1.1274-1(b)(1). (Since the interest is payable semiannually the interest does not compound.) Bernice includes the interest when she receives it.

E. THE CASH METHOD OF ACCOUNTING

Reading: §§61, 83, 451(a); Reg. §§1.451-1(a), 1.446-1(c)(1)(i), 1.451-2.
Taxpayers who use the cash method of accounting generally must include an item of income when they receive it. §451(a). Inclusion is required whether the item of income is received in the form of cash, property, or services. Reg. §1.446-1(c)(1)(i). Although an unfunded, unsecured promise to pay money in the future is not treated as property generally, a promise to pay is treated as the "equivalent of cash" and immediately included if the promise to pay is unconditional, not subject to set-offs, and readily transferable. Cowden v. Commissioner, 289 F.2d 20 (5th Cir. 1961). Cash method taxpayers generally deduct an item of expense when it is paid. Reg. §1.446-1(c)(1)(i). However, where the payment of an expense creates an asset with a useful life that extends substantially beyond the close of the year in which the expense is incurred, the cash method taxpayer cannot simply deduct the entire expense; instead, the expense must be capitalized. (For a discussion of capitalization and depreciation of business assets, see Chapter 5.)

Under the general inclusion rule stated above, a cash method taxpayer who sells property on December 1, year one, and is paid on that day will include the gain from the sale in income in year one. Can the taxpayer defer inclusion until year two by arranging to defer receipt of the year one payment until year two? No, he cannot because a cash method taxpayer is deemed to have received an item if it is *constructively received*. In other words, a cash method taxpayer includes an item of income on the earlier of actual or constructive receipt of the item. Reg. §§1.451-1(a), 1.446-1(c)(1)(i). An item of income is constructively received if it is made available to the taxpayer, so that he could receive it, but he chooses not to receive it. Reg. §1.451-2. Under the doctrine of constructive receipt, the taxpayer in our example will be deemed to have received income in year one, the year in which the payment was made available to him, even if he defers actual receipt of the payment until year two.

On the other hand, if the original sale contract had provided for payment to be made in year two, the constructive receipt doctrine would not apply because under the terms of the contract the taxpayer has no right to the payment until year two. Courts will not "look through" the contract to determine whether the payment date was insisted upon by the taxpayer or his purchaser. See, e.g., Schniers v. Commissioner, 69 T.C. 511 (1977). If the taxpayer qualifies for the installment method, described earlier in this chapter, inclusion of the gain would be deferred until year two.

The doctrine of constructive receipt, and the point that constructive receipt can be avoided through contract, both apply to payment for services as well as goods. Thus, an employee whose salary is made available to her on December 1, year one, must recognize taxable income in year one, even if she does not pick up her paycheck until year two. On the other hand, an employee who contracts ahead of time to be paid on January 1, year two, will not include the income until year two. In other words, an employee can defer compensation income if she enters into the deferral agreement before she earns the income. Rev. Rul. 60-31 (which describes several deferred compensation arrangements and explains why each of them would or would not result in income deferral). (Note that, in deferred compensation arrangements such as those described in the ruling, the employer will not be able to deduct the compensation until the employee includes it. §404(a)(5). Also note that certain deferred compensation arrangements can trigger §409A, which accelerates inclusion of deferred compensation and imposes interest and penalties if nonqualified deferred compensation plans do not meet certain requirements.)

Online gaming, including online gaming in virtual worlds, raises an interesting timing issue for cash method taxpayers: If a cash method taxpayer plays an online game and wins game credits or prizes, does the taxpayer have to include the game winnings when they are credited to the taxpayer's game account, under the cash equivalence doctrine or constructive receipt doctrine, or can the taxpayer defer inclusion until the credits or prizes are actually redeemed for cash? The IRS has not answered this question and commentators disagree about the answer, which may depend in part on the nature of the winnings and the terms of the taxpayer's contract with the gaming website.

(If the player is required to include the winnings from game play, the player may be allowed to deduct certain game play costs. The deductibility of game play costs depends on various factors, such as: (i) whether the game play is characterized as a trade or business, an activity entered into for profit, or a personal activity; and (ii) whether the game play constitutes gambling. The §165(d) deduction for gambling losses is discussed in Chapter 2.)

If the players of an online game win credits that can be redeemed for cash, the credits may constitute a cash equivalent or constructive receipt of the cash value of the credits when credited to the taxpayer's account. If the contract between the taxpayer and the gaming website meaningfully restricts redemptions or creates a significant risk of forfeiture of the winnings, however, these features may prevent current inclusion of the credits.

Consider the features of Worldwinner's online gaming website, for example. Worldwinner credits player accounts with play dollars if a player wins an online game tournament. The play dollars can be used to pay for additional game play on the website or can be redeemed for real dollars. (Worldwinner highlights this cash redemption feature in its advertising.) Absent additional facts, the play dollars may be a cash equivalent, or the ability to redeem the play dollars for real dollars may constitute constructive receipt of the equivalent real dollars. However, the contract between players and the Worldwinner website gives Worldwinner the right, at its "sole discretion," to unilaterally "void" the winnings in a player's account. In addition, the contract makes the play dollars in a player's account nontransferable and imposes a fee on redemptions of less than $10. Commentators disagree whether these features of the contract prevent current inclusion of winnings from game play; some commentators take the position that these terms preclude cash equivalence and constructive receipt, but other commentators suggest that these terms do not preclude cash equivalence or constructive receipt if Worldwinner exercises these contractual rights only infrequently (such as when a player violates the website's policies, for example, by hacking the website to alter a player account or using the website's IM feature to send spam). In a 2005 private letter ruling, the IRS ruled that an online gaming business must send a Form 1099-MISC to each of its players whose annual net income from online gaming is at least $600. Priv. Ltr. Rul. 200532025.

A similar issue is raised if the online game website credits a player's account with "virtual" dollars that cannot be redeemed for real dollars but can be sold to third parties for real dollars. Does the player have to include the value of the virtual dollars when they are credited to the player's game account, or can the player defer inclusion until the virtual dollars are sold? The intuition of most people is that Monopoly money is not a cash equivalent and a Monopoly player is not in constructive receipt of income as a result of winning Monopoly money, but that is because Monopoly money cannot readily be converted into real dollars. Whether the result is the same for receipt of an online virtual currency may depend on whether there is active trading of the virtual currency for real dollars. For example, Linden dollars in the Second Life virtual world can be used for Second Life game play and to buy goods and services in that virtual world, but cannot be redeemed for real dollars. Linden dollars can be converted into real dollars, however, by selling them to a third party via exchange facilities maintained by Second Life or others. The ability to convert a virtual currency into real dollars may trigger inclusion of the cash value of the virtual currency when it is credited to a cash method player's account.

If winnings from online gaming cannot be redeemed for cash and are not readily convertible into cash, the winnings probably do not trigger an inclusion under the cash method of accounting. This category includes online equivalents of Monopoly money.

The doctrine of constructive receipt is closely related to the *economic benefit doctrine*, which is the product of case law. Under the economic benefit doctrine, a cash method taxpayer recognizes income as soon as a payor irrevocably sets aside funds for the taxpayer in a manner that prevents the payor's creditors from being able to reach the amount set aside. See, e.g., Pulsifer v. Commissioner, 64 T.C. 245 (1975). Inclusion is required despite the fact that the cash method taxpayer has not actually received the amount set aside. However, if the funds set aside for the taxpayer's benefit can be reached by the payor's creditors, the taxpayer does not have to include the funds set aside. Suppose, for example, that in year one a cash method taxpayer, Teresa, renders services for her employer in exchange for the employer transferring $20,000 to an irrevocable trust with Teresa as the sole beneficiary. If the employer's creditors could not reach the trust assets (if, for example, the employer later defaulted on its debts), Teresa will have to include the $20,000 in year one despite the fact that she has not received the money. On the other hand, she can defer inclusion of the $20,000 set aside in year one if the employer's creditors can reach the funds set aside. In addition, the economic benefit doctrine does not require inclusion in year one if the employer makes an unsecured promise to pay her the $20,000 in year two instead of transferring the funds to the trust. Rev. Rul. 60-31.

Deferring compensation by contract, in the manner discussed above, has two drawbacks. First, the employee runs the risk that the employer will not be able to make the deferred payment when it is due. If the employer and employee structure the deferred compensation so that the employee does not run the risk of nonpayment, the employee will not be able to defer the income. Second, an employer cannot deduct deferred compensation until the employee includes it, so the tax advantage gained by deferral of the employee's income is offset by the loss of the employer's deduction. §404(a)(5). In most cases, therefore, deferral of compensation by contract is not desirable. Occasionally, however, such deferral is advantageous. One well-publicized industry in which deferral is common is professional athletics. Professional sports teams often lose money and so are in the zero percent tax bracket. Such teams are often owned, however, by wealthy individuals, and are unlikely to default on contractual obligations. An employee of such a team can defer compensation without fear of default, and the team can give up its tax deduction without cost. For this and other reasons, compensation for professional athletes is frequently deferred by contract.

The two drawbacks of deferring income by contract can be avoided if the deferred compensation takes the form of a qualified pension or profit-sharing plan. Under such a plan, funds are set aside (usually through a trust or annuity contract) for the irrevocable benefit of employees. The employer is able to deduct the current payment and the employee is not taxed on the contributions, or the interest earned on the contributions, until she receives the funds upon retirement or separation from service. A form of qualified retirement plan can be utilized by self-employed persons: The amounts set aside can be deducted from business earnings and are not taxable until withdrawn.

Why doesn't all deferred compensation take the form of qualified retirement plans? One reason is that such plans must comply with certain nondiscrimination provisions designed to ensure retirement coverage for low-paid employees. In general, if an employer provides high-paid employees with retirement benefits equal to, say, 10 percent of their annual salary, the employer must provide low-paid employees with retirement benefits equal to 10 percent of their salary. Another reason is that the amount that can be set aside for an employee in a qualified retirement plan is subject to statutory limits. §415. Finally, high penalties apply if the employee withdraws her interest in such plans prior to retirement or separation from employment. See, e.g., §72(t). Thus, such plans generally are not used to defer compensation for only a year or two.

An individual who wishes to set aside money for retirement also can establish her own individual retirement account (IRA). §408. Section 219(b)(5)(A) limits annual IRA contributions to $5,000, although that amount is adjusted annually for inflation. §219(b)(5)(D). For example, the 2013 IRA contribution limit was $5,500. IR News Release 2012-77 (2012). Individuals who turn 50 before the end of the taxable year can also deduct annual "catch-up contributions" of $1,000. §219(b)(5)(B). The IRA contribution deduction is unavailable, however, to individuals who are covered under a qualified retirement plan and have adjusted gross income above a certain amount. §219(g). If an individual is not an active participant in a qualified retirement plan but that individual's spouse is an active plan participant, the nonparticipant spouse can make a deductible IRA contribution unless the couple's combined adjusted gross income exceeds a certain amount. Id. No tax is levied on the contributions, or the interest earned on the contributions, until the amounts are withdrawn. Penalties generally apply to withdrawals made by the taxpayer prior to retirement. §72(t). Individuals who are unable to deduct their IRA contributions (because they are covered by a qualified retirement plan and have a relatively high adjusted gross income) may still wish to establish an IRA because the interest earned on the nondeductible contributions is not taxed until it is withdrawn.

An alternative type of IRA, known as a *Roth IRA*, provides tax benefits that are "back-loaded." §408A. Although contributions to a Roth IRA are not deductible, income earned on the account is not taxed and distributions from the account are not taxed if the distribution is a "qualified distribution." §408A(d). A distribution is "qualified" if the distribution (i) is made no sooner than the end of the fifth tax year after the first contribution to the Roth IRA, and (ii)(a) is made on or after the individual reaches age 59½, (b) is made to a beneficiary after the death of the individual, (c) is made on account of the individual becoming disabled, or (d) is a special purpose distribution — for example, a distribution to enable a taxpayer to buy her first home. §§408A(d)(2), (5) and 72(t)(2)(F). (A qualified distribution to a first-time home-buyer is capped at $10,000. §72(t)(8).) The annual limit on contributions to a Roth IRA is the same as the annual deduction limit on traditional IRA contributions, but the Roth IRA contribution limit is reduced by any contributions made to traditional IRAs. §408A(c)(2).

Examples

21. In year one, Andrew, a cash method taxpayer, sells real property, which has a basis of $40,000, to Roberta for $100,000. Under which, if any, of the following circumstances would the doctrines of constructive receipt or economic benefit require that Andrew be taxed on his property gain in year one?

    a. The sale closes on December 1, year one. On that date, the property is transferred to Roberta and she sends Andrew a certified check for the sale proceeds. Andrew does not accept the certified check until January 1, year two.

    b. During the sale negotiations, Roberta tells Andrew that she would prefer to close the deal and receive the property on December 1, year one. However, Andrew counters that for tax reasons he does not want the sale to close until January 1, year two. Roberta agrees to time the transaction as Andrew prefers. On January 1, year two, the property is transferred to Roberta, she gives Andrew a certified check for the sale proceeds, and he cashes the check.

    c. During the sale negotiations, Roberta tells Andrew that she would prefer to close the deal and receive the property on December 1, year one. Andrew would like to defer the tax on the gain until year two. However, he is not sure whether Roberta will still be able to make the $100,000 payment in year two, so he would like for her to actually make the payment in year one. They work out a compromise. On December 1, year one, Andrew transfers the property to Roberta and she places the $100,000 of sale proceeds in an irrevocable trust, naming Andrew the sole beneficiary of the trust. Roberta's creditors cannot reach the trust assets. The $100,000 in the trust will be distributed to Andrew on January 1, year two.

22. On January 1, year one, executive Ellen and BigCo sign an employment contract that contains the following terms: Ellen agrees to work for BigCo from January 1, year one, to December 31, year one. BigCo agrees to pay Ellen $5,000 a month during year one. BigCo also agrees to pay Ellen $36,000 on January 30, year two. In order to fund the year two payment to Ellen, BigCo agrees to purchase an annuity contract that will pay BigCo $36,000 on January 30, year two. Is Ellen taxed on the $36,000 deferred payment in year one? (Assume that §409A does not apply.) Can BigCo deduct the cost of the annuity in year one?

23. Is each of the following statements true or false?
    a. An employer currently can deduct amounts set aside for employees in a qualified pension or profit-sharing plan.
    b. Amounts contributed to a qualified pension or profit-sharing plan by an employer will be currently taxable to the employees because the employer's creditors cannot reach the amounts contributed.
    c. An employer may adopt a qualified pension or profit-sharing plan that covers only a few "key" employees.
    d. Withdrawals from qualified pension or profit-sharing plans prior to retirement or separation from employment are subject to substantial penalties.
    e. An employee who is covered by a qualified pension or profit-sharing plan cannot establish an IRA.
    f. Contributions to traditional IRAs and Roth IRAs are deductible in the year in which the contribution is made.

Explanations

21. a. Andrew will be taxed on the gain in year one, under the constructive receipt doctrine. He constructively received the sale proceeds in year one because the check was made available to him in year one but he chose not to receive it until year two. §451(a), Reg. §§1.451-1(a), 1.451-2, 1.446-1(c)(1)(i).
    b. Andrew will not be taxed on the gain in year one. The contract did not permit Andrew to receive payment in year one. The constructive receipt doctrine does not apply because the sale proceeds were not made available to Andrew in year one. Reg. §1.451-2. The fact that the contractual deferral of payment benefits Andrew and was his idea is irrelevant. In situations such as this, the tax law will not rewrite a contract to eliminate a tax benefit to one of the parties.

c. Andrew must include the property gain in year one. Roberta transferred the sale proceeds in year one to an irrevocable trust with Andrew as the sole beneficiary, and the trust assets were beyond the reach of Roberta's creditors. Under the economic benefit doctrine, Andrew will be treated as though he received in year one the $100,000 that was transferred to the trust. Pulsifer v. Commissioner, 64 T.C. 245 (1975). Note that §453 does not defer inclusion of the gain until year two because the transfer here of $100,000 to the trust is treated as a "payment" under §453. Reg. §15a.453-1(b)(3).

22. Under the doctrine of economic benefit, the deferred payment would be taxable in year one only if it were funded and irretrievably dedicated to Ellen in a manner that secured it from BigCo's creditors. Here, the purchase of the annuity should guarantee that BigCo will have funds with which to make the deferred payment. However, there is no guarantee that BigCo will use the funds to pay Ellen. Moreover, because BigCo is the beneficiary of the annuity contract, the contract is an asset of BigCo and is probably subject to the claims of its creditors. As a result, the doctrine of economic benefit does not require Ellen to include the deferred payment in year one. See Rev. Rul. 60-31. (Similarly, Ellen has received only an unfunded, unsecured promise to pay $36,000 in year two, which is not "property" subject to §83, which is discussed in the next section of this book.) Because Ellen does not take the deferred payment into income in year one, BigCo cannot receive a deduction for the payment in year one. §404(a)(5).

23. a. True. An employer may deduct qualified pension or profit-sharing plan contributions in the year in which the contributions are made.
    b. False. Employees are not taxed on amounts contributed on their behalf to qualified pension or profit-sharing plans until those amounts are withdrawn.
    c. False. A plan will not qualify for tax-favored treatment unless it covers low-paid, as well as high-paid, employees.
    d. True. Premature withdrawals from a qualified retirement plan are subject to immediate taxation and to a 10 percent "penalty" tax under §72.
    e. False. Any individual may establish an IRA. However, contributions to an IRA are deductible only for those individuals who are not covered by a qualified pension or profit-sharing plan or who are covered by such a plan but have an adjusted gross income below a certain amount. §219.
    f. False. Contributions to traditional IRAs are deductible up to an individual's annual contribution limit, which is $5,500 in 2013. (Individuals who are 50 or older can also deduct annual catch-up contributions of $1,000.) If an individual is an active participant in a qualified retirement plan, the individual may not be able to deduct

any of the IRA contribution. Contributions to a Roth IRA are not deductible, but the income earned on the account and distributions from the account are not taxed if the distribution is a "qualified distribution."

F. SECTION 83 TRANSFERS

Reading: §§83, 421, 422; Reg. §§1.83-3, -7, 1.61-2(d)(2).
Some of the case law that established the economic benefit doctrine has been supplanted by §83, which applies to compensatory transfers of property. For example, if an employer irrevocably transfers cash or property to a trust for the employee's benefit, and the trust assets are beyond the reach of the employer's creditors, §83 requires the employee to include the amounts set aside in the year in which they are transferred to the trust. §83(a), Reg. §1.83-3(e). However, transfers outside the employment context are not subject to §83 and may be subject to the economic benefit doctrine.

Section 83 applies to transfers of property in connection with the performance of services. (Although §83 applies to service providers, which would include employees and independent contractors, assume for the purposes of this explanation that the compensatory transfer is made to an employee.) For purposes of §83, the term *property* does not include money or an unfunded, unsecured promise to pay money in the future, but does include real and personal property or a beneficial interest in assets transferred to a trust or escrow account if the assets are beyond the reach of the transferor's creditors. Reg. §1.83-3(e). Under §83(a), the employee must include income from the transfer in the first year in which the transferred property vests, which means that it is either *transferable* or no longer *subject to a substantial risk of forfeiture*. Rights in the transferred property are subject to a substantial risk of forfeiture if the person's rights in the property are conditioned on the future performance of substantial services by the employee. §83(c)(1). Rights in property are transferable only if the employee can transfer the property to someone else who would not be subject to a substantial risk of forfeiture (which does not generally happen if the employee is subject to a substantial risk of forfeiture). §83(c)(2). The amount included under §83(a) is (i) the value of the transferred property *at the time that it vests* less (ii) the amount (if any) that the employee paid for the property. Since the amount included is compensation for services, it is taxed at ordinary income rates, not the special capital gain rates. The employee's basis in the property is the value of the property at the time of inclusion under §83. Reg. §1.61-2(d)(2). The employer deducts the compensation only when the employee includes it. §83(h).

Section 83(a) does not apply if an employee makes an election under §83(b). If a §83(b) election is made, the employee includes, in the year in which the property is transferred, (i) the value of the property *at the time of the transfer* less (ii) the amount (if any) that the employee paid for the property. Throughout this book, we stress that taxpayers prefer to defer income. Why would a taxpayer make a §83(b) election? Because, under some circumstances, making a §83(b) election will save the taxpayer money. Amounts included under either §83(a) or (b) constitute ordinary income so they do not qualify for the special capital gain rates. However, appreciation in the property following the §83 inclusion does qualify for the special capital gain rates (assuming that the property transferred, which is often stock, is a capital asset). If §83(a) applies, at the time of vesting the employee will be taxed at ordinary rates on all prior appreciation in the property. If §83(b) applies, the employee will be taxed (i) in the year of the transfer, at ordinary income rates on the difference between the value of the property and the amount the employee paid for it, and (ii) on a subsequent sale of the property, at the appropriate capital gain rate, on the appreciation in the property after the transfer to the employee. In effect, a taxpayer making a §83(b) election is betting that the tax cost of accelerating the §83 ordinary income inclusion will be more than made up by the tax savings from converting ordinary income on appreciation in the property into capital gain.

The following example will illustrate the §83 rules. A start-up company called Minicomp is recruiting Steve, a young computer wizard. Minicomp cannot afford to pay Steve as much cash compensation as he wants, but offers to let him buy 100 shares of Minicomp stock, which has a value of $200,000 ($2,000 a share), for $100,000. If Steve works for Minicomp for five years, he can keep the stock. If Steve leaves Minicomp before the five years are up, he must sell the stock back to Minicomp for $100,000. Steve accepts their offer, goes to work for Minicomp, and immediately buys the stock. After five years, Steve is still working for Minicomp and the stock that he bought has appreciated in value to $2.1 million. After the stock vests, Steve sells it for $2.1 million. (To simplify the example, assume that Steve's tax rate in years one through five is 40 percent, and that gain from the sale of the stock does not qualify for the §1202 "small business stock" exclusion.)

Section 83 applies to the transfer of the stock to Steve. The stock is transferred in connection with the performance of services because Steve is allowed to buy the stock at a discount. Reg. §1.83-3(f). Steve's rights in the stock are subject to a substantial risk of forfeiture because retention of the stock is conditioned on Steve working for Minicomp for five years. §83(c)(1). If Steve does not make a §83(b) election in year one, §83(a) will apply. In year one, there is no inclusion because the stock is nontransferable and subject to a substantial risk of forfeiture. §83(a). However, in year five, the year in which the stock vests, Steve will have an income inclusion of $2 million, which is (i) the $2.1 million value of the stock at the time that it vests less (ii) the $100,000 amount that Steve paid for the stock in year one. He will owe $800,000 of tax (40 percent of the inclusion because it is ordinary income) in year five.

If Steve makes a §83(b) election in year one, he will include in year one $100,000, which is (i) the $200,000 value of the stock at the time of the transfer less (ii) the $100,000 that he paid for the stock. He will owe $40,000 of tax (40 percent of the inclusion, which is ordinary income) for year one. His basis in the stock is $200,000, the value of the stock at the time of inclusion. In year five, when the stock vests, §83(a) does not apply. §83(b)(1) (flush language). When Steve sells the stock, he will realize capital gain of $1.9 million ($2.1 million amount realized less the $200,000 basis in his stock). Assume that the appropriate capital gain rate is 20 percent. He will owe $380,000 of tax (20 percent of $1.9 million) for year five. Summarizing these results, Steve will either (i) apply §83(a) and owe $800,000 of tax for year five or (ii) make a §83(b) election and owe $40,000 for year one and $380,000 for year five. Assume that the present value of the $800,000 year-five tax is $491,130 and the present value of the $380,000 year-five tax is $233,280. By making the election, Steve saves $217,850, which is $491,130 less $273,280 ($40,000 plus $233,280).

Special rules apply under §83 if an employee receives *stock options*, instead of stock. A stock option gives the employee the right to buy stock of the employer at a specified price (referred to as the *strike price* or *exercise price*) for a specified period of time. For example, an employee of Growth Company may be given the right to buy Growth Company stock at $10 a share at any time during the next five years. The value of such an option depends on the current and future value of the stock. (Although the value of the option depends in part on other factors as well, we will disregard those other factors for now.) If Growth Company stock now sells for $12 a share, the employee can exercise the option, buying the stock for $10 a share, then sell it for $12 a share, making a $2 a share profit. If, as in this example, the stock price exceeds the exercise price, the option is said to be *in the money*. Even if the stock now sells for $8 a share, the option has value because the stock price may rise above $10 a share during the five-year period of the option. If, as in this variation of the example, the stock price is less than the exercise price, the option is said to be *out of the money*. If the stock price equals the exercise price, the option is said to be *at the money*.

In the following discussion of the application of §83 to the grant and exercise of stock options, assume that all options are out of the money or at the money on the date the options are granted. There are two reasons for making this assumption. First, in the real world most compensatory stock options are out of the money or at the money on the date the options are granted. Second, making this assumption prevents the grant of the options from triggering §409A, which accelerates deferred compensation and imposes interest and penalties in certain circumstances. Section 409A applies to the grant of an option that is in the money on the date the option is granted, but does not apply to an option that is out of the money or at the money on the date the option is granted. §409A(a)(1), Reg. §1.409A-2. (Note that the §409A distinction between in-the-money options and out-of-the-money or at-the-money options increases the stakes for valuing the underlying stock, especially nonpublicly traded stock, on the date the options are granted.)

The §83 tax treatment of the grant and exercise of a stock option depends on whether the option has a readily ascertainable fair market value; §83 applies to the grant of an option with a readily ascertainable fair market value, but does not apply to the grant of an option that does not have a readily ascertainable fair market value. §83(e)(3). Why does §83 make this distinction? If we permitted an employee to make a §83(b) election on the grant of an option that does not have a readily ascertainable fair market value, the employee may understate the value of the option to reduce or eliminate the tax cost of making the §83(b) election. (Of course, an employee receiving stock in a closely held corporation, instead of an option, might also underestimate the value of the stock, but the potential for valuation understatement is even worse with options.) The §83(b) election would then permit the conversion of the appreciation in the stock after the grant of the option into capital gain, at little or no tax cost. This potential for abuse in the valuation of options is reduced if the option has a readily ascertainable value, so §83 draws a distinction between options with and without a readily ascertainable fair market value.

Regulation §1.83-7(b) provides that the value of an option is generally not ascertainable unless the option is actively traded on an established securities market. An option that is not actively traded has an ascertainable fair market value if the taxpayer can establish that several conditions are satisfied; however, taxpayers generally cannot satisfy these conditions.

Section 83 does not apply to the grant of an option that does not have a readily ascertainable fair market value; instead, §83(a) and (b) will apply to the subsequent transfer of stock on the exercise of the option. §83(e)(3), Reg. §1.83-7(a). If the option is sold, instead of being exercised, §83 applies to the money or property received for the option. Reg. §1.83-7(a).

If an option has a readily ascertainable fair market value, §83(a) and (b) apply to the grant of the option. Reg. §1.83-7(a). If such an option is not subject to a substantial risk of forfeiture, the employee is taxed on the value of the option in the year of receipt. §83(a). In effect, the employee is treated as if she had received cash and used it to purchase the stock option. If the employee later exercises the option and purchases the stock, §83 does not apply to the transfer of the stock on exercise. §83(e)(4). The employee's basis in the stock received on exercise is the sum of (i) the amount she included in income under §83(a) on receipt of the option plus (ii) the price she pays for the stock when she exercises the option. Reg. §1.61-2(d)(2). If the employee does not exercise the option (because the stock price is below the option price), she can, subject to certain limitations, deduct the amount previously taken into income. §§1234, 1211. The rationale for the deduction is that the employee has acquired an asset, the stock option, that has become worthless. In keeping with this rationale, the deduction may be limited by the capital loss limitations discussed in Chapter 8.

The following example illustrates the §83 rules for options with a readily ascertainable fair market value. On January 1, year one, Frank receives a stock option in High Company stock. The option allows Frank to purchase 100 shares of stock at $10 a share at any time during the next five years. The option is nonforfeitable and is a type of option that is traded on an established securities market. The price of High Company stock on January 1, year one, is $10 a share. The option is valuable because (i) if the stock rises to, say, $15 a share, Frank will be able to buy the stock for $5 less than its value and (ii) if the stock price does not rise above $10, or falls, Frank loses nothing. Assume that the value of the option on January 1, year one, is $100 ($1 for every share of stock Frank can purchase under the option). Frank is taxed as if he had in year one received $100 cash and purchased the stock options. In other words, he has an ordinary income inclusion of $100 in year one and a $100 basis in the option. On January 1, year two, High Company stock has risen in value to $25 a share, and Frank exercises the option, paying $10 a share for 100 shares, for a total of $1,000. Frank receives a basis in the stock of $1,100 ($100 included in year one plus $1,000 paid for the stock in year two on exercise), or $11 a share. If Frank now sells the stock for $25 a share, or $2,500, he will recognize $1,400 of gain. This makes sense: The stock option has made Frank $1,500 richer — he paid only $1,000 for stock he sold for $2,500. Frank recognizes $1,500 total gain, $100 upon receipt of the option and $1,400 upon sale of the stock.

If retention of an option with an ascertainable value is conditioned on the employee continuing to work for the employer for some specified period of time, the option is subject to a risk of forfeiture. In that case the employee is not taxed in the year in which the option is granted; instead, the employee is taxed, in the year in which the restriction lapses, on the value of the option at the time of inclusion. If the fair market value of an option is expected to increase greatly between the time it is granted and the time the risk of forfeiture will lapse, the employee might benefit from making a §83(b) election.

There is one final twist to the tax treatment of stock options: Section 83 does not apply to the so-called *incentive stock option* (ISO). An ISO is an employee stock option that satisfies certain conditions set forth in §422. Employees are not taxed on the grant or exercise of an ISO. §421(a). A taxpayer's basis for stock received on the exercise of an ISO equals the amount paid for the stock on exercise. If an ISO had to be included in income, the stock basis would be increased by the amount included in income; not taxing an ISO therefore decreases the basis for the stock and increases the gain realized on the subsequent sale of the stock. Nonetheless,

ISOs are advantageous to employees because they defer tax. On the other hand, the employer receives no deduction for the issuance of an ISO. §421(a)(2). Under many plausible assumptions, the disadvantageous treatment of ISOs to the employer outweighs the advantageous treatment of ISOs to the employee. The issuance of ISOs can actually increase the parties' combined tax burden.

As is perhaps obvious, the tax treatment of stock options is quite complex; indeed, the above discussion ignores some hard issues and is incomplete in other ways. Even experienced tax attorneys find this area of the law requires careful attention to detail.

Examples

24. a. In year one Biotech Breakthroughs Inc. (BB Inc.) hires Anna. Anna receives year one compensation of $300,000. In addition, BB Inc. gives her BB Inc. stock worth $100,000, for which she pays nothing. If Anna works for BB Inc. until the end of year five, she can keep the stock. If Anna leaves BB Inc. before the five years are up, she has to give the stock back to BB Inc. In year five Anna is still working for BB Inc. and her stock is worth $1 million. What are the tax consequences to Anna and BB Inc. of the transfer of the stock?
    b. What tax advice would you give Anna if you are her lawyer in year one?

25. On January 1, year one, Gary receives a stock option to purchase up to 10 shares of Sybex Company stock for $20 a share. The Sybex options are publicly traded, so Gary's option has a readily ascertainable value. The option is nonforfeitable and may be exercised at any time during the next 10 years. The value of Sybex Company stock on January 1, year one, is $20 a share. Which, if any, of the following statements are true?
    a. Gary is taxed in year one on the fair market value of the option on the date he received it, January 1, year one.
    b. Gary includes no income upon receipt of the option because the exercise price of the option is as high as the stock price and so the option has no value.
    c. Sybex Company may deduct the value of the option in the year in which Gary exercises the option and purchases stock.
    d. If the Sybex options were not traded, Gary would be taxed, in year one, on the fair market value of the option on the date he received it, January 1, year one.

26. On January 10, year one, Harriet receives a stock option to purchase 1,000 shares of Tirex Company stock for $10 a share. The option cannot be exercised prior to January 10, year three, and is forfeited if Harriet should voluntarily terminate her employment prior to that time. The option has

an ascertainable fair market value. How much income does Harriet include, in years one and three, as a result of the grant of the option?

27. On January 1, year one, Irene receives a stock option to purchase 1,000 shares of HiLo Company stock for $300 a share. On that date the value of HiLo Company stock is $290 a share. The option is nonforfeitable, has an ascertainable value of $30,000 ($30 a share), and may be exercised at any time during the next five years. Irene exercises the option on January 1, year four, when the stock is worth $400 a share. On March 1, year six, Irene sells her 1,000 shares of HiLo Company stock for $500 a share, or $500,000.
    a. How much, if any, income does Irene include upon receipt of the stock option in year one?
    b. How much, if any, income does Irene include upon exercise of the stock option in year four?
    c. How much income does Irene include upon sale of the HiLo Company stock in year six?

28. On January 1, year one, John receives a stock option to purchase 1,000 shares of Uber Company stock for $10 a share. The option is a qualified incentive stock option within the definition of §422. On January 1, year four, John exercises the option; the price of Uber Company stock at that time is $50 a share. On January 2, year five, John sells the Uber Company stock for $50 a share.
    a. How much, if any, income does John recognize upon receipt of the option?
    b. How much, if any, income does John recognize upon exercise of the option?
    c. How much, if any, income does John recognize upon sale of the stock?
    d. What are the tax consequences to Uber Company?

Explanations

24. a. Section 83 applies to the transfer of the stock to Anna. The stock is transferred in connection with the performance of services because Anna paid nothing for the stock. Reg. §1.83-3(f). Anna's rights in the stock are subject to a substantial risk of forfeiture because retention of the stock is conditioned on Anna working for BB Inc. for five years. §83(c)(1). If Anna does not make a §83(b) election in year one, §83(a) will apply. In year one there is no inclusion because the stock is nontransferable and subject to a substantial risk of forfeiture. §83(a). However, in year five, the year in which the stock vests, Anna will have an income inclusion of $1 million, which is the

$1 million value of the stock at the time that it vests. (Anna did not pay anything for the stock.) Anna will pay tax on that inclusion at her ordinary income rate.

If Anna makes a §83(b) election in year one, she will include in year one $100,000, which is (i) the $100,000 value of the stock at the time of the transfer less (ii) the amount that she paid for the stock, zero. She will pay tax on that amount at her ordinary income rate. Her basis in the stock will be $100,000, the value of the stock at the time of inclusion. In year five, when the stock vests, §83(a) will not apply. §83(b)(1) (flush language). If Anna later sells the stock, she will realize a capital gain in an amount equal to the value of the stock at the time of the sale less her $100,000 basis in the stock.

b. I would advise Anna to consider whether she should make a §83(b) election in year one. Anna has two choices. She can either (i) apply §83(a) and owe tax for year five, at ordinary income rates, on the value of the stock in year five, or (ii) make a §83(b) election and owe tax (a) for year one, at ordinary income rates, on the $100,000 value of the stock and (b) at the lower capital gain rate tax on the appreciation over years one through five. If she is in the 40 percent bracket in year one, she would owe $40,000 of tax on the $100,000 inclusion. If the BB Inc. stock will appreciate substantially during years one through five, making the election would allow her to convert a large amount of ordinary income, which would be taxed at ordinary income rates, into capital gain taxed at a lower rate. (In addition, if she does not sell the stock in year five, she can defer the capital gain until she sells the stock.) If the present value of the tax savings from converting the ordinary income in year five into capital gain is more than $40,000, she should consider making the election.

25. a. True. An employee is taxed on the grant of stock options if the options have an ascertainable value and are nonforfeitable. §83(a), Reg. §1.83-7. The amount included is the value of the option on the date the employee received it (less any amount that the employee paid for the option, here zero). §83(a).

b. False. Although the exercise price is as high as the current stock price, the option is still valuable. If the stock rises in value, Gary can exercise the option and buy the stock for less than its value. Even if the stock price remains constant, the option provides a time-value-of-money benefit because Gary can wait up to 10 years to invest the $20 per share of Sybex Company stock, and in the interim he can earn a return on an alternative investment of the $20. If the stock price falls, Gary loses nothing.

c. False. Under §83, the treatment of the employer and employee is symmetrical. Gary includes income under §83 in the year in which the option is granted, year one, so Sybex Company receives a deduction in that same year. §83(h).

d. False. Nontraded options do not generally have a readily ascertainable fair market value and §83 does not apply to the grant if an option does not have a readily ascertainable fair market value. Gary would instead be taxed on the exercise of the option. §83(e)(3), Reg. §1.83-7(a).

26. Section 83 applies to the option because it has an ascertainable value. However, the option is forfeitable until year three, so Harriet will not have to include any income in year one as a result of the grant of the option. §83(a). In year three, when the risk of forfeiture lapses, Harriet will include income in an amount equal to the value of the option on the date that the restriction lapses. If the option is not very valuable upon receipt but Harriet believes that it will be quite valuable on January 10, year three, she will probably want to make a §83(b) election. If she makes the election, she will include in year one the value of the option on the date she receives it. Section 83 would then not apply in year three when the restriction lapses. §83(b) (flush language).

27. a. Section 83 applies to the option because it has an ascertainable value. The option is nonforfeitable, so Irene will have to include the $30,000 value of the option in year one, the year in which the option is granted. §83(a).

b. The option has an ascertainable value, so §83 does not apply to the exercise of the option. §83(e)(4). Irene has no inclusion in year four.

c. Irene includes $170,000 of gain ($500,000 amount realized less her $330,000 basis in the stock) in year six. Irene included $30,000 upon receipt of the option. This gives her a $30,000 basis in the option. When she exercises the option, her basis in the option is transferred to the shares. Her basis for the stock also includes the price she paid for the stock when she exercised the option, $300,000 ($300 a share). Thus, her total basis is $330,000.

28. a. John includes no income upon receipt of the incentive stock option.

b. John includes no income upon exercise of the incentive stock option.

c. John recognizes $40 per share upon sale of the stock — the difference between the exercise price of $10 and the sale price of $50. Note that since John included no income upon receipt of the stock option, he has no basis in the option, so his basis for the stock is $10 per share, the amount he paid for the stock on exercise of the option.

d. Uber Company receives no deduction at any time. §421(a)(2).

G. THE ACCRUAL METHOD OF ACCOUNTING

Reading: §§446, 448, 451, 456, 461; Reg. §§1.451-1, -5, 1.461-1, -2, -4, -5, -6.

Earlier in this chapter we saw that taxpayers using the cash method of accounting must generally include income in the year in which they receive it. (Of course, this rule is limited by the doctrines of constructive receipt and economic benefit and the special rules that apply to various forms of deferred compensation.) In contrast, taxpayers using the accrual method include items of income "when all the events have occurred which fix the right to receive [the] income and the amount thereof can be determined with reasonable accuracy." Reg. §1.451-1(a).

The accrual method of accounting is generally thought to be a more accurate measure of income and expense than the cash method of accounting, and most companies use the accrual method to keep their books. Companies using the accrual method of accounting to keep their books ordinarily must use the accrual method for tax purposes. §446(a). Regulation §1.446-1(c)(2)(i) also provides that companies that sell goods generally must use the accrual method. In addition, some taxpayers are required to use the accrual method because §448 prevents them from using the cash method.

As a simple example illustrating the difference between the cash and accrual methods of accounting, assume that an automotive repair shop performs services for a customer in November, year one. The customer and the shop agree that the bill for the services will be $100. The shop bills the customer in December, year one, and the customer pays the bill in year two. If the repair shop is on the accrual method, it will include the $100 of income in year one. It is in that year that the *all events test* is met; the events needed to establish the right to income (the provision of services) have occurred, and the amount of income can be determined with reasonable accuracy. In contrast, if the repair shop is on the cash method of accounting, it will not include the $100 of income until year two. Most students will agree that the accrual method more closely tracks the time at which the income is in fact earned.

Suppose, instead, that a customer pays $100 in December, year one, for services to be rendered in January, year two. Under generally accepted accounting principals (GAAP), which govern accounting for nontax purposes, an accrual method taxpayer would not include prepaid income for services until the services were performed. Thus, under GAAP, the $100 of income would be included in year two, not year one; the fact that the accrual method business receives cash prior to that time is irrelevant. However, in American Automobile Association v. United States, 367 U.S. 687 (1961), the Supreme Court concluded that tax accounting does not have to follow GAAP. The issue in that case was whether the taxpayer had to include, in year one, dues paid by members in year one for services to be provided in year two. The taxpayer argued that the all events test was not met until the services were provided in year two and that GAAP would not require inclusion until year two. The Court held that for tax purposes prepaid income is taxable in the year in which it is received by an accrual method taxpayer, despite the fact that GAAP would defer inclusion until a later year. The decision in the *American Automobile Association* case effectively requires an accrual method taxpayer to use the cash method for prepaid income. There is a sort of "heads, the government wins; tails, the taxpayer loses" aspect to this rule. When an accrual method taxpayer performs services before receiving cash, he is taxed as soon as he performs services. Under the all events test, the liability is fixed as soon as the services are rendered. However, when the taxpayer receives cash before performing services, he is taxed as soon as he receives cash.

The one-sided rule established by the *American Automobile Association* case has been limited by subsequent developments. Soon after the decision was announced, Congress enacted §456, which permits membership organizations to include prepaid dues ratably as services are performed. Thus, the holding in *American Automobile Association* no longer requires the American Automobile Association to include prepaid dues in the year received. Perhaps more importantly, the Service has exercised its administrative discretion to allow an accrual method taxpayer who receives payment in one year to defer inclusion of income until the following year under certain circumstances.

Various types of prepaid income can qualify for deferral. Regulation §1.451-5 permits deferral of prepaid income for certain goods (e.g., inventory). Rev. Proc. 2004-34, modifying and superseding Rev. Proc. 71-21, significantly expanded the availability of deferral. The deferral method specified in the revenue procedure applies to payments for: (i) services; (ii) goods (other than goods covered by Regulation §1.451-5); (iii) the use of intellectual property; (iv) the occupancy or use of property that is ancillary to the provision of services (such as rental of a booth at a trade show); (v) the sale, lease, or license of computer software; (vi) certain guaranty or warranty contracts; (vii) certain subscriptions; (viii) certain membership fees; or (ix) any combination of the other items listed. A taxpayer qualifies for deferral of these types of prepaid income if some or all of the prepayment will be included in a later year for financial accounting purposes. In the year of the prepayment, the portion of the prepayment included in income for financial accounting purposes also is included for tax purposes. In the following year, the taxpayer must include the remainder of the prepayment for tax purposes, regardless of when the rest of the prepayment will be included for financial accounting purposes. This deferral method also applies to advance payments received by a taxpayer on the sale of gift cards that can be redeemed for goods or services, including those that are to be provided by a third party merchant, pursuant to an agreement between the taxpayer and the merchant. Rev. Proc. 2011-18 (2011) (modifying and clarifying Rev. Proc. 2004-34).

In addition, some, though by no means all, courts have rebelled at the seeming unfairness of the *American Automobile Association* holding and have found ways to allow accrual method taxpayers to defer inclusion of income until the provision of services. See, e.g., Artnell Co. v. Commissioner, 400 F.2d 981 (7th Cir. 1968) (where a baseball team was permitted to defer inclusion of prepaid season ticket sales until the year in which the games were to be played since the time for future performance was relatively certain). Accrual method taxpayers who do not fall within one of the statutory or administrative exceptions and who do not find a sympathetic court will be subject to the holding in *American Automobile Association* and taxed on prepaid income in the year in which they receive it.

The "all events" standard for deduction under the accrual method is similar to the standard for including an item in income; deduction is allowed only when all events have occurred to determine the fact of liability and the amount of the liability can be determined with reasonable accuracy. Reg. §1.461-1(a)(2)(i). This standard may be illustrated by again considering the company that provides repair services for a client in November of year one and is paid in January of year two. The appropriate time for the client to receive a deduction (assuming that the repair is a business expense) is year one, the year in which the liability is fixed and determinate.

The application of the all events test to payments to be made far in the future raises difficult questions. For example, suppose someone is injured on company grounds, and the company agrees to pay the victim $10,000 a year for 25 years. Assuming a 9 percent discount rate, the present value of the obligation is about $100,000. The company could fund the obligation by setting aside $100,000 today, or by making future payments that total $250,000. Interpreted literally, the all events test seems to allow the company to deduct the entire $250,000 in the year of settlement. After all, the liability is fixed and determinate, and there is no provision that requires taxpayers to reduce this sort of deduction to present value. If the expense is deductible, and the company is in the 40 percent combined state and federal income tax rate, the deduction will save the company $100,000 in taxes (40 percent of $250,000). That is equal to the amount the company must set aside to pay the obligation. In effect, the company's tort liability has been paid by the government.

This loophole could have been closed by limiting the amount deductible under the all events test to the present value of the future obligation. However, Congress instead chose to adopt §461(h), which provides that an accrual method taxpayer cannot deduct a future expense unless the all events test has been met *and economic performance* has occurred. In the case of a deferred payment in settlement of a tort liability, §461(h)(2)(C) provides that economic performance does not occur until the liability is paid. Thus, in the above example the company gets no deduction in the year of settlement, but may deduct the $10,000 annual payments when they are made.

Section 461(h) also applies more generally to limit deductions for future expenses in connection with services and properties received by the taxpayer or provided by the taxpayer. For example, suppose a company sells a piece of machinery and, as part of the sale, obligates itself to service the machinery once a year for three years. The cost of servicing the machinery, even if determinate, cannot be deducted until economic performance occurs, which is at the time that the machinery is actually serviced. §461(h)(2)(B).

Section 461(h)(3) and Regulation §1.461-5(b)(1) provide an exception to the §461(h) economic performance requirement. Under this exception (generally referred to as the *recurring item exception*), an item may be deducted notwithstanding the absence of economic performance, provided that the following conditions are satisfied:

i. the all events test is otherwise met;
ii. economic performance with respect to the item occurs by the earlier of (a) the date that the taxpayer files a timely return for that year (taking into account any extensions of the time to file) or (b) eight and a half months following the close of the tax year in which the deduction is taken;
iii. the item is recurring in nature and the taxpayer consistently reports the item in accordance with the all events test; and
iv. either (a) the item is not material or (b) accruing the item under the all events test provides better matching of income and expense than the economic performance standard would provide.

Examples

29. Office Cleaners Inc. and Accountants Inc. are both accrual method taxpayers. In each of the following situations, state the year in which Office Cleaners Inc. includes income and the year in which Accountants Inc. receives a deduction.
    a. Office Cleaners Inc. provides office cleaning services for Accountants Inc. in November, year one, and is paid for those services in January, year two.
    b. Office Cleaners Inc. agrees to, and does, provide a fixed and determinate amount of office cleaning for Accountants Inc. in January, year two. Accountants Inc. prepays the cleaning expense in December, year one.

30. Ventana Ranch Inc., an accrual method taxpayer, is an exclusive health spa in Southern California. On January 1, year one, 50 people each pay

the spa $20,000 for the right to use the spa facilities for five years. How does Ventana Ranch Inc. report the income received for financial accounting and tax accounting purposes?

31. On December 31, year one, Consumers Inc., an accrual method taxpayer, sells a television set to Joe's Bar. As part of the sale, Consumers Inc. agrees to service the television set for four years. Consumers Inc. has determined that the average cost of providing such service will be $10 a year, for a total expected cost of $40. May Consumers Inc. deduct the $40 cost in year one?

Explanations

29. a. Office Cleaners Inc. must include income in year one, the year in which the services were performed and the liability became fixed. Accountants Inc. will receive a deduction in that same year.

   b. Under the holding in *American Automobile Association*, Office Cleaners Inc. would be required to include the prepaid income in the year in which it receives the payment, year one. Office Cleaners Inc. nonetheless probably can defer inclusion until year two because the service income will be earned, for financial accounting purposes, entirely in year two. Rev. Proc. 2004-34.

   Accountants Inc. may or may not be able to deduct the expense of office cleaning in year one. The all events test is met in year one since the liability for cleaning expenses is fixed and determinate in that year. However, Accountants Inc. cannot deduct the expense until the economic performance requirement of §461(h) is also met. With respect to services to be provided to the taxpayer, economic performance occurs when the services are provided, so economic performance occurs in year two. §461(h)(2)(A)(i). Section 461(h)(1) precludes Accountants Inc. from deducting the expense in year one.

30. This transaction falls within the ambit of *American Automobile Association*, but Ventana Ranch Inc. probably can qualify for limited deferral of the prepaid income. The deferral method in Rev. Proc. 2004-34 can apply to prepayments for (i) services and (ii) use of property that is ancillary to the provision of services. Here, the prepayment is for spa services and use of the spa facilities so the deferral method can apply. A taxpayer qualifies for deferral of these types of prepaid income if some or all of the prepayment will be included in a later year for financial accounting purposes. In the year of the prepayment, the taxpayer includes the same amount for tax and financial accounting purposes. The remainder of the

prepayment must be included in the following year. For financial accounting purposes, Ventana Ranch Inc. will include $200,000 (1/5 of the $1 million prepayment) in year one and $800,000 (4/5 of the $1 million prepayment) in years two through five. For tax purposes, Ventana Ranch Inc. will include $200,000 in year one and $800,000 in year two.

31. No. Section 461(h) provides that an accrual method taxpayer cannot deduct an item until the later of (i) satisfaction of the all events test or (ii) economic performance. Section 461(h)(2)(B) provides that, where liability arises from the provision of services by the taxpayer, economic performance occurs when the services are provided. Hence, Consumers Inc. will be able to deduct the cost of the service contract only as it provides service. (The recurring item exception of §461(h)(3) *might* permit Consumers Inc. to take a year one deduction for the expense of services provided prior to the date in year two on which it files its year one tax return. See, e.g., Reg. §1.461-5(e), Example 1. The recurring item exception cannot apply, however, if Consumers Inc. uses the deferral method to report the service income received in year one. A portion of the sale price of the television set is allocable to the service warranty. For financial accounting purposes, that service income will be earned in later years. For tax purposes, Consumers Inc. can defer inclusion of that prepaid service income until year two. Rev. Proc. 2004-34, Example 5. If Consumers Inc. uses the deferral method to report the prepaid service income, there is better matching of income and expense if the deduction for the cost of the services is taken in year two, the year in which the prepaid service income is included for tax purposes. In that event, the recurring item exception matching requirement would not be satisfied in year one and Consumers Inc. could not take the deduction in that year.)

Personal Deductions, Exemptions, and Credits

The deductions, exemptions, and credits examined in this chapter are called *personal* because they are largely unrelated to the cost of earning income. Personal deductions, exemptions, and credits often are designed to reflect differences in ability to pay. This is the primary function, for example, of the deduction for extraordinary medical expenses and the exemption for dependents. Other personal deductions and credits are designed to encourage certain forms of behavior. Section 170, for example, provides a deduction for charitable contributions.

Section A of this chapter introduces the standard deduction, examines some of the issues surrounding personal and dependent exemptions, and briefly describes personal credits. Sections B through F look at the deductions for extraordinary medical expenses, casualty losses, charitable contributions, home mortgage interest, and state and local taxes.

A. INTRODUCTION

Reading: §§22, 24, 31, 32, 63, 67, 151, 152.
Personal deductions are subtracted from adjusted gross income in determining taxable income. A taxpayer may take either (i) *itemized* personal deductions or (ii) a *standard deduction*. §63(b). What qualifies as an itemized personal deduction is the subject of this chapter; the largest itemized deductions are the home mortgage interest deduction and the deduction for state and local taxes.

An otherwise qualifying itemized deduction may be lost entirely or in part due to statutory limits imposed by §§67 and 68 and under the

Alternative Minimum Tax (discussed in Chapter 5). Section 67(a) provides that itemized deductions, other than the ones listed in §67(b), are allowed only to the extent they exceed 2 percent of the taxpayer's adjusted gross income. Fortunately, most major itemized deductions — including all the itemized deductions discussed later in this chapter — are listed in §67(b) and thus are not subject to the 2 percent floor. The deductions for unreimbursed employee business expenses and certain investment-related fees, such as the cost of subscribing to the Wall Street Journal, are subject to the 2 percent floor. In addition, under the Alternative Minimum Tax, the miscellaneous itemized deductions that are subject to the 2 percent floor of §67 are disallowed. §56(b)(1)(A)(i).

Section 68 imposes an overall limitation on the itemized deductions of high-income taxpayers. The §68 limitation (which is commonly referred to as "Pease" for historical reasons) applies to taxpayers with adjusted gross income in excess of the inflation-adjusted "applicable amount." §68(b). For 2014, the inflation-adjusted applicable amount was $254,200 for individuals and $305,050 for married taxpayers filing a joint return. Rev. Proc. 2013-35. Section 68 applies to all itemized deductions other than deductions for medical expenses, investment interest, casualty losses, theft losses, and gambling losses. §68(c). If §68 applies, the taxpayer's aggregate itemized deductions are reduced by the lesser of 3 percent of the taxpayer's adjusted gross income in excess of the applicable amount or 80 percent of the taxpayer's itemized deductions. For example, assume that an individual taxpayer has $554,200 of adjusted gross income and $80,000 of itemized deductions. Assume also that the "applicable amount" is $254,200. Section 68 reduces the taxpayer's itemized deductions by the lesser of (1) $9,000 (3 percent of the taxpayer's $300,000 of adjusted gross income in excess of the $254,200 applicable amount) or (2) $64,000 (80 percent of the taxpayer's $80,000 of itemized deductions). Section 68 thus limits the taxpayer's itemized deductions to $81,000 ($90,000 itemized deductions less the $9,000 reduction under §68).

Section 63(c)(2) sets forth the standard deduction amounts, which are adjusted annually for inflation. §63(c)(4). For 2014, the inflation adjusted standard deduction was $6,200 for an unmarried taxpayer and $12,400 for a married couple filing a joint return. Rev. Proc. 2013-35. (In addition, §63(f) provides small additional inflation-adjusted standard deductions for the elderly and the blind.) For most taxpayers who are not paying interest on a home mortgage, the standard deduction will generate a larger deduction than would itemized deductions.

Personal exemptions are also subtracted from a taxpayer's adjusted gross income and may be taken in addition to itemized deductions or the standard deduction. §63(b), (d). Each taxpayer receives a *personal exemption* and an additional *dependent exemption* for each dependent. §151(b), (c). Although §151 provides that the exemption amount for both personal and dependent exemptions is $2,000, that amount is adjusted for inflation under §151(d)(4). In 2014, the personal and dependent exemption amount was $3,950. Rev. Proc. 2013-35.

The rules for determining who is a *dependent* for purposes of the exemption are surprisingly complex. The term *dependent* is defined in §152(a) as a "qualifying child" or a "qualifying relative." A *"qualifying child"* is a person who: (i) is the taxpayer's child or sibling, or the descendant of the taxpayer's child or sibling; (ii) is 18 or younger (or 23 or younger if the person is a student); (iii) has "the same principal place of abode" as the taxpayer for more than half the year; and (iv) has not provided more than half of his own support for the year. §152(c). A *"qualifying relative"* is a person: (i) who either (A) is the taxpayer's child or child's descendant, parent or parent's ancestor, sibling, aunt, uncle, niece, nephew, cousin, or in-law, or (B) has "the same principal place of abode as the taxpayer and is a member of the taxpayer's household"; (ii) whose gross income for the year is less than the §151 personal exemption amount (e.g., $3,950 in 2014); (iii) who receives more than half of her support from the taxpayer; and (iv) who is not a qualifying child of the taxpayer. §152(d). Note that a person who is not related to a taxpayer can be the taxpayer's "qualifying relative" if the taxpayer lives with and supports the person. For example, if a taxpayer's same-sex partner is not treated as the taxpayer's "spouse" under federal income tax law (as it is evolving), the same-sex partner nonetheless may qualify as the taxpayer's "dependent" if the taxpayer supports the partner.

High-income taxpayers' personal and dependent exemptions are subject to a phase-out (commonly referred to by the acronym "PEP" for personal exemption phase-out). If a taxpayer's adjusted gross income exceeds the "threshold phase-out amount," the taxpayer's exemptions are reduced 2 percent for each $2,500 increment (or fraction thereof) of adjusted gross income in excess of the inflation-adjusted threshold phase-out amount. §151(d)(3), (4)(B). For 2014, the inflation-adjusted threshold phase-out amount was $305,050 for married taxpayers filing a joint return and $254,200 for unmarried individuals. Rev. Proc. 2013-35. Consider the following example: Jack and Jill, married taxpayers who file a joint return, have one young child who qualifies as a dependent. In 2014, Jack and Jill were entitled to three $3,950 exemptions (one each for Jack, Jill, and their child), which totaled $11,850. Assume that their 2014 adjusted gross income was $377,600, so it exceeded the $305,050 threshold amount by $72,550. For purposes of computing the phase-out, there were 30 full or partial $2,500 increments (29 full increments of $2,500, totaling $72,500 and 1 partial increment of $50). Their $11,850 exemption amount was reduced 2 percent for each of the 30 increments, or 60 percent. The reduction thus was $7,110 (60 percent of $11,850), leaving them with an exemption amount of $4,740 (original $11,850 exemption amount minus the $7,110 reduction). Note that the exemption amount is fully phased out if the excess of a taxpayer's adjusted gross income over the threshold phase-out amount is more than $122,500, because there are 49 full increments of $2,500 in $122,500; any excess that is greater than $122,500 is 50 full or partial $2,500 increments. A reduction of 2 percent per increment, with 50 increments, leads to a 100 percent reduction in the exemption amount.

In effect, both the Pease and PEP limitations constitute tax rate increases for the high-income taxpayers whose deductions are reduced. The limitations increase the progressivity of the tax system, by limiting the deductions of high-income taxpayers who (arguably) need them the least, but not limiting the deductions of taxpayers with less income; the limitations increase the complexity of an already complex tax system, however. Congress temporarily eliminated the Pease and PEP limitations, during the presidency of George W. Bush, but added them back to the Code as part of the American Taxpayer Relief Act of 2012. P.L. 112-240 §101(b)(2).

Unlike deductions and exclusions, which reduce a taxpayer's taxable income, tax credits reduce a taxpayer's tax liability dollar for dollar. Thus, for a taxpayer in the 40 percent marginal tax bracket, a $100 deduction reduces taxable income by $100 and reduces tax liability by $40; a $100 credit, by contrast, would reduce tax liability by $100.

The most generally applicable credit is the §31 credit for income taxes withheld by an employer from an employee's wages. This credit is refundable, meaning that a taxpayer is entitled to a refund to the extent that this credit exceeds the taxpayer's income tax owed for the year.

The most significant credit premised on concern about "ability to pay" is the earned income credit, designed to reduce the tax burden on low-income workers. If the credit amount exceeds the taxpayer's tax liability, the excess amount is refundable. As the taxpayer's income increases, the credit is phased out. The precise calculation of the credit is complex and subject to frequent modification. We suggest students just skim the following brief (!) description of its operation.

The §32 credit equals the credit percentage of an eligible taxpayer's earned income up to the earned income amount. §32(a)(1). For 2014, the *credit percentage* was (i) 34 percent if the taxpayer had one qualifying child, (ii) 40 percent if the taxpayer had two qualifying children, (iii) 45 percent if the taxpayer had three or more qualifying children, and (iv) 7.65 percent if the taxpayer had no qualifying children. §32(b)(1)(A),(3)(A). The term *qualifying child* is defined as in §152(c), without the support requirement of §152(c)(1)(D). §32(c)(3)(A). *Earned income* includes wages, salaries, tips, and any other employment compensation and income from self-employment, but does not include pensions or annuities. §32(c)(2). The amount of earned income that may be taken into account, for purposes of computing the credit, is limited to the *earned income amount*. §32(a)(1).

In 2014, the earned income amount was: (i) $9,720 if the taxpayer had one qualifying child; (ii) $13,650 if the taxpayer had more than one qualifying child; and (iii) $6,480 if the taxpayer had no qualifying children. §32(b)(2)(A), (j), Rev. Proc. 2013-35. The maximum earned income tax credit for 2014 was thus: (i) $3,305 (the 34 percent credit percentage multiplied by the $9,720 earned income amount) for a taxpayer with one qualifying child; (ii) $5,460 (the 40 percent credit percentage multiplied by the $13,650 earned income amount) for a taxpayer with two qualifying children; (iii) $6,143 (the 45 percent credit percentage multiplied by the $13,650 earned income amount) for a taxpayer with three or more qualifying children; and (iv) $496 (the 7.65 percent credit percentage multiplied by the $6,480 earned income amount) for a taxpayer with no qualifying children. Rev. Proc. 2013-35. Also, the earned income credit is subject to a complex phase-out that ensures that the benefits of §32 go only to the "working poor."

Sound complicated? It is. Few taxpayers could hope to determine the §32 credit without an accountant or tax lawyer — a luxury those eligible for the credit are unlikely to be able to afford. Fortunately, for the working poor who file returns, the amount of the credit can be and is calculated automatically by the Service in their computerized review of returns.

Section 22, another ability-to-pay credit, provides a nonrefundable credit for taxpayers who either are at least 65 years old or are retired because of permanent and total disability. The maximum credit is $750 (15 percent of $5,000) for unmarried taxpayers or married taxpayers where only one spouse qualifies for the §22 credit. §22(a), (c)(2)(A)(i). If married taxpayers both qualify for the credit and file a joint return, the maximum credit is $1,125 (15 percent of $7,500). §22(a), (c)(2)(A)(ii). The credit is reduced if the taxpayer receives certain types of government pension, annuity, or disability payments. §22(c)(1), (3). The credit is also subject to a phase-out based on the taxpayer's adjusted gross income. §22(d).

Section 24 provides a $1,000 child tax credit for each "qualifying child" for which the taxpayer is allowed a §151 dependent exemption. §24(a). (EGTRRA, the 2001 tax act, increased the credit from $500 to $1,000 through 2010, and subsequent legislation extended EGTRRA through 2012. P.L. 111-312 §101(a)(1).) The term *qualifying child* is defined as a §152(c) "qualifying child" who is 16 or younger. §24(c)(1). The credit is reduced by $50 for each $1,000 (or fraction thereof) by which the taxpayer's adjusted gross income (with a few modifications) exceeds the "threshold amount," which is $110,000 for married taxpayers filing a joint return and $75,000 for single taxpayers. §24(b)(1), (2). The credit is generally refundable up to a maximum of 15 percent of the taxpayer's earned income above $3,000 (through 2017). §24(d), P.L. 112-240 §103(b), Rev. Proc. 2013-35. Taxpayers with three or more qualifying children may be able to qualify for a larger amount of refundable credit. §24(d)(1)(B)(ii).

The Code also includes various other specific nonrefundable and refundable personal credits, such as credits for adoption expenses, the cost of alternative energy vehicles, and the cost of certain health insurance premiums. If you need to research specific tax credits, you must read the applicable Code sections very carefully. Note whether the credit is non-refundable, partially refundable, or fully refundable (both under the regular income tax and the Alternative Minimum Tax, discussed in Chapter 5). Be aware of phase-outs based on adjusted gross income, and pay particularly close attention to statutory amendments (which can be layered and complex) and effective dates.

Congress frequently amends the tax credit provisions and sometimes renumbers the Code section for specific tax credits or changes the refundability of the credits. These amendments may be temporary or permanent and may take effect immediately or may have deferred effective dates. In addition, more than one tax credit provision might potentially apply to a category of credit. For example, several specific tax credits all relate to the purchase of "green" vehicles.

(If you would like to peruse a list of the various credits in the Code, the table of contents for Part IV of Chapter 1 of the Code provides a convenient list, although it includes some credits that are temporary or have deferred effective dates.)

Examples

1. Peter and Martina are married and have three children. Each child receives more than half of his or her support from them. The youngest, Alex, age 13, lives at home and earns $2,000 per year as a child actor in advertisements. Alex is adopted. Betsy, age 16, lives with her aunt in New York so that she can attend a special high school for young musicians. Carl, age 21, lives with a friend in an apartment two miles from his parents' home. Carl earns about $5,000 per year as a member of a struggling rock band. Peter and Martina file a joint return and have combined adjusted gross income of $120,500. (Assume the §151(d)(3) personal exemption phase-out does not apply.)

   a. How many personal and dependent exemptions may be taken by Peter and Martina?

   b. Would your answer in part (a) change if Carl were a part-time student at the local community college?

   c. Suppose that Martina and Peter also paid more than half of the support for Anna, Martina's niece. Anna, who lives in New York with her mother, Martina's sister, earns no income during the year. May Peter and Martina take a dependent deduction for Anna?

   d. For what amount of child tax credit can they qualify under §24?

2. Debby's best friend, Emily, is disabled in a skiing accident. Debby invites Emily to live with her and provides more than half of her support. Emily's income drops to less than the exemption amount. (Assume the

§151(d)(3) personal exemption phase-out does not apply.) Will Debby be entitled to a dependent exemption for Emily?

3. Mom's daughter Greta, age 22, is attending law school. Her annual expenses are $20,000 for tuition and books, $10,000 for food and lodging, and $5,000 for other expenses. Greta meets these expenses as follows:

$18,000	Scholarship from the law school
$ 4,000	Summer earnings
$ 3,000	Student loans
$10,000	Support from Mom

(Assume the §151(d)(3) personal exemption phase-out does not apply.) Will Mom be entitled to a dependent exemption for Greta?

4. Harry and Sally are married and have twin toddlers. Sally works full time in a fast-food restaurant. Harry stays at home with the two children. In 2014, Harry and Sally file a joint return and have combined adjusted gross income of $20,000. All of their income is attributable to Sally's wages. For what type and amount of tax credits might Harry and Sally qualify? Are these credits refundable under the regular income tax?

Explanations

1. a. They may take two personal exemptions, one each for Peter and Martina, and two dependent exemptions, one each for Alex and Betsy. They may not take a dependent exemption for Carl. The §151 definition of "dependent" cross-references the definition of "dependent" in §152. §151(c). Under §152, the term *dependent* includes a "qualifying child" and a "qualifying relative." The term *qualifying child* includes a child of the taxpayer who: (i) is 18 or younger (or 23 or younger if the person is a student); (ii) has "the same principal place of abode" as the taxpayer for more than half the year; and (iii) has not provided more than half of his or her own support for the year. All three kids are Peter and Martina's children. Adopted children, like Alex, are treated the same as the taxpayers' biological children. Alex and Betsy satisfy the age requirement. Carl flunks the age requirement because he is 21 and is not a student. He also flunks the residency requirement because he lives in an apartment, not in his parents' home. The residency requirement is met for Alex and Betsy. Although Betsy lived with her aunt in New York during the 10-month school year, the legislative history of §152 indicates that a temporary absence from home to attend school is disregarded for purposes of the residency requirement. The support

test probably is met for all three kids. Although Alex earned $2,000 and Carl earned $5,000, the amounts they earned probably were less than half of their support for the year.

Carl also is not a "qualifying relative." A "qualifying relative" includes the taxpayers' child if the child (i) is not a qualifying child; (ii) has gross income for the year that is less than the §151 personal exemption amount (e.g., $3,950 in 2014); and (iii) receives more than half of his support from the taxpayer. Carl flunks the gross income test.

b. No. "Student" is defined in §152(f)(2) to include only full-time students.

c. Yes. Anna is not a qualifying child because she flunks the residency test. She is, however, a "qualifying relative." A niece is one of the relationships that qualifies under the §152(d)(2) "qualifying relative" test. Anna has no income so the gross income requirement is satisfied. Peter and Martina pay over half of Anna's support so the support requirement also is satisfied.

d. Peter and Martina qualify for a §24 tax credit. Only two of their children, Alex and Betsy, are qualifying children for purposes of §24. Carl is not a qualifying child, for purposes of §24, because (i) he is not a qualifying child, for purposes of §152, and (ii) he is older than 16. §24(c)(1). Peter and Martina are entitled to a $1,000 credit for each of the two qualifying children. §24(a). That $2,000 amount will be reduced, however, because Peter and Martina's adjusted gross income exceeds the $110,000 threshold amount. §24(b)(2)(A). The amount of the credit is reduced by $50 for each increment of $1,000 by which the taxpayer's income exceeds the threshold amount. §24(b)(1). Peter and Martina's $120,500 of adjusted gross income exceeds the $110,000 threshold amount by $10,500. Treating a partial increment as a full increment, there are 11 $1,000 increments in excess of the threshold amount ($10,500/$1,000). The $2,000 credit amount is reduced by $550 (11 × $50), so Peter and Martina qualify for a $1,450 credit under §24.

2. Yes. Under the §152 definition of "dependent," a non-relative cannot be a "qualifying child" but, paradoxically, can be a "qualifying relative." A non-relative is a "qualifying relative" if that person: (i) has "the same principal place of abode as the taxpayer and is a member of the taxpayer's household"; (ii) has gross income for the year that is less than the §151 personal exemption amount (e.g., $3,950 in 2014); (iii) receives more than half of her support from the taxpayer; and (iv) is not a qualifying child of the taxpayer. §152(d). Emily lives with Debby and is a member of Debby's household. Debby provides over half of Emily's support. Emily's gross income is below the personal exemption amount and Emily is not a qualifying child.

3. Probably. Greta: (i) is Mom's child, (ii) is under 24 years of age and is a full-time student; and (iii) does not provide more than half of her own support for the year. (The scholarship is not treated as support provided by Greta.) The question here is whether Greta satisfies the residency test. Greta pays $10,000 for food and lodging, so it seems as though she does not live with Mom. Temporary absence from home to attend school is disregarded for purposes of the residency test, however. If Greta "has the same principal place of abode" as Mom for more than half the year, Greta is a "qualifying child" and Mom can take a dependent exemption for Greta.

4. Harry and Sally will be allowed a refundable credit for any income tax withheld from Sally's wages by her employer. §31. They also will qualify for the maximum amount of the earned income credit, $5,460, which is 40 percent (the applicable percentage for a taxpayer with two qualifying children) of the 2014 maximum earned income amount for a taxpayer with two or more children, $13,650 (which is less than Sally's $20,000 of earned income). §32(a), (b), (c), Rev. Proc. 2013-35. The earned income credit is refundable. In addition, Harry and Sally will qualify for a child tax credit of $2,000 ($1,000 for each of their two young children). The child tax credit also is fully refundable because $2,000 is less than the maximum refundable amount in 2014, $2,550, which is 15 percent of their $17,000 of earned income in excess of $3,000. §24(a), (c), (d)(1)(B)(i), (4); P.L. 112-240 §103(b), Rev. Proc. 2013-35.

B. CASUALTY LOSSES

Reading: §165; Reg. §§1.165-1, -7, -8.

A taxpayer can deduct net *personal casualty losses* (personal casualty losses less personal casualty gains) to the extent that the aggregate losses during the taxable year exceed 10 percent of the taxpayer's adjusted gross income, after reducing each loss by $100. §165(h). Personal casualty losses are losses of "property not connected with a trade or business or a transaction entered into for profit, if such losses arise from fire, storm, shipwreck, or other casualty, or from theft." §165(c)(3). Losses of property used in a business or profit-seeking activity are deductible whether or not they are due to casualty or theft. §165(c)(1), (2).

The rationale for the personal deduction for casualty losses can be illustrated by the following example. Suppose Martha, a young San Francisco lawyer, receives a $5,000 end-of-year bonus from her law firm and uses the money to purchase a set of fine china. One day after the purchase, the china is destroyed in an earthquake. Supporters of the casualty deduction contend that Martha is in the same economic position after the earthquake that she would have been in had she never received the bonus and purchased the china. A casualty loss deduction thus is necessary to ensure that her taxable income accurately reflects her "ability to pay." Opponents of the casualty loss deduction point out that Martha could have avoided a loss by purchasing earthquake insurance or, perhaps, by taking additional measures to protect the china. If she decided not to purchase such insurance or to take such care, they argue, the government should not subsidize part of her loss through a tax deduction.

Under current law, a casualty loss deduction is permitted only to the extent that the loss is not reimbursed by insurance or otherwise. §165(a). In general, the deduction is permitted in the taxable year in which the loss occurs or, in the case of theft, in the taxable year in which the taxpayer discovers the loss. §165(e), Reg. §§1.165-1(d)(1), 1.165-8(a)(1), (2). If the taxpayer has a claim for reimbursement of a casualty loss, the loss may not be deducted until the taxable year in which the amount that will be reimbursed can be ascertained. Reg. §1.165-1(d)(2).

In some circumstances, a taxpayer may have gain from a personal casualty. For example, assume that a taxpayer's basis in lost property is $50,000, but the taxpayer receives $75,000 from the insurance company because the property was insured for its replacement cost. The taxpayer will recognize $25,000 of gain on the involuntary conversion (assuming that the nonrecognition rule of §1033 is inapplicable). If a taxpayer's personal casualty gains exceed the taxpayer's personal casualty losses, the personal casualty gains and losses are treated as capital gains and losses. §165(h)(2)(B). In these circumstances, the personal casualty loss would not be an itemized deduction; instead it would offset the taxpayer's gain from the personal casualty. §165(h)(5)(A). If, on the other hand, the taxpayer's personal casualty losses exceed the taxpayer's personal casualty gains, the net personal casualty loss is an itemized deduction. §165(h). (This itemized deduction is not subject to the limitations of §67 or §68. §§67(b)(3), 68(c)(3).)

The amount of a casualty loss is determined by comparing the fair market value of the damaged property before and after the casualty. Reg. §1.165-7(a)(2)(i), (b)(1). However, the loss cannot exceed the taxpayer's adjusted basis in the property. §165(b), Reg. §1.165-7(b)(1). (The amount of the loss claimed as a deduction reduces the taxpayer's basis in the damaged property. Reg. §1.165-1(c)(1).) In addition, the loss from each casualty is allowed only to the extent that it exceeds $100. §165(h)(1). The deduction for net personal casualty losses (personal casualty losses in excess of personal casualty gains) also is limited to the net casualty losses that exceed 10 percent of the taxpayer's adjusted gross income. §165(h)(2). Thus, a deduction is provided only for losses that have a substantial impact on a taxpayer's financial well-being, distinguishing casualty losses from the ordinary mishaps of daily life. The 10 percent threshold simplified the Code by effectively eliminating the deduction for most losses. However, casualty losses continue to raise interesting theoretical issues.

If a taxpayer's loss of personal property is caused by an event other than fire, storm, shipwreck, or theft, the taxpayer may deduct the loss only if it was caused by a casualty. §165(c)(3). Defining the term *casualty* presents difficult line-drawing problems. The Service's position is that only an event that is "sudden, unexpected, and unusual" qualifies as casualty. Rev. Rul. 72-592. For example, the Service has taken the position that gradual termite damage does not qualify as a casualty loss because it is not sudden. Rev. Rul. 63-232. The "unexpected" requirement is illustrated in Dyer v. Commissioner, 20 T.C.M. (CCH) 705 (1961), where the taxpayer claimed a casualty loss deduction for a $100 vase that was destroyed by a cat suffering a fit. The Tax Court denied the deduction because breakage of household goods by a family pet is not unexpected.

Courts do not always apply the "sudden, unexpected, and unusual" standard consistently. This inconsistency is illustrated in numerous decisions involving casualty loss deductions for lost or destroyed diamond rings. Compare, e.g., Keenan v. Bowers, 91 F. Supp. 771 (E.D.S.C. 1950) (where the taxpayer was denied a casualty loss deduction for two diamond rings that were wrapped in a tissue and mistakenly flushed down a toilet) with Carpenter v. Commissioner, 25 T.C.M. (CCH) 1186 (1966) (where the taxpayer was allowed a casualty loss deduction for a diamond ring that had been left in a glass of ammonia and water for cleaning and was later poured into the kitchen sink and destroyed by the garbage disposal).

A taxpayer may take a casualty loss deduction for property destroyed due to the taxpayer's negligence. However, a casualty loss deduction is not allowed if the loss is caused by gross negligence or a willful act by the taxpayer. See, e.g., Blackman v. Commissioner, 88 T.C. 677 (1987), (where the taxpayer was denied a casualty loss deduction for his destroyed home because of his gross negligence in failing to put out the fire he started), Reg. §1.165-7(a)(3)(i) (denying a casualty loss deduction if the loss is due to the willful act or willful negligence of the taxpayer).

Examples

5. In year one the contents of Susan's rented apartment are destroyed by a fire. Susan suffers a $20,000 loss from the destruction of her personal belongings in the fire. The property lost had a basis of $35,000. Susan's year one adjusted gross income is $100,000.
   a. If Susan had no renter's insurance, how much of her $20,000 loss is deductible?
   b. How, if at all, would your answer in part (a) change if Susan had renter's insurance that covered $8,000 of her loss?

6. In year one Jack has adjusted gross income of $40,000. On March 1, year one, his car is stolen. Jack's basis in the car is $20,000, but it is worth only $5,000. On July 1 a flood in his apartment destroys his stereo, worth $500, and his television set, worth $200. Jack has a $1,000 basis in the stereo and an $800 basis in the television. Jack will not be reimbursed for the stolen car or the lost stereo and television. How large a casualty deduction is Jack entitled to take in year one?

7. In year one Mickey, who has adjusted gross income of $50,000, loses a painting worth $12,000 in a storm. Mickey's basis in the painting is $10,000. The painting was not insured. How large a casualty deduction will Mickey be entitled to take in year one?

8. In year one Nell's uninsured car is destroyed in a flood. Prior to the flood, the car had a basis of $8,000 and a fair market value of $7,000. Nell's year one adjusted gross income is $20,000.
   a. How large a casualty deduction is Nell allowed if the car is her personal car?
   b. How large a deduction is Nell allowed if the car was used exclusively in her business?

9. a. In year one Maria, who has adjusted gross income of $100,000, loses her home and her car in an earthquake, which unfortunately occurs just one hour after she closes on the purchase of her home. From various insurance policies, she recovers $250,000 for the loss of her home, which has an adjusted basis of $220,000. Her car, which has an adjusted basis of $15,000 and is worth $10,000, is uninsured. How much is her casualty loss deduction in year one?
   b. How, if at all, would your answer in part (a) change if Maria's basis in her home at the time of the earthquake is instead $243,000?
   c. How, if at all, would your answer in part (b) change if, at the time of the earthquake, Maria's car is worth $35,000 and her basis in the car is $40,000?

Assume, for purposes of the examples below, that the losses incurred are not reimbursed by insurance or otherwise and that the casualty losses stated already take into account the $100 and 10 percent of adjusted gross income floors.

10. Tim suffered a $15,000 loss when his sailboat was destroyed in a storm. Briefly state the arguments for and against allowing Tim a deduction for the loss.

11. Buck lost his home in a flash flood on January 20 of year one. It was unclear whether Buck had let his insurance policy lapse. After the insurance company refused his claim, Buck filed a lawsuit against the company seeking payment. In which year or years can Buck take a casualty loss deduction?

12. Tim keeps a snowmobile at his vacation cabin in the mountains. Tim's snowmobile was stolen on October 15 of year one, but Tim did not discover the theft until January 15 of year two. In which year or years can Tim take the casualty loss deduction for the stolen snowmobile?

13. Pyro lit a bonfire in his living room. He mistakenly believed that he could contain the fire because when he was young he was a Boy Scout. He was wrong and suffered a $30,000 loss. Is Pyro's loss deductible?

14. a. Giovanni suffers a $7,000 loss when his kitchen floor suddenly collapses due to termite damage. Is Giovanni's loss deductible?
    b. Would your answer change if Giovanni's kitchen floor collapses when his furnace explodes?

15. Wendy's car suffers $5,000 of damage due to her negligent driving. Is her loss deductible?

16. Bill suffers a $4,000 loss due to his negligent driving. Bill has auto insurance, but decides not to file a claim because he does not want his rates raised. Can Bill still deduct his loss?

17. In each of the following cases, determine whether Dusty will be allowed a casualty loss deduction for the loss of his wedding ring:
    a. The ring slips off his finger while he is skiing.
    b. The ring is lost when he runs into a tree while skiing.
    c. Dusty wraps his ring in tissue and puts it on his night stand. His wife flushes the tissue with the ring down the toilet.
    d. The ring is inadvertently dropped into the kitchen sink and is destroyed by the garbage disposal.
    e. A burglar steals the ring.
    f. The ring is lost when a friend accidentally slams a car door on Dusty's finger.

18. Donna's uninsured automobile was destroyed in a stock car race. Can Donna deduct the loss?

Explanations

5. a. Susan will be allowed a $9,900 casualty loss deduction. Susan's adjusted gross income is $100,000. A taxpayer is allowed a deduction for net personal casualty losses (reduced by $100) in excess of 10 percent of adjusted gross income. §165(c)(3), (h). Susan's personal casualty loss is $20,000. That amount is first reduced by $100, to $19,900. §165(h)(1). Susan's adjusted gross income is $100,000 and 10 percent of that amount is $10,000. Thus, she can deduct $9,900 ($19,900 loss less $10,000). §165(h)(1), (2)(A).

b. Susan will be allowed a $1,900 casualty loss deduction. A deduction is permitted for casualty losses only to the extent that they are not reimbursed. §165(a). If Susan lost $20,000 in the fire and was reimbursed for $8,000, her loss is reduced to $12,000. That amount is further reduced by $100, to $11,900. §165(h)(1). Her deduction is thus $1,900, which is $11,900 less $10,000 (10 percent of her adjusted gross income). §165(h)(1), (2)(A).

6. Jack is allowed a $1,500 casualty loss. Losses resulting from the same event are combined for purposes of the $100 floor, so the flood generates a $700 loss that exceeds the $100 floor by $600. Reg. §1.165-7(b)(4). The amount of the theft loss is the $5,000 value of the car since this amount is less than Jack's basis in the car. §165(b), Reg. §1.165-7(b)(1), (3), Example 2. The loss from the car theft exceeds the floor by $4,900, so the total loss from the two events is $5,500. Ten percent of Jack's $40,000 adjusted gross income is $4,000. Jack is allowed a casualty loss of $1,500, which is $5,500 less $4,000. §165(c)(3), (h)(1), (2).

7. Mickey is allowed a $4,900 casualty loss. The amount of the casualty loss is $10,000, which is the lesser of the $12,000 value of the painting destroyed or Mickey's $10,000 basis in the painting. That $10,000 loss is reduced by $100 to $9,900. Mickey is allowed to deduct $4,900, which is $9,900 less $5,000 (10 percent of his $50,000 adjusted gross income). §165(c)(3), (h)(1), (2).

8. a. Nell is allowed a $4,900 casualty loss. The amount of the casualty loss is the $7,000 value of the car destroyed since this amount is less than Nell's adjusted basis. After taking into account the $100 and 10 percent of AGI floors, Nell would be able to deduct $4,900, which is $6,900 ($7,000 less $100) less $2,000 (10 percent of her $20,000 adjusted gross income).

b. Business losses, which are taken under §165(c)(1) rather than §165(c)(3), are not subject to the $100 and 10 percent floors imposed by §165(h). Nell would be allowed a business loss of $8,000, the adjusted basis of the car. Taxpayers whose personal property is totally destroyed in a casualty are allowed a loss equal to the lesser of the basis or the fair market value of the property. On the other hand, taxpayers whose business property is totally destroyed are allowed a loss equal to the adjusted basis of the property even if that basis is greater than the fair market value of the property. Reg. §1.165-7(b)(1).

9. a. Maria would not be allowed an itemized deduction for her losses. Instead, she would have a $30,000 capital gain and a $9,900 capital loss. §165(h)(2)(B), (4), (5)(A). Maria has a personal casualty gain

of $30,000 on her home because the $250,000 of insurance proceeds received for her home exceed her $220,000 basis in the home by $30,000. §165(h)(4)(A). She cannot exclude the gain under §121 because she does not meet the ownership and residency requirements of that section. Maria also has a personal casualty loss of $9,900 on her car ($10,000 less $100) since the $10,000 value of the car is less than her $15,000 basis in the car. If casualty gains exceed casualty losses, the gains are treated as capital gains and the losses are treated as capital losses. §165(h)(2)(B). Therefore, Maria would have a $30,000 capital gain and a $9,900 capital loss. In other words, the casualty loss is netted against the casualty gain and is not allowed as an itemized deduction.

b. Maria is not allowed a casualty loss deduction and does not have to include her casualty gain in income. If Maria's basis in her home is $243,000, her casualty gain is reduced to $7,000 ($250,000 insurance proceeds less her $243,000 basis in her home). Maria's casualty loss on the car is still $9,900. Maria thus has a $2,900 net personal casualty loss. This net casualty loss does not exceed 10 percent of her $100,000 adjusted gross income, so she will not be allowed to take a deduction in year one for the net loss. §165(h)(2)(A). However, she is permitted to net the loss (up to the amount of the gain) against the gain, so she will not have to include the gain. §165(h)(5)(A). In this example, the reporting mechanics are determined by §165(h)(2) and Form 4684, the form on which taxpayers report casualty gains and losses. On Form 4684, taxpayers list casualty gains and losses and net the gains and losses. If casualty gains exceed casualty losses, the taxpayer reports the difference on Schedule D, the capital gains and losses schedule. If the losses exceed the gains, the taxpayer reduces the net loss by 10 percent of AGI and reports the allowable loss as an itemized deduction on Schedule A, the itemized deduction schedule. In this example, Maria would complete Form 4684, but the reduction of the net casualty loss by 10 percent of her AGI leaves her with no allowable loss to report as an itemized deduction on Schedule A.

c. Maria is allowed a $17,900 personal casualty loss deduction. §165(c)(3), (h). As in part (b), Maria's personal casualty gain is $7,000. Her personal casualty loss here is $34,900 ($35,000 value of the lost car less $100). Thus, Maria has a net personal casualty loss of $27,900 ($34,900 personal casualty loss less $7,000 personal casualty gain). She is allowed to deduct $17,900 ($27,900 net casualty loss less $10,000, which is 10 percent of her $100,000 adjusted gross income) as an itemized deduction. §165(h)(2)(A), Form 4684.

10. The basic argument in favor of granting Tim a deduction is as follows: A casualty loss represents a reduction in wealth just like a loss of income. If Tim makes $50,000 and suffers a $15,000 casualty loss, he is in the same financial position as a person who makes $35,000 and suffers no damage. Thus, he should bear the same tax burden as a person who makes $35,000. This can be achieved by allowing Tim a casualty loss deduction.

    The basic arguments against granting Tim a deduction are as follows: It is difficult to draw the line between extraordinary, unforeseeable losses and random but predictable losses. Perhaps the loss due to the storm ought to be considered one of the costs of owning a boat, just as the costs of plumbing repairs or the replacement of a worn out furnace are considered nondeductible costs of home ownership. Most individuals probably consider the risk of storm damage as one of the predictable costs of boat ownership and insure against the risk. Free partial insurance in the form of a tax deduction from the government discourages the purchase of private insurance, since the casualty loss deduction is lost to the extent that an individual is reimbursed through insurance. The free partial insurance provided by a casualty loss deduction also subsidizes individuals who engage in risky activities and, accordingly, may reduce their incentives to take care of their property.

11. A casualty loss deduction is not permitted for any loss that reasonably might be reimbursed. Reg. §1.165-1(d)(2)(i). Thus, Buck will not be permitted a casualty loss deduction until the taxable year in which it becomes clear how much reimbursement, if any, he will receive. This is likely to be the year in which the lawsuit is settled or adjudicated.

12. Losses due to theft are deductible in the taxable year in which they are discovered. §165(e). Thus, Tim is allowed a theft loss deduction in year two.

13. Pyro's loss is probably not deductible. A taxpayer is not allowed a deduction for casualty losses suffered through his own willful act or gross negligence. Losses caused by a taxpayer's ordinary negligence, however, may be deducted. Pyro's actions probably constitute a willful act or gross negligence and thus he would not be allowed a deduction for any portion of his loss. See Blackman v. Commissioner, 88 T.C. 677 (1987). See also Regulation §1.165-7(a)(3)(i), which states that a taxpayer is entitled to a casualty loss for damage to his automobile that results from his faulty driving, but not for damage that is due to a willful act or willful negligence.

14. a. Giovanni will probably not be allowed a casualty loss deduction. The Service contends that a casualty loss deduction is only permitted for "sudden" losses like those caused by the fires, storms, and

shipwrecks explicitly listed in §165(c)(3). Rev. Rul. 72-592. Since termite damage occurs over a period of years, the Service has taken the position that a loss caused by termite damage is not deductible as a casualty loss. Rev. Rul. 63-232. In addition, courts generally do not treat a loss caused by termite damage as a deductible casualty loss, reasoning that such damage occurs over a period of many years, not "suddenly." United States v. Rogers, 120 F.2d 244 (9th Cir. 1941); Fay v. Helvering, 120 F.2d 253 (2d Cir. 1941); Dodge v. Commissioner, 25 T.C. 1022 (1956).

b. Giovanni is allowed a casualty loss deduction. The damage caused by an exploding furnace is a casualty because it meets the "suddenness" requirement.

15. Yes. Although damages caused by willful negligence are not deductible, casualty loss deductions are permitted for damages resulting from ordinary negligence. Reg. §1.165-7(a)(3)(i).

16. No. An insured taxpayer must file a timely claim with his insurance company in order to qualify for the casualty loss deduction. §165(h)(5)(E).

17. a. The ring cases demonstrate that the suddenness requirement can lead to differing results depending upon whether there is the "intervention of any sudden or destructive force." Stevens v. Commissioner, 6 T.C.M. (CCH) 805 (1947) (where the taxpayer was denied a casualty loss deduction for a ring lost in muddy water while the taxpayer was duck hunting). Dusty probably cannot deduct this loss because there is no intervening destructive force.

b. Dusty will probably be allowed to deduct the loss because the skiing accident is a sudden, destructive force. Kielts v. Commissioner, 42 T.C.M. (CCH) 238 (1981) (where the taxpayer was allowed a deduction where it appeared that a diamond fell out of its ring setting because of a sudden blow to the ring).

c. Here there is no sudden, destructive force. In a similar case, the court denied the deduction. Keenan v. Bowers, 91 F. Supp. 771 (E.D.S.C. 1950).

d. On similar facts, a court permitted the deduction. Carpenter v. Commissioner, 25 T.C.M. (CCH) 1186 (1966).

e. The deduction would be allowed as a loss due to theft. §165(c)(3).

f. The deduction probably would be allowed because the slamming door was sudden and destructive. See White v. Commissioner, 48 T.C. 430 (1967).

18. No. Crashes are not unexpected in automobile racing. Priv. Ltr. Rul. 8227010.

C. EXTRAORDINARY MEDICAL EXPENSES

Reading: §§105, 106, 213, 223; *Reg.* §1.213-1(e).

Under §213(a), a taxpayer can deduct amounts spent on medical care for the taxpayer and the taxpayer's spouse and dependents to the extent that the medical expenses exceed 10 percent of the taxpayer's adjusted gross income. The 10 percent floor makes the medical deduction available only to a small portion of taxpayers. On the other hand, medical benefits provided by an employer are fully excluded from an employee's income. §§105(b), 106. The exclusion has the same effect as (i) requiring the employee to include the employer-provided benefits then (ii) allowing the employee to deduct 100 percent of the expense. Thus, the taxation of medical expenses paid by a taxpayer is much less favorable than the treatment of employer-provided medical benefits.

The argument in favor of the medical expense deduction is similar to the argument for the casualty loss deduction: A taxpayer who becomes ill and incurs substantial medical expenses is in a similar financial situation as a healthy taxpayer with a lower salary. Thus, a medical deduction is needed to ensure that the two taxpayers bear the same tax burden. The arguments against the medical deduction are: (i) following the enactment of Obamacare (PPACA), insurance is available for most illnesses, so if an individual chooses to forgo such insurance there is no reason for the government to provide it through the tax code; (ii) it is often difficult to distinguish between deductible "medical" expenses and other nondeductible forms of consumption that improve the health of taxpayers or simply make them feel better; and (iii) the medical deduction seems to invite claims that sometimes border on the fraudulent.

Medical care generally is defined as amounts paid for the "diagnosis, cure, mitigation, treatment, or prevention of disease, or for the purpose of affecting any structure or function of the body." §213(d)(1)(A). If an expense improves the health of the taxpayer, but is not directed at diagnosing, curing, mitigating, treating, or preventing a disease, it is nondeductible. For example, if a doctor tells a patient who is showing signs of stress to take a vacation, the cost of the vacation is not a "medical" expense even if it improves the patient's health. Reg. §1.213-1(e)(1)(ii) (last sentence). Similarly, if a doctor tells a patient who is overweight but not sick to join a gym, the cost of the gym membership is not deductible even though exercise will improve the health of the patient. Rev. Rul. 79-151. On the other hand, the Service has ruled that an obese patient may deduct the cost of a weight loss program because obesity is recognized clinically as a disease. Rev. Rul. 2002-19. If a taxpayer incurs costs for a medical item (other than over-the-counter drugs) not specifically recommended by her doctor, she may be able to deduct the cost of the item, but will have a difficult time establishing that she bought the item primarily for medical reasons.

See, e.g., Rev. Rul. 76-80 (where the taxpayer was denied a deduction for the cost of a vacuum cleaner, allegedly purchased for health reasons, because the vacuum was not specifically recommended by her doctor and she could not establish that she had bought it primarily for medical care).

Amounts spent on property improvements for medical purposes are deductible only to the extent that the cost of the improvement exceeds the increase in the value of the property. Reg. §1.213-1(e)(1)(iii). For example, if a taxpayer, on the advice of his doctor, installs a home swimming pool that costs $50,000 and adds $40,000 to the value of his home, the taxpayer's medical expense deduction is limited to $10,000. Reg. §1.213-1(e)(1)(iii). However, even that deduction will not be allowed if the taxpayer has access to a nearby pool. Evanoff v. Commissioner, 44 T.C.M. (CCH) 1394 (1982) (where a medical expense deduction for a home pool was not allowed because, but for a personal religious objection to boys swimming in the same pool with girls, the taxpayer's daughter could have used a nearby community pool). In addition, if a home pool built for medical reasons is extravagantly expensive, the taxpayer will not be permitted to deduct the entire difference between the cost of the pool and the value it adds to the home; instead, the taxpayer is allowed to deduct only the average cost of a home pool less the value added to a home by such a pool. Ferris v. Commissioner, 582 F.2d 1112 (7th Cir. 1978) (where a taxpayer who needed to use a pool for medical reasons was not allowed to deduct all of the $194,660 cost of adding an elaborate luxury pool to her home). The Service has ruled that certain improvements made to the taxpayer's residence to accommodate a sick or impaired member of the taxpayer's household do not improve the value of the residence. For example, the ruling states that installing ramps, railings, lifts, and hardware, and modifying doorways, hallways, stairs, electrical outlets, and kitchen cabinets do not generally improve the value of a personal residence. Rev. Rul. 87-106.

If an expense is for cosmetic surgery, §213 allows a deduction for the expense only if the surgery is necessary to correct a congenital deformity or an abnormality arising from injury or disease. §213(d)(9). The costs of insulin and prescription drugs are deductible, but no deduction is allowed for over-the-counter drugs. §213(b).

Deductible medical expenses also include the costs of medical insurance, hospital lodging, and transportation incurred "primarily for and essential to medical care." §213(d)(1). However, the cost of lodging while away from home for the primary purpose of obtaining medical care by a physician in a licensed hospital or equivalent medical care facility is deductible only up to $50 per night, and then only if the lodging is not lavish and has no significant element of personal pleasure, recreation, or vacation. §213(d)(2). If medical treatment is available where the taxpayer lives, but the taxpayer chooses to travel to another area (for example, a resort area) to receive the care, the costs of traveling to receive the care are not deductible. Reg. §1.213-1(e)(1)(iv). In addition, if a taxpayer travels on a doctor's orders to a more hospitable climate, the costs of travel may be deductible, but the costs of meals and lodging are nondeductible even if the taxpayer sees a doctor from time to time in the area visited. Polyak v. Commissioner, 94 T.C. 337(1990).

The costs of nursing home care may qualify for the §213 deduction. Amounts paid for "qualified long-term care" services and certain premiums for "qualified long-term care insurance" are treated as medical expenses for purposes of §213. §213(d)(1)(C), (10). *Qualified long-term care services* are defined in §7702B(c) to include various medical, rehabilitative, mainte-nance, and personal care services that are performed for a chronically ill person and that have been provided pursuant to a plan of care prescribed by licensed medical personnel. A person is considered to be "chronically ill" if he (i) cannot perform at least two activities of daily living, such as eating and dressing, for a period of at least 90 days; (ii) is disabled; or (iii) must be supervised in order to avoid harm resulting from his severe cognitive impairment. §7702B(c)(2). Section 7702B(b) sets forth a multi-part test for qualifying long-term care insurance.

Although educational costs are not generally deductible, the cost of special schooling designed to rehabilitate an ill or disabled individual is deductible as a medical expense. Reg. §1.213-1(e)(1)(v)(a). For example, the cost of a special school where Braille is taught to blind students is a deductible medical expense. Id. A taxpayer is also allowed a deduction for the extra cost of Braille books and the costs of a seeing eye dog or human guide for a blind person. Reg. §1.213-1(e)(1)(iii), Rev. Rul. 75-318, Rev. Rul. 64-173. If a sick spouse stays at home and sends her children away to boarding school to facilitate her recovery, the costs of the boarding school are not deductible. Ochs v. Commissioner, 195 F.2d 692 (2d Cir. 1952).

In 2003 Congress created a new type of tax-favored medical savings account, called a *Health Savings Account* (HSA). HSAs are designed to encourage taxpayers to purchase health insurance with a high annual deductible. The rationale is that patients who have health insurance with a low deductible use more health care than they would if they had to pay the entire cost of their care. Low deductible health insurance thus increases the demand for health care and ultimately its cost.

To qualify for an HSA, the taxpayer must not be covered by Medicare and must have a *High Deductible Health Plan* (HDHP) and no other health insurance (other than ancillary coverage, such as accident, disability, dental care, vision care, or long-term care). §223(c)(1). In 2014, a health insurance plan is a HDHP if: (i) the annual deductible is not less than $1,250, for individual coverage, or $2,500, for family coverage; and (ii) the annual combined deductible and out-of-pocket expenses are not more than $6,350, for individual coverage, or $12,700, for family coverage. §223(c)(2), (g), Rev. Proc. 2013-25.

Taxpayers can take an above-the-line deduction for amounts they contribute to an HSA and can exclude employer contributions to an HSA. §223(a). Section 223(b) caps the contributions that may be made to an HSA. For 2014, the annual contribution was capped at $3,300 for individual coverage, or $6,550 for family coverage. §223(b)(2), (g), Rev. Proc. 2013-25. If the taxpayer is 55 or older, the dollar caps are increased to $4,300 for individual coverage, and $7,550 for family coverage. §223(b)(3).

Income earned on the HSA is not included in the taxpayer's income and distributions from the account are not included in the taxpayer's income if the distributions are used to pay unreimbursed medical expenses. §223(f)(1). The definition of medical expenses under §223 tracks the §213(d)(1)(A) definition of medical expenses. §223(d)(2).

Examples

In the examples below, assume that any medical expenses are incurred in 2014.

19. a. In year one Randy receives $96,000 in salary and $4,000 worth of medical benefits under an employee health plan. Is Randy taxed on the $4,000 value of the medical benefits?
    b. Assume, instead, that Randy receives $100,000 in salary from his employer and spends $4,000 on §213 medical expenses. Is Randy allowed a deduction for the $4,000 of medical expenses he pays in year one?

20. a. Betty's adjusted gross income is $50,000. If Betty spends $6,000 on medical expenses qualifying under §213, what portion of those expenses would be deductible?
    b. How, if at all, would your answer in part (a) change if Betty were reimbursed for her medical expenses by an insurance company?

21. Susan says: "Even if medical expenses should be deductible, a deduction should be permitted only to the extent that the expenses exceed a certain floor." What is the best argument for a floor on medical deductions?

For the remaining examples in this section, assume that the expenses exceed the 10 percent of adjusted gross income floor.

22. The costs of which of the following qualify as medical expenses under §213?
    a. Psychotherapy for a successful, but nervous, comedy director.
    b. Hair transplants for a balding opera singer.

    c. Cosmetic surgery to improve the appearance of a lawyer born with a harelip.

    d. Extra-large doorways, ramps, and an elevator for a banker confined to a wheelchair.

    e. Membership in a yoga studio for a former smoker whose family has a history of heart disease.

    f. Braces for a taxpayer's daughter.

23. a. Robert's daughter, Celia, is blind. In the current year he spends $10,000 on tuition for a school for the blind, $5,000 on a seeing eye dog, and $600 on Braille books. An ordinary private school would cost $6,000 and a regular printed edition of the books would cost $200. How much of these expenditures qualify as medical expenses subject to §213?

    b. Assume that, instead of sending Celia to a school for the blind, Robert sends Celia to public school and pays someone $10,000 a year to accompany and guide Celia while she is at school. Is the $10,000 cost of Celia's human guide deductible under §213?

24. Jerry, a Maine resident, has a chronic respiratory infection. His doctor recommends that he spend a few weeks in a warm and dry climate. Jerry flies to New Mexico for three weeks. While in New Mexico he sees a doctor twice for checkups. His expenses are as follows: $500 for the plane ticket, $1,500 for lodging, $800 for meals, and $200 for doctor's fees. Which of these expenses, if any, qualify as medical expenses under §213?

25. a. George suffered injuries in an automobile accident, and his doctor recommended swimming as a form of therapy. In keeping with the style of his Beverly Hills estate, George paid $250,000 for the construction of an elaborate swimming pool with marble tiles and a waterfall. The pool increased the value of the house by $100,000. An average swimming pool costs about $50,000 and would increase the value of the home by $30,000. How much, if any, of the cost of the swimming pool would be deductible?

    b. How, if at all, would your answer in part (a) change if the Beverly Hills community pool is two blocks from George's mansion and George can swim at the community pool?

26. Jackie suffered injuries from an automobile accident and was hospitalized for seven days. During that time, she paid $53,000 for a private suite in the best hospital in town, nursing care, medical tests, X-rays, and the care of the best (and most expensive) doctors. The average cost for a seven-day hospital stay in a non-private room with average doctors is $10,000. How much of Jackie's hospital bills are deductible?

27. Which of the following costs qualify as medical expenses under §213?
    a. The cost of aspirin taken to relieve arthritis pain on the advice of a physician.
    b. The costs of a vasectomy or legal abortion undertaken solely for contraceptive purposes.
    c. The costs of a babysitter hired to enable an individual to visit a doctor.
    d. The costs of an annual medical examination.
    e. The costs of attending a clinic to stop smoking.
    f. The costs of breast reconstruction surgery following a cancer diagnosis and mastectomy.
    g. The costs of sex reassignment surgery, hormone therapy, and breast augmentation surgery.

28. Pam is a busy executive who is suffering from stress related to her job. At the advice of her psychiatrist, she joins a private tennis club. During year one, she spends $2,000 for court time, $1,000 for lessons, and $800 on tennis clothing and equipment. Are any of these expenses deductible?

29. Without consulting a doctor, Linda purchases a humidifier and air cleaner to help relieve a sinus condition. Are the expenses deductible under §213?

30. Marion's son, James, has performed poorly in school and has been difficult to control at home. On the recommendation of a psychiatrist, Marion enrolls James in a military school with a highly structured environment. Are the costs of the military school tuition, room, and board deductible under §213?

31. John, a Vermont resident suffering from an unusual illness, is advised by his doctor to get help from Dr. Xerxes, a specialist in Seattle. He flies to Seattle and receives outpatient medical care for a month. John rents a hotel room close to the hospital and visits the hospital for treatment every other day. His travel expenses are: $800 for the plane ticket, $1,350 for the hotel ($45 per night), and $750 for food ($25 per day). What portion of these travel expenses can John deduct under §213?

32. After a car accident that left Alice paralyzed from the waist down, she buys a custom-made van specifically designed to accommodate her impairment. The van enables Alice to maintain her mobility and independence. Is any portion of the van's cost deductible?

33. While in Oregon with her mother, eight-year-old Yolanda, a California resident, is seriously injured in a car accident and admitted to a Portland hospital. She remains in intensive care and undergoes three operations over the next six weeks until she can be moved back to Los Angeles.

On the recommendation of the doctor, Yolanda's mother, Anne, stays at a Portland hotel during Yolanda's treatment. Are Anne's lodging expenses deductible?

Explanations

19. a. No. Medical benefits provided by an employer are excluded from income. §§105, 106.

   b. No. Under §213(a), medical expenses are deductible only to the extent such expenses exceed 10 percent of adjusted gross income. Randy's adjusted gross income is $100,000, so only medical expenses in excess of $10,000 would be deductible.

20. a. Betty is allowed a $1,000 §213 deduction. Betty can deduct her medical expenses only to the extent that they exceed $5,000, which is 10 percent of her $50,000 adjusted gross income. §213(a). Thus, she can deduct $1,000 ($6,000 medical expenses less the $5,000 floor).

   b. Only uncompensated expenses are deductible under §213(a), so Betty would not be able to deduct any amount of the reimbursed medical expenses.

21. The basic argument for permitting a deduction for medical expenses is that such expenses are involuntary expenditures that reduce wealth much like a reduction in income. This is similar to the argument in favor of allowing a casualty loss deduction. However, nearly all taxpayers incur some low level of medical expenses. If a deduction were permitted for all medical expenses without a floor, it would be necessary for all taxpayers to keep track of these costs. Since most taxpayers would receive a deduction of a similar amount, a general reduction in the tax rate would have the same impact as the deduction. Thus, it might be argued, a medical deduction should be permitted only for extraordinarily high medical expenses.

22. a. Costs of psychiatric treatment are medical expenses under §213. Reg. §1.213-1(e)(1)(ii).

   b. The costs of cosmetic surgery are medical expenses only if the surgery is performed to repair a congenital defect or an abnormality caused by an accident or deforming disease. §213(d)(9). Male pattern baldness is not considered to be a disease, so the costs of these hair transplants are not medical expenses.

   c. This cost is a medical expense. The costs of cosmetic surgery are medical expenses if the surgery is performed to repair a congenital defect. §213(d)(9).

  d. The costs of capital improvements to property for qualifying medical purposes are medical expenses to the extent that the costs of the improvements exceed the value that the improvements add to the home. Ramps and extra-large doorways presumably add no value to a home and thus the costs of these improvements are medical expenses. Rev. Rul. 87-106. The cost of the elevator is a medical expense to the extent its cost exceeds the value it adds to the home. Reg. §1.213-1(e)(1)(iii).

  e. The membership fee is not a medical expense. Expenses that help a person who is not ill to maintain or improve his health are not deductible. Reg. §1.213-1(e)(1)(ii).

  f. The cost of the braces is a medical expense. Dental work is considered a medical expense under §213. Reg. §1.213-1(e)(1)(ii). A taxpayer can deduct the medical expenses of his or her spouse and dependents. §213(a).

23. a. The special school tuition and the cost of the seeing eye dog are fully deductible. Reg. §1.213-1(e)(1)(iii), (v)(a). The cost of an ordinary school is irrelevant. Reg. §1.213-1(e)(1)(v)(a). The cost of Braille books is deductible to the extent that the cost exceeds that of the regular printed editions, so Robert is allowed to deduct $400 of the costs of the books. Rev. Rul. 75-318.

  b. The Service has ruled that the cost of such a companion is deductible under §213 because it is designed to "alleviate the child's physical defect of blindness." Rev. Rul. 64-173.

24. Only the cost of the transportation and the doctor's fees qualify as medical expenses under §213. The cost of food and lodging while away from home for medical treatment is not deductible unless the taxpayer is residing at a licensed hospital or equivalent facility. Thus, Jerry may only deduct the $500 for the plane ticket and the doctor's fees. Reg. §1.213-1(e)(1)(iv). The fact that Jerry visited a doctor while in New Mexico makes no difference since the main purpose of the trip was to stay in an area with a better climate. Polyak v. Commissioner, 94 T.C. 337 (1990).

25. a. In the case upon which these facts are based, the court held that costs above those that are necessary to produce a functionally adequate swimming pool are not incurred for medical care. See Ferris v. Commissioner, 582 F.2d 1112 (7th Cir. 1978). The taxpayer probably is not limited to buying the cheapest pool, but it is unclear how much more than the minimum may be spent and still be considered deductible. Assuming it is necessary for George to have a pool at his home, George probably would be allowed to deduct at least $20,000, the average cost of a pool less the increase in property value from such a pool.

b. George would likely be denied any deduction for the cost of his home pool since he can swim in the nearby community pool. In Evanoff v. Commissioner, 44 T.C.M. (CCH) 1394 (1982), the court denied a deduction for the cost of building a pool where the taxpayer could have used the nearby community swimming pool for $250 a year. The taxpayers decided to build a pool because their religion forbade their daughter from swimming in the same pool as boys. The court held that this reason made the expenditure personal in nature, not medical, and therefore not deductible.

26. The cost of conventional medical care at hospitals, including food and lodging costs, is fully deductible even if the taxpayer pays more than is necessary for adequate care. Therefore, Jackie may deduct the full $53,000. Reg. §1.213-1(e)(1)(v).

27. a. Not a medical expense. Only the costs of prescription drugs and insulin are medical expenses. §213(b).
b. Medical expense. Rev. Rul. 73-201.
c. Not medical expenses. Costs of child care are considered personal expenses, even if incurred to enable an individual to receive medical treatment. Ochs v. Commissioner, 195 F.2d 692 (2d Cir. 1952).
d. Medical expenses. Costs of an annual diagnostic checkup are medical expenses even though they are not designed to treat a specific illness. Reg. §1.213-1(e)(1)(ii).
e. Medical expenses. The Service at one point took the position that the costs of smoking cessation were not medical expenses. Rev. Rul. 79-162. The Service has since changed its position, however, and ruled that smoking cessation costs are medical expenses because nicotine causes disease and is addictive. Rev. Rul. 99-28.
f. Medical expenses. Breast reconstruction surgery is performed by a plastic surgeon and would seem to be a form of "cosmetic surgery." The costs of "cosmetic surgery or other similar procedures" are not "medical care" and thus are not deductible. §213(a), (d)(1), (9). There is an exception to the general definition of cosmetic surgery, however, for a surgery or procedure that "is necessary to ameliorate a deformity arising from, or directly related to [a] disfiguring disease." §213(d)(9)(A). In this example, the disfiguration is caused by the surgical removal of the breast to treat the cancer, not the disease itself. The legislative history of §213(d)(9) specifically states, however, that the costs of breast reconstruction following a cancer diagnosis and mastectomy are deductible medical expenses, not nondeductible cosmetic surgery expenses.
g. The costs of the sex reassignment surgery and hormone treatment probably are medical expenses, but the costs of the related breast augmentation surgery probably are not medical expenses. Doctors in

the United States follow specific treatment guidelines for patients who receive a diagnosis of gender identity disorder. Under these guidelines, gender identity disorder must be medically documented before a doctor prescribes sex change hormones and before a plastic surgeon will perform sex reassignment surgery. In the case on which this example is based, a majority of the U.S. Tax Court held that the taxpayer could deduct the costs of hormone therapy and sex reassignment surgery but could not deduct the costs of the breast augmentation surgery. O'Donnabhain v. Commissioner, 134 T.C. No. 4 (2010) (reviewed decision). The majority concluded that the hormone therapy and sex reassignment surgery treated the disease of gender identity disorder, but the breast augmentation surgery was not required to treat the disease because the taxpayer had developed "B" cup breasts (as a result of the hormone therapy) without any surgery.

28. No. Expenses that improve the general health of an individual are not deductible. Reg. §1.213-1(e)(1)(ii). Thus, the taxpayer must meet a heavy burden of proof to deduct the expenses of ordinary personal activities, like tennis, that provide general health benefits. In this case, Pam's stressed condition might not qualify as a mental defect or disease for purposes of §213. Even if her condition is viewed as an illness, she will probably not be able to establish that tennis is needed to reduce her stress since running or other less expensive forms of exercise might provide her with the same benefits. See Altman v. Commissioner, 53 T.C. 487 (1969) (where the taxpayer was denied a deduction for his costs of playing golf, despite the fact that the taxpayer's doctor had recommended that the taxpayer play golf as treatment for his emphysema).

29. Yes, if she can establish that she bought the items primarily for medical care. A doctor's recommendation is not required for an expense to be deductible under §213. In this case, the purchase of the humidifier and air cleaner is designed to relieve a medical condition and thus should be deductible. Although a doctor's recommendation is not required under §213, it may enable a taxpayer to demonstrate that a medical purpose underlies an expense that normally would be considered personal such as the construction of a swimming pool. Here, Linda can take a deduction for the cost of the humidifier and air cleaner if she can establish that she purchased those items primarily for her medical care. Compare Rev. Rul. 76-80 (where the taxpayer was denied a deduction for the cost of a vacuum cleaner, allegedly purchased for health reasons, because it was not specifically recommended by her doctor and she could not establish that she had bought it primarily for medical care).

30. Probably not. Private school tuition generally is deductible only if the school treats a specific medical problem such as blindness or deafness. Reg. §1.213-1(e)(1)(v). See also Fay v. Commissioner, 76 T.C. 408 (1981); Grunwald v. Commissioner, 51 T.C. 108 (1968).

31. John can deduct the full amount of the plane ticket since it is transportation primarily for and essential to his medical care. §213(d)(1)(B). Under §213(d)(2), a taxpayer can also deduct up to $50 per night for lodging away from home in situations where he travels to receive outpatient medical care. Since John receives medical care at the hospital of Dr. Xerxes and there is no significant element of recreation in his trip, he can deduct the $45 per day cost of the hotel room. John gets no deduction, however, for any amount spent on meals.

32. Alice can deduct the cost of the van to the extent that it exceeds the cost of a comparable ordinary automobile. Reg. §1.213-1(e)(1)(iii), Rev. Rul. 70-606.

33. The expenses probably are deductible up to $50 per night. In the letter ruling on which this question is based, the hospital requested that parents of minor patients in intensive care remain nearby. Priv. Ltr. Rul. 8516025. The Service noted that the "transportation costs of a family member traveling with the taxpayer have been allowed as a medical expense deduction where the presence of the family member was necessary to enable [the] taxpayer to obtain medical care." Transportation costs include associated lodging, subject to a $50 per day limitation. Although Anne did not incur any actual transportation expenses because she was already in Portland, her lodging expenses should remain deductible since they were necessary for her daughter's medical treatment.

D. CHARITABLE CONTRIBUTIONS

Reading: §§170, 501, 6115, 6662(e), (h).

An itemized deduction for charitable contributions is permitted under §170(a)(1). Charitable contributions are defined in §170(c) as contributions to or for the use of certain listed nonprofit enterprises:

    i.   the United States government, a state government or any other political subdivision of the United States, including local governments and United States territories if the contribution is made for exclusively public purposes. §170(c)(1).

ii. a charitable corporation, trust, community chest, fund, or foundation if the organization is operated exclusively for religious, charitable, scientific, literary, or educational purposes, to foster national or international amateur sports competition, or for the prevention of cruelty to children or animals. §170(c)(2).

iii. a fraternal order or lodge, but only if the gift is to be used exclusively for charitable purposes. §170(c)(4).

iv. an organization of war veterans or a nonprofit cemetery company or corporation. §170(c)(3), (5).

Contributions to an organization are not deductible, however, if any part of the net earnings of the donee organization benefit any private shareholder or individual or if the donee organization attempts to influence legislation or political campaigns. §170(c)(2)(C), (D).

Section 170 determines the extent to which donors may deduct contributions to charitable organizations. Sections 501–528 determine the tax treatment of charities receiving contributions. Section 501 generally exempts from tax the organizations listed in §501(c). The §501(c) list of organizations is substantially broader than the list of organizations in §170(c). Business leagues, labor unions, and nonprofit recreational clubs, for example, can qualify for tax-exempt status under §501(c), but donors contributing to those organizations generally cannot qualify for a charitable contribution deduction under §170(c). On the other hand, if donors' contributions qualify for the §170 charitable contribution deduction, the organization receiving the contribution will almost always qualify for tax-exempt status under §501. Qualifying exempt organizations are not taxed on income from contributions, fees for services related to their charitable purpose, and income from passive investments. §501(a), (b). However, if an exempt organization earns income from a business that is unrelated to the organization's charitable purpose, the exempt organization is taxed on the income from that business. §§501(b), 511–514. In addition, exempt status will be denied any §501(c)(3) organization that engages in racial discrimination or terrorist activity or supports terrorist activity. Bob Jones University v. United States, 461 U.S. 574(1983) (holding that the test for exempt status includes a requirement that the organization serve a public purpose and not operate in a manner that is contrary to public policy), §501(p).

A §170 deduction for the full amount contributed is allowed only if the donor receives no substantial benefit from the contribution. Ottawa Silica Co. v. United States, 699 F.2d 1124 (Fed. Cir. 1983). If the donor receives a substantial benefit as a result of the contribution, for purposes of §170 the donor's contribution is reduced by the benefit received. For example, if a charity hosting a fund-raising dinner charges $300 for a dinner that has a value of $50, a donor paying $300 for a ticket to the dinner would be entitled to deduct only $250 ($300 paid to the charity less the $50 value of the dinner), even if the donor decided not to attend the dinner. Rev. Rul. 67-246. What constitutes a "substantial" benefit? In *Ottawa Silica*, the Federal Circuit Court of Appeals stated that benefits received by a donor are "substantial" if the benefits received by the donor "are greater than those that inure to the general public from transfers for charitable purposes." 699 F.2d at 1131 (citing Singer Co. v. United States, 449 F.2d 413, 423 (Cl. Ct. 1971)). Ottawa Silica had donated real property for a high school to a school district that qualified as a §170(c)(1) organization. The plans for the new high school required the school district to construct two access roads to the new school. These access roads provided a benefit to Ottawa Silica because the company owned much of the land in the area around the proposed new school and intended to develop it. The court held that the increase in value of the land that Ottawa Silica did not contribute constituted a substantial benefit to the company, so it was not allowed a §170 deduction for the land contributed.

Section 170(l) sets forth a special rule that applies where a donor makes a contribution to a college or university and the contribution gives the donor the right to buy preferred seating tickets for athletic events at the school. In these circumstances, the donor's deduction is limited to 80 percent of the contribution. §170(l)(1).

The Service has ruled that fixed payments to churches or synagogues for pew rents, dues, or to attend specific services are deductible under §170 despite the fact that the contribution would appear to confer a specific benefit on the donor. Rev. Rul. 70-47. On the other hand, in Hernandez v. Commissioner, 490 U.S. 680 (1989), members of the Church of Scientology were denied a deduction for amounts "donated" to the church for "training" and "auditing." A member could not receive these services without paying a donation that was set by a schedule, so the majority concluded that the payment for these services was "a quintessential quid pro quo exchange" and was thus not deductible under §170. Justices Scalia and O'Connor dissented, noting the Service's longstanding practice of allowing deduction of fixed payments to churches. The Service later issued Rev. Rul. 93-73, in which it reversed the position it had previously taken and stated that it would allow deductions for amounts "donated" to the Church of Scientology. See also §6115(b).

A donor may contribute services, cash, or property to a §170(c) charity. The tax consequences to the donor under §170 turn, in part, on the type of contribution made by the donor. If a donor contributes her services, she will not be allowed a §170 deduction for the services. Reg. §1.170A-1(g). However, her unreimbursed expenses incurred in rendering those services (other than child care expenses) are deductible. Id. Child care expenses incurred to enable the taxpayer to donate charitable services are considered nondeductible personal expenses. Rev. Rul. 73-597.

If a taxpayer contributes cash, the §170 deduction is subject only to the general deduction limitations in §170(b)(1)(A), (B), and (2), which limit a taxpayer's charitable contribution deduction to a percentage of the taxpayer's "contribution base" (generally the taxpayer's adjusted gross income). Taxpayers typically make their charitable contributions to the common types of charities listed in §170(b)(1)(A) (so-called "A" charities). A taxpayer's §170 deduction for a contribution to an "A" charity is limited to 50 percent of the taxpayer's adjusted gross income in that year. Any contribution in excess of that limitation is carried forward five years and may be taken in those years as a charitable contribution. §170(d). If a taxpayer makes a contribution to one of the less common types of charities described in §170(b)(1)(B) (so-called "B" charities), a less favorable limitation rule applies.

The §170 deduction for corporate taxpayers is limited to 10 percent of the corporation's taxable income, determined without regard to its charitable contributions and certain other items (such as net operating loss carrybacks and the §243 deduction for dividends received by a corporate taxpayer that is a shareholder in another corporation). §170(b)(2). In addition, several other special rules in §170 apply to determine a corporate taxpayer's §170 deduction. See, e.g., §170(a)(2), (c)(2), (d)(2), (e)(3).

Donors of appreciated property deduct the *value* of property they contribute, despite the fact that neither the taxpayer nor the exempt organization will ever pay tax on the appreciation in the property. However, this extremely favorable tax treatment of contributions of appreciated property to charities is limited by a series of special rules in §170(e), (b)(1)(C), and (D). First, if the property contributed would have produced ordinary income or short-term capital gain had it been sold (because the property is not a capital asset or has not been held by the donor for at least a year), the donor may deduct only her adjusted basis in the contributed property. §170(e)(1)(A). (For a discussion of the distinction between ordinary assets and capital assets, and between short-term and long-term capital gain, see Chapter 8.) Consider the following example, which illustrates the §170(e)(1)(A) limitation. Assume that Lonnie, an art dealer, owns a painting worth $20,000 that he bought for $3,000. If Lonnie donates the painting to an art museum, his §170 deduction will be limited to $3,000, his basis in the painting, because the painting would have produced ordinary income if Lonnie, a dealer in art, had sold it.

Second, even if a sale of the contributed property by the donor would have produced long-term capital gain, the donor's §170 deduction is limited to the donor's adjusted basis in the property if: (i) the contributed property is tangible personal property (for example, works of art, antiques, stamp or coin collections, and books) and the donee charity's use of the property is unrelated to the organization's charitable purpose; (ii) the property is donated to certain private foundations; or (iii) the contributed property is a patent or certain other intellectual property, including specific types of copyrights and software, trademarks, trade names, trade secrets, know-how, or similar property. §170(e)(1)(B). (If the donee subsequently earns income from contributed intellectual property that is subject to the §170(e)(1)(B) limitation, the donor in some circumstances will be entitled to take additional charitable contribution deductions. §170(m).) For example, assume that Connie, a professional actress, bought a painting for $10,000 in year one. By year 10, Connie's painting had appreciated in value to $300,000. In year 10, when Connie has adjusted gross income of $800,000, she contributes the painting to her church. Connie's year 10 §170 deduction is limited to $10,000, her basis in the painting, because the painting is tangible property and the use of the painting by the church is not related to its charitable purpose. If Connie instead gives the painting to an art museum, the §170(e)(1)(B) limitation does not apply because the charity's use of the painting is related to its exempt purpose. (However, her deduction is then subject to the §170(b)(1)(C) limitation, described below.)

Third, if a donor contributes property that would have produced long-term capital gain had the donor sold it, and the §170 (e)(1)(B) limitation described above does not apply, the limitation of §170(b)(1)(C) will generally apply to the contribution. If the donor contributes the property to an "A" charity, as is generally the case, her §170 deduction for the contribution is limited to 30 percent of her adjusted gross income. §170(b)(1)(C)(i). Any excess contribution is carried forward for five years. §170(b)(1)(C)(ii). The donor can elect to apply §170(e) instead of the 30 percent of adjusted gross income limitation. §170(b)(1)(C)(iii). If this election is made, the donor's §170 deduction is limited to the donor's basis in the contributed property. (A donor may want to make this election if the value of the contributed property exceeds 30 percent of the taxpayer's adjusted gross income and the basis of the property is the same as or not much less than the value of the contributed property.) Again, a less favorable limitation applies to contributions of capital gain property to "B" charities, such as private foundations. §170(b)(1)(D).

For example, assume that Ronnie bought a piece of raw land, as a long-term investment, for $20,000 in year one. In year 10, he contributes the land (which is still held for investment), to a university, which is an "A" charity. The land is worth $300,000 at the time of the contribution. Ronnie's year 10 adjusted gross income is $700,000. A sale of the land by Ronnie would have produced long-term capital gain, so §170(e)(1)(A) does not apply. Section 170(e)(1)(B) does not apply either because (i) the land is not tangible personal property and (ii) Ronnie did not give the land to a private foundation listed in §170(e)(1)(B)(ii). However, §170(b)(1)(C) will limit Ronnie's year 10 §170 deduction to $210,000, which is 30 percent of his $700,000 adjusted gross income. The $90,000 excess contribution ($300,000 contribution less $210,000 allowed as a deduction in year one) is carried forward to the next tax year.

Despite these limitations, the charitable contribution deduction rules are very favorable to taxpayers who contribute appreciated property to charities. Aggressive taxpayers trying to gain the tax benefit of large charitable contribution deductions often claim inflated values for the property contributed. Thus, the valuation of appreciated property contributed to a charity is an issue that is frequently litigated. For example, in Isbell v. Commissioner, 44 T.C.M. (CCH) 1143 (1982), the taxpayer claimed a $15,000 deduction (which was later increased to $50,000 on an amended return) on the charitable contribution of a damaged Han dynasty jar that was valued at $800 by a government expert and was sold by the charity in an auction for $360! Congress and the Service have taken several steps to curb overvaluation of appreciated property contributed to charities.

Section 6662 imposes an "accuracy-related" penalty for valuation overstatement if a taxpayer claims that the value of property contributed to a charity is 150 percent or more of the actual value of the property. §6662(e). The penalty is 20 percent of the tax deficiency that results from the valuation overstatement (provided that the deficiency is at least $5,000 for an individual). §6662(a), (e). If a taxpayer claims a value that is 200 percent or more of the actual value of the property, the penalty is 40 percent of the deficiency related to the overstatement. §6662(h).

Congress has increased the statutory substantiation requirements for charitable contributions, to curtail common taxpayer abuses. The precise substantiation rules applicable to a contribution depend on the amount of the claimed contribution and the type of property contributed. If the amount of the contribution is $250 or more, the donor must substantiate the contribution with a contemporaneous written acknowledgment of the contribution, prepared by the donee charity. §170(f)(8). Contributions of more than $500 generally are subject to more formal and elaborate substantiation requirements, often including a qualified appraisal. §170(f)(11). Special substantiation rules apply to contributions of cars, boats, and airplanes (other than inventory) if the claimed value of the contributed vehicle is more than $500. §170(f)(12). (Section 170(f)(8) does not apply if §170(f)(12) applies. §170(f)(12)(A).)

If donors receive something of benefit (other than intangible religious benefits) in exchange for their contributions, §6115 requires donee charities to provide donors with an estimate of the value of property received by the donors in the exchange, if the contribution exceeds $75. In addition, if a donor contributes property (other than publicly traded securities) valued at more than $5,000 and the donee charity sells it within three years of the date of contribution, the donee must file a special return with the Service giving them information about the donor, the contribution, and the subsequent disposition of the property. §6050L.

If a taxpayer makes a donation to charity using a credit card, for tax purposes the contribution occurs at the time the charge is incurred, not when the charge is later paid by the taxpayer. Rev. Rul. 78-38.

A complete discussion of the complex rules on charitable contribution is beyond the scope both of this book and, we suspect, of most introductory courses in income taxation. In the questions that follow, we will explore the basic structure of the charitable contribution deduction rules and a few of the more important details.

Examples

Assume that the taxpayers in the examples below can satisfy the substantiation requirements in §170, except where the facts specifically indicate that substantiation is an issue.

34. State whether contributions to the following individuals or organizations are deductible.
    a. the city of Los Angeles, California;
    b. Harvard University;
    c. the Girl Scouts;
    d. the Elks Club;
    e. the Lutheran Church;
    f. the Republican Party;
    g. a homeless individual living at a government shelter;
    h. a local professional basketball team;
    i. the city of Bombay, India;
    j. a private university that has a racially discriminatory admissions policy.

35. a. In year one Bridget has $100,000 of adjusted gross income and contributes $38,000 to the Red Cross. She makes no other contributions during the year. How much does she deduct under §170 in year one?
    b. How, if at all, would your answer in part (a) change if Bridget is instead Bridget Inc., a corporation, with $100,000 of taxable income?

36. The Metropolis Children's Center provides aid to abused and runaway children.
    a. Suppose that the Children's Center receives $10 million in contributions during the taxable year. On what amount of contributions will the Center have to pay tax?
    b. Suppose that the Children's Center operates a chain of greeting card stores that earns $5 million per year. On what amount of that income will the Center be taxed?
    c. Assume that the Children's Center invests $10 million in corporate stock and bonds and earns $1 million in interest and dividends. On what amount of those earnings will the Center be taxed?

37. If an organization is exempt from taxation on contributions, are such contributions to the organization necessarily deductible by the donor?

38. Maria purchases two seats to an all-star concert to benefit the homeless. The seats cost $200 each. Similar seats at concerts not benefiting charitable organizations cost $30 each. Maria tells her friends that she would have paid $200 each for the seats even if the proceeds were not for the benefit of charity.
    a. How much of the $400 cost of the concert tickets is deductible?
    b. Would your answer in part (a) change if the only reason Maria purchased the tickets was to aid the charity and she never attended the concert?

39. Pasqual donated $2,000 to Grunt University's athletic program, which has one of the top college football teams in the United States. Anyone who donates $2,000 or more to the program is made a member of the Grunters Club, which permits the member to purchase two season tickets in a preferred section at the 50-yard line for $600 each. Individuals who are not members of the Grunters Club can purchase season tickets at the same price, but the seats are much less desirable. How much of the $2,000 contribution may Pasqual deduct?

40. Bill's son has applied for admission to Posh College, a private college. One week after Bill makes a large donation to the college, his son is accepted for admission. Is the donation deductible under §170?

41. Cindy, a gym teacher, volunteered to work for a week with handicapped children at an athletic event sponsored by a charitable organization. Cindy spent $40 on transportation to the event and paid $100 for child care to enable her to attend. If Cindy had been paid her normal fee for her services, she would have received $500. What amount can Cindy deduct as a charitable contribution?

42. Bill owns a sporting goods store. If Bill contributes inventory (shoes, baseballs, and so forth) with an adjusted basis of $600 and fair market value of $1,000 to a public charity, how much can he deduct under §170?

43. Carlos bought stock in year one for $1,000. In year three, when the stock is worth $10,000, he donates the stock to Alma Mater Law School. Carlos has $300,000 of adjusted gross income in year three. How much gain does Carlos realize on the contribution and how much does he deduct under §170 in year three? Assume that Carlos is subject to a 30 percent marginal tax rate on ordinary income and a 20 percent tax rate on capital gain. (Also assume that Carlos would not be allowed to exclude any gain from a sale of the stock.) What is the after-tax cost to Carlos of donating the stock instead of selling it and using the proceeds for personal consumption?

44. Jin owns a Chinese snuff bottle from the 19th century that she found in a trunk in her attic. Assume that Jin is in the 30 percent tax bracket and has adjusted gross income of $250,000. Assume also that gain from the sale of the bottle would be taxed at the 28 percent capital gain rate applicable to gain from the sale of a "collectible." §§1(h), 408(m).

    a. What would be the tax consequence to Jin if she sells the bottle for $1,000?

    b. What would be the tax consequence to Jin if she donates the bottle to a museum, for inclusion in their porcelain collection, and establishes that the value of the bottle is $3,000 at the time of her contribution? Will Jin be wealthier here, or in part (a) above?

    c. How, if at all, would your answer in part (b) change if Jin instead donates the bottle to a hospital?

    d. Assume the facts in part (b), except that Jin, in a fit of naive optimism, claimed on her year one return that the bottle was worth $20,000, when it was actually worth $3,000. (Ignore the qualified appraisal requirements of §170(f)(11)(c) for now.) If the Service later challenges the valuation, and Jin fails to establish that the value of the bottle exceeded $3,000 in year one, what are the tax consequences to her?

45. Larry, a caterer who happens to be a good judge of modern art, buys a painting in March of year one for $10,000. In December of year one, he donates the painting to a contemporary art museum. Two qualified independent appraisers value the painting at $28,000 at the time of contribution. Larry's year one adjusted gross income is $200,000. How much can he deduct as a year one charitable contribution?

46. In year one Kevin bought raw land as an investment. He paid $80,000 for the property. In year three, when the land is worth $95,000, he contributes it to his church. The church will not use the land in its activities, but expects to sell the property within the next several years to raise funds for a renovation of other church property. Kevin's adjusted gross income in year three is $200,000. How much can Kevin deduct under §170 in year three?

47. Robert, a real estate developer in Phoenix, Arizona, contributes to the city of Phoenix the streets and sewers of a residential subdivision he is developing. The city will maintain the streets and sewers after the contribution. May Robert deduct the value of the streets and sewers as a charitable contribution?

48. In December, year one, Elizabeth phones the AIDS Project of Los Angeles and charges a $1,000 donation to the organization on her Mastercard. She pays that charge in March, year two. In which year is Elizabeth allowed to deduct her contribution?

49. Mona says: "It costs a low-income taxpayer more to make a donation to charity than it costs a high-income taxpayer." Is Mona correct? Explain.

50. Ned says: "The charitable deduction is unfair because it treats taxpayers who donate money to charity more favorably than it treats taxpayers who donate their own services. Taxpayers who donate money can deduct the amount donated, but taxpayers who donate services can't deduct the value of their services." Is Ned correct? Explain.

Explanations

34. a. Deductible. Section 170(c) sets forth the list of the organizations to which deductible contributions may be made. This list includes a political subdivision of a state or territory of the United States. §170(c)(1). The city of Los Angeles is a political subdivision of the State of California.

    b. Deductible. A charitable deduction is permitted for contributions to organizations operated exclusively for educational purposes. §170(c)(2)(B). Colleges and universities clearly fall within this provision.

    c. Deductible. The Girl Scouts qualify as an organization devoted to charitable purposes under §170(c)(2)(B).

    d. The answer depends on how the money is to be used. The Elks Club qualifies as a "domestic fraternal society" under §170(c)(4). Contributions made to such organizations are considered charitable contributions only if the contribution is to be used *exclusively* for religious, charitable, scientific, literary, or educational purposes, or for the prevention of cruelty to children or animals. §170(c)(4). Thus, general contributions to such organizations usually are not deductible. It is common, however, for fraternal societies to establish separate funds devoted exclusively to charitable purposes, and contributions to such funds are deductible.

    e. Deductible. Contributions to religious organizations are within §170(c)(2)(B).

    f. Not deductible. A political party does not qualify as a charitable organization under any of the provisions of §170 (c). Moreover, an organization otherwise qualifying for deductible contributions under §170(c)(2) as devoted exclusively to charitable purposes will lose its qualification if it participates or intervenes in any political campaign on behalf of or in opposition to any candidate. §170(c)(2)(D).

    g. Not deductible. Contributions to particular individuals, even if needy, are not deductible. A contribution to the shelter, however, would be deductible. §170(c)(2)(B).

h. Not deductible. A professional basketball team is not a charitable organization under §170(c).

i. Not deductible. Contributions to foreign governments and political subdivisions of foreign governments are not listed in §170(c), so such contributions are not deductible.

j. Not deductible. The Supreme Court has read the test for tax-exempt status under §501(c) to include a requirement that the organization serve public policy and not act in a manner contrary to public policy. In Bob Jones University v. United States, 461 U.S. 574 (1983), the majority held that an organization that maintains a policy of racial discrimination cannot qualify for tax-exempt status under §501(c). The §170(c) test would most likely be interpreted to include a similar requirement.

35. a. All of it is deductible because it does not exceed the 50 percent of adjusted gross income limitation in §170(b)(1)(A), which applies because the cash was donated to an "A" charity.

b. Bridget Inc. may deduct only $10,000 in year one. A corporation is permitted to deduct contributions only to the extent of 10 percent of its taxable income, so Bridget Inc.'s year one deduction is limited to $10,000. §170(b)(2). The $28,000 excess contribution is carried forward. §170(d)(2).

36. a. The Center will not be taxed on any of the contributions. Under §501(a), contributions received by organizations described in §501(c) or (d) are exempt from taxation. The Metropolis Children's Center falls within the description of §501(c)(3) as a corporation organized and operated exclusively for charitable purposes.

b. The Center will be taxed on all of the income from the stores. Under §§511–514, income from business operations that are unrelated to an organization's tax-exempt purpose is subject to tax. The $5 million would constitute "unrelated business taxable income" and would be subject to tax in its entirety. §501(b).

c. The Center will not be taxed on any of the investment earnings. "Passive investment income" earned from investments such as stocks, bonds, and annuities is not considered unrelated business taxable income and thus is not subject to tax when received by a charity. §512(b).

37. No. Some nonprofit organizations, such as political parties, pension plans, labor unions, and social clubs, are tax-exempt under §501(c), but donations to those organizations do not qualify for the §170 deduction.

38. a. $340. A taxpayer who purchases tickets to a concert or other event will be permitted a deduction in an amount equal to the difference

between the amount contributed and the fair market value of the tickets. Maria contributed $400 and received tickets worth $60, so she may deduct only $340 as a charitable contribution. The subjective value of the tickets to Maria is irrelevant. Rev. Rul. 67-246.

b. Even if Maria does not attend the concert, she would be permitted to deduct only $340 if she retained the tickets. Rev. Rul. 67-246. However, Maria would be permitted to deduct the full $400 if she refused the tickets or returned them to the charitable organization.

39. $1,600. A taxpayer is allowed a §170 deduction only to the extent that the taxpayer did not receive a benefit in return for the donation. A special rule exists, however, for contributions in return for the right to purchase tickets to athletic events. Under §170(l), if a contribution by an individual to a college or university otherwise would be deductible, but the individual receives the right to purchase tickets to an athletic event in return for the contribution, 80 percent of the amount donated will be deductible. Thus, Pasqual may deduct 80 percent of $2,000 or $1,600.

40. If, as appears to be the case, his son was admitted because of the contribution, then Bill received something of value for his gift and it would not be deductible. On the other hand, if his son's acceptance did not depend on the donation, then a charitable deduction probably would be allowed. See, e.g., Rev. Rul. 83-104.

41. $40. A taxpayer cannot deduct the value of the services donated to a charity. Reg. §1.170A-1(g). (On the other hand, a taxpayer is not taxed on the imputed value of those services.) A taxpayer can deduct unreimbursed expenses incurred in connection with services performed for charitable organizations. However, child care expenses incurred to enable the taxpayer to donate charitable services are considered nondeductible personal expenses. Rev. Rul. 73-597. Thus, only the $40 transportation expense is deductible.

42. The §170 deduction for a contribution of ordinary income property is limited to the donor's adjusted basis in the contributed property, so Bill can deduct only $600. §170(e)(1)(A). Ordinary income property is any property that would have produced ordinary income had the donor sold it. This includes inventory held for sale in the taxpayer's trade or business.

43. Carlos realizes no gain because making a gift or contribution is not treated as a realization event for the donor. Carlos is entitled to a deduction of $10,000, the value of the contributed property. Since he is in the 30 percent bracket, this reduces his tax liability by $3,000. If Carlos had

sold the stock, he would have realized and recognized a gain of $9,000 and paid a tax of $1,800. This would have left him $8,200 ($10,000 received less $1,800 tax) to spend after taxes. Since Carlos is allowed a deduction worth $3,000 by donating the stock, the after-tax cost of the donation is $5,200.

44. a. Jin's amount realized is $1,000 and she appears to have a basis in the bottle of zero. Jin will realize and recognize a gain of $1,000 and pay tax of $280. Thus, Jin will have an extra $720 to spend.

   b. If the bottle is donated, Jin will get a deduction of $3,000. This deduction will reduce her tax liability by 30 percent of $3,000, or $900, so she will have an extra $900 to spend. Thus, Jin would be $180 wealthier if she donates the bottle rather than selling it. The keys to this result are: (i) Jin is permitted to deduct the fair market value of the tangible personal property, not her zero basis in the property, because the use by the museum relates to its charitable purposes (so that §170(e)(1)(B)(i) does not apply) and (ii) Jin can substantiate the $3,000 value.

   c. If Jin donates the bottle to a hospital, she will lose her $3,000 deduction. Here, she is donating tangible personal property and the charity donee's use of the property is unrelated to its charitable purpose, so §170(e)(1)(B)(i) applies, limiting her §170 deduction to her basis in the contributed property, which appears to be zero.

   d. Here, in year one, Jin substantially overstated the value of the bottle. She claimed a $20,000 year one deduction under §170, which reduced her tax for that year by $6,000. Jin is actually allowed a $3,000 deduction for year one (which saves her $900 of tax), so she will have to pay $5,100 of additional tax for year one, plus interest on the deficiency. §6601. The year one deficiency exceeds $5,000 and the value she claimed was more than twice the value of the bottle, so Jin will also be liable for an accuracy-related penalty of $2,040 (40 percent of the $5,100 understatement). §6662(e), (h). (Under the §170(f)(11)(c) substantiation rule, Jin could not have claimed a $20,000 deduction, because the appraised value of the bottled would have been only $3,000.)

45. The limitation of §170(e)(1)(A) applies because the sale of the painting, which Larry owned for less than a year, would have produced short-term capital gain had Larry sold it. Larry's deduction is thus limited to his $10,000 basis in the painting.

46. Kevin can deduct $60,000 in year three, unless he elects to be treated under §170(e), in which case he can deduct $80,000. Absent an election under §170(b)(1)(C)(iii), the §170(e)(1)(A) and (B) limitations do not apply because (i) a sale of the property would have produced

long-term capital gain, (ii) the property is not tangible personal property, and (iii) Kevin did not donate the property to the type of foundation specified in §170(e)(1)(B)(ii). On the other hand, the §170(b)(1)(C) limitation applies because Kevin donated capital gain property to an "A" charity. Section 170(b)(1)(C) limits Kevin's year three §170 deduction to $60,000, which is 30 percent of his $200,000 adjusted gross income. The $35,000 excess contribution is carried forward to year four. §170(b)(1)(C)(ii). If Kevin elected under §170(b)(1)(C)(iii) to be treated under §170(e), he would deduct $80,000, his basis in the land, in year three.

47. No. Robert is not entitled to a charitable deduction. The transfer benefits the lots in the subdivision, which are still owned by Robert. This substantial benefit received by Robert precludes him from taking a §170 deduction for the contribution. Ottawa Silica Co. v. United States, 699 F.2d 1124 (Fed. Cir. 1983). In addition, the transfer relieves Robert of the legal responsibility of maintaining the transferred property. McConnell v. Commissioner, 55 T.C.M. (CCH) 1284 (1988).

48. Year one. If a taxpayer makes a donation to charity using a credit card, the §170 deduction is taken in the year in which the charge is incurred, not the year in which the charge is later paid by the taxpayer. Rev. Rul. 78-38.

49. Mona is correct. A charitable deduction is more valuable to a high-income taxpayer because she is subject to a higher marginal tax rate than a low-income taxpayer. A wealthy taxpayer in the 40 percent tax bracket who donates $100 to charity will reduce the amount of tax she owes by $40, so the after-tax cost of the donation is only $60. A low-income taxpayer in the 15 percent tax bracket who donates $100 to charity will reduce the amount of tax she owes by only $15, so the after-tax cost of the donation is $85. In addition, the charitable deduction is available only to those who itemize their deductions and many low-bracket taxpayers take the standard deduction rather than itemizing.

50. Ned's statement is incorrect. It is true that donations of cash are deductible and donations of services are not deductible. This difference in treatment is necessary, however, to ensure that donors of cash and services bear the same tax burden. Suppose, for example, that Doctor Debby and Lawyer Larry each can earn $1,000 per day providing services. Doctor Debby works for pay four days per week and spends one day providing free medical services to the poor. Debby will have taxable income of $4,000. Lawyer Larry works for pay five days per week and earns $5,000, but he donates one day's earnings, $1,000, to a charitable organization that provides free medical services to the poor. If Larry is permitted to deduct his cash donation, he will have taxable income of $4,000, the same as Debby, who donated services.

E. PERSONAL INTEREST

Reading: §163.

The tax treatment of interest paid by a taxpayer varies according to the purpose of the borrowing. Interest on amounts borrowed in connection with a trade or business (*business interest*) and on amounts borrowed for investment purposes (*investment interest*) generally are deductible in calculating net income, subject to certain limitations to prevent tax avoidance. §163. (The deduction of business interest and investment interest is discussed in Chapter 5 of this book.)

Prior to the Tax Reform Act of 1986, interest on money borrowed for personal reasons, such as the purchase of a home, automobile, or vacation, also was deductible, although only as an itemized deduction. The 1986 Act generally eliminated the deduction for personal interest, with an exception for *qualified residence interest*. §163(h). Qualified residence interest is defined as interest paid on either "acquisition indebtedness" or "home equity indebtedness" with respect to a "qualified residence" of the taxpayer. §163(h)(3). A *qualified residence* is the taxpayer's principal residence and one other residence of the taxpayer. §163(h)(4)(A). A dwelling that the taxpayer rents to others is a qualified residence only if, during the year, the taxpayer uses the dwelling for personal reasons for longer than the greater of (i) 14 days or (ii) 10 percent of the number of days that it is rented. §§163(h)(4) (A)(i)(II), 280A(d)(1).

Acquisition indebtedness is any indebtedness that is secured by the residence and is incurred in acquiring, constructing, or substantially improving the residence. §163(h)(3)(B)(i). Acquisition indebtedness also includes any indebtedness, secured by the residence, from refinancing qualified acquisition indebtedness, but only up to the amount of current indebtedness that was refinanced. Id. The aggregate amount of acquisition indebtedness cannot exceed $1 million. §163(h)(3)(B)(ii). If spouses file separately, the limit for each spouse is $500,000. Where the principal residence is co-owned by two unmarried taxpayers (who might be an opposite-sex couple or a same-sex couple), the $1 million limit also is applied on a per-residence basis (not on a per-taxpayer basis). Sophy v. Commissioner, 138 T.C. 204 (2012). The $1 million limit is allocated based on the percentage of the mortgage interest paid by each unmarried co-owner (not based on each co-owner's percentage ownership interest). Id. Each co-owner taxpayer is allowed to deduct the product of (1) the interest paid by the taxpayer on the acquisition indebtedness, multiplied by (2) $1 million divided by the average balance of the acquisition indebtedness for the year. Id. For example, assume that unmarried taxpayers Sam and Terry co-own a personal residence and share the payments on the residence, which include interest payments on acquisition indebtedness. During the year, the average balance on the acquisition indebtedness was $2,500,000, and total interest paid on that indebtedness was $180,000; Sam paid $100,000 of the interest and Terry paid $80,000 of the interest.

Sam is allowed to deduct $40,000 of acquisition indebtedness interest, which is the product of multiplying (1) the $100,000 of interest Sam paid during the year, by (2) 40 percent ($1 million acquisition indebtedness limit/ $2,500,000 average balance on the acquisition indebtedness during the year). Terry is allowed to deduct $32,000 of acquisition indebtedness interest, which is the product of multiplying (1) the $80,000 of interest Terry paid during the year by (2) 40 percent.

Home equity indebtedness is any indebtedness, other than acquisition indebtedness, secured by a qualified residence. §163(h)(3)(C)(i). Home equity indebtedness is subject to two limitations. First, the total of (i) home equity indebtedness plus (ii) acquisition indebtedness cannot exceed the fair market value of the qualified residence. Id. Second, home equity indebtedness cannot exceed $100,000 (or $50,000 if spouses file separately). §163(h)(3)(C)(ii). (The $100,000 limit also is applied on a per-residence basis; interest on home equity indebtedness is allocated between unmarried co-owners of a qualified residence in the same manner as interest on acquisition indebtedness is allocated. Sophy v. Commissioner, 138 T.C. 204 (2012).)

Debt secured by a qualified residence and incurred before October 13, 1987, is treated as acquisition indebtedness and is not subject to the $1 million limitation. However, such indebtedness will reduce the $1 million limitation (but not below zero) for any additional loans (other than qualified refinancing). §163(h)(3)(D).

Points are amounts a lender requires a borrower to pay, usually on the closing of the loan, in lieu of charging the borrower a higher interest rate on the loan. Points paid in connection with a loan generally must be capitalized and are deducted over the term of the loan. §461(g)(1). However, §461(g)(2) provides an exception to that rule for points paid on indebtedness secured by the taxpayer's principal residence and incurred to purchase or improve the principal residence, provided that (i) the payment of points is an established business practice in the area in which the indebtedness is incurred and (ii) the points paid do not exceed the amount generally charged in the area. If the requirements of §461(g)(2) are met, the points are deducted in the year in which they are paid. Note that points paid to refinance an existing home mortgage are not within the §461(g)(2) rule and cannot be immediately deducted in the year in which they are paid. Instead, the points are deducted over the term of the loan.

In addition, §163(h)(3)(E) provides that taxpayers can treat the cost of premiums for home mortgage insurance (which protects the lender in the event of a subsequent default by the taxpayer-borrower) as home mortgage interest. This rule is subject to a phase-out, based on adjusted gross income, and is scheduled to sunset at the end of 2013, although future legislation might extend it. P.L. 112-240 §204(a).

As a policy matter, the home mortgage deduction can be best defended as a method of encouraging home ownership or, more persuasively, as necessary to prevent individuals who have purchased homes in reliance on the deduction from suffering large losses. One important argument against the home mortgage deduction is that it seriously undermines the repeal of the deduction for other personal interest. Homeowners can deduct interest on loans secured by their residence (up to $100,000) even if the amounts are borrowed for purposes unrelated to home ownership, such as for the purchase of a new car. More important, the home mortgage deduction has been criticized for encouraging individuals to overinvest in housing.

The following examples explore some of the details of the deduction for qualified residence interest. Unless stated otherwise, assume that all debts are incurred after October 13, 1987.

(The deduction for interest on student loans is discussed in Chapter 6.)

Examples

51. In year one Alice purchases property to be used as a principal residence for $400,000, using $50,000 of savings and borrowing $350,000 from the Friendly Bank. The loan is secured by the property. In year three the residence is worth $500,000. What portion, if any, of the interest paid on the following alternative loans can be deducted?

    a. Alice borrows an additional $60,000 from the Friendly Bank, secured by her residence. She uses the money to add an additional room to her home.

    b. Assume the same facts as in part (a) except that Alice uses the loan proceeds to purchase a luxury automobile.

    c. Assume the same facts as in part (a) except that the loan is not secured by Alice's home.

    d. Alice borrows $120,000 from the Friendly Bank, secured by her residence, and uses the money to purchase a luxury automobile and take a trip around the world.

    e. Alice borrows $120,000 from the Friendly Bank and uses the proceeds to add a home theater and a pool to her residence.

52. a. In July of year one Jim purchases a home that he will occupy as a principal residence for $220,000, using $20,000 of his savings and borrowing the other $200,000. At the closing, Jim pays $250 in filing fees and $2,000 in "points" on the mortgage. During the remainder of year one, Jim pays $8,000 of interest on the mortgage. What is Jim's deductible interest for year one?

    b. Suppose that by year five interest rates have dropped and Jim's home is worth $400,000. Jim decides to refinance his loan, which has an outstanding principal amount owed of $180,000. He borrows $320,000 and uses $180,000 of the amount to repay the original loan. He also pays $6,000 in "points" on the new mortgage, which runs for 25 years. He uses the remainder of the amount borrowed to purchase an automobile and boat and pay for his daughter's college education. During year five Jim makes monthly interest payments totaling $15,000. What is Jim's deductible interest in year five?

53. Eve has a mortgage of $800,000 on her principal residence, which is worth $1,200,000. What portion of the interest on the following alternative additional loans can be deducted?
   a. In year one Eve purchases a vacation beach house on Cape Cod for $500,000, using $100,000 of savings and borrowing $400,000. The loan is secured by the beach house.
   b. In year one Eve instead purchases a smaller beach house for $250,000 and also purchases a ski chalet in Vermont for $250,000. On each vacation home she puts $50,000 down and borrows $200,000. The loan on the beach house is secured by the beach house and the loan on the chalet is secured by the chalet.
   c. How, if at all, would your answers in parts (a) and (b) change if Eve purchased her principal residence in 1986? If she purchased all the homes in 1986?

54. Fay purchased a home in 1970 for $30,000. The mortgage has been completely repaid and the home is now worth $300,000. In year one Fay borrows $160,000, secured by her home, and purchases a pickup truck, speed boat, and a trailer costing a total of $160,000.
   a. What portion of the interest paid in year one on the $160,000 loan is deductible?
   b. Suppose, instead, that in year one Fay sold her home for $300,000, used $160,000 of the proceeds to purchase the truck, boat, and trailer, and at the same time purchased a new home for $300,000, using $140,000 of the proceeds from the sale of her old home and borrowing $160,000. What portion of the interest paid in year one on the $160,000 loan is deductible?

Explanations

51. a. Interest on the loan is fully deductible. Qualified residence interest, which includes interest on acquisition indebtedness, is deductible. §163(h)(2)(D), (3)(A). Acquisition indebtedness includes amounts borrowed to finance a substantial home improvement if the debt is secured by the home. §163(h)(3)(B)(i).
   b. Interest on the loan is fully deductible. Qualified residence interest is deductible. §163(h)(2)(D). Here, the interest is qualified residence interest because the debt is home equity indebtedness. The amount borrowed is not acquisition indebtedness because the loan proceeds

were not used to purchase, build, or substantially improve her home. However, the loan qualifies as home equity indebtedness because (i) it is secured by her home; (ii) the home equity indebtedness, when added to the acquisition indebtedness, does not exceed the fair market value of her home; and (iii) the total amount of home equity indebtedness does not exceed $100,000. §163(h)(3)(C).

c. Not deductible. The deduction for qualified residential interest is only available for loans secured by the taxpayer's residence.

d. Interest on only $100,000 of the $120,000 borrowed is deductible. Qualified residence interest, which includes interest on acquisition indebtedness and home equity indebtedness, is deductible. §163(h)(2)(D), (3)(A). The amount borrowed is not acquisition indebtedness because the loan proceeds were not used to purchase, build, or substantially improve her home. However, the interest paid on $100,000 of the debt qualifies as deductible home equity indebtedness because (i) it is secured by her home, and (ii) the home equity indebtedness, when added to the acquisition indebtedness, does not exceed the fair market value of her home. §163(h)(3)(C)(i). Section 163(h)(3)(C)(ii) limits the total home equity indebtedness to $100,000. The interest on the $20,000 of debt in excess of the $100,000 limit is not qualified residence interest and thus is not deductible. §163(h)(1), (2).

e. Interest on the loan is fully deductible. In this part of the example, unlike part (d), the loan qualifies as acquisition indebtedness because it is used to improve her home substantially. §163(h)(3)(B)(i)(I). Acquisition indebtedness is subject to a $1 million limit, instead of the $100,000 limit imposed on home equity indebtedness. The interest on the entire $120,000 of debt is deductible qualified residence interest.

52. a. $10,000 — $8,000 interest and $2,000 points. The interest on Jim's principal residence is qualified residence interest. §163(h)(3)(A)(i), (B). Points paid on the original financing of the purchase of a principal residence are treated as interest that can be deducted in the year in which they are paid, provided the other requirements of §461(g)(2) are met. Filing fees and similar closing costs do not constitute deductible interest.

b. In year five Jim deducts $13,125 of the $15,000 of monthly interest payments and $240 of the points he paid. Qualified residence interest, which includes interest on acquisition indebtedness and home equity indebtedness, is deductible. §163(h)(2)(D), (3)(A). Amounts borrowed to refinance a loan on a qualified residence are considered acquisition indebtedness only up to the amount refinanced. §163(h)(3)(B) (flush language). Thus, $180,000 of the amount borrowed is acquisition indebtedness. The other $140,000 borrowed is not acquisition indebtedness. However, $100,000 of that remaining $140,000 of debt is home equity indebtedness. §163(h)(3)(C). Thus, interest on $280,000 of the $320,000 mortgage would be deductible, or 87.5 percent (7/8) of the $15,000 interest paid. In year five Jim will also deduct $240 of the $6,000 of points paid on the refinancing. Although amounts paid for points on the original mortgage on a taxpayer's principal residence are immediately deductible, points on amounts borrowed in connection with refinancings, second mortgages, and purchases of second homes must be amortized over the life of the loan. Thus, on a 25-year loan, 4 percent of the $6,000 paid for points would be deductible each year. §461(g)(1), Rev. Rul. 87-22, Rev. Proc. 87-15.

53. a. Interest on $300,000 of the additional $400,000 borrowed is deductible, but the rest of the interest is not deductible. Qualified residence interest, which includes interest on acquisition indebtedness and home equity indebtedness, is deductible. §163(h)(2)(D), (3)(A). Amounts borrowed to purchase a second home qualify as acquisition indebtedness, provided that the second home is a "qualified residence." §163(h)(3)(B)(i)(I), (4)(A)(i)(II). However, total acquisition indebtedness is limited to $1 million. §163(h)(3)(B)(ii). Eve already has an $800,000 mortgage on her principal residence, so only $200,000 of the amount borrowed to purchase the beach house is acquisition indebtedness. However, of the remaining $200,000 of indebtedness on the beach house, $100,000 qualifies as "home equity indebtedness" because (i) it is secured by her home and (ii) the home equity indebtedness, when added to the acquisition indebtedness, does not exceed the fair market value of her home. §163(h)(3)(C). Section 163(h)(3)(C)(ii) limits total home equity indebtedness to $100,000. The interest on the remaining $100,000 of debt is not qualified residence interest and is not deductible. §163(h)(1), (2).

b. Deductible qualified residence interest includes acquisition indebtedness on a qualified residence and home equity indebtedness on a qualified residence. The term *qualified residence* includes the taxpayer's principal residence and one additional residence of the taxpayer's choice. §163(h)(4)(A)(i). Thus, only one of the vacation homes is a qualified residence. Eve can deduct interest on the indebtedness on the vacation home that is a qualified residence. All of the $200,000 borrowed on that residence will be deductible as acquisition indebtedness since the $1 million limitation is not exceeded. However, none of the interest paid on the indebtedness on the other vacation home can be deducted. §163(h)(1), (2).

c. A "grandfather clause" exists for indebtedness incurred on qualifying residences purchased before October 13, 1987. §163(h)(3)(D)(i). However, the $1 million limitation on acquisition indebtedness is reduced (but not below zero) by the amount of grandfathered debt. Thus, the results in parts (a) and (b) would not change if Eve had purchased only her principal residence in 1986.

If Eve had purchased all the residences in 1986, however, the result in part (a) would change. On these facts, both Eve's principal residence and her beach house are qualifying residences, so all interest paid on amounts outstanding before October 13, 1987, would be deductible. §163(h)(3)(D). In part (b), on the other hand, only one of the vacation homes would be considered a qualifying residence, so the interest paid on the loan used to purchase Eve's second vacation home would remain nondeductible.

54. a. 62.5 percent (5/8) of the interest paid will be deductible. Qualified residence interest, which includes interest on acquisition indebtedness and home equity indebtedness, is deductible. §163(h)(2)(D), (3)(A). Here, none of the amount borrowed is acquisition indebtedness because the loan is not incurred to acquire, construct, or improve her residence. §163(h)(3)(B)(i)(I). However, $100,000 of the $160,000 borrowed qualifies as home equity indebtedness because (i) it is secured by her home and (ii) the home equity indebtedness, when added to the acquisition indebtedness, does not exceed the fair market value of her home. §163(h)(3)(C). Section 163(h)(3)(C)(ii) limits total home equity indebtedness to $100,000, so the interest on the remaining $60,000 of debt in excess of the $100,000 of home equity indebtedness is not qualified residence interest and is not deductible. §163(h)(1), (2). Fay can deduct 62.5 percent ($100,000 home equity indebtedness/$160,000 total indebtedness) of the interest she paid in year one.

b. Here, all of the interest paid in year one is deductible. On these facts, the entire amount borrowed qualifies as acquisition indebtedness because the debt is incurred to buy the new home.

F. TAXES

Reading: §164; *Reg.* §§1.164-3, 1.1001-1(b).

A personal itemized deduction is permitted under §164 for state and local income taxes and taxes on real and personal property. (Section 164 also permits a deduction for certain foreign taxes, but individuals subject to foreign taxation generally take the §901 foreign tax credit instead.)

Until 1986, §164 allowed a deduction for sales tax, but that provision in §164 was repealed as part of the Tax Reform Act of 1986. Note that states vary in the degree to which they rely on income taxes, property taxes, and sales taxes to raise revenue. Following the repeal of the sales tax deduction, a taxpayer who was a resident of a state that relied heavily on sales tax for revenue paid more federal tax than a taxpayer with equal income who was a resident of a state that relied more heavily on income and property taxes. Congress subsequently amended §164 to allow taxpayers an election to take a sales tax deduction in lieu of a deduction for state and local income taxes. §164(b)(5). Taxpayers who live in states with an income tax generally will not elect to take the sales tax deduction because their deduction for state and local income taxes generally will exceed the deduction for state and local sales taxes. Taxpayers who live in states with a sales tax but no income tax (including Alaska, Florida, Nevada, New Hampshire, South Dakota, Tennessee, Texas, Washington, and Wyoming) will elect to take the sales tax deduction. Taxpayers electing to take the sales tax deduction can use either of two methods to determine the amount of their sales tax deduction. They can deduct either: (i) the amount indicated in state sales tax tables prepared by the IRS; or (ii) the sales taxes they actually paid (provided they kept receipts). §164(b)(5)(H). (The amendment sunsets at the end of 2013 but may be extended by future legislation.). Taxpayers cannot generally deduct federal taxes paid.

Amounts charged for government services are considered "fees" rather than "taxes." Such fees do not qualify for the §164 personal deduction for state and local taxes. They may be deductible, however, as ordinary and necessary business expenses or as expenses incurred in the production of income. Rev. Rul. 72-608. In addition, assessments on real property owners for local benefits, such as sidewalks, are not treated as real property taxes for purposes of §164 and are not deductible. Reg. §1.164-4.

The §164 personal deduction for state and local taxes is taken as an itemized deduction. (Under the Alternative Minimum Tax, discussed in Chapter 5, this itemized deduction is disallowed. §56(b)(1)(A)(ii).) On the other hand, taxes incurred in a business or in connection with the production of income are deductible under §162 or §212 in the calculation of adjusted gross income. Consistent with the principle that the expenses of earning income should be deductible, state and local excise, sales, and other taxes, as well as income and property taxes, incurred in the production of income, are deductible in the calculation of adjusted gross income. Federal taxes, however, generally remain nondeductible.

A current §164 deduction is not permitted for taxes paid in connection with the acquisition of property. If paid by the buyer, such transfer taxes must be treated as part of the buyer's cost of the property, whether or not incurred in a business context. Similarly, taxes incurred by a seller in connection with the sale of property are not deductible, but instead reduce the amount realized on the sale. §164(a) (flush language).

When real property is sold, the property taxes for the year of the sale must be allocated between the buyer and the seller. §164(d)(1). Under §164(d), the property taxes are allocated based on the part of the year the property was owned by each. For the purpose of making this allocation, the buyer is treated as the owner of the property on the date the property was sold. §164(d)(1). For example, assume that Sela sells Whiteacre to Betty in year one. Sela owns the property for 1/4 of that year (91 days Sela owned the property/365 days in the year) and Betty owns the property for 3/4 of that year (274 days Betty owned the property/365 days in the year). If the property tax on Whiteacre for year one is $4,000, Sela is allocated $1,000 of the year one property tax and Betty is allocated the other $3,000 of the property tax. This allocation method determines the amount of property tax that the buyer and seller may deduct under §164.

If the buyer pays property taxes allocable to the seller, the seller's property taxes paid by the buyer increase the seller's amount realized and the buyer's basis in the property acquired. If, on the other hand, the seller pays property taxes allocable to the buyer and is reimbursed for the taxes by the buyer, the property taxes allocable to the buyer and reimbursed by the buyer reduce the seller's amount realized and the buyer's basis in the property acquired. Reg. §1.1001-1(b).

Examples

55. State whether the following amounts are deductible under §164.
    a. Alice pays a $2,000 per year local real property tax on the home she lives in.
    b. Carlos recently graduated from dental school. He purchases a building to use as an office for $150,000. He is required to pay a state transfer tax of $1,000 on the purchase.
    c. To play tennis on the new public courts of Centerville, residents must purchase an annual pass. Tim pays $100 for a pass.
    d. Ernest must pay a motor vehicle fee of 1 percent of the value of his car each year. The fee in year one is $150.
    e. Karen pays $4,000 of state and local sales tax when she buys a new recreational sailboat for $60,000.
    f. Greta is a cigarette smoker. She calculates that she pays $150 per year in federal cigarette excise taxes and $200 per year in state cigarette excise taxes.

56. On January one of year two, Harry purchases Blackacre from Irving. At the time of the purchase, Irving owes $4,000 in property taxes on

Blackacre for year one. Harry pays the year one taxes Irving owes in order to obtain clear title to the property. Can Harry deduct all $4,000 of year one tax that he pays in year two?

57. Jane purchases Whiteacre from Karl on January 31 of year one for $300,000. Karl had already paid $3,650 of property taxes on Whiteacre for all of year one. Will Jane receive a tax deduction for any portion of the taxes paid?

58. The City of Oceanview assesses beachfront property owners for the construction of jetties to protect shoreline property from the destructive effects of ocean storms. Is the assessment deductible by the property owners?

Explanations

55. a. Alice can deduct the taxes. Local property taxes are deductible as itemized personal deductions. §164(a)(1).

   b. Carlos cannot deduct the taxes in the year in which they are paid. A tax that is paid in connection with an acquisition of property is treated as part of the cost of the acquired property. §164(a) (flush language). Thus, Carlos could not immediately deduct the tax paid, but would include the amount paid in the basis of the property acquired, giving him a basis of $151,000.

   c. Tim cannot deduct the $100 cost of the pass. User fees for state and local services are not considered taxes and thus are not deductible under §164. Rev. Rul. 72-608.

   d. Ernest can deduct the $150 "fee." A motor vehicle fee is a deductible personal property tax under §164(a)(2). Reg. §1.164-3(c).

   e. If Karen pays this sales tax in 2013, she can elect to take a deduction for state and local sales taxes in lieu of a deduction for state and local income taxes. §164(b)(5). She will take a deduction for the greater of: (i) the state and local sales taxes; or (ii) the state and local income taxes. If she pays the sales tax in a later year, the answer depends on whether Congress has extended the sales tax deduction to later years.

   f. Greta is not entitled to a deduction. Excise taxes are not deductible under §164.

56. No. The §164 deduction for taxes paid is applicable only to taxes owed by the taxpayer. In this case, Irving, not Harry, owed the year one property taxes. Harry would not be able to deduct the $4,000 of Irving's taxes that he paid, but he would be able to add the $4,000 payment to his basis in Blackacre. Irving would include in the amount realized on the sale the $4,000 of tax paid on his behalf

241

by Harry and would take a §164 deduction in the same amount. Reg. §1.1001-1(b).

57. Yes, Jane can deduct $3,350 as year one property taxes. On the sale of property, real estate taxes are allocated between the buyer and seller according to the number of days the property was owned by each. §164(d). Here, the seller would have owned the property for 30 days and the buyer for 335 days. Thus, Jane would be permitted a §164 deduction of $3,350 ($3,650 multiplied by 335/365) for the year one property taxes. Jane's basis in Whiteacre is $296,650 ($300,000 contract price less $3,350 of property taxes allocable to Jane). Reg. §1.1001-1(b).

58. Probably not. As a general rule, real property taxes do not include amounts assessed for local benefits that increase the value of the assessed property. §164(c)(1), Reg. §1.164-4. Building jetties will increase the value of the assessed beachfront property. Thus, the amount of the assessment is not deductible, but is added to the adjusted basis of the taxpayer's property.

Deductions for the Costs of Earning Income

Business and investment expenses are subtracted from gross income in order to determine net income. Section 162(a) provides that a taxpayer is allowed to deduct "all the ordinary and necessary expenses paid or incurred during the taxable year in carrying on any trade or business." Section 212 also allows a deduction for expenses incurred in connection with investment activities. However, a number of Code sections and judicial doctrines limit the deductibility of certain types of business and investment expenses or require that certain types of expenses be capitalized and deducted over a number of years.

In this chapter, we will first consider the basic statutory framework for deducting the costs of earning income. Second, we will consider the rules for determining whether a business deduction is deducted in the year in which it is incurred or instead is deducted over a number of years. Current expenses of a business can be deducted immediately, while capital expenses — those that create a benefit that extends substantially beyond the close of the year in which the expense is incurred — must be deducted over the time that the expenses produce benefits. As we will see, however, it is often far from obvious whether an expense is a current or capital expense.

Third, we will explore several limitations on the deduction of certain types of business expenses. Fourth, we will consider the rules for determining a taxpayer's deductions for the cost of tangible and intangible depreciable property used in the taxpayer's trade or business or held for investment.

Fifth, we will examine a number of issues that arise in connection with *tax shelters*. A tax shelter is an investment that generates tax losses that can be used to shield other income from taxation. This chapter explains the complex judicial and statutory responses to abusive tax shelters. Sixth, this chapter concludes with a brief introduction to the Alternative Minimum Tax, which supplements the regular income tax. The AMT has a broader base but lower rates than the regular income tax.

A. THE STATUTORY FRAMEWORK

Reading: §§62, 63, 67; Reg. §§1.62-1T(d), 1.162-17(b), 1.67-1T.
A basic principle of the federal income tax is that individuals are taxed only on their net income. Thus, individuals generally are permitted to deduct costs associated with earning income.

Section 162 provides a deduction for "ordinary and necessary" expenses incurred in carrying on a trade or business. Under this section, a taxpayer who owns and operates a housecleaning business could deduct, for example, the costs of renting office space, utilities and other office expenses, advertising, and wages paid to employees of the business. The computational effect of a business expense depends, in part, on whether the taxpayer who incurred the expense is an employee, because an employee is not considered to be engaged in a trade or business for purposes of computing adjusted gross income under §62. Reg. §1.62-1T(d). If business expenses are incurred by a taxpayer who is not an employee of a firm (for example, a law firm partner who is considered to be self-employed), the business expenses are subtracted from gross income to determine adjusted gross income under §62(a)(1). (Deductions taken into account in computing adjusted gross income are referred to as *above-the-line* deductions because they are taken above the adjusted gross income line on a tax return.)

On the other hand, if business expenses are incurred by an employee (for example, an associate in a law firm) and are not reimbursed by the employer, the expenses are subtracted from adjusted gross income to determine taxable income. §§62(a)(1), 63(a). (Deductions taken into account in computing taxable income are called *below-the-line* deductions because they are taken below the adjusted gross income line on a tax return.) Employee business expenses that are not reimbursed by the employer are subject to §67, which generally limits a taxpayer's itemized deductions to her aggregate deductible expenses in excess of 2 percent of her adjusted gross income. §67(a). The 2 percent floor eliminates the business expense deduction for most employee taxpayers. In addition, even if a taxpayer's unreimbursed employee business expenses exceed the 2 percent floor, the taxpayer is allowed to take a deduction for the excess over the floor only if the taxpayer itemizes deductions. A taxpayer taking the standard deduction, instead, is precluded from deducting any of the employee business expenses. §63(b). Thus, unreimbursed employee business expenses (which are below-the-line deductions, are subject to the 2 percent floor, and can only be deducted if the taxpayer does not take the standard deduction) are treated less favorably than nonemployee business expenses, which are fully deductible and are above-the-line deductions.

Reimbursed employee business expenses are treated like nonemployee business expenses. Thus, they are above-the-line deductions and not subject to §67. §62(a)(2)(A), Reg. §1.67-1T(a)(1). If the amount reimbursed by the employer is equal to the employee business expense, Regulation §1.162-17(b) allows the employee, for reporting purposes, to net the reimbursement (which would otherwise be included in income) and the business expense (which would otherwise be an above-the-line deduction). The result is that the employee does not have an income tax inclusion or deduction with respect to the reimbursed expense.

Expenses incurred in earning income from sources other than a trade or business are deductible under §212. For example, this section permits an individual with investment income from stocks and bonds to deduct her brokerage fees and the cost of a subscription to the *Wall Street Journal*. Section 212 expenses are generally below-the-line deductions and thus subject to the §67 limitation. An exception is the deduction for §212 expenses attributable to property held for the production of rents or royalties, which is an above-the-line deduction. §62(a)(4).

Example

1. Sally is an employee of Yaba Corporation. As the chief financial officer of the corporation, she subscribes to several business and finance newspapers and magazines. The annual cost of these subscriptions is $500. In year one Sally has adjusted gross income of $200,000, §67 miscellaneous itemized deductions (determined without regard to the $500 subscription cost) of $1,000, and no other itemized deductions. Explain the tax treatment, in year one, of the $500 subscription cost in the following alternative circumstances.
   a. Sally pays the $500 cost of the subscriptions and is not reimbursed by Yaba Corporation.
   b. Sally pays the $500 cost of the subscriptions and is reimbursed by Yaba Corporation.

Explanation

1. a. The $500 cost of the subscriptions is a deductible expense of earning income. The deduction is not an above-the-line deduction, however, because (i) Sally is an employee of Yaba Corporation and (ii) Yaba Corporation did not reimburse her for the cost of the subscriptions. Thus, the $500 cost is a below-the-line itemized deduction and is subject to §67. That section limits Sally's itemized deductions to her deductible expenses in excess of 2 percent of her adjusted gross income. §67(a). The $500 cost of the subscriptions plus her other miscellaneous itemized deductions total $1,500, which is less than 2 percent of her $200,000 adjusted gross income. In effect, the §67 floor eliminates her deduction for the $500 cost of the subscriptions. (In addition, the standard deduction exceeds her itemized deductions.)

   b. Sally does not have to include the amount reimbursed in income because the employer reimbursement equals the employee expense. Reg. §1.162-17(b). (But for this administrative reporting rule, Sally would have been required to include the reimbursement in income but would have had an above-the-line deduction for the employee expense. §62(a)(2)(A).)

B. CURRENT EXPENSES VERSUS CAPITAL EXPENDITURES

Reading: §§263, 263A; *Reg.* §§1.162-3, 1.263(a)-1, -2, -3, -4, -5, 1.263A-1, -2
Current business expenses are deductible in the year in which they are incurred. The cost of a business asset with a useful life that extends beyond the year in which the expense is incurred, on the other hand, must be *capitalized*. §263. The object of the capitalization requirement is to accurately reflect the taxpayer's true income for each year by matching an expense with the income to which it relates. See, e.g., Encyclopaedia Britannica v. Commissioner, 685 F.2d 212 (7th Cir. 1982). If a taxpayer is required to capitalize a business expense, how does the tax system provide for this matching?

The cost of an asset with a useful life that extends beyond the year in which the expense is incurred is deducted as *depreciation* over the useful life of the asset, provided the asset has a determinable useful life. §167. Suppose, for example, that a donut shop purchases a new donut-making machine that is expected to produce donuts for 10 years and then be worthless. Under a theoretically pure income tax, the cost of the machine would be deducted over the 10-year period with an annual depreciation deduction equal to the annual reduction in value of the machine. Under current law, however, annual deductions for the cost of business assets are determined by reference to bright-line statutory rules rather than by reference to the actual decline in the value of the asset. §§167, 168.

Section 167 allows a deduction "for the exhaustion, wear and tear" of property used in a trade or business or for the production of income. Both tangible property, such as a machine or building, and intangible property, such as a patent, are eligible for the deduction. Reg. §§1.167(a)-2, -3. The term *amortization*, rather than depreciation, typically is used to describe deductions for the cost of intangible property. Under §168, most tangible property with a limited useful life is depreciated under the accelerated cost recovery system (ACRS). ACRS permits a taxpayer to deduct the cost of the asset over a period of time that is shorter than the actual useful life of the asset. (The rules for calculating a taxpayer's depreciation deductions on business assets are discussed in more detail later in this chapter.)

A depreciable asset is *not a capital asset*, despite the fact that the cost of the depreciable asset must be *capitalized*. §1221(a)(2). Depreciable assets are instead "section 1231 assets." Gain or loss from the sale of section 1231 assets may be capital or ordinary. Capital gain and loss, capital assets, and section 1231 assets are discussed further in Chapter 8. For now, note that, even if the cost of a business asset must be capitalized, the asset may not be (and, in fact, usually is not) a capital asset. Students often incorrectly assume that an asset is a capital asset if the taxpayer has to capitalize its cost. "Capitalization" and "capital asset" sound similar, but remember that the two terms express different concepts in the tax law.

Property with an unlimited useful life, such as land, cannot be depreciated or amortized. Reg. §§1.167(a)-2, -3. Instead, with a few statutory exceptions, the costs of such property may be recovered only when the property is sold (by subtracting the taxpayer's adjusted basis from the amount realized on the sale).

Section 263 generally requires capitalization of amounts paid to acquire, produce, or improve: (i) real or personal property, including land, buildings, machinery, and equipment; or (ii) intangibles. §263(a), Reg. §§1.263(a)-1, -2, -3, -4. In addition, taxpayers must capitalize transaction costs incurred to facilitate an acquisition or certain other transactions. Reg. §§1.263(a)-1, -2, -5.

The Code and regulations provide for certain limited exceptions to the capitalization requirement. For example, §179 (discussed later in this chapter) allows taxpayers to immediately deduct certain costs of acquiring property. In addition, Regulation §1.263(a)-1(f) provides a de minimis exception to the capitalization requirement, in some circumstances, if the taxpayer's deduction of certain relatively minor expenditures is consistent with the taxpayer's treatment of the expenditures for financial accounting purposes.

Although taxpayers must generally capitalize amounts paid to acquire or produce property, under §263(a), there is an exception for "materials and supplies." Reg. §§1.162-3(a), 1.263(a)-2(c)(2). The regulations define the term "materials and supplies" to include certain tangible property that is not inventory and is used or consumed in the taxpayer's business operations, including property that (i) costs $200 or less, or (ii) has a useful life of 12 months or less. Reg. §1.162-3(c)(1). Taxpayers deduct the cost of "incidental" materials and supplies (goods carried on hand for which no record of consumption is kept, such as a law firm's legal pads and pens) in the year in which the costs of these supplies are paid or incurred, and deduct the cost of "non-incidental" materials and supplies in the year in which the supplies are used or consumed. Reg. §1.162-3(a). The regulation provides that the cost of a rotable part (i.e., a part that a taxpayer can remove for repair and reinstall after repair) or a temporary spare part may be deducted in the year in which the taxpayer disposes of the part. Reg. §1.162-3(a)(3).

The capitalization requirement applies to amounts paid for intangible assets. For example, if a taxpayer prepays an expense that is attributable to later years, the expense must be capitalized. In Commissioner v. Boylston Market Association, 131 F.2d 966 (1st Cir. 1942), a cash method taxpayer that prepaid three years of insurance premiums had to allocate that expense over the three years and deduct a portion in each year. (Recall that accrual method taxpayers are generally not allowed to deduct prepaid expenses, despite the fact that the all events test may be met in the year in which the expense is prepaid, because of the economic performance requirement of §461(h).)

In Commissioner v. Lincoln Savings and Loan Association, 403 U.S. 345 (1971), the Supreme Court held that a taxpayer must capitalize an expense that creates or enhances a separate and distinct asset. In a later case, INDOPCO, Inc. v. Commissioner, 503 U.S. 79 (1992), the Supreme Court held that the capitalization requirement also applies to expenses that produce significant future benefits, even if the benefits are intangible and the expenses do not create a separate and distinct asset. The taxpayer in INDOPCO took a deduction for investment banking and legal fees incurred during the year in connection with a friendly takeover. The record indicated that the takeover produced significant long-term benefits for the taxpayer's shareholders. The Court held that the investment banking and legal fees had to be capitalized, despite the fact that the expense did not create a separate asset; it observed that the creation of a separate and distinct asset was sufficient to require capitalization, but was not necessary for an expense to require capitalization.

The "significant future benefit" test articulated in INDOPCO created a great deal of uncertainty, controversy, and litigation about the scope of the capitalization requirement. Eventually, in 2004, the IRS and Treasury promulgated final regulations that attempted to clarify the scope of the capitalization requirement for costs of acquiring or creating intangibles. T.D. 9107 (2004), Reg. §§1.263(a)-4, -5. The regulations retain the precise holding of INDOPCO, but reduce the scope of the "significant future benefit" test and generally reinstate the "separate and distinct asset" test of *Lincoln Savings*, on the grounds that the latter test is more certain and administrable.

Regulation §1.263(a)-4 provides that taxpayers must capitalize amounts paid to: (i) acquire intangibles described in -4(c); (ii) create intangibles described in -4(d); (iii) create or enhance a separate and distinct intangible asset; (iv) create or enhance a future benefit (but only as specified in other administrative guidance, which to date has been quite limited); and (v) facilitate the acquisition or creation of intangibles. Reg. §1.263(a)-4(b)(1). A *separate and distinct intangible asset* is a property interest, protected by law, that can be transferred separately from a trade or business. Reg. §1.263(a)-4(b)(3).

Regulation §1.263(a)-4(c) defines "acquired intangibles" and §1.263(a)-4(d) defines "created intangibles." Both (c)(1) and (d)(2) define "intangibles" to include the following *financial* interests: (i) ownership interests in corporations, partnerships, limited liability companies, and other entities; (ii) debt instruments and other debt intangibles; (iii) financial instruments; (iv) annuity and insurance contracts; and (v) nonfunctional currency. For purposes of (c)(1) (acquired intangibles), the term intangibles also includes: (i) leases; (ii) patents and copyrights; (iii) franchises, trademarks, and trade names; (iv) an assembled workforce; (v) goodwill; (vi) customer lists; (vii) servicing rights; (viii) customer-based intangibles; and (ix) certain computer software. (The capitalized costs of several types of acquired intangibles in this latter grouping can be amortized, under §197, over a 15-year period, or under §167, over the remaining useful life of the asset. Amortization of the cost of intangibles is discussed later in this chapter.) Regulation §1.263(a)-4(d) also provides that "created intangibles" include: (i) prepaid expenses, such as prepaid insurance; (ii) fees for memberships and privileges, such as hospital privileges; (iii) certain rights granted by a government agency, such as a business license; (iv) costs of creating or renewing certain contracts; (v) certain contract termination costs; (vi) certain costs of real property transferred to another or produced for another; and (vii) costs of defending or perfecting title to intangible property. Reg. §1.263(a)-4(d)(3)–(9). (Rules regarding amortization of the costs of certain types of self-created intangibles are discussed later in this chapter.)

In addition to narrowing the application of the INDOPCO significant future benefit test, Regulation §1.263(a)-4 provides various special rules that are favorable to taxpayers. For example, in applying the transaction cost rule, a taxpayer may disregard de minimis costs (costs aggregating $5,000 or less), compensation paid to the taxpayer's employees, and overhead expenses. Reg. §1.263(a)-4(e)(4). In addition, the regulations allow taxpayers to currently deduct costs of acquiring or creating intangibles if the rights acquired or created do not extend beyond 12 months after the taxpayer realizes the right. Reg. §1.263(a)-4(f). These special rules allow taxpayers to currently deduct various expenses that would be capitalized under the INDOPCO future benefit test.

Regulation §1.263(a)-5 provides specifically that taxpayers must capitalize amounts paid to facilitate the acquisition of a business or to change the capital structure of a business. The regulation retains the significant future benefit test of INDOPCO, but limits its application to specific circumstances. In addition, the regulation provides that taxpayers may disregard de minimis costs (costs aggregating $5,000 or less), compensation paid to the taxpayer's employees, and overhead expenses. Reg. §1.263(a)-5(d).

In general, an amount is paid to facilitate a transaction if it is paid in the process of investigating or otherwise pursuing the transaction. Reg. §1.263(a)-5(b)(1). Whether an amount is paid to investigate or otherwise pursue a transaction is based on a facts-and-circumstances analysis. Id. Amounts paid regarding certain covered transactions only facilitate the transaction if they are paid on or after the earlier of (i) the date on which the taxpayer executed a letter of intent, exclusivity agreement, or similar written communication, or (ii) the date on which the material terms of the transaction are agreed upon by the taxpayer's board of directors (or comparable managers, if the taxpayer is not a corporation). Reg. §1.263(a)-5(e). Covered transactions include (i) taxable acquisitions of assets constituting a trade or business, (ii) certain taxable acquisitions of ownership in a business entity, and (iii) certain tax-deferred reorganizations. (Certain corporate acquisitions can qualify for nonrecognition of gain realized, in a manner similar to the §1031 nonrecognition rule applicable to like-kind exchanges, discussed in Chapter 3.) Notwithstanding this taxpayer-friendly cutoff date, certain costs are deemed inherently facilitative and must be capitalized regardless of when they are paid or incurred. These include amounts paid to: secure an appraisal, formal written evaluation, or fairness opinion on the transaction; negotiate the structure of the transaction; obtain tax advice on the structure of the transaction; prepare and review documents that effect the transaction; obtain regulatory approval; obtain shareholder approval; and convey property between the parties.

Amounts paid to terminate an agreement to enter into a transaction are an amount paid to facilitate a second transaction if the two are mutually exclusive. Reg. §1.263(a)-5(c)(8). These payments generally arise when a target corporation agrees to be sold to a buyer, but a second buyer makes a better offer. To prevent this, the first buyer typically contracts to be paid a termination fee if the target corporation wants to get out of the acquisition agreement. If the second offer is more attractive than the first, even after taking into account the termination fee, the board of directors of the selling corporation typically has a fiduciary duty to agree to the better deal for their shareholders.

The IRS concluded that these types of termination fees facilitate the second deal. At least one court, however, applying the INDOPCO test to a tax year before the regulations came into effect, found that a termination fee did not provide the selling corporation a significant future benefit. Santa Fe Pacific Gold Co. v. Commissioner, 132 T.C. 12 (2009). In *Santa Fe Pacific Gold* a large mining corporation was interested in purchasing the taxpayer, a smaller competitor, because it owned valuable land. Fearing that the large mining corporation would take over the taxpayer's land, lay off its employees, and shut down its business, the taxpayer sought to merge with a similar-sized company. The taxpayer found a willing company and reached an agreement that contained a termination fee. Thereafter the large mining corporation made an even better offer for the taxpayer. The board of directors of the taxpayer reluctantly decided to accept the better deal. The tax court held that the taxpayer did not have any significant long-term benefits from paying the fee because any synergies from the merger benefited only the large mining corporation. As it turned out, the taxpayer's fears of layoffs and a shutdown of its business came to fruition. According to the Court, the taxpayer did not pay the fee in hopes of attaining some future benefit, but rather as a mandatory cost of the board of directors complying with their fiduciary duty to accept the better deal for the shareholders.

Costs incurred to maintain or repair tangible assets also raise complex capitalization issues. Taxpayers must capitalize the costs of improving property, but can currently deduct the cost of incidental repairs. §§162(a), 263(a), Reg. §1.162-4, 1.263(a)-3. The distinction between repairs and improvements is explored in the next section of this chapter.

If a taxpayer incurs expenses that would otherwise be deductible business expenses (for example, wages paid to employees) in constructing a building or machinery, the otherwise deductible expenses must be capitalized. For example, in Commissioner v. Idaho Power Co., 418 U.S. 1 (1974), a power company had to capitalize expenses for wages and depreciation on trucks used to construct a capital facility with a 30-year useful life. The effect was that the taxpayer was required to recover the cost of the trucks over the 30-year life of the facility, not the shorter useful life of the trucks. The holding in *Idaho Power* was codified in 1986 when Congress enacted the §263A uniform capitalization (UNICAP) rules.

The UNICAP rules apply to manufacturers, wholesalers, retailers, and any other taxpayers who produce real or tangible property for sale or acquire real or personal property (tangible or intangible) for sale to customers in the ordinary course of their business. §263A(b), Reg. §1.263A-3(a)(1). *Tangible property* is defined to include books, films, and sound recordings. §263A(b) (flush language). However, §263A does not apply to freelance authors, photographers, and artists. §263A(h). In addition, §263A applies to a taxpayer who acquires personal property for resale only if the taxpayer's average annual gross receipts from sales, over a three-year period, exceed $10 million. §263A(b)(2)(B).

If §263A applies, it requires the taxpayer to recover the expenses of producing or selling goods held for sale to customers when the goods are sold, by including those expenses in the taxpayer's "cost of goods sold" (which is the term for the taxpayer's inventory cost for the year). §263A(a)(1). (Inventory accounting is discussed in more detail later in this chapter.) The UNICAP rules apply to the "direct costs" of producing and selling goods and the portion of "indirect costs" that is allocable to the goods sold. §263A(a)(2).

The regulations define the terms direct cost and indirect cost and specify which indirect costs must be allocated to the goods sold. Reg. §1.263A-1(e), (g). Direct costs include the cost of materials and wages of employees who produce or sell goods. Reg. §1.263A-1(e)(2)(i), (g)(1), (2). Indirect costs can include the following types of costs: the costs of repair and maintenance of equipment or facilities; utility costs; rent on equipment, facilities, or land; indirect labor costs; indirect material costs; purchasing costs; the costs of tools and equipment, if such costs are not otherwise capitalized; certain taxes; depreciation on equipment or facilities; depletion; the costs of certain administrative or support departments or functions; compensation paid to officers; insurance premiums; contributions to deferred compensation plans; bidding expenses; and certain interest costs. Reg. §1.263A-1(e)(3)(i), (e)(4)(ii). However, the regulations provide that the taxpayer's expenses for marketing, advertising, and general business and financial planning do not have to be capitalized. Reg. §1.263A-1(e)(3)(iii), (4)(iv)(B), (C). As you can tell from reading §263A and Reg. §§1.263A-1 and -2, the UNICAP rules are complicated.

Most research and experimental expenses do not have to be capitalized even though they provide a benefit extending beyond the taxable year. §§174, 263A(c)(2). However, the costs of researching a book (along with preproduction costs such as editing and illustrating) may have to be capitalized. Reg. §1.263A-2(a)(2)(ii)(A)(1). (Section 263A does not apply to freelance writers, however. §263A(h).) Farmers generally do not have to capitalize expenditures for soil or water conservation, for the prevention of erosion, or for endangered species recovery. §175. Section 198 also allows taxpayers to deduct certain costs of environmental remediation at designated sites that are contaminated by hazardous substances. Remediation costs incurred for depreciable property are not deductible under §198. (Although §198 sunsets at the end of 2013, future legislation may extend it.)

Examples

2. Briefly explain whether each of the following expenses may be deducted currently or must be capitalized.
   a. purchase of the copyright to the song "Stormy Weather;"
   b. purchase of a copying machine that will be used in a law firm;
   c. purchase of paper used in the copying machine described in part (b);
   d. incidental repair and maintenance of the copying machine described in part (b);
   e. legal fees incurred in purchasing the property on which the taxpayer's business is located;
   f. the costs of a feasibility study on overseas expansion incurred by a chain of fast food restaurants;
   g. the commission paid to a stockbroker on the purchase of 100 shares of stock.

3. Pete's Big Business, Inc. outgrows the office building it has occupied for the last several years. Rather than buy or lease an existing structure, Pete commissions an architect to design a new office building. The architect's fees are $120,000. The building costs $15 million to construct. The office furniture and fixtures cost an additional $1.2 million. How much of these expenditures are currently deductible?

4. In year one the Admiral Byrd Refrigerator Company made the following expenditures: $4 million for materials used in the production of refrigerators, $5 million for labor, and $900,000 for warehousing costs, all of which are allocable to the production and sale of refrigerators. The company had $20 million of gross sales in year one. Will the company be able to deduct all of the year one expenditures in year one?

5. Wilma's Widget Company manufactures widgets that are generally not sold until at least a year after they are produced. Determine which of the following expenditures must be capitalized and included in the cost of the widgets produced.
   a. The company spent $120,000 on salaries for the production line employees.
   b. The company bought a widget manufacturing machine for $1 million.
   c. The company spent $20,000 to insure the widget machine.
   d. The company spent $1,200 on repairs for the widget machine.
   e. The company spent $30,000 on research and development of improved widgets.
   f. The company spent $50,000 on advertising its new line of widgets.

6. Bob's Publishing Company publishes the Surfer's Almanac yearly. The costs of publishing the book are incurred at least a year before the books

are sold. For example, in year five the company worked exclusively on the year six edition. The company's year five expenditures included $25,000 for the salary of Cathy, Bob's research assistant, $15,000 for secretarial services, $5,000 for the copyright to a surfer's manuscript, and $10,000 for printing and binding. How much of these expenses must be capitalized under §263A?

7. Sarah writes articles and novels that she sells to different publishing companies. In year one she worked on two projects: an article about Portugal for a travel magazine and a romance novel for Jester Romance Books Company. She incurred $5,000 in expenses related to the article and $10,000 in expenses related to the novel. How much of her expenditures must be capitalized under §263A?

8. a. Jose has a national chain of balloon retail outlets. He buys the balloons wholesale rather than manufacturing them himself. In year one his business had gross sales of $16 million and incurred the following expenses: $1 million on salaries for his purchasing agents; $50,000 on payroll taxes; $80,000 on general business planning; $2 million on rent for the balloon stores; and $8 million on wholesale balloons. How much of these expenditures must be capitalized under §263A?

   b. How, if at all, would your answer in part (a) change if Jose's business had average annual gross sales of $9 million?

Explanations

2. a. The copyright to "Stormy Weather" has a useful life of more than one year, so the cost of purchasing the copyright must be capitalized. §263(a), Reg. §1.263(a)-4(c)(1)(vii).

   b. A photocopying machine has a useful life of more than one year, so the cost of purchasing the machine must be capitalized. §263, Reg. §1.263(a)-2.

   c. The cost of the paper may be deducted currently. Supplies that are used up in the taxable year in which they are purchased are immediately deductible because they provide no benefit beyond the current taxable year. Taxpayers who do not keep track of when incidental supplies are used are allowed to deduct the cost of such supplies even if they are not actually used up during the taxable year. Reg. §§1.162-3, 1.263(a)-2(c)(2). This rule is designed to simplify matters for taxpayers who do not perform a year-end inventory of supplies.

   d. The cost of the incidental repairs and maintenance may be deducted currently, even though the benefit may extend over several years. Reg. §§1.162-4, 1.263(a)-3.

   e. The costs of acquiring the property, including these legal fees, must be capitalized. Reg. §1.263(a)-2(f).

f. The decision to expand overseas might be expected to produce benefits over many years. Costs of planning such an expansion, therefore, might logically be treated as capital expenditures.

   The capitalization of general planning costs, however, would raise a number of difficult issues. Should the restaurant chain be allowed to depreciate the expansion study costs? Should a portion of the costs be allocated to each overseas restaurant and be recovered if and when the restaurant is sold? Or should the costs be recoverable only on the sale of the entire overseas operation? Mindful of these issues, courts generally have allowed a current deduction for the costs of such studies. See, e.g., Young & Rubicam, Inc. v. United States, 410 F.2d 1233 (Ct. Cl. 1969) (permitting current deduction of salaries paid to employees to investigate a possible expansion into foreign markets).

   The Preamble to T.D. 9107 notes a concern, expressed by commentators, that Regulation §§1.263(a)-4 and -5 should be consistent with the business expansion cases. The regulations appear to require capitalization of some investigatory costs, however. The regulations provide generally that taxpayers must capitalize the transaction costs of facilitating (i) the acquisition or creation of intangible assets, (ii) the acquisition of a trade or business, or (iii) a change in the capital structure of a business entity. Regulation §§1.263(a)-4(e)(1) and -5(b) both state "an amount is paid to facilitate [a capital transaction] if the amount is paid in the process of investigating or otherwise pursuing the transaction." However, Regulation §1.263(a)-4(e)(1)(iii) states that an amount is not capitalized if it relates to activities performed prior to negotiations with other parties or the preparation of a bid, and Regulation §1.263(a)-5(e) provides a similar rule with respect to business acquisitions. In addition, the regulations provide that employee compensation and general overhead expenses are not treated as amounts that facilitate a transaction. Reg. §§1.263(a)-4(e)(4), -5(d).

g. The costs of commissions paid to acquire securities must be capitalized. Reg. §1.263(a)-4(e)(1), -4(e)(4)(iii)(B).

3. None of these expenditures are currently deductible. The costs associated with erecting a building, including architect's fees, and the cost of furniture and fixtures, must be capitalized. Reg. §1.263(a)-2(d)(1). These are all costs associated with the acquisition or construction of property with a useful life that extends beyond the close of the year in which the costs were incurred. However, beginning in the year in which the building is placed in service, Pete's Big Business, Inc. could recover its investment in the building (for tax purposes) by taking annual depreciation deductions over the useful life of the building.

4. No. This company is subject to the §263A UNICAP rules because it produces goods for sale to customers. Section 263A requires capitalization of expenditures associated with the production of goods for sale. Such expenses are reflected in the taxpayer's inventory costs (i.e., cost of goods sold), so they are deducted when the refrigerators are sold. Unless there are no refrigerators left in the company's inventory at the end of year one, §263A will prevent the company from fully deducting all of the year one expenditures. The costs of materials and labor incurred in producing the goods are "direct costs" and the warehousing costs are "indirect costs" allocable to the goods. §263A, Reg. §1.263A-1(e)(2)(i)(A), (B), (3)(ii)(H).

5. a. Direct labor costs must be capitalized, so these costs will be part of the taxpayer's inventory costs (i.e., cost of goods sold). Reg. §1.263A-1(e)(2)(i)(B).
   b. Since the widget machine has a useful life of many years, it must be capitalized under §263(a). The taxpayer will then take depreciation deductions with respect to the machine. The depreciation deductions will be part of the taxpayer's inventory costs. Reg. §1.263A-1(e)(3)(ii)(I).

      Suppose, for example, that the widget machine costs $100,000 and has a useful life of 10 years. If straight line depreciation were taken over the 10-year period, the company could depreciate $10,000 of the cost each year. The $10,000 of depreciation could not, however, be deducted immediately. Instead, it would be capitalized and recovered as part of the "cost of goods sold" when the widgets are sold.
   c. Insurance on machinery or equipment used to produce goods for resale must be capitalized and can be recovered as part of the taxpayer's cost of goods sold. Reg. §1.263A-1(e)(3)(ii)(M).
   d. The costs of repairing machinery used to produce goods for resale must be capitalized and can be recovered as part of the taxpayer's cost of goods sold. Reg. §1.263A-1(e)(3)(ii)(O).
   e. Research and development costs generally are currently deductible. §§174, 263A(c)(2).
   f. Advertising costs do not have to be capitalized and are thus currently deductible. Reg. §1.263A-1(e)(3)(iii)(A). (The cost of advertising is currently deductible even if the purpose of the advertising is to create goodwill.)

6. Section 263A applies to property produced by the taxpayer only if the property is real or tangible property. §263A(b)(1). Tangible property, however, includes books, films, and sound recordings so all of the expenditures must be capitalized. Although research costs generally are currently deductible, the costs of researching the year six almanac have to be capitalized. The publisher's costs for the copyright, direct labor costs, and direct costs of producing the year six almanac must also be capitalized.

§263A(a), Reg. §1.263A-2(a)(2)(ii)(A)(1). Thus, all of the costs will be included in the publisher's cost of goods sold when the year six almanac is sold.

7. Section 263A does not apply to freelance authors, photographers, and artists, so she does not have to capitalize her expenses and can deduct them currently. §263A(h).

8. a. All of the costs except the $80,000 expense for general business planning. Salaries of purchasing agents, payroll taxes, costs of acquiring goods for resale, and rent are all inventory costs. All of these expenditures relating to the resale of the balloons must be capitalized. Reg. §1.263A-1(e)(2), (3)(ii)(K). Costs that are not incurred in connection with the resale of the balloons, such as general business planning costs, can be deducted currently. Reg. §1.263A-1(e)(4)(iv)(B).
   b. Section 263A does not apply to wholesalers and retailers with average annual gross receipts of less than $10 million. §263A(b)(2)(B).

C. REPAIR AND MAINTENANCE EXPENSES

Reading: Reg. §§1.162-4, 1.263(a)-3.

The fundamental principle of capitalization is easily stated: Expenditures that produce a benefit that does not extend beyond the year in which the expenses were incurred do not have to be capitalized, but expenses that produce a benefit that has a useful life that extends beyond the year in which the expenses were incurred must be capitalized. Applying the rule is more difficult.

One of the most perplexing problems is distinguishing between repairs and capital improvements. Suppose a business replaces the leaky roof on its office building with a new one. Is the cost of the new roof a capital expenditure because it will last for many years? Or is it a current expenditure because it restores the building to its prior operating condition?

The determination of whether a particular expenditure is a deductible repair is made on a facts-and-circumstances basis. The cases on this issue (and other capitalization issues) are often difficult to reconcile. Consider, for example, the following two cases.

In Midland Empire Packing Co. v. Commissioner, 14 T.C. 635 (1950), the taxpayer used the basement of its meat packing plant to store and cure meats. In the tax year at issue, oil from a newly constructed refinery began to seep through the walls of the plant basement, creating a health hazard that caused federal meat inspectors to threaten to shut down the plant. In order to avoid a plant shutdown, the taxpayer paid about $5,000 to line the basement walls with concrete. The Tax Court concluded that the addition of the concrete lining was a repair, not a capital improvement, because adding the lining merely permitted the taxpayer to keep doing what it had been doing for 25 years before the oil seepage occurred.

In contrast, in Mt. Morris Drive-In Theatre Co. v. Commissioner, 25 T.C. 272 (1955), the taxpayer was denied a current deduction for the cost of a drainage system it installed to stop runoff to nearby land. The runoff had increased as a result of clearing land during construction of the taxpayer's drive-in theater. The taxpayer argued that installation of the drainage system was a repair and that the cost of the system was therefore currently deductible. However, the court concluded that the need for the drainage system was foreseeable at the time the taxpayer constructed the drive-in theater, so the cost of the drainage system had to be capitalized.

In September 2013, the IRS and Treasury issued final regulations, under §§162 and 263(a), that synthesized various tests and factors courts have considered for purposes of distinguishing between repairs and improvements. (Note that the term "amounts paid," as used in these regulations, incorporates a requirement that the liability paid has accrued under the taxpayer's method of accounting. Reg. §§1.162-3(c)(5), 1.263(a)-1(c)(1), -3(b)(1). In other words, the amounts deductible by an accrual method taxpayer are subject to the economic performance requirement of §461(h), discussed in Chapter 3.)

The regulations provide a safe harbor for "routine maintenance," which the regulations define as recurring activities (e.g., inspection, cleaning, testing, and replacement of component parts) that a taxpayer expects to perform to maintain the property in its "ordinarily efficient operating condition." Reg. §1.263(a)-3(i). (Note that costs that are deductible under the safe harbor will, in some circumstances, have to be capitalized nonetheless under the separate capitalization requirement of §263A.) The following factors are relevant for purposes of determining whether amounts are paid for routine maintenance: (i) the recurring nature of the activity; (ii) industry practice; (iii) manufacturer's recommendations; and (iv) the taxpayer's experience with similar or identical property. Id. Maintenance is "routine" only if a taxpayer expects to perform the activities more than once during the class life of the property. Id. The safe harbor applies to maintenance performed on rotable parts and temporary spare parts, but a taxpayer generally cannot deduct the costs of *acquiring* such parts until they are discarded. Reg. §§1.162-3(a), 1.263(a)-3(i)(2).

If the maintenance activities do not qualify for the safe harbor, they are subject to a three-part "improvement" test. Regulation §1.263(a)-3 provides that costs "improve" property, and must be capitalized, if the amounts paid: (i) result in a "betterment" of the property; (ii) "restore" the property; or (iii) adapt the property to a new or different use. Reg. §1.263(a)-3(d).

The regulation provides that an amount paid results in the *betterment* of property only if the amount paid: (i) ameliorates a material condition or defect that existed at the time the taxpayer acquired the property or the property was produced; (ii) results in a material addition (i.e., enlargement, expansion, or extension) to the property; or (iii) results in a material increase in productivity, efficiency, strength, or quality of the property or its output. Reg. §1.263(a)-3(j)(1). The determination of whether an amount paid results in a betterment is made by comparing: (i) the condition of the property just before the event (either normal wear and tear or a particular event) that made the maintenance necessary; and (ii) the condition of the property after the maintenance. Reg. §1.263(a)-3(j)(2)(iv). If a replacement part is not available and a taxpayer replaces the defective part with a similar but better part, that fact alone will not result in a material increase in the value of the property. Reg. §1.263(a)-3(j)(2)(iii).

An amount paid "restores" property and must be capitalized if the amount paid: (i) is for a component the cost of which the taxpayer has deducted as a loss or as a basis offset to gain; (ii) is to repair property for which the taxpayer has taken a §165 casualty loss; (iii) returns the property to its ordinarily efficient operating condition, if the property no longer can function for its intended use; (iv) results in the rebuilding of the property to a like-new condition following the end of its useful life; or (v) is to replace "a major component or a substantial structural part" of the property. Reg. §1.263(a)-3(k)(1). The regulations define a major component as a non-incidental part or combination of parts that performs a discrete and critical function in the operation of the unit of property. Reg. §1.263(a)-3(k)(6)(i)(A). A substantial structural part is a part or combination of parts that comprises a "large portion" of the physical structure of the unit of property.

Regulation §1.263(a)-3 also provides that taxpayers must capitalize the costs of adapting property to a new or different use. Reg. §1.263(a)-3(l). A use is "new or different" if it varies from the taxpayer's original use of the property. Id.

Before applying these tests, the taxpayer must first determine the appropriate "unit of property" to which the rules in the regulations are to be applied. Reg. §1.263(a)-3(e). The unit of property affects the characterization and deductibility of maintenance expenses; the larger the unit of property, the less likely it will be that maintenance performed on components of that property will result in improvement of the property. The regulation generally adopts a "functional interdependence" test to determine the appropriate unit of property; under this test, "[c]omponents of property are functionally interdependent if the placing in service of one component by the taxpayer is dependent on the placing in service of the other component by the taxpayer." Reg. §1.263(a)-3(e)(3)(i).

The regulation provides several exceptions to the general rule. A component is treated as a separate unit of property if the depreciation method used to depreciate the component is different from the depreciation method used to depreciate the property of which the component is a part. Reg. §1.263(a)-3(e)(5)(i). Also, a special rule provides that buildings and the structural components of buildings (other than a lessee's leasehold improvements) comprise a single unit of property. Reg. §1.263(a)-3(e)(2). In addition, a special rule applicable to plant property provides that a component or group of components that perform a discrete and major function or operation can comprise a separate unit of property. Reg. §1.263(a)-3(e)(3)(ii)(B).

The costs of repairs that are deductible under §§263(a) and 162 may have to be capitalized under §263A (discussed in the previous section of this chapter). Repair costs are generally classified as indirect costs and are allocable to inventory or produced property if the costs directly benefit production activities or are incurred by reason of production or resale activities. Reg. §1.263A-1(e)(3)(i), (ii)(O). Repair costs that are not allocable to inventory or produced property do not have to be capitalized under §263A. The §263A capitalization rule also can apply to the costs of improvements that must be capitalized under §263(a). Reg. §1.263(a)-3(c)(1).

Examples

9. Dr. Tan, an acupuncturist, owns the business office building in which his acupuncture practice is located. The building, which was built in the traditional Craftsman style, has a wooden shingle roof. At the beginning of the current year, wind and rain from a storm damaged the roof of the building. Determine whether each of the following expenditures incurred with respect to the building is currently deductible as a repair or maintenance expense.

   a. The cost of replacing the roof shingles with new wooden roof shingles

   b. The cost of replacing the roof shingles with new asphalt shingles, which must be used in place of the wooden shingles because the original wooden shingles are no longer available

   c. The cost of replacing all of the roof sheathing, which had rotted, and some weakened roof rafters, along with the cost of replacing the roof shingles with new wooden roof shingles

10. Friendly Skies Airline (FSA) maintains a fleet of commercial aircraft to transport passengers and cargo. When FSA purchases an aircraft, it purchases the aircraft engine separately. The engine manufacturer provides FSA with a separate warranty and written maintenance policy for

the engine. For financial accounting purposes, FSA keeps separate accounts for each type of aircraft frame and engine in its fleet. The FAA mandates regular maintenance on the aircraft frames and engines. One type of FAA-mandated maintenance is an engine shop visit (ESV), which is performed on FSA's engines every four years.

FSA purchased an aircraft frame and engine in year one. In year five, FSA removes the engine from the aircraft and ships the engine to a vendor who performs the ESV. During the ESV, the vendor disassembles the engine, checks the component parts, and repairs defective parts, if possible. If a timely repair is not possible, the vendor replaces the defective part with a used part from FSA's customer stock of used parts or a used part from the vendor's inventory.

Another regularly scheduled maintenance visit is a heavy mainte-nance visit (HMV), which is performed on FSA's aircraft frames every eight years. During the HMV, the entire aircraft frame is disassembled and all of its major and minor component parts are checked. Many minor structural parts are lubricated, repaired, or replaced. In addition, the interior passenger area of the aircraft frame is cleaned and repaired and the aircraft frame is painted.

In year 24, when the aircraft frame is due for an HMV, FSA decides to substantially modify the frame of the aircraft; the maintenance includes replacement of fuselage panels, wiring, metal supports, rivets, passenger seats, overhead bins, partitions, carpeting, windows, galleys, lavatories, and ceiling panels. In addition, FSA pays for installation of a cabin smoke and fire detection system, a ground proximity warning system, new avionics and cockpit equipment, and new paint on the aircraft exterior. At the same time, FSA pays for the scheduled mainte-nance work that would ordinarily be performed during an HMV.

a. Is FSA allowed to currently deduct the cost of the ESV in year five?
b. Is FSA allowed to currently deduct the cost of the aircraft modifica-tions in year 24?
c. Is FSA allowed to currently deduct the cost of the HMV in year 24?

Explanations

9. a. Dr. Tan does not have to capitalize the cost of replacing the wooden shingles. The appropriate unit of property is the building and its struc-tural components. Reg. §1.263(a)-3(e)(2). Dr. Tan must capitalize the cost of the new wooden roof shingles under §263(a) if the replace-ment shingles "improve" the building. The new wooden shingles improve the building if they: (i) result in a "betterment" of the prop-erty; (ii) "restore" the property; or (iii) adapt the property to a new or different use. Reg. §1.263(a)-3(d).

An amount paid results in the betterment of property only if the amount paid: (i) ameliorates a material condition or defect that existed at the time the taxpayer acquired the property or the property was produced; (ii) results in a material addition (i.e., enlargement, expansion, or extension) to the property; or (iii) results in a material increase in productivity, efficiency, strength, or quality of the property or its output. Reg. §1.263(a)-3(j)(1).

To determine whether the new shingles result in a betterment of the building, Dr. Tan compares the condition of the building immediately after installation of the new shingles with the condition of the building just before the storm, the external event that necessitated the roof repair. Reg. §1.263(a)-3(j)(2)(iv)(A). The building was functioning for its intended use before the storm. The amounts paid to replace the wooden roof shingles did not ameliorate a preexisting condition or defect and did not result in a material addition to the property or a material increase in the productivity, or quality of the property. The amounts paid thus did not result in a betterment of the property. Reg. §1.263(a)-3(j)(3), Example 13.

The new wooden roof does not restore the building to a like-new condition (provided that Dr. Tan did not take a casualty loss deduction for the storm damage) and does not prolong the building's useful life. Reg. §1.263(a)-3(k). The roof shingles do not constitute a major structural component of the building. In addition, the new shingles do not adapt the property for a new or different use; thus the cost of the replacing the wooden roof shingles does not have to be capitalized under §263(a). Reg. §1.263(a)-3(l).

b. The result is the same as in part (a). If an exact replacement part is not available and the taxpayer substitutes a comparable but slightly better part, that substitution does not result in an improvement of the property. Reg. §1.263(a)-3(j)(2)(iii).

c. In this example, the sheathing and rafters are replaced, in addition to the shingles. Regulation §1.263(a)-3(k)(1) provides that taxpayers must capitalize amounts paid to restore property, which includes replacing "a major component or a substantial structural part of the unit of property." The entire roof structure, which includes the shingles, sheathing, rafters, and joists, seems to be a substantial structural part of a building. Under the regulations, the roof is both a major component, because it performs a discrete and critical function in the operation of the building (keeping out the rain), and a substantial structural part because it comprises a large portion of the building. Reg. §1.263(a)-3(k)(7), Example 14. The regulations require that the cost of repairing a "significant portion" of a major component of a building must be capitalized. Reg. §1.263(a)-3(k)(6)(ii)(A). On these facts it seems likely that a significant portion of the roof is being repaired. Thus, the cost of replacing most of the roof is a restoration and must be capitalized.

10. a. The facts of this example are based on FedEx Corp. v. United States, 291 F. Supp. 2d 699 (W.D. Tenn. 2003), aff'd, 412 F.3d 617 (6th Cir. 2005). In the FedEx case, the court held that the unit of property was the aircraft and FedEx could currently deduct the cost of the ESV as a repair.

Regulation §1.263(a)-3 includes examples based on the FedEx ESV fact pattern. The regulation also reaches the conclusion that the airline does not have to capitalize the cost of the ESV. Reg. §1.263(a)-3(i)(6), Example 1. The regulation treats the entire aircraft as the appropriate unit of property and the aircraft engine as a rotable component part. The regulation concludes that the ESV is within the Regulation §1.263(a)-3(i) safe harbor for routine maintenance because: (i) the ESVs involve routine maintenance activities (e.g., disassembly, inspection, cleaning, repair, and replacement of parts with comparable parts); (ii) the airline expects to perform the ESVs more than once during the class life of the aircraft; and (iii) the airline performs the ESVs to keep the aircraft in ordinarily efficient working condition.

b. The facts of this example are based on Rev. Rul. 2001-4, Situation 3. In the Revenue Ruling, the IRS ruled that capitalization was required because the substantial modifications resulted in the replacement of major structural elements of the aircraft frame with new parts and upgraded and added major components. The result is probably the same under the regulations. The modifications are not within the routine maintenance safe harbor and probably "improve" the property under the three-part improvement test. The extensive modifications constitute a "betterment" of the property because they result in a material increase in the quality of the property. Reg. §1.263(a)-3(j)(1). In addition, the modifications may "restore" the property because they may either rebuild the property to a like-new condition or replace a major component or a substantial structural part of the property. The frame is a major component because it performs a discrete and critical function of the aircraft. In addition, it is also likely a substantial structural part because it is a large portion of the structure of the aircraft.

c. The analysis of the HMV for the aircraft frame, as a separate maintenance procedure, is similar to the analysis of the ESV for the aircraft engine in part (a). If the HMV had been performed at a different time than the modifications, FSA would not have to capitalize the cost of the HMV because the HMV is within the routine maintenance safe harbor. Reg. §1.263(a)-3(i)(6), Example 1, Rev. Rul. 2001-4, Situation 1. The fact that the routine maintenance is performed near or even beyond the end of the aircraft's useful life does not change the result. Reg. §1.263(a)-3(i)(6), Example 2.

In this example, the HMV is performed in conjunction with modifications that probably constitute an improvement of the aircraft frame, which may alter the deductibility of the amounts paid for the HMV. Section 263A applies to property "produced" by the taxpayer, and an improvement is treated as production. §263A(b)(1), (g)(1). The cost of the aircraft frame improvement is subject to 263A. Furthermore, Rev. Rul. 2001-4 provides that the deductible HMV repair costs must be capitalized, as "indirect costs" *of the aircraft improvements*, under the separate capitalization rules of §263A, to the extent the HMV repair costs directly benefit or are incurred by reason of the improvement to the aircraft frame. The airline does not have to capitalize the rest of the amounts paid for the HMV.

D. INVENTORY ACCOUNTING

Reading: §§446, 471, 472; Reg. §§1.446-1, 1.471-1, -2, -3, -4, 1.472-1, -2.

As we saw earlier in this chapter, a taxpayer may deduct the costs of incidental materials and supplies, such as paper for a copying machine, in the year they were purchased. However, a taxpayer who keeps an inventory of goods for sale must capitalize the costs of supplies and materials instead of immediately deducting them; the costs are added to the taxpayer's inventory costs and deducted when the inventory is sold.

Taxpayers must use inventories for tax purposes if use of inventories is necessary to clearly reflect the taxpayer's income. §471(a). The idea is to match income with the expense of producing that income. Regulation §1.471-1 requires a taxpayer to use inventories if (i) the taxpayer produces, purchases, or sells merchandise and (ii) the production, purchase, or sale of such merchandise is an income-producing factor. *Merchandise* is defined as property held for sale to customers. For example, in Wilkinson-Beane, Inc. v. Commissioner, 420 F.2d 352 (1st Cir. 1970), the court held that an undertaker that sold complete funeral packages at fixed prices (around 15 percent of which was attributable to the cost of the casket) had to use inventories to account for its sales of caskets because the caskets were merchandise and the sale of the caskets was an income-producing factor in the taxpayer's business.

Section 471 and Regulation §1.471-1 thus require manufacturers, wholesalers, and retailers to use inventories. Taxpayers who must use inventories are also required to use the accrual method of accounting with respect to purchases and sales. Reg. §1.446-1(c)(2)(i). There are some exceptions to the general rule that requires use of inventories and the accrual method of accounting. For example, there is an exception for certain small taxpayers, including: (i) taxpayers with average annual gross receipts of $1 million or less and (ii) taxpayers, in specific industries, with average annual gross receipts of $10 million or less. See, e.g., Rev. Proc. 2001-10 and Rev. Proc. 2002-28 (both amplified and modified, in part, by various subsequent technical revenue procedures on changes in accounting methods). In addition, taxpayers who are required to account for their inventory purchases and sales using the accrual method of accounting may still be able to use the cash method of accounting for other types of income or costs or for separate businesses. Reg. §1.446-1(c)(1)(iv), (d).

Recall that §61(a)(2) provides that gross income includes "gross income derived from business." For a taxpayer who uses inventories, gross income derived from business equals gross receipts from sales less the taxpayer's *cost of goods sold*. Reg. §1.61-3(a). Cost of goods sold is equal to the cost of the inventory at the beginning of the taxable year (*opening inventory*), plus the cost of goods purchased during the year (*purchases* or, if goods are produced, the cost of such goods, *additions*), less the cost of the inventory remaining at the end of the year (*closing inventory*). The idea is to match the cost of goods sold by the taxpayer with the income from the sale of those goods. Expressed as formulae, cost of goods sold and gross income from inventory sales are calculated as follows:

$$
\begin{array}{l}
\text{Opening inventory} \\
+ \ \underline{\text{Purchases/additions during the year}} \\
\text{Goods available for sale}
\end{array}
$$

$$
\begin{array}{l}
\text{Goods available for sale} \\
- \ \underline{\text{Closing inventory}} \\
\text{Cost of goods sold}
\end{array}
$$

$$
\begin{array}{l}
\text{Gross receipts from sales} \\
- \ \underline{\text{Cost of goods sold}} \\
\text{Gross income from inventory sales}
\end{array}
$$

Opening inventory equals the value of the closing inventory from the previous year. Purchases/additions for the year are taken into account at their cost, determined from invoices. Merchandise is reflected in inventory when the taxpayer has title to the merchandise. Inventory costs that are capitalized under the §263A UNICAP rules (for example, warehousing costs, selling costs, direct labor costs, and indirect labor costs allocated to production or sales activities) are also added to the cost of the merchandise.

In order to compute the value of closing inventory, a taxpayer must first count the number of units in the inventory at the close of the tax year. The taxpayer can either physically count the units or use "book inventories," provided that the book inventories are verified by physical inventories at reasonable intervals. Reg. §1.471-2(d). The taxpayer must then determine the cost of the units in the closing inventory. If the taxpayer's costs for inventory were constant, the taxpayer could just count the units and multiply the number of units by the constant cost. However, inventory costs fluctuate, so the taxpayer must determine the cost of the units in the closing inventory by using one of several methods.

If a taxpayer can identify the actual cost for the goods in closing inventory, the taxpayer can calculate the cost of the closing inventory on that basis. For example, a fine jewelry store with one-of-a-kind items in its inventory may be able to use this method. However, taxpayers cannot typically use the specific identification method because the inventory includes too many fungible items.

Typically a taxpayer determines the cost of its closing inventory by applying either the *first-in-first-out* (FIFO) method or the *last-in-first-out* (LIFO) method. Both of these methods are fictions; they are simply conventions that are used to determine the value of the taxpayer's closing inventory. The FIFO method applies unless a taxpayer makes an election to apply LIFO. §472. A taxpayer who uses LIFO for tax purposes must also use it for financial reporting purposes. §472(c).

The FIFO method assumes that the items sold during the year are the earliest items purchased, and that the items left in closing inventory at the end of the year are the most recently purchased items. A taxpayer using FIFO may compute the value of its closing inventory using the *lower of cost or market* method to value the inventory. Reg. §1.471-2(c). A taxpayer who uses the lower of cost or market method would: (i) calculate the cost of the units in the closing inventory, using FIFO; (ii) calculate the "market" price (generally replacement cost) of the units in closing inventory; and (iii) use the lower amount as the value of the closing inventory. Reg. §1.471-4.

What is the effect of using the lower of cost or market method on the taxpayer's cost of goods sold and gross income? If inventory prices have risen, the lower of cost or market will be the cost, so the use of the lower of cost or market method will not have any effect on the taxpayer's cost of goods sold or gross income. On the other hand, if inventory prices have declined so that the market value of the inventory is less than its cost, using the market value reduces the closing inventory, which increases the taxpayer's cost of goods sold and, in turn, reduces the taxpayer's gross income. In effect, allowing a taxpayer to use the lower of cost or market method, in conjunction with FIFO, permits the taxpayer to anticipate a loss on the inventory before it is sold.

The market value of the inventory is generally the replacement cost of the inventory. Reg. §1.471-4. However, the general replacement cost rule does not apply if: (i) goods are defective or obsolete or (ii) there have been offers to sell and actual sales at a price that is less than the replacement cost (in which case the goods should be valued at the price at which the goods are actually sold). Reg. §§1.471-2(c), -4(b). In Thor Power Tool Co. v. Commissioner, 439 U.S. 522 (1979), the taxpayer valued its inventory using the lower of cost or market method. The taxpayer decided that it had "excess" inventory and reduced its closing inventory to "net realizable value" (in effect, scrap value), which resulted in a $900,000 write-down of the inventory. The write-down amount was calculated by management of the taxpayer, based on their business expertise, not on the replacement cost of the inventory. The taxpayer kept the excess inventory on hand and did not reduce the price at which it sold the inventory. The Service disallowed the inventory write-down, arguing that the taxpayer's inventory method did not clearly reflect income under §§446(b) and 471. The taxpayer offered no objective evidence to support the write-down; in fact, the taxpayer continued to sell the inventory at its original price. However, the write-down taken by the taxpayer did conform to financial accounting principles. After noting that financial accounting rules do not control the tax treatment of inventories, the Court held that the Commissioner had not abused his discretion in disallowing the writedown because the write-down appeared to be based on the subjective estimates of management of the taxpayer.

The LIFO method assumes that the items sold are the most recently purchased items and that the items in closing inventory are the earliest items purchased. A taxpayer using LIFO is not permitted to use the lower of cost or market method; the taxpayer must use cost to determine the closing inventory. §472(b), Reg. §1.472-2(b). Using LIFO in a period of rising inventory costs decreases the taxpayer's closing inventory, which increases the taxpayer's cost of goods sold and, in turn, decreases the taxpayer's gross income. In other words, in a period of rising prices, LIFO produces more favorable tax results than FIFO. However, the vast majority of taxpayers with inventories use FIFO because §472(c) requires that taxpayers who use LIFO for tax purposes also use LIFO for financial accounting purposes (for example, in reports to shareholders and creditors). For financial accounting purposes, taxpayers want high gross income so they frequently do not want to use LIFO if inventory costs are rising. There are pending proposals to repeal use of LIFO, for tax purposes, in part to raise more tax revenue. Even if use of LIFO is not repealed, it may become uncommon if U.S. financial accounting rules (i.e., Generally Accepted Accounting Principles) converge with International Financial Reporting Standards, which prohibit the use of LIFO for financial reporting.

Examples

11. Is each of the following statements true or false?
    a. Taxpayers who keep inventories generally may use either the cash or accrual method of accounting.
    b. Inventory purchases are currently deductible as a cost of earning income.

12. On January 1, year two, Jack's Piano Palace had $100,000 worth of pianos in inventory. During the year, Jack purchased pianos for $400,000. On December 31, year two, Jack's Piano Palace had $30,000 of inventory left. Jack's gross receipts for year two totaled $850,000. Determine the cost of goods sold and Jack's gross profit for year two.

13. M&M Enterprises, a commodity and institutional food services company, purchases 100,000 bushels of wheat for $200,000 in December, year one. In January, year two, M&M Enterprises purchases another 100,000 bushels of wheat for $300,000. In June, year two, M&M Enterprises sells 100,000 bushels of wheat for $350,000.
    a. Assume M&M Enterprises uses the LIFO method. Determine the amount of M&M Enterprises' cost of goods sold and gross income from sales for year two.
    b. Assume M&M Enterprises uses the FIFO method. Determine the amount of M&M Enterprises' cost of goods sold and gross income from sales for year two.
    c. Would you advise M&M Enterprises to use LIFO or FIFO?

14. a. In January of year one Products Inc. commences operations and purchases 20,000 widgets for $200,000 ($10 per widget). In March of year one Products Inc. purchases another 20,000 widgets for $300,000 ($15 per widget). In May of year one Products Inc. sells 30,000 widgets for $600,000 ($20 per widget). Developments in the second half of year one cause the value of widgets to fall. The 10,000 widgets left in inventory at the close of the year have a wholesale value of only $50,000 ($5 per widget). Assume that Products Inc. uses FIFO and does not value closing inventory at the lower of cost or market. Determine the company's year one cost of goods sold and gross income from widget sales.
    b. How, if at all, does your answer in part (a) change if Products Inc. uses the lower of cost or market method?
    c. What effect does use of the lower of cost or market method have on the year one gross income from sales?

15. Is each of the following statements true or false?
    a. The LIFO method of inventory accounting will result in higher taxable income in a period in which the cost of inventory is rising.

b. Taxpayers using either the FIFO or LIFO methods may choose to determine closing inventory using the lower of cost or market method.

c. Taxpayers who use the LIFO method for tax purposes must also use the LIFO method for financial accounting purposes such as in reports to shareholders and creditors.

16. Willie's Widget shop opened early in year one. During year one Willie bought 10,000 widgets for $100,000 ($10 per widget) and sold 5,000 widgets for $75,000. In year two Willie bought 20,000 widgets for $300,000 ($15 per widget) and sold 15,000 widgets for $300,000.

   a. Determine Willie's gross income from sales in year one and year two using the FIFO method.

   b. Determine Willie's gross income from sales for year one and year two using the LIFO method.

17. Tammy's Thingamajig Emporium opened for business in year one. In January of year one Tammy bought 20,000 thingamajigs for $40,000 ($2 per unit). In March of year one Tammy sold 8,000 thingamajigs for $28,000. After March, a glut in the thingamajig market caused the market value of thingamajigs to fall to $1 per unit, and Tammy sold no more thingamajigs for the rest of the year.

   a. Determine Tammy's gross income from sales for year one using the FIFO method.

   b. Determine Tammy's gross income from sales for year one using the LIFO method.

Explanations

11. a. False. Regulation §1.446-1(c)(2) generally requires use of the accrual method for taxpayers who keep inventories.

    b. False. Inventory purchases constitute a nondeductible capital expenditure. The cost of inventory is deductible as an offset against sales proceeds.

12. Cost of goods sold equals opening inventory plus inventory purchases less closing inventory.

Opening inventory	$100,000
Plus inventory purchases	+$400,000
Less closing inventory	−$ 30,000
Cost of goods sold	$470,000

Gross income from sales equals gross receipts less the cost of goods sold.

Gross receipts	$850,000
Less cost of goods sold	−$470,000
Gross income from sales	$380,000

13. a. Under the LIFO method, sales are first attributed to the most recent purchases. Here, the most recent purchase of 100,000 bushels of wheat cost $300,000; M&M Enterprises is treated as having sold that wheat for $350,000. Thus, the closing inventory is the older wheat that was purchased for $200,000. M&M Enterprises' cost of goods sold is therefore $300,000, and its gross income from sales is $50,000. Represented another way:

Opening inventory	$200,000
Plus inventory purchases	+$300,000
Less closing inventory	−$200,000
Cost of goods sold	$300,000
Gross receipts	$350,000
Less cost of goods sold	−$300,000
Gross income from sales	$ 50,000

b. Under the FIFO method, sales are first attributed to the earliest purchases. Here, the earliest purchase costs $200,000; M&M Enterprises is treated as having sold that wheat for $350,000. Thus, the closing inventory is the newer wheat that was purchased for $300,000. M&M Enterprises' cost of goods sold is therefore $200,000, and its gross income from sales is $150,000. Represented another way:

Opening inventory	$200,000
Plus inventory purchases	+$300,000
Less closing inventory	−$300,000
Cost of goods sold	$200,000
Gross receipts	$350,000
Less cost of goods sold	−$200,000
Gross income from sales	$150,000

c. It depends on whether M&M would prefer to have (i) higher gross income for both tax and financial accounting purposes or (ii) lower gross income for both tax and financial accounting purposes. As we saw in parts (a) and (b), where the price of inventory is rising, the taxpayer's gross income from sales is lower using LIFO because LIFO increases the cost of goods sold. However, M&M may not want to use LIFO for tax purposes because it would then have to use LIFO for financial accounting purposes. §472(c). A business may prefer to use FIFO in order to show larger gross profits to shareholders and lenders, such as banks, even if it means paying higher taxes.

14. a. Cost of goods sold is determined by adding opening inventory to inventory purchases and subtracting closing inventory. Using FIFO, the earliest purchased items are the ones deemed sold, and the most recently purchased items are the ones deemed to be in the closing inventory. Here, the closing inventory includes 10,000 of the 20,000 widgets Products Inc. purchased in March of year one for $15 per widget.

   The closing inventory is $150,000 (10,000 widgets at $15 cost per widget), the cost of goods sold is $350,000, and the gross income from sales is $250,000.

Opening inventory	$ 0
Plus inventory purchases	+$500,000
Less closing inventory	−$150,000
Cost of goods sold	$350,000
Gross receipts	$600,000
Less cost of goods sold	−$350,000
Gross income from sales	$250,000

   b. As explained in part (a), the closing inventory is $150,000 (10,000 widgets at $15 cost per widget) if the taxpayer does not use the lower of cost or market method. The market value of the widgets left in closing inventory is $5 per widget, which is less than their $15 per widget cost, so here closing inventory will be determined using the $5 per widget market value.

   Here, the closing inventory is $50,000 (10,000 widgets at $5 market value), the cost of goods sold is $450,000, and the gross income from sales is $150,000.

Opening inventory	$ 0
Plus inventory purchases	+$500,000
Less closing inventory	−$ 50,000
Cost of goods sold	$450,000
Gross receipts	$600,000
Less cost of goods sold	−$450,000
Gross income from sales	$150,000

c. Using the lower of cost or market method to value closing inventory reduces the taxpayer's gross income from sales by $100,000. In effect, this method allows Products Inc. to deduct the unrealized decline in the value of the closing inventory before that inventory is sold.

15. a. False. Under LIFO, the more recent purchases are included in the cost of goods sold. In a period of rising prices, recent purchases will be more expensive than prior purchases. The LIFO method will therefore produce a higher cost of goods sold and lower gross income from sales.

   b. False. The election to value closing inventory at the lower of cost or market is only available to taxpayers who use the FIFO method. §472(b), Reg. §1.472-2(b).

   c. True. §472(c). This is the main reason taxpayers do not use LIFO, even though using LIFO would reduce their gross income from sales in periods of rising prices.

16. a. The FIFO method assumes that the first goods acquired for resale are the first goods sold so that closing inventory consists of the most recently purchased goods.

   For year one Willie's cost of goods sold equals $50,000, and his gross income from sales is $25,000.

Opening inventory	$ 0
Plus inventory purchases	+$100,000
Less closing inventory	−$ 50,000
Cost of goods sold	$ 50,000
Gross receipts	$ 75,000
Less cost of goods sold	−$ 50,000
Gross income from sales	$ 25,000

At the beginning of year two Willie's opening inventory is his closing inventory from year one, $50,000. The FIFO method assumes that these widgets are sold before any widgets that Willie purchased in year two. Therefore, of the 15,000 widgets sold in year two for $20 per widget, 5,000 were purchased in year one for $10 per widget and 10,000 were purchased in year two for $15 per widget. Said another way, the closing inventory at the end of year two is $150,000 (10,000 widgets at a cost of $15 per widget). The cost of goods sold in year two is $200,000, and the gross income from sales in year two is $100,000.

Opening inventory	$ 50,000
Plus inventory purchases	+$300,000
Less closing inventory	−$150,000
Cost of goods sold	$200,000
Gross receipts	$300,000
Less cost of goods sold	−$200,000
Gross income from sales	$100,000

b. For year one the closing inventory, cost of goods sold, and gross income from sales are the same as in part (a). The LIFO method assumes that the last goods acquired for resale are the first goods to be sold so that closing inventory is assumed to consist of the earliest purchased goods. Willie has no beginning inventory in year one and all of the goods purchased during year one were purchased at the same cost, so his closing inventory using LIFO is the same as his closing inventory using FIFO. This, in turn, means that Willie's cost of goods sold and gross income from sales for year one are also the same using LIFO.

At the beginning of year two, Willie has opening inventory of $50,000 (5,000 widgets in stock, each of which cost Willie $10). Since the LIFO method assumes that the most recently purchased goods are sold first, the widgets that Willie purchased in year two, at a cost of $15 per widget, are deemed to be sold before any of the widgets purchased in year one are deemed to be sold. Therefore, the 15,000 widgets sold in year two for $20 per widget all come from the stock purchased by Willie in year two for $15 per widget. Said another way, the closing inventory at the end of year two is $125,000 (5,000 unsold widgets that were purchased in year two at a cost of $15 per widget plus 5,000 unsold widgets that were purchased in year one at a cost of $10 per widget). The cost of goods sold in year two is $225,000 and the gross income from sales in year two is $75,000.

Opening inventory	$ 50,000
Plus inventory purchases	+$300,000
Less closing inventory	−$125,000
Cost of goods sold	$225,000
Gross receipts	$300,000
Less cost of goods sold	−$225,000
Gross income from sales	$ 75,000

17. a. A taxpayer using FIFO may value the inventory using either (i) cost or (ii) the lower of cost or market, provided that the same valuation method is used consistently. Reg. §§1.471-2.

If Tammy uses cost in valuing inventory, year one gross income from sales is $12,000.

Opening inventory	$ 0
Plus inventory purchases	+$40,000
Less closing inventory	−$24,000
Cost of goods sold	$16,000

Gross receipts	$28,000
Less cost of goods sold	−$16,000
Gross income from sales	$12,000

If Tammy uses the lower of cost or market method, year one gross income from sales is zero.

Opening inventory	$ 0
Plus inventory purchases	+$40,000
Less closing inventory	−$12,000
Cost of goods sold	$28,000

Gross receipts	$28,000
Less cost of goods sold	−$28,000
Gross income from sales	$ 0

b. Taxpayers using LIFO must use cost; they are not permitted to use the lower of cost or market method. §472(b).

If Tammy uses the LIFO method, gross income for year one will be $12,000, the same as in part (a) where cost was used to value the closing inventory, because all of the units purchased or left in closing inventory were purchased at the same price per unit.

E. RENT PAYMENTS VERSUS INSTALLMENT PURCHASE

If a taxpayer makes a series of payments in exchange for the use of business property, the series of payments may be characterized as either (i) an installment purchase of the business property or (ii) rental or lease payments for the property.

If the payments are characterized as an installment purchase of the business property, the purchaser of the property deducts (i) depreciation on the property and (ii) the portion of the installment payments that represents interest. §§163(a), 167, 168. The seller of the business property includes (i) the income from the sale of the property and (ii) the portion of the installment payments that represents interest. §§61(a)(2), (4), 453, 1001.

If the payments are characterized as lease payments, the lessee deducts the lease payment made and the lessor includes the lease payment in income. §§61(a)(5), 162.

Which treatment is more favorable to the taxpayer using the property and the taxpayer providing the property? It depends on a number of factors such as the taxpayers' tax brackets and the period of time over which the property would be depreciated. In some circumstances, installment purchase treatment reduces the combined tax owed by the two taxpayers. In other circumstances, lease treatment reduces the combined tax burden. Taxpayers often label their transaction a "lease" or an "installment purchase" according to which treatment produces the lower tax burden. The Service may challenge the taxpayer's characterization on the theory that the substance, not the form, of the transaction determines the tax consequences of the transaction.

In Starr's Estate v. Commissioner, 274 F.2d 294 (9th Cir. 1959), the taxpayer took the position that it had leased a fire sprinkler system that a sprinkler company had installed in the taxpayer's plant. The "lease" agreement provided that the taxpayer would pay the lessor $1,240 a year in years one through five (for a total of $6,200) and, if the taxpayer renewed the lease, $32 a year in years six through ten. The lease provided that, if the taxpayer did not renew the lease, the lessor would remove the property from the taxpayer's plant. The lease did not say what would happen beginning in the eleventh year. The taxpayer deducted the entire $1,240 of rent paid each year as a §162 expense.

The Service took the position that the "lease" was, in fact, an installment purchase of the sprinkler system and disallowed the taxpayer's deduction for the $1,240 annual lease payments. In the Service's view, the taxpayer was required to capitalize the cost of the property, $6,200, instead of deducting each payment. The useful life of the sprinkler system was 23 years, so under this approach the taxpayer would have been entitled to an annual deduction of around $270 ($6,200 cost of the property/ 23-year useful life).

The Ninth Circuit Court of Appeals held that the transaction was a sale, based on several facts. First, although the lease did not transfer title to the taxpayer, the court was skeptical that the lessor would ever retrieve the system, since sprinkler systems are typically made to fit a specific location and the salvage value of the system would therefore have been negligible. Second, in similar prior transactions, the lessor had not reclaimed the leased property after the lease term although the useful life of the property extended far beyond the original five-year term of the lease. Third, the amount of "rent" to be paid in years six through ten (after the original five-year term of the lease) was nominal. (The court characterized the $32 a year payment in years six through ten as a service charge for maintaining the system.)

The court did not, however, agree with the Commissioner that all of the $6,200 of payments had to be capitalized. The court instead concluded that a portion of the "lease" payments represented the purchase price of the system and a portion represented interest on the deferred payments. The sprinkler system typically was sold for $4,960, so the court treated that amount as the purchase price of the system and characterized the remainder of the payments, $1,240 ($6,200 less $4,960), as interest. The $4,960 deemed purchase price for the system had to be capitalized; because the system had a 23-year useful life, the annual depreciation deduction was around $216 ($4,960/23 years).

Since the annual payments were level, each of the payments included a partial payment of the $4,960 of principal owed and interest on the unpaid balance. Taking into account this amortization, the implicit interest rate was 7.93 percent and the year one interest was around $393. Thus, the taxpayer's total deductions for year one were $609 ($393 of interest plus $216 of depreciation), instead of the $1,240 amount that the taxpayer originally deducted as lease payments.

Under the taxpayer's original characterization of the transaction as a lease, the sprinkler company that installed the system would have included the lease payments in income and deducted depreciation based on the 23-year useful life of the property. If the sprinkler company had instead treated the transaction as a sale, it would have been able to deduct its costs for the system over a five-year period instead of over the longer useful life of the property. Thus, the tax benefits to Starr's Estate from characterizing the transaction as a lease were offset, at least to some extent, by a tax cost to the sprinkler company. Tax benefits to a lessee-purchaser and tax costs to a lessor-seller would generally offset each other to some extent, but in many cases they would not fully offset each other. For example, if the lessor/seller and the lessee/purchaser were in different tax brackets, the combined tax burden of the parties could be reduced by characterizing the transaction in the manner that assigns the largest possible tax deductions to the higher bracket taxpayer.

We will further develop this discussion later in this chapter when we examine the tax consequences of sale and leaseback transactions. For now, consider the following examples, which illustrate the principles discussed in this section.

Examples

18. An exclusive restaurant called Ma Grande Bouche leases a commercial refrigerator from Fanny's House of Refrigerators. The lease contract calls for rental payments of $700 per year for three years, at which time title to the refrigerator will be transferred to Ma Grande Bouche. (Assume that the useful life of the refrigerator is five years.) Will the lease be recharacterized as an installment purchase?

19. At the beginning of year one, Frieda's Flowers, Inc. leases a custom-built commercial greenhouse from AgriCo. This type of greenhouse has a useful life of 10 years and costs $40,000 to purchase. Assume that a taxpayer purchasing such a greenhouse would be entitled to take $4,000 a year of straight line depreciation on the greenhouse. The cost of maintaining the greenhouse is $1,000 per year. The lease contract calls for rental payments of $10,000 per year in years one through five with an option to renew the lease for $1,000 a year in years six through ten. Under the lease, AgriCo is responsible for maintaining the greenhouse. If Frieda's Flowers, Inc. does not exercise its option to renew the lease, AgriCo has three weeks to remove the greenhouse. The lease is silent as to what happens after the second five-year term.

    a. How much of the $10,000 of rent would Frieda's Flowers, Inc. deduct in year one if the lease is not recharacterized as an installment purchase?

    b. How much of the $10,000 of rent would Frieda's Flowers, Inc. be able to deduct in year one if the lease is recharacterized as an installment purchase?

    c. Will the lease be recharacterized as an installment purchase?

Explanations

18. This purported lease is fairly obviously a sale in substance since title passes to the restaurant at the end of the rental period and the useful life of the refrigerator extends beyond the lease term. Ma Grande Bouche will be deemed to be making an installment purchase and will not be able to deduct the "rental" payments. The restaurant will, however, be able to deduct imputed interest on the installment payment and depreciation on the refrigerator. See Oesterreich v. Commissioner, 226 F.2d 798 (9th Cir. 1955).

19. a. Frieda's Flowers, Inc. would deduct the entire $10,000 of rent as a §162 business expense.

    b. The deemed purchase price for the greenhouse is $40,000 and the greenhouse has a 10-year useful life, so Frieda's Flowers, Inc. could deduct $4,000 a year of straight line depreciation on the greenhouse. The flower company could also deduct interest on the unpaid balance of the purchase price. A portion of the $50,000 of payments to be made in years one through five would be characterized as interest. A greenhouse of this type usually sells for $40,000, so there is $10,000 of interest on the deferred payments. Since the annual payments were level, each of the five $10,000 payments would be deemed to include a partial payment of the $40,000 of principal owed and an interest payment on the unpaid balance. Frieda's Flowers, Inc. would take a total year one deduction of the portion of the $10,000 of interest allocable to year one plus $4,000 of depreciation instead of the $10,000 amount that Frieda's would otherwise deduct as lease payments.

c. Here title does not pass automatically to Frieda's Flowers, Inc. at the end of the rental period. In fact, the contract is silent as to what happens at the end of the rental period. However, some factors weigh in favor of recharacterizing the lease as an installment purchase: First, the entire rental cost is about the same as the purchase price plus interest. Second, the useful life of the greenhouse exceeds the initial five-year term of the lease. Third, the "rent" in years six through ten is nominal and seems to represent a service payment for maintaining the greenhouse. These facts look very similar to the facts in Starr's Estate v. Commissioner, 274 F.2d 294 (9th Cir. 1959), where the lease was recharacterized as a sale. The facts here differ from the facts in that case in one respect. In *Starr's Estate*, the court concluded that, despite the fact that the sprinkler company could remove the system if the lease were not renewed, the sprinkler company would probably not remove the sprinkler system because its salvage value was negligible. Here, it is not clear whether a used greenhouse has a negligible salvage value. However, the greenhouse here was "custom-built," so it may have little value to another user. On balance it seems likely that the lease would be recharacterized as an installment purchase.

F. GOODWILL AND OTHER INTANGIBLE ASSETS

Reading: §197; Reg. §1.167(a)-3.

In the famous case, Welch v. Helvering, 290 U.S. 111 (1933), the taxpayer claimed a §162 deduction when he paid his employer's debts that had been discharged in a bankruptcy proceeding. The taxpayer paid the discharged debts to improve his business reputation so that he could continue to work in the same profession. The court held that the taxpayer could not take a §162 deduction for the amounts paid on the discharged debts. Although much of the opinion is framed in terms of the §162 "ordinary and necessary" requirement, the strongest rationale for the holding in the case is that amounts paid by the taxpayer had to be capitalized because repayment of the discharged debts produced benefits to the taxpayer that extended beyond the year in which the payments were made. In other words, the taxpayer's expenditures were for goodwill.

Until 1993, no deduction or amortization was allowed for the acquisition and maintenance of goodwill. One explanation for this was the difficulty in determining the useful life over which goodwill should be amortized. The cost of advertising, on the other hand, traditionally has been immediately deductible even though advertising often increases residual goodwill. See, e.g., Rev. Rul. 92-80.

Section 197 (added to the Code in 1993) provides that "§197 intangibles" can be amortized ratably over a 15-year period regardless of their actual useful lives. Section 197 intangibles include goodwill, going-concern value, know-how, information bases, customer-based intangibles, supplier-based intangibles, governmental licenses, trademarks, covenants not to compete, and similar items. §197(d). Intangibles that are created by the taxpayer (rather than purchased) generally cannot be amortized, however, unless they are created in connection with a transaction or series of transactions involving the acquisition of assets constituting a trade or business or a substantial portion of a trade or business. §197(c)(2), (d)(1). The rule for self-created intangibles does not apply, however, to government licenses, covenants not to compete acquired in connection with the acquisition of a trade or business, or any franchise, trademark, or trade name. Id. The costs of creating a new trade name for an existing business thus could be amortized over a 15-year period.

On the other hand, §197 specifically excludes from the definition of a §197 intangible: (i) an interest in a corporation, partnership, trust or estate; (ii) an interest in a financial contract; (iii) an interest in land; (iv) computer software; (v) certain interests or rights (e.g., an interest in a film, book, copyright, or certain contract rights) if not acquired in connection with the acquisition of other assets constituting a trade or business or a substantial portion of a trade or business; (vi) certain interests under leases and debt instruments; (vii) mortgage servicing rights if not acquired in connection with the acquisition of other assets constituting a trade or business or a substantial portion of a trade or business; and (viii) professional fees and transaction costs in certain corporate reorganizations. §197(e).

Although the capitalized costs of most self-created intangibles cannot be amortized under §197, the costs of some types of intangibles can be amortized under §167. Section 167(f) and Regulation §1.167(a)-14 provide for amortization of the costs of some specific types of intangibles that are listed in §197(e). In addition, amortization may be allowed under §167(a) and Regulation §1.167(a)-3 (which was revised in conjunction with the promulgation of Regulation §§1.263(a)-4 and -5, discussed earlier in this chapter). Regulation §1.167(a)-3(a) provides that the costs of an intangible can be amortized if the useful life of the intangible can be estimated with reasonable accuracy. A new safe harbor allows a taxpayer to assume that the useful life of intangibles is generally 15 years. Reg. §1.167(a)-3(b)(1). The combination of Regulation §1.167(a)-3(a) and -3(b) allows taxpayers to amortize the cost of certain self-created intangibles over 15 years, in a manner comparable to §197 amortization.

There are several exceptions to the safe harbor. First, if the useful life of the self-created intangible can be determined with reasonable accuracy, the taxpayer can amortize the cost of the intangible over its useful life. Reg. §1.167(a)-3(a), (b)(1)(iii). For example, prepaid expenses, such as insurance prepayments, are deducted over the period to which the prepayment relates. Second, the safe harbor does not apply to intangibles for which the Code, Regulations, or other administrative pronouncements provide a specific amortization period. Reg. §1.167(a)-3(b)(1)(i). For example, the specific §167(f) amortization rules applicable to certain intangibles trump the safe harbor rule. In addition, Regulation §1.167(a)-3(a) provides that the costs of self-created goodwill cannot be amortized under §167, although the costs of acquired goodwill can be amortized under §197. Third, the safe harbor does not apply to the self-created financial intangibles listed in Regulation §1.263(a)-4(d)(2) and costs that must be capitalized under Regulation §1.263(a)-5 (discussed earlier in this chapter). Reg. §1.167(a)-3(b)(1)(ii), (2). The safe harbor can apply to the other types of self-created intangibles listed in Regulation §1.263(a)-4(d)(3) — (9) (although a special 25-year amortization period applies to the cost of real estate intangibles described in Regulation §1.263(a)-4(d)(8)). Reg. §1.167(a)-3(b)(1)(iv).

Examples

20. a. Monroe owns a travel agency. He gives a quote of $800 to his best client, Rich, for a luxury cruise. The quote was based on an outdated brochure. When Monroe goes to book the cruise, he finds the cruise now costs $2,000. Because he values Rich's patronage, Monroe pays the $1,200 difference to avoid losing Rich as a client. How much of the $1,200 may Monroe deduct?

    b. Suppose that Monroe must capitalize the goodwill expenditure. When, if ever, will Monroe recover his expenditure?

21. Early this year, Global News Company acquired a chain of newspapers for $350 million, $70 million of which was allocable to the cost of the newspaper chain's list of current subscribers and $20 million of which was allocable to goodwill. The useful life of the subscriber list is 20 years. When, if ever, will Global News Company recover the $70 million expenditure for the subscriber list and the $20 million expenditure for goodwill?

22. Kooky Cola is seeking to expand its overall market share by expanding into lemonade. One option is to acquire Snappy, a popular brand of

lemonade. Another option is to acquire Tartco, a small regional brand, and use a marketing blitz to increase customer awareness of the brand. What advice would you give Kooky Cola as to the tax consequences of these two alternatives?

Explanations

20. a. Courts are split as to the treatment of such "goodwill" payments. The Service may argue that the expenditure is designed to purchase goodwill and that goodwill is a nondeductible capital asset. Welch v. Helvering, 290 U.S. 111 (1933). On the other hand, Monroe's payment was made to retain existing goodwill rather than to purchase the goodwill of a new business. Thus, Monroe might argue, the expenditure is much like deductible advertising designed to maintain the good reputation of a business. Monroe might also argue that it is common for travel agents to make up the difference if they misquote prices. For cases supporting the deduction of specialized goodwill payments, see M.L. Eakes Co. v. Commissioner, 686 F.2d 217 (4th Cir. 1982); Pepper v. Commissioner, 36 T.C. 886 (1961), acq., 1962-2 C.B. 5; Dunn & McCarthy, Inc. v. Commissioner, 139 F.2d 242 (2d Cir. 1943). Monroe's expenditures would not fall under §197 because they were not incurred in connection with the acquisition of assets constituting a trade or business.

    b. Unless §197 applies, goodwill cannot be amortized because it does not have a determinable useful life. Reg. §1.167(a)-3(a).

21. These facts are similar to the facts in Newark Morning Ledger Co. v. United States, 507 U.S. 546 (1993), in which the Supreme Court held that the purchaser of a subscription list could amortize the cost of the list over its expected useful life, which is 20 years here. However, since Global News Company acquired the newspaper chain after the enactment of §197, that section determines the timing and amount of Global News Company's deductions. The subscriber list and goodwill purchased by Global News Company are both §197 assets. §197(c), (d)(1)(A), (C)(ii). Global News Company will deduct the $90 million cost ratably over 15 years, or $6 million a year for 15 years, regardless of the actual useful life of the subscription list and goodwill. §197(a).

22. All other things equal, Kooky Cola is probably better off acquiring Tartco. Advertising costs incurred to increase customer awareness of the Tartco brand would be deductible currently. On the other hand, the cost of acquiring Snappy's goodwill would be amortizable over a 15-year period under §197.

G. "ORDINARY AND NECESSARY" EXPENSES

1. The Scope of "Ordinary and Necessary"

Business expenses are deductible under §§162 and 212 only if they are "ordinary and necessary." The complexity and variety of business dealings make it impossible to develop clear rules for deciding when an expenditure has met this requirement. In addition, courts are often reluctant to question the business judgment of a taxpayer. Thus, taxpayers generally are permitted to deduct business expenditures even if they appear unusual and unnecessary.

However, in some limited circumstances, the expenses will not be deductible because they are thought to be personal in nature. For example, in Gilliam v. Commissioner, 51 T.C.M. 515 (CCH) (1986), the taxpayer was denied a deduction for expenses incurred to settle lawsuits arising out of a business trip. On that trip the taxpayer, who suffered from a mental condition, had a bad reaction to a prescription drug during an airplane flight, became irrational, tried to exit the plane, and subsequently injured another passenger. The court held that, although the incident would not have occurred but for the business trip, the costs that the taxpayer incurred in connection with the altercation were not ordinary expenses of the taxpayer's trade or business (apparently because the court also thought that the altercation would not have occurred but for the taxpayer's mental condition). Although the Gilliam opinion frames the issue in terms of the ordinary or extraordinary nature of the expense, the issue would have been better framed as one involving the distinction between personal and business expenses (which is discussed in more detail in Chapter 6).

(For a discussion of Welch v. Helvering, 290 U.S. 111 (1933), the case typically cited for the "ordinary and necessary" standard, see the previous section of this chapter.)

Examples

23. Jack flies first class to all of his business meetings at a cost of $20,000 per year. He could fly business class for only $10,000 per year. How much of his transportation cost is deductible under §162?

24. Acme Dynamite Company does business in 35 states. The company maintains a private airplane to transport top executives to meetings. Because the president's hobby is flying, the president usually pilots the plane whenever possible. The cost of operating the plane is $50,000 per year. The cost of sending the same employees by commercial airlines

would be $40,000 per year. How much of the transportation cost is deductible under §162?

25. The Beverly Hills Dermatology Group, a professional corporation of physicians, owns and maintains a plane in case one of the doctors has to fly to another city to treat a patient. The plane has not been used for this purpose, but the doctors, who are all licensed pilots, fly the plane to keep up their licenses. The cost of operating the airplane is $50,000 per year. Is the cost of operating the airplane deductible?

26. Ronald owns a chain of 10 donut shops. During the past three years the profits of the shops have declined sharply. Ronald consults a psychic to determine what to do about his reduced profits. On the advice of his psychic he pays $10,000 for 10 custom-made doormats, which he places in front of the entrance to each of his stores. The psychic tells him that the doormats will bring luck to his businesses for the rest of the year. Is the cost of the doormats deductible?

Explanations

23. All $20,000 is deductible. If the trip itself has a good business purpose, the entire cost of transportation is deductible even though it is more luxurious than necessary. It is common, moreover, for top executives to travel first class.

24. Businesses are allowed a deduction for "reasonable and necessary" traveling expenses. Reg. §1.162-2(a). The fact that the president is getting a certain amount of personal value from operating the plane is probably irrelevant because the plane is used solely to transport employees to business meetings, that is, for business purposes. The cost of the transportation is $10,000 more than if the company used commercial airlines, which makes it seem that the entire expenditure is not "necessary." However, Acme can argue that the plane is necessary since the meetings are often spur-of-the-moment and commercial airline schedules are often inadequate. The entire $50,000 is probably deductible.

25. In this example, none of the expenditure is deductible. There does not seem to be any business reason for a local medical group to maintain a private airplane. In the event that one of the doctors had to travel to treat a patient, the doctor could fly on a commercial scheduled flight or a charter flight. The doctors, who are licensed pilots, appear to be using the plane for personal reasons, so the expense is not deductible. See, e.g., Harbor Medical Corp. v. Commissioner, 38 T.C.M. (CCH) 1144 (1979) (holding that the expense of purchasing and operating an

airplane was not an ordinary or necessary expense of the taxpayer corporation's medical practice, which was limited to one geographic area).

26. Probably not. Although courts generally do not question the business judgment of a taxpayer, purchasing magic doormats is so unusual that it probably would not be considered a deductible expenditure. Compare Gilliam v. Commissioner, 51 T.C.M. 515 (1986). Even if Ronald incurred the expense because he genuinely believed that it would help his business, the expense will likely be nondeductible because courts tend to use an objective approach to distinguish between ordinary business expenses and personal expenses. See, e.g., Trebilcock v. Commissioner, 64 T.C. 852 (1975), acq. 1976-2 C.B. 3, aff'd, 557 F.2d 1226 (6th Cir. 1977) (denying a §162 deduction for the cost of hiring a minister to give the taxpayer and his employees spiritual guidance).

2. Reasonable Compensation

Reading: §162(a)(1), (m); *Reg.* §§1.162-7, -8.

Section 162(a)(1) specifically allows a taxpayer to deduct a "reasonable allowance for salaries or other compensation." On the other hand, unreasonable compensation paid to an employee is not deductible. Reg. §1.162-7(b)(3). The Service has generally taken the position that compensation is unreasonable and nondeductible only if the compensation arrangement between the employee and employer involves tax avoidance.

What standard is used to determine whether compensation is reasonable or unreasonable? The test is a facts-and-circumstances test that takes into account a number of factors, including: (i) the employee's qualifications; (ii) the nature of the employee's work; (iii) the employer's history of paying or not paying dividends; (iv) the compensation paid to comparable employees by comparable employers; (v) the amount the employer has paid the employee in previous years; (vi) the results of the employee's efforts; (vii) general and local economic conditions; and (viii) the profitability of the employer after the compensation has been paid. See Mayson Manufacturing Co. v. Commissioner, 178 F.2d 115 (6th Cir. 1949); Elliotts, Inc. v. Commissioner, 716 F.2d 1241 (9th Cir. 1983).

A publicly held corporation is allowed to deduct compensation paid to its most highly compensated employees only to the extent that the compensation does not exceed $1 million. §162(m)(1). The $1 million cap does not apply to any portion of the employee's compensation that is based on commissions or the financial performance of the employer. §162(m)(1), (4), Reg. §1.162-27. (Also, certain employers that received federal aid under TARP, the Troubled Assets Relief Program, are denied a deduction for compensation in excess of $500,000 that was paid to chief executive officers or highly compensated employees. §162(m)(5). In addition, a $500,000 deduction limitation applies to certain health insurance issuers with respect to compensation paid to officers and employees. §162(m)(6).)

Examples

27. Randy is the sole shareholder and president of Randy's Place, Inc., a successful country and western music hall in Branson, Missouri. Randy's Place, Inc. has been in business for six years. Randy has "zeroed out" the corporation in each of those years by paying himself compensation in an amount equal to whatever is left after paying all of the corporation's expenses other than his own compensation. The corporation has paid no corporate tax because, after taking into account Randy's compensation, the corporation has had zero taxable income. In addition, the corporation has never paid a dividend. In year six of operations, Randy's compensation was $3.8 million. How much of that compensation will Randy's Place, Inc. be able to deduct under §162?

28. Intelligence, Inc., a publicly traded corporation, pays its chief executive officer (C.E.O.) annual fixed compensation of $3 million a year. The company is consistently profitable, did not receive any federal aid under TARP, and is not a health insurance issuer. What advice would you give the company as to the effect of §162(m) on the company's ability to deduct the compensation?

Explanations

27. It depends. Two facts indicate that a portion of the $3.8 million of compensation may be nondeductible "unreasonable" compensation: First, the corporation has no profits after paying Randy's compensation. Second, the corporation has never paid a dividend. Thus, a portion of the compensation may be recharacterized as a disguised dividend, in which case the dividend amount could not be deducted by Randy's Place, Inc. See Reg. §§1.162-7, -8; Elliotts, Inc. v. Commissioner, 716 F.2d 1241 (9th Cir. 1983). However, we cannot conclude that a portion of the compensation would be recharacterized as a dividend without considering a number of other factors not mentioned here. For example, if the presidents of other comparable music halls are typically paid compensation in the neighborhood of $3.8 million, that fact would weigh against recharacterization of the compensation. See Mayson Manufacturing Co. v. Commissioner, 178 F.2d 115 (6th Cir. 1949). The §162(m) salary limitations do not apply to these facts.

   (Whether the payment of compensation in lieu of a dividend reduces the aggregate tax paid by the corporation and its shareholders depends on the tax rates of the corporation and its shareholders. The maximum tax rate on dividends received by shareholders currently is 20 percent. Shareholder-employees pay tax on compensation income at their ordinary income rate.)

28. I would advise Intelligence, Inc. to pay the C.E.O. a fixed base salary of $1 million and performance-based salary that would make up the rest of the salary usually paid to the C.E.O. If Intelligence, Inc. pays fixed salary in excess of $1 million, the compensation in excess of $1 million is nondeductible under §162(m). However, if the company pays the C.E.O. a fixed salary of $1 million or less, plus performance-based compensation (that is, compensation based on the financial fortunes of the company), §162(m) will not disallow the compensation in excess of $1 million. Using performance-based compensation still enables the company to pay the C.E.O. something on the order of the usual amount of salary because Intelligence, Inc. is very profitable.

3. Costs Associated with Illegal or Unethical Activities

Reading: §§162 (c), (f), (g), 280E.

Income obtained illegally is taxable (even if the taxpayer-criminal is required to return the funds to the victim). James v. United States, 366 U.S. 213 (1961). A basic principle of our tax system is that net rather than gross income is taxed. Since the income from illegal or unethical activities is taxable, are the costs of earning that income deductible?

Prior to the passage of the Tax Reform Act of 1969, courts used a frustration-of-public-policy test to determine whether the expenses of an illegal activity were deductible. Under this test, courts allowed a deduction for the expenses of an illegal activity unless allowing the deduction would frustrate a clearly defined state or national public policy, "evidenced by some governmental declaration." The scope of this frustration-of-public-policy test was uncertain and the test fostered a great deal of litigation. For example, in Tank Truck Rentals v. Commissioner, 356 U.S. 30 (1958), the Court denied the taxpayer a deduction for the fines it paid for intentionally violating state law that set maximum weight limits for trucks operating in the state. The Court concluded that the fines were intended to discourage the behavior in which the taxpayer engaged and that allowing the taxpayer to deduct the fines would dilute their intended effect and frustrate public policy. However, in Commissioner v. Tellier, 383 U.S. 687 (1966), the Court allowed a securities dealer to deduct the legal fees he incurred in unsuccessfully defending himself against charges of securities and mail fraud. The Court concluded that allowing the deduction would not frustrate public policy severely enough to warrant disallowance.

In 1969 Congress attempted to clarify the law by adding language to §162 that explicitly provides that the following expenses cannot be deducted: most bribes and kickbacks, fines and penalties; and the punitive damages portion of criminal antitrust violations. §162(c), (f), (g). The legislative history of these provisions indicates that they were intended to be all-inclusive and preempt the case law public policy doctrine. S. Rep. No. 91-552, 91st Cong., 1st Sess. 274 (1969), 1969-3 C.B. 423, 597. Thus, expenses of illegal activities are deductible unless §162 explicitly provides that the expenses are nondeductible. (Section 280E specifically provides, however, that expenses incurred in drug trafficking are nondeductible.)

Examples

29. Tom runs an illegal bookie operation for an organized crime ring. Last year he spent $14,500 on rent and utilities for his gambling operation and an additional $20,000 to hire a thug to break the legs of customers who did not pay their gambling debts. Are these expenses deductible?

30. The delivery trucks of Pizza Shack often have to park illegally to deliver their pizzas on time. As a consequence, Pizza Shack pays approximately $7,000 per year in parking fines. Is this expense deductible?

31. Bill ran a moonshining business before the authorities caught up with him. Is he allowed to deduct the following expenses?
    a. The cost of the corn and bottles used in making the moonshine.
    b. Bribes paid to local police to let him run his moonshine operation.
    c. Fees paid to a local defense attorney who unsuccessfully defended him on the moonshining charges.

Explanations

29. All $34,500 of Tom's expenses probably are deductible since they do not fall into any of the categories specifically disallowed by §162.
    It is true that the government has repeatedly declared "war" against organized crime, most recently with the enactment of RICO. Hiring a thug to maim people is a very serious crime. For this reason, Tom's deductions probably would have failed the frustration-of-public-policy test. The Tax Reform Act of 1969, however, essentially replaced this test with a specific list of nondeductible expenditures.

30. Section 162(f) specifically disallows deductions for fines or similar penalties paid to the government for the violation of any law. Thus, it appears that Pizza Shack cannot deduct any fines paid.

31. a. The cost of the bottles and corn should be allowed as an ordinary cost of moonshining since they are not disallowed by §162.
    b. Bribes to a government official are nondeductible under §162(c).
    c. Business-related costs of defending oneself against criminal charges are deductible, so Bill is allowed to deduct his legal expenses. The fact that Bill was convicted is irrelevant. Commissioner v. Tellier, 383 U.S. 687 (1966).

H. DEPRECIATION AND THE ACCELERATED COST RECOVERY SYSTEM

Reading: §§167, 168, 179, 1016, 1245, 1250.

The cost of a business asset with a useful life greater than one taxable year cannot be immediately deducted, but must be capitalized. If the asset declines in value over time, the taxpayer will be entitled to recover the cost of the asset (less the salvage value of the asset when it can no longer be used in the business) by taking depreciation deductions in the years in which the asset is expected to be used in the business. In order to determine a taxpayer's depreciation deductions for an asset, we must determine (i) the useful life of the asset, (ii) the salvage value of the asset, and (iii) the method for allocating the cost of the asset (less the salvage value of the asset) over its useful life.

To illustrate the basic principles (but not the actual rules in §168), assume that a taxpayer who owns a flower delivery service buys a delivery van for $21,000. The taxpayer expects to use the van in her business for five years, then sell it for its salvage value of $1,000. One way to determine the taxpayer's annual depreciation deductions would be to use the *straight line method*. Under this method, we would allocate the $20,000 cost (net of the $1,000 salvage value) ratably over the five years in which the taxpayer expects to use the van in her business. The taxpayer would deduct $4,000 of depreciation in each of the five years. The depreciation deductions, which represent recovery of the cost of the van, would reduce her basis in the van so that at the end of the five years her adjusted basis would be $1,000. If she sold the van for $1,000, she would have no gain or loss on the sale of the van and would have recovered her entire $21,000 cost of the van (through $20,000 of depreciation and $1,000 of basis, which permitted her to receive $1,000 for the van tax-free). Although this example illustrates the basic concept of depreciation, it does not illustrate the actual §168 depreciation rules that apply to tangible business or investment property. We now turn to those rules.

Section 167(a) provides generally that a taxpayer is allowed to take depreciation deductions for business or investment property, provided that the property has a limited useful life. Depreciation on intangible assets is determined under §167 (or, in some circumstances, under §197). Depreciation on tangible business or investment property generally is determined under §168. §§167(b), 168(a). The §168 system of depreciation is generally referred to as the *accelerated cost recovery system* (ACRS) (or is more specifically referred to as the *modified accelerated cost recovery system* (MACRS)). ACRS accelerates the taxpayer's depreciation deductions in three ways: (i) it uses recovery periods that are substantially shorter than the actual useful lives of the property; (ii) it allows the use of accelerated depreciation methods; and (iii) it assumes that the salvage value of the property is zero, permitting deduction of the entire cost of the property. §168(b), (c), and (e).

Under §168, a taxpayer's annual depreciation deductions are determined using (i) the *applicable depreciation method*, (ii) the *applicable recovery period*, and (iii) the *applicable convention*. §168(a)(1), (2), and (3).

The *applicable recovery period* for tangible property is determined under §168(c) and (e). The recovery periods are generally based upon the class life (determined by the Secretary of the Treasury) for the property. The recovery period specified in §168(c) and (e) for an asset is often shorter than the class life of the asset. For example, property with a nine-year class life has a five-year recovery period. §168(e)(1).

Section 168(e)(3) gives the classification for certain types of property. For example, it provides that a car or light general purpose truck is "5-year property." §168(e)(3)(B)(i). Section 168(c), in turn, provides that the recovery period for five-year property is five years. Section 168(c) also provides that the recovery period for residential rental property is 27.5 years and the recovery period for nonresidential real property is 39 years. If a taxpayer purchases a business asset that is not real property and is not one of the types of assets listed in §168(e)(3), the recovery period of the property generally is determined under §168(e)(1), based on the class life of the asset as determined by the Secretary of the Treasury.

The *applicable convention* is determined under §168(d). This subsection determines the date on which the depreciable property is deemed to have been placed in service by the taxpayer. (The date on which the property is placed in service, not the date on which the taxpayer acquires the property, is used to determine when the depreciation deductions begin.) If the asset is not real property, a "half-year convention" generally applies so the asset is deemed to have been placed in service on the date that is halfway through the year. §168(d)(1), (4)(A). This convention creates some potential for abuse, however, because a crafty taxpayer could place property in service at the end of the year and still take half a year's depreciation. To discourage this type of abuse, a mid-quarter convention applies (instead of the half-year convention) if a disproportionate amount of depreciable property is placed in service in the last three months of the year. §168(d)(3). If the mid-quarter convention applies, the property is deemed to have been placed in service on the date that is halfway through the quarter in which the property is actually placed in service. §168(d)(4)(C). A mid-month convention applies to depreciable real property, so real property is deemed to have been placed in service on the date that is halfway through the month in which the property is actually placed in service. §168(d)(2), (4)(B).

The *applicable depreciation method* is determined under §168(b). The simplest method is the *straight line method*. As we saw in the illustration at the beginning of this section, straight line depreciation allocates the total cost of an asset ratably to each year of the useful life of the asset. For example, if the useful life of an asset were five years, 20 percent of the cost could be deducted each year. A taxpayer must use the straight line method to depreciate real property and may elect to use the straight line method to depreciate other types of property. §168(b)(3), (5). If the property is not real property and the taxpayer does not elect to use the straight line method, one of two accelerated depreciation methods will apply: If the property is 15-year property or 20-year property, the *150 percent declining balance method* will apply; if the property is any other type of property, the *200 percent declining balance method* (also known as the *double declining balance method*) generally will apply (unless the taxpayer elects to apply the 150 percent declining balance method, under §168(b)(2)(D)). §168(b)(1), (2).

Under a *declining balance* depreciation method, the *percentage* deduction that would be allowed for the property under the straight line method is calculated and *multiplied by the specified percentage*, either 150 percent or 200 percent. This amount of depreciation is then subtracted from the basis of the depreciable property. For example, if a taxpayer places in service five-year property, with a five-year recovery period, the taxpayer would be allowed to deduct 20 percent (1/5) of the cost of the property each year (disregarding the conventions) under the straight line method, so the taxpayer would be allowed to deduct 40 percent of the cost of the property under the 200 percent declining balance method. (However, we would then have to apply the appropriate convention to determine the taxpayer's actual year one depreciation deduction.) The taxpayer's basis in the property is then reduced by the amount of depreciation taken in year one, and the taxpayer's year two depreciation deduction equals 40 percent (200 percent of the 20 percent straight line percentage) of that adjusted basis.

If we kept deducting 40 percent of an ever-decreasing adjusted basis, we would never fully depreciate the asset, so §168 provides that we switch over to straight line deductions in the first year in which the straight line deduction is more than the deduction computed using the declining balance method. §168(b)(1)(B). However, in this context, the straight line deduction in a given year is calculated based on: (i) the adjusted basis of the property in that year and (ii) the *remaining* useful life of the property. (Students often make the mistake of assuming that the straight line amount in this context is the straight line deduction on the original basis determined in the year in which the property is placed in service.)

To illustrate the §168 rules, suppose that Tom pays $20,000 for a delivery van that he will use in his business. He places the van in service in September of year one. The van is five-year property and has a five-year recovery period. §168(c), (e)(3)(B)(i). Under the straight line method, the depreciation deduction would be 20 percent (1/5) each year for five years. Under the double or 200 percent declining balance method, the percentage deduction would be 200 percent of 20 percent, or 40 percent, of the $20,000 cost of the van, which equals $8,000 in year one. The double declining balance method applies in this illustration. §168(b)(1), (2). The half-year convention also applies, however, so Tom's year one depreciation deduction is $4,000. §168(d). This deduction reduces Tom's adjusted basis in the van to $16,000. §1016(a)(2).

In year two Tom's double declining balance depreciation deduction is 40 percent of the $16,000 adjusted basis, which equals $6,400. Straight line deductions on a cost of $16,000 over a recovery period of 4.5 years (the remaining useful life of the property) would be $3,556, which is less than the $6,400 double declining balance deduction, so Tom deducts $6,400. This reduces Tom's adjusted basis to $9,600.

In year three Tom's double declining balance depreciation deduction is 40 percent of $9,600, which equals $3,840. Straight line deductions on a cost of $9,600 over a recovery period of 3.5 years (the remaining useful life of the property) would be $2,743, which is less than the $3,840 double declining balance deduction, so Tom deducts $3,840. This reduces Tom's adjusted basis to $5,760.

In year four Tom's double declining balance depreciation deduction is 40 percent of $5,760, which equals $2,304. Straight line deductions on a cost of $5,760 over a recovery period of 2.5 years (the remaining useful life of the property) would be $2,304, which equals Tom's double declining balance deduction, so Tom deducts $2,304. This reduces Tom's adjusted basis to $3,456.

In year five Tom's double declining balance depreciation deduction is 40 percent of $3,456, which equals $1,382. Straight line deductions on a cost of $3,456 over a recovery period of 1.5 years (the remaining useful life of the property) would be $2,304, which exceeds Tom's double declining balance deduction, so Tom deducts $2,304. This reduces Tom's adjusted basis to $1,152. Tom also will use the straight line method to compute his depreciation deduction in year six. He will deduct the remaining $1,152 of adjusted basis in that year. He will then have a zero basis in the property. The following chart summarizes these calculations:

Year	Basis	200 percent method	S.L. method	Depreciation deduction
1	$20,000	$4,000	$2,000	$4,000
2	16,000	6,400	3,556	6,400
3	9,600	3,840	2,743	3,840
4	5,760	2,304	2,304	2,304
5	3,456	1,382	2,304	2,304
6	1,152	461	1,152	1,152
7	0			

Which depreciation method most accurately measures a taxpayer's income? The most accurate method is neither the straight line nor the accelerated method; instead, the most accurate method is the *economic depreciation method*. Under this method the taxpayer would take an annual depreciation deduction equal to the decline, during that year, of the value of the property. How would we determine the decline in the value of the property? In some cases the decline in value could be determined from market transactions, or books or indexes that reflect such transactions. For example, used car prices are compiled and published monthly. We might give a taxpayer a depreciation deduction for a car used in business equal to the decline in the amount for which she could sell the car.

In other cases the decline in value can be determined by discounting expected income streams. To see how this latter approach may be used to determine depreciation, consider the following example: Assume that a taxpayer bought a piece of business equipment for $4,975. The property is expected to produce $2,000 of income a year for three years, and no income thereafter. A $4,975 investment invested at a rate of return of about 10 percent would yield $2,000 a year for three years. If we use this rate to discount to present value the three $2,000 income streams, the sum of the present values must equal $4,975. We can determine the loss in the value of the property in each of the three years by comparing the sum of the present values of the future income streams (i) at the beginning of the year and (ii) at the end of the year, using the 10 percent rate to compute the present values.

Continuing with our example, at the beginning of year one the sum of the present values of the income streams equals $4,975, which is the sum of (i) the $1,818 present value of the $2,000 income stream due in year one,[1]

---

1. Recall from Chapter 1 that the formula for computing present value is:

$$PV = \frac{FV}{(1+r)^n}$$

Here, $\$1,818 = \$2,000/(1.1)^1$.

(ii) the $1,653 present value of the $2,000 income stream due in year two,[2] and (iii) the $1,504 present value of the $2,000 income stream due in year three.[3] At the end of year one, the sum of the present values of the income streams equals $3,471, which is the sum of (i) the $1,818 present value of the $2,000 income stream due in year two (that is, one year later) and (ii) the $1,653 present value of the $2,000 income stream due in year three (that is, two years later). The decline in the value of the property in year one thus is $1,504 ($4,975 less $3,471).

The sum of the present values of the income streams at the beginning of year two is $3,471 (as computed in the last paragraph). The present value of the $2,000 income stream due in year three (one year later) is $1,818. The decline in the value of the property in year two thus is $1,653 ($3,471 less $1,818).

At the beginning of year three the present value of the year three income stream is $1,818 (as computed in the last paragraph). The present value at the end of year three is zero, so the decline in the value of the property in year three is $1,818 ($1,818 less zero).

To summarize, the taxpayer in our example would take depreciation deductions of $1,504 in year one, $1,653 in year two, and $1,818 in year three. Note that, using the economic method to determine the depreciation for this piece of business equipment, the taxpayer's depreciation deductions are *back-loaded* (starting out low and increasing over time). In fact, economic depreciation will always produce back-loaded depreciation deductions for investments that produce a level stream of income. Recall that straight line deductions are level over time and so-called accelerated method depreciation deductions are (*front-loaded*), starting out high and decreasing over time. For assets that produce a level stream of income, both of those methods overstate depreciation deductions and understate income in the early years of use of the property and have the opposite effect in the later years of the use of the property.

So why do we not require taxpayers to use the economic method to compute depreciation deductions? One reason is that it may be very difficult to estimate the income streams that the asset would produce; if we cannot estimate the income streams, we cannot determine the annual decline in the sum of the present values of the income streams. Even where a market in used equipment exists, valuation may be difficult, in part because businesses may disproportionately sell badly manufactured equipment. If buyers know or suspect this, the used equipment market may undervalue superficially similar equipment not offered for sale. To return to an earlier example, car owners may systematically unload their "lemons." If this is true, and car

_____

2. $1,653 = \$2,000/(1.1)^2$.

3. $1,504 = \$2,000/(1.1)^3$. (The amounts of the three present values are rounded so that the sum of the three present values equals $4,975.)

buyers know this, the price of a used car is to some extent the price of a "used lemon." Cars not offered for sale may be expected to perform better, and to decline in value in a different fashion.

Another reason is that we may want to encourage investment in business assets as a matter of fiscal policy. Allowing taxpayers to use accelerated methods provides an incentive to invest in business assets.

In some limited circumstances, depreciation is computed by reference to the predicted income stream from the property (for example, a motion picture). However, this method is beyond the scope of this book.

Section 168(g) also provides an alternate depreciation system for the types of property specified in §168(g)(1). Property subject to this alternate system has a longer recovery period and is depreciated using the straight line method. §168(g)(2).

As property is depreciated or amortized, its adjusted basis is reduced by the amount of the deductions taken. §1016(a)(2). These basis reductions increase the gain realized by the taxpayer when the property is later sold. Under §1231, gain from the sale of a depreciable asset can be capital gain. §1231(a)(3). (Section 1231, which is discussed in Chapter 8, provides that a taxpayer's gains and losses from the sale of section 1231 property are generally capital if, in the current year, the taxpayer's gains from the sale of section 1231 property exceed the taxpayer's losses from the sale of section 1231 property.) However, depreciation deductions are ordinary deductions. Therefore, the portion of any gain, on the sale of depreciable property, that is attributable to having taken depreciation deductions is recharacterized as ordinary gain under the *depreciation recapture* rules of §1245. For example, if property acquired for $1,000 is fully depreciated, then sold for $1,200, the taxpayer would realize $1,200 of gain on the sale, $1,000 of which would be ordinary gain and $200 of which would be capital gain. §1245(a)(1) — (3).

For real property, depreciation is recaptured only to the extent that the depreciation taken is greater than straight line. §1250. This seldom occurs since straight line depreciation is required for almost all real property. (The capital gain tax rate that applies to some or all of the gain from the sale of depreciable property may be higher than the capital gain tax rate that applies to the sale of some other types of capital assets, however. Chapter 8 discusses the capital gain rules.)

In an effort to encourage investment in income-producing assets, Congress from time to time has enacted various provisions that allow taxpayers to deduct immediately some or all of the cost of certain income-producing property. The most significant current tax incentives are §168 bonus depreciation and §179 expensing.

In addition to regular depreciation deductions (described earlier), taxpayers can deduct additional "bonus" depreciation on property with a recovery period of 20 years or less if the property was acquired between 2008 and 2013 and placed in service by the end of 2013. §168(k), as amended by 2012 TRA, P.L. 112-240 §331. (Congress may or may not extend the temporary §168(k) bonus depreciation in the future.) Depending on when the property was acquired and placed in service, the bonus depreciation is either 50 percent or 100 percent of the taxpayer's basis in the property. §168(k)(1), (5). The taxpayer's basis in the property is reduced by the amount of the bonus depreciation. If the 50 percent bonus depreciation rule applies, the taxpayer also deducts regular depreciation on the property, but the taxpayer's regular depreciation deduction reflects the taxpayer's reduced basis in the property. To illustrate this rule, assume that, in our previous example, Tom purchased the van and placed it in service in 2013, when the 50 percent bonus depreciation rule was in effect. The bonus depreciation for 2013 equals $10,000, which is 50 percent of Tom's $20,000 basis in the van. The bonus depreciation reduces Tom's basis in the van to $10,000. Tom's regular depreciation deduction for 2013 equals $2,000, which is 50 percent (due to the half-year convention) of 40 percent (double the straight line 20 percent deduction) of Tom's remaining $10,000 basis in the van. Tom's 2013 depreciation deduction for the van equals $12,000, which is the sum of the $10,000 bonus depreciation and the $2,000 regular depreciation.

Under §179, a taxpayer also can elect to expense (i.e., deduct immediately) the cost of "section 179 property" placed in service in the current year. §179(a). The amount of this deduction is capped and is subject to a phase-out if the taxpayer places more than a limited amount of section 179 property in service during the year. Beginning in 2013, the maximum §179 deduction is $25,000 and is not adjusted for inflation. §179(b)(1)(C). In addition, the taxpayer's §179 deduction is reduced one dollar for each dollar of section 179 property placed in service, during the year, in excess of a threshold amount provided in §179(b)(2). Beginning in 2013, the §179(b)(2) threshold is $200,000 and is not adjusted for inflation. §179(b)(2)(C).

In addition, §179(b)(3)(A) provides that the taxpayer's §179 deduction cannot exceed the taxable income from the taxpayer's business in the year in which the property is placed in service. (Any excess deduction is carried over to the next year. §179(b)(3)(B).) Section 179 property is defined generally as depreciable tangible personal property, which is acquired by purchase for use in an active trade or business. §§179(d)(1), 1245(a)(3). Section 179 applies only if the taxpayer elects to apply it. Making the election reduces the taxpayer's depreciable basis in the property by the amount deducted under §179. §179(a). If the property is later sold at a gain, a §179 deduction is treated like a depreciation deduction and may be recaptured as ordinary income under §1245. §1245(a), Reg. §1.1245-2(a)(3).

As noted earlier, depreciation deductions also reduce the taxpayer's basis in the depreciable property. §1016(a)(2). The taxpayer's basis is reduced by the amount of depreciation allowed or allowable, so the basis of depreciable property is reduced even if the taxpayer does not take the depreciation deductions permitted under §§167 and 168. The taxpayer's original depreciable basis of property is generally determined under §1012, which provides that the basis is the cost of the property. As we saw earlier, a taxpayer's basis includes the portion of the cost financed with debt. If the taxpayer improves the property, the cost of the improvements increases the taxpayer's basis. §1016(a)(1). There are several exceptions to the general cost basis rule: First, the basis of property acquired by bequest generally is the fair market value of the property at the decedent's death. §1014. Second, the basis of property acquired by gift generally is the donor's basis or, in some cases, the value of the property at the time of the gift. §1015. Third, the basis of property received in a nonrecognition transaction (for example, a transaction subject to §1031) is a substituted basis (potentially with some adjustments).

Examples

In the examples that follow, disregard §179 unless the example specifically asks you to determine the amount the taxpayer can expense. Also disregard bonus depreciation unless the example indicates that bonus depreciation is in effect.

32. A depreciation or amortization deduction may be taken for which, if any, of the following assets?
    a. a copyright;
    b. an office building;
    c. land on which an office building sits;
    d. a valuable original painting placed in the office building lobby;
    e. an owner-occupied residence.

33. Farmer John bought a tractor for $5,000. He plans to use the tractor for 11 years and then sell it as scrap metal, figuring he will receive about $300 for it. After 11 years, Farmer John scraps the tractor for $400. What is the salvage value of the tractor for purposes of determining Farmer John's depreciation deductions?

34. Is each of the following statements true or false?
    a. Section 168(c) and (e) establish six different general recovery periods for tangible personal property and two general recovery periods for tangible real property.
    b. The recovery period for an asset generally is based upon the class life for the asset as determined by the Secretary of the Treasury.
    c. The recovery period for an asset is frequently shorter than the class life of the asset.

35. State the applicable recovery period for the following types of property.
    a. residential rental real property;

   b. nonresidential real property;

   c. an automobile or light truck.

36. Which depreciation method would a taxpayer use to depreciate the following types of property?

   a. residential rental property or nonresidential real property;

   b. an automobile or light truck.

37. On December 20, year one, Joan pays $10,000 for a tangible asset that she will use in her business. She places the asset in service on May 5, year two. The asset has a five-year recovery period.

   a. What amount of depreciation will Joan deduct in year one?

   b. What amount of depreciation will Joan deduct in years two through seven?

   c. How, if at all, would your answer in part (b) change if 50 percent bonus depreciation applies, under §168(k), to depreciable tangible assets that are placed in service in year two?

   d. How, if at all, would your answer in part (b) change if Joan elects to use the 150 percent declining balance method instead of the double declining balance method?

   e. How, if at all, would your answer in part (b) change if Joan elects to use the straight line method instead of the double declining balance method?

38. a. In 2014 Tad buys $195,000 of tangible personal property and places it in service in his business. May Tad elect to expense, rather than depreciate, a portion of the cost of the property?

   b. How, if at all, would your answer in part (a) change if the cost of the property were $205,000?

39. Assume that patents are granted for 20 years. Progress Company spends $100,000 to purchase a new patent. May Progress Company amortize the patent and, if so, how will Progress Company determine its annual amortization deductions for the patent?

40. In year one Paddy's Pork Rinds Company buys and places in service equipment that costs $20,000. Using the straight line method, the company deducts $1,000 in year one (because of the half-year convention) and $2,000 per year in years two and three. In year four Paddy's Pork Rinds does not take a depreciation deduction because it wants to show a high earnings report to Petunia's Pork Products, which may acquire Paddy's. What is the equipment's adjusted basis at the end of year four?

41. a. Early in year one, Out Damn Spot Company, a laundry business, bought a dry-cleaning machine for $10,000. Assume that in years one and two the company took depreciation deductions on the machine totalling

$3,000. At the end of the second year the company sold the machine for $9,000. What are the tax consequences of the sale of the machine?

b. What are the tax consequences if the company sells the machine for $11,000?

42. a. On January 1, year one, Chubby Candy Company bought and placed in service an office building, at a cost of $936,000. What is the building's basis at the end of year two?

b. How, if at all, would your answer in part (a) change if Chubby Candy Company placed the property in service on January 1 of year two?

43. Jim, who owns and runs a fine shoe boutique, is an antiques expert. At a yard sale he buys an antique chair worth $10,000 for only $1,000. Jim places the chair in his store. What is Jim's basis in the chair?

44. Carol wishes to purchase Blackacre for use in her business. To pay the $50,000 purchase price, she uses $10,000 of her savings and borrows $40,000 from a bank. What is Carol's basis in Blackacre?

45. Is each of the following statements true or false?
    a. The cost of making improvements in property increases the basis of the property.
    b. The cost of making incidental repairs on property increases the basis of the property.

46. Amy purchases a machine for $100,000 and places it in service in her business at the beginning of year one. Assume that, in year one, Amy takes a $10,000 depreciation deduction for the machine. The actual value of the machine, however, increases by $5,000 during that year so at the end of the year the machine has a fair market value of $105,000. If Amy sold the machine for $105,000, what would be the tax consequences of the sale? (Disregard the §168(d) applicable convention.)

47. Is the §168 allowance for depreciation during the first few years of an item's useful life generally less or more than the actual decline in value of the item?

48. Assuming one of the goals of the income tax laws is to accurately measure income:
    a. State the reasoning behind the allowance of deductions for depreciation.
    b. Explain the method of determining depreciation that conforms with this goal and state why this method is generally not used.

49. Under a cash-flow consumption tax, individuals would be taxed only on their personal (as opposed to business) expenditures. What depreciation schedule would be consistent with a cash-flow consumption tax?

Explanations

32. a. A copyright is an intangible wasting asset and may be amortized under §167 (or §197).
    b. An office building is depreciable under §168.
    c. Land is a non-wasting asset and may not be depreciated.
    d. Valuable original artwork would not appear to have a limited useful life and so would not be depreciable.
    e. Only assets used in a trade or business or held for the production of income are depreciable. An owner-occupied residence is treated as an asset that does not produce income and is therefore not depreciable.

33. For purposes of determining §168 depreciation deductions, salvage value is treated as zero, regardless of the depreciation method used. As this example illustrates, this rule is favorable to the taxpayer. See §168(b)(4).

34. a. True. The "general" rules of §168(c) and (e) establish recovery periods of 3, 5, 7, 10, 15, and 20 years for tangible personal property and 27.5 and 39 years for real property.
    b. True.
    c. True. The recovery periods are *based upon,* but *not equal to,* the class life periods. For example, five-year recovery property is generally defined as property with a class life midpoint of more than four years and less than ten years. Seven-year property is defined as property with a class life midpoint of ten or more years but less than sixteen years. §168(e)(1).

35. a. 27.5 years. §168(c).
    b. 39 years. §168(c).
    c. Five years. §168(c), (e)(3)(B)(i).

36. a. The straight line method. §168(b)(3).
    b. The double declining balance method, switching to straight line in the first year in which the straight line deduction for the year exceeds the double declining balance deduction. §168(b). The property is five-year property. §168(c), (e)(3)(B)(i). A taxpayer can elect to apply the straight line method or 150 percent declining balance

method (in lieu of the default double declining balance method) to depreciate five-year property. §168(b)(1), (2)(D), (3)(D), (5).

37. a. Depreciation does not begin until an asset is placed in service. Thus, Joan receives no depreciation deduction in year one.

b. Joan is allowed to deduct depreciation in year two because the property is placed in service in that year. The applicable recovery period is five years. The property is not real estate and she does not place a disproportionate amount of depreciable property in service during the last three months of year two, so the mid-month and mid-quarter conventions do not apply. §168(d)(2), (3). The applicable convention is thus the half-year convention, so Joan is deemed to have placed the property in service halfway through year two. §168(d)(1), (4)(A). Joan receives one half-year's depreciation in year two. The other half-year's depreciation is tacked on to the end of the recovery period.

The applicable depreciation method is the double declining balance unless Joan elects to apply either the straight line method or 150 percent declining balance method. §168(b)(1). Applying the double declining balance method and the half-year convention, Joan's year two depreciation deduction equals $2,000. The straight line percentage on five-year property would be 20 percent and 200 percent of that percentage is 40 percent. The double declining deduction thus is $4,000 (40 percent of Joan's $10,000 basis in the property). However, after applying the half-year convention, Joan's deduction is $2,000 (half of the $4,000 double declining balance deduction). This depreciation deduction reduces Joan's basis in the property to $8,000.

In year three Joan's double declining balance depreciation deduction equals 40 percent of the $8,000 adjusted basis, or $3,200. The straight line deduction on a cost of $8,000 over a recovery period of 4.5 years (the remaining useful life of the property) would be $1,778, which is less than the $3,200 double declining balance deduction, so Joan deducts $3,200. This reduces Joan's adjusted basis to $4,800.

In year four Joan's double declining balance depreciation deduction equals 40 percent of $4,800, or $1,920. The straight line deduction on a cost of $4,800 over a recovery period of 3.5 years (the remaining useful life of the property) would be $1,371, which is less than the $1,920 double declining balance deduction, so Joan deducts $1,920. This reduces Joan's adjusted basis to $2,880.

In year five Joan's double declining balance depreciation deduction equals 40 percent of $2,880, or $1,152. The straight line deduction on a cost of $2,880 over a recovery period of 2.5 years (the remaining useful life of the property) would be $1,152, which equals Joan's double declining balance deduction, so Joan deducts $1,152. This reduces Joan's adjusted basis to $1,728.

In year six Joan's double declining balance depreciation deduction equals 40 percent of $1,728, or $691. The straight line deduction on a cost of $1,728 over a recovery period of 1.5 years (the remaining useful life of the property) would be $1,152, which exceeds Joan's double declining balance deduction, so Joan deducts $1,152. This reduces Joan's adjusted basis to $576. Joan will also use the straight line method to compute her depreciation deduction in year seven. She will deduct the remaining $576 of adjusted basis in that year. She will then have a zero basis in the property.

c. The asset has a five-year recovery period. The §168(k) bonus depreciation rule applies because Joan places the asset in service in year two. The bonus depreciation equals $5,000, which is 50 percent of Joan's $10,000 basis in the asset. §168(k). Joan's basis in the asset is reduced to $5,000. Joan calculates her regular depreciation deductions as in part (b), except that the basis being depreciated is $5,000 instead of $10,000. The annual regular depreciation deductions in this part are half the annual depreciation deductions in part (b). For example, her year two depreciation deduction in part (b) was $2,000; in this part, her year two regular depreciation deduction equals $1,000, which is 50 percent (due to the half-year convention) of 40 percent (double the straight line 20 percent deduction) of Joan's remaining $5,000 basis in the asset. Joan's year two depreciation deduction equals $6,000, which is the sum of the $5,000 bonus depreciation and the $1,000 regular depreciation deduction.

d. The straight line percentage for five-year property would be 20 percent, and 150 percent of that percentage is 30 percent. The depreciation would be calculated using the 150 percent declining balance method until the year in which the deduction using the straight line method exceeds the 150 percent declining balance deduction. However, because of the half-year convention, Joan's deduction in year two, the year in which the property is placed in service, is half of the amount computed using the 150 percent declining balance method. Applying the 150 percent declining balance method and the half-year convention, Joan's depreciation deductions are as follows:

Year	Basis	150 percent method	S.L. method	Depreciation
2	$10,000	$1,500	$1,000	$1,500
3	8,500	2,550	1,889	2,550
4	5,950	1,785	1,700	1,785
5	4,165	1,250	1,666	1,666
6	2,499	750	1,666	1,666
7	833	250	833	833

e. The straight line percentage for five-year property would be 20 percent. The cost of the property is $10,000, so the annual straight line deduction equals $2,000 a year. However, the half-year convention applies in year two, the year in which Joan places the property in service, so the deduction for that year is $1,000. (On the other end of the recovery period, Joan also deducts $1,000 in year seven.) Applying the straight line method and the half-year convention, Joan's depreciation deductions are as follows:

Year	Basis	S.L. method depreciation
2	$10,000	$1,000
3	9,000	2,000
4	7,000	2,000
5	5,000	2,000
6	3,000	2,000
7	1,000	1,000

38. a. Yes. In 2014 Tad may elect to expense $25,000 of the cost of the property under §179. §179(b)(1). Tangible personal property is §179 property. §§179(d), 1245(a)(3).

   b. The option to expense the first $25,000 of §179 property is phased out, on a dollar-for-dollar basis, as the amount of §179 property placed in service in 2014 rises above $200,000. §179(b)(2). Here, the amount of §179 property in excess of $200,000 is $5,000. Thus, a taxpayer who places in service $205,000 of §179 property during 2014 and makes a §179 election may expense $20,000 ($25,000 less $5,000) of the cost of such property. The remaining cost of the property must be capitalized and depreciated.

39. Progress Company can amortize the newly acquired patent, despite the fact that §168 does not apply to intangible assets. Progress Company determines its annual depreciation deductions with respect to the patent under either §167 or §197. Section 197 applies if the patent was acquired as part of an acquisition of a trade or business. §197(a) — (c), (d)(1)(C)(iii), (e)(4)(C). Otherwise §167 applies. §167, Reg. §1.167(a)-14(a).

If §167 applies, Progress Company will probably amortize the patent ratably over its remaining useful life. Regulation §1.167(a)-14(c)(4) provides that a taxpayer amortizes a patent ratably over the remaining useful life of the patent, unless: (i) a special income forecast method in §167(g) applies; or (ii) the taxpayer's annual payments to the seller of the patent are based on the use of the patent or the revenue the taxpayer derives from the patent, in which case the taxpayer's amortization deduction equals the amount the taxpayer paid the seller that year. The recovery period is not clear, based on the facts given. The fact that a patent has a 20-year life might establish a *prima facie* case for a 20-year recovery period. Reg. §1.167(a)-3(a). However, the taxpayer might be able to establish a shorter recovery period if it provides evidence that the useful life of a particular patent is likely to be less than 20 years.

If §197 applies, Progress Company would deduct the $100,000 cost of the patent ratably over a 15-year period, so Progress Company's annual amortization deduction would be $6,667. §197(a).

40. The basis is reduced by *allowable* depreciation deductions, even if the deductions are not actually taken. §1016(a)(2). Since Paddy's Pork Rinds is allowed to take a $2,000 depreciation deduction in year four, the equipment's basis must be reduced by that amount. Therefore, the basis at the end of year four is $13,000, which is the $20,000 cost less allowed or allowable depreciation of $7,000 ($1,000 depreciation in year one and $6,000 of depreciation in years two through four). (Note that Paddy's may be violating federal securities law by misreporting its depreciation on its financial reports.)

41. a. The company's adjusted basis in the machine is $7,000 ($10,000 cost less $3,000 depreciation), therefore, the gain realized on the sale is $2,000 ($9,000 amount realized less $7,000 basis). Gain on the sale of depreciable business assets is often capital. §1231. However, the §1245 depreciation recapture rule states that gain on the sale of depreciable personal property is ordinary income to the extent of the prior depreciation deductions taken with respect to the property. §1245(a). This rule makes sense because depreciation deductions offset ordinary income, not capital gain, and are based on an estimate of the asset's decrease in value. Any gain on the sale of the asset shows that the depreciation was overestimated. By including the gain in ordinary income, the government is, in effect, recovering the excess ordinary deductions taken in the earlier years. The $2,000 of gain is ordinary because Out Damn Spot Company was allowed $3,000 of depreciation deductions on the machine.

   b. The company's adjusted basis in the machine is $7,000 ($10,000 cost less $3,000 depreciation), so the gain realized is $4,000 ($11,000 amount realized less $7,000 basis). Section 1245 mandates the inclusion in ordinary income of the amount by which the lower of (i) original basis (the basis before any depreciation deductions were taken) or (ii) the amount realized exceeds the adjusted basis of the property. §1245(a)(1), (2). In this instance the original basis ($10,000) is lower than the amount realized ($11,000), therefore, Out Damn Spot must include $3,000 as ordinary income ($10,000 original basis less $7,000 adjusted basis). The rest of the gain ($1,000) is probably capital gain. §1231. Put differently, a taxpayer's gain on depreciated equipment will be taxed as ordinary income to the extent of the depreciation previously taken, but any additional gain probably will be taxed as capital gain.

42. a. For nonresidential real property, the straight line method over a recovery period of 39 years must be used. §168(b)(3)(A), (c). The annual straight line deduction is thus $24,000 ($936,000/39). The applicable convention is a mid-month convention. §168(d)(2). Chubby Candy will be deemed to have placed the property in service in the middle of January, year one, so the company will deduct 23/24 of the annual straight line amount, or $23,000 ($2,000 per month for 11 months plus $1,000 for January), in year one. In year two the depreciation deduction is $24,000. The total depreciation for years one and two is thus $47,000, which reduces the adjusted basis in the property to $889,000 ($936,000 basis less $47,000 depreciation). §1016(a)(2).

 b. Depreciation begins when property is placed in service. The acquisition date is irrelevant. Therefore, Chubby Candy Company cannot take a depreciation deduction for year one. The year two deduction here is $23,000 (for the same reasons that the year one deduction in part (a) was $23,000). The adjusted basis at the end of year two is $913,000 ($936,000 cost less $23,000 depreciation).

43. $1,000. The basis of a purchased item is equal to the amount paid for the item. §1012.

44. $50,000. It is irrelevant that Carol borrowed part of the funds used to purchase the property.

45. a. True. §1016(a).
 b. False. Incidental repairs are currently deductible under §162, so they do not increase the basis of the property repaired.

46. Her basis at the end of the year is $90,000 ($100,000 cost less the $10,000 of year one depreciation). She would realize and recognize $15,000 of gain on the sale of the machine ($105,000 amount realized less $90,000 adjusted basis), $10,000 of which would be ordinary

income under §1245, and $5,000 of which would probably be capital gain under §1231. The depreciation recapture amount is limited to the depreciation taken on the property sold.

47. More. The §168 depreciation deductions allowed are generally much larger than the decline in value of the property, for several reasons. First, the recovery period for most assets is less than the actual useful life of the asset. Second, taxpayers are generally allowed to use accelerated depreciation methods that bunch the deductions in the early years of the asset's useful life. Third, the salvage value of the asset is deemed to be zero.

48. a. If accurate measurement of income is a concern, then income must accurately reflect the cost of assets that produce the income. For this reason, the cost of a "wasting asset" should not be fully deductible in the year of purchase. The asset would still have substantial value at the end of the year and the taxpayer's income would be understated. Since the decline in value of a wasting asset is a cost of earning income, the most accurate reflection of true income requires capitalization of the cost of the asset, then the deduction of depreciation over the useful life of the asset to reflect the decline in value of the asset.

b. In order to truly measure income, the depreciation method must reflect the asset's *actual* decline in value for the year. This method is referred to as the *economic depreciation* method. This method entails determining the asset's value at the beginning of the year and subtracting its value at the end of the year. The annual cost of the asset equals the decline in the present value of the income that will be earned on the asset in the future. Under this method, depreciation generally is *back-loaded, increasing* each year. Under the straight line method, depreciation deductions are even. Under the accelerated depreciation methods allowed under §168, depreciation *is front-loaded, decreasing* each year. In other words, both the straight line and accelerated depreciation methods overstate deductions and understate income in the early years of use of the property and have the opposite effect in the later years of the use of the property.

There are a couple of reasons why we do not use the economic depreciation method to compute depreciation for tax purposes. The main reason is that the economic depreciation method is impractical. Often it is impossible to determine an asset's value without selling the asset. We also might prefer to use straight line or accelerated depreciation instead of economic depreciation to encourage capital investments such as investment in equipment and machinery. Many people believe the current accelerated depreciation rules encourage such investment.

49. Deducting the full cost of a business or investment asset in the year in which it is placed in service. The cost of this type of asset is not an item of personal consumption, so the cost should be excluded from the taxable base.

I. DEPLETION DEDUCTIONS

Reading: §§263(c), 611, 612, 613, 613A, 616, 617.

Deductions may be taken for the depletion of certain natural resources, including mineral deposits, oil, gas, and timber. §§611–613A. There are two important methods of depletion: cost depletion and percentage depletion.

Cost depletion allocates the cost of the property among the estimated number of units of raw materials that will be recovered from the property. Thus, if the cost of the property were $1,000 and it is estimated that 100 tons of ore will be recovered, $10 of basis will be allocated to each ton.

Percentage depletion, on the other hand, permits a taxpayer simply to deduct a stated percentage of its gross income as a depletion allowance. Under this method, there is no need to estimate the number of recoverable units. Moreover, percentage depletion continues *even after the taxpayer's entire cost has been recovered.* The permitted depletion percentage ranges from 5 percent to 22 percent, depending on the type of natural resource. However, generally it may not exceed 50 percent of the taxable income from the property, computed without allowance for depletion. (Special income limitations apply to oil and gas depletion deductions.)

Examples

50. Describe the two main methods of determining depletion deductions.

51. Woody bought 30 acres of timber land for $3 million. He estimates that he will eventually take 500,000 tons of timber on the land. In the first year he cuts down and sells 80,000 tons of timber. Determine Woody's depletion deduction in the first year using the cost method.

52. Mr. Match buys a sulphur mine for $2 million. He estimates that there are about 500,000 tons of sulphur in the mine. In year one Mr. Match recovers 60,000 tons and his gross income is $1.2 million. In year two Mr. Match recovers 90,000 tons and his gross income is $1.8 million. In year three he recovers 30,000 tons and his gross income is $750,000. The depletion percentage for sulphur is 22 percent.
   a. Determine Mr. Match's depletion deductions for year one, year two, and year three under the cost depletion method.

b. Determine Mr. Match's depletion deductions for year one, year two, and year three under the percentage depletion method.

53. Ursula owns a sulphur mine and uses the percentage depletion method to determine her depletion deductions. The depletion percentage for sulphur is 22 percent. In year one Ursula has $1 million of gross income and $800,000 of expenses (other than the depletion). Determine Ursula's year one depletion deduction.

Explanations

50. One method of determining depletion deductions is cost depletion, which is based on the cost of the property being depleted. With this method, the taxpayer estimates the number of units of the resource that can be recovered and allocates the adjusted basis of the property to the units as they are sold. The estimate of recoverable units may be revised if it is later ascertained that the estimate was erroneous. §§611, 612.

The second method of determining depletion deductions is called percentage depletion. With this method, the taxpayer may deduct a percentage of gross income for depletion. Because the same percentage is used each year and there is no limitation on the number of years, the taxpayer may end up taking aggregate deductions that exceed the cost of the property. Section 613(b) lists the percentages applicable to the particular resources. §613.

51. Woody's basis in the timber property is $3 million. Since he estimates that 500,000 tons of timber are recoverable from the land, the cost per ton is $6 ($3 million/500,000 tons). In the first year Woody cuts down and sells 80,000 tons. Therefore his depletion deduction is $480,000 (80,000 tons multiplied by $6/ton).

52. a. Mr. Match's basis in the sulphur mine is $2 million. Since he estimates that 500,000 tons of sulphur are recoverable from the mine, the cost per ton is $4 ($2 million/500,000 tons). In year one Mr. Match recovers 60,000 tons so his cost depletion deduction is $240,000 (60,000 tons multiplied by $4/ton). In year two Mr. Match recovers 90,000 tons, so his cost depletion deduction is $360,000 (90,000 tons multiplied by $4/ton). In year three Mr. Match recovers 30,000 tons, so his cost depletion deduction is $120,000 (30,000 tons multiplied by $4/ton).

b. Under the percentage depletion method, sulphur mines are allowed a 22 percent deduction from gross income. §613(b)(1)(A). Therefore, in year one Mr. Match's percentage depletion deduction is $264,000 ($1.2 million multiplied by 22 percent). In year two his percentage depletion deduction is $396,000 ($1.8 million multiplied by 22 percent). In year three Mr. Match's percentage depletion deduction is $165,000 ($750,000 multiplied by 22 percent).

53. The maximum depletion deduction is limited to 50 percent of the *taxable* income from the property. §613(a). Since Ursula's gross income is $1 million and her costs are $800,000, her taxable income is $200,000. Ursula's depletion allowance is $220,000 ($1 million multiplied by 22 percent). Ursula is only allowed to deduct that allowance to the extent of one-half of her taxable income, or $100,000.

J. TAX SHELTERS

1. The Characteristics of Tax Shelters

The tax law has always favored certain forms of investments. We have earlier noted that specific Code provisions make certain kinds of investments (for example, municipal bonds, life insurance, deferred annuities, and qualified retirement plans) tax-favored. In addition, the realization requirement defers the taxation of gain from appreciation in an asset until the asset is sold, which encourages investment in such tax-deferred assets. Consider, for example, an investment in a growth stock that appreciates for many years and is then sold. The annual appreciation is not taxed until the time of sale, so the present value of the tax on the investment is much less than the tax paid on an equally profitable investment that is taxed currently. Preferential capital gains rates also encourage investment in capital assets. Some investments are also tax-favored because they permit taxpayers to accelerate expenses. For example, taxpayers can take accelerated depreciation deductions on depreciable property, which reduce the current tax due and increase the tax due in later years. The effect of accelerating expenses is to defer taxes, which reduces the tax due in present value terms.

Taxpayers who make such tax-favored investments have not done anything wrong; indeed, taxpayers who take advantage of benefits provided in specific Code provisions are presumably doing exactly what Congress wanted them to do when it enacted the provisions. Suppose, though, a taxpayer combines provisions that defer or do not fully tax annual investment income with other provisions that allow accelerated deductions of annual investment expenses. By creating a mismatch of income and expense, the taxpayer has an investment that may be quite profitable, on a before-tax basis, but that produces an annual tax loss that can be used to shelter (i.e., reduce) the tax the investor owes on other forms of income (including active business income). In extreme cases, the tax savings from the deferral of income and acceleration of expenses may convert an investment with a before-tax loss into a profitable investment after-tax. Investments like these that package deferred tax or no tax on income with accelerated deduction of expenses are often referred to as *tax shelters*, particularly if the investments are packaged and marketed by promoters.

Many tax shelters in the 1970s were built around real estate. Consider the following investment: Amy borrows $1 million at 9 percent and purchases an apartment building. The loan is nonrecourse and requires current payment of interest, but no payment of principal, for 30 years. Amy pays $90,000 of interest each year and receives $90,000 of rent each year; in addition, Amy claims $30,000 of depreciation each year. Amy incurs no out-of-pocket costs (since the rent and interest offset each other) but claims a $30,000 tax loss each year until the property is fully depreciated. The depreciation deduction is statutory and does not reflect the expected decline in value. In fact, the apartment building does not decline in value and is sold in year 30 for $1 million, with the sale proceeds being used to pay off the principal owed on the debt. Until 1986, Amy could use the $30,000 annual tax loss to shelter a like amount of salary income. If her tax rate were 50 percent, her tax savings would be $15,000 a year. In year 30, Amy would recognize $1 million in gain (because depreciation had reduced her basis to zero), but she would still be ahead, tax-wise. She would take large deductions, beginning in year one, for about 30 years, and have a large gain in year 30. The present value of the tax savings from the deductions would be much greater than the present value of the tax on the gain, which would not be realized until year 30.

Real life tax shelters differed from the example above in a number of ways. Typically, the investors had to contribute some of their own money to help finance the purchase of the property. Also, investments were generally not owned by a single individual. Instead, tax shelter promoters put together partnerships and sold interests in the partnerships to investors. The partnership then bought the property — often from the tax shelter promoters. The investors shared the annual losses from the partnership. The investors' tax shelter losses offset the investors' income from other sources and reduced the tax they owed. (Of course, the investors had to include gain on the back-end of the shelter, but they still came out ahead in present value terms because the shelter permitted them to defer tax.)

An even simpler tax shelter might involve financial assets. For example, suppose a taxpayer borrows at 9 percent and uses the funds to purchase an asset, such as annuity or growth stock, that is expected to and does provide an 8 percent return. If the interest on the loan is deductible each year as paid, but the annual appreciation on the asset is not taxed, the taxpayer can make money on an investment that would otherwise make no sense economically.

Congress could have limited the tax shelters described above, and other shelters as well, by adopting a more uniform tax on capital. Congress could, for example, have moved toward a more pure Haig-Simons tax base by taxing all or most forms of annual appreciation, by eliminating the low rate of tax on so-called capital gain, and by eliminating accelerated forms of depreciation. Instead, Congress has enacted a variety of complex statutory provisions that were crafted to discourage tax shelter investments. In addition, courts have tried to limit some of the more aggressive tax shelters by adopting general doctrines that look beyond literal compliance with specific tax-favored Code provisions.

2. The Judicial Response to Tax Shelters

Tax shelters based on clear statutory authority are impervious to IRS challenge. The government's only recourse is to convince Congress to change the law. The garden variety real estate tax shelter described above, for example, was widely marketed to high income taxpayers. The taxpayers who bought into such shelters benefited from the tax law in effect at that time. Occasionally, however, a promoter or taxpayer will come up with a tax shelter in an area in which the law is not settled, or will push settled law "too far" — at least in the government's mind. This type of aggressive tax shelter may be challenged by the IRS and struck down by the courts. Sometimes the court will conclude that the shelter simply does not meet the literal language of the law. Other times the court will conclude that the shelter complies with the literal language of the statute, but does not comply with the intent that underlies the statute. Still other times the court bases its decision on long-standing, extra-statutory judicial doctrines such as the *business purpose doctrine*, the *sham transaction doctrine*, and the *economic substance doctrine*. These doctrines are used to deny tax benefits in transactions that do not fall squarely within the letter and intent of the statute, are solely tax-motivated, and are without economic substance. Needless to say, the use of these judicial doctrines is controversial.

In Knetsch v. United States, 364 U.S. 361 (1960), the Supreme Court considered whether a taxpayer who had borrowed to fund a deferred annuity should be allowed to deduct the interest on the debt. Simplifying the facts of the *Knetsch* case, the taxpayer bought a $4,004,000 annuity from an insurance company for $4,000 of his own money and the proceeds of a $4 million nonrecourse loan from the insurance company. The yield on the annuity was 2.5 percent and the interest rate on the debt was 3.5 percent, so, before taking into account the tax consequences, the taxpayer lost money on the transaction. Each year that the loan was outstanding, the taxpayer was required to prepay $140,000 of interest on the debt. However, the annuity value increased each year and the taxpayer was permitted to borrow (again nonrecourse) the value of the annuity in excess of the $4 million of debt. In year one the taxpayer borrowed $100,000 against the increase in the value of the policy and prepaid $3,500 of interest on that new debt. The taxpayer did not have to include in income the increase in the value of the annuity, but claimed a $143,500 interest deduction for year one.

In the year at issue in the case, the top marginal rate was 91 percent. Assume that the taxpayer's rate was 91 percent, so the claimed interest deduction would have saved the taxpayer around $130,000 in tax. The taxpayer's out-of-pocket cost for year one would have been $47,500 — $40,000 ($140,000 of prepaid interest less the $100,000 the insurance company loaned the taxpayer), plus $4,000 cash paid for the annuity, plus $3,500 prepaid interest on the extra $100,000 borrowed. Thus, the taxpayer's net savings from the transaction in year one would have been $82,500. The Service disallowed the taxpayer's interest deduction and the trial court agreed with the Service, concluding that the purported debt was not true indebtedness.

The Supreme Court affirmed the disallowance of the interest deductions, calling the transaction a "sham." The Court concluded that the form of the transaction was a fiction; that the $100,000 "loan" on the increase in the value of the annuity was "in reality" a rebate of $100,000 of the $140,000 of interest prepaid on the $4 million loan. In addition, the Court characterized the taxpayer's $47,500 out-of-pocket cost as a fee paid to the insurance company for providing the tax shelter.

The outcome in *Knetsch* may be correct, considering the obvious tax avoidance motivation for the transaction and its artificial nature. However, it is not clear where legitimate tax reduction ends and "sham" characterization begins. In many cases in which the Service has urged a court to apply the sham transaction doctrine, the court has refused to do so. For example, in Fabreeka Products Co. v. Commissioner, 294 F.2d 876 (1st Cir. 1961) (and the related cases), the court concluded that taxpayers who had entered into various tax avoidance schemes that involved the deduction of "premium" paid for bonds were allowed their deductions, despite the fact that the tax avoidance motivation for the transactions was obvious.

The taxpayers in *Fabreeka* and the two companion cases had purchased bonds at a "premium," meaning that the price they paid exceeded the amount payable on the debt. At the time of the case, the entire bond premium could be deducted against ordinary income in the year in which the bond was purchased. Fabreeka Products and the two taxpayers in the related cases incorporated the bond premium deduction into various tax avoidance schemes. Fabreeka Products borrowed $100, bought bonds for $115, deducted the $15 of bond premium, and distributed the bonds to its shareholders. The shareholders then sold the bonds, paid the debt, and were left with $15. The shareholders had to include a $15 dividend on the distribution. A corporation is not allowed to deduct dividends it pays its shareholders, so the scheme effectively converted a $15 nondeductible dividend into a $15 bond premium deduction. In one of the related cases, the taxpayer took an ordinary deduction for the bond premium, then sold the bonds six months later, generating capital gain that was taxed at a lower rate than ordinary income. In the other related case, the taxpayer bought the bonds and donated them to charity. She took a deduction for the bond premium and a charitable contribution deduction for the donation of the bonds. The tax-exempt charity sold the bonds, netting the premium.

The Service argued that the taxpayers' bond premium deductions should be disallowed because the taxpayers had no investment motive when they acquired the bonds; instead, the sole motivation was tax avoidance. However, the court, noting that the taxpayers bore the economic risk of loss while they owned the bonds, refused to characterize the transactions as shams because the transactions involved "actual investments," instead of "paper proceedings" without any economic substance.

The opinion in *Fabreeka* is difficult to reconcile with the opinion in Goldstein v. Commissioner, 364 F.2d 734 (2d Cir. 1966). In the *Goldstein* case, the taxpayer won $140,000 in the Irish Sweepstakes in 1958. Her son, an accountant, devised a strategy to minimize the tax due on her winnings in that year. Simplifying somewhat, the taxpayer borrowed $465,000 in 1958 from a bank at a 4 percent interest rate, prepaying $52,000 of interest on that debt. With the loan proceeds, she purchased U.S. Treasury notes that yielded 1.5 percent interest and were due in 1961. She repeated these steps with a second bank. Her economic (that is, nontax) loss on the bonds was expected to be $18,500. However, the tax savings from the transactions exceeded that economic loss because: (i) in 1958 her interest deductions offset the ordinary income from her winnings, dramatically reducing the tax for that year; (ii) she was in a lower tax bracket when she earned the interest on the notes in later years; and (iii) she converted ordinary income, from her winnings in 1958, into capital gain on the redemption of the bonds in 1961. The Service disallowed the interest deductions for 1958. The Second Circuit noted that, absent tax consequences, a taxpayer would not borrow at 4 percent to buy an investment that yields 1.5 percent. In light of the strong tax-avoidance motive and the lack of other business motivation for the transaction, the court concluded that the interest was not deductible under §163.

The *Goldstein* and *Fabreeka* decisions can be reconciled, but not easily. One difference between the facts in the two cases may be significant: The court in *Fabreeka* thought that people would acquire bonds at a premium for reasons other than the current deduction of the bond premium, but the court in *Goldstein* expressed the view that no one would borrow at 4 percent to earn 1.5 percent. (The sham transaction doctrine is also discussed in the context of corporate tax shelters later in this chapter.)

The attractiveness of tax shelters in real estate and other fields often depends on the depreciation that is available to the investor. One way to increase the amount of depreciation is to arrange to purchase the property at an inflated price — with a real down payment up front and a large payment scheduled, but never made, sometime in the distant future. If the scheme works, the investor gets a basis equal to the total purchase price (the up front payment plus the unrealistically large payment to be made in the future). The investor then takes inflated depreciation deductions on the inflated basis for the property. Eventually, the basis is reduced to zero and the investor defaults on the loan. Under *Tufts*, the balance of the loan is treated as having been received upon sale or foreclosure. The investor then has to recognize income and, in effect, "give back" the depreciation taken in the earlier years. The default and gain occurs after many years of depreciation deductions have been taken, however, which makes the present value of the tax savings from the annual depreciation deductions much greater than the present value of the tax cost on foreclosure.

Estate of Franklin v. Commissioner, 544 F.2d 1045 (9th Cir. 1976), illustrates one of the judicial approaches to this type of problem. A partnership (Associates) "purchased" an inn from the Romneys for $1.2 million purchase money nonrecourse debt (meaning that the sellers took back a note) bearing 7.5 percent interest. At the closing, Associates prepaid $75,000 of interest on the debt. Associates was to make monthly payments to the Romneys of $9,000 (part of which was interest and part of which was repayment of principal). After 10 years, Associates was to make a balloon payment of any remaining balance, approximately $975,000. Associates then leased the motel back to the Romneys in exchange for $9,000 a month of rent. Since the $9,000 monthly payments owed by each party to the other offset each other, no cash (other than the initial $75,000 payment) was to pass between the parties until the balloon payment was due in 10 years. The lease was a net lease, meaning the Romneys paid all of the expenses of owning the motel.

The partners in Associates took interest deductions on the debt and depreciation deductions calculated on $1.2 million of basis, which included the debt, under the *Crane* case. The deductions produced large partnership losses that the partners used to offset their earnings as doctors. The Commissioner disallowed the losses claimed by the partners. The Tax Court held that the transaction was not a debt transaction, but was instead the purchase of an option to acquire the inn. The Ninth Circuit Court of Appeals concluded that, at the time the inn was purchased, the value of the inn (which was in the neighborhood of $600,000) was significantly less than the $1.2 million of nonrecourse debt on the property. Based on that fact, the court further concluded that the nonrecourse debt was not genuine indebtedness, so the debt should not have been included in basis and did not produce interest or depreciation deductions.

Although many courts have followed the *Franklin* approach, some courts have adopted a different approach to inflated nonrecourse debt. For example, in Pleasant Summit Land Corp. v. Commissioner, 863 F.2d 263 (3d Cir. 1988), the court allowed the taxpayer basis for the inflated nonrecourse debt, but only up to the fair market value of the property. In that case, a partnership bought real property for $500,000 in cash plus $7.2 million of nonrecourse debt. The seller of the property (which was related to the partnership) had paid $4.2 million for the property plus the land it was on just the year before the partnership bought it. The taxpayer, a partner in the partnership, took $760,000 of deductions (for depreciation and interest) with respect to the property, but the Commissioner disallowed the deductions. The Tax Court judge found that the value of the property was not in excess of $4.2 million and concluded that the nonrecourse debt was not real indebtedness, so the debt could not support any of the deductions. On appeal, the court held that, where nonrecourse debt exceeds the value of the property subject to the debt, the nonrecourse debt is includible in basis only up to the value of the property. The court reasoned that a borrower would not default on nonrecourse debt if the debt did not exceed the value of the property, so a taxpayer should get basis credit for that portion of the debt. The court added that any cash paid by the taxpayer should also be included in the taxpayer's basis for the property. In other words, the basis would include both the $4.2 million portion of the $7.2 million of nonrecourse debt that did not exceed the value of the property and the $500,000 of cash paid for the property.

The judicial approach to limiting deductions in egregious tax shelters did not stop the proliferation of tax shelters. The fact that many high income taxpayers avoided paying tax by investing in tax shelters angered middle and low income taxpayers and threatened taxpayer morale. Eventually, in the early 1980s, the press began to focus on the public perception that permitting high income taxpayers to avoid tax by investing in tax shelters was unfair. This prompted Congress to launch a frontal assault on tax shelters, which culminated in the enactment, in 1986, of new and expanded statutory limitations on tax shelters.

Examples

54. Daisy, a highly compensated investment banker, is in the 40 percent tax bracket. In year one she buys a limited-edition photograph of a Picasso painting and the worldwide rights to reproduce the photograph in any media (for example, posters and calendars). Two appraisers recommended by the seller, who is a tax shelter promoter, appraised the photograph "package" at around $700,000, but provided no support for their appraisals. Government experts estimated that the package was worth only $5,000. Daisy paid $550,000 for the package, $50,000 of which was cash and $500,000 of which was from nonrecourse debt. Daisy claimed year one interest and depreciation deductions totaling $90,000. Daisy unsuccessfully attempted to market the package.

The Commissioner disallows Daisy's year one deductions and Daisy has decided to litigate the case. Will a court agree with the disallowance of the deduction?

55. Adam acquired Blackacre in year one for $200,000 of cash and $800,000 of nonrecourse debt. (At the time, Blackacre was probably only worth $700,000.) In year one Adam took deductions for $80,000 of interest on the nonrecourse debt and $35,000 of depreciation (calculated by reference to a $1 million basis for the property).

The Commissioner disallows Adam's year one deductions and he decides to litigate the case. Will a court agree with the disallowance of the deductions?

Explanations

54. A court would probably not allow the deductions. However, this is a tough call because it is impossible to discern a clear standard for determining when a transaction entered into to reduce taxes will be recharacterized for tax purposes.

Here, it may be possible to characterize the transaction as a "sham," given that Daisy paid so much more for the package than government experts estimated it was worth. One could argue that, as in Knetsch v. United States, 364 U.S. 361 (1960), Daisy's interest deductions should be disallowed since her transaction had no economic substance; absent tax considerations, no rational person would have entered into the transaction because, on an economic basis, it lost money. Further, a court might characterize Daisy's $50,000 cash payment for the painting as a fee paid for the tax shelter, just as the Court in *Knetsch* did with respect to the taxpayer's year-one, $47,500 out-of-pocket costs.

On the other hand, a court might refuse to apply the sham transaction doctrine, as the court refused to do in Fabreeka Products Co. v. Commissioner, 294 F.2d 876 (1st Cir. 1961) (and the related cases). Despite the seemingly obvious tax avoidance motive, the court might find that people buy paintings for reasons other than tax avoidance and that buying the painting exposed Daisy to changes in its value. In this sense, the court might rule that the purchase of the painting is similar to the purchase of bonds in *Fabreeka* and that the deductions should thus be allowed.

Even if Daisy can avoid the sham label, some courts have disallowed deductions from transactions that were not shams because of the taxpayer's patent tax avoidance motive for entering into the transaction. For example, in Goldstein v. Commissioner, 364 F.2d 734 (2d Cir. 1966), the court disallowed the taxpayer's deduction for interest she prepaid on a loan bearing 4 percent interest, which she incurred to acquire bonds yielding 1.5 percent. Although, on an economic basis, the transaction lost money, the transaction was profitable after taking into account the tax savings from the transaction. The Second Circuit noted that, absent tax consequences, a taxpayer would not borrow at 4 percent to buy an investment that yields 1.5 percent. In light of the strong tax avoidance motive and the lack of other business motivation for the transaction, the court concluded that the interest was not deductible under §163.

Here, it is theoretically conceivable that someone could earn substantial amounts by exploiting a photograph of a famous work of art. However, the facts do not establish the profitmaking potential of the photograph package. It appears that Daisy bought something worth $5,000 on an economic basis, for $50,000 of cash and $500,000 of debt. The $500,000 of debt is also nonrecourse and it seems very likely that Daisy would have defaulted on the debt (which also raises an Estate of Franklin issue). In sum, these facts indicate that this transaction is one that people would not enter into for economic reasons, but would enter into for tax avoidance reasons. The facts of this example are loosely based on the facts in Rose v. Commissioner, 88 T.C. 386 (1987), in which the court agreed with the Commissioner's disallowance of the deductions from the Picasso photograph tax shelter.

55. A court would probably view this case as distinguishable from Estate of Franklin v. Commissioner, 544 F.2d 1045 (9th Cir. 1976), for the reasons described below, and thus would not apply that approach to disallow the deductions. However, if a court applies the approach adopted in Pleasant Summit Land Corp. v. Commissioner, 863 F.2d 263 (3d Cir. 1988), the basis attributable to the nonrecourse debt will be limited to the $700,000 value of the property so Adam's depreciable basis for the property would be $900,000 instead of $1 million.

The Service may argue that the nonrecourse debt is not true indebtedness, citing Estate of Franklin, so the deductions must be disallowed. The Franklin approach is used by some but not all circuits. For example, the Third Circuit would apply the approach adopted in Pleasant Summit. In other words, the approach taken by a court might depend on where the taxpayer lives and where the taxpayer litigates. If the taxpayer litigates in the Tax Court or a district court, the court will apply the precedent of the circuit in which the taxpayer resides. If the taxpayer litigates in the Court of Federal Claims, the court will apply precedent from the Federal Circuit Court of Appeals.

If Franklin applies, none of the $800,000 of nonrecourse debt would be included in Adam's depreciable basis for the property. Here, as in Franklin, the property subject to the debt has a value that is less than the amount of the debt. However, this case may be distinguishable from *Franklin* for two reasons. First, in *Franklin*, the taxpayers paid only 6 percent of the "purchase price" in cash, so the court concluded that the taxpayers had not made "an investment" in the property, but instead had purchased something akin to an option. Here, on the other hand, Adam paid 20 percent of the purchase price in cash, which may make a difference. Second, in *Franklin*, the nonrecourse debt on the property was twice the likely value of the property. Here, the nonrecourse debt exceeded the value of the property by around 15 percent. In sum, this transaction does not look nearly as egregious as the transaction in *Franklin*, and some courts might view the *Franklin* approach as extreme, so it seems unlikely that a court would hold that the debt was not true debt.

Under the *Pleasant Summit* approach, Adam's depreciable basis in the property would be $900,000 — the $200,000 of cash Adam paid plus the $700,000 portion of the nonrecourse indebtedness that does not exceed the value of the property. This would reduce his year one depreciation, but would not reduce it nearly as much as the extreme *Franklin* approach.

3. The Congressional Response to Tax Shelters

As we said earlier, Congress could have limited tax shelter investments by adopting a more uniform approach to capital taxation, but instead enacted a variety of complex statutory provisions that were designed to discourage tax shelter investments. Some of the provisions enacted in 1986 were new and some reinforced older, more specific anti-abuse limitations in the Code (a few of which we will discuss below). The combination of the old and new anti-tax shelter provisions has virtually eliminated the individual tax shelter industry.

In addition to the limitations discussed in this section, taxpayers who invest in tax shelters can be subject to §6662 accuracy-related penalties (discussed in Chapters 1 and 4). Various other Code sections also impose penalties on tax shelter promoters and require additional information reporting for tax shelters. See, e.g., §§6111, 6112, 6662A, 6700, 6701, 6707, 6707A, 6708.

In this section, we will consider the following anti-tax shelter provisions: (i) the investment interest limitation of §163(d); (ii) the passive loss limitation of §469; (iii) the at-risk limitation of §465; and (iv) the interest deduction limitations of §§264 and 265. (In Chapter 6 we will consider another anti-tax shelter provision, the so-called "hobby loss" limitation of §183.)

You can categorize these various limitations by asking yourself two questions: First, what type of *investments* (for example, active business investments, passive business investments, portfolio investments, or investments in insurance products or tax-exempt bonds) are affected by the limitation? Second, what type of *deductions* (for example, depreciation, interest, or other deductions) are affected by the limitation?

a. The Investment Interest Limitation of §163(d)

Reading: §163(d).

The §163 investment interest limitation is designed to prevent the misstatement of income and mismatching of items of income and expense, both of which can result from using borrowed funds to invest in property that is expected to appreciate.

Suppose, for example, that in year one Joan borrows $500 and uses the proceeds to purchase "growth" stock that does not pay a high rate of dividends but is expected to rise in value. During year one the interest on the loan is $50 and the stock appreciates $50, so that its value at the end of year one is $550. The investment does not produce any economic loss since the $50 interest expense is offset by the $50 rise in value. However, because Joan has not realized any gain from the stock through a sale or taxable exchange, the rise in value will not be subject to current tax. If Joan is allowed to deduct the interest expense, the deduction will be offset against her ordinary income for the year, reducing her tax for the year. If Joan sells the stock in year two for $550, she will pay tax on the gain in that year. In other words, Joan will have reduced her tax in year one and increased her tax in year two, which benefits Joan because of the time value of money; the present value of the year two tax payment is less than the present value of the immediate tax savings.

If Joan retains the stock until her death, the tax treatment of the transaction will be even more favorable. Joan will deduct the loss in year one, but, under §1014, her heirs will receive a basis in the property equal to its fair market value at the time of death. If the property is worth $550 at the time of death, the $50 in gain will never be taxed.

Section 163(d) provides that the amount allowed as a deduction for investment interest shall not exceed net investment income. Investment interest is defined as interest on indebtedness allocable to property held for investment. §163(d)(3)(A). However, qualified residence interest and interest taken into account in calculating the §469 passive loss limitation are not within the definition of investment interest. §163(d)(3)(B). Investment income is defined, generally, as the net income (gross income less expenses) from investments that produce interest, dividends, annuities, or royalties not derived in the ordinary course of a trade or business. §§163(d)(4), (5), 469(e)(1). (Since 1986 rent has not been treated as investment income.) Long-term capital gain (gain on the sale of a capital asset held by the taxpayer for more than a year) from investments (also certain dividend income) is taken into account in computing investment income only if the taxpayer elects to not apply preferential capital gain rates to the gain and dividends. §§163(d)(4)(B), 1222(11), 1(h)(11)(B), Reg. §1.63(d)-1(a). Interest in excess of the §163(d) limitation is carried forward and treated as investment interest in the next year. §163(d)(2). Note that the §163(d) investment interest limitation does not apply to corporations that are subject to the §11 entity level corporate tax. §163(d)(1).

Examples

56. What is the purpose of the limitation on the deduction allowed for investment interest?

57. a. On January 1, year one, John borrows $100 and uses the loan proceeds to purchase $100 of Rise Company stock. The loan used to purchase the stock is nonrecourse. On December 31, year one, the value of the Rise Company stock is $110. On that same day, John pays $10 of interest on the loan used to purchase the stock. The stock pays no dividends and John has no other investment income or interest expense. How much, if any, of the investment interest expense may John deduct?

  b. How, if at all, would your answer in part (a) change if the loan used to purchase the stock is recourse?

  c. How, if at all, would your answer in part (a) change if the value of the stock on December 31, year one, is only $100?

  d. How, if at all, would your answer in part (a) change if, on December 31, year one, John sells the stock for $115?

  e. Is John allowed to deduct the $10 of interest he paid in year one if, on January 2, year two, he sells the stock for $110?

  f. How, if at all, would your answer in part (a) change if, on December 31, year one, John sells the stock for $95?

  g. How, if at all, would your answer in part (a) change if, in year one, John includes $6 in interest income from a corporate bond?

  h. Assume the same set of facts as in part (a) except that, in year two, John pays another $10 of interest on the loan used to purchase the Rise Company stock and includes $15 of dividends from the Rise Company stock. How much, if any, interest may John deduct in years one and two?

  i. Assume the same set of facts as in part (a) except that, in year one, John receives $20 of dividends from the Rise Company stock, and, in year two, John pays $10 of interest but receives no dividends from Rise Company stock. How much, if any, of the interest is John allowed to deduct in years one and two?

j. How, if at all, would your answer in part (a) change if, in year one, John recognizes $10 of rental income?

Explanations

56. The §163(d) investment interest limitation is designed to prevent the misstatement of income and mismatching of items of income and expense, both of which can arise from using borrowed funds to invest in property that is expected to appreciate.

57. a. John is not allowed to deduct investment interest in excess of his net investment income. §163(d). Here, John has $10 of investment interest expense but no investment income. Thus, John will not be able to deduct any of the $10 of investment interest.
   b. As in part (a), John will not be able to deduct any of the investment interest. The fact that the loan is recourse is irrelevant.
   c. Recall that the purpose of §163(d) is to prevent the deduction of interest on investments that are expected to produce unrealized gain. Here, there is no unrealized gain: John has suffered an economic loss equal to the amount of the $10 interest payment. Nonetheless, under §163(d), John will not be allowed to deduct any portion of the interest in year one.
   d. John may deduct the $10 of interest. Investment income is defined to include short-term capital gain (gain on the sale of a capital asset held by the taxpayer for a year or less) from the disposition of investment property. (Note that short-term capital gain is not taxed at preferential rates.) John has $15 of net investment income, so he is allowed to deduct the full $10 of investment interest. §163(d)(4)(B)(i).
   e. As in part (a), John cannot deduct the $10 of interest in year one. However, John carries the $10 of investment interest forward to year two. The $10 of capital gain on the sale of the stock is long-term capital gain, so it is treated as investment income only if John elects to forgo the preferential capital gain rate on the gain. §163(d)(4)(B)(iii). If John makes this election, he has $10 of investment income and can deduct the $10 of interest in year two. If he does not make this election, he cannot deduct the interest because his investment income is zero.
   f. Here, John has suffered an economic loss on the investment and there is no possibility that the investment will ever produce an economic gain. Nonetheless, John will not be able to deduct any portion of the $10 interest expense since his investment income for year one is zero. John will, however, be able to carry the $10

investment interest deduction forward to year two. He can deduct that interest in year two to the extent of his year two investment income.

g. John may deduct $6 of the interest expense. Interest expense may be deducted in an amount equal to all investment income, including income from investment property that was not purchased with borrowed funds. Here, John has $6 of investment income from the corporate bond and may therefore deduct $6 of investment expense. The other $4 of year one interest is carried forward to year two.

h. The answer depends on whether John elects to forgo preferential capital gain rates. As in part (a), John has no investment income in year one and therefore cannot deduct the $10 of interest in that year. The $10 interest expense that cannot be deducted in year one carries forward to year two and is treated as interest expense in that year. In year two John has $15 of dividend income and $20 of investment expense ($10 current expense and $10 that is treated as a current expense under §163(d)(2)). The dividend income will be treated as investment income only if John elects to forgo the preferential tax rate applicable to qualified dividend income. §163(d)(4)(B)(iii), Reg. §163(d)-1(a). If John makes this election, he can deduct $15 of interest in year two. The remaining $5 of interest is carried forward to year three. If he does not make this election, John cannot deduct the $20 of interest in year two and that interest is carried forward to year three.

i. As in part (h), the answer depends in part on whether John forgoes the preferential tax rate on the dividend income. If he makes that election, the $20 of dividend income received in year one is treated as investment income and John can deduct the entire $10 of interest expense. In year two John cannot deduct any interest expense, even if he makes the election.

j. John may not deduct any portion of the interest. Prior to 1986, certain forms of rental income were considered investment income. Currently, however, rental income is not treated as investment income. §§163(d)(5), 469(e)(1). Thus, John has no investment income and therefore cannot deduct any of the interest expense.

b. The Passive Loss Rules of §469

Reading: §469.

Tax shelters are designed to exploit the mismatching of deductions and inclusions in order to permit the taxpayer to defer tax and, in some cases to convert ordinary income into capital gain. Recall our earlier illustration of a real estate tax shelter, in which a taxpayer buys real estate for nonrecourse debt. The depreciation and interest deductions in excess of the amount of rental income from the property offset the taxpayer's income from other sources (for example, from the active conduct of a trade or business such as the practice of medicine). However, the appreciation in the property is not taxed until the property is sold or exchanged. Even if the tax saved in the early years of the investment exactly equals the tax that will be owed in the later years of the investment, the taxpayer benefits significantly from deferral of tax. Section 469 destroys the tax deferral benefit of shelters by disallowing the deductions from the shelter until the income from the shelter is realized.

The §469 passive loss limitation is designed to prevent a taxpayer from using deductions from "passive activities" to offset the taxpayer's income from either portfolio investment or an active trade or business. In order to accomplish this goal, §469 segregates the taxpayer's income and loss for the year into three baskets: (i) *passive*, (ii) *portfolio*, and (iii) *active trade or business*. A passive activity loss is deductible only to the extent of the taxpayer's passive income; it cannot be used to offset the taxpayer's portfolio income (for example, interest or dividends) or active business income. Passive activity losses disallowed under §469 are carried forward to the next tax year and are again subject to §469 in that year. §469(b). When a taxpayer ultimately disposes of her entire interest in a passive activity (in a transaction other than a nonrecognition transaction), the taxpayer can generally deduct the remaining losses from that activity that were carried forward from earlier years. §469(g).

A *passive activity loss* is defined, in general, as the net loss from activities (i) that involve the conduct of a trade or business and (ii) in which the taxpayer does not "materially participate." §469(c), (d). The determination of whether an activity is active or passive usually turns on whether the taxpayer materially participates in the activity. *Material participation* is defined as participation that is "regular, continuous, and substantial." §469(h)(1). Temporary Regulation §1.469-5T(a) provides that a taxpayer is deemed to have materially participated in an activity in a given year only if the taxpayer can satisfy one of the following seven tests set forth in the regulation:

1. The individual participates in the activity for more than 500 hours during the year;
2. The taxpayer's participation in the activity during the year constitutes substantially all of the participation in such activity of all individuals, including non-owners;
3. The individual participates in the activity for more than 100 hours during the year and no one else had greater participation in the activity;
4. The activity is a "significant participation activity" (defined in Temporary Regulation §1.469-5T(c) as a trade or business activity in which the taxpayer "significantly participates") and the taxpayer's

aggregate participation in all significant participation activities during the year exceeds 500 hours;

5. The taxpayer materially participated in the activity for any five taxable years in the 10-year period that immediately precedes the current tax year;

6. The activity is a "personal service activity" (defined in Temporary Regulation §1.469-5T(d) as an activity involving the performance of personal services in the fields of health, law, engineering, architecture, accounting, actuarial science, performing arts, consulting, or any other trade or business in which capital is not a material income-producing factor) and the taxpayer materially participated in the activity for any three taxable years (whether or not consecutive) preceding the taxable year; or

7. The taxpayer participates in the activity over 100 hours during the taxable year and, based on all of the facts and circumstances, the taxpayer participates in the activity on a regular, continuous, and substantial basis during the year. Temp. Reg. §1.469-5T(b). (For purposes of applying this last test, time spent managing an activity counts toward participation only if the taxpayer spends more time than anyone else managing the activity and no other person is paid to manage the activity.)

Section 469(h)(2) provides that a limited partner is not deemed to materially participate in the activities of the partnership. However, Temporary Regulation §1.469-5T(e)(2) provides that, if the limited partner can satisfy the material participation tests of §1.469-5T(a)(1), (5), or (6) (described above) with respect to an activity, the passive loss limitation does not apply to the limited partner's losses from that activity.

A *rental activity*, which is an activity in which payments are principally for the use of tangible property, is generally treated as a passive activity. §469(c)(2), (j)(8). (However, Temporary Regulation §1.469-1T(e)(3)(ii) provides that some activities in which property is rented are not treated as rental activities.) There are several exceptions to the general rule that rental activities are passive. For example, this general rule does not apply to a rental real estate activity if: (i) more than half of the personal services performed in trades or businesses by the taxpayer are performed in real property trades or businesses in which the taxpayer materially participates and (ii) the taxpayer performs more than 750 hours of services during the year in real property trades or businesses in which the taxpayer materially participates. §469(c)(7)(B).

In addition, if the rental real estate activity is passive, an individual taxpayer who "actively participates" in the rental real estate activity during the year is allowed to deduct up to $25,000 of the taxpayer's passive losses from the activity despite the general disallowance rule. §469(i)(1), (2).

This $25,000 exemption is reduced by 50 percent of the taxpayer's adjusted gross income (with a few modifications) over $100,000. §469(i)(3). The term *active participation* is not defined in the statute, which says only that the active participation standard is not met unless the taxpayer owns at least 10 percent of the value of the activity. §469(i)(6). The legislative history of §469 states that active participation can be established through managerial functions such as deciding on rental terms and approving tenants or capital outlays. It also clarifies that the standard for active participation is less than the standard for material participation.

If a passive activity involves the use of a dwelling unit and the limitation of §280A(c)(5) (discussed in Chapter 6) applies, the income, deduction, gain, or loss allocable to such use is disregarded for purposes of §469. §469(j)(10). A working interest in any oil and gas property is not a passive activity if the taxpayer has unlimited liability with respect to the property. §469(c)(3).

The term *activity* is defined in Regulation §1.469-4, which provides that trade or business or rental activities may be treated as a single activity if the activities to be grouped together are "an appropriate economic unit" for purposes of applying §469. The determination as to whether activities constitute an appropriate economic unit is based on a facts and circumstances test, but the following factors are given the greatest weight: (i) the similarities and differences in the types of trades or businesses; (ii) the extent of common control or ownership of the activities; (iii) the geographical location of the activities; and (iv) any interdependencies among the activities. Reg. §1.469-4(c)(2). Under this test, business or rental activities that are conducted at the same location and are owned by the same person are generally treated as a single activity.

The §469 passive loss rules apply only to individuals, estates, trusts, closely held C corporations, and personal service corporations. §469(a)(2). A *closely held C corporation* is defined as a corporation, 50 percent of the stock of which is held, directly or indirectly, by five or fewer individuals. §§469(j)(1), 465(a)(1)(B), 542(a)(2). A corporation is a *personal service corporation* if its principal activity is the performance of personal services and the services are substantially performed by employees who own stock of the corporation either directly or indirectly. §269A(b).

Examples

58. On January 1, year one, Ann borrows $80,000 and uses the proceeds of the loan, together with $20,000 of her own money, to open a bicycle shop. The loan is recourse and Ann does not materially participate in the management of the shop. In year one the bicycle shop shows a net loss on operations of $30,000. In each of the following situations, state the

amount of loss that Ann may deduct and the year in which Ann may deduct the loss.

a. Ann has no other investments.

b. Ann receives $20,000 of dividends from stock.

c. Ann also owns a restaurant and works there full-time. Her year one taxable income from the restaurant is $30,000.

d. Ann also owns a restaurant, but does not materially participate in the management of the restaurant. Her year one taxable income from the restaurant is $30,000.

e. Ann also owns a restaurant, but does not materially participate in the management of the restaurant. In the year before year one, Ann's taxable income from the restaurant is $30,000. In year one the restaurant has no taxable income.

f. Ann also owns a restaurant, but does not materially participate in the management of the restaurant. In year one the restaurant has no taxable income. In year two Ann's taxable income from the restaurant is $40,000, and the bicycle shop has zero income or loss.

g. Ann sells the bicycle shop for $130,000 on December 31, year one.

h. Ann sells the bicycle shop for $90,000 on December 31, year one.

i. On December 31, year one, Ann sells a restaurant she owns for $130,000. Ann's basis in the restaurant is $100,000 and Ann does not materially participate in the management of the restaurant. The restaurant shows no taxable income or loss from operations in year one.

j. Assume the same facts as in part (i), except that Ann sells the restaurant for $70,000.

k. Assume the same facts as in part (i), except that the loan is nonrecourse, and in year one Ann recognizes $30,000 of income from another passive activity.

59. Roger's auto repair shop shows a taxable loss of $25,000 in year one. State the amount, if any, of that loss that would be deductible in each of the following situations.

a. Year one is the first taxable year for the repair shop. The shop has five full-time employees. Roger, however, works at the shop only 450 hours each year.

b. How, if at all, would your answer in part (a) change if Roger works at the shop for 1,050 hours?

c. How, if at all, would your answer in part (a) change if Roger works at the shop for 550 hours?

d. Roger works at the shop for only 150 hours in year nine. The shop has five full-time employees. Roger has owned the store for the past eight years. During four of those years, Roger worked at the shop for less than 300 hours; during the remaining four years, Roger worked at the shop for over 1,500 hours.

60. On January 1, year one, Shannon starts a consulting business.
    a. During year one Shannon works at the business for 150 hours and the only other employee works at the business for 100 hours. Does Shannon materially participate in the activity in year one?
    b. During year one Shannon works at the business for 75 hours and there are no other employees who participate in the management of the business. Does Shannon materially participate in the activity in year one?
    c. During year one Shannon works at the business for 75 hours and employs two other employees who work full-time at the activity. Does Shannon materially participate in the activity in year one?
    d. Shannon works full-time in the business in years one through three. In year four she works at the business 75 hours and employs two other employees who work full-time in the activity. Does Shannon materially participate in the activity in year four?
    e. Shannon works full-time in the business in years one through three. In year four she does not work at the business at all. Does Shannon materially participate in the activity in year four?

61. On January 1, year one, Juan purchases an apartment building. The apartment building shows a net loss for the year of $30,000. Juan has a full-time employee manage the building; however, Juan interviews all prospective tenants and makes the final decision on major repairs. Juan spends about 110 hours a year on the building and has no other investments. How much, if any, of the loss may Juan use to offset his salary income?

62. In year one Tissy has an $18,000 loss from an investment in a goat's milk frozen yogurt shop. She did not materially participate in the business. In the same year, she has $10,000 of income from a limited partnership, made $30,000 in wages as an environmental analyst, and made $15,000 in the stock market. What are the tax consequences?

63. Describe the special provisions of §469, if any, that apply to the following investments.
    a. losses recognized by large, publicly held corporations;
    b. losses recognized by limited partners;
    c. losses recognized by general partners in a limited partnership;
    d. losses recognized by trusts;
    e. losses recognized on working interests in oil and gas properties;
    f. losses recognized on rental of a vacation home.

64. Under what circumstances would a taxpayer want to *avoid* material participation in a particular trade or business?

Explanations

58. a. Section 469 prevents the deduction of any "passive activity loss." §469(a)(1). A passive activity loss generally is defined as the net loss from all activities that involve the conduct of a trade or business and in which the taxpayer does not materially participate. §469(c), (d). Here, Ann has a passive activity loss and will not be able to deduct any portion of that loss in year one. Instead, that loss may be deducted in subsequent years when and if Ann has passive activity income or disposes of the bicycle shop in a taxable transaction.

    b. Investors with losses from passive activities may offset those losses against gains from other passive activities. However, passive activity losses may not offset portfolio income or trade or business income. The stock dividends constitute so-called "portfolio" income, so no portion of Ann's passive activity loss will be deductible in year one.

    c. Here, Ann has income from a nonpassive activity — the restaurant at which she works on a full-time basis. Ann's passive activity loss from the bicycle shop may only offset passive income, however. Ann may not use the bicycle shop loss to offset this nonpassive income.

    d. Here, the restaurant is a passive activity because Ann does not materially participate in the activity. Ann has $30,000 of income from a passive activity, so the entire $30,000 bicycle shop loss may be deducted against that income.

    e. The passive loss rules permit taxpayers to carry forward any net passive losses and apply those losses against passive activity income in subsequent years. §469(b). However, the rules do not permit taxpayers to carry back any net passive losses and apply those losses against passive activity income in past years. Here, Ann has past but no current passive activity income and therefore cannot deduct the loss in year one.

    f. Ann will not be able to deduct any portion of the year one loss. Instead, that loss will carry over to year two. Since Ann has $40,000 of passive activity income in year two, she may deduct the entire $30,000 loss against that income in year two.

    g. Ann will recognize gain or loss on the sale of the shop in an amount equal to the difference between the $130,000 sale price and her adjusted basis. Ann may deduct the entire year one loss at the time the bicycle shop is sold. §469(g).

    h. Ann may deduct the entire year one loss at the time the bicycle shop is sold. §469(g). The deduction of that earlier loss is not dependent upon the sale price. In year one Ann will also recognize gain or loss equal to the difference between the $90,000 sale price and her adjusted basis.

i. Gain from the sale of a passive activity is treated as passive activity income and can be offset against otherwise unusable passive activity loss. Ann has year one passive income of $30,000, so she will be able to deduct the entire loss from the bicycle shop. Note that while the sale of the bicycle shop would allow Ann to deduct the bicycle shop loss *regardless of whether or not Ann recognized gain on the sale*, the sale of the restaurant allows Ann to deduct the bicycle shop loss only to the extent that gain was recognized on the sale.

j. Ann recognizes a loss on the sale of her restaurant, so there is no passive income from the sale. Since she has no passive activity income in year one, she cannot deduct any of the passive activity loss from the bicycle shop. Note that if Ann had sold the bicycle shop, rather than the restaurant, at a loss, she would have been able to deduct the year one losses from the bicycle shop. To review: Loss from a passive activity may be deducted against gain from other passive activities or at the time *the passive activity that generated the loss* is sold.

k. Section 469 will not prevent deduction of the loss: The fact that the loan used to finance the passive activity is nonrecourse does not affect the operation of §469. The use of nonrecourse debt may, however, prevent any loss from being recognized pursuant to the "at-risk" rules of §465, which are discussed in the next section of this chapter.

59. a. Roger will be able to deduct the loss only if he materially participates in the repair shop. §469(c). The term *material participation* is statutorily defined to require involvement in the activity that is regular, continuous, and substantial. §469(h). Under Temporary Regulation §1.469-5T, a taxpayer is treated as having materially participated only if she meets one of the following tests: (1) she participates in the activity for more than 500 hours; (2) her participation in the activity constitutes substantially all of the participation in the activity of all individuals; (3) she participates in the activity for more than 100 hours and as much as anyone else; (4) she participated in the activity by meeting other participation tests for five of the past ten taxable years; (5) the activity is a personal service activity (such as a law practice) and she has materially participated in the activity by meeting other participation tests for three prior years; or (6) facts and circumstances show material participation.

Finally, there is a class of activities referred to as significant participation activities. These are activities in which the taxpayer participates for more than 100 hours but which do not, in themselves, constitute activities in which the taxpayer materially participates. If the sum of the hours of significant participation activities exceeds 500, then the taxpayer is treated as having materially participated in all such activities.

Here, Roger fails the first test because he does not participate for over 500 hours; he fails the second and third tests because he does not participate as much as other employees. Tests based on prior years are not applicable (since this is his first year of operations) and, since he has no other activities, he cannot qualify under the significant participation activity test. The facts and circumstances test is not yet fully defined. Unless he qualifies under this test (which seems unlikely), Roger will not be deemed to have materially participated in the activity, and his loss will be disallowed as a passive activity loss and carried forward to year two.

b. Here, Roger participates in the activity for over 500 hours and qualifies under the first material participation test of Temporary Regulation §1.469-5T(a).

c. Here, Roger participates in the activity for over 500 hours and qualifies under the first material participation test of Temporary Regulation §1.469-5T(a).

d. The issue raised here is whether an individual who materially participates in an activity during four of the preceding eight years is treated as materially participating in an activity during the current year. The answer to that question depends on whether the activity is a personal service activity.

If the activity is not a personal service activity, the material participation standard is met only if the taxpayer materially participated in the activity (as determined under other tests) for five of the preceding ten years. If it is a personal service activity then the material participation standard is met so long as the taxpayer materially participated in the activity (as determined under other tests) for three prior years. Temporary Regulation §1.469-5T(d) defines a personal service activity as an activity in the field of health, law, engineering, architecture, accounting, actuarial science, performing arts, consulting, or any other trade or business in which capital is not a material income-producing factor. If, as seems likely, capital is a material income-producing factor in an auto repair shop, then Roger will not meet the material participation test based on participation in prior years.

60. a. Shannon works at the business for over 100 hours and more than any other employee. Thus, Shannon meets the material participation test of Temporary Regulation §1.469-5T(a)(3).

b. Shannon's participation constitutes substantially all of the participation in the activity and Shannon therefore meets the material participation test of Temporary Regulation §1.469-5T(a)(2).

     c. Unless Shannon somehow meets the facts and circumstances test (which seems highly unlikely), she will not be treated as having materially participated in the activity.

     d. The consulting business is a personal service activity under Temporary Regulation §1.469-5T(d). (See the explanation for example 59(d).) Shannon has worked full-time at the activity during three previous years and thus met the material participation standard in those years. Because she has materially participated in the activity during three prior years, she will be treated as having materially participated in the activity in year four.

     e. Shannon will be treated as having materially participated in the activity in year four because she met the material participation standard (based on over 500 hours a year participation) in three prior years. The fact that she has not participated in the activity in more recent years is irrelevant.

61. Juan does not materially participate in the management of the building. (See discussion of the material participation tests in the explanation for example 59, above.) Moreover, under §469(c)(2), rental activities are treated as per se passive. However, §469(i) permits the deduction of the first $25,000 of losses from rental real estate activities provided the taxpayer actively participates in the activity. The deduction is reduced by 50 percent of the taxpayer's adjusted gross income in excess of $100,000. For example, a taxpayer with an adjusted gross income of $140,000 may deduct a maximum of only $5,000 of such losses, which is $25,000 less $20,000 (50 percent of $40,000).

    The term *active participation* is not defined in the statute, which says only that the active participation standard is not met unless the taxpayer owns at least 10 percent of the value of the activity. §469(i)(6). The §469 legislative history states that active participation can be established through managerial functions such as deciding on rental terms and approving tenants or capital outlays. It also indicates that the standard for active participation is less than the standard for material participation. Since Juan owns 100 percent of the value of the building and makes broad managerial decisions concerning the building, it seems likely that Juan will be treated as actively participating in the management of the building. If that is the case, and Juan's adjusted gross income is less than $100,000, Juan will be able to deduct the first $25,000 of the loss. The remaining loss will be treated as a passive activity loss and may be carried forward and deducted against passive activity income in later years or deducted at the time the building is sold.

62. The §469 passive activity loss rules prevent Tissy from offsetting losses from passive activities against gains from active activities or portfolio income. Under §469(h)(2), limited partnerships are presumed to be

passive activities; therefore, $10,000 of the $18,000 loss from the yogurt shop may offset the $10,000 income from the limited partnership. The remaining $8,000 of loss is carried forward. Her year one taxable income is $45,000, which includes $30,000 of wages plus $15,000 of portfolio income.

63. a. The passive loss rules apply only to individuals, estates, trusts, closely held C corporations, or personal service corporations. §469(a)(2). A closely held C corporation is defined as a corporation, 50 percent of the stock of which is held, directly or indirectly, by five or fewer individuals. §§469(j)(1), 465(a)(1)(B), 542(a)(2). Thus, losses recognized by publicly held corporations are not subject to the §469 passive loss restrictions.

    b. Section 469(h)(2) provides that, unless otherwise stated in the regulations, limited partners are not treated as materially participating in an activity. Thus, limited partners in a trade or business are subject to the passive loss restrictions. However, Temporary Regulation §1.469-5T(e)(2) provides that, if the limited partner can satisfy the material participation tests of §1.469-5T(a)(1), (5), or (6) (described above) with respect to an activity, the passive loss limitation does not apply to the limited partner's losses from that activity.

    c. Losses recognized by general partners in a limited partnership are treated like any other form of losses and are subject to the passive loss rules if the partnership engages in a trade or business and the general partners do not meet the material participation standard.

    d. Losses recognized by trusts are treated like any other form of losses and are subject to the passive loss rules if the trust engages in a trade or business and the beneficiaries do not meet the material participation standard.

    e. Losses recognized on working interests in oil and gas properties may be deducted even if the investor does not materially participate in the activity, provided that the taxpayer has unlimited liability with respect to the activity. §469(c)(3).

    f. Losses recognized on the rental of a vacation home are subject to the limitation of §280A(c)(5) (discussed in Chapter 6) and not §469. §469(j)(10).

64. A taxpayer will want to avoid material participation in a trade or business if the business is profitable and the taxpayer has other passive activities that are unprofitable. Suppose, for example, a taxpayer owns a restaurant and does not participate in the management of the restaurant. The restaurant has a taxable loss of $50,000. Suppose, further, that the taxpayer owns a printing shop that has a taxable income of $50,000. If the taxpayer actively participates in the printing shop, she

will have taxable income of $50,000 from that shop and a passive activity loss that she cannot currently deduct. Her current net taxable income from the two activities will be $50,000. If, instead, the taxpayer does not materially participate in the printing shop, she will have $50,000 of passive income from that shop and $50,000 of passive loss from the restaurant. Now she will be able to net the passive income and passive loss and show no net taxable income from the two activities. Remember, a passive loss cannot be used to offset non-passive income, but can be used to offset passive income. So taxpayers who already have otherwise unusable passive losses will want future taxable income to be passive rather than active.

c. The At-Risk Rules of §465

Reading: §465.

Section 465 limits the deduction of losses from trade or business activities to the amount of the taxpayer's at-risk investment. §465(a)(1). Losses disallowed under §465 are carried forward to the next year. §465(a)(2).

A taxpayer's *at-risk amount* includes cash contributed by the taxpayer to the activity, the basis of property contributed by the taxpayer to the activity, and debt for which the taxpayer is personally liable or that is secured by assets of the taxpayer (other than assets used in the activity). §465(b). The taxpayer's at-risk amount is reduced by any money distributed by the activity to the taxpayer and by the amount of losses that are allowed under §465 based on the taxpayer's at-risk amount. Prop. Reg. §§1.465-22(c)(2), 1.465-23(c). The at-risk amount is increased by income from the activity that the taxpayer includes but does not withdraw from the activity. Prop. Reg. §1.465-22(c).

A taxpayer's at-risk amount from a real estate activity also includes "qualified nonrecourse financing," which is generally financing (i) borrowed from a "qualified person" and (ii) secured by the real property used in the activity. §465(b)(6). A *qualified person* is defined as an unrelated lender who did not sell the taxpayer the property or obtain a fee with respect to the taxpayer's investment in the property. §§465(b)(6)(D), 49(a)(1)(D)(iv). Attribution rules apply to determine whether the taxpayer and lender are related. §§465(b)(3)(C), (6)(D)(i), 49(a)(1)(D)(iv), 267(b), 707(b)(1). For example, if a lending bank is owned and controlled by the taxpayer, the taxpayer and the bank are related so the lender is not a qualified person. If a taxpayer borrows from a party that is not a "qualified person," the debt is still qualified nonrecourse financing if the terms of the financing are commercially reasonable and similar to the terms of loans made to unrelated borrowers. §465(b)(6)(D)(ii).

If, at the close of the year, the taxpayer's at-risk amount is a negative number (which could result from distributions being made during the year), the taxpayer must include in income the absolute value of the negative at-risk amount. §465(e). In effect, this rule provides for "recapture" of losses, previously allowed under §465, that would not have been allowed under §465 had the distributions preceded the losses deducted by the taxpayer. The amount included under §465(e) is treated as a deduction allocable to the activity in the next year. §465(e)(1)(B).

Individuals are subject to the at-risk rules of §465. §465(a)(1)(A). The at-risk rules also apply to a C corporation if more than 50 percent of the stock of the corporation is directly or indirectly owned by five or fewer individuals. §§465(a)(1)(B) and 542(a)(2).

The at-risk rules are applied before the §469 passive loss limitation. In other words, the §469 limitation applies only to losses allowed under §465.

Examples

65. Siskel N. Ebert, a prominent movie critic, buys a motion picture for $500,000. He puts up $50,000 of his own money and $450,000 from a nonrecourse loan. In the first year of distribution, the movie loses $80,000. What are the tax consequences?

66. On January 1, year one, Arnold borrows $100,000 from a local savings and loan. The loan is nonrecourse. Arnold uses the $100,000 of loan proceeds, together with $20,000 of his own funds, to purchase a travel agency that rents space in a downtown office building. In year one, the travel agency has a taxable loss of $30,000; Arnold pays interest on the $100,000 loan but does not make any principal payments on the loan. In year two, the travel agency has a taxable loss of $20,000; Arnold pays interest on the $100,000 loan and makes a $25,000 principal payment on the loan so that at the end of the year the loan balance is $75,000. Arnold materially participates in the travel agency in year one and year two.
    a. How much, if any, of the travel agency loss may Arnold deduct in year one?
    b. How much, if any, of the travel agency loss may Arnold deduct in year two?
    c. How, if at all, would your answer in part (a) change if the travel agency that Arnold purchased were located in a separate building, and if the building, and the land on which the building was located, were included in the purchase price and secured the loan?

67. On January 1, year one, Maria borrows $70,000 from a commercial bank and uses the loan proceeds, together with $30,000 of her own funds, to purchase the food and souvenir concession at a local ballpark. The loan is nonrecourse. In year one the concession has a taxable loss of $40,000. In year two the concession has taxable income from

operations of $25,000. Maria does not contribute or withdraw any funds from the operation in year one or year two. Maria materially participates in the activity during both years.

a. How much, if any, of the concession loss may Maria deduct in year one?

b. How much, if any, of the concession income must Maria report in year two?

c. Assume the same facts as in part (a), except that the $70,000 loan is recourse. How much, if any, of the year one loss may Maria deduct?

68. On January 1, year one, David borrows $150,000 from a commercial bank and uses the loan proceeds, together with $50,000 of his own funds, to purchase an apartment building. The loan is nonrecourse. In year one the apartment building has a taxable loss of $60,000.

a. How much, if any, of the loss may David deduct?

b. Assume the same facts as in part (a), except that the loan is made by David's brother. How much, if any, of the loss may David deduct?

69. On January 1, year one, Nancy borrows $90,000 and uses the proceeds, together with $10,000 of her own funds, to purchase an apartment building. The loan is nonrecourse and is made by the seller of the property. In year one the building generates a taxable loss of $15,000, and her basis in the building is reduced to $85,000 (for depreciation). On January 1, year two, Nancy sells the building for $95,000; she receives $5,000 and the buyer takes the building subject to the mortgage of $90,000. Describe the tax consequences of the investment in year one and year two.

70. On January 1, year one, wealthy socialite Mary purchases 10 pieces of art from a local artist for $500 apiece. During the next few years, Mary purchases another 20 pieces of art for an average of $500 apiece. On January 1, year four, Mary borrows $40,000 from a bank and uses the proceeds, together with the art she has collected, to open an art gallery. Mary's basis in the art is $15,000; the fair market value of the art on January 1, year four, is $100,000. The bank loan is nonrecourse and is secured by the artwork. The art gallery shows a taxable loss in year four of $20,000. Mary materially participates in the operation of the art gallery. How much, if any, of the year four loss may Mary deduct?

71. On January 1, year one, publicly traded High Corporation borrows $800,000 and uses $200,000 of its own funds to purchase an apartment building. The loan is nonrecourse and is financed by the seller of the property. In year one High Corporation recognizes a taxable loss on

the building of $210,000. What portion, if any, of the loss may the corporation deduct?

The following two examples illustrate the interaction of §§163(d), 465, and 469.

72. On January 1, year one, prominent surgeon Leslie purchases Large Company stock for $100,000. On January 2, year one, Leslie borrows $50,000 and uses the proceeds, together with $50,000 cash, to purchase Small Company stock. The loan is nonrecourse and is secured by the Small Company stock. Leslie is appointed to the Board of Directors of Small Company and maintains a keen interest in her investment in that company. The Small Company Board of Directors meets twice a year to exercise oversight regarding company management. (Other than serving on the Board of Directors, Leslie is not involved in managing Small Company or its business operations.) Leslie learns of developments in Large Company only through her broker. Between year one and year 10, Leslie pays $60,000 in interest expense on the debt incurred to purchase the Small Company stock and includes in income $60,000 of dividend income from the Large Company stock. How much, if any, of the interest expense may Leslie deduct?

73. Your client, Daniel, is a doctor who lives and practices in the resort community of Seaview. On January 1, year one, Daniel purchases a restaurant for $400,000. The purchase price includes the real property (land and building) on which the restaurant is located. No portion of the purchase price is paid with borrowed funds. On January 5, year one, Daniel completes construction of a bakery on a valuable parcel of commercial property that he purchased many years ago for only $10,000. The value of the property is $500,000. The costs of construction total $290,000 and are financed through a nonrecourse loan that is secured by the property. The bakery sells both to the public and to other grocery stores and restaurants, including, of course, the restaurant that Daniel owns. Daniel's sister manages the bakery; Daniel's son-in-law manages the restaurant.

    On July 1 Daniel informs you that the restaurant will show a profit of $50,000 for the year but the bakery will show a taxable loss of $80,000. In order to meet the expenses of the bakery, Daniel is considering an additional $50,000 nonrecourse loan on the bakery property. Daniel says that he spends about 10 hours a week supervising restaurant operations and only one or two hours a week supervising the bakery operations. Daniel asks you what portion of the expected loss of the bakery he may deduct, and what, if anything, he might do to increase his chances of deducting that loss.

Explanations

65. Because of the at-risk rules, Siskel may only deduct losses from the activity to the extent of his financial stake in the deal, or the amount that he is personally at risk of losing. Therefore, Siskel may only deduct $50,000 of the first year's loss. Siskel is not at risk for the $450,000 loan because it is nonrecourse. The $30,000 disallowed loss may be carried forward to the next year to offset any income from the movie in that year. §465(a), (c).

66. a. Section 465 limits the deductions from trade or business activities to the amount of the taxpayer's at-risk investment. A taxpayer's at-risk amount includes cash contributed by the taxpayer, here $20,000. §465(b). The $100,000 of debt is not included in Arnold's at-risk amount because Arnold is not personally liable on the debt and the debt is not "qualified nonrecourse financing." §465(b)(2), (b)(6). In year one Arnold's at-risk amount is thus $20,000, so Arnold will be able to deduct only $20,000 of the $30,000 loss. The $10,000 of loss disallowed under §465 is carried forward to year two. §465(a)(2).

    b. The $10,000 loss not allowed in year one will carry over to year two. In year two the travel agency loses another $20,000, so the potential loss allowable in year two is $30,000. The deduction of this loss, however, will be limited to Arnold's at-risk amount. Here, the at-risk investment at the start of the year is zero ($20,000 original at-risk amount less $20,000 of loss allowed in year one under §465). §465(b)(5). The $25,000 of cash Arnold contributes to pay down the loan increases his amount at-risk, so his amount at-risk for year two is $25,000. Thus, he is allowed to deduct $25,000 of the $30,000 of losses. The $5,000 of loss disallowed in year two is carried forward to year three. In years one and two Arnold has contributed $45,000 and has been allowed to deduct $45,000 of losses.

    c. Although nonrecourse debt does not generally increase the taxpayer's amount at-risk, nonrecourse debt that is "qualified nonrecourse financing" does increase the amount at-risk "in the case of an activity of holding real property." §465(b)(6). Qualified nonrecourse financing is financing (i) borrowed from a "qualified person" and (ii) secured by the real property used in the activity. §465(b)(6). A qualified person is defined as an unrelated lender who did not sell the taxpayer the property or obtain a fee with respect to the taxpayer's investment in the property. §§49(a)(1)(D)(iv), 465(b)(6)(D).

Here, part of the nonrecourse financing was attributable to the real estate that was included in the purchase price. Arnold might argue that, under §465(b)(6), his year one amount at-risk includes some portion of the nonrecourse debt. Neither the statute nor the regulations directly define "an activity of holding real estate." If part of the nonrecourse debt is treated as qualified nonrecourse financing because it is attributable to a real estate activity, that portion of the debt would increase his year one amount at-risk and would allow him to deduct part or all of the $10,000 of year one loss in excess of his $20,000 cash contribution. This would, in turn, reduce the amount of year one loss to be carried forward to year two.

67. a. Maria's at-risk amount is $30,000, the amount of cash she contributed to the activity. The $70,000 of debt is not included in Maria's at-risk amount because Maria is not personally liable on the debt and the debt is not qualified nonrecourse financing. §465(b)(2), (b)(6). In year one Maria's at-risk amount is thus $30,000, so she will be able to deduct only $30,000 of the $40,000 loss. The $10,000 of loss disallowed under §465 is carried forward to year two. §465(a)(2).

b. The $10,000 loss that Maria could not deduct in year one is treated as an allowable deduction in year two, provided that Maria has a sufficient amount at-risk in that latter year. §465(a)(2). The amount at-risk is increased by income included and not withdrawn from the activity. Prop. Reg. §1.465-22(c). Thus, Maria has $25,000 at-risk in year two, and can deduct the $10,000 of loss carried forward from year one. In year two Maria's net income from the activity will be $15,000 — the $25,000 of operating income less the $10,000 loss carried forward from year one. Maria's at-risk amount at the end of year two will be $15,000.

c. Maria's amount at-risk includes both the $30,000 of cash contributed and the $70,000 of debt for which she is personally liable. §465(b)(1), (2). Since her amount at-risk in year one is $100,000, she is allowed to deduct the entire $40,000 loss in year one.

68. a. David has contributed $50,000 cash; the question here is whether any portion of the borrowed funds will increase his at-risk amount and thereby increase the amount of allowable deduction. As noted above, funds borrowed on a nonrecourse basis generally do not increase a taxpayer's at-risk amount. However, §465(b)(6) provides a special exception for nonrecourse financing used to finance the activity of holding real property. Such borrowed funds increase the taxpayer's at-risk amount provided that the funds are borrowed

from a "qualified person." A qualified person is defined as an unrelated lender who did not sell the taxpayer the property or obtain a fee with respect to the taxpayer's investment in the property. §§49(a)(1)(D)(iv), 465(b)(6)(D). If the property is purchased from a related party, such as the taxpayer's sister or controlled business, nonrecourse funds increase the at-risk amount only if the loan is commercially reasonable and on substantially the same terms as loans involving unrelated persons. §465(b)(6)(D)(ii).

Assuming the debt is qualified nonrecourse financing, David's at-risk amount includes his $50,000 cash contribution plus the $150,000 of nonrecourse debt. He can deduct the entire $60,000 loss in year one.

b. Here, the loan is made by a related party. As a result, the loan will increase the at-risk amounts only if it is made at commercially reasonable rates and on substantially the same terms as loans made to unrelated persons. If the loan meets these requirements, David can deduct the entire loss, as in part (a). If not, his at-risk amount is limited to his cash contribution and he can deduct only $50,000 of the $60,000 loss.

69. Nancy's at-risk amount includes the $10,000 of cash she contributed to the activity. As noted above, although funds borrowed on a nonrecourse basis generally do not increase a taxpayer's at-risk amount, §465(b)(6) provides a special exception for nonrecourse financing that is used to finance the activity of holding real property. Such borrowed funds increase the taxpayer's at-risk amount provided the loan is from a qualified person and the debt is secured by the property. Here, the seller of the property is not a qualified person, so the debt here is not qualified nonrecourse financing. §49(a)(1)(D)(iv)(II).

In year one Nancy is allowed to deduct $10,000 of the $15,000 loss because her at-risk amount is $10,000. In year two Nancy recognizes $10,000 of gain ($95,000 amount realized less $85,000 adjusted basis) and deducts the $5,000 loss from year one that is carried forward to year two. Note that Nancy recognizes a total loss on the transaction of $5,000 — the sum of the $10,000 year one loss allowed as a deduction in year one, the $5,000 year one loss allowed as a deduction in year two, and $10,000 of gain recognized in year two. This corresponds to Nancy's out-of-pocket loss of $5,000. At the time an activity subject to §465 is sold, the aggregate tax losses will mirror the out-of-pocket losses.

70. Mary's year four at-risk amount includes the $15,000 basis of the artwork she contributed to the activity. §465(b)(1)(A). Her at-risk amount does not include the nonrecourse debt, which is secured by property used in the activity. §465(b)(2)(B). Since her year four at-risk

amount is $15,000, she is allowed to deduct $15,000 of the $20,000 year four loss. The $5,000 of year four loss that is disallowed is carried forward to year five.

71. The at-risk rules apply only to corporations that are closely held. Other corporations are not subject to the at-risk rules. §§465(a)(1)(B), 542(a)(2). High Corporation is not closely held and therefore may deduct the entire loss unimpeded by the at-risk rules. Note that if the taxpayer here were an individual, the loss would be limited to the $200,000 cash investment. This transaction would not qualify for the qualified nonrecourse financing exception because, while the investment is in real estate and the loan is commercially reasonable, the lender here is the seller of the property.

72. The answer to this question turns, in part, on whether Leslie's investment in Small Company is thought to be subject to the §163 interest deduction limits for portfolio investments, or the §465 and §469 limits on trade or business losses. Sections 163(d) and 469(e) explicitly place interest incurred to carry stock under the ambit of §163 and subject it to the investment interest, rather than passive loss, restrictions. Section 465 does not explicitly address the issue, but it seems that the active management of a personal stock portfolio (as opposed to active management of the *business*, not the portfolio) does not comprise a trade or business activity and so is not subject to §465. Cf. Van Suetendael v. Commissioner, 3 T.C.M. 987 (1944). The answer also turns on whether Leslie elects to forgo the preferential tax rate on the dividend income. If she makes the election, the dividend income is investment income. §§163(d)(4)(B), 1(h)(11)(B). Section 163 would not limit Leslie's $60,000 of interest deduction because she received $60,000 of investment income during the same period. On the other hand, if the dividends do not qualify for a preferential tax rate or if Leslie has not made the election, her dividend income is not investment income and the §163 limitation would prevent her from deducting the $60,000 of interest during the 10-year period.

73. The deductibility of the bakery loss will be limited by both the §469 passive loss restrictions and the §465 at-risk rules. The at-risk limitation is applied first.

    Under §465, losses from a trade or business activity are limited to the amount "at risk" in that activity. The term *activity* is not really defined by statute or regulations; on these limited facts it is not clear whether the bakery and the restaurant will be treated as a single activity. If they are treated as separate activities, the at-risk rules will limit Daniel's deduction for the $80,000 loss from the bakery. Daniel has contributed no nonborrowed funds to the bakery business and has contributed property worth only $10,000. Further nonrecourse borrowing on the contributed property will not increase the at-risk amount. Thus, absent an increase in the at-risk amount, Daniel's deduction from the bakery will be limited to $10,000.

Is there any way for Daniel to get around the at-risk limitation? Daniel could increase his at-risk amount by contributing nonborrowed funds or by obtaining a nonrecourse or recourse loan using his restaurant property as security. Nonrecourse debt secured by property that is not used in the activity will increase the at-risk amount to the extent of the cash investment in the property. Here, Daniel has a $400,000 cash investment in the restaurant property, so a loan secured by the property will be considered a cash investment.

If the bakery and the restaurant are treated as one activity, Daniel's amount at risk is $410,000 ($400,000 of cash invested in the restaurant and $10,000 of property contributed to the bakery), and §465 will not disallow his deduction for the $30,000 net loss ($50,000 of income less the $80,000 loss) from the activity.

If Daniel's loss is not disallowed by the §465 at-risk rules, he still must get past the §469 passive loss limitation. His $80,000 loss will be suspended under the passive loss limitation if (i) for purposes of §469, the bakery is considered a separate activity from the restaurant and (ii) Daniel meets the material participation standard for the restaurant and not the bakery.

Daniel might, of course, argue that the restaurant and bakery comprise a single activity. In that case, it looks as if Daniel spends about 12 hours a week on that single activity. That would be sufficient to meet the 500 hours a year material participation test. The loss would then not be a passive loss and Daniel would therefore be allowed to use the bakery loss to offset the restaurant and other sources of income.

Will the bakery and the restaurant be considered a single activity? The term *activity* is defined in Regulation §1.469-4. That regulation provides that trade or business or rental activities may be treated as a single activity if the activities to be grouped together are "an appropriate economic unit" for purposes of applying §469. The determination as to whether activities constitute an appropriate economic unit is based on a facts and circumstances test, with the following factors having the greatest weight: (i) the similarities and differences in the types of trades or businesses; (ii) the extent of common control or ownership of the activities; (iii) the geographic location of the activities; and (iv) any interdependencies among the activities.

Here, the bakery and the restaurant are both owned by Daniel. The facts do not indicate whether they are located in the same geographic area. The businesses are similar in that both prepare and sell food; however, the restaurant, unlike the bakery shop, probably involves serving customers food and drinks at tables on the premises. There may be interdependencies between the two businesses, for example, if the restaurant buys all of its baked goods from the bakery. The answer is not clear on the facts given in the example.

If Daniel is not able to treat the bakery and the restaurant as a single activity, and he continues to work at the restaurant and not the bakery, the gain from the restaurant will not be passive and the loss from the bakery will be passive. As a result, Daniel will not be able to currently deduct any of the loss.

Daniel could avoid this result by reducing his hours at the restaurant. If, for example, Daniel works only six hours a week at the restaurant, then both the restaurant and the bakery will be passive, and Daniel will be able to use the bakery loss to offset the restaurant income. If Daniel works nine hours a week at the restaurant and two hours a week at the bakery, then both the bakery and restaurant will be "significant participation activities." Since the total hours of significant participation activities will exceed 500, neither activity will be considered passive. (Note that if Daniel works more than 500 hours at the restaurant, the restaurant will be nonpassive but will not be a significant participation activity and the hours worked at the bakery cannot be combined with the hours worked at the restaurant.)

d. The Limitations of §§264 and 265

Reading: §§264, 265.

A number of anti-abuse provisions prevent taxpayers from deducting interest on debt incurred to purchase certain types of assets on which income is either exempt or deferred. For example, §265(a)(2) provides that a taxpayer is not allowed to deduct interest on debt incurred or carried to purchase obligations that are exempt from tax under §103. This rule prevents a taxpayer in the 35 percent bracket from making an after-tax profit by borrowing at 10 percent (for an after-tax cost of 6.5 percent) to purchase tax-exempt bonds that yield 7 percent.

As another example, §264(a)(2) provides that a taxpayer is not allowed to deduct interest on debt incurred or carried to purchase a single premium life insurance policy or annuity contract. A policy or contract is treated as a single premium contract or policy if substantially all of the premiums due on the policy or contract are paid within four years of the date on which it was purchased. §264(c).

Similarly, §264(a)(3) disallows a deduction for interest incurred to purchase or carry a life insurance policy pursuant to a plan that contemplates systematic borrowing. However, §264(d) overrides §264(a)(3) and allows deductions for interest paid pursuant to a plan of systematic borrowing if four of the first seven annual premiums are paid with funds that have not been borrowed.

Examples

74. On January 1, year one, Xavier borrows $80,000 and uses the proceeds, together with $20,000 of his own funds, to purchase tax-exempt municipal bonds. The loan is nonrecourse. In year one Xavier receives $7,000 of interest on the bonds and pays $8,000 interest on the loan used to purchase the bonds. How much, if any, of the interest expense may Xavier deduct?

75. On January 1, year one, Carol borrows $90,000 and uses the proceeds, together with $10,000 of her own funds, to purchase a single premium life insurance policy that pays $1 million upon Carol's death. Carol's life expectancy at the time of the purchase is 35 years. In year one Carol pays $8,100 interest on the loan. How much, if any, of the interest is deductible?

76. On January 1, year one, Carl purchases a so-called "level payment whole life insurance policy" that requires Carl to pay $5,000 a year in return for payment of $500,000 upon Carl's death. If Carl lives to his life expectancy, his total premiums will aggregate $150,000. The $500,000 payment to his beneficiaries will represent a return on investment of about 8 percent.

    Carl pays the first 10 premiums with funds that were not borrowed. The $5,000 premium for the 11th year, however, is paid with funds loaned to Carl from the insurance company. If Carl dies before repaying the loan, the insurance company will reduce the amounts paid to Carl's beneficiaries by the amount of the loan. The interest rate on the loan from the insurance company is 10 percent. In the 12th year, Carl again borrows the amount of the premium from the insurance company. Carl borrows an additional amount from the insurance company to cover the $500 of interest owed on the loan from the prior year. Carl continues this practice for the next eight years, so that in years 11 through 20, all funds paid to the insurance company are borrowed. During that time, the principal on his debt continues to grow, as do the interest payments he owes on that debt. The total interest Carl "pays" to the insurance company during those years is about $10,000.

    a. How much, if any, of the interest may Carl deduct?
    b. Assume the same facts as in part (a), except that Carl borrows the funds needed to pay the premiums and interest on prior loans from

savings institutions rather than the insurance company. How much, if any, of the interest is deductible?

Explanations

74. In this example, Xavier is paying $8,000 to earn $7,000. This otherwise irrational behavior is tax-motivated. The $7,000 income is tax-free; if Xavier is in the 35 percent marginal tax bracket and can deduct the $8,000 interest expense, his after-tax interest expense will be only $5,200. A before-tax loss of $1,000 would turn into an after-tax profit of $1,800 ($7,000 less $5,200). Unfortunately for Xavier, §265(a)(2) prohibits any deduction for interest on indebtedness incurred to purchase or carry tax-exempt bonds, so he will not be allowed to deduct his interest expense.

75. Section 264(a)(2) prohibits the deduction of any amount paid on indebtedness incurred to purchase or carry a single premium life insurance contract. The reason for this rule is that such contracts present the same kind of mismatching of income and expense as tax-exempt bonds. Each year, as Carol grows older, the value of the life insurance policy increases; at the time of Carol's death, the contract will be worth $1 million. There is no tax on the annual increase in value and, under §101, no tax on the eventual payout of the contract to the beneficiaries of the contract. Some life insurance policies permit the policyholder to borrow some of the increase in value and, in some cases, no tax will be levied on such borrowing. (Section 72(e) will treat certain loans to policyholders as income.)

    Absent §264, Carol could borrow at 9 percent to fund a policy that increased in value (when measured by the difference between purchase price and payout at expected age of death) by 8 percent. The policy would show a before-tax loss and, if the interest were deductible, an after-tax gain. As it turns out, though, §264(a)(2) disallows any deduction for interest incurred or continued to purchase or carry a single premium life insurance, endowment, or annuity contract. Thus, Carol will not be allowed to deduct any of the interest expense associated with the policy.

76. a. Carl is borrowing at 10 percent to earn 8 percent. However, the appreciation of the policy is not taxed. If the interest on the loan is deductible, Carl will make an after-tax profit on the transaction so long as his tax rate is above 20 percent. If, for example, Carl is in the 25 percent tax rate, the after-tax cost of the loan will be only 7.5 percent, which is 10 percent less 2.5 percent (25 percent of 10 percent). As noted in the previous explanation, §264(a)(2)

disallows any deduction for interest incurred in connection with the purchase of a single premium life insurance contract. Carl's contract requires annual payments and is not a single premium life insurance contract. (Note, however, that under §264(c)(1), a life insurance policy on which substantially all of the premiums are paid in the first four years is treated as a single premium policy.)

Section 264(a)(3) disallows any deduction for interest incurred to purchase or carry a life insurance policy pursuant to a plan that contemplates systemic borrowing. However, §264(d) provides an exception to §264(a)(3) and allows deductions for interest paid pursuant to a plan of systematic borrowing if four of the first seven annual premiums are paid with funds that have not been borrowed. Since Carl has met this latter condition, the interest on the loans will not be limited by §264.

b. For tax purposes, the fact that Carl borrows the funds from outside sources, rather than the insurance company, is irrelevant. All of the interest will be deductible.

4. Sale and Leaseback Transactions

Suppose that a low bracket or exempt taxpayer plans to buy a significant amount of depreciable property. Since the tax to be saved from depreciation deductions increases as the taxpayer's tax bracket increases, the low bracket taxpayer may attempt to reduce its cost for the property by shifting the depreciation to a higher bracket taxpayer. For example, a low bracket taxpayer might sell depreciable property to a high bracket taxpayer in exchange for the proceeds of a loan incurred by the high bracket taxpayer, and then lease the property back from the high bracket taxpayer. In such a sale-leaseback transaction (also referred to as a "leveraged lease"), the low bracket taxpayer would retain use of the property, but the high bracket taxpayer would nominally own the property and obtain large depreciation deductions.

The taxpayers' characterization of a lease may not be respected, however. Courts may recharacterize a lease payment as a loan or a conditional installment purchase like the one we saw earlier in this chapter in *Starr's Estate*. Recharacterization is most likely where (i) the length of the lease is greater than the useful life of the property, (ii) the lessee bears the risk of damage to the property, or (iii) the lease payments equal the purchase price, plus interest, of the leased property and the lessee has the option to renew the lease for a nominal amount. However, the lease transaction will usually be respected if there is a business purpose for the transaction and the lessor retains sufficient burdens and benefits of owning the leased property.

Leveraged lease transactions can be quite complex and the characterization of a leveraged lease may turn on a variety of factors. However, the

Service will issue an advance ruling that a transaction constitutes a lease if certain requirements, including the following, are met: (i) the lessor must have at least 20 percent of the cost of the leased property at risk unconditionally; (ii) the lessee may not have the option to purchase the leased property for less than the value of the property; (iii) the lessor may not have the right to require the lessee to purchase the property on the expiration of the lease; (iv) the lessee may not furnish any part of the cost of the leased property or loan the lessor any of the funds used to purchase the property; (v) the lessor must expect the lease transaction to generate a positive cash flow without regard to the tax consequences of the transaction; and (vi) the useful life of the leased property must be greater than the term of the lease. Rev. Proc. 2001-28, Rev. Proc. 2001-29. However, if the leased property is property that can be used only by the lessee (referred to as "limited use property"), the transaction will not be treated as a lease. Rev. Proc. 2001-28, Rev. Proc. 2001-29.

Even if the transaction cannot meet the advance ruling requirements, the transaction may still qualify as a lease under case law. Courts appear to examine each transaction using a facts and circumstances test and to interpret that test rather loosely in the taxpayer's favor. A transaction that leaves at least some of the indicia of ownership in the hands of the ostensible lessor will be treated as a bona fide lease.

For example, in Frank Lyon Co. v. United States, 435 U.S. 561 (1978), a lessor was allowed to deduct depreciation on property subject to a leveraged lease because the Court concluded that the lessor retained some incidents of ownership of the leased property. Simplifying the facts in that case somewhat, Worthen Bank, the lessee, was in a rush to build a new bank headquarters but discovered that bank regulations would not allow it to build the structure as it had planned. The bank then structured the following leveraged lease transaction: Worthen constructed the new building and sold it to Frank Lyon Co. (a home appliance distributor run by a member of the Worthen board) for $7.6 million, $500,000 of which was funded by Frank Lyon Co. and $7.1 million of which was borrowed from a third party lender, New York Life. Worthen then leased the building back from Frank Lyon Co. in exchange for annual rent of $580,000, which equaled the annual amounts Frank Lyon Co. was required to pay New York Life on the building loan. The New York Life loan would be fully repaid after 25 years, at which time the lease payments would drop to $300,000 a year. In addition, Worthen had the option of repurchasing the building for an amount that equaled Lyon's $500,000 investment in the building plus a 6 percent return on that investment. The lease was a net lease, so Worthen paid the costs of maintaining the building.

Frank Lyon Co. included the rent it received from Worthen in income, deducted the interest it paid to New York Life, and claimed large depreciation deductions on the building. The Commissioner disallowed the deductions on the theory that Worthen, not Frank Lyon Co., owned the building.

The Commissioner recharacterized the transaction as one in which Worthen borrowed $500,000 from Frank Lyon Co., at 6 percent interest, and borrowed $7.1 million from New York Life, with Frank Lyon Co. acting as a conduit through which the New York Life loan proceeds passed. This recharacterization was based on several factors: (i) the rent due from Worthen to Frank Lyon Co. equaled the amounts Frank Lyon Co. owed New York Life; (ii) Worthen had the option to buy the building by repaying Frank Lyon Co. its investment plus a 6 percent return; (iii) as soon as the New York Life loan was repaid, the rent dropped by almost 50 percent; (iv) the lease was a net lease, so Worthen paid the costs of maintaining the building; and (v) Worthen built the building.

However, the Supreme Court majority refused to recharacterize the sale-leaseback transaction and held that Frank Lyon Co. was entitled to deduct the depreciation on the building. The Court reached this decision based on several factors: (i) bank regulations prevented Worthen from owning the building itself (so it did not appear that Worthen entered into the transaction for a tax avoidance motive); (ii) the transaction involved three parties (not two parties, as is the case in some sale-leaseback transactions); and (iii) Frank Lyon Co. ran the risk that Worthen would default on the lease before the New York Life loan had been repaid. (The Court also erroneously assumed that Frank Lyon Co. and Worthen Bank were in comparable tax brackets, so that attributing the depreciation to Worthen instead of Frank Lyon Co. would not have raised revenue. Worthen Bank was in fact subject to a lower rate than Frank Lyon Co.)

Example

77. Sky Airlines Inc. has significant net operating losses from operations in previous years, so it is taxed at a zero rate. The airline needs to add a new plane to its fleet. If the airline leased the plane directly from the manufacturer, the airline would have to pay the manufacturer $2.1 million a year for 20 years (for a total of $42 million) and, at the end of the 20-year lease term, would have the option to buy the airplane for its value at that time.

    Instead of leasing the plane from the manufacturer, Sky Airlines will lease the airplane from Top Gun Leasing Partnership, in which the four partners (who each materially participate in the partnership) are in the 35 percent tax bracket. The Top Gun Leasing partnership will acquire the plane from the manufacturer for $25 million, $5 million of which it will fund and $20 million of which will be funded by a recourse loan from an insurance company. Top Gun Leasing will make annual payments of $2 million on the debt for 20 years (for total payments of interest and principal of $40 million).

Sky Airlines will lease the plane from Top Gun Leasing on the following terms: (i) the initial term of the lease will be 20 years; (ii) during that lease term, Sky Airlines will pay Top Gun annual lease payments of $2 million (for a total of $40 million during the initial 20-year term of the lease); (iii) on the expiration of the initial lease term, Sky Airlines has the option to renew the lease for another 10 years for an annual lease payment of $50,000 a year; (iv) on the expiration of the initial lease term, Sky Airlines also has the option to purchase the airplane for $30,000; and (v) Sky Airlines will provide all maintenance and insurance on the airplane. The useful life of the airplane is 20 years. Will the partners in the Top Gun Leasing partnership be treated as the owners of the airplane, for purposes of determining who is entitled to depreciation deductions on the airplane?

Explanation

77. This is a tough call. This transaction could be characterized as either of the following: (i) a sale of the plane by the manufacturer to Top Gun Leasing and a lease of the plane from Top Gun to Sky Airlines (in which case Top Gun Leasing owns the plane) or (ii) a sale of the plane by the manufacturer to Sky Airlines, with Top Gun acting as a conduit through which the payments from Sky Airlines to the insurance company lender pass (in which case Sky Airlines owns the plane).

The Service will issue an advance ruling that states that a leveraged lease transaction constitutes a lease if certain requirements are met. Rev. Proc. 2001-28, Rev. Proc. 2001-29. One of the requirements is that the lessor has at-risk at least 20 percent of the purchase price. That requirement is met here because the partners have either paid or assumed personal liability for the full purchase price of the plane. Another requirement is that the useful life of the property must be greater than the term of the leasehold interest. That requirement is not met here. Another requirement is that the transaction generates positive cash flow without regard to the tax consequences of the transaction. This requirement is not met here because the transaction will lose money on a before-tax basis.

The transaction here would not constitute a lease under the advance ruling test since the requirements of the revenue procedures are not satisfied. However, the transaction may still qualify as a lease under case law. Courts appear to examine each transaction on a facts and circumstances test and to interpret that test rather loosely in the taxpayer's favor. A transaction that leaves at least some of the indicia of ownership in the hands of the ostensible lessor will likely be treated as a bona fide lease. See Frank Lyon Co. v. United States, 435 U.S. 561 (1978).

The factors indicating that Sky Airlines purchased the airplane, using Top Gun as a financing conduit, are the following: (i) the initial 20-year lease term coincides with the useful life of the airplane; (ii) the lease is a net lease; (iii) the annual lease payments drop significantly after the initial 20-year lease term; and (iv) Sky Airlines can acquire title to the airplane by paying a nominal amount on the expiration of the initial lease term.

However, some of the facts here are reminiscent of the Frank Lyon case, in which the court refused to recharacterize the lease. Here, the Top Gun Leasing Partnership invested $5 million of its own money and assumed personal liability on the entire amount of debt used to finance the purchase of the plane. In other words, Top Gun was exposed to economic risk of loss with respect to the property. As in Frank Lyon, the transaction here is not a two-party transaction. (In addition, the seller here is a third party manufacturer, not the lessee, as was the case in Frank Lyon.) On the other hand, the motive for the lease transaction here is likely tax avoidance. Taking into account all of the factors here, it is unclear whether a court would recharacterize this lease.

5. Corporate and Individual Tax Shelters of the 1990s

Anti-tax shelter measures such as the passive loss rules and investment interest limitations killed the real estate shelters described earlier in this chapter, as well as many similar shelters. By 1990, however, a new form of shelters came onto the scene. These shelters were marketed to publicly traded companies or individuals of extremely high net-worth. (Publicly traded companies are not subject to the passive loss and related anti-tax shelter measures. High net-worth individuals are subject to these anti-tax shelter measures. However, they have many sources of income and, for that and other reasons, are not constrained by these measures.) The shelters were generally packaged by investment banks, accounting firms, or "tax shelter" shops. The shelters typically involved financial assets rather than tangible assets and were much more aggressive than the individual shelters described earlier in this chapter. Often the shelters made use of a zero-bracket taxpayer, such as a tax-exempt entity, a company with unusable net operating losses, or, most commonly, a foreign person not subject to U.S. tax. The parties entered into a transaction in which income was misallocated; the zero-bracket taxpayer absorbed taxable income far in excess of its economic return, leaving the domestic corporation with a taxable loss on a break-even investment.

Perhaps the most well known corporate shelter was that sold by Merrill Lynch to Colgate-Palmolive. The deal, somewhat simplified, was as follows. Colgate entered into a partnership with a zero-bracket taxpayer (the "Dutch Bank"). Partnerships are not taxable entities; partnership gain and loss is allocated to the partners in accordance with their partnership agreement. The parties agreed that virtually all of the gain or loss recognized by the partnership would go to the Dutch Bank. Colgate contributed $180 million to the partnership and the partnership used the funds to purchase publicly traded debt of Citicorp. The partnership sold the debt a few weeks later on an installment sale basis. The installment note provided that the partnership was to receive $140 million in cash in year one and payments over the following five years that were contingent upon prevailing interest rates. The expected value of the future payments was $40 million, leaving the expected total sales price at $180 million. The transaction produced no economic gain or loss and no gain or loss for financial accounting purposes. The transaction also involved little or no risk for the parties. The partnership did not hold the Citicorp debt for more than a brief period, and the parties hedged their exposure to risks during that period.

Under the installment sale regulations, basis on a sale with contingent payments is recovered in equal amounts over the years in which payments were to be made. Taxpayers are allowed to petition out of the regulations if these rules produced an uneconomic accrual of income in early years. Under the regulations, the partnership was allowed to recover 1/6 of its basis each year, or $30 million a year. The problem was that the partnership received nearly 5/6 of its expected sales proceeds the first year. The result was income during the first year of $110 million — the $140 million sales proceeds less the $30 million basis. This gain was allocated to the Dutch Bank, which, as noted above, was not subject to U.S. tax.

The same basis recovery rules that produced too much income in early years produced too much loss in later years. The partnership still had 5/6 of its basis, or $150 million, left to recover in years two through six. But the partnership was expected to receive only $40 million in sales proceeds over those years — just a bit over 1/6 of the total sales proceeds. So there was $110 million of "built-in" loss to be recognized by the partners — the difference between its $150 million basis and the $40 million sales proceeds.

Had the Dutch Bank stayed in the partnership, it would have recognized this taxable loss. Instead, after absorbing the $110 million in taxable income in the first year, the Dutch Bank sold out to a subsidiary of Colgate. The $110 million loss would now go to Colgate and its subsidiary.

In effect, Colgate turned a break-even, no-risk transaction into a $110 million tax loss. It recognized none of the $110 million taxable income during the first year, and all of the $110 million loss during the following years. The shelter Colgate entered into was marketed by Merrill Lynch and was virtually identical to the shelter sold to ten other large corporations. Allied Signal used the shelter to produce a tax loss of approximately one-half billion dollars on a break-even investment.

The flaw exploited by the shelter was a portion of the contingent sales rules, which provided that when payments were contingent and spread over a number of years, the seller could offset the payments with an equal amount of basis each year. Reg. §15a.453-1(c)(3). This ratable recovery of basis rule accurately measured income only where the payments were equal each year. Since taxpayers were allowed to petition out of the regulations, the regulations were not necessarily anti-taxpayer and had gone unchallenged for many years. What the drafters of the regulation had not foreseen was that taxpayers would structure contingent deals so as to receive most of their income in the first post-sale year. The level recovery of basis rule produced taxable income in that year far in excess of economic income; the taxable income was allocated to a zero-bracket party, leaving the actual shelter participant to recognize a taxable loss in excess of economic loss in later years.

(At the time the facts of this case arose, the §453 regulations permitted the taxpayer, but not the Service, to argue that the ratable basis allocation rule inappropriately defers basis. Reg. §15a.453-1(c)(7)(ii). When the government learned of the shelter, it issued Notice 90-56, in which it announced that it would amend the §453 regulations to provide that the Service can require an alternative method of basis recovery where the ratable basis recovery rule inappropriately defers basis — as it did in the shelter.)

The denial of losses to Colgate was upheld by the Tax Court and the Court of Appeals for the Third Circuit. ACM Partnership v. Commissioner, 157 F.3d 231 (1998). The appellate court based its decision on the "economic substance" doctrine. As its name implies, that doctrine nullifies the intended tax consequences of transactions that lack economic substance. After its victory in ACM, the government used the economic substance doctrine aggressively to attack many shelters.

In 2010, the economic substance doctrine was codified and a strict liability penalty of 20 percent (40 percent for undisclosed transactions) was enacted for transactions that lack economic substance. §§6662, 7701(o). One of the reasons for codification was to clarify just what economic substance means. (Another reason was to raise revenue.) Under §7701(o)(1), a transaction has economic substance only if (i) it changes in a meaningful way the taxpayer's economic position; and (ii) the taxpayer has a substantial purpose (apart from saving on federal income taxes) for entering into the transaction. If a taxpayer relies on expected profit to support a transaction, it must show that the present value of the expected profit was substantial in relation to the present value of the tax benefits. The Joint Committee on Taxation explanation of the measure clarifies that it is not intended to be used to deny benefits from transactions that Congress intends to be tax-driven (such as investments that qualify for the low-income housing investment tax credit).

While the new statute removes some of the uncertainty over the reach of the doctrine, other questions remain. For example, it is not clear how large expected profits have to be in order to be "substantial" in relation to tax benefits. It will often be unclear as to whether a transaction falls within the protected ambit of congressionally blessed tax-driven transactions. And in some cases, questions will arise whether a transaction that is purely tax-driven can be cleansed by the fact that it is part of a larger series of transactions that have substantial economic effect.

The economic substance transaction has always been controversial. Some tax practitioners and scholars feel that it leaves too much discretion to the IRS or the courts. Others support the doctrine as a necessary evil. If taxpayers can exploit flaws in the law with transactions without economic substance, there is no practical limit to the amount of loss the fisc can realize before the government discovers and fixes the flaw.

Since the decision in ACM, the government has used the economic substance doctrine to attack shelters in scores of cases. The government has also attacked these shelters through changes in reporting requirements (not covered here) and an increase in penalties. These efforts have succeeded in greatly reducing the market for these kinds of shelters.

Example

81. Review the set-up of the Colgate contingent installment sale shelter, described above. Discuss whether the following variants of the transaction would lack economic substance.
    a. Colgate holds the Citicorp debt for a year, and the interest on the debt is sufficient to pay Merrill Lynch its fee, cover all other expenses, and provide for a 2 percent before-tax return on its $180 million investment. Colgate invests most of its money in long-term projects that are slated to return at least 12 percent. However, Colgate keeps roughly $100 million in short-term Treasury notes. The return on those notes varies with changes in the inflation rate. The average annualized one-year return is between 3 percent and 4 percent but has dropped to as low as 1 percent.
    b. Colgate has been in a partnership with a Dutch distributor to operate a toothpaste factory in Europe. It hires Merrill Lynch to help it find a buyer for the factory. Merrill Lynch finds a buyer for the factory, and then advises Colgate that the sale can be structured so as to produce a

huge tax loss to Colgate. Colgate pays Merrill a substantial fee to structure the deal so as to produce the tax benefits.

Explanation

81. a. This question explores a central ambiguity in the economic substance doctrine; how much return does a transaction need to escape the reach of the doctrine, and how do you define return?

    The government will argue that the before-tax return is actually negative — it is less than the taxpayer would have gotten without setting up the partnership, paying Merrill Lynch a fee, and so on. In effect, the government will be determining return as compared to the investment the taxpayer would have otherwise made, or the most similar investment that an ordinary taxpayer might have made. The government will also argue that the return is not substantial in relation to the tax benefits and that (because the return is below the otherwise available return) the transaction lacked a non-tax purpose.

    Colgate may argue that its alternative investment would not have been taxable Treasury notes. Instead, it might have made a tax-favored investment in low-income housing. That latter investment (because it is tax-favored) would be expected to have a lower risk-adjusted return.

    b. This question explores another ambiguity in the economic substance doctrine: what exactly is the "transaction" that must have substance? Here, the operation and sale of the toothpaste factory has economic substance, but the structuring of the deal is solely tax-motivated. Most practitioners believe that the transaction, in this case, is the sale of a toothpaste factory, and that transaction will have economic substance since it involves a real asset used in a trade or business.

K. ALTERNATIVE MINIMUM TAX

Reading: §§55–58.

The alternative minimum tax (AMT) is a separate system for computing income tax liability. Taxpayers must compute their tax liability under the regular income tax and the AMT and pay the higher amount. §55(a). (The AMT applies to both individual and corporate taxpayers, but our discussion here addresses only individual taxpayers.)

The AMT imposes tax on the taxpayer's *taxable excess*, which is the taxpayer's *alternative minimum taxable income* (AMTI) less the AMT *exemption amount*.

To compute AMTI, taxpayers start with their taxable income, as computed under the regular income tax, and add amounts to reflect various adjustments required by §§56–58. For example, personal and dependent exemptions, state and local taxes, miscellaneous itemized deductions, and the standard deduction are included in the broader AMT base. §56(b)(1)(A), (E). (This is why large families and taxpayers who live in high-tax states such as California and New York are often subject to the AMT.)

The taxpayer subtracts from AMTI the relevant inflation-adjusted AMT exemption amount. For example, the 2014 exemption amounts were: (i) $82,100 for married taxpayers filing a joint return and (ii) $52,800 for individual taxpayers. §55(b)(1)(A), (d)(1), (d)(4), Rev. Proc. 2013-35 §3.10. The taxpayer's AMT exemption amount is reduced by 25 percent of the amount by which the taxpayer's AMTI exceeds the amounts specified in §55(d)(3), adjusted annually for inflation. The inflation-adjusted §55(d)(3) amounts for 2014 were (i) $156,500 for married taxpayers filing a joint return and (ii) 117,300 for individual taxpayers. §55(d)(3), (d)(4), Rev. Proc. 2013-35 §3.10.

Under this phase-out rule, the AMT exemption is reduced to zero if (i) married taxpayers filing a joint return have $484,900 or more of AMTI, and (ii) individual taxpayers have $328,500 or more of AMTI.

Section 55(b)(1)(A) provides that a 26 percent rate applies to the first $175,000 of a taxpayer's taxable excess, and a 28 percent rate applies to taxable excess above $175,000. These statutory rate brackets are adjusted annually for inflation. §55(d)(4)(B)(i). For example, in 2014, the 26 percent rate applies to the first $182,500 of a taxpayer's taxable excess, and the 28 percent rate applies to taxable excess above $182,500. Rev. Proc. 2013-35 §3.10. (Long-term capital gain is taxed at reduced rates, instead of the 26 percent and 28 percent rates, under the AMT. §55(b)(3).) The AMT rates are lower than the top nominal tax rate under the regular income tax, but higher than the marginal regular tax rate applicable to most taxpayers.

The future of the AMT is uncertain. Congress originally enacted the AMT to prevent very wealthy taxpayers from eliminating their tax liability by taking advantage of tax preferences that are available under the regular income tax. Under current law, however, taxpayers with the very highest income are less likely to be affected by the AMT than taxpayers in the upper-income range, because the highest income taxpayers have more income that is taxed at the highest regular tax rate.

The AMT increases the progressivity of the tax system. On the other hand, commentators have criticized it on efficiency grounds because the AMT increases marginal tax rates for taxpayers who are subject to it. In addition, the AMT significantly raises compliance costs and has been criticized because it disproportionately affects families with many children and taxpayers who live in high-tax states.

Example

82. In 2014 Sandy and Bob, married taxpayers who file a joint return, have $300,000 of income from wages. For purposes of computing their regular tax liability, their personal exemptions and deductions (including, for example, state income and property taxes) total $100,000, so their taxable income is $200,000. (Assume, for purposes of computing their regular tax liability, that they are taxed at a flat 30 percent rate.) For purposes of computing their alternative minimum tax liability, assume that their deductions and exemptions are zero because of various adjustments provided in §§56–58. Also assume, for purposes of computing their tentative minimum tax, that they are taxed at (i) a 26 percent rate on the first $182,500 of taxable excess and (ii) a 28 percent rate on any additional taxable excess. How much tax do they owe for 2014?

Explanation

82. Sandy and Bob owe $67,407 of tax for 2014. Their regular tax liability for 2014 is $60,000 (30 percent of $200,000 of taxable income). However, under §55, their 2014 tax liability is $67,407.

Sandy and Bob owe §55 alternative minimum tax if their tentative minimum tax is more than their $60,000 regular tax liability. §55(a). In order to compute their tentative minimum tax, we must first determine their AMTI and exemption amount. Their AMTI equals their $200,000 taxable income, adjusted upward under §§56–58 to $300,000. The 2014 inflation-adjusted exemption amount for married taxpayers filing a joint return is $82,100. §55(d)(1)(A), (d)(4)(B)(ii), Rev. Proc. 2013-35 §3.10. However, that exemption amount is reduced by 25 percent of their AMTI over $156,500. §55(d)(3), (d)(4)(B)(iii), Rev. Proc. 2013-35 §3.10. Their $300,000 of AMTI exceeds $156,500 by $143,500. Their $82,100 exemption amount is reduced by 25 percent of $143,500, which is $35,875. After this reduction, their exemption amount is $46,225 and their taxable excess (AMTI in excess of the exemption amount) is $253,775. The first $182,500 of taxable excess is taxed at a 26 percent rate and the remaining $71,275 of taxable excess is taxed at a 28 percent rate. §55(b)(1)(A)(i), (d)(4)(B)(i), Rev. Proc. 2013-35 §3.10. Their tentative minimum tax for 2014 is $67,407, which is the sum of $47,450 plus $19,957. Their tax liability for 2014 is $67,407, because their $67,407 tentative minimum tax exceeds their $60,000 regular tax for 2014. Technically, they will owe regular tax of $60,000 and an additional $6,407 under §55, for a total 2014 tax of $67,407. If Sandy and Bob have a §31 credit for $60,000 of income tax withholding for 2014 (and do not qualify for any additional credits), they must pay $7,407 (surprise!) of additional tax for 2014.

Mixed Personal and Business Expenditures

In contrast to §§162 and 212, §262 provides that no deduction is permitted for personal expenses. The tax law therefore requires that we distinguish between business and personal expenses. It is often difficult to draw a clear line between personal and business expenses. Many expenses are incurred partly for personal reasons and partly for business reasons. For example, a lawyer may purchase art for her office, in part because she enjoys looking at it and in part because she thinks that it will impress her clients.

This chapter will explore the tax treatment of a number of common mixed personal and business expenses. In determining the treatment of some types of mixed personal and business expense, the tax law adopts a black-and-white approach and requires that the mixed motive expense be treated entirely as either a personal expense or business expense. In determining the treatment of other types of mixed motive expense, the tax law requires an allocation of the expense between the business portion and the personal portion. We will see that a number of the rules applicable to mixed motive expenses are anti-abuse provisions designed to prevent taxpayers from converting nondeductible personal expenses into deductible business expenses.

A. CONTROLLING THE ABUSE OF BUSINESS DEDUCTIONS

1. Hobby Losses

Reading: §183; Reg. §1.183-1, -2.

Individuals often engage in activities that are enjoyable and offer an opportunity to produce income. The fact that an individual enjoys an income-producing activity generally will not affect the deductibility of the expenses associated with that activity. However, some business activities, such as breeding race horses, painting landscapes, writing books, and farming, tend to combine significant elements of personal pleasure with a low probability of profitability. Although some individuals earn their livelihood from such ventures, others engage in these activities for personal reasons, without regard for whether the activity will be profitable.

The tax treatment of losses generated by such "hobby" businesses is governed, in part, by §183. That section distinguishes between activities that are "not engaged in for profit" and activities that are engaged in for profit.

If an activity is engaged in for profit, §183 does not alter the tax consequences of any of the expenses from the activity. If an activity is not engaged in for profit, the effect of §183 on a deduction depends on whether the deduction is one that is allowed without regard for whether the expense is a personal expense. Recall from Chapter 4 that taxpayers are allowed various personal deductions, including, for example, the §164 deduction for property tax paid. Section 183 does not alter taxpayers' deductions for these types of expenses, which are deductible without regard to whether the activity is personal. §183(b)(1). Some expenses, however, are deductible in full only if the activity is engaged in for profit. If an activity is not engaged in for profit, these expenses are deductible only to the extent that the gross income from the activity exceeds the deductions permitted under §183(b)(1). §183(b)(2). In effect, §183(b)(2) prevents taxpayers from using hobby losses to shield other income.

Section 183 (c) defines an *activity not engaged in for profit* as any activity other than one with respect to which deductions are allowable under §162 ("ordinary and necessary" business expenses) or under §212 (expenses related to the production of income). This less-than-helpful definition is fortunately supplemented by §183(d) and the regulations. Section 183(d) creates a rebuttable presumption that an activity is engaged in for profit if, in three or more of the last five consecutive years, the activity earns a profit (that is, the gross income from the activity exceeds the deductions attributable to the activity). If the activity is horse breeding, the presumption applies if the activity generates a profit in two or more of the last seven consecutive years.

Under §183(e), a taxpayer can elect to wait to determine whether the presumption is met until the close of the fifth year in which the taxpayer engages in the activity. If the taxpayer makes the election, the statute of limitations on assessment, for the first four years in which the taxpayer engages in the activity, is extended until two years after the return for year five is due. If the activity is horse breeding, the election defers the determination until the seventh year and extends the statute of limitations for years one through six of the activity until two years after the year seven return is due.

If a taxpayer fails to satisfy the test for the presumption, that failure does not necessarily result in characterization of the activity as a non-profit-motivated activity. The taxpayer may still try to establish that the activity was engaged in for profit. Reg. §1.183-1(c). Courts have held that the determination turns on whether the taxpayer engaged in the activity for the purpose of making a profit, not whether, considering the activity objectively, it was likely to make a profit. For example, in Nickerson v. Commissioner, the court stated that taxpayers "need only prove their sincerity rather than their realism." 700 F.2d 402 (7th Cir. 1983). Regulation §1.183-2(a) provides that "[i]n determining whether a [profit-making] objective exists, it may be sufficient that there is a small chance of making a large profit," but adds that "greater weight is given to objective facts than to the taxpayer's mere statement of his intent."

Regulation §1.183-2(b) states that the determination of whether an activity is engaged in for profit is made in light of all the facts and circumstances. The regulation goes on to list nine factors that should be considered:

1. Whether the taxpayer carries on the business in a businesslike manner and keeps complete and accurate books and records.
2. The degree to which the taxpayer has prepared for the activity, either by study or consultation with experts.
3. The time and effort expended by the taxpayer in carrying on the activity.
4. The taxpayer's expectation that assets used in the activity will appreciate in value.
5. The success or failure of the taxpayer in carrying on similar activities.
6. The history of income and losses with respect to the activity. (The regulation states that losses in the start-up phase of the activity do not necessarily indicate that the activity is not engaged in for profit.)
7. The amount of occasional profits, if any, that are earned, as compared with the taxpayer's investment in and losses from the activity.
8. The financial status of the taxpayer. (The regulation provides that the fact that a taxpayer is of modest means may indicate that the activity is

engaged in for profit. Conversely, the fact that a taxpayer is wealthy may indicate that the activity is not engaged in for profit, especially if the activity generates substantial tax benefits and involves recreational elements.)

9. The degree to which the activity is recreational or for personal pleasure.

No one factor is dispositive. Instead, they are all considered. For example, in Nickerson the court of appeals held that a taxpayer's farming activity was engaged in for profit. In that case, several factors indicated that the activity might not have been engaged in for profit, including the following: (i) The farming activity lost a significant amount of money in the first two years of operation, the years at issue in the case; (ii) during those two years, the taxpayer had a full-time job in a city that was a five-hour drive from the farm, so he visited the farm only on weekends; and (iii) the taxpayer did not have a concrete plan for making the farm profitable and had little expertise in farming. On the other hand, several factors also indicated that the activity might have been engaged in for profit: (i) The farm was never used for entertainment and lacked recreational facilities; (ii) the taxpayer and his family performed strenuous manual labor when they were at the farm; (iii) the taxpayer was not wealthy; and (iv) during the two years at issue in the case, the taxpayer attempted to learn more about farming by reading magazines and government publications. After weighing all these factors, the court concluded that taxpayer's farming activity was engaged in for profit.

Examples

1. Upon retirement from his law firm, Donald purchased a second home and small vineyard in Napa Valley. Donald spends approximately four months a year working at the vineyard. The simplified tax returns for the years one through five are as follows. (Add "000" to each of the dollar amounts.)

	Year 1	Year 2	Year 3	Year 4	Year 5
Gross income	$ 1	$10	$19	$80	$ 6
Property taxes	$ 3	$ 3	$ 3	$ 3	$ 3
Labor and supplies	$20	$20	$20	$20	$20
Net income (loss)	($22)	($13)	($4)	$57	($17)

   a. Is Donald's vineyard presumed to be an activity engaged in for profit under §183?

   b. If Donald's vineyard is not an activity engaged in for profit, which expenses can he deduct in year one?

2. Andi is a successful New York City tax attorney who, believing that the fast-paced world of tax law is "a young woman's game," decides to invest

some of her free time and money in the manufacture of chic sweaters for dogs. Although Andi can scarcely conceal her distaste for all things canine, she feels that dogs will be the trendy pet of the next decade. Andi derived much greater enjoyment from her previous successful business producing "designer" cat bowls.

Andi keeps careful records of her dog sweater business operations and looks for ever-cheaper methods of production. She has taken several classes at the local fashion institute in product design and merchandising and spends several hours each week looking at fashion magazines so that she can adapt the latest sweater styles to dachshund and poodle sizes. Although Andi is optimistic that she will be able to retire from tax law when the business takes off, she has lost between $3,000 and $5,000 in each of the four years she has been in business. Fortunately, earning $250,000 a year as a lawyer allows her to pay her living expenses and subsidize the dog sweater business until it becomes profitable. Will Andi be able to deduct the expenses of her dog sweater activity as business losses?

3. Lita, an accountant for a large corporation, used her weekends and evenings to write a mystery novel, Blood on the Balance Sheet, featuring a crime-solving accountant, B. Lance Sheet. After her manuscript was rejected by commercial publishers, she ignored the advice of her friends and published it herself. "There are plenty of accountants who would love to read my novel," she said. Unfortunately, the novel was a critical and commercial failure and Lita lost $15,000 on the venture.

Undaunted, the next year Lita wrote and published a second novel, A Cruel Method of Accounting, again featuring B. Lance Sheet. "The problem with my first novel was that my audience was not aware of it," she reasoned. This time she spent a large sum advertising the novel in the accounting trade magazines. Nonetheless, A Cruel Method of Accounting also failed and Lita lost an additional $25,000. Can Lita deduct the losses she incurred writing, publishing, and advertising the novels?

4. Jasmine raises, shows, and sells Siamese cats as a hobby. In 10 years of raising Siamese cats she has never earned a profit. In year 10, her gross income from the sale of Siamese kittens is $1,600. Although her records of the expenses incurred in the breeding activity are spotty, she can establish that in year 10 she spent $1,000 on transportation and lodging to attend cat shows, $400 on cat food, $700 on veterinary expenses, and $300 on grooming, for a total of $2,400.
   a. How much of these costs, if any, can she deduct in year 10?
   b. Suppose instead that Jasmine's year 10 gross income from the sale of the kittens is $4,000. How much can she deduct?

5. When Abraham turned 30, he unexpectedly inherited a large sum of money from a rich uncle. Freed from financial worry, he decided to

quit his job as a tax associate in a major law firm and become a performance artist. During each of the next five years, he presented an off-Broadway show. The shows received mixed critical reviews and limited commercial success. A summary of the earnings from the shows follows. (Add "000" to each of the dollar amounts.)

Year	Show	Run in Weeks	Gross Income	Costs	Profit/ (Loss)
1	My Best Home Videos	2	$ 3	$ 28	($25)
2	Plato and Babe Ruth Go Fishing	10	$ 22	$ 21	$ 1
3	A Pie in the Face	15	$ 30	$ 27	$ 3
4	IRS Follies: A Musical	30	$ 50	$ 48	$ 2
5	An Evening of Mime	1	$ 1	$ 26	($25)
	Totals	58	$106	$150	($44)

In year five, will Abraham's performance art be considered an "activity not engaged in for profit" under §183?

Explanations

1. a. No, the vineyard is not presumed to be an activity engaged in for profit. Section 183(d) provides that an activity that is profitable in three out of the last five consecutive years is presumed to be an activity engaged in for profit. In this case, a profit was earned in only one of the five years. The fact that the activity has produced a net $1,000 profit over the five-year period does not establish a presumption that it was engaged in for profit.

   b. Section 183 does not alter the taxpayer's deductions for expenses that are deductible without regard to whether the activity is personal. §183(b)(1). Here, the property taxes are deductible without regard to whether the property is used in a profit-making enterprise. §164. Thus, Donald can deduct the $3,000 of property taxes despite the fact that the activity is not engaged in for profit. If the activity is not engaged in for profit, Donald's deduction for the other expenses will be eliminated under §183(b)(2) because the $1,000 of year one gross income from the activity does not exceed the $3,000 of property taxes that are deductible without regard to whether the activity was engaged in for profit.

2. Andi probably will be permitted to deduct her expenses. She cannot satisfy the §183(d) test for the presumption because her business has not been profitable in any of the four years of operation. However, failure to qualify for the presumption does not establish that the activity was not engaged in for profit. Reg. §1.183-1(c). Even without the advantage of

the presumption, Andi may show a profit motive under the nine factors listed in Regulation §1.183-2(b).

The following factors indicate that Andi may have had a profit motive:

1. Andi keeps careful records and looks for ways to make production cheaper;
2. Andi has taken classes to increase her knowledge of merchandising pet products;
3. Andi spends hours each week studying emerging trends in sweater designs;
4. Andi has had success in a similar venture; and
5. a profit motive is more likely when the activity is not enjoyable to the taxpayer, and Andi derives little pleasure from making dog sweaters.

The following factors indicate that Andi may not have had a profit motive:

1. The business has shown steady losses;
2. there have been no profits; and
3. Andi has high income from working as a lawyer. However, the tax benefits of the losses from the activity are not large compared to her income.

A court weighing these factors would likely conclude that her dog sweater business is an activity engaged in for profit. See Nickerson v. Commissioner, 700 F.2d 402 (7th Cir. 1983).

3. This is a close call. A good argument can be made that Lita will be able to deduct the losses. Under §183, the test is not whether it was likely that the taxpayer would earn a profit, but whether the taxpayer entered into the activity with the *purpose* of making a profit. Dreicer v. United States, 665 F.2d 1292 (D.C. Cir. 1981). Lita apparently believed that her novels would be profitable and changed her advertising strategy for her second novel in an attempt to increase its sales. The fact that her judgment was poor is irrelevant if her intent was to earn a profit. Although Lita may enjoy writing her novels, writing may or may not be an activity that would generally be viewed as recreational. Lita is not wealthy and it seems unlikely that she is publishing the novels primarily for personal reasons unrelated to earning a profit.

Nevertheless, other factors suggest that this is not an activity engaged in for profit. There is no evidence that Lita has writing expertise, although she does have expertise as an accountant. She has no history of making a profit as a novelist and she was advised that the activity would be likely to show a loss. However, on balance (no pun intended), it is likely that Lita will be entitled to a deduction.

4. a. Jasmine can deduct $1,600. The following factors indicate that Jasmine did not have a profit motive:

    1. The business has shown steady losses;
    2. there have been no profits;
    3. breeding Siamese cats and attending cat shows is an activity that many cat-lovers enjoy; and
    4. Jasmine does not maintain complete records in a businesslike manner.

    Thus, the activity is not engaged in for profit and §183 (a) and (b) apply. Here, none of the expenses are the type that are deductible without regard to whether the activity was engaged in for profit. All of the expenses here are deductible only to the extent of her gross income from the activity, which is $1,600. §183(b)(2).

  b. Jasmine will be allowed to deduct all $2,400 of her expenses. Section 183 does not limit the deduction of the expenses since her gross income from the activity, $4,000, exceeds her expenses. §183(b)(2).

5. The performance art activity meets the §183(d) test since Abraham has earned a profit in three of the last five consecutive years in which he has engaged in the activity. The activity is thus presumed to be engaged in for profit even though he has suffered an aggregate loss. The fact that Abraham could have made a larger amount of money by practicing law is irrelevant so long as he intended to make a profit from his performance art. The §183(d) presumption is rebuttable, but the facts here, on balance, do not indicate that the Service could successfully rebut the presumption. Although Abraham does seem to be wealthy, it does not appear that he is engaging in the performance art activity to shelter his other income.

2. Rental of a Dwelling Used by the Taxpayer

Reading: §280A.

If a taxpayer owns rental property that is not used by the taxpayer for personal purposes at any time during the taxable year, the taxpayer is entitled to deduct all expenses associated with the property, including depreciation, repairs, utilities, property taxes, and interest. (See Chapter 5 of this book for a discussion of business deductions and Chapter 4 for a discussion of the deduction for property taxes.) However, if the taxpayer's property is rented for part of the year and used by the taxpayer for part of the year, allowing the taxpayer to deduct the expenses of the rental property creates potential for abuse. In 1976 Congress enacted §280A to address this potential abuse. Section 280A applies only if the taxpayer uses the rental property for "personal purposes" during the year.

A dwelling unit is deemed used for personal purposes if it is occupied by the taxpayer, certain relatives of the taxpayer (including the taxpayer's spouse, siblings, ancestors, and lineal descendants), or by any person who does not pay a fair rental. §§267(c)(4), 280A(d)(2). A dwelling unit also is deemed used for personal purposes if the use of the unit by another individual gives the taxpayer the right to use another dwelling unit. §280A(d)(2)(B). Rental of the dwelling at a fair rent to a relative who uses the dwelling as a principal residence, however, is not considered personal use. §280A(d)(3). Occupation of the dwelling unit by the taxpayer for the purpose of making repairs also is not deemed use for a personal purpose. §280A(d)(2).

Under §280A, a taxpayer's deductions for the expenses of a dwelling unit rented by the taxpayer during the year turn on (i) the number of days during the year that the taxpayer used the dwelling unit for personal purposes and (ii) the number of days during the year that the dwelling unit was rented.

If the taxpayer rents the dwelling and does not use it for personal purposes at all during the year, §280A does not limit the taxpayer's deductions for the expenses of the rental property (although other provisions, such as §469, discussed in Chapter 5, may limit the deductions).

If, during the year, the taxpayer rents the dwelling and uses it for personal purposes on one or more days, §280A(e) and (b) limit the taxpayer's deductions for the expenses of the dwelling to the sum of (i) the deductions that are allowed without regard to whether the dwelling was used in a trade or business or income-producing activity ("non-profit-motivated expenses") such as deductible property taxes and home mortgage interest plus (ii) the portion of the other expenses ("profit-motivated expenses") that are allocable to the period during which the property was rented. The profit-motivated expenses are allocated to the rental period based on the ratio of (i) the number of days the property was rented to (ii) the number of days the property was used either by the rental tenant or by the taxpayer for personal reasons. Days on which the property was not used are disregarded. Thus, the profit-motivated expenses allocated to the rental use of the property equal the product of multiplying the profit-motivated expenses for the year by the following fraction:

$$\frac{\text{Number of Rental Days}}{\text{Total Number of Days Used}}$$

What types of expenses constitute non-profit-motivated expenses? In a typical case, they are home mortgage interest and property taxes on the dwelling, both of which are generally deductible without regard to profit motive. §§163(h)(2)(D), 164. However, note that home mortgage interest is deductible as qualified residence interest only if the debt is acquisition indebtedness or home equity indebtedness on a "qualified residence."

The determination of whether a home is a qualified residence is made as the mortgage interest accrues. §163(h)(3)(A). (The deduction for home mortgage interest is discussed in Chapter 4.) A qualified residence is defined as either the taxpayer's principal residence or a second home that the taxpayer uses "as a residence." §163(h)(4)(A). A second home is used as a residence if, during the year, the taxpayer uses it for personal reasons for more than 14 days (or, if greater, 10 percent of the days during the year that the home is rented at a fair rental). §280A(d).

If the taxpayer does not use a second home enough to make the home a qualified residence, the mortgage interest on that home is not deductible as qualified residence interest. However, the portion of the mortgage interest allocable to the days during the year that the second home was rented may still be deductible as a profit-motivated expense. In other words, the interest may have to be allocated between personal and rental use of the property.

The property taxes paid by the taxpayer on the rented dwelling are deductible without regard to whether the taxpayer had a profit motive. §164. However, the effect of taking the deduction depends on whether the property taxes were expenses of an income-producing rental activity: Property taxes are taken as an above-the-line deduction to the extent that they are incurred with respect to an income-producing rental activity. Any remaining property taxes are taken as a below-the-line itemized deduction. §62(a)(4). In other words, the property taxes paid during the year must be allocated between the rental use and personal use of the property, despite the fact that the property taxes are non-profit-motivated expenses.

The Service takes the position that the allocation of non-profit-motivated expenses to rental use of the dwelling is done in the same way as the allocation of the profit-motivated expenses, using the formula given above (the "percentage-of-days-used" formula). Prop. Reg. §1.280A-3(d). However, a number of courts have adopted a more pro-taxpayer formula and allocated the non-profit-motivated expenses by comparing the number of days that the property was rented to the number of days in the entire year (the "percentage-of-days-in-the-year" formula). This method allocates a smaller portion of the non-profit-motivated expenses to the rental use and allows the taxpayer to deduct against rental income a higher amount of profit-motivated expenses allocable to the rental use of the property. See, e.g., Bolton v. Commissioner, 77 T.C. 104 (1981), aff'd, 694 F.2d 556 (9th Cir. 1982); McKinney v. Commissioner, 732 F.2d 414 (10th Cir. 1983).

Although §280A(e) generally requires allocation of the profit-motivated expenses if the taxpayer uses the dwelling on one or more days during the year, a special rule in §280A(g) applies if, during the year, the taxpayer uses the dwelling as a residence and rents the dwelling for less than 15 days. If this special rule applies, the taxpayer is not allowed to deduct any of the expenses of the dwelling rented, other than non-profit-motivated expenses, such as mortgage interest and property taxes. §280A(g)(1). In other words,

§280A(g)(1) disallows the taxpayer's deductions for the profit-motivated expenses allocable to the rental use of the property. On the other hand, the taxpayer does not have to include in income the rent paid by the tenant. §280A(g)(2).

If the taxpayer rents the dwelling and uses it as a residence during the year (that is, uses it for the greater of 14 days or 10 percent of the number of days on which the property is rented), the taxpayer's deductions for the profit-motivated expenses of the dwelling (e.g., depreciation and mainte-nance costs) will be limited by both §280A(e) and (c)(5). In these circum-stances, §280A(c)(5) limits the taxpayer's deduction of these expenses in a given year to (i) the gross income from the rental of the dwelling less (ii) the non-profit-motivated expenses allocable to the rental use of the dwelling (under either the percentage-of-days-used formula or the percentage-of-days-of-the-year formula, described above).

Proposed Regulation §1.280A-3(d) also provides an ordering rule for applying the §280A(c)(5) limitation based on whether the profit-motivated expenses allocable to the rental use of the dwelling result in an adjustment of the basis of the dwelling (for example, depreciation) or do not result in an adjustment of the basis of the dwelling (for example, utilities or insurance). Under this rule, depreciation deductions are allowed last, after the deductions for profit-motivated expenses that do not reduce the taxpayer's basis in the dwelling. Any expenses allowed under §280A(e) but limited by §280A(c)(5) are carried forward to the next year. §280A(c)(5) (flush language).

Examples

6. Jade owns a beach house in South Carolina. She rents the house to her brother Mike year-round for its fair rental value of $1,000 per month. Can Jade deduct the depreciation, repairs, interest, and other expenses of owning and renting the house?

7. Belle lives year-round in a two-bedroom ranch house in Claremont. During July, the International Frozen Yogurt Festival is held in Claremont. Wanting to escape the masses that would converge on the town and knowing that she stands to make a large profit, Belle rents her house to festival-goers and flees Claremont for the duration of the festival. The rent amounts to $3,000 for 10 days. Is Belle allowed to deduct non-profit-motivated expenses (for example, mortgage interest and property taxes) and profit-motivated expenses (for example, insurance, utilities, and depreciation) that are allocable to the period during which her house is rented?

8. Billie owns a beachfront vacation condominium in a resort community in Florida. During year one she uses the condominium for 20 days and rents it for 300 days, for which she receives a fair rent of $15,000. During the year she pays the following expenses with respect to the condo: property

taxes of $4,800, mortgage interest of $12,000 (10 percent interest on a $120,000 mortgage), and $1,600 of maintenance charges. The year one depreciation on the condo is $3,200. The mortgage on her principal residence is $500,000.

a. What is the tax treatment of Billie's year one expenses?
b. How, if at all, would your answer in part (a) change if she uses the condominium for 60 days and rents it out for 260 days at a fair rent of $15,000?

Explanations

6. Yes. Section 280A limits deductions on a rented dwelling only if the taxpayer has used the dwelling for personal purposes during the year. If the taxpayer has not used the unit for personal purposes, repair expenses, interest, and other expenses are deductible, subject to the limitations on passive activity and hobby losses.

   Although occupancy by a taxpayer's relative usually is considered personal use by the taxpayer, an exception applies where the relative uses the dwelling as a principal residence and pays a fair rental. Note that if Jade visits her brother briefly, her visit will not be considered personal use of the house. Prop. Reg. §1.280A-1(e)(2).

7. Belle is not allowed to deduct any of the profit-motivated expenses because her house is rented for fewer than 15 days during the year. §280A(g)(1). Belle has no reason to complain, however. She is allowed to deduct the non-profit-motivated expenses such as home mortgage interest and property taxes. In addition, Belle does not have to include in income any of the $3,000 of rent she receives because she rented the home for fewer than 15 days. §280A(g)(2).

8. a. During year one the condominium is used for both personal and rental purposes during the taxable year, so §280A will limit Billie's deduction of the year one expenses. Billie is allowed to deduct the $4,800 of property taxes because such property taxes are deductible regardless of profit motive. §164. The property tax will have to be allocated between personal and rental use, despite the fact that it is a non-profit-motivated expense, in order to determine which portion of the tax is an above-the-line deduction and which portion is a below-the-line itemized deduction. §62(a)(4). The Service's position is that non-profit-motivated deductions should be allocated based on the per-centage-of-days-used formula. Prop. Reg. §1.280A-3(d)(3). This method has been rejected, however, by the Tax Court and the Ninth and Tenth Circuits, which have held that non-profit-motivated expenses should be allocated based on the percentage-of-days-in-the-year formula.

Bolton v. Commissioner, 77 T.C. 104 (1981), aff'd, 694 F.2d 556 (9th Cir. 1982); McKinney v. Commissioner, 732 F.2d 414 (10th Cir. 1983). Here, if we apply the courts' allocation method to the $4,800 of property taxes, Billie will take an above-the-line deduction of $3,945 (300/365 of the $4,800 of property taxes) and a below-the-line deduction of $855 ($4,800 less $3,945) (assuming that she itemizes).

Home mortgage interest is generally deductible under §163(h)(3) as qualified residence interest. However, here the mortgage will not be deductible as qualified residence interest. Mortgage interest can be qualified residence interest only if it is paid with respect to a qualified residence. §163(h)(3)(A). If a dwelling is not used "as a residence," the dwelling is not a qualified residence. §163(h)(4)(A)(i)(II). Section 280A(d)(1) provides that a second home is used "as a residence" only if the taxpayer uses it for the greater of 14 days or 10 percent of the days that the dwelling is rented. Billie does not use the condominium as a residence in year one because she did not use it for more than 30 days (which is the greater of 14 days or 10 percent of the 300 days that the dwelling was rented). The mortgage interest is thus not deductible as qualified residence interest. Recall from Chapter 4 that personal interest other than qualified residence interest is nondeductible. §163(h)(1), (2). Even though the mortgage interest is not deductible as qualified residence interest, the portion of the interest that is allocable to the rental use of the dwelling may still be deductible as a profit-motivated expense allocable to the rental use of the dwelling.

The $12,000 of mortgage interest, $1,600 of maintenance charges, and $3,200 of depreciation are profit-motivated expenses that must be allocated between the personal and rental use of the property. §280A(e). Profit-motivated expenses are allocated to the rental use pro rata by comparing the number of days the property was rented (300 days) to the total number of days the property was used (320). Here, 300/320 (or 15/16 or 93.75 percent) of the interest, maintenance, and depreciation expenses are allocable to the rental use of the property. Thus, §280A(e) limits Billie's deduction for the interest, maintenance charges, and depreciation to $15,750 ($11,250 of interest, $1,500 of the maintenance charges, and $3,000 of the depreciation).

Billie's $15,750 year one deduction for interest, maintenance charges, and depreciation is not limited by §280A(c)(5) because Billie does not use the dwelling as a residence in year one.

b. Here, Billie uses the residence for personal purposes for more than 26 days (which is the greater of 14 days or 10 percent of the 260 days that the dwelling is rented). The dwelling is thus a qualified residence and the mortgage interest is qualified residence interest, which is deductible without regard to profit motive. §163(h)(3), (4)(A)(i)(II). Because the mortgage interest is a non-profit-motivated expense, it is deductible without regard to the §280A(e) limitation.

As in part (a), the $1,600 of maintenance charges and $3,200 of depreciation are profit-motivated expenses that must be allocated between the personal and rental use of the property. §280A(e). Here, however, the portion of these expenses allocable to the rental use is different than in part (a). Profit-motivated expenses are allocated to the rental use by comparing the number of days the property was rented (here, 260 days) to the total number of days the property was used (320). Thus, 260/320 or 81.25 percent of the maintenance and depreciation expenses are allocable to the rental use of the property. Section 280A(e) limits Billie's deduction for the maintenance charges and depreciation to $3,900 ($1,300 of the maintenance charges and $2,600 of the depreciation).

Billie's $3,900 year one deduction for maintenance charges and depreciation may be limited further by §280A(c)(5). Billie is using the dwelling in year one for more than 26 days (10 percent of the 260 days that the condo was rented), so she is using the condominium as a residence and her year one deductions are thus subject to §280A(c)(5). This will limit her year one deductions for the profit-motivated expenses allocable to the rental use of the property to (i) the year one rental income less (ii) the year one non-profit-motivated deductions allocable to the rental use.

Section 280A does not specify the proper method of allocating non-profit-motivated deductions to the rental use of the dwelling. As noted in part (a), the Service's position is that non-profit-motivated deductions should be allocated based on the percentage-of-days-used formula, but the Tax Court and the Ninth and Tenth Circuits have held that non-profit-motivated expenses should be allocated based on the percentage-of-days-in-the-year formula. Using the latter method to determine the §280A(c)(5) limitation allocates a smaller portion of the non-profit-motivated expenses to the rental use and allows the taxpayer to deduct a higher amount of the profit-motivated expenses allocable to the rental use of the dwelling.

Billie has $16,800 of non-profit-motivated expenses ($12,000 of mortgage interest deductible under §163(h)(2)(D) and $4,800 of property taxes deductible under §164, regardless of the taxpayer's profit motive). Assuming that the pro-taxpayer allocation method endorsed by the courts is followed, Billie's non-profit-motivated deductions would be allocated as follows:

Non-profit-motivated deductions: $16,800

Days of rental use: 260 days

Days in the year: 365 days

Rental use portion: 260/365 × $16,800 = $11,967

Billie receives $15,000 of rent. This amount exceeds the $11,967 of non-profit-motivated deductions allocable to rental use of the property by $3,033. Thus, Billie can deduct $3,033 of the $3,900 of year one profit-motivated deductions allocable to rental use of the dwelling. §280A(c)(5). Where the entire amount of profit-motivated expenses cannot be currently deducted, expenses other than depreciation are taken first. In year one Billie will take a $1,300 deduction for the maintenance charges and a $1,733 deduction for depreciation. The portion of the $3,900 expense that cannot be deducted in year one, $867 ($3,900 less $3,033) is carried forward to year two.

3. Home Offices, Computers, and Automobiles

Reading: §§280A, 280F.

Many taxpayers work sometimes at home, and home computers and personal automobiles are often used part of the time for business purposes. Permitting deductions for these expenses, however, might enable aggressive taxpayers to take deductions for expenses that are primarily personal. On the other hand, denying a deduction would be unfair to individuals who genuinely incur these types of expenses for business reasons. Thus, current law permits deductions for these expenses, but adopts special restrictions to prevent abuse.

Section 280A(a) provides that an individual is not allowed a deduction for use of his dwelling unless one of a number of special rules in §280A applies. Section 280A(c)(1), one of those special rules, allows a deduction for an office in the taxpayer's home (or a separate structure not attached to the home) only where the taxpayer uses the home office exclusively on a regular basis: (i) as the principal place of business for any trade or business of the taxpayer; (ii) as a place of business that is used by patients, clients, or customers in meeting or dealing with the taxpayer in his business; or (iii) in connection with the taxpayer's business if the office is in a separate structure that is not attached to the taxpayer's home. In addition, if the taxpayer is an employee (as opposed to being self-employed), he is allowed the home office deduction only if his use of the home office is for the "convenience of the employer." §280A(c)(1) (flush language). An employee's use of a home office is for the convenience of the employer if the employer does not provide the employee with an office at all, or if the employer has not provided adequate office space in which the employee can effectively carry out employment duties. Weissman v. Commissioner, 751 F.2d 512 (2d Cir. 1984). If the employer has provided the employee with adequate office space, the home office is for the convenience of the employee, not the employer, even if the office is used exclusively for business purposes. Cadwallader v. Commissioner, 919 F.2d 1273 (7th Cir. 1990).

A taxpayer can qualify for one of the three parts of the §280A(c)(1) test only if she is engaged in a "trade or business." If a taxpayer spends most of her time managing her investments from a home office, is the investment activity a trade or business for the purpose of applying §280A(c)(1)? In Moller v. United States, 721 F.2d 810 (Fed. Cir. 1983), the taxpayers deducted the expenses of the home office in which they worked full-time managing their investments. In determining whether the Mollers were engaged in a trade or business, the court distinguished between "investing" and "trading." Investors buy securities for the long-term and their income from investing is primarily dividend and interest income. Traders, on the other hand, invest for the short-term and their income from trading is primarily gain from the sale of securities. Although trading is a trade or business, managing investments, even full-time, is not a trade or business. The court concluded that the Mollers were investors, not traders, and thus were not engaged in a trade or business and could not deduct the expenses of their home office.

In Commissioner v. Soliman, 506 U.S. 168 (1993), the Supreme Court articulated a standard for determining whether a home office is the "principal place of business" for purposes of applying §280A(c)(1)(A). In that case, the taxpayer was an anesthesiologist who spent 30 to 35 hours a week seeing patients at three hospitals. He did not have any office space at the hospitals, so he spent 10 to 15 hours a week in a home office doing various tasks related to his practice, including billing, professional reading, and speaking on the telephone. The Service took the position that the home office was not the taxpayer's principal place of business and disallowed the deduction he had taken for it. The Supreme Court stated that the "principal place of business" is the most important or significant place for the business. The Court added that the test requires consideration of (i) the relative importance of the activities performed in each of the taxpayer's places of business and (ii) the amount of time spent at each of the places of business. The Court added that great weight must be given to the place of business where the taxpayer delivers goods or services. Dr. Soliman spent 30 to 35 hours a week at the hospitals treating patients and 10 to 15 hours a week in his home office doing ancillary activities related to his practice, so the Court held that the home office was not his principal place of business.

Congress responded to the decision in *Soliman* by amending §280A. As amended, the flush language of §280A(c)(1) provides that the term *principal place of business* includes the taxpayer's home office if it is exclusively and regularly used to conduct substantial administrative or management activities for a trade or business of the taxpayer and the taxpayer does not conduct substantial administrative or management activities at any other fixed location of the trade or business. Under the amended test, the taxpayer in *Soliman* would have qualified for the deduction. (The test articulated in *Soliman* would still apply, however, where the taxpayer taking the home office deduction is arguing that the home office is the principal place of business and the office is not used for administrative or management activities.)

Section 280A(c)(1)(B) allows a deduction for the home office if it is "used by patients, clients, or customers in meeting or dealing with the taxpayer in the normal course of his trade or business." Speaking on the telephone with patients, clients, or customers does not constitute "meeting or dealing" with them. Rather, the clients must be physically present in the office, and their use of the taxpayer's home must be substantial and integral to the conduct of the taxpayer's business. Green v. Commissioner, 707 F.2d 404 (9th Cir. 1983), Prop. Reg. §1.280A-2(c), IRS Publication 587 (2012), at 6.

A home office deduction permitted under one of the three parts of §280A(c)(1) is subject to the §280A(c)(5) limitation discussed in the preceding section of this book. That section limits a taxpayer's home office deduction to the taxpayer's gross income derived from the use of the home office less the deductions allowed for the taxpayer's non-profit-motivated expenses of the home office (such as property taxes and deductible qualified residence interest).

In 2013, the Service created a new optional safe harbor to simplify the calculation of certain types of §280A(c) deductions, including the §280A(c)(1) home office deduction. Rev. Proc. 2013-13. Under the new safe harbor, a taxpayer may deduct the product of multiplying the "prescribed rate" (currently $5) times the square footage of the taxpayer's home office (but not to exceed 300 square feet). Id. Taxpayers electing to use the safe harbor can still deduct non-profit-motivated deductions (e.g., qualified residence interest and property tax deductions) as itemized deductions, and can still deduct business expenses that are unrelated to the taxpayer's use of the home, such as business expenses for advertising, wages, and supplies. Id. Electing taxpayers cannot deduct depreciation or other expenses (e.g., insurance and utilities) for the portion of the home used for business. Id. The safe harbor deduction is allowed only to the extent that gross income from the business for the year exceeds the sum of (1) the taxpayer's non-profit-motivated deductions (which are taken as itemized deductions) plus (2) the deductible business expenses that are unrelated to the taxpayer's use of the home. §280A(c)(5), Rev. Proc. 2013-13. Each year, taxpayers are free to use the safe harbor deduction or to calculate their actual expenses for business use of their home. Rev. Proc. 2013-13. The Revenue Procedure provides coordination rules for taxpayers who change from using the safe harbor deduction to actual expenses or vice versa; this type of change does not require approval from the Service. Id. A taxpayer irrevocably elects to use the safe harbor deduction in a given year by filing a timely return for that year using the safe harbor deduction. Id. The Revenue Procedure also provides an allocation method where a portion of the taxpayer's home is used for business during part of the year but not the entire year. Id.

Section 280F imposes additional limitations on a taxpayer's business deductions for certain listed property that is especially subject to abuse. *Listed property* is defined in §280F(d)(4)(A) to include computers, cars or other transportation vehicles, and any property generally used for entertainment or recreation. However, a computer is not listed property if it is: (i) used exclusively at a regular business establishment, including a home office that meets the test of §280A(c)(1); and (ii) owned or leased by the person operating the business establishment. §280F(d)(4)(B). Section 280F(d)(4)(C) and (5)(B) also except from the definition of listed property certain types of cars and vehicles, such as delivery vehicles, moving vans, and cars used in business to transport passengers (for example, by a limousine service).

If a taxpayer does not use listed property for business purposes more than 50 percent of the time, the taxpayer's depreciation deduction, for the portion of the cost of the property allocable to the business use of the property, is not eligible for accelerated depreciation (discussed in Chapter 5); instead the taxpayer is limited to straight line depreciation deductions on the property. §§168(g)(1), (2)(A), 280F(b). This reduces the taxpayer's depreciation deductions in the earlier years in which the taxpayer owns and uses the property. The §280F(b) (more than 50 percent business use) limitation also applies for purposes of determining the taxpayer's §179 deduction with respect to listed property. §280F(d)(1).

Additional complications arise if, in an earlier year, a taxpayer took accelerated depreciation deductions on listed property because the taxpayer used the listed property for business more than 50 percent of the time that year, and, in a subsequent year, the taxpayer's business use of the listed property drops to 50 percent or less. If that occurs, the taxpayer must recapture the excess depreciation deduction from the earlier year by including in gross income, in the subsequent year, the difference between the accelerated depreciation deduction taken on the listed property in the earlier year and a straight line deduction on the listed property for the earlier year. §280F(b)(2).

Finally, any use of listed property by an employee (rather than a self-employed individual) is not treated as use in a trade or business (and thus is not eligible for any depreciation) unless such use is (i) for the convenience of the employer and (ii) required as a condition of employment. §280F(d)(3).

Examples

Assume, in all of the examples below, that the taxpayer uses the home office exclusively for business.

9. Mercedes inherited a $5 million investment portfolio from her parents. She receives almost all of her income from dividends and interest on the securities in the portfolio and spends over 30 hours per week monitoring the portfolio. She maintains an office in her home that she occupies from 9:00 A.M. to 4:00 P.M. each day and that is the principal place from which she manages her investments. Is Mercedes allowed to take a home office deduction?

10. a. June is employed as a therapist at a counseling center. She has an office at the center where she meets with patients, but she spends only about half her workday there. She spends the rest of her workday (totaling 20 to 25 hours each week) in an office in her home doing work related to her practice, including billing, professional reading, and returning phone calls. Is June entitled to a home office deduction?

    b. How, if at all, does your answer in part (a) change if June owns the counseling center and is self-employed instead of being an employee of the center?

    c. How, if at all, does your answer in part (b) change if June sees patients and takes care of billing, professional reading, and returning phone calls at her center office, which takes 30 to 35 hours a week, and uses her home office for 10 to 15 hours a week in the evenings to speak on the phone to patients who cannot come to her office during the day?

11. Alfred, a professor at Eastman University, maintains a laboratory in a detached garage next to his home because the university does not provide laboratory space for him to engage in the scientific experiments that are the subject of his scholarly writing. He spends 20 hours each week working in his home laboratory and 30 hours each week at the university in the classroom and in his university office where he writes and sees students. Is Alfred entitled to a home office deduction?

12. Mabel, a lawyer, is an associate in a large urban law firm. One or two days a week and most evenings, Mabel works at home in an office that she set up in a spare bedroom of her home. She uses her home personal computer to research cases through Lexis and Westlaw and to write drafts of briefs and memos. Is Mabel allowed to deduct her home office and computer expenses?

13. Bob is an elementary school teacher. On evenings and weekends he operates a mail-order comic book service, buying and selling rare comic

books. He sets up an office in his home that he uses exclusively for running the comic book business. His annual gross income from the comic business is $4,000 and his teacher's salary is $40,000. Bob uses a home computer exclusively to maintain customer lists. Is Bob allowed a deduction for his home office and computer?

Explanations

9. No. A taxpayer is allowed a home office deduction only if she is engaged in a "trade or business." In Moller v. United States, 721 F.2d 810 (Fed. Cir. 1983), the Federal Circuit held that a couple who managed their investment portfolio full-time were not allowed to take a home office deduction because long-term investing (as opposed to trading) is not a trade or business. Mercedes, who derives most of her investment income from dividends and interest, not from gain on the sale of securities, is an investor rather than a trader, so she is not engaged in a trade or business and is not allowed a home office deduction.

10. a. June is an employee of the center, so she cannot take a home office deduction unless the home office is maintained for the convenience of her employer. §280A(c)(1) (flush language). She has an adequate office at the center, so the home office is not for the convenience of her employer. Cadwallader v. Commissioner, 919 F.2d 1273 (7th Cir. 1990).

b. June is not an employee of the center, so the limitation discussed in the explanation to part (a) is inapplicable. June can take a deduction for the home office if it is her "principal place of business." §280A(c)(1)(A). Under the post-Soliman amendments to §280A, "a principal place of business" includes a home office that is used exclusively and regularly for substantial administrative or management activities. §280A(c)(1) (flush language). June's activities in her home office are regular and administrative (being similar to the anesthesiologist's activities in Soliman, the case that prompted the amendment), so the home office would be considered a principal place of business and a home office deduction would be allowed.

Each year in which June uses the home office exclusively for business, she can deduct either her actual costs for the home office or the safe harbor amount (the product of multiplying $5 times the square footage of her home office). The home office deduction is allowed only to the extent that gross income from the business for the year exceeds the sum of the taxpayer's non-profit-motivated deductions plus the deductible business expenses that are unrelated to the taxpayer's use of the home. §280A(c)(5), Rev. Proc. 2013-13.

c. Is the home office still June's "principal place of business"? The home office is no longer used for substantial administrative matters, so the amendment to §280A does not apply. Under the test articulated in *Soliman*, the taxpayer's "principal place of business" is the most important or significant place for the taxpayer's business, taking into account the relative importance of the activities performed in each place of business and the amount of time spent in each place. The Court also said that the place where the taxpayer delivers services must be given great weight. Counseling patients is the service June delivers, and it is her most important business activity, but she counsels patients both in her center office and from her home office. However, she spends twice as much time in her center office, so her home office would not be considered her "principal place of business" for purposes of §280A.

Could June qualify for the deduction by arguing that her home office is "a place of business which is used by patients . . . in meeting and dealing with [June] in the normal course of [her] trade or business," under §280A(c)(1)(B)? June does counsel patients from her home office, but a home office is used by patients "in meeting and dealing" with the taxpayer only if the patients actually visit the taxpayer's home office; talking to patients on the phone is not sufficient, so June will not qualify for the home office deduction. Green v. Commissioner, 707 F.2d 404 (9th Cir. 1983); Prop. Reg. §1.280A-2(c).

11. Probably. The Code provides that an employee may only deduct a home office that is used for the convenience of the employer. §280A(c)(1) (flush language). The Second Circuit has held, however, that where an employer has not provided space in which an employee can effectively carry out his employment duties, a home office is for the convenience of the employer. Weissman v. Commissioner, 751 F.2d 512 (2d Cir. 1984). Although the university provides Alfred an office in which he can talk with students and write, the university does not provide him with laboratory space in which he can perform other essential duties of his employment. Alfred's use of the garage thus is probably for the convenience of his employer.

The garage is a separate structure and is used in connection with Alfred's trade or business, so it satisfies §280A(c)(1)(C). A separate structure need not be the principal place of business or a place where clients are met. Alfred thus is allowed to take a home office deduction.

12. Mabel will not be able to receive any business deductions for either the home office or the computer. Section 280A(c)(1) allows deductions for the cost of a home office only if the office is used exclusively on a regular basis: (i) as the taxpayer's principal place of business; (ii) as

a place of business where clients meet the taxpayer; or (iii) in a structure separate from the rest of the house. Mabel cannot satisfy any of these three tests because: (i) her principal place of business is the law firm; (ii) she does not meet clients in her home; and (iii) the spare bedroom is not a separate structure.

Moreover, §280A(c)(1) states that, for employees, the cost of a home office is deductible only if it is used for the convenience of the employer. Since Mabel presumably has an adequate office at work, the home office would be deemed used for her own convenience and not for the convenience of her employer. See Cadwallader v. Commissioner, 919 F.2d 1273 (7th Cir. 1990).

Computers are "listed property" and thus subject to the limitations imposed under §280F. §280F(d)(4)(A)(iv). An employee is allowed to deduct the cost of a home computer only if the computer is used for the convenience of the employer and is required as a condition of employment. §280F(d)(3)(A). There is no indication that Mabel is required by her law firm to purchase a computer or to work at home, so she will not be able to deduct the cost of her computer.

13. Yes. The office is the principal place of business for the comic book business. Thus, Bob is allowed a home office deduction under §280A(c)(1)(A). Note, however, that §280A(c)(5) could potentially limit Bob's home office deduction since his gross income from the comic business is only $4,000.

Section 280F does not limit Bob's deduction for his computer; the computer is not "listed property" because it is used exclusively for business purposes in a qualifying home office. §280F(d)(4)(B).

B. TRAVEL AND ENTERTAINMENT EXPENSES

Reading: §§162, 274.

Taxpayers are allowed to deduct the ordinary and necessary expenses incurred in carrying on a trade or business. §162(a). Travel and entertainment expenses associated with a business have an inherent element of personal consumption and have been subject to substantial taxpayer abuse. Thus, §§162(a)(2) and 274 place a number of restrictions on the deductibility of such expenses. The goal is to permit deductions for travel and entertainment expenses that serve a genuine business purpose while restricting the deductibility of expenses that are incurred primarily for personal reasons. This section summarizes the §162(a)(2) test and some of the most important provisions of §274.

Section 162(a) provides generally that a taxpayer is allowed to deduct the ordinary and necessary expenses paid or incurred in carrying on a trade or business. (For a discussion of the terms *ordinary* and *necessary*, see Chapter 5 of this book.) Section 162(a)(2) allows a taxpayer to deduct travel expenses, including the costs of meals and lodging, if the following three requirements are met: (i) the travel expenses are reasonable and appropriate; (ii) the expenses are incurred while the taxpayer is away from home; and (iii) the expenses are motivated by the exigencies of the taxpayer's business, not the taxpayer's personal preferences. For purposes of this test, a taxpayer is "away from home" only if the taxpayer is away overnight. United States v. Correll, 389 U.S. 299 (1967).

Usually, the location of the taxpayer's "home" will be obvious because the taxpayer will live and work in the same area. However, if the taxpayer lives in one location and works in a different location, is the taxpayer's "home" the place where the taxpayer lives or works? A number of courts have refused to adopt a bright-line test on this issue. Instead they have considered all of the facts and circumstances to determine whether the expense is motivated by the exigencies of the taxpayer's business rather than the taxpayer's personal preferences. Hantzis v. Commissioner, 638 F.2d 248 (1st Cir. 1981). If a taxpayer maintains two residences and incurs duplicate living expenses because of the exigencies of the taxpayer's business, the expenses are likely to be deductible. On the other hand, if a taxpayer maintains two residences for personal reasons (for example, because the taxpayer must work in one location but simply prefers for personal reasons to live in another area), the duplicate expenses incurred at the work location are not deductible.

For example, in *Hantzis*, the court upheld the Service's disallowance of a law student taxpayer's costs of living in New York City during a 10-week summer law firm clerkship despite the fact that she and her husband lived in Boston. Ms. Hantzis was not engaged in a trade or business in Boston, where she lived and attended law school, but was engaged in a trade or business in New York, where she worked, so the court concluded that her "home," for purposes of §162(a)(2), was New York. The court also concluded that Ms. Hantzis did not meet the "exigencies of the business" test because she chose to live in Boston for personal reasons, not business reasons. Since she could not satisfy the requirements of §162(a)(2), she could not deduct the costs of living in New York as "away from home" travel expenses.

Some taxpayers have no "home" so they cannot be "away from home" for purposes of §162. In Rosenspan v. United States, 438 F.2d 905 (2d Cir. 1971), the taxpayer traveled for business most of the year. He voted and filed income tax returns from his brother's home, but rarely spent the night with his brother because he feared he would wear out his welcome there. The Second Circuit held that the taxpayer could not deduct his travel expenses under §162(a)(2) because he had no home from which to be away.

Certain meal, recreation, and entertainment expenses incurred in a business setting may be deducted even if the taxpayer is not away from home. However, the costs of such business entertainment or recreation (including meals) may be deducted only if: (i) the item was "directly related to" the active conduct of the taxpayer's trade or business (as opposed to the creation of goodwill); or (ii) the item preceded or followed a "substantial and bona fide business discussion" and was "associated" with the taxpayer's trade or business. §274(a)(1). See also Reg. §1.274-2(c)(3). Under the second part of the §274(a)(1) test, a taxpayer may be able to deduct the cost of taking a client to a concert or sporting event that is not directly related to the taxpayer's business, simply by holding a business discussion at a restaurant before or after the event.

Section 274(e) provides a number of specific exceptions to §274(a) for certain expenses. For example, §274(e) provides that §274(a) does not limit an employer's deduction for expenses associated with a bona fide business meeting of employees, stockholders, partners, or directors. A meeting held principally to discuss business, not for social purposes, is a bona fide business meeting. §274(e)(5), Reg. §1.274-2(f)(2)(vi).

Even if a business meal deduction is not limited by §274, the deduction will be limited under §162 if the expense of the meal does not appear to be an ordinary and necessary business expense. For example, in Moss v. Commissioner, 758 F.2d 211 (7th Cir. 1985), a partner in a law firm was denied a §162 deduction for the expense of daily lunches at a restaurant where the taxpayer and the other partners in his small firm met to discuss and coordinate their work. The court noted that having the partners eat lunch together every day probably fostered camaraderie and facilitated business, but concluded that such frequent lunches were not necessary to coordinate such a small number of partners. The expense of the daily lunches was not, in the court's view, a deductible §162 ordinary and necessary business expense.

Deductions for meal and entertainment expenses are limited to 50 percent of the amount spent. §274(n). If an employer reimburses an employee for such expenses, and does not treat the reimbursement as additional compensation paid to the employee, the employee can deduct all of the expense as an offset against the reimbursement, for a net inclusion by the employee of zero; the employer, on the other hand, will only be able to deduct 50 percent of the expenses. §274(e)(3), (n)(2)(A), Reg. §1.274-2. If, instead, the employer treats the reimbursement as additional compensation paid to the employee, the employer will be able to deduct the full amount of the reimbursement as salary, but the employee will have to include the full reimbursement in income and will only be able to deduct 50 percent of the expenses. Reg. §1.274-2. The 50 percent limitation does not apply to expenses for food and beverages that would be excludable by the recipient as a de minimis fringe benefit under §132(e) (discussed in Chapter 2). §274(n)(2)(B).

Except for certain charitable sports events, deductions for entertainment tickets are limited to the face value of the tickets. §274(l)(1). Deductions for luxury skyboxes generally are limited to the cost of seats in non-luxury boxes. §274(l)(2).

Dues or fees paid to athletic, sporting, or social clubs generally are not deductible. §274(a)(2)(A). In addition, a taxpayer may not deduct fees paid to other types of clubs unless the taxpayer "establishes that the facility was used primarily for the furtherance of the taxpayer's trade or business and that the item was directly related to the active conduct of such trade or business." §274(a)(2)(C). Even if this standard is met, however, no deduction may be taken for membership dues "in any club organized for business, pleasure, recreation, or other social purpose." §274(a)(3). A club is within the §274(a)(3) limitation if the club's principal function is to entertain its members (for example, country clubs and airline clubs). Reg. §1.274-2(a)(2)(iii). On the other hand, the §274(a)(3) limitation does not apply to trade or professional organizations (for example, bar associations). Id. Even if the club dues are deductible under §274(a), any portion of the dues that is for meals is subject to the §274(n) 50 percent limitation.

Business gifts generally are deductible only up to $25 per year per recipient. §274(b).

Business travel often is mixed with personal sightseeing or visiting friends and relatives. If the primary purpose of mixed business-personal travel is personal, the taxpayer is not allowed to deduct any part of the travel costs, even if the taxpayer conducts some business activity while on the trip. Reg. §1.162-2(b)(1), Noz v. Commissioner, T.C. Memo 2012-272 (2012). (Other trade or business expenses incurred while on a trip that is primarily personal may be deductible, despite the fact that none of the travel expenses are deductible.) If, on the other hand, the primary purpose of mixed business-personal travel is business, the amount of travel expenses that the taxpayer can deduct depends on (1) whether the travel is domestic or foreign and (2) how much of the total travel time is spent on personal activities. If the business travel is domestic, the taxpayer can deduct all of the travel costs other than any additional (incremental) costs that are attributable to the personal activities. A stricter allocation rule applies to foreign travel if the travel time exceeds one week and 25 percent or more of the total travel time is spent on personal activities. §274(c). If this limitation applies, the taxpayer must allocate all of the travel costs, including airfares, between the personal and business components of the trip.

To illustrate, assume that a taxpayer who lives in New York takes a trip to Alaska that is primarily a business trip; the taxpayer spends the entire first week of the trip doing business and extends the trip by an extra week to explore Alaska. The taxpayer would be able to deduct the entire amount of her airfare and the cost of lodging and meals (subject to the §274(n) limitation) for the first week, but not the costs of lodging and meals for the second week. If the destination instead were Paris, meals and lodging would be treated identically, but the cost of the airfare would have to be allocated between the business and nonbusiness uses. Only half of the cost of the airfare would be deductible.

No expenses for attending a convention outside of the North American area may be deducted unless the taxpayer is able to show that it is reasonable to hold the meeting outside of North America. §274(h)(1). Deductions also are limited for conventions held on cruise ships and for other luxury water transportation. §274(h)(2), (m)(1). No deduction is permitted for travel as a form of education. §274(m)(2).

No deduction or credit is permitted for traveling, entertainment, or recreation expenses, or business gifts (or for certain listed property such as computers) unless the taxpayer substantiates the expense by adequate records, preferably made at or near the time of the expenditure, as specified in the regulations. §274(d), Temp. Reg. §1.274-5T. The regulations allow exceptions to the substantiation requirement for reimbursed employee expenses and expenses under $75 (other than lodging). Temp. Reg. §1.274-5T(f)(2)(i), Reg. §1.274-5(c)(2)(iii). In addition, the regulations permit taxpayers to take specified deductions for certain business expenses such as automobile travel and meals. Reg. §1.162-17(b)(3). For travel by automobile, for example, taxpayers are permitted to deduct a specified amount (which changes from year to year) per mile instead of keeping records of their actual expenses. Temp. Reg. §1.274-5T(b)(6)(i)(B). Taxpayers may also take meal deductions based on per diem amounts (subject to the 50 percent limitation of §274(n)) without having to substantiate their actual expenses. §274(d), Reg. §1.274-5(j)(3), Rev. Proc. 2011-47.

Examples

14. Is each of the following statements true or false?
    a. A deduction is permitted for 50 percent of the cost of food and entertainment if the expense is incurred in the active conduct of the taxpayer's trade or business and a business discussion occurs before, during, or after the meal or entertainment.
    b. If an employer reimburses an employee for a business meal, the reimbursement is not included in the employee's income, and the employer receives a deduction for 50 percent of the cost of the meal.

15. A management consulting firm holds an annual three-day February "retreat" at an exclusive resort for the employees of the firm. The firm sponsors the following activities: Friday and Saturday night

banquets; Saturday and Sunday golf and tennis tournaments; and Sunday horseback riding. A two-hour firm meeting is held from noon to 2 P.M. Saturday. Attendance at the retreat is encouraged, but not required.

a. Assume that each individual employee pays his or her own expenses. Are the expenses deductible?

b. Assume that the firm pays all of the employees' expenses. Will those who attend be taxed on their pro rata share of the expenses?

16. Vivien, an executive with Shark Corporation, purchased tickets to Major League Baseball's All-Star Game. During the hour prior to the game and during the seventh-inning stretch, she laid the groundwork for a multimillion-dollar business deal with the client who accompanied her. Shark Corporation reimburses Vivien for the cost of the tickets and the hot dogs and sodas that Vivien and the client consumed during the game. (Shark Corporation does not treat the reimbursement as additional compensation to Vivien.) What are the tax consequences to Vivien and Shark Corporation?

17. Ross is a member of the Maple Creek Country Club and pays annual membership dues of $12,000. He plays golf at the club two or three times a week. About twice a month he meets with clients at the club, either for a round of golf or for dinner. Ross says he would have joined a club costing only $6,000 per year if he were only interested in golf, but that the business advantages of Maple Creek justified the additional $6,000 fee. How much of the $12,000 country club dues can Ross deduct?

18. Lou is a college professor of American History and a member of the Society for the Study of United States History. Lou traveled to Venice, Italy, to present a paper at the Society's annual convention. Is the cost of travel to the convention deductible?

19. Kitty is a partner in a Los Angeles law firm with 10 partners and 14 associates. The firm found it convenient to hold meetings during lunch three times a week in a meeting room at the inexpensive Dino's Diner. The meetings consist only of partners and associates at the firm. The luncheon conversation focuses on legal strategy and other topics related to the business of the law firm. Can Kitty deduct the cost of her meals?

20. Laura is assistant manager of Stereo Lab, a Miami, Florida, store selling high-quality audio and video equipment. In July she attends a consumer electronic show in Chicago. She spends six days at the show and the next eight days visiting (and staying) with her parents who live in a Chicago suburb. Her round-trip first-class airfare of $1,400 and her $200 per day of meal and lodging expenses while at the show are paid by Stereo

Lab. Are all of the expenses deductible by Stereo Lab? Are any of the expenses paid by Stereo Lab taxable to Laura?

21. Wendy owns The Surf Shop, a California store specializing in surfing clothing and equipment. Wendy is considering whether to take a trip to Hawaii to attend a surfing convention at a cost of $1,000. Wendy is in the 40 percent tax bracket. Wendy believes that attending the convention has no business value, but that the personal value of the trip to Hawaii is worth $700 to her.
    a. Will Wendy attend if she can deduct all of the cost of the trip?
    b. Will Wendy attend if she cannot deduct the cost of the trip?
    c. Is it efficient for Wendy to attend the convention?
    d. How, if at all, would your answers in parts (a) through (c) change if Wendy believed that attending the convention would increase the earnings of The Surf Shop by $200?

Explanations

14. a. Statement (a) is true. See §274(a)(1), (n).
    b. Statement (b) is true. An employee reimbursed by his employer for a business meal does not have to include the reimbursement (in effect, because the income would be offset by the employee's deduction of that expense). §274(e)(3). The employer will be able to deduct 50 percent of the reimbursed amount. §274(n).

15. a. A deduction is permitted under §274(a)(1)(A) for travel and entertainment expenses only if such expenses directly relate to or directly precede or follow a substantial and bona fide business discussion, including business meetings. Expenses would be deductible under §274(a) only to the extent they directly related to, preceded, or followed the Saturday meeting. It is hard to imagine how the Friday dinner and Sunday horseback riding (among other activities) would meet this standard.

    More generous rules, however, are provided under §274(e) for certain expenses, including those associated with an employee business meeting. §274(e)(5). Under Regulation §1.274-2(f)(2)(vi), a complete deduction is permitted for expenses associated with "bona fide" business meetings. A business meeting held primarily for social purposes, however, is not considered a bona fide business meeting. The expenses for the firm retreat, therefore, would be deductible under §274(e) only if the weekend is considered to serve primarily a business rather than a social purpose. This seems unlikely.

b. The analysis is identical to that outlined in (a) above. Since the retreat appears to have been held primarily for social purposes, the value of the retreat would be taxable compensation to the employees and would be deductible to the firm like any other form of compensation. In practice, employers and employees seldom report the value of employer-sponsored retreats as income, even where it is clear that the purpose of the retreat is primarily social.

16. Vivien is not taxed on the value of the tickets and meals. §274(e)(3). Shark Corporation can deduct 50 percent of the expenses. Section 274(a)(1)(A) allows a deduction of the cost of entertainment expenses that are "associated with" business and directly precede or follow a "substantial and bona fide business discussion." Because there was a business discussion before the game, the cost of tickets and meals is deductible. However, under §274(n), a deduction for meals and entertainment is limited to 50 percent of the cost.

17. Ross cannot deduct any of the dues. Dues or fees paid to a club are deductible only if the club is used by the taxpayer primarily for business purposes. §274(a)(2). The taxpayer's actual use of the club, not his purpose in joining, determines its primary use. Ross plays golf at the club eight to 12 times a month and meets clients at the club about twice a month, so this test is not met.

Even if the Maple Creek Country Club were used primarily for business purposes, under §274(a)(3), no deduction is permitted for membership dues in any club organized for business, pleasure, recreation, or other social purpose. Since the payments Ross made were membership fees, they would not be deductible.

18. Probably not. Travel to a convention outside the "North American area" is not deductible unless "it is as reasonable for the meeting to be held outside the North American area as within." §274(h)(1). The convention Lou attended was for a society dedicated to United States history, so it probably is more reasonable to hold the convention in North America.

19. Probably not. Under similar facts, the Seventh Circuit in Moss v. Commissioner, 758 F.2d 211 (7th Cir. 1985), disallowed a deduction for the expenses of the partner's daily lunch meetings. The court concluded that, although having the eight partners in the firm eat together every day may have facilitated business, the expense of the daily meetings was not an ordinary and necessary expense since the work of eight lawyers

could have been coordinated with less frequent meetings. Here, the meetings are less frequent than in *Moss*, and there are more lawyers to coordinate than in *Moss*. However, on balance, the meetings are probably still too frequent to permit deduction of the expense.

20. None of the expenses are taxable to Laura. All of the airfare and lodging and 50 percent of the meal expenses are deductible by Stereo Lab. The primary purpose of the trip seems to be attendance at the consumer electronics show even though more than half of Laura's stay in Chicago was spent visiting her parents. Thus, all of the expenses will be considered incurred for business reasons and will be deductible by Stereo Lab and received tax-free by Laura under §132(d) as a working condition fringe benefit. Stereo Lab's deduction for Laura's meals, however, is limited by §274(n) to 50 percent of the expense. Note that business-related first-class air travel and reasonably luxurious hotel accommodations are permitted as ordinary and necessary business expenses.

21. a. Wendy is in the 40 percent tax bracket, so deducting the cost of the $1,000 trip will reduce her taxes by $400. The after-tax cost of the trip is $600 and the trip is worth $700 to her, so she will attend the convention.

    b. If Wendy cannot deduct the cost of the trip, it will have an after tax cost of $1,000. The trip is only worth $700 to her, so she will not attend the convention.

    c. The convention has no business value and a personal value of $700 for a total value of $700. The $1,000 cost of the trip is greater than its total value, so it is not efficient for Wendy to attend the convention. This example demonstrates that inefficiency can result if expenditures with no business value are permitted to be deducted as business expenses.

    d. Attending the convention will cost $1,000 and will increase the earnings of The Surf Shop by $200. The net pre-tax cost of the trip is $800. Deducting the $1,000 cost of the trip will reduce her taxes by $400. Taxes on the $200 of additional earnings arising from the trip will be $80. The net tax saving from attending the convention is $320. The after-tax cost of the trip, therefore, is $800 minus $320 or $480. This is less than the $700 personal value of the trip, so Wendy will attend the convention if she can deduct the cost of the trip.

       If Wendy cannot deduct the cost of the trip, it will have an after-tax cost of $880. The $1,000 cost of the trip will be offset by the $200 of increased earnings from attending the convention. However, the $200 of increased earnings will be subject to a tax of $80. Since the $700 personal value of the trip is less than its $880 after-tax cost, Wendy will not take the trip.

The convention has a $200 business value and a personal value of $700 for a total value of $900. The $1,000 cost of the trip is still greater than its total value, so it is not efficient for Wendy to attend the convention. This example demonstrates that inefficiency can result from permitting a deduction for expenditures with both a business value and a personal value if the combined business and personal value is less than the cost of the expenditure.

C. CHILD CARE EXPENSES

Reading: §§21, 129.

In Smith v. Commissioner, 40 B.T.A. 1038 (1939), aff'd without opinion, 113 F.2d 114 (2d Cir. 1940), the Board of Tax Appeals held that the child care costs of a two-earner couple were not deductible because such child care expenses were inherently personal. After *Smith*, a limited deduction for child care costs was added to the Code, but in 1976 the deduction was replaced by a credit.

Under §21, a taxpayer is allowed a credit for certain household and dependent care services incurred to enable the taxpayer to work. Section 21(a) provides that, if the taxpayer's household includes one or more "qualifying individuals," the taxpayer is allowed a credit in an amount equal to the "applicable percentage" of the "employment-related expenses" the taxpayer paid during the taxable year.

A *qualifying individual* is: (i) a dependent who is under the age of 13, or (ii) a dependent or spouse who is physically or mentally incapable of caring for himself. §21(b)(1). The term *dependent* is defined in §152(a)(1). (The §152 definition of dependent is described in Chapter 4.) *Employment-related expenses* are expenses incurred for the care of a qualifying individual, but only if such expenses are incurred to enable the taxpayer to work. §21(b)(2). The amount of employment-related expense that may be taken into account in computing the credit is limited to: (i) $3,000 if there is only one qualifying individual in the taxpayer's household, or (ii) $6,000 if there are two or more qualifying individuals in the taxpayer's household. §21(c). Section 21(d) provides that the eligible employment-related expenses cannot exceed the earned income (for example, wages) of the taxpayer, or in the case of a married taxpayer, the lesser of the earned income of the taxpayer or the taxpayer's spouse. §21(d)(1). A special rule permits a credit where the taxpayer's spouse is disabled or a full-time student. §21(d)(2).

The *applicable percentage* is 35 percent, but is reduced by one percentage point for each $2,000 (or fraction thereof) by which the taxpayer's adjusted gross income for the year exceeds $15,000. §21(a)(2). For example, suppose a taxpayer's 2012 adjusted gross income is $29,500. The taxpayer's adjusted gross income exceeds $15,000 by $14,500. There are eight full or partial $2,000 increments in $14,500. Thus, the applicable percentage is reduced by eight percentage points, from 35 percent to 27 percent. The percentage cannot be reduced below 20 percent. Id. (The applicable percentage for any taxpayer with adjusted gross income in excess of $43,000 is 20 percent because a taxpayer with $43,001 or more of adjusted gross income has at least 15 full or partial $2,000 increments of adjusted gross income in excess of $15,000.)

The maximum credit for a taxpayer with one qualifying individual and adjusted gross income of over $43,000 is thus $600, which is 20 percent of the $3,000 of employment-related expenses that may be taken into account. If the taxpayer has a second qualifying individual, the maximum credit increases to $1,200, which is 20 percent of the $6,000 of employment-related expenses that may be taken into account.

Section 129 also provides an exclusion for employee child care expenses reimbursed by an employer pursuant to a written "dependent care assistance program" as defined in §129(d). The requirements for a §129 program are similar to the requirements under §21 for the child care credit except that, under §129, the employer reimburses the employee for the expense. The amount that may be excluded under §129 is limited to $5,000 a year. §129(a)(2)(A). Any amount excluded under §129 reduces the employment-related expenses that may be taken into account under §21(c) for purposes of computing the §21 credit. §21(c). For example, a taxpayer who has one child and excludes $5,000 under §129 is precluded from taking a §21 credit. A taxpayer who would prefer to take the credit may do so if she does not avail herself of the employer's dependent care assistance program. In other words, if the taxpayer's employer maintains a dependent care assistance program, the taxpayer must choose between the §129 exclusion and the §21 credit.

Recall that a credit is different from a deduction or exclusion. A credit is a direct reduction in tax while a deduction or exclusion is a reduction in taxable income; the tax saving from a credit is the amount of the credit, while the tax saving from a deduction or exclusion is the amount of the deduction or exclusion multiplied by the taxpayer's tax rate.

Consider the following example, which illustrates this distinction in the context of §§21 and 129. Tom, a single parent, is an associate at a big Chicago law firm. In year one, he pays a babysitter $20,000 to take care of his three-year-old child. Tom's year one adjusted gross income is $100,000 and he is in the 25 percent tax bracket. Tom's child is a qualifying individual and his $20,000 of child care expenses are employment-related expenses. However, only $3,000 of the employment-related expenses may be taken into account in computing the credit. §21(c). Tom earns more than $43,000 a year, so the applicable percentage is 20 percent. Tom's §21 credit equals 20 percent of $3,000, or $600.

Assume instead that Tom avails himself of a dependent care assistance program offered by his employer. His employer reimburses him for $5,000 of his child care expenses, which he excludes from income under §129. That $5,000 exclusion saves Tom $1,250 of tax because he is in the 25 percent tax bracket. The $5,000 exclusion precludes Tom from taking a §21 credit. §21(c). However, the $1,250 of tax saved by taking the §129 exclusion more than makes up for the loss of the $600 credit.

Examples

22. Leslie and Guy have four children. Leslie earns $65,000 a year as an attorney. Leslie's salary alone places the family in the 25 percent marginal tax bracket. Guy has stayed at home and provided child care, but is now thinking of accepting a job as a secretary. Child care to enable Guy to work will cost $20,000 a year. The secretarial position pays $25,000 a year (after taking into account Social Security taxes and Guy's work-related expenses other than child care). Guy will accept the secretarial position if it increases the family's after-tax income. Which, if any, of the following statements are true?
    a. Guy will accept the secretarial position even if the child care cost is not deductible.
    b. If Guy's secretarial income is exempt from all taxation, Guy will accept the secretarial position.
    c. Guy will accept the secretarial position if the child care costs are eligible for the dependent care credit under §21.
    d. Guy will accept the secretarial position if his employer reimburses him for $5,000 of the expenses and the reimbursement is eligible for the §129 exclusion.
    e. Guy will accept the secretarial position if the child care costs are deductible.

23. Kim and Mike, who are married and have one child, each earn $10,000 for a total annual income of $20,000. The cost of child care required to enable Mike to work is $2,000.
    a. What amount of tax credit will Kim and Mike be allowed to take under §21?
    b. How, if at all, would your answer in part (a) change if they each earned $25,000 per year?
    c. Assume the same facts as in part (b) except that Kim and Mike also care for Kim's elderly mother, who lives with them and is unable to

work, support herself, or care for herself. In order to work, they incur $2,000 for the care of their child and $4,000 for the care of Kim's mother. Again, assume that they each earn $25,000. What amount of credit can they claim under §21?

d. Assume the same facts as in part (c), except that Kim makes $47,000 and Mike makes $3,000. What amount of credit can they claim under §21?

Explanations

22. a. This statement is false. The secretarial position will increase the family's before-tax income by $5,000, the difference between the $25,000 salary and the $20,000 cost of child care. However, if the costs of child care are not deductible, the family's tax burden will increase by $6,250 (25 percent of Guy's $25,000 of income). Thus, the total costs of accepting the secretarial position are $26,250 ($20,000 for child care plus $6,250 of tax). The salary is only $25,000, so the family will be $1,250 poorer, after paying taxes and child care expenses, if Guy accepts the secretarial position. Guy has replaced tax-free imputed household income with taxable income earned as a secretary. The newly created tax burden more than offsets the higher income earned outside of the home.

b. This statement is true. If Guy's earnings are exempt from taxation, the secretarial position increases the family's income by $5,000 a year, the difference between his $25,000 salary and the $20,000 cost of child care.

c. This statement is false. Leslie and Guy's combined income is greater than $43,000, so they will receive a 20 percent credit for their child care expenses up to $6,000. §21(a)(2), (c). This produces a $1,200 credit (20 percent of $6,000) under §21. If Guy accepts the secretarial position, the net change in family income is calculated as follows: $25,000 income from employment less $20,000 child care expenses less $6,250 of tax on the income plus $1,200 child care credit equals $50. Guy would suffer a $50 net loss by accepting employment, so he will not take the position.

d. This statement is true. If the employer reimburses Guy for $5,000 of the family's child care expenses, Guy can exclude the $5,000 reimbursement from income under §129. He will accept the secretarial position because the net change in family income is $3,750, calculated as follows: $25,000 income from employment less $20,000 child care expenses plus $5,000 reimbursed less $6,250 of tax on the $25,000 of income equals $3,750.

e. This statement is true. If Guy receives a deduction for child care costs incurred while working as a secretary, his taxable income will be only $5,000 a year. If that sum is taxed at a 25 percent rate, his tax liability will be $1,250. He will accept the secretarial position because the net change in family income is $3,750, calculated as follows: $25,000 income from employment less $20,000 child care expenses less $1,250 of tax on the $5,000 of income equals $3,750.

23. a. Kim and Mike are entitled to a tax credit of $640. The child care tax credit is a percentage of expenses, which is reduced from 35 percent (but no lower than 20 percent) by one point for every $2,000 (or fraction thereof) by which the taxpayer's income exceeds $15,000. §21(a)(2). Kim and Mike have a combined income of $20,000, which exceeds $15,000 by $5,000. There are three full or partial increments of $2,000 in that $5,000 amount. Thus, Kim and Mike are entitled to a credit of 32 percent (35 percent less 3 percent). Their §21 credit is $640 (32 percent of the $2,000 of employment-related expenses).

   b. Here, Kim and Mike are entitled to a tax credit of $400. For taxpayers with income in excess of $43,000, the child care credit is 20 percent of eligible expenses. §21(a)(2). The credit is thus $400 (20 percent of $2,000).

   c. Kim and Mike are entitled to a tax credit of $1,200. Kim's mother is a qualifying individual because she is a dependent unable to care for herself. §21(b)(1)(B). The $4,000 expense of caring for Kim's mother is an employment-related expense. §21(b)(2)(A). The maximum amount of employment-related expenses that a couple with two or more qualifying individuals can claim is $6,000. Therefore, Kim and Mike are entitled to a credit of $1,200 (20 percent of $6,000).

   d. Kim and Mike are entitled to a tax credit of $600. For purposes of computing the credit, the employment-related expenses are limited to the income of the lower-earning spouse. §21(d)(1)(B). Mike's income is $3,000 so the credit is $600 (20 percent of $3,000).

D. COMMUTING EXPENSES

Taxpayers would not incur the commuting expenses of traveling to and from their jobs if they did not work. If a taxpayer lives close to the place where he works, however, he incurs little or no commuting costs. If, on the other hand, the taxpayer chooses to live some distance from the place where he works, he may incur substantial commuting costs. Thus, commuting costs are thought to result from the taxpayer's personal choice of where to live and are generally treated as nondeductible personal expenditures. Reg. §§1.262-1(b)(5), 1.162-2(e), Commissioner v. Flowers, 326 U.S. 465 (1946).

There are a few exceptions to the general rule of nondeductibility of commuting expenses. If a taxpayer has a regular work location but takes a temporary assignment at a different location, the taxpayer can deduct his costs of traveling to and from the temporary job site. Rev. Rul. 99-7. (The deduction is a §162(a) deduction, not a §162(a)(2) deduction.)

In addition, if the taxpayer is "away from home," within the meaning of §162(a)(2), the costs of commuting to and from work (as well as lodging and meals, subject to §274(n)) are deductible if the expense is required by the exigencies of the taxpayer's business. Recall that §162(a)(2) allows a taxpayer to deduct travel expenses if the taxpayer is away overnight and the travel expenses are: (i) reasonable and appropriate; (ii) incurred while the taxpayer is away from home; and (iii) motivated by the exigencies of the taxpayer's business, not the taxpayer's personal preferences. As we saw earlier in this chapter, in the discussion of travel expenses, a taxpayer claiming to be "away from home" has to establish his *business* connection both to the location he calls "home" and the place where he is temporarily working. Hantzis v. Commissioner, 638 F.2d 248 (1st Cir. 1981). As we also saw earlier, a taxpayer with no "home" cannot be "away from home." Rosenspan v. United States, 438 F.2d 905 (2d Cir. 1971).

There is also a limited exception to nondeductibility of commuting expenses if a taxpayer's job requires her to transport job-related tools to and from work. In that case, the taxpayer may be able to deduct her extra commuting costs that are attributable to transporting the tools. Fausner v. Commissioner, 413 U.S. 838 (1973). For example, assume that a taxpayer's work requires her to carry heavy tools to and from work. If the taxpayer did not have to transport the tools, she would commute to and from work on public transportation at a cost of $2 a day. In order to transport the tools, she drives her car to and from work and carries the tools in a trailer attached to the car. If she drove without the tools, her commute would cost $3 a day, but with the tools the commute costs $8 a day. On these facts, the Service ruled that the taxpayer could deduct $5 a day (the $8 cost of commuting in the car with the trailer less the $3 cost of commuting in the car without the trailer), not $6 a day (the $8 cost of commuting in the car with the trailer less the $2 cost of commuting on public transportation). Rev. Rul. 75-380.

Transportation costs while on the job are generally deductible even though the costs of travel between the taxpayer's home and principal place of business generally are not deductible. Reg. §1.162-2. Thus, for example, an insurance adjuster can deduct the costs of driving to accident sites to assess losses. Applying this rule, courts have held that a taxpayer whose home is also her principal place of business can deduct transportation costs between her home and another regular workplace. See, e.g., Curphey v. Commissioner, 73 T.C. 766 (1980).

Examples

24. Glen, who lives with his family in Santa Barbara, works full-time for a Los Angeles law firm. When he was hired, the firm wanted him to move with his family to Los Angeles, but he refused. After some negotiations, they worked out an arrangement; Glen works three days a week in the office of the firm and three days a week in office space in Santa Barbara that is sublet from another law firm. Can he deduct his commuting expenses to and from Los Angeles?

25. Regional manager Barbara spends $10 a day commuting to and from her office in the headquarters of her corporate employer. She spends another $15 a day traveling between the headquarters and branch offices and calling on customers. What portion, if any, of her transportation expenses are deductible?

26. David works as a traveling salesman for a number of clothing manufacturers. David is on the road five months a year; in the remaining months, he works out of his Chicago home.
    a. Are David's "on-the-road" transportation expenses deductible? Are the expenses of his travel-related meals and lodging deductible?
    b. Assume instead that David is on the road 11 months a year; in the remaining month David rents a vacation home in various locations and spends a week or so visiting his brother and sister-in-law. Are David's business travel expenses for transportation, meals, and lodging deductible?

Explanations

24. A deduction is permitted under §162(a)(2) for business expenses incurred while away from home in the pursuit of a trade or business. However, case law and regulations deny deductions for commuting expenses incurred while traveling to and from one's principal place of business. Reg. §§1.262-1(b)(5), 1.162-2(e). The facts here are similar to the facts in Commissioner v. Flowers, in which a taxpayer was denied a deduction for the costs of traveling between his home (and part-time work location) in Jackson, Mississippi, and his principal place of business in Mobile, Alabama, because, in the court's view,

the expense was motivated by the taxpayer's personal decision to live in Jackson. Here, Glen's costs of commuting to Los Angeles are probably similarly attributable to his personal preference as to where to live, so he probably would be denied a §162(a)(2) deduction.

25. Barbara can deduct only the $15 per day expenses of traveling to branch offices. The expenses of commuting to work are nondeductible, but taxpayers are permitted to deduct business transportation expenses other than commuting costs under §162. Reg. §1.162-2.

26. a. David is allowed to deduct his business travel expenses for transportation under §162. He is also allowed to deduct the costs of meals and lodging incurred while away from home and in the pursuit of a trade or business. §162(a)(2). Here, the meal and lodging expenses are incurred in connection with business-related travel to locations other than his principal place of business. David's deductions for meal and entertainment expenses are limited to 50 percent of the expenses. §274(n).

    b. The costs of David's transportation expenses are still deductible under §162(a). However, a deduction is permitted under §162(a)(2) for other travel-related expenses only if they are incurred "away from home" and a taxpayer with no "home" cannot be "away from home." Rosenspan v. United States, 438 F.2d 905 (2d Cir. 1971). It seems likely that David has no "home" and is thus not allowed to deduct his other travel expenses such as food and lodging costs.

    Should a taxpayer in David's position receive a deduction? The basic policy underlying the deduction is that an individual traveling on business incurs higher expenses than an individual who does not have to travel for work. Thus, a deduction should be permitted for the additional expenses incurred due to business-related travel, for example, the costs of paying for motel lodging to the extent that they exceed the costs of maintaining a year-round residence. In one sense, the taxpayer here does not face such additional costs; he is not required to maintain two households. In another sense, of course, a taxpayer like David does face additional costs since motel lodging and restaurant meals are more expensive than the average taxpayer's food and lodging.

E. CLOTHING EXPENSES

An employee is allowed to take an itemized deduction for the unreimbursed cost of clothing worn exclusively at work if: (i) the employer requires, as a condition of employment, that employees wear the clothes at work; and (ii) the clothing is not suitable for general use. Rev. Rul. 70-474. An objective test is used to determine whether clothing is suitable for general use. In Pevsner v. Commissioner, 628 F.2d 467 (5th Cir. 1980), the manager of an Yves Saint Laurent (YSL) clothing boutique was denied a deduction for the cost of YSL clothes that she bought to wear at work at the urging of her employer. Ms. Pevsner did not wear the YSL clothes when she was not working because she led a simple lifestyle and wanted the clothes to last longer. However, the Fifth Circuit held that an objective approach must be used to determine whether clothing is suitable for general use, so her subjective views about the clothing were irrelevant. The court concluded that the taxpayer could not deduct the cost of the YSL clothes because they were suitable for general use. If the cost of work clothing is deductible and is reimbursed by the employer, the employee does not have to include the reimbursed amount in her gross income. §62(a)(2)(A).

Examples

27. Sam works at the Enrico Arpaci men's clothing boutique in Beverly Hills, earning $30,000 per year. He is required as a condition of his employment to wear Enrico Arpaci suits, which cost $1,500 each. Sam purchases five new suits each year. He never wears the suits except at work because he does not want to wear them out and because he seldom goes to places where they would be appropriate. Can Sam deduct the costs of the suits?

28. Mary is a tennis pro at a posh country club. Can she deduct the cost of her tennis clothing and tennis shoes?

29. Chuck earns $10,000 per year as a mascot for the Happyville Dogs, a minor league baseball team. He creates goodwill for the club by appearing at public events dressed as a bloodhound. He purchased the costume with his own funds at a cost of $1,000. Not only does he wear his costume at public events but, priding himself on being the life of the party, he wears it at private, neighborhood social gatherings. Can Chuck deduct the cost of his costume?

30. Terri is a flight attendant for Northern American Airlines. She is required to wear a uniform to work. The uniform, which is manufactured by a specialty company that makes uniforms, consists of a Navy blue suit jacket, either navy blue pants or a skirt, a white shirt, and a red scarf. The airline uniform shop charges Terri $1,000 for the uniform. Can she deduct the cost of her uniform?

Explanations

27. Probably not. These facts are similar to those in Pevsner v. Commissioner, 628 F.2d 467 (5th Cir. 1980). In that case a designer boutique manager who was required to wear expensive designer clothing at work was denied a deduction for the cost of the clothing even though she wore the clothing only at work because she wanted it to last longer and it was not appropriate for her after-work lifestyle. The court denied a deduction because, applying an objective test, the clothing was suitable for general use.

28. Probably not, again because the clothing is suitable for general use. These facts are similar to those in Mella v. Commissioner, 52 T.C.M. (CCH) 1216 (1986). In that case the court denied a deduction for the costs incurred by a nationally ranked tennis pro for clothing and shoes because such apparel is worn for a wide variety of sport and leisure activities.

29. No. Although. Chuck's costume would not be considered adaptable to general use, he actually did wear it outside of his employment, so no deduction will be allowed.

30. Yes. An employee is allowed to take an itemized deduction for the unreimbursed cost of clothing worn exclusively at work if: (i) the employer requires, as a condition of employment, that employees wear the clothes at work; and (ii) the clothing is not suitable for general use. Rev. Rul. 70-474. No self-respecting flight attendant is going to wear her uniform as street clothes, but, as we saw in the *Pevsner* case, we do not take into account the taxpayer's subjective view as to whether the clothing is suitable for general use; instead, we apply an objective test. Here, Terri's uniform is a navy blue suit, which, at least theoretically, could be worn for general use. However, it is manufactured by a uniform company, not a company that makes clothes for general usage. Ms. Pevsner could have proudly worn her YSL clothes to social events, but she chose not to because of her lifestyle. On the other hand, it would be odd for a flight attendant to wear her navy blue uniform, which many people would recognize as a Northern American Airlines uniform, to a social event, so this case probably is distinguishable from the *Pevsner* case. It seems likely that a court applying the objective test would agree that, even though the uniform may resemble other general use business clothing, a standard, readily identifiable airline uniform is probably not suitable for general use.

F. LEGAL EXPENSES

Reading: §212(3); Reg. §1.263(a)-1, -2, -5.

An individual may deduct legal fees that are incurred in a trade or business or related to the production of income, under §162 or §212, respectively. Legal fees incurred in a business context must be capitalized, however, if they are incurred in connection with the acquisition of property that has a useful life extending substantially beyond the close of the year in which the legal expense is incurred. Reg. §§1.263(a)-2, -5.

Personal legal fees, on the other hand, are nondeductible personal expenses. Certain legal fees, such as those arising out of a divorce, can be incurred in part for personal reasons and in part to protect business or investment interests. The deductibility of such legal fees depends on the "origin" of the claim, not on the potential consequences of the claim. If the origin of the claim is personal, legal fees are nondeductible even if they also protect the taxpayer's business or investment interests. For example, in United States v. Gilmore, 372 U.S. 39 (1963), a taxpayer who ran a family business was denied a deduction for legal fees that he incurred, during his divorce, to defend against his wife's claim on his controlling interest in the business. The taxpayer argued that his litigation costs were deductible under §212 because they were incurred to conserve income-producing property. However, the Supreme Court disagreed, holding that the origin of the divorce claim was personal and that the litigation costs were, therefore, not deductible.

Note that §212(3) permits a deduction for expenses incurred "in connection with the determination, collection, or refund of any tax." This provision sometimes allows a taxpayer to deduct legal fees incurred in exchange for personal tax advice, even tax advice given with respect to a divorce. Zmuda v. Commissioner, 79 T.C. 714 (1982).

As the examples in this section demonstrate, however, it often is far from clear how to determine the "origin" of a claim.

(As discussed in Chapter 2, §62(a)(20) provides for an above-the-line deduction for legal fees in discrimination cases. Deductions for legal fees paid in other types of suits may be limited by §§67, 68, and the AMT.)

Examples

31. State whether each of the following legal expenses is deductible.
    a. Legal fees incurred by the sole proprietor of a donut shop in connection with a contract dispute with a distributor regarding supplies.
    b. Legal fees incurred by an individual taxpayer in obtaining an injunction against a noisy and obnoxious neighbor.

    c. Legal fees incurred in defending the taxpayer, who is a clinical psychologist, against an assault claim filed by the taxpayer's neighbor. The taxpayer is spending large amounts to defend himself in the lawsuit because he fears that the charge will damage his business reputation.

    d. Legal fees incurred by a taxpayer, an employee of MaltCo., in defending against a wrongful death action arising out of a car accident after the MaltCo. company Christmas party, which all employees are encouraged to attend. At the time of the accident, the taxpayer, who was very intoxicated, was on his way home from the party and was driving a company car. The plaintiff in the case has filed suit against both the employee and MaltCo.

32. a. Karen had spent years building up a profitable discount jewelry store when her husband George filed for divorce. George claimed he should be awarded a controlling interest in the store. Karen incurred $100,000 of legal expenses in successfully fighting George's claim. Can she deduct the legal expenses as a §212 expense incurred for the conservation of income-producing property?

    b. Two years later Karen purchased a larger building to house her discount store. The building was expected to last many years and to expand Karen's share of the market. Karen incurred $15,000 in legal expenses in connection with the acquisition of the new building. Can she deduct the legal expenses?

Explanations

31. a. These legal expenses are deductible. A taxpayer may deduct only those legal expenses that are deductible under §162 or §212. In other words, legal expenses are deductible only if they arise in connection with a taxpayer's trade or business or in connection with the production of income. Legal fees incurred with respect to a business-related contract dispute are deductible.

    b. A dispute with a noisy neighbor is a personal matter, so associated legal expenses are not deductible.

    c. The taxpayer may argue that the legal fees are deductible, under §162, because he is defending his reputation for business reasons. However, we must look to the "origin of the claim" in order to determine whether the legal fees are deductible. United States v. Gilmore, 372 U.S. 39 (1963). This standard requires that we focus on the reason that the claim arose, not on whether the claim could harm the taxpayer's business. Here, the alleged assault does not appear to have anything to do with the taxpayer's business, so the legal fees would be nondeductible.

d. This is a close call and the *Gilmore* "origin of the claim" test does not clearly resolve it one way or the other. The taxpayer may argue that the legal fees are deductible as a §162 business expense because the accident occurred in a business context — while he was driving a company car and as a result of drinking at the work-related function. However, the amount that the taxpayer drank at the party was a personal decision, so a court might conclude that these legal fees were nondeductible. Even if the taxpayer can establish that the origin of the claim was business, a court may conclude that this expense is not an "ordinary or necessary" business expense and thus is not deductible under §162. (For a discussion of what constitutes an "ordinary and necessary" business expense, see Chapter 5.)

32. a. Karen cannot deduct the legal fees associated with the divorce action. These facts are similar to the facts in United States v. Gilmore, 372 U.S. 39 (1963). As in *Gilmore*, the origin of the claim here is personal because it arises in a divorce proceeding, so no deduction is allowed even though the legal fees are necessary to preserve Karen's business.

b. Karen's legal expenses are directly related to her business. However, the expenses here must be capitalized (added to her basis in the new building) because the legal expenses are incurred in connection with the acquisition of property having a useful life substantially beyond the taxable year. Reg. §1.263(a)-2(d)(2), Example 6, -2(f).

G. EDUCATIONAL EXPENSES

Reading: §§25A, 127, 135, 162, 221, 222, 529, 530; Reg. §1.162-5.
The cost of a college education is generally nondeductible because courts consider the cost to be a personal expenditure. See, e.g., Carroll v. Commissioner, 418 F.2d 91 (7th Cir. 1969) (in which a police detective was denied a deduction for the costs of his college tuition because the court concluded that the college education was a personal expense, not an expense of being in the profession of being a detective). On the other hand, an individual is allowed to deduct educational expenses if the education either: (i) maintains or improves skills required by the individual in his trade or business; or (ii) meets express requirements of the individual's employer or legal requirements imposed by applicable law or regulations as a condition of doing work of the type performed by the taxpayer. Educational expenses incurred to meet the minimum educational requirements of a new trade or business are nondeductible. Reg. §1.162-5(a) and (b).

Congress has, however, enacted a bewildering variety of specific provisions that affect the tax treatment of education expenses. These specific provisions include: (1) the §25A Hope Scholarship/American Opportunity Tax Credit (the "Modified Hope Credit"); (2) the §25A Lifetime Learning Credit; (3) the §221 deduction for interest on student loans; (4) the §222 deduction for certain higher education expenses; (5) the §530 Coverdell Education Savings Account deferral and exclusion provisions; (6) the §529 Qualified Tuition Program deferral and exclusion provisions; (7) the §135 exclusion for income from certain U.S. savings bonds used to pay higher education expenses; (8) the §127 exclusion for employer-provided education assistance; (9) the §117 exclusion for qualified scholarships (discussed in Chapter 2); and (10) the §108(f) exclusion for income from the discharge of student loans where the student performs public service work. The complexity in this area is attributable to several factors (beyond the sheer number of specific provisions). Several of these specific provisions are extremely complex, standing alone. Some of the provisions create an above-the-line deduction or a credit, which may or may not be refundable; other provisions permit the deferral or exclusion of income. The definition of qualifying education expenses even varies from section to section. Several of these provisions also phase out at certain income levels, but again the precise phase-out rules vary from section to section and some of the phase-out rules are subject to annual inflation adjustments. In addition, to make matters worse, the interactions of these various provisions are governed by specific statutory operating rules that make the tax treatment of education expenses unusually complex.

In this section, we will briefly discuss the first eight provisions listed above. Given the complexity of this material, we have simplified somewhat to make the discussion more understandable.

The §25A Modified Hope Credit provides a 100 percent partially refundable credit on the first $2,000 of "qualified tuition and related expenses" and a 25 percent credit on the next $2,000 of such qualified expenses. §25A(b)(1)(A), (B), (i)(1), (6). The maximum annual credit thus is $2,500.

Section 25A defines the term *qualified tuition and related expenses* to include tuition, mandatory fees, and course materials such as textbooks, but not room and board, other fees, or insurance that is unrelated to the student's course of study. §25A(f)(1), (i)(1). Education expenses related to sports, games, or hobbies are not qualified expenses unless the activities are part of the student's degree program. §25A(f)(1)(B). The creditable education expenses are reduced by scholarships that are excluded from income and certain forms of educational assistance (e.g., grants). §25A(g)(2). A student qualifies for the Modified Hope Credit only if the student is enrolled on at least a half-time basis at a qualified education institution (which includes accredited post-secondary schools that award bachelor's degrees, associate's degrees, and certain vocational credentials). §25A(b)(2)(B), (b)(3), (f)(2). The credit can be taken only for the first four years of post-secondary education (and may be claimed no more than four times for any student). §25A(b)(2)(A), (C), (i)(2). The credit is disallowed if the student is convicted of a federal or state felony drug offense. §25A(b)(2)(D).

The §25A *Lifetime Learning Credit* is a nonrefundable credit equal to 20 percent of up to $10,000 of qualified tuition and related expenses paid by the taxpayer. §25A(c)(1). Thus, the maximum annual credit is $2,000. The creditable education expenses are reduced by scholarships that are excluded from income and certain forms of educational assistance (e.g., grants). §25A(g)(2). Unlike the Hope Credit, the Lifetime Learning Credit can be taken for each year of undergraduate education and for graduate education.

The Modified Hope Credit is determined on a student-by-student basis. §25A(b)(1). The Lifetime Learning Credit is not determined on a student-by-student basis, because the dollar limitation on the amount of creditable expenses is not affected by the number of eligible students in the family. §25A(c)(1).

If a student is not claimed as a dependent on his parents' tax return, the student can claim the credit. If a student is claimed as a dependent on his parents' tax return, the student's parents, not the student, take the credit. In that case, any qualified tuition and related expenses that were paid by the student are treated as though his parents paid them. §25A(g)(3).

The Modified Hope Credit is phased out for individual taxpayers with modified adjusted gross income between $80,000 and $90,000 and joint filers with modified adjusted gross income between $160,000 and $180,000. §25A(d)(2), (i)(4). In 2014, the Lifetime Learning Credit is phased out for individual taxpayers with modified adjusted gross income between $54,000 and $64,000 and joint filers with modified adjusted gross income between $108,000 and $128,000. §25A(d)(2), (h)(2), Rev. Proc. 2013-35 §3.05(2). If the requirements for §25A are satisfied, that section applies unless the taxpayer elects to waive both the Modified Hope Credit and the Lifetime Learning Credit. §25A(e). Although both credits may not be claimed for the same student in the same year, the Modified Hope Credit may be claimed for a student in one year and the Lifetime Learning Credit may be claimed for the same student in a different year. The Hope and Lifetime Learning Credits are claimed for the year in which the expenses are actually paid, subject to the requirement that the education commence or continue in that year or during the first three months of the following year. §25A(g)(4).

Section 221 sets forth the rules for deducting student loan interest. It provides that the taxpayer can deduct interest payments on a "qualified education loan." §221(a). The deduction is an above-the-line deduction that may be taken even if the taxpayer does not itemize deductions. §62(a)(17). The maximum deduction allowed is $2,500. §221(b)(1).

The deduction is phased out for individual taxpayers with modified adjusted gross income between $65,000 and $80,000 and for joint filers with modified adjusted gross income between $130,000 and $160,000. §221(b)(2)(B), (f), Rev. Proc. 2013-35 §3.26. The deduction is not available to any individual who may be claimed as a dependent on another taxpayer's tax return. §221(c).

The term *qualified education loan* means any indebtedness incurred to pay "qualified higher education expenses." §221(d)(1). *Qualified higher education expenses* include tuition, books, fees, supplies, and equipment required for attendance at an eligible educational institution (e.g., an accredited college or junior college). The education expenses must relate to a period when the taxpayer is enrolled on at least a half-time basis and must have been incurred on behalf of the taxpayer, the taxpayer's spouse or dependents, determined as of the time the debt was incurred. §221(d)(1)(A), (d)(3). Qualified higher education expenses are reduced by (i) scholarships that are excluded from income and certain forms of educational assistance, and (ii) education expenses excluded under §127, 135, 529, or 530. §221(d)(2). A qualified education loan does not include any indebtedness owed by the taxpayer to a person who is related to the taxpayer. §221(d)(1).

Section 222 allows an above-the-line deduction for qualified higher education expenses. §62(a)(18). Under §222, the term *qualified tuition and related expenses* has the same meaning as in §25A(f), discussed above, with some additional limitations. §222(d)(1).

The §222 deduction is capped at $4,000. The maximum deduction is reduced if the taxpayer's modified adjusted gross income exceeds certain amounts. The maximum §222 deduction is reduced to: (1) $2,000 where an individual taxpayer's modified gross income exceeded $65,000 but did not exceed $80,000 or joint filers' modified adjusted gross income exceeded $130,000 but did not exceed $160,000; and (2) zero where an individual taxpayer's modified gross income exceeded $80,000 or joint filers' modified adjusted gross income exceeded $160,000. §222(b)(2)(B). In addition, for purposes of §222, the amount of qualified tuition and related expenses is reduced by any amounts excluded under §135, 529, or 530.

Married taxpayers filing separately and taxpayers who may be claimed as a dependent on another taxpayer's return are not allowed to take the deduction. §222(c)(3), (d)(4). A taxpayer cannot take a §222 deduction and a Modified Hope Credit or Lifetime Learning Credit in the same year. §222(c)(2)(A). Also, §222 sunsets at the end of 2013, although future legislation may extend it.

Sections 135, 529, and 530 tax favor certain methods for saving to fund education expenses. Section 530 sets forth the rules for *Coverdell Education Savings Account* (ESA), also known as an education IRA. Contributions made to an ESA are not deductible, but ESA earnings are tax exempt and distributions made from the ESA are excluded by the beneficiary to the extent of the beneficiary's "qualified education expenses." §530(a), (d)(2)(A). Section 530 permits aggregate annual ESA contributions of up to $2,000. §530(b)(1)(A)(iii). The $2,000 annual permitted contribution is gradually phased out (i) for individual taxpayers with modified adjusted gross income between $95,000 and $110,000 and (ii) for joint filers with modified adjusted gross income between $190,000 and $220,000. §530(c). Also, no contributions may be made to an ESA after the beneficiary reaches the age of 18. §530(b)(1)(A).

The term *qualified education expenses* includes qualified higher education expenses and qualified elementary and secondary education expenses. §530(b)(2)(A). *Qualified higher education expenses* include tuition, books, fees, dormitory costs, supplies, and equipment required for attendance at an eligible educational institution (e.g., an accredited college or junior college). §§529(e)(3), 530(b)(2)(A)(i). *Qualified elementary and secondary education expenses* include expenses for tuition, fees, academic tutoring, books, supplies, computers, Internet access, room and board, uniforms, transportation, and supplementary items and services (including extended day programs) that are required or provided by a public, private, or religious school in connection with the student's education. §530(b)(3)(A).

A taxpayer taking a tax-free distribution from an ESA can claim either the Modified Hope Credit or the Lifetime Learning Credit, but the distribution from the ESA cannot be used for the same expenses for which the credit is claimed. In other words, there is no double counting of education expenses. §530(d)(2)(C)(i).

Section 529 sets forth the rules for a *Qualified Tuition Program* (QTP), also known as *529 Plans*. A QTP is a plan offered by a state or private educational institution to allow families to either prepay a beneficiary's future tuition or to contribute to an account that will be used in the future to pay a beneficiary's education expenses. Until 2002, only states could set up QTPs, but private educational institutions can now also set up QTPs. Contributions made to a QTP are not deductible, but QTP earnings are tax exempt. In addition, distributions made from a QTP are excluded by the beneficiary to the extent of the beneficiary's qualified higher education expenses. §529(a), (c)(3)(B). The term *qualified higher education expenses* includes tuition, fees, books, supplies, equipment required for enrollment or attendance at an eligible education institution (e.g., a university, college, or junior college) and reasonable room and board for a beneficiary who is at least a half-time student. §529(e)(3). The qualified higher education expenses are reduced by scholarships that are excluded from income and certain forms of educational assistance (e.g., grants). §§25A(g)(2), 529(c)(3)(B)(v)(I). A taxpayer taking a tax-free distribution from a QTP can also claim either the Modified Hope Credit or the Lifetime Learning Credit, but the distribution from the QTP cannot be used for the same expenses for which the credit is claimed. §529(c)(3)(B)(v)(II).

Very substantial amounts can be contributed to a QTP because §529 permits contributions on behalf of a beneficiary up to the amount necessary to fund the qualified higher education expenses of the beneficiary. §529(b)(6). On the other hand, a contribution to a QTP is treated as a gift to the beneficiary from the contributor for gift tax purposes (and the gift tax treatment can also have estate tax implications), so potential contributors should consider the income tax, gift tax, and estate tax consequences of making a QTP contribution.

Section 135 allows qualifying taxpayers to exclude income from certain U.S. savings bonds if the proceeds are used to pay qualified higher education expenses, which are narrowly defined to include tuition and fees. §135(a), (c). Section 135 has yet another phase-out rule, keyed to the taxpayer's modified adjusted gross income. §135(b)(2).

Section 127 also allows employees an annual exclusion of up to $5,250 of qualified employer-provided educational assistance benefits. §127(a).

(Also note that the penalty tax on early withdrawals from a traditional IRA or Roth IRA does not apply if the withdrawal is made to pay higher education expenses for the taxpayer or the taxpayer's children or grandchildren.)

Examples

Examples 33–39 address the §162 rules regarding the deductibility of educational expenses. Examples 40–43 address the specific education incentives discussed above.

33. Which, if any, of the following educational expenses are deductible under §162?
    a. An individual currently working as a social worker pays tuition in connection with earning a graduate degree in business administration.
    b. An individual currently working as a detective incurs expenses in connection with a graduate degree in law enforcement.

34. Teri, a third-year law student, earned $10,000 working as a full-time clerk during the summer prior to her third year and continues to work as a part-time law clerk during the school year. May Teri deduct her third-year law school tuition as a §162 business expense?

35. a. Pierre is hired as an instructor at the Acme School for French Chefs in Cleveland, Ohio. Pierre is considered a member of the Acme School's faculty and has completed the four-year undergraduate course offered by the school. He is working on a graduate degree, specializing in snails and flaming desserts. The school requires that its instructors obtain graduate degrees in some area of French

cooking within five years after beginning employment. Can Pierre take a §162 deduction for the graduate degree expenses?

b. The Acme School offers a limited number of graduate courses, and, as a result, the only place that offers the class in snail sauces that Pierre needs to obtain his degree is a cooking school in Paris, France. Can he deduct his tuition costs and travel expenses under §162?

c. Suppose Pierre wants to visit France so that he can tour French restaurants and get a better idea of regional variations in French food preparation. Can he deduct his travel expenses under §162?

36. Doug has finished one semester of his two-semester clown school program. Desperate to fill an unexpected vacancy, the Two-Ring Circus hires Doug, conditioning his continued employment on his completing the second semester of clown school and passing the Twelve Clowns in a Car and Pie Throwing examinations necessary for the state license as a clown. Doug tours with the circus for six months (under a temporary state permit) and then returns to finish clown school. Under §162, can Doug deduct his expenses for the second semester of school and for the clown examination review course?

37. Catherine, the managing partner in a major law firm, decides to enter a one-year program leading to a degree as a licensed animal trainer, in the hope that the principles that apply to lions can be used in dealing with other attorneys. Catherine intends to continue practicing law and does not plan to do any work in the animal training field. Can she take a §162 deduction for the expenses incurred in her animal training education?

38. Richard taught macrame classes at the adult education center, but his heart belonged to folded-paper swans, so he took courses that would enable him to teach origami instead. Can Richard deduct his educational expenses under §162?

39. Rita is a clerk in the Woods Department Store. The store encourages its employees to get college degrees and work their way up into management. Rita is getting her bachelor's degree from Eastman University in the hope that the education will help her move up in the company. The course is a general liberal arts curriculum. Can Rita deduct her college expenses under §162?

40. a. Armon is enrolled full-time in a four-year college program at Able University. In year one, Armon's second year of college, his tuition at Able University is $14,000. Armon receives a $13,000 tuition scholarship and his parents pay the remaining $1,000 of his tuition for the year. Armon's parents also pay $5,000 during the year for Armon's dormitory room and food. Armon pays $800 for his books and $200 to participate in intramural soccer. Armon's

parents have adjusted gross income of $30,000, file a joint return, and claim Armon as a dependent. Armon's adjusted gross income is $5,000. What amount of Hope Scholarship Credit or Lifetime Learning Credit can be claimed with respect to Armon's various education expenses and who would claim the credit?

b. How, if at all, would your answer in part (a) change if Armon is in his fourth year of college?

c. How, if at all, would your answer in part (a) change if Armon's parents do not claim him as a dependent on their tax return?

d. How, if at all, would your answer in part (a) change if Armon's parents have adjusted gross income of $200,000?

e. How, if at all, would your answer in part (a) change if $4,000 of the $6,000 Armon's parents paid came from a Coverdell Education Savings Account?

f. How, if at all would your answer in part (a) change if, during the year, Armon were convicted of vehicular manslaughter, a felony offense punishable by up to 10 years in state prison?

41. Is each of the following statements true or false? Please explain your answers.

a. Thomas has two children. Thomas establishes a Coverdell Education Savings Account for each child. The most that Thomas can contribute to each ESA is $1,000.

b. Debby's father Frank has established an ESA for her and makes a $2,000 contribution to the ESA each year. Debby's grandmother, Grace, can establish a second ESA for Debby and contribute $2,000 per year to it.

c. Contributions to an ESA are not deductible from adjusted gross income, but withdrawals used to pay education expenses are not taxed.

d. Abel has three children: Robert, age 12; Casey, age 5; and Brian, age 20. Four years ago Abel established an ESA for each child. This year Abel can legally contribute a *total* of $6,000 to the ESAs.

e. In year one, Matt and Jackie have a 13-year-old daughter, Eva. Jackie and Matt plan to start saving for Eva's college expenses. Their accountant suggested that they participate in ScholarShare, California's §529 College Savings Plan, a state Qualified Tuition Plan. Jackie and Matt plan to contribute $15,000 to the QTP in year one with Eva as the beneficiary. They are allowed, under §529, to contribute $15,000 to the QTP in year one. The earnings from the QTP and distributions from the QTP to pay Eva's qualified higher education expenses are tax-free.

42. In year one, Gloria pays $3,600 of interest on her student loans from college. On her tax return for year one, Gloria takes the standard

deduction instead of itemizing. Explain the tax treatment of her student loan payments.

43. a. Dan, a single parent with modified adjusted gross income of $35,000 per year, has twin daughters, Alice and Betty. In 2013, each daughter enters Delta University as a freshman. Dan pays $15,000 in tuition for each daughter. How should Dan use the Modified Hope and Lifetime Learning Credits to minimize his tax liability? Should Dan take a §222 higher education expense deduction?

    b. How might Dan's tax strategy change if Dan's modified adjusted gross income was instead $200,000?

Explanations

33. a. The social worker's educational expenses probably are not deductible because a degree in business administration trains the social worker for a new field rather than improving her skills in her current profession. Reg. §1.162-5(b)(3). In a recent case, however, a nurse whose hospital job focused on quality management and patient outcomes was allowed to deduct the cost of getting an MBA, which improved her skills for the work she already did instead of training her for a new profession. Singleton-Clarke v. Commissioner, T.C. Summary Opinion 2009-182 (2009) (but note that summary opinions cannot be cited as precedent under §7463(b)). If the social worker in the example does full-time clinical care, however, the MBA trains her for a new profession.

    b. The detective will be permitted to deduct the expenses of a degree in law enforcement because it improves or maintains her skills in her current profession. Reg. §1.162-5(a)(1).

34. Only those educational expenses that are incurred primarily for the purpose of maintaining or improving skills in connection with a present occupation are deductible. Reg. §1.162-5; Carroll v. Commissioner, 418 F.2d 91 (7th Cir. 1969). Teri would argue that she meets this test because the educational expenses of her third year in law school are incurred for the purpose of improving her performance at the law firm.

    Unfortunately for the readers of this book, this argument would fail. Education that is necessary to meet the minimum requirements for entry into a trade or business is nondeductible. Reg. §1.162-5(b)(2). An example in the regulations deals explicitly with a situation like Teri's and states that law school tuition is nondeductible because it is required to meet minimum educational requirements for working as a lawyer. Reg. §1.162-5(b)(2)(iii), Example 3.

35. a. Pierre's education expenses will be deductible under §162. The minimum educational requirements for a position in an educational institution are considered to have been met once the individual becomes a member of the faculty of that institution. Reg. §1.162-5 (b)(2)(ii). Thus, the additional training would be deductible because it improves Pierre's skills at his current employment.

    b. Pierre will be able to deduct both his tuition and travel expenses under §162. His tuition is deductible for the reasons stated in the answer to part (a). He will be able to deduct the travel expenses in spite of §274(m)(2), which specifically disallows any deduction for travel as a form of education. This provision is intended to disallow a deduction, for example, where a French teacher travels to France to maintain a general familiarity with the French language and culture. The rule is not intended to apply to travel in connection with an activity that qualifies for a business deduction. For example, a scholar of French literature who travels to France to take courses offered only at the Sorbonne in Paris would be permitted to deduct her expenses.

    c. Pierre will not be permitted to deduct his travel expenses. No deduction is allowed for expenses of travel as a form of education. §274(m)(2).

36. Doug cannot deduct any of his clown school or clown examination preparation expenses. The courses constitute education required to meet the minimum educational requirements for qualification in Doug's trade or business and are not deductible under Regulation §1.162-5(b)(2). The fact that Doug is already employed as a clown does not establish that he has met the minimum educational requirements for clowning.

37. Catherine cannot deduct any of her animal training courses. Expenditures that will qualify the taxpayer for a new trade or business are not deductible even if the taxpayer does not intend to practice in the new field. Reg. §1.162-5(b)(3).

38. Richard will be permitted to deduct the educational expenses associated with learning origami. Although expenditures that qualify the taxpayer for a new trade or business are not deductible, all teaching and teaching-related duties are considered to involve the same general type of work. Even a teacher who takes courses to prepare him for certification as a school administrator is entitled to deduct the costs of the education. Reg. §1.162-5(b)(3)(i).

39. Probably not. There probably is not a sufficient relationship between a general liberal arts education and the particular job skills required of a department store employee. Carroll v. Commissioner, 418 F.2d 91 (7th Cir. 1969).

40. a. Armon's parents would claim an $1,800 Modified Hope Credit. They are eligible for either the Modified Hope Credit or the Lifetime Learning Credit. Both credits are computed by reference to a student's "qualified tuition and related expenses," but that term is defined more broadly for purposes of the Modified Hope Credit than for the Lifetime Learning Credit. §25A(f)(1), (i)(3). For purposes of the Modified Hope Credit, Armon's tuition and books are qualified expenses, but his room and board and sports expenses are not. Id. The creditable education expenses are reduced by scholarships that are excluded from income, in this case, $13,000. §25A(g)(2). The qualified tuition and related fees, for purposes of the Modified Hope Credit, are thus $1,800 ($14,000 tuition plus $800 for books less $13,000 scholarship), so the Modified Hope Credit would be $1,800 (100 percent of the qualified tuition and related expenses). The Lifetime Learning Credit would be $200 (20 percent of the $1,000 qualified tuition and related expenses). §25A(b)(1), (c)(1). Armon's parents would be eligible to claim the credit because Armon is a dependent on their tax return. The adjusted gross income phase-out provisions applicable to the two credits do not apply. Armon's parents can claim only one of the two credits. The Modified Hope Credit is greater than the Lifetime Learning Credit, so they would elect the Modified Hope Credit.

    b. The answer is the same as in part (a). The §25A Modified Hope Credit, as amended in 2009, applies to four years of post-secondary education (although the original Hope Scholarship Credit applied to just two years of post-secondary education).

    c. Armon would claim the Modified Hope Credit since he is not a dependent on his parents' tax return. Armon's adjusted gross income is only $5,000, but the $1,800 credit is partially refundable.

    d. Armon's parents cannot claim a credit. The credit that they could otherwise claim is reduced to zero by the phase-out provision of §25A(d).

    e. Armon's parents can claim one of the two credits and can exclude the distribution from the Coverdell Education Savings Account. They would claim the $1,800 Modified Hope Credit, as explained above. They would then need to compute the amount of the ESA distribution that can be excluded from income under §530. Even though the §530 exclusion can be claimed in conjunction with the Modified Hope Credit or the Lifetime Learning Credit, no education expense may be double counted. §530(d)(2)(C)(i). Thus the $1,800 cost of tuition and books reduces the "qualified education expense" for purposes of calculating the ESA exclusion. Section 530, however, defines qualified higher education expense more broadly than §25A and treats the costs of room and board as qualified higher education expenses. §529(e)(3). Armon's room and board expense totals $5,000, so Armon's parents would be allowed to exclude the full $4,000 distributed out of the ESA, in addition to claiming the $1,800 Modified Hope Credit.

f. The answer would not change. The Modified Hope Credit is only disallowed for students convicted of a felony drug offense. §25A(b)(2)(D). Armon was not convicted for drug possession or distribution.

41. a. False. A taxpayer is allowed to contribute a maximum of $2,000 per beneficiary. §530(b)(1).

b. False. The annual ESA contribution is limited to $2,000 per beneficiary. §530(b)(1).

c. True. §530(d)(2)(A).

d. False. A taxpayer cannot make contributions for a beneficiary who has reached the age of 18. §530(b)(1)(A). Thus Abel can contribute a total of $4,000 only — $2,000 for each child under the age of 18.

e. True. Section 529 permits contributions to a Qualified Tuition Program on behalf of a beneficiary up to the amount necessary to fund the qualified higher education expenses of the beneficiary. §529(b)(6). Said another way, parents saving for a child's education by participating in a QTP can save very large amounts of money on a tax-favored basis. (In fact, ScholarShare, California's §529 College Savings Plan accepts contributions until the account balance for a beneficiary is well over $100,000!) Earnings from the QTP and distributions from the QTP are tax-free. §529(a), (c)(3)(B). Contributors to a QTP should, however, consider the potential gift tax and estate tax consequences of making the QTP contribution.

42. Gloria can take a $2,500 above-the-line deduction for her student loan interest. Section 221 allows an annual deduction of up to $2,500 of student loan interest. The fact that she does not itemize deductions is irrelevant because the §221 deduction is an above-the-line deduction. §62(a)(17).

43. a. Dan should elect the Modified Hope Credit for both daughters. The maximum Modified Hope Credit is $2,500 (100 percent of the first $2,000 of qualifying expenses and 25 percent of the next $2,000). The maximum Lifetime Learning Credit is $2,000 (20 percent of the qualifying education expenses up to a maximum of $10,000 of expenses).

Dan can take the $2,500 maximum Modified Hope Credit with respect to each of his two daughters because the limitation on the Modified Hope Credit is a "per student" limitation. §25A(b)(1). (The annual $2,000 limitation on the Lifetime Learning Credit is determined without regard to whether there is more than one student in the family because the Lifetime Learning Credit limitation is a "per taxpayer" limitation. §25A(c)(1).)

With $35,000 of modified adjusted gross income, Dan probably will have credits left over after paying his taxes. The Modified Hope Credit is partially refundable, however. §25A(i)(6).

Dan should not deduct any of the education expenses under §222 because the credits save Dan more in taxes than the deduction would. A taxpayer claiming a §25A credit cannot also take the §222 higher education expense deduction. §222(c)(2)(A).

b. Dan cannot claim either type of §25A credit and cannot claim a §222 higher education deduction; with modified adjusted gross income of $200,000, the §25A credits and the §222 deduction are fully phased out. §25A(d)(2), (h)(2), (i)(4), §222(b)(2), Rev. Proc. 2013-35 §3.05(2).

Income Shifting

The chapter number "7" appears as a large stylized graphic in the left margin with "CHAPTER" written vertically.

A. INCOME FROM SERVICES AND PROPERTY

Reading: §1.

As we have noted throughout this book, the federal income tax is *progressive*; persons with high income pay a higher percentage of that income to the government in the form of taxes than do persons with low income. (A tax that requires all taxpayers to pay an equal percentage of income is *proportionate* and a tax that requires low-income taxpayers to pay a higher percentage of their income is *regressive*.) The progressivity of the income tax encourages high-bracket individuals to shift some of that income to family members, relatives, or close friends in lower tax brackets. Suppose a taxpayer has a marginal income tax rate of 40 percent. She will pay $1,200 of tax on an additional $3,000 of income. Her son, in contrast, may be in the zero percent marginal tax bracket and owe no tax if the $3,000 is attributed to him.

In practice, loss of tax revenue due to income shifting is limited by a number of statutory provisions, three of which deserve special mention. First, virtually all married couples will find their tax liability minimized through filing a joint return, on which all income is combined. The attribution of income between married persons is therefore irrelevant. Federal tax law now recognizes the marriages of same-sex couples that were married in a state that recognizes same-sex marriage (even if a couple currently lives in a state that does not recognize same-sex marriage). Rev. Rul. 2013-17. On the other hand, the Service has asserted that unmarried Registered Domestic Partners and Civil Union Partners are not married for purposes of federal tax law. Id. (Later in this chapter we discuss these and other recent developments regarding the federal taxation of same-sex couples.)

Second, if the "kiddie tax" applies, the net unearned income of a child is taxed at the greater of the child's marginal rate or her parents' marginal rate. §1(g). The "kiddie tax" applies only if the child: (1) is under age 18; or (2) is age 18 (or age 19-23 *and* a full-time student) and the child's earned income (e.g., wage income) does not exceed half of the child's support for the year. §§1(g), 152(c)(3)(A). *Unearned income* is that portion of income not attributable to personal services. §§1(g), 911(d)(2). *Net unearned income* is, to simplify a bit, unearned income in excess of twice the §63(c)(5) limited standard deduction available to an individual who is claimed as a dependent on another taxpayer's return (in 2014, $1,000). §1(g)(4)(A)(ii)(I), Rev. Proc. 2013-35 §3.02. To illustrate the operation of §1(g), suppose that in 2014 a married couple gave their infant daughter a bond that paid $10,000 of interest each year, and the daughter had no other source of income and no itemized deductions. The daughter would have net unearned income of $8,000, which is $10,000 less twice the minimum standard deduction of $1,000. That $8,000 of net unearned income would be taxed at the parents' rate. The remaining $2,000 of the daughter's gross income would be reduced by the §63(c)(5) $1,000 standard deduction. The remaining $1,000 of income would be taxed at the daughter's individual rate. (Note that the daughter is not allowed a personal exemption because her parents are allowed to take a dependent exemption for her on their return. §151(d)(2).)

Third, the tax law is less progressive than it once was. For many years the maximum marginal rate on unearned income was 70 percent and the maximum rate on personal service income was 50 percent. The maximum rates are lower today and the payoff for income shifting is less.

Notwithstanding these and other statutory provisions, income shifting is often advantageous. Income shifting can reduce the combined tax liability of unmarried individuals living as domestic partners, parents and children who are not subject to the kiddie tax, and wealthy individuals and nonfamily members. And while past marginal rates of 70 percent and upward may be gone forever, the tax law is still progressive.

The basic rules governing attempts to shift personal service income are simple enough. Such income is taxed to the person who performs the services and cannot be shifted to a lower-bracket taxpayer. Lucas v. Earl, 281 U.S. 111 (1930) (assignment to the taxpayer's wife of half of the taxpayer's income from personal service did not shift that income to his wife); Helvering v. Eubank, 311 U.S. 122 (1940) (assignment to a family trust of commissions to be received in the future for service rendered in the past by the taxpayer did not shift the commission income to the assignees). To illustrate this rule, suppose a high-income executive gives her 25-year-old daughter a one-half interest in her next year's salary. Suppose, further, that the gift is legally enforceable. Notwithstanding the gift, the executive will be taxed on her entire salary. The same result would be obtained if the executive gave a one-half interest in payment due for services already performed.

The prohibition against shifting income from personal services does not apply to the value of services provided free of charge to a third party. (See the discussion of imputed income in Chapter 2.) Consider a carpenter in the 30 percent marginal tax bracket who gives his cousin $1,000 of his earnings to pay for household improvements. The carpenter is taxed on the $1,000. By contrast, the carpenter would not be taxed on the value of his services if, instead, he builds cabinets worth $1,000 for his cousin. Indeed, in this example, no one would be taxed on the $1,000 value. The performance of free services has the same effect as shifting $1,000 of income from the 30 percent to the zero percent tax bracket.

Similar advantages are reaped by contributing services to a §501(c)(3) charity such as the Red Cross. A lawyer is taxed on that portion of her salary she gives to such organizations and may deduct her donation, subject to the annual deduction limitations of §170. Contributions of money to certain other nonprofit organizations, such as political parties, are nondeductible. (See the discussion of §170 in Chapter 4.) In contrast, the lawyer is not taxed on the value of the services she provides directly to the organization free of charge. Again, working for no pay for the nonprofit organization, as opposed to working for a paying client and donating the proceeds, has the effect of shifting income to a taxpayer in the zero percent bracket.

In the preceding examples, the donee is the end user of the donor's services. Suppose, instead, that the donee sells the services to unrelated parties. For example, suppose a charity holds a benefit concert featuring a popular entertainer who has donated her services. Must the entertainer declare the value of her services as income and then deduct the gift only as permitted by law? In fact, services donated to charitable and political organizations are treated as untaxed imputed income even if the organization sells the services to the public and the value of the service is easy to ascertain. (On the other hand, if the services are donated to an individual and then sold to an unrelated party, the tax treatment is much less clear. For example, a parent who provides legal services to his daughter's law firm, which in turn charges out his services to its clients, may well be thought to be in partnership with his daughter and taxed on the income attributable to his services.)

For taxpayers who wish to offer free services without recognition of income, form is all important. An entertainer avoids taxation on the proceeds from a charity or political benefit only if the benefit is arranged by the organization or its agent. Suppose, instead, that the benefit is arranged by a for-profit promoter not acting as a charitable organization's agent and the entertainer directs the value of her services to a charity. In that event, the entertainer will be taxed on the net proceeds of the event and be left to struggle with the §170 limitations on charitable deductions. A similar emphasis on form is present in gifts of services to family members or friends. A real estate broker can sell her daughter's home free of commission without paying tax on the commission forgone. But a broker who sells her daughter's home, collects a commission, and returns that commission to her daughter the following day will be taxed on that commission.

In contrast to personal service income, which (with the exception of imputed income from services) cannot be shifted, income from property can be shifted by transferring the income-producing property. Thus, a parent with rental property can shift the rental income to his 26-year-old son by giving the son the property. A parent with appreciated property can have that appreciation taxed at his 26-year-old son's rate by giving him the property prior to sale. (See the discussion of gifts in Chapter 2.)

Here, too, form is important. A transaction in which a donor negotiates a sale of appreciated property and then, a moment before the sale is consummated, transfers the property to a donee who completes the sale, may be recharacterized as a sale of property by the donor, followed by a gift of the sale proceeds to the donee. Under that characterization, it is the donor who must pay tax on the gain.

Perhaps the most difficult set of issues raised in this area concern gifts of partial interests in property. Suppose a parent gives her 25-year-old daughter a one-tenth undivided interest, as a tenant in common, in an apartment building. Has the parent succeeded in shifting one-tenth of the yearly rental income to her daughter? Or suppose a parent gives her daughter the rights to the rental income for the next five years and (to make the examples here parallel) that rental income represents one-tenth of the value of the building. Has the parent here succeeded in shifting rental income to her daughter during the next five years?

It is useful to begin discussion of these issues on a definitional note. An interest in property that is coterminous in time with the donor's interest is often referred to as a *horizontal interest*. A 10 percent undivided interest in property is a horizontal interest, as it extends as far in time as the donor's remaining interest in the property. A gift of a horizontal interest in property shifts the income from that interest to the donee. Blair v. Commissioner, 300 U.S. 5 (1937). Thus, if a parent gives her 27-year-old son a half-interest in income-producing property, half the net income from the property and half the proceeds from sale will be taxed to the son.

A gift of property that is not coterminous in time with the interest retained by the donor, but that reverts back to the donor, is often referred to as a *vertical interest*, or a *carved-out interest*. Suppose a donor gives her son the rental income on an apartment building for the next five years, but retains the rental income after the next five years or other incidents of ownership thereafter. The donor has given a vertical or carved-out interest in the property, which does not shift income to the donee. Helvering v. Horst, 311 U.S. 112 (1940). The donor will be taxed on the next five years' rental income on the rationale that, notwithstanding the form of the transaction, she has effectively maintained control of the underlying property.

Some gifts may be both horizontal and vertical. For example, a parent might give her son a one-half interest in property for five years with the parent regaining sole control of the property thereafter. Such gifts are taxed in the same manner as gifts of vertical interests: The parent is taxed on the entire income from the property.

The basic rules on income shifting are as follows: Personal service income cannot be shifted except by the performance of gratuitous services. Income from property can be shifted provided there is a complete transfer of the income-producing property, and the donee does not receive a carved-out or vertical interest. One final complication, implicit in the above description, concerns the hazy line between services and property. An artist might use personal efforts to produce a piece of tangible property such as a sculpture. In both a colloquial (and legal) sense, a composition, patent, or book is also seen as property, albeit property of a more intangible nature. Indeed, even the right to payment for past or future personal services can be seen as property, in the sense that such a right can be bought and sold. For tax purposes, the transfer of tangible self-created property is seen as the transfer of property rather than services and is effective to shift income from the property to the transferee. A sculpture that is transferred by an artist to a relative and then sold by the relative is seen as property of the relative at the time of sale. Gain from the sale is taxed to the relative rather than the artist. At the other extreme, the transfer of the right to payment for personal services by the service provider is not seen as a transfer of property such that the gain is recognized by the transferee. Instead, as noted above, the gain is taxed to the provider of the services.

The transfer of rights to intangibles such as copyrights or patents occupies a middle ground. Here, as elsewhere, form is all important. An author can shift income from a work by transferring her copyrighted manuscript to a donee and having the donee negotiate a contract with the publisher. Suppose, instead, the author signs a publishing contract and then assigns her royalties under the contract to a donee. While the assignment may be legally binding for state law purposes, it is ineffective for tax purposes. The author, and not the donee, will be taxed on the royalty income. Compare Wodehouse v. Commissioner, 178 F.2d 987 (4th Cir. 1949) (novelist P.G. Wodehouse taxed on royalty income notwithstanding assignment of contract rights) with Cory v. Commissioner, 23 T.C. 775 (1955) (assignment of manuscript by philosopher George Santayana effective to shift income to assignee).

Examples

1. State whether the following taxes are progressive, proportionate, or regressive. Assume all individuals fall into the same filing category (for example, that they are all single individuals):
   a. Daniel has taxable income of $50,000 and pays $5,000 of tax. Sarah has taxable income of $40,000 and pays $4,000 of tax.

b. Daniel has taxable income of $100,000 and pays $8,000 of tax. Sarah has taxable income of $50,000 and pays $5,000 of tax.

2. a. Barbara, who earns $100,000 a year as an attorney, signs a binding contract that requires her to pay half of her future earnings to her 25-year-old daughter. On what portion of her future earnings will Barbara be taxed?

   b. Assume the same facts as in part (a), except that Barbara signs a binding contract to pay her daughter one-half of what she collects from legal work that has already been performed and billed. On what portion of those previously billed amounts will Barbara be taxed?

3. High-income taxpayer Mary gives 1,000 shares of Bigco stock to her 10-year-old daughter, Nancy (who has no income from other sources). The stock pays an annual dividend of $10 per share. Is each of the following statements true or false?

   a. Nancy will be taxed on the dividends.

   b. The tax on the net unearned income attributable to the dividends will be equal to the tax that would have been paid on the dividends had the stock been retained by Mary.

   c. Unearned income consists of income that is not attributable to wages, salaries, and professional fees.

   d. If Nancy receives stock from her uncle, Tom, the net unearned income attributable to the stock will be taxed at Tom's marginal rate.

   e. If Mary gives the stock to her 19-year-old son, David (who has no income from other sources), the net unearned income attributable to the stock will be taxed at Mary's marginal rate.

4. a. Fred owns 100 acres of rental property. He gives his 26-year-old son, Sam, 50 acres. The 50 acres are worth $50,000. In the year immediately following the gift, the 50 acres are rented out for $5,000, with the rent being paid to Sam. Who pays tax on the rent?

   b. Assume the same facts as in part (a), except that Fred gives his son the right to all of the rental income from all 100 acres for nine years. The present value of that right is $50,000. In the year immediately following the gift, the 100 acres are rented out for $10,000, with the rent being paid to Sam. Who pays tax on the rent?

5. Tom gives Peter the following gifts. State whether each gift creates a carved-out interest.

   a. A 30 percent interest in a business. Tom retains the remaining 70 percent interest.

   b. A five-year right to the income from a 30 percent interest in a business. Tom retains all the other rights to the business.

   c. A five-year right to the income from a business. Tom retains all other rights to income from the business.

  d. The right to the next two years' rent on an apartment building. Tom retains the right to the rentals in succeeding years.

6. Barbara gives her son a sculpture she has just completed. One year later, the son sells the sculpture for $200,000. Who is taxed on the gain from the sale?

7. Real estate broker Ed sells his daughter's home in Redwood City for $200,000.
  a. Ed waives his commission, thereby saving his daughter $4,000. Is Ed taxed on the $4,000?
  b. The total commission on the sale is $12,000 and is collected by the real estate company that employs Ed. Ed's share of the commission is $4,000. The company charges Ed's daughter the full $12,000 commission and gives $4,000 of the commission to Ed, who gives the $4,000 back to his daughter. Is Ed taxed on the $4,000?

8. Discuss the tax consequences of the following transactions:
  a. In year one Douglas buys Blackacre for $100,000. On December 30, year four, Tom offers Douglas $200,000 for Blackacre. Douglas immediately transfers the property to his 25-year-old son, Sonny. Douglas then informs Tom that the property is owned by Sonny but that he, Douglas, will negotiate the sale on Sonny's behalf. Douglas next informs Tom that Sonny will agree to sell the property for $210,000. Tom issues a counteroffer at $205,000. Acting on his father's advice, on December 31, year four, Sonny accepts the offer. The terms of the December 31 agreement call for payment and transfer of title on January 30, year five. On January 30, year five, Sonny receives $205,000.
  b. Assume the same facts as in part (a), except that Douglas negotiates the sale and signs the December 31, year-four agreement on his own behalf. On January 1, year five, Douglas transfers title to the property to Sonny. Sonny takes title subject to the sale agreement; that is, Sonny is obligated to sell the property on the terms specified in the agreement. The property is in fact sold pursuant to the agreement. On January 30, year five, Sonny receives $205,000.

9. a. Alan accepts a job with Wagner, Inc., which has a long-standing policy to make college more affordable for its employees' children. Under that policy, each year the company pays each college-age child of each employee the lesser of (i) the child's college tuition or (ii) $5,000. Wagner, Inc. pays Alan's child, Donna, $5,000 in year one. Alan received no parental support from his parents and refuses to provide any parental support for Donna. Alan did not know of Wagner's policy when he accepted the job. Discuss the tax consequences of the $5,000 transfer to Donna.

b. Wagner maintains and operates on-premises athletic facilities that are available to its employees, their spouses, and their children. Alan's daughter, Donna, uses those facilities. The cost of similar facilities at a private health club is $500 a year per person. Before accepting his job at Wagner, Alan refused to give his daughter the $500 a year necessary to join a private health club with similar athletic facilities. Is Alan taxed on the value of the facilities made available to Donna?

10. Accountant Amy normally charges $100 an hour for her time. Discuss the tax consequences of the following events:
   a. Amy spends 10 hours preparing her cousin's tax return. Amy does not receive any form of compensation for her work.
   b. Amy spends 10 hours preparing her church's tax returns. Amy does not receive any form of compensation for her work.
   c. Amy spends 10 hours preparing her dentist's tax returns. In return, her dentist provides Amy and her family with approximately $1,000 of dental work.

11. Pop star Paula receives $20,000 per performance from concert promoters. Paula performs at the following events for no compensation. Discuss the tax consequences of these events.
   a. Paula performs at a Democratic Party victory celebration. Seats are free but are available only to party workers, politicians, or past contributors.
   b. Paula performs at a fund-raiser for the Democratic Party. The event nets the Democratic Party $20,000.
   c. Paula organizes a concert and gives the net proceeds of $20,000 to the Democratic Party.

Explanations

1. a. The tax is proportionate. Daniel faces a higher absolute amount of tax liability, but both taxpayers pay 10 percent of their income to the government. A tax that requires all taxpayers to pay an equal percentage of income is proportionate; a tax that requires high-income taxpayers to pay a higher percentage of their income is progressive; a tax that requires low-income taxpayers to pay a higher percentage of their income is regressive.
   b. The tax is regressive. Again, Daniel pays more tax. However, Daniel pays a lower percentage of his income to the government than does Sarah. Here, taxes comprise 8 percent of Daniel's income and 10 percent of Sarah's income.

2. a. Barbara will be taxed on all of her earnings. The Supreme Court has held that assignments of personal service income do not shift

the tax levied upon that income. Lucas v. Earl, 281 U.S. 111 (1930); Helvering v. Eubank, 311 U.S. 122 (1940).

   b. Barbara will be taxed on all of her earnings. Here, the income assigned is attributable to past services. This assignment is in some sense more complete than the assignment discussed in the preceding question because Barbara's work has already been performed. The daughter's interest does not depend on Barbara's willingness to continue work. The Supreme Court has held, however, that assignments of personal service income attributable to past services, like assignments of personal service income attributable to future services, do not shift the tax levied upon that income from the service provider. Helvering v. Eubank.

3. a. True. Income from property, unlike income from personal services, can be shifted by transferring the income-producing property. (However, due to the "kiddie tax," most of the income will be taxed at the mother's marginal rate. See part (b), below.)

   b. True. Although the net unearned income attributable to the stock will be taxable to the daughter, the income will be taxed at the mother's tax rate under the "kiddie tax" of §1(g).

   c. True. Unearned income is defined in §1(g)(4) as income that is not earned income under §911(d)(2). That latter section states that "[t]he term 'earned income' means wages, salaries, or professional fees, and other amounts received as compensation for personal services actually rendered. . . ."

   d. False. The net unearned income will be taxed at her parent's tax rate. §1(g)(1). The fact that the income is attributable to a gift from her uncle is irrelevant.

   e. False, if David is not a full-time student; true, if David is a full-time student. Section 1(g)(2)(i) provides that the §1(g) kiddie tax applies to a child under the age of 18. However, §1(g)(2)(ii) also provides that the kiddie tax applies to a child who meets the age requirements of §152(c)(3)(A). A child meets the §152 age requirements if the child is (i) under age 19, or (ii) a full-time student under the age of 24. Putting these rules together, the kiddie tax applies to a child (i) under age 19, or (ii) a full-time student over 18 but under 24.

4. a. Sam. The gift of the underlying property interest shifts the tax from Fred to his son.

   b. Fred. The nine-year right to income constitutes a carved-out interest. Fred is regarded as having maintained the underlying property ownership and simply shifted the right to income.

5. a. No carved-out interest is created. The interest assigned is a permanent interest. The 30 percent interest will never revest in,

or revert back to, Tom. Thus, although the 30 percent interest is a partial interest, it is not a carved-out interest.

b. A carved-out interest is created. Here, Tom retains a reversionary interest in the 30 percent interest in the business; it is the presence of the reversion that creates a carved-out interest.

c. A carved-out interest is created because Tom retains a reversionary interest in the business.

d. A carved-out interest is created because Tom retains a reversionary interest in the rentals.

6. The son. The gift of personally created property will shift the income from such property to the donee. However, if the gift had been made immediately prior to the sale, *and* Barbara had arranged the sale, the Service might argue that Barbara controlled the sculpture up to the time of sale and attribute the sale proceeds to Barbara.

7. a. No, here the waived commission would be treated as nontaxable imputed income.

b. Yes. In similar situations, a number of courts have ruled that taxpayers are taxed on their personal service income even if that income is "rebated" back to the family members.

8. a. As noted throughout this chapter, a high-bracket individual may transfer property to a low-bracket donee. Gain from the sale of the property is taxed to the donee rather than the donor. On the other hand, a high-bracket individual who sells appreciated property and then transfers the proceeds is taxed on the gain. The primary question raised by this example is whether this transaction is properly described for tax purposes as a transfer of property followed by a sale of the property by the donee or a sale of the property by the donor followed by a transfer of sale proceeds to the donee. The law in this area is far from clear. In general, however, a high-bracket individual can shift income from appreciated property by transferring the property prior to the sale, provided that the terms of the sale agreement have not been agreed upon. Here, the property is in fact transferred before an agreement is reached. Most probably, therefore, Sonny, rather than Douglas, will be taxed on the sale proceeds. The fact that Douglas negotiates for his son clouds the issue somewhat but should not alter the final result.

How much gain does Sonny recognize? As discussed in Chapter 2 of this book, for purposes of computing gain, Sonny receives a basis in property received by gift equal to the donor's basis in the property. §1015. If we assume there are no selling expenses and that Douglas has neither added to the basis of the property since purchase (through improvements) nor reduced the basis (through depreciation), Sonny recognizes gain of $105,000 — the sale price of $205,000 less his basis of $100,000.

This hypothetical raises an interesting — if slightly off topic — timing issue. Is the sale complete in year four, when the sale agreement is signed, or in year five, when the sale "closes"? In fact, property is generally treated as sold for tax purposes in the year in which the sale closes and title is transferred.

b. Here, the terms of the sale agreement are fixed prior to the transfer of the property. Douglas may argue that under state law the sale is not finalized until title passes. Indeed, for some purposes, even the tax law does not treat the sale as final until title passes. For example, as noted in the explanation for part (a), gain is realized in the year in which the transaction closes rather than the year in which the sale agreement is reached. (Whether gain is included in that year depends on the installment sale rules, discussed in Chapter 3 of this book. Here, all payments are received in year five, so gain will be included in that year.) Unfortunately for Douglas, a donor who enters into a binding agreement to sell property and then transfers the property subject to the agreement is generally treated as if he had first sold the property and then transferred the proceeds. For this purpose, the tax law treats the donor as the seller of the property, notwithstanding the fact that under state law title to the property has passed to the donee prior to completion of the sale.

9. a. In general, it seems reasonable to assume that most employees feel the $5,000 tuition given their children is as valuable as an additional $5,000 salary. Otherwise, why wouldn't Wagner junk the tuition program and raise salaries? Presumably, Wagner is interested solely in attracting and retaining employees. Of course, some employees, such as Alan, will find the benefit of little value. The tax law is caught in a dilemma. It is impossible to determine and then tax the idiosyncratic value of the tuition benefit to each employee. If the benefit is taxed to the employee at its cost, some employees will be overtaxed. If the benefit is tax-free to employee and child, most or all employees will be undertaxed. If the child, rather than the parent, is taxed on the benefit, the result for most employees, who value the benefit at cost, is that some personal service income is shifted to a lower bracket family member. With respect to this type of benefit, the tax law has chosen the first approach — Alan will be taxed on the full $5,000. Armantrout v. Commissioner, 67 T.C. 996 (1977), aff'd per curiam, 570 F.2d 210 (7th Cir. 1978).

b. The issue is analytically identical to the issue in part (a). However, this fringe benefit is subject to special legislative treatment. Section 132, discussed in Chapter 2 of this book, excludes from taxation the value of on-premises athletic facilities, provided that substantially all of the use of the facilities is by employees and their spouses and dependents. §132(j)(4). Neither Alan nor his daughter is taxed on the value of the facilities.

10. a. The value of Amy's services provided free of charge to her cousin is not subject to tax.
   b. The value of Amy's services provided free of charge to the church is not subject to tax.
   c. Here, Amy is receiving valuable compensation for her services. Amy will be taxed on that compensation. The fact that the compensation is in the form of services rather than cash is irrelevant. See, e.g., Rev. Rul. 79-24 (individuals taxed on services or property received under barter arrangements).

11. a. Paula is not taxed on the imputed value of her services.
   b. Here, Paula's services are "sold" by the Democratic Party. One might imagine that Paula could be treated as if she had performed for her usual compensation and then given that sum to the Democratic Party. In that event, Paula would be taxed on the $20,000; contributions to political parties are nondeductible. §170(c). In fact, however, Paula will escape taxation on the value of her services so long as she neither receives the profits directly nor organizes the event.
   c. Here, Paula has crossed the line between providing free services and contributing personal service income. She will be taxed on the $20,000; the contribution is not deductible. §170(c).

B. SAME-SEX COUPLES, JOINT RETURN FILING, AND THE RELATIONSHIP BETWEEN STATE LAW AND FEDERAL TAX LAW

Reading: §§1(a)–(d), 6013.

This section explores some of the federal tax issues that same-sex couples must address as they prepare and file their tax returns. Throughout this book, we have assumed that spouses file joint returns because filing jointly generally allows them to pay less tax than if they file separately. A brief history of the federal authorization of joint return filing by opposite-sex married couples can help us consider how the tax law should address current issues regarding the federal taxation of same-sex couples.

Until 1948, spouses filed separate federal tax returns because federal law did not allow joint filing. Events leading up to the 1948 authorization of federal joint return filing illustrate the interaction of state property law and federal tax law.

The property rights of spouses are determined under applicable state law, not federal tax law. Federal law, however, determines the federal tax consequences of the ownership or transfer of property by spouses. Before federal joint filing was allowed, the aggregate federal tax for married couples varied from state to state, depending on the property rights of the spouses under state law, including community property law. If a married couple lived in a community property state, the spouses were required to split their income for federal income tax purposes, with each spouse reporting half of the income on his or her separate tax return. Poe v. Seaborn, 282 U.S. 101 (1930). The rationale was that under state community property law, each spouse had a legal right to half of the income of the other spouse. As a result of such income-splitting, married couples in community property states typically paid less federal tax than married couples in non–community property states.

Following the decision in *Poe v. Seaborn*, several states enacted new community property laws to reduce the federal tax liability of married couples living in the state. Litigation continued as courts addressed the federal tax implications of new state community property laws. For example, the Supreme Court held that income-splitting did not apply in states in which spouses had to elect into the state's new community property system. Commissioner v. Harmon, 323 U.S. 44 (1944). State-by-state disparities in the federal income tax treatment of married couples attributable to variations in state law continued until Congress enacted the joint return rules in 1948.

In recent years, questions surrounding the federal tax allocation of income and property between spouses again have become prominent as a result of new state laws that either recognize same-sex marriages or provide for domestic partnerships or civil unions with legal rights that are similar to marriage for state law purposes. We will use the term *same-sex union* to denote same-sex relationships that are legally recognized by states and use the term DPs/CUs to denote the subset of same-sex unions that are not marriages.

States that recognize same-sex unions and have an income tax require same-sex unions to file joint state income tax returns, as opposite-sex married couples do. Until recently, all same-sex unions were prohibited from filing federal joint returns, however, because (for purposes of federal law) §3 of the federal Defense of Marriage Act (DOMA) defined "marriage" to include only marriages of opposite-sex couples and defined "spouse" as a person married to a person of the opposite sex. In 2013, however, the U.S. Supreme Court held that §3 of DOMA was unconstitutional, in a case in which a surviving same-sex spouse, Edith Windsor, had been denied an estate tax marital deduction. U.S. v. Windsor, 570 U.S. __ (2013). Interpreting the *Windsor* decision, Revenue Ruling 2013-17 subsequently concluded that, for federal tax purposes: (1) same-sex married couples are treated as "married" if the state in which the marriage was celebrated recognizes same-sex marriages—even if the couple currently resides in a state that does not recognize same-sex marriage; (2) the terms "spouse," "husband," and "wife," apply to married same-sex couples; and (3) unmarried same-sex couples, including DPs and CUs, are not treated as "married" for federal tax purposes.

These recent developments clarified some but not all of the federal tax treatment of married same-sex couples. In the future, expect to see numerous administrative pronouncements on the application of specific tax rules to same-sex married couples, as well as transition rules to move from the old DOMA federal tax system to the post-*Windsor* federal tax system. See, e.g., Notice 2014-1 (providing post-*Windsor* rules and transition rules with respect to various employee benefits and health savings accounts).

There still is a great deal of complexity and uncertainty regarding the federal tax law as applied to DPs/CUs, because such unions are not treated as marriages under Revenue Ruling 2013-17. Although DPs/CUs are required to file a joint return for state income tax purposes, federal tax law continues (as of March 2014) to prohibit DPs/CUs from filing a joint return.

In some states, however, certain information that must be reported on the state joint return is derived from the taxpayer's federal joint return. As a result, DPs/CUs often must prepare two sets of federal returns: the single (or head of household) returns that they each actually file with the IRS and a "dummy" federal joint return that is used to prepare the couple's state joint return.

The IRS has provided guidance on some, but by no means all, of the federal tax issues that partners in DPs/CUs must consider. For example, the IRS has announced that DP/CU partners who live in community property states must split their income, under *Poe v. Seaborn*, for federal tax reporting purposes. Chief Counsel Advisory Memorandum 201021050. In addition, the IRS has taken a position that, if DP/CU partners co-own their personal residence, (1) each partner's home mortgage interest deduction is based on the interest paid by each partner (not their ownership interests in the property), and (2) the acquisition indebtedness cap of $1 million is applied on a per-residence basis, not on a per-taxpayer basis, and the allowable interest is allocated between the partners. Many other federal tax issues remain uncertain, however. For example, it is unclear what effect community property laws have on property transfers incident to the dissolution of same-sex unions, whether §1041 applies to any division of property, and whether alimony payments made incident to the dissolution will be treated as alimony for federal tax purposes. Uncertainty about how to report various kinds of items on tax returns has significantly increased compliance costs and complexity for taxpayers in same-sex unions. In addition, some IRS personnel have been unaware of the new positions that the IRS has adopted with respect to same-sex unions and have acted punitively towards taxpayers who have filed amended returns based on *Windsor* and the revised IRS positions. National Taxpayer Advocate 2013 Annual Report to Congress, available at http://www.taxpayeradvocate.irs.gov/userfiles/file/2013Full Report/DEFENSE-OF-MARRIAGE-ACT-IRS%2C-Domestic-Partners%2C-and-Same-Sex-Couples-Need-Additional-Guidance.pdf.

Example

12. Jennifer and Sarah, a long-term committed couple with no children, have lived together for 15 years. In 2014, Jennifer works full time and earns $140,000 of wage income. Sarah works part time and earns $10,000 of wage income.

   a. Assume that Jennifer and Sarah live in Massachusetts and are married under state law. Massachusetts is not a community property state. Briefly describe how their marriage affects their filing status for their 2014 federal and state tax returns and the amount of gross income reported on their tax returns.

   b. How, if at all, would the answer in part (a) change if Jennifer and Sarah were married in Massachusetts but in 2014 reside in California, which is a community property state?

   c. Assume that Jennifer and Sarah live in California and are registered domestic partners under state law. Briefly describe how their status as domestic partners affects their 2014 federal and state tax returns.

   d. Assume that Jennifer and Sarah live in California but have not registered as domestic partners. Instead, they have entered into enforceable mutual contracts by which each promises to share equally in all income and property with the other partner forever. How, if at all, do these facts change the answer in part (c)?

Explanation

12. a. Jennifer and Sarah are married under Massachusetts law. Federal tax law recognizes their marriage under the "state of celebration" rule. Rev. Rul. 2013-17. Jennifer and Sarah will file a joint 2014 federal tax return and a joint 2014 Massachusetts state tax return. They will aggregate their $150,000 of joint income on those returns.

   b. The answer in part (a) does not change. Jennifer and Sarah will report combined income of $150,000 on their federal and California joint tax returns.

   c. Although federal tax law recognizes same-sex marriage, it does not treat a DP as marriage. Rev. Rul 2013-17. Although Jennifer and

Sarah will file a joint 2014 state tax return, they will have to file separate federal tax returns. On their federal returns, they will split their 2014 wage income because California domestic partners have the same community property rights and obligations as married spouses under California law. Chief Counsel Advisory Memorandum 201021050.

d. Chief Counsel Advisory Memorandum 201021050 does not apply because Jennifer and Sarah are not California-registered domestic partners. As discussed earlier in this chapter, income from personal services cannot be shifted by contract. Lucas v. Earl, 281 U.S. 111 (1930). On their separate federal tax returns, Jennifer and Sarah each must include in gross income her own wage income. In addition, Jennifer and Sarah each must report her own income on separate California state income tax returns.

C. TRUSTS

Reading: §§1(e), 641–643, 651, 652, 661, 662.

We saw earlier in this chapter that a gift of property effectively shifts income derived from the property from the donor to the donee. Taxpayers with young or irresponsible family members, however, may not wish to make outright gifts of property. An alternative for such taxpayers is to transfer income-producing property to a trust set up for the benefit of family members.

The trust is a separate legal entity under state law; the transferor-donor is the trust *grantor*; the donee family members are the trust *beneficiaries*. The fiduciary who manages the trust is the *trustee*; the trust property is the *trust corpus*. The taxation of trusts is in many ways quite complicated. The following description of trust taxation is designed to provide students with a brief overview of the subject.

A *simple trust* is a trust that is required to annually distribute current income (and only current income) to the beneficiaries, and that does not distribute or set aside any amounts to charity.[1] Thus, a grandparent who transfers stock to a trust with instructions that all dividends be distributed annually to her son and, upon the son's death, the stock be distributed to her

---

1. A simple trust may accumulate items, such as capital gain and stock dividends, that constitute income for tax purposes, but for trust purposes are seen as part of the corpus. §643(b).

granddaughter has set up a trust that is a simple trust (except in the final year of the trust, during which the corpus will be distributed). Such a trust is (nominally) taxed on its income but receives a deduction for distribution of that income.[2] §651. Thus, a simple trust does not itself generally pay tax. Instead, income from a simple trust is taxed directly to the beneficiaries.[3] §§61(a)(15) and 652(a).

Any trust that is not a simple trust is a *complex trust*. For example, a trust whose governing instrument (the *deed of trust*) allows, but does not require, the trustee to retain income earned in a given year and distribute that income in a later year is a complex trust. A complex trust, like a simple trust, is able to deduct current income that is distributed to the beneficiaries; the beneficiaries are then taxed on that income. §661(a). Suppose, however, a complex trust does not distribute all of its income in one year. In that event, the trust is taxed on its undistributed current income under the rate schedule set forth in §1(e). That rate schedule has the same maximum marginal rate as the rate schedule that applies to individuals. However, the maximum marginal rate applies to nearly all of the trust's earnings. Moreover, net income for trusts, unlike net income for individuals, is determined without regard to certain deductions. For example, the trust receives no deduction for medical care and no personal or dependency deductions.[4]

The beneficiaries of a complex trust are taxed on undistributed or accumulated income in the year in which it is finally distributed. §662. The trust in that year receives no deduction for the distribution. However, under a complicated system of "throwback" rules, the tax paid in prior years by the trust on that income is credited to the beneficiaries. §§667(b)(1), 668(b). In most cases, that credit offsets any tax owed by the beneficiary.[5] The tax paid by the complex trust on accumulated income thus bears some resemblance to the tax withheld by an employer on an employee's salary. In both cases the

---

2. More precisely, the trust receives a deduction equal to the lesser of the taxable income distributed or its "distributable net income." That latter term is defined, generally, as taxable income as determined without regard to the de minimis deduction granted in lieu of the personal deduction or items such as capital gain properly seen as part of the trust corpus. §643(a). For the purposes of this overview, we will assume, somewhat simplistically, that distributable net income is always equal to taxable income.

3. As noted in note 1, above, the trust may accumulate certain items such as capital gains that for trust purposes are treated as part of the corpus. In that case, to simplify just a bit, the trust receives a deduction only for the income distributed, and the beneficiaries are taxed only on the income distributed.

4. The trust does receive a small deduction in lieu of personal and dependent deductions. See §642(b).

5. If the tax paid by the trust exceeds the tax owed by the beneficiaries, the beneficiaries owe no tax but receive no refund. In such situations, the income from the trust is taxed only once, but at the trust's tax rate.

government collects tax first from the paying entity (the trust or the employer). The government then collects tax from the recipient (beneficiary or employee) on the gross amount earned but allows an offset for the tax already paid by the entity.

To summarize, income of a simple or complex trust is taxed only once. In the case of a trust that distributes its entire current income, and only its current income, the income is taxed to the beneficiaries in the year earned. In the case of a complex trust that accumulates income, the income is taxed to the trust in the year it is earned and then taxed again to the beneficiaries when distributed. However, the tax owed by the beneficiaries is offset by the prior tax paid by the trust.

Examples

13. On January 1, year one, Sandy transfers $100,000 to a trust. The deed of trust appoints Sandy's attorney, Able, as trustee. Able is required by the deed of trust to invest the trust funds in a money market account and to distribute all of the annual income to Sandy's cousin, Max. Upon Max's death, the $100,000 is to be distributed to Max's daughter, Lisa.

    a. Assume that in year one, the trust has interest income of $5,000. Assume further that the trust has no expenses and qualifies for no deductions other than the deduction provided by §651(a). After taking into consideration §651(a), what is the trust's taxable income?

    b. Assume that in year one the trust distributes $5,000 to Max. Is Max taxed on that income?

14. On January 1, year one, Daniel transfers $100,000 to a trust. The deed of trust appoints Daniel's attorney, Able, as trustee. Able is required by the deed of trust to invest the trust funds in a money market account, to accumulate all income for year one, and then, on January 1, year two, to distribute that income, together with the trust corpus of $100,000, to Daniel's son, Greg.

    a. Assume that, in year one, the trust has interest income of $5,000. Assume further that the trust has no expenses and qualifies for no deductions other than the deductions set forth in §§651(a) and 661(a), which may or may not apply. What is the trust's taxable income?

    b. Assume that on January 1, year two, the trust distributes its year one income to Greg, together with the trust corpus. Discuss the tax consequences of that distribution to the trust and to Greg.

Explanations

13. a. The trust receives a deduction for the amount distributed so it is left with no taxable income. §651.

    b. Max is taxed on the $5,000 he receives. §652.

14. a. The trust has taxable income of $5,000. Section 651(a) does not apply because the trust is not a simple trust. Section 661(a) does not apply because the trust does not distribute its current income.

    b. The trust receives no deduction because it has not distributed any current income. Greg is taxed on last year's income at the time of the distribution but receives a credit for the amount of taxes paid by the trust.

      The computations of the tax liability are somewhat complicated. A portion of the year one income went to pay the taxes due that year. As a result, in year two, the trust will distribute the $100,000 corpus and the $5,000 income less tax paid on that income. Assume that both the trust and Greg are in the 35 percent marginal tax bracket. In that case, the trust pays $1,750 of tax in year one so the total distribution is $103,250. The $100,000 represents the distribution of the corpus and is tax-free to Greg. For tax purposes, the remaining $3,250 is increased by the $1,750 tax paid by the trust. Greg is treated as having received the entire income included by the trust in year one. In financial argot, the distribution is "grossed up" by the taxes paid by the trust. Greg is taxed on $5,000. His tax liability is $1,750 (35 percent of $5,000) but he receives credit for the $1,750 paid by the trust, so he ends up with no tax liability on the $5,000 deemed distributed — he ends up, then, with after-tax income of $3,250.

      The "gross up" feature of the law may be easier to understand if it is compared with the treatment of employer withholding. Assume an employee and an employer are both in the 35 percent tax bracket. The employee earns $5,000; $1,750 tax is withheld by the employer and so the employee receives only $3,250 cash. For tax purposes, however, the employee is treated as having received gross pay of $5,000 — the $3,250 take home pay plus the $1,750 tax withheld by the employer. The employee is taxed on the gross pay but receives a credit for the tax withheld. The net result is that the employee is in the same situation as if he had gotten the full $5,000 and then paid tax directly. The same is true here. Greg ends up with $100,000 corpus and after-tax earnings of $3,250 — the same amount he would have received had the trust paid no tax and made a current distribution of the full income of $5,000, and had that amount been taxed directly to Greg.

      If the trust is in a higher tax bracket than the beneficiary, the beneficiary will not get a refund for the difference between the tax paid by the trust and the tax owed by the beneficiary. In this and other ways, the treatment of complex trusts only approximates a single-tax system in which income is taxed only once, and at the beneficiary's tax rate.

D. GRANTOR TRUSTS

Reading: §§671–678.

In the previous section, we discussed the treatment of complete and unequivocal transfers to a trust. We noted that, in general, income of such trusts is taxed only once and at the beneficiary's tax rate. We did not discuss, however, situations in which the grantor transfers property to a trust but retains certain control over the property. Suppose, for example, that the grantor transfers an apartment building to a trust with the income each year to go to his daughter and the building to be transferred outright to his daughter upon his death, but he retains the power to revoke the transfer and reclaim the property. Has the grantor succeeded in shifting the annual income from the building to his daughter? Or is the transfer subject to the common law rules governing partial transfers of property, discussed at the start of this chapter?

In fact, these sorts of partial transfers to trusts are subject to a special set of rules in the Code governing *grantor trusts*. As discussed below, these rules have substantially the same effect as the rules governing partial gifts that do not involve a trust. These rules make trusts a poor vehicle with which to shift income. In cases in which the grantor retains control over property transferred to a trust, it is the grantor, not the beneficiary, who is taxed on the trust income.

Section 673 applies to property that is placed in trust for a period of years and later reverts back to the grantor. Under §673(a), if the value of the reversionary interest exceeds 5 percent of the value of the property, income from the property is taxed to the grantor. (Section 673(a) does not apply to reversionary interests that occur only in the event that a lineal descendant beneficiary dies before attaining the age of 21. §673(b).) The reversionary interest is valued as of the time of contribution, using federal tables that take into account the prevailing interest rates and, if applicable, the life expectancy of beneficiaries. To illustrate the operation of §673, suppose that attorney Able places income-producing property in trust for her niece, and the terms of the trust provide that the trust terminates, and the property reverts back to Able in 18 years. Assume further that the appropriate discount rate is 4 percent. In that case, the federal tables will show that Able's reversionary interest is worth about 50 percent of the value of the interest. Accordingly, Able will be treated as if she owns the property outright, and she, not her niece, will be taxed on the income.

As is perhaps evident, §673 is similar in effect to the common law rules governing gifts of carved-out interests. In the first part of this chapter, we discussed the tax treatment of an individual who, outside of the trust context, gives his child the right to income from property for a number of years but retains a reversionary right in the property thereafter. We noted that this form of gift is referred to as a vertical or carved-out interest and does not shift taxes from the donor. Section 673 provides the same result for taxpayers who use trusts to make a temporary gift of property income, but who, in the deed of trust, retain a reversionary interest in the income-producing property.

Section 676 generally provides that a grantor who transfers property to a trust but retains the right to revoke the transfer and regain title to the property is taxed on the income from the property. The same result occurs if a third party is given the power to revest title to the property in the grantor unless the third party has a substantial interest in the trust as beneficiary or power of appointment over the trust. §§672, 676(a).[6]

Section 675 generally treats the grantor as the owner of any property in respect to which he retains certain prohibited administrative powers, such as the power to purchase the property at less than full consideration. (A grantor who is characterized as the "owner" of trust property is taxed on the income from that property.) Section 675 also taxes the grantor on any amounts he has borrowed from the trust unless the loan carries adequate security and interest and meets certain other requirements.

Section 677 generally treats the grantor as the owner of any portion of a trust property the income of which may be distributed or accumulated for the benefit of the grantor's spouse or used to pay life insurance premiums on the life of the grantor or the grantor's spouse.

Section 674 is perhaps the most complex of the grantor trust provisions. Generally speaking, this section treats a grantor as the owner of property if, after the initial transfer of the property to a trust, the grantor or her spouse retains the right to change the mix of income received by the trust beneficiaries or to add certain new beneficiaries. §674(a). However, a grantor may escape taxation by vesting such power in an independent trustee. §674(c). An independent trustee is defined, generally, as anyone other than a close relative, employee, or close business relation. §672(c). Thus, a grantor will not be taxed on trust income merely because she gives an

---

6. As noted in the preceding text, §673 allows a grantor to retain a reversionary interest in trust property and escape tax on the income from such property, provided that at the time of the original transfer, the reversionary interest represents no more than 5 percent of the value of the property. Section 676(b) provides that the grantor may retain a power to revoke a transfer upon the occurrence of an event, provided that the event is sufficiently distant in the future so that the value of the certain exercise of that power, measured at the time of original transfer, does not exceed 5 percent of the value of the property.

independent trustee the power to change the distribution of income among beneficiaries. The same result obtains if such power is given to a non-independent trustee (other than a spouse), such as a sister, provided that such power is limited by a reasonably definite external standard. §674(d). One example of a reasonably definite external standard is an instruction to the trustee that funds are to be distributed in accordance with educational needs. Reg. §1.674(b)-1(b)(5)(i).

The grantor trust rules treat the grantor as the owner of property with respect to which she retains certain rights or powers. Similarly, a trustee is treated as the owner of trust property as she is given certain rights or powers with respect to the property. For example, suppose that Grandmother appoints her son, Sonny, as trustee of a trust set up for the benefit of her grandson. The trust instrument provides that Grandson is to receive all income but the trustee, Sonny, has the power to revoke the trust at will; upon revocation, title to the property is to vest in Sonny. Such trusts are often referred to as *Mallinckrodt trusts.* (Mallinckrodt was the taxpayer in an earlier case involving the taxation of such trusts. Mallinckrodt v. Nunan, 146 F.2d 1 (8th Cir. 1945).) Under §678, the trust income will be taxed to the trustee rather than the beneficiary.

Taxpayers with modest resources will find trusts a burdensome and expensive way of exercising control over property, the benefit of which they wish to go to their beneficiaries. This is particularly true with respect to small gifts given to minor children. Generally such taxpayers may instead rely upon the Uniform Transfers to Minors Act, variants of which have been enacted in nearly all states. That Act allows a donor who wishes to give property to a minor to appoint herself or a member of the minor's family as custodian of the property. The custodian is given discretion to use such property, or the income from such property, for the benefit of the minor. The minor receives any remaining property, or income from such property, when she attains the age of 21. The Service has ruled that, generally speaking, the income from the property will be taxed to the minor. However, if and to the extent the property is used to discharge a legal obligation to support the minor, income from the property will be taxed to the person with the support obligation. Rev. Rul. 59-357.

Parents sometimes open up savings accounts in their own name but as trustees for their children (or other individuals). For example, an account may be opened in the name of "Gary Metro as Trustee for Henry Metro." The treatment of such accounts depends on their status under state law. In many states, unless other steps have been taken to evidence a formal trust, the parent-depositor retains the authority to reclaim the funds. In that event, the depositor, rather than the named beneficiary, will be taxed on any interest income. Rev. Rul. 62-148. Savings account trusts that allow the depositor to reclaim funds are sometimes referred to as *Totten trusts.*

Examples

15. State whether retention of the following powers by the grantor will result in the grantor being taxed on the trust income.
    a. Reversion of the trust corpus to the grantor after 15 years. The value of the reversion at the time the property is transferred to the trust is 30 percent of the value of the property.
    b. The power to change the mix of income received by the trust beneficiaries.
    c. The power to switch trust investments.

16. Assume a grantor-appointed trustee is given the power to revoke the trust and return the trust corpus to the grantor. Does this power trigger grantor trust treatment?

17. Larry wants to set up a trust for the graduate school education of his children. Larry does not want to earmark any of the income for any particular child; instead he wants the income used as needed to provide educational support. How can Larry achieve his objective?

18. A non-grantor trust that gives a third party the right to revoke the trust and receive the trust corpus is called a *Mallinckrodt* trust. Is income from such a trust taxed to the grantor?

19. Sam is the grantor of trust X. The trust agreement of trust X provides that income from the trust is to be distributed to Sam's niece, Jill; however, Jill's father, Bill, is given the power to revoke the trust and take the trust income. Who is taxed on the trust income?

20. Nancy sets up a savings account for her minor daughter. The account is in the daughter's name, but Nancy retains the power to withdraw the funds and use them for her own benefit.
    a. Who is taxed on the annual income?
    b. What name is often used to describe this sort of trust?

Explanations

15. a. The grantor will be taxed on the trust income. The grantor's reversionary interest triggers grantor trust treatment where the reversionary interest, measured at the time of transfer, is worth more than 5 percent of the value of the property transferred. §673.
    b. The grantor will be taxed on the trust income. The grantor's retention of the power to change the income mix for the beneficiaries triggers grantor trust treatment. §674(a). However, if the

power to change the income mix is lodged in a person who is not subordinate to the grantor, the trust is not treated as a grantor trust. §674(c). In addition, a power vested in any trustee (whether or not subordinate), other than the grantor or the spouse of the grantor to apportion income within a class of beneficiaries, will not result in grantor trust treatment if the power to apportion is limited by a reasonably definite standard. §674(d).

c. In general, a grantor may appoint herself as trustee and control trust investments without triggering grantor trust treatment. However, a grantor will be held taxable on trust income if she retains administrative powers proscribed by §675, such as the power to borrow from the trust without giving the trust adequate interest or security. §675(2).

16. Yes. Generally, a power that a nonbeneficiary can exercise on behalf of the grantor is treated as a power retained by the grantor. §§672, 676(a). This rule is necessary to prevent grantors from appointing friends or relatives as trustees, and (through such trustees) retaining control over the trust corpus while at the same time escaping tax on trust income.

17. Larry should give the power to distribute income to someone he trusts, such as a close friend, with a stipulation that the funds be used for his children's education. If Larry himself retains the power to control beneficial enjoyment, he will be taxed on the trust income under §674. However, Larry will not be taxed on trust income if the power to control beneficial enjoyment is given to an independent trustee, that is, someone who is not a related party and who is not an employee or otherwise economically subordinate to Larry. §674(c). Larry will also escape grantor trust treatment if the power to control beneficial enjoyment is given to anyone but his spouse, provided that the exercise of that power is limited by a "reasonably definite external standard." §674(d). If Larry gives the power to a close friend, he is doubly secure against grantor trust treatment — he has given the power to an unrelated party and the power is subject to what is arguably a reasonably definite external standard.

18. No. Income from a Mallinckrodt trust is not taxed to the grantor; it is taxed to the third party who controls the trust. §678.

19. Bill. §678.

20. a. Nancy is taxed on the trust income.
    b. Such trusts are often referred to as "Totten" trusts.

E. FAMILY PARTNERSHIPS

Reading: §704(e).

By this time in the course, most students will have encountered one or two cases involving business operations or investments carried out by partnerships. For example, the real estate in Commissioner v. Tufts, 461 U.S. 300 (1983), was owned and managed by a partnership; Tufts was a partner in that partnership. A partnership is not a taxable entity; although a partnership is required to file tax returns, the partnership does not itself pay tax. Instead, the income or losses of a partnership are allocated to the partners, who report their share of partnership income or loss on their individual tax returns.

Many service businesses are carried out by partnerships. Most law firms are partnerships. (As an irrelevant aside, so are many rock bands.) Partners in a law firm often are paid no formal salary but instead split the year's profits under some previously agreed upon formula. Suppose a partner in a law firm gives one-half of her partnership interest to her 25-year-old daughter. If the gift were respected for tax purposes, then, under the normal rules of partnership tax, one-half of the income attributable to that interest would be taxed to the daughter. The partner would thus be able to shift one-half of her service income — something she could not do if she realized the income as a salaried employee.

In a series of influential early cases, the Supreme Court developed various standards designed to prevent this sort of income shifting. Under those standards, whether a gift of a partnership interest to a family member succeeded in shifting partnership income to that family member depended on a number of factors, most notably the services or oversight provided by the donee.

Notwithstanding certain ambiguities, the standards generally produced sensible results in cases involving the transfer of interests in service partnerships to family members. The standards would not, for example, respect the transfer of the law firm partnership interest described above. Instead, the lawyer-donor would be taxed as before on the income attributable to her entire interest, including that portion of the interest ostensibly transferred to her daughter.

Suppose, however, the lawyer-parent described above owned a one-half interest in a partnership that itself owned an apartment building, and that the parent provided no services to the partnership. Income from this form of partnership is attributable to capital rather than services. We saw earlier that a parent can shift income from capital simply by making a gift of the income-producing capital. For example, a parent who owns an interest in an apartment building can shift income from that interest by giving away the building. The interposition of a partnership between the parent and the apartment building should not change this result. A parent who owns an interest in a partnership that owns an apartment building should be able to shift income from her partnership interest by giving away that interest. Since the income in question is attributable to capital, rather than services, the fact that the donee performs no services to the partnership should be irrelevant. The parent-donor performed no services, either! Unfortunately, the standards set forth in early cases seemed to apply to all forms of partnerships. Those cases suggested that transfer of a partnership interest did not shift the income from that interest even if the partnership held significant assets, and the transferor himself performed no services to the partnership.

To avoid this latter construction, Congress passed §704(e), which provides that a transfer of partnership interest to a family member will be respected for tax purposes provided that capital (property) is a material income-producing factor in the partnership. Thus, just as the transfer of property to a low-bracket family member will shift income to that family member, so will the transfer of an interest in a partnership that holds property.

What about partnerships whose income is attributable to both capital and the donor's services? The general rule of §704(e) still applies, but under §704(e)(2) the donor is taxed on the share of partnership income that reflects the value of services rendered to the partnership by the donor. Section 704(e) applies only if and to the extent that the interest transferred to the family member is an interest in partnership capital, that is, an interest such that, upon liquidation of the partnership, the family member would receive some portion of the partnership assets.

Suppose that a transfer does not qualify for the safe harbor of §704(e) because capital is not a material income-producing factor in the partnership. In that case, the standards described at the beginning of this section still apply. As noted above, under those standards, the transfer is generally not respected unless the donee-transferee performs significant services for the partnership.

Examples

21. Donald is one of 10 partners in an advertising firm. The firm has a number of employees who are not partners. Substantially all of the firm's revenues are attributable to the efforts of its employees. The partnership agreement provides that all items of income and loss are to be divided equally among the partners. Donald gives his son one-half of his partnership interest on January 1, year one. The partnership reports $1 million of income in year one. Donald reports $50,000 of income from the partnership and his son reports the same amount. Each of the other nine partners report $100,000 of income. Is each of the following statements true or false?

    a. The transfer of the partnership interest and the allocation of income to Donald's son will be respected for tax purposes.

    b. The transfer will not qualify for the safe harbor provided by §704(e) because capital is not a material income-producing factor in the partnership.

    c. Donald will be taxed on $100,000 of income from the partnership.

22. Monica is a partner in a two-person accounting firm. The partners have agreed, in the partnership agreement, to share equally in all items of income and expense. On January 1, year one, Monica sells her entire partnership interest to her son for $1,000. The partnership earns $80,000 in year one. How much, if any, of the income will be attributed to Monica?

23. Sarah and David are partners in a clothing store. Neither Sarah nor David work in the store. The partnership agreement provides that profit and loss are to be shared equally between them. On January 1, year one, Sarah gives her daughter, Mary, her partnership interest. The partnership earns $100,000 in year one.

    a. Will the transfer of the partnership interest be respected for tax purposes? Will the gift be effective in shifting $50,000 of income to Mary?

    b. Suppose that Sarah and David both work in the store and that the fair market value of each of their services is $30,000 a year. Neither draws a salary. Discuss the income tax consequences of the transfer.

Explanations

21. Statement (a) is false and statements (b) and (c) are true. Section 704(e) provides a safe harbor for transfers of interests in a partnership in which capital is a material income-producing factor. The rationale for this provision is that, as we have seen earlier in this chapter, an individual can shift income from property by transferring ownership of that property. It seems logical, therefore, that a person can shift income from capital investments (or what amounts to the same thing, property) owned by a partnership by transferring her ownership interest in that partnership. This partnership earns its revenue from personal services rather than ownership of property. Thus, this transfer does not qualify for the safe harbor of §704(e).

    Transfers of partnership interests that do not qualify for the safe harbor are subject to the case law and administrative guidelines discussed in the text. In a case such as this one, where the transferee provides no services or management expertise, the putative transfer will be ignored for tax purposes, and the full income will be taxed to the transferor, Donald.

22. The safe harbor of §704(e) applies to sales of partnership interests in addition to donative transfers of those interests. As noted in the text and in the explanation of the previous example that safe harbor does not apply to partnerships in which capital is not a material income-producing factor. It seems clear from the facts that the income of this partnership is attributable to services and capital is not a material income-producing factor. This transfer will not qualify for the safe harbor of §704(e). Moreover, under the case law and administrative rulings, it is almost certain that the sale would be treated as a sham. Thus, Monica would be taxed on her full share of partnership profits.

    Note: It is not obvious how the $1,000 payment will be treated. It may be most equitable to simply ignore the payment for tax purposes on the assumption that the sum will be returned to the son.

23. a. Capital is a material income-producing factor in this partnership. As a result, under §704(e)(1) the transfer of the partnership interest will be effective for tax purposes. Here, Mary, the donee, will be taxed on $50,000 of income.

    b. A significant portion of the income of the store is attributable to capital, so capital is a material income-producing factor in this partnership. As noted above, to be consistent with common law rules on income shifting, the law should allow Sarah to shift this income by transferring her interest in the partnership. Here, however, some of the partnership income is attributable to the personal services Sarah rendered to the partnership. It would be inconsistent with other areas of the tax law to allow Sarah to shift this form of income. The value of Sarah's services is $30,000 a year. Section 704(e) provides that where capital is a material income-producing factor, the donee of a partnership interest is allocated all income attributable to that interest except to the extent that such income is determined without allowance of reasonable compensation for the donor's services. Here, that section requires Sarah to include $30,000 of income attributable to services in her income; Mary will be taxed on the remaining $20,000 of income from the partnership.

F. BELOW-MARKET LOANS

Reading: §7872.

For many years, high-bracket taxpayers with excess cash were urged by their tax advisors to make short-term, no-interest loans to low-bracket family members. Investment income attributable to the cash loaned would then be realized by the low-bracket family members and taxed to those family members. Section 7872 now severely limits this form of income shifting.

Section 7872 applies not only to the type of "gift" loan described above (from one family member to another), but also to no-interest (or low-interest) loans from corporations to shareholders and from employers to employees. We focus here on the application of §7872 to gift loans and, even with that limited focus, ignore some of the complexities of the statute.

Section 7872 applies to a loan if (i) the loan is a *below-market loan*, (ii) the loan is one of the types of loans within the scope of §7872(c), and (iii) none of the exceptions to §7872 apply. §7872(c), (e)(1). In general, a loan is a below-market loan if it is interest-free or provides for interest at a rate that is less than *the Applicable Federal Rate* (AFR). The AFR is an interest rate that is set monthly by the Service pursuant to §1274(d) and is based on prevailing interest rates for U.S. government bonds. Under §1274(d), there are different AFRs for short-term loans (with a term of up to three years), mid-term loans (with a term of over three years up to nine years) and long-term loans (with a term of over nine years). If a loan is a *demand loan* (that is, a loan payable in full upon demand of the lender), the short-term AFR applies. If the loan is a *term loan* (that is, a loan that is not a demand loan), the appropriate AFR (short-term, mid-term, or long-term) depends on the term of the loan. §7872(f)(2).

If the loan is a below-market loan, the next step is to determine whether it is one of the types of loans subject to §7872. Below-market gift loans are within the scope of §7872. §7872(c)(1)(A).

If the loan is a below-market loan, and is one of the types of loans listed in §7872(c), the loan is subject to §7872 unless one of a number of exceptions apply. In the case of a gift loan, a relevant exception might be §7872(c)(2), which excludes from the ambit of §7872 gift loans of up to $10,000 between individuals.

Assume a particular gift loan is covered by §7872. In that event, the statute subjects the loan to three fictions. The first fiction is that the loan bears a market rate of interest. §7872(e)(2). The second fiction (referred to as the "deemed transfer") is that the lender gives the borrower sufficient funds to enable the borrower to pay the lender the market rate of interest. §7872(a)(1)(A). The third fiction (referred to as the "deemed retransfer") is that the borrower pays the lender a market rate of interest on the loan. §7872(a)(1)(B). The deemed transfer from the lender to the borrower and the deemed retransfer from the borrower to the lender both occur on the last day of the calendar year. §7872(a)(2). The net effect is to leave the high-bracket lender with interest income and, depending on the nature of the borrower's investment, to possibly give the low-bracket borrower a corresponding interest deduction.

An example may be helpful here. Wealthy attorney Amy loans her 26-year-old son, Bob, $200,000 on January 1 of year one. The loan is interest-free and must be repaid in two years. Assume that the AFR for such a short-term loan on that date is 10 percent, compounding semiannually.

Amy is in the 40 percent income tax bracket; Bob is in the 15 percent income tax bracket. Bob invests the $200,000 in bonds that pay annual interest income of $22,000. Absent §7872, all of the $22,000 would be taxed at Bob's low marginal rate. Amy would pay no tax on the transaction.

Under §7872, the $200,000 loan will be treated as a loan bearing interest at the AFR of 10 percent, compounding semiannually. The annual interest on the loan is $20,500, which is the sum of $10,000 of interest (5 percent of $200,000) for the first six months of the year plus $10,500 of interest (5 percent of $210,000) for the second six months of the year. At the end of years one and two, the $20,500 of annual forgone interest on the loan is deemed transferred, as a gift, from Amy to Bob, and is then deemed retransferred, as an interest payment, from Bob to Amy. The deemed transfer does not have any income tax consequences here because donors do not deduct gifts and donees do not include gifts in income. §102. However, Amy will have to include $20,500 of interest income as a result of the deemed retransfer. That amount will be taxed at her 40 percent rate. Bob will be able to deduct the $20,500 of interest deemed retransferred to Amy, subject to the restrictions on "investment interest" discussed earlier in Chapter 5. The net result is that Amy will have to include most of the income she would have included had she made the investment in the bonds herself. Thus, §7872, to some extent, prevents taxpayers from using interest-free loans to shift income. A taxpayer who makes an interest-free loan is taxed on the forgone interest (at the AFR) on that loan. The lender's imputed interest inclusion may be more or less than the actual income earned by the borrower on the loan principal.

Examples

24. Ed lends his daughter, Sandy, $150,000 on January 1, year one. The loan has a two-year term and is interest-free. Sandy invests the $150,000 and earns $15,000 of interest in year one. The AFR is 10 percent compounding semiannually. How are Ed and Sandy taxed in year one?

25. Wendy lends her sister Zelda $150,000 on January 1, year one. The loan has a two-year term and is interest-free. Zelda uses the proceeds to speculate in commodities and earns $1.5 million in year one. The AFR is 10 percent compounding semiannually. How are Wendy and Zelda taxed in year one?

26. A carved-out interest can be thought of as a short-term no-interest loan of income-producing property. Are gifts of no-interest cash loans treated like gifts of carved-out interests?

27. A gift between individuals of an interest-free loan with an outstanding balance of less than $20,000 is not subject to the rules of §7872. True or false?

Explanations

24. This term loan is a below-market loan because it is interest-free. It appears to be a gift loan, so it is subject to §7872. The income tax consequences of the loan are determined under §7872(a). Ed and Sandy are treated as if (i) Ed had loaned the money to Sandy at the AFR of 10 percent compounding semiannually; (ii) Ed had given Sandy enough extra money to pay that market rate of interest; and (iii) Sandy had then used that money to pay Ed interest at the market rate. On the deemed transfer, which is treated as a gift, Ed receives no deduction and Sandy has no inclusion. §102. The deemed retransfer is treated as an interest payment made by Sandy to Ed. The amount of the deemed transfer and retransfer is the amount of forgone interest for the year, computed at the AFR. Here, the forgone interest is $15,375, which is the sum of $7,500 (5 percent of $150,000) in the first six months of year one plus $7,875 (5 percent of $157,500 in the second six months of year one). (Note that §7872(d)(1) does not apply because the loan exceeds $100,000. If the amount loaned were $ 100,000 or less, the amount of the deemed transfer generally would be limited to the borrower's net investment income.)

    On the deemed retransfer: (i) Ed must include $15,375 of constructively received interest and (ii) Sandy has $15,375 of interest expense. Under §163(d), she will be able to deduct only $15,000 of that interest expense. Sandy is then taxed on her investment earnings — here also $15,000. The net result is that in year one Sandy breaks even for tax purposes on the transaction, but Ed is taxed on $15,375.

25. The analysis and calculations are the same as in the explanation of the previous example, except that Zelda has much larger investment income: Wendy is treated as if she had loaned the money to Zelda at the AFR of 10 percent compounding semiannually. Wendy receives no deduction for the deemed transfer and is taxed on $15,375 of interest income from the deemed retransfer. Zelda has no inclusion from the deemed transfer, which is a gift, and may deduct the $15,375 of interest deemed retransferred to Wendy. Zelda is taxed on her investment earnings — here $1.5 million.

26. Almost but not quite. A taxpayer who makes a gift of a carved-out property interest is taxed on all income from that interest. A taxpayer who makes an interest-free loan of cash is taxed on the imputed interest (at the AFR) on that loan. The imputed interest taxed to the donor may be higher or lower than the actual income earned by the donee on the investment made with the borrowed cash.

27. False. The threshold amount is $10,000, and the exception for no-interest loans of $10,000 or less does not apply if the loan proceeds are invested in income-producing assets. §7872(c)(2)(B).

441

Capital Gains and Losses

A. THE TAX TREATMENT OF CAPITAL GAINS AND LOSSES

Reading: §§1(h), 1201, 1202, 1211, 1212, 1222.

Historically, capital gain has been taxed at lower rates than so-called ordinary income (income other than capital gain). Today the maximum marginal rates on capital gains recognized by individuals, estates, and trusts are significantly lower than the maximum marginal rate on ordinary income. §1(h). However, capital gain recognized by corporations does not receive favorable treatment. §1201(a).

The flip side of favorable treatment for capital gains is unfavorable treatment of capital losses. Both corporate and noncorporate taxpayers can deduct the capital losses they recognize during a given year to the extent of the capital gains they recognize during that year. §1211. Corporate taxpayers are not allowed to deduct their capital losses in excess of their capital gains. §1211(a). However, they may carry the excess capital loss back three years and forward five years. §1212(a)(1). Noncorporate taxpayers are allowed to deduct up to $3,000 of their capital losses in excess of their capital gains in a given year and carry forward indefinitely the excess capital losses disallowed. §§1211(b), 1212(b)(1). However, if the capital loss is large, the $3,000 a year allowance may seem paltry. For example, if a taxpayer recognizes a $900,000 capital loss and no capital gain in the current or future years, §1211 allows the taxpayer to deduct the entire $900,000, but only at a rate of $3,000 a year — at that rate, it would take 300 years for the taxpayer to deduct the full $900,000!

The Code draws a distinction between long-term and short-term capital gain; long-term capital gain is taxed at the §1(h) preferential rates, but short-term capital gain is taxed at ordinary income rates. Capital gain (or loss) is long-term if the taxpayer held the capital asset for more than one year and short-term if the taxpayer held the capital asset for a year or less. §1222(1)–(4). Both short-term and long-term capital losses are subject to the §1211 limitation described above.

The current §1(h) capital gain rules are inordinately complex as a result of a whole series of amendments, which began with a substantial revision of the §1(h) rules in 1997 and have continued to the present. (We have simplified the mechanics of the rules in order to make the following discussion comprehensible.) In fact, these capital gain rules are so complex that commentators, tax lawyers, and members of Congress have called for simplification of the rules.

Prior to the 1997 amendment, long-term capital gain was taxed at a 28 percent rate if the taxpayer's marginal ordinary income rate was higher. The 1997 Act amendments replaced the single 28 percent rate with a variety of long-term capital gain rates.

Capital gains are grouped into three categories: (i) the 28 percent group; (ii) the 25 percent group; and (iii) the other gain group. Long-term capital gain in the 28 percent group is taxed at the lower of 28 percent or the taxpayer's marginal ordinary income rate. §1(h)(1). The 28 percent group includes (i) capital gain from the sale or exchange of "collectibles," and (ii) in some cases, a portion of the capital gain on the sale of "§1202 stock." §§1(h)(4), (5), (7), 1202(a)(1), (b). Collectibles include artwork, antiques, rugs, gems, metal, stamps, wines, and coins. §§1(h)(5)(A), 408(m).

Section 1202(a)(1) provides that a taxpayer can exclude from income 50 percent of the gain from the sale or exchange of "qualified small business stock" held by the taxpayer for more than five years. The §1202(a)(1) exclusion percentage is increased from 50 percent to (i) 75 percent if the taxpayer acquired the qualified small business stock in the period from February 18, 2009 through September 27, 2010; and (ii) 100 percent if the taxpayer acquired the qualified small business stock in the period from September 28, 2010 through December 31, 2013. §1202(a)(3), (4), Creating Small Business Act of 2010, P.L. 111-240 §2011(b)(2), 2012 TRA, P.L. 112-240 §324(a). Qualified small business stock is defined as stock: (i) issued by a domestic "C" corporation with assets of $50 million or less (although stock of corporations engaged in certain types of businesses, such as law, accounting, health, consulting, athletics, brokerage services, mining, banking, and farming, does not qualify); and (ii) acquired by the taxpayer (or a person who transfers the stock to the taxpayer by gift, bequest, or in a tax-free exchange) when the stock originally was issued. (Qualified small business stock is sometimes referred to as "founders' stock.") §1202(c)–(f), (h). The amount of §1202 gain to which the §1202(a)(1) exclusion applies may be limited by §1202(b), however. In that case, the amount of gain to which the §1202(a)(1) exclusion applies less the excluded amount is in the 28 percent group, and the taxable portion of the gain to which the §1202(b) limitation applies is in the other gain group. §1(h)(4), (7).

Here is an example. Sullivan realizes $300,000 of gain in 2013 from the sale of §1202 qualified small business stock that he acquired in 2008. Assume that the §1202(b) limitation prevents Sullivan from applying the §1202(a)(1) exclusion to $60,000 of the gain, but Sullivan can apply the exclusion to $240,000 of the gain; he can exclude $120,000 of the gain (50 percent of $240,000). (The §1201(a)(4) 100 percent exclusion does not apply in this example because §1201(a)(4) applies to qualified small business stock that was *acquired* by the taxpayer in 2013, not sold in 2013. The §1202(a)(1) 50 percent exclusion applies because Sullivan acquired the stock in 2008.) Sullivan includes $180,000 of gain from the sale of the §1202 stock. Of that amount, $120,000 (the taxable portion of the gain equal to the amount excluded) is in the 28 percent group. The remaining $60,000 of gain is in the other gain group. (If, instead, Sullivan had acquired the stock in 2011, he would have been able to exclude 100 percent of the gain on the sale of the stock.)

Long-term capital gain in the 25 percent group is taxed at the lower of 25 percent or the taxpayer's marginal ordinary income rate. §1(h)(1). In order to explain the type of gain that is in this category, we must first mention §1231. Later in this chapter we will discuss §1231 and the special rules applicable to gain from the sale or exchange of depreciable property. For purposes of this capital gains discussion, you need to know that gain from the sale of depreciable real property can be characterized as capital gain. Long-term capital gain from the sale of depreciable real property held for more than one year is in the 25 percent category to the extent that the capital gain is attributable to *unrecaptured depreciation*, which is the straight line depreciation that the taxpayer has taken on the real property. §1250.

The tax rate on long-term capital gain in the other gain group (also called *adjusted net capital gain*) varies with the taxpayer's marginal ordinary income tax rate. The capital gain rate on this type of gain is: (1) 20 percent if the taxpayer's marginal ordinary income rate is 39.6; (2) 15 percent, if the taxpayer's marginal ordinary income rate is at least 25 but less than 39.6 percent; or (3) zero percent, if the taxpayer's marginal ordinary income rate is less than 25 percent. Gain in the other gain group includes (i) any long-term capital gain that is not in the 28 percent group or the 25 percent group and (ii) qualified dividend income. §1(h)(3). (A dividend received by the taxpayer is a qualified dividend if the taxpayer can satisfy a holding period requirement for the stock on which the dividend is paid.[1]) Although dividend income is ordinary income, not capital gain, dividend income is taxed at the preferential capital gain rates by including the dividend income in the other gain group under §1(h)(3).

Recall that all capital losses are subject to the §1211 limitation described above. What happens if in a single tax year a taxpayer recognizes both capital gains and losses? The taxpayer must net the capital gains and losses as provided in §1222. There are a number of steps in the netting process. First, the taxpayer's capital gains and losses are divided into four categories: (1) short-term capital gain and loss; (2) capital gain and loss in the 28 percent group; (3) capital gain in the 25 percent group; and (4) capital gain and loss in the other gain group.

Second, the taxpayer computes her *net short-term capital gain* or *loss* by netting her short-term capital gains and losses.

Third, the taxpayer computes her *net long-term capital gain* or *loss*. The taxpayer nets the gains and losses within the 28 percent group and the other gain group (the 25 percent group will only have gain in it), then nets the gains and losses in the 28 percent, 25 percent, and other gain groups. (Long-term capital loss carryovers from other tax years are netted in the 28 percent group. Notice 97-59.) If there is a net loss in the 28 percent group, that loss is applied first to reduce any gain in the 25 percent group, then to reduce any net gain in the other gain group. If there is a net loss in the other gain group, that loss is applied first to reduce any net gain in the 28 percent group, then to reduce any gain in the 25 percent group. Notice 97-59.

If, after that netting process, the taxpayer has both a net long-term gain and a net short-term gain, or both a net long-term loss and a net short-term loss, the results are straightforward. In the case of two net gains, the taxpayer has a *net capital gain* in an amount equal to the net long-term capital gain, which is taxed at the capital gain rates specified in §1(h). §1222(11). The short-term gain is taxed at ordinary income rates. In the case of two net losses, a non-corporate taxpayer can deduct up to $3,000 of the excess losses (losses in excess of gains) in the current year. §1211. Any remaining loss, referred to as a *net capital loss*, is carried forward to subsequent years, with the character of its short-term and long-term components preserved. §§1212(b)(1), 1222(10). (The §1211 deduction is applied first to reduce short-term capital losses, then to reduce long-term capital losses. Reg. §1.1212-1(b)(2)(ii).)

If, after the initial netting process, the taxpayer has a net long-term gain and a net short-term loss, or a net short-term gain and a net long-term loss, additional computations are required. In either case, the taxpayer must net the gain and the loss. If the taxpayer's net long-term gain exceeds the

---

1. A dividend is not a qualified dividend if the taxpayer held the stock on which the dividend is paid for 60 days or less during the 121-day period beginning on the date that is 60 days before the stock becomes ex-dividend. §§1(h)(11)(B)(iii), 246(c)(1).

taxpayer's net short-term loss, the taxpayer has a *net capital gain*, which is taxed at the capital gain rates specified in §1(h). (The net short-term loss is applied first to reduce any net long-term gain in the 28 percent group, then to reduce any long-term gain in the 25 percent group, and finally to reduce any net long-term gain in the other gain group.) If, instead, the taxpayer's short-term gain exceeds the long-term loss, the resulting excess gain is a short-term capital gain and is taxed at the ordinary income rates.

Alternatively, if the short-term loss exceeds the long-term gain, or if the long-term loss exceeds the short-term gain, a non-corporate taxpayer may deduct up to $3,000 of this excess loss in the current year under §1211. The remaining net capital loss is carried forward, with its character as short-term or long-term preserved. §1212(b)(1).

The following example may help to illustrate the netting system. Taxpayer Dale's marginal ordinary income rate is 39.6 percent. In 2013 Dale recognizes the following capital gains and losses: (i) $90,000 of capital gain from the sale of land held for 22 months; (ii) $25,000 of capital gain from the sale of an antique dresser held for 10 years; (iii) $30,000 of capital gain from the sale of §1202 stock held for six years (all of which qualifies for the 50 percent §1202(a)(1) exclusion); (iv) $50,000 of capital gain from the sale of depreciable real property held for seven years, $40,000 of which is attributable to depreciation deductions the taxpayer took on the property; (v) $80,000 of capital loss from the sale of DEF Co. stock held for 10 months; and (vi) $60,000 of capital gain from the sale of XYZ Co. stock held for one week. Dale also has a $90,000 long-term capital loss carryover.

Dale's 2013 capital gains and losses are divided into the following four categories: (i) short-term capital gains and losses; (ii) long-term capital gains and losses in the 28 percent group; (iii) long-term capital gains in the 25 percent group; and (iv) long-term capital gains and losses in the other gain group.

Short-term capital gains and losses include gains and losses from the sale or exchange of capital assets held for a year or less. The short-term capital gain and loss category includes (i) the $80,000 capital loss on the sale of the DEF Co. stock, and (ii) the $60,000 capital gain on the sale of the XYZ Co. stock.

The 28 percent group includes (i) the $90,000 long-term capital loss carryover; (ii) the $25,000 capital gain from the sale of the antique dresser, which is a collectible; and (iii) $15,000 of the capital gain from the sale of the §1202 stock.

The 25 percent group includes the $40,000 of unrecaptured depreciation from the depreciable real property.

The other gain group includes (i) the $90,000 of capital gain from the sale of the land and (ii) $10,000 of the $50,000 of capital gain from the sale of the depreciable real property.

Dale nets her short-term capital gains and losses to compute her net short-term capital gain or loss, which produces a $20,000 net short-term capital loss ($80,000 short-term capital loss less $60,000 short-term capital gain).

Dale then computes her net long-term capital gain or loss. She first nets the long-term capital gains and losses within each group, which produces the following net gains and losses: (i) a $50,000 net loss in the 28 percent group ($90,000 loss carryover less $40,000, which is the sum of the $25,000 collectibles gain and the $15,000 §1202 gain); (ii) a $40,000 gain in the 25 percent group; and (iii) a $100,000 net gain in the other gain group (the $90,000 gain from the sale of the land plus $10,000 of the gain from the sale of the depreciable real property). The next step is to net the gains and losses in the three categories. The $50,000 net loss in the 28 percent group is applied first to reduce the $40,000 gain in the 25 percent group to zero. The remaining $10,000 of net loss in the 28 percent group is then applied to reduce the net gain in the other gain group from $100,000 to $90,000.

Dale then nets the $90,000 net long-term capital gain and the $20,000 net short-term capital loss, which yields a net capital gain of $70,000. That $70,000 net capital gain is taxed at a 20 percent rate since (i) the net capital gain is in the other gain group, and (ii) Dale's marginal ordinary income rate is 39.6 percent.

Now suppose, instead, that Dale recognizes a $180,000 loss on the sale of the DEF Co. stock. Dale's net short-term capital loss is $120,000 ($180,000 short-term capital loss less $60,000 short-term capital gain) and her $120,000 net short-term capital loss exceeds her $90,000 net long-term capital gain by $30,000. She has a net loss of $30,000, which is subject to the §1211 loss limitations discussed earlier.

Consider another example, which illustrates the operation of §1(h) where the taxpayer's marginal ordinary income rate is less than the otherwise applicable capital gain rate. Assume that the following ordinary income rate schedule (which is a fictitious, simplified version of the real §1 rate schedule) applies to unmarried individuals:

If taxable income is:	The tax is:
Not over $10,000	10 percent of taxable income
Over $10,000	$1,000 (10 percent of $10,000) plus 15 percent of the excess over $10,000
Over $50,000	$7,000 ($1,000 plus $6,000, which is 15 percent of the $40,000 of taxable income between $10,000 and $50,000) plus 30 percent of the excess over $50,000
Over $400,000	$112,000 ($7,000 plus $105,000, which is 30 percent of the $350,000 of taxable income between $50,000 and $400,000) plus 40 percent of the excess over $400,000

Taxpayer Evan earns $15,000 a year of salary from his job as a gardener. Evan recognizes $500,000 of long-term capital gain from the sale of an antique he has owned for 25 years. The gain from the sale of the antique is in the 28 percent group because the antique is a collectible. The first $10,000 of Evan's ordinary income is in the 10 percent ordinary income rate bracket, and the next $5,000 of Evan's ordinary income is in the 15 percent ordinary income rate bracket, so $35,000 of Evan's capital gain will be taxed at the 15 percent rate, completely filling the 15 percent rate bracket. (The 15 percent rate bracket applies to the $40,000 of income between $10,000 and $50,000. Evan fills the 15 percent rate bracket with $5,000 of his ordinary income and $35,000 of his capital gain.) But for the preferential capital gain rate, the tax rate applicable to $350,000 of the remaining $465,000 of Evan's gain (the $350,000 between $50,000 and $400,000) would be 30 percent, and the tax rate on the last $115,000 of Evan's capital gain would be 40 percent. Both the 30 percent ordinary income rate and the 40 percent ordinary income rate exceed the 28 percent long-term capital gain rate applicable to gain from the sale of collectibles, however. Thus the remaining $465,000 of Evan's capital gain is taxed at a 28 percent rate. (If a taxpayer has long-term capital gain in more than one capital gain group, the capital gain is applied to the unused portion of the ordinary income bracket in the following order: (i) capital gain in the 25 percent group; (ii) capital gain in the 28 percent group; and (iii) capital gain in the other gain group.)

Examples

In examples 1 and 2, assume that the following ordinary income rate schedule (which is a fictitious, simplified version of the real §1 rate schedule) applies to unmarried individuals:

If taxable income is:	The tax is:
Not over $10,000	10 percent of taxable income
Over $10,000	$1,000 (10 percent of $10,000) plus 15 percent of the excess over $10,000
Over $50,000	$7,000 ($1,000 plus $6,000, which is 15 percent of the $40,000 of taxable income between $10,000 and $50,000) plus 30 percent of the excess over $50,000
Over $400,000	$112,000 ($7,000 plus $105,000, which is 30 percent of the $350,000 of taxable income between $50,000 and $400,000) plus 40 percent of the excess over $400,000

1. a. Liz earns $150,000 a year from her job. Liz recognizes the following capital gains and losses during the year: (i) $90,000 of capital gain from the sale of land held for three years; (ii) $30,000 of capital gain from the sale of stamps held for two years; (iii) $30,000 of capital gain from the sale of depreciable real property held for three years, $20,000 of which is attributable to depreciation deductions Liz took on the property; (iv) $10,000 of capital gain from the sale of ABC Co. stock held for 20 months; (v) $70,000 of capital loss from the sale of DEF Co. stock held for 10 months; and (vi) $50,000 of capital gain from the sale of XYZ Co. stock held for three days. Liz also has a $100,000 long-term capital loss carryover. Explain the tax treatment of her capital gains and losses.

   b. Assume the same facts as in part (a), except that Liz recognizes a $200,000 loss on the sale of the DEF Co. stock.

2. a. Novelist John earns $12,000 during the year from book royalties. He also recognizes $20,000 of capital gain from the sale of depreciable real property he held for four years. All of that $20,000 gain is attributable to straight line depreciation deductions John has taken on the property. Explain the tax treatment of John's capital gain.

   b. Assume the same facts as in part (a), except that John receives $20,000 of qualified dividend income instead of $20,000 of capital gain.

Explanations

1. a. Liz's capital gains and losses are divided into the following four categories: (i) short-term capital gains and losses; (ii) long-term capital gains and losses in the 28 percent group; (iii) long-term capital gains in the 25 percent group; and (iv) long-term capital gains and losses in the other gain group.

      Short-term capital gains and losses include gains and losses from the sale or exchange of capital assets held for a year or less. The short-term capital gain and loss category includes (i) the $70,000 capital loss on the sale of the DEF Co. stock, and (ii) the $50,000 capital gain on the sale of the XYZ Co. stock.

      The 28 percent group includes (i) the $100,000 long-term capital loss carryover and (ii) the $30,000 capital gain from the sale of the stamps, which are collectibles.

      The 25 percent group includes the $20,000 of unrecaptured depreciation from the sale of the real property.

      The other gain group includes (i) the $90,000 of capital gain from the sale of the land, (ii) $10,000 of the $30,000 of capital gain from the sale of the depreciable real property, and (iii) the $10,000 of capital gain from the sale of the ABC Co. stock.

Liz nets her short-term capital gains and losses to compute her net short-term capital gain or loss, which produces a $20,000 net short-term capital loss ($70,000 short-term capital loss less $50,000 short-term capital gain).

Liz then computes her net long-term capital gain or loss. She first nets the long-term capital gains and losses within each group, which produces the following net gains and losses: (i) a $70,000 net loss in the 28 percent group ($100,000 loss carryover less the $30,000 collectibles gain); (ii) a $20,000 gain in the 25 percent group; and (iii) a $110,000 net gain in the other gain group ($90,000 gain from the sale of the land, plus $10,000 gain from the sale of the depreciable real property, plus $10,000 gain from the sale of the ABC Co. stock).

The next step is to net the gains and losses in the three categories. The $70,000 net loss in the 28 percent group is applied first to reduce the $20,000 gain in the 25 percent group to zero. The remaining $50,000 of net loss in the 28 percent group is then applied to reduce the net gain in the other gain group from $110,000 to $60,000.

Liz then nets the $60,000 net long-term capital gain and the $20,000 net short-term capital loss, which yields a net capital gain of $40,000. That $40,000 net capital gain is taxed at a 15 percent rate since (i) the $60,000 of net long-term capital gain is in the other gain group, and (ii) Liz's marginal ordinary income rate (30 percent) is at least 25 percent but less than 39.6 percent.

b. Liz's net short-term capital loss is $150,000 ($200,000 short-term capital loss less $50,000 short-term capital gain) and her $150,000 net short-term capital loss exceeds her $60,000 net long-term capital gain by $90,000, so she has a net capital loss of $90,000. The $90,000 net capital loss is subject to the §1211 loss limitations. Liz can deduct only $3,000 of the loss in the current year. The rest of the loss is carried forward.

2. a. There is $20,000 of unrecaptured depreciation on the sale of the depreciable real property. That $20,000 of gain is in the 25 percent group. However, John has only $2,000 of ordinary income in the 15 percent rate bracket ($10,000 of the ordinary income is in the 10 percent rate bracket and the remaining $2,000 of ordinary income is in the 15 percent rate bracket), so all of the $20,000 of John's capital gain is taxed at the 15 percent rate. (The 15 percent rate bracket applies to a maximum of $40,000 of income over $10,000. Here, there is $22,000 of income — $2,000 of ordinary income and $20,000 of capital gain — above $10,000, so all of the capital gain is taxed at a 15 percent rate.)

b. As in part (a), $10,000 of John's ordinary income is in the 10 percent rate bracket and $2,000 of his ordinary income is in the 15 percent

451

rate bracket. Although the $20,000 of qualified dividend income is technically ordinary income, it is treated like capital gain that is in the other gain group. §1(h)(3), (h)(11). The $20,000 of qualified dividend income is taxed at a zero percent rate because the dividend income is in the other gain group and John's marginal ordinary income tax rate is 15 percent (i.e., less than 25 percent).

B. POLICY RATIONALE FOR THE TREATMENT OF CAPITAL GAIN AND LOSS

Why have we historically taxed long-term capital gain at a preferential rate? Over the years, a number of arguments have been made to support the preferential capital gains rate. (A number of these arguments made more sense when the top marginal ordinary income rate was much higher than it is now.)

One argument in favor of the special capital gain rate is that capital gain should be taxed at a lower rate because the gain included in the year in which the asset is sold may throw the taxpayer into a higher tax bracket than the taxpayer would have been in had the gain been taxed over a number of years. However, most capital gain is realized by taxpayers who are already in the top rate bracket, without regard to their capital gain, and these taxpayers still benefit from the preferential capital gains rate. In addition, allowing income averaging would be a much more precise way to solve the bunching problem for taxpayers who are generally taxed at lower rates.

Capital gain proponents have also argued that capital gain should be taxed at a lower rate because the gain realized on the sale of a capital asset reflects both true economic gain from the asset, which should be taxed, and inflationary gain from the asset, which should not be taxed. Suppose, for example, that taxpayer Mike bought a share of BigCo stock in year one for $5,000. Fifty years later, Mike sold the share of stock for $205,000. For tax purposes, Mike has a $200,000 realized gain on the sale of the stock. Assume that $160,000 of that gain reflects true economic gain on the stock, but that the remaining $40,000 of gain is due to inflation (that is, because prices for goods have increased, a dollar buys less than it did 50 years earlier).

The argument is that it is unfair to tax Mike on the full $200,000 of realized gain at the normal tax rates, so we should allow Mike to pay a lower rate of tax on the gain. Extending this argument, the rate should then vary depending on how long the taxpayer held the asset and the inflation rate during the time the taxpayer held the asset. However, the rate applied to capital gain does not generally reflect the length of time the taxpayer held the property (other than the holding period distinction between short-term and long-term capital gain) and does not reflect the actual inflation rate during the time the asset was held. In other words, the current capital gain rules are a very gross way of solving the inflation problem. The problem could be solved more precisely by indexing the tax basis of assets to reflect inflation, then taxing gain from the sale of the assets at ordinary tax rates.

Capital gain proponents have also argued that capital gain should be taxed at a lower rate in order to mitigate the "lock-in" effect and improve the mobility of capital. The idea is that since taxpayers can defer the tax on gain until the gain is realized, they will refuse to sell assets that they would sell but for having to pay tax on the sale; this lock-in effect causes immobility of capital and inefficient uses of capital. The special capital gain rate may reduce the lock-in effect. However, it does not eliminate the lock-in effect because the realization requirement and §1014 (the stepped-up basis at death rule) both deter taxpayers from selling their assets. If we wanted to improve liquidity of investment assets, we could enact more liberal nonrecognition rules along the lines of §1031. However, the logical extension of taking this approach would be to replace the income tax with a consumption tax.

Another argument is that dividends and capital gain on the sale of stock should be taxed at lower rates because corporate earnings, unlike most other investments, are double-taxed; corporate income is taxed first at the corporate level and again at the shareholder level when the corporation pays shareholders dividends or shareholders sell appreciated stock. Many tax experts believe that corporate income should not be double-taxed, but completely eliminating the double tax would cost the government a large amount of revenue, so it is not politically viable. Taxing dividends and gain from the sale of stock at lower rates ameliorates the double tax. However, note that the double-tax argument is not applicable to the extent a corporation finances its operations with retained earnings or debt.

Capital gain proponents have also argued that the tax rate for capital gain should be lower than the ordinary rate in order to encourage saving and investment. In order to fund a reduction in rates for capital gain, the rate of tax on income from labor would be increased. The argument is that increased savings and investment would stimulate economic growth, and that the efficiency gains from reducing the rate of tax on investments would more than offset any reductions in efficiency that would result from taxing labor at a higher rate. There may be more precise solutions to this problem. In addition, converting consumption into savings, which shifts consumption to future generations, may deprive poor taxpayers of current consumption.

Capital gain proponents have also argued that the tax rate for capital gain should be lower than the ordinary rate in order to encourage investments in risky start-up businesses that may generate new jobs. If gains from those investments are not taxed at a more favorable rate, investors would require higher pre-tax returns on those investments. However, one might ask whether we should be encouraging businesses that would not survive

without special tax breaks. In addition, if we choose to encourage investment in new and risky businesses, we could tax favor those specific types of
investments instead of tax favoring all capital gain. We could also encourage
investment in risky new businesses by relaxing the §1211 limitation on
the utilization of capital losses.

If §1211 discourages investment in risky new businesses, why does the
section limit the deductibility of capital losses? The limitation is designed to
prevent taxpayers from manipulating the timing of capital gain and loss.
Absent such a limitation, a taxpayer with wage income of $100,000,
$100,000 of unrealized capital loss and $100,000 of unrealized capital
gain could sell the loss asset, eliminating his tax liability for the year in
spite of the fact that the taxpayer could defer the gain on the other capital
asset until the taxpayer decided to sell it in a later year. However, the loss
limitation applies even where such manipulation is impossible because the
taxpayer does not own any appreciated capital assets.

C. THE DEFINITION OF "CAPITAL ASSET"

Reading: §1221.

What is capital gain or loss? In common parlance, capital gain is used as a
synonym for gain on investment, as opposed to operating income from a
business, dividends, interest, or salary income. This simple (and simplistic)
definition will give the right answer most of the time, but ignores many
hard issues that arise in tax practice. As is obvious from the discussion below
and the cases assigned for your tax course, the definitional issues surrounding capital gain and loss are complex. Indeed, the distinction between capital
and ordinary gains and losses has historically been one of the most trou-
blesome, and hotly litigated, issues in tax law.

The Code defines capital gain or loss as gain or loss on the sale or
exchange of a "capital asset." Section 1221(a) defines the term *capital asset*
as "property" that does *not* fall within any of the following eight ordinary
asset categories:

1. inventory or property held for sale to customers in the ordinary
   course of business;
2. depreciable or real property used in the taxpayer's trade or business;
3. certain copyrights or literary, musical, or artistic properties;
4. accounts receivable or notes receivable acquired in the ordinary
   course of a trade or business;
5. certain United States government publications;
6. certain commodities derivative financial instruments held by a commodities derivative dealer;

7. hedging transactions that are identified as such in advance;
8. supplies of a type regularly used or consumed by the taxpayer in the ordinary course of business.

We will see that courts have limited the capital asset definition by reading these ordinary income asset categories in §1221 very broadly.

The first category of ordinary assets, listed in §1221(a)(1), consists of "stock in trade . . . or other property of a kind which would properly be included in . . . inventory . . . or property held by the taxpayer primarily for sale to customers in the ordinary course of his trade or business." (Whew!) This category encompasses the shoe store's shoes, the smoke shop's cigarettes, and the coffee shop's coffee. Profit from the sale of these items generates ordinary income, not capital gain.

In some cases, determining whether an item falls within §1221(a)(1) can be quite difficult. This difficulty is particularly evident with respect to real estate, where one can support oneself with just a few sales per year. Consider, for example, a teacher who, in an effort to supplement her income, buys a home on the outskirts of what she feels is a growing vacation area. During weekends she paints and does other minor repairs on the home. She neither uses nor rents out the home, but instead allows a college-age child of a close friend to live in the home on a month-to-month basis. She sells the home two years after purchase, and soon thereafter purchases another home in the same area and repeats the process. Over a 10-year period, she makes as much on her real estate activities as she does in salary from teaching. Is the teacher in the trade or business of buying, repairing, and selling old homes? Are the homes held for sale in the ordinary course of that business? If so, the homes are noncapital assets by virtue of §1221(a)(1) and gain on the sale is ordinary income rather than capital gain. Does the answer to these questions change if the teacher retires but continues her real estate activities as before, so that the profits from those activities constitute a predominant source of her income? If some of the homes the teacher purchases after retirement require structural repairs? If the teacher obtains a broker's license to facilitate her real estate activities? If the teacher employs or has long-term working relationships with architects, contractors, and painters?

The best the courts have been able to do with situations similar to this is to agree on a number of relevant factors and, based on those factors, to decide the issue on a case-by-case approach. Factors that point toward inclusion in §1221(a)(1) and hence ordinary income or loss treatment include (i) frequent or numerous sales, (ii) significant improvements, (iii) brokerage activities, (iv) advertising, (v) purchase and retention of the property with a goal to short-term resale, and (vi) the importance of the activity in relation to the taxpayer's other activities and sources of income. See, e.g., Biedenharn Realty Co. v. United States, 526 F.2d 409 (5th Cir. 1976) (ordinary income on the sale of farm property bought as an investment that was later subdivided and sold in lots). In the above example, the teacher's preretirement activities probably do not meet the "ordinary course of trade or business" standard of §1221(a)(1) and thus do not preclude capital asset status. But as the relative and absolute importance of the teacher's real estate activities grows after retirement, so does the likelihood the homes will be characterized as noncapital assets by virtue of §1221(a)(1).

One might expect that similar factors would be used to distinguish investment from business activity in stock and commodities so that an individual who spent all of his time and realized all of his income from "playing the market" would recognize ordinary income or loss from that activity. In an early case, however, one court held that individual stock trading, no matter how frequent or central to one's livelihood, did not generate ordinary income or loss. Van Suetendael v. Commissioner, 3 T.C.M. 987 (1944), aff'd, 152 F.2d 654 (2d Cir. 1945). The taxpayer in *Van Suetendael* recognized losses on stocks and bonds and treated the losses as ordinary, reasoning that the assets were noncapital under §1221(a)(1). The court held that the assets did not fit within the §1221(a)(1) category because the assets were not held primarily for sale to "customers," but were sold through brokers to unknown persons. The court thus held that the losses were capital.

The rationale articulated by the court is hard to swallow. In general, the fact that sales are made to regular clients or known parties is irrelevant for purposes of distinguishing between capital and ordinary assets. The holding of the case, however, is now established law. See, e.g., Swartz v. Commissioner, 876 F.2d 657 (8th Cir. 1989) (holding that securities were capital assets in the hands of a full-time commodities trader). Only securities sales conducted by entities such as commercial brokerages will meet the *Van Suetendael* standard and generate ordinary income and loss under §1221(a)(1).[2] The government's victory in *Van Suetendael* proved Pyrrhic. In the long run, due to inflation and other factors, stock held for investment is generally sold at a gain. The government savings from forcing taxpayers such as Van Suetendael to recognize capital loss on the sale of stock at a loss has been more than offset by the cost to the government of allowing more successful speculators to recognize capital gain when stock is sold at a profit.

One final issue deserves mention before leaving §1221(a)(1). Until 1999, the tax treatment of certain "hedging transactions" was determined by reference to §1221(a)(1). We'll first explain the §1221(a)(1) "inventory" issue that existed, prior to the amendment of §1221 in 1999, then explain the effect of the amendment. Taxpayers in some industries may experience considerable fluctuation in the cost of inventory or goods used to produce inventory. Such taxpayers may be

---

2. Under §1236, securities dealers can still avoid §1221(a)(1) characterization by segregating securities held for investment, as opposed to business, purposes.

able to hedge against the risk of a price increase in their raw materials, or hedge against certain other business risks, by buying futures on the commodities market. Are these and similar hedge-related investments capital assets, like investments in other securities? Or are these investments part of the cost of acquiring inventory, and excluded from capital asset treatment under §1221(a)(1)? Most taxpayers who purchase these sorts of hedges are corporations. Such taxpayers will generally prefer noncapital treatment since, as noted above, corporate taxpayers do not qualify for the capital gain preference and cannot deduct capital losses except to the extent of capital gains.

An example may help illuminate the issue. Agri Corp buys oats to process into animal feed. On July 1 oats are selling for $4 a bushel. At that price the company is able to make $1 for every bushel it purchases. To guard against the possibility of an increase in the price of oats, the company buys futures contracts that obligate it to take delivery of a given number of bushels of oats in September at a price of $4 a bushel. The price of a bushel of oats falls to $3 a bushel by September 1. If Agri Corp takes delivery of the oats it purchased in July, the oats cost $4 a bushel, so it will earn $1 a bushel from processing the oats into animal feed.

Suppose, however, that Agri Corp finds it somewhat more convenient not to take delivery of the oats but instead to "close out" its futures contracts by paying $1 for every bushel it would otherwise have the obligation to purchase. In effect, Agri Corp pays to be relieved of its obligation to purchase oats at a price that is higher than the current market price. This frees up the company to purchase oats at their current market price of $3. At that price the company makes $2 a bushel on the sale of animal feed. However, it loses $1 a bushel on the futures contracts.

Agri Corp earns a net profit of $1 a bushel, regardless of whether it takes delivery of the oats. If the company takes delivery of the oats, it obviously earns $1 a bushel of ordinary income. Assume the company does not take delivery of the oats. Must it recognize $2 a bushel ordinary income on the sale of oats and report the loss on the futures contract as a capital loss — deductible only against capital gain?

In a famous case arising out of a similar fact pattern, Corn Products Refining Co. v. Commissioner, 350 U.S. 46 (1955), the Supreme Court held that these sorts of hedge investments generate ordinary income or loss. In a more recent case, the Court restated *Corn Products* as standing for the following limited proposition: Net proceeds from hedging transactions that are an integral part of a business's inventory-purchase system are treated as proceeds from the sale of inventory and generate ordinary income or loss. Arkansas Best Corp. v. Commissioner, 485 U.S. 212(1988).

These days, the classification of hedging transactions as capital or noncapital is much clearer than it used to be. The Treasury issued final regulations in 1994 that enabled a taxpayer to characterize a hedging transaction as noncapital by electing noncapital treatment of the hedging transaction at the time the taxpayer entered into the hedge. Under those regulations, a taxpayer could generally ensure noncapital asset treatment of certain hedges entered into to reduce business risks. Such hedges included contracts entered into to reduce risk due to possible fluctuations in interest rates or currency exchange rates, or in the cost of supplies or inventory.

In 1999, Congress amended §1221 to specifically provide that certain hedging transactions, which are identified as such before being entered into, are noncapital assets. §1221(a)(7). The legislative history of this amendment indicates that Congress thought that business hedges that reduce risk or manage risk should qualify for noncapital treatment. The characterization of certain hedging transaction as noncapital requires that the property being hedged is noncapital property. Congress also amended §1221 in 1999 to make clear that supplies of a type regularly used or consumed by the taxpayer in the ordinary course of business are noncapital assets. §1221(a)(8). (Congress also specified in §1221(a)(6) that certain types of hedging transactions entered into by commodities derivatives dealers are also characterized as noncapital.)

An important statutory exclusion from the category of capital asset is found in §1221(a)(2), which encompasses real or depreciable property used in a trade or business. Such property is excluded from the class of capital assets under §1221(a)(2) only to be subject to a still more favorable set of rules under §1231. Generally speaking, property in this category has the happy quality of generating capital gain when sold at a profit and ordinary loss when sold at a loss. The definition and treatment of §1221(a)(2) property is discussed more fully, in connection with §1231, below.

The remaining statutory exceptions are less generally applicable. Section 1221(a)(3) provides that the term "capital asset" does not include "a copyright, a literary, musical, or artistic composition, a letter or memorandum, or similar property" if the asset is held by (i) the person who created the asset (or the person for whom a letter or memo was prepared), or (ii) a transferee of the asset, if the transferee's basis in the asset is determined by reference to the creator–transferor's basis. Under the first part of this rule, an artist's self-created copyrighted work is not a capital asset in the hands of the artist who created the work. If an artist makes a gift of a self-created copyrighted work, the asset is not a capital asset in the hands of the donee either, under the second part of this rule, because the donee's basis in the asset is determined by reference to the donor's basis, under §1015. If the same work is instead transferred at death and the beneficiary's basis is determined under §1014, the asset is not within §1221(a)(3) and is a capital asset in the hands of the beneficiary.

Section 1221(a)(4) excludes from capital asset status accounts or notes receivable and §1221(a)(5) prevents persons who receive United States government publications at a price less than charged to the public from claiming those publications as capital assets.[3]

Examples

3. Stan spends substantially all of his time buying and selling stocks, bonds, and other securities for his own account. He subscribes to scores of financial newspapers and magazines and has an online account with a national brokerage firm. At any given time, Stan may have well over $1 million invested in securities. Last year Stan earned $80,000 in interest from his securities and $250,000 in profit from the sale of securities. This year Stan has earned $75,000 from interest and dividends from his securities but has lost $150,000 on securities sales. Discuss the tax treatment of Stan's current income and losses.

4. Carl Conard owns 8,000 acres of land that is used primarily for raising beef and dairy cattle. Carl also sells a small amount of produce he grows on the land that is not used in his beef and dairy operations. Until year 10, Carl also owned approximately 200 acres of land in Sproutsville; the Sproutsville land was used in Carl's dairy operations. Sproutsville was for many years a small, rural town; its character and size changed, however, after the opening of a nearby auto plant in year one. During the next decade, residents of Sproutsville expressed increasing dissatisfaction at the noise and odor generated by the dairy operations.

    In year seven a motion to rezone the Sproutsville property to prohibit its then-present use was narrowly defeated. In year eight, after fighting to keep his Sproutsville operations intact for many years, Carl negotiated an agreement with local officials. Under that agreement, Carl discontinued dairy operations and gave 100 acres of his 200 acres of land to the City of Sproutsville. On the 100 acres it received, Sproutsville built roads, parks, and schools. The 100 acres that Carl kept were rezoned; 40 acres were zoned mixed residential and commercial, and the remaining 60 acres were zoned residential. Subdivision into one-acre parcels was allowed. In year 10 Carl sold all 60 acres zoned residential to a single developer for a profit of $1 million. In that same year Carl listed the remaining 40 acres with a local real estate broker. The acres were sold to 40 separate buyers over five years. Carl himself did no promotion or advertising for the parcels and did not improve the

---

3. Section 1221(a)(5) was adopted in response to reports that several legislators donated their free copies of the Congressional Record to libraries and took a charitable deduction equal to the value of the publications. As discussed in Chapter 4 of this book, taxpayers may claim a charitable deduction equal to fair market value only for capital assets. Otherwise, the charitable deduction is limited to the taxpayer's basis. Since the Congressional Record is received free of charge, the publication has no basis in the hands of legislators, and the donation of that publication would now generate no charitable deduction.

land by bringing in utility lines or building roads. Carl recognized $1.5 million of gain from these sales, which represented approximately 60 percent of Carl's income over the relevant five-year period. Carl had no other sales or exchanges during that five-year period.

What arguments might Carl make in favor of capital gain treatment of the $1.5 million profit? What arguments might the Service make in favor of ordinary income treatment?

5. Attorney Andy and his law partner, Perry, purchase a 64-unit apartment building for $3 million. Four years after the purchase, they convert the building to condominiums. The conversion requires $150,000 in improvements. The 64 units are listed with a broker and sell quickly. Each of the two partners realizes a net profit of $1 million on the investment. Neither partner has any other real estate investments or any other sales or exchanges in the year of sale. Discuss the likely tax positions of Andy and his partner, on the one hand, and the Service, on the other hand.

6. Your tax client, Gloria, is a highly successful architect. Gloria pays $1 million for a large, dilapidated, and nearly vacant office building located near the downtown area. Gloria's purchase was based on the assumption that the downtown area would expand and that, with some renovation, the building would become highly desirable. Unfortunately, in the year following the purchase, the downtown area shrinks and the assessed value of the building falls to $750,000. Gloria tells you that she is not sure what she should do with the property. She may carry out her envisioned but postponed renovations and then sell the building; or she may renovate and then rent the office space in the building. She has asked you to advise her as to the tax consequences of both an immediate sale and a future sale of the building. Apart from her home and assets in her pension fund, Gloria owns no other significant assets.

7. Information Inc. publishes a weekly newsmagazine and five daily newspapers. The company owns two large paper mills that it uses to process timber into paper for its magazine and newspapers. In order to guard against an increase in the price of timber, Information Inc. pays $7 million for 70 percent of the stock of Timber Company, a large timber producer. In fact, the price of timber does rise, and so does the price of newsprint. In theory Information Inc. could avoid the negative effect of the increase in the price of newsprint by using the timber it has already purchased through the acquisition of Timber Company. In practice, Information Inc. finds it more convenient and slightly more profitable to sell the Timber Company stock at a gain and then purchase newsprint from its regular supplier. Information Inc. sells the Timber Company stock for a profit of $3 million and

then pays an additional $2,950,000 for newsprint. The additional cost of newsprint reduces the company's operating income by $2,950,000. Is the stock of Timber Company a capital asset in the hands of Information Inc.?

8. Northern Company is a large shipping company that operates out of 50 ports throughout the world. The company's profits are extremely sensitive to the price of crude oil, which has fluctuated widely over the past two decades. In order to hedge against an increase in the price of fuel, on January 1, Northern Company enters into a contract on a commodities exchange pursuant to which it will take delivery of a certain quantity of crude oil, on July 1, at the January 1 crude oil price. Between January 1 and July 1, the price of oil falls rather than rises. In retrospect, the oil contract is a burden rather than a benefit to the company. In theory the company could take delivery of the fuel under the terms of the contract. If it does so, the cost of its oil would be $3 million more than it would have been had the company bought it at the July 1 price; this increased oil cost would reduce the company's income from operations to $7 million. In fact, the company finds it more convenient and profitable to pay to get out of the contract and purchase oil more cheaply on the open market. The company pays $3 million to get out of the contract and, due to its lower than expected cost of fuel, earns income from operations (other than the oil contract) of $10 million. Is the $3 million loss on the oil contract capital or ordinary?

Explanations

3. The $75,000 of interest and dividend income is ordinary, although some or all of the dividends may qualify to be taxed at preferential capital gain rates, as discussed earlier in this chapter. The $150,000 loss is capital. Stan might consider himself in the trade or business of buying and selling securities. It may seem natural to him to consider the securities a form of stock in trade or property held primarily for sale to customers in the course of business and to deduct the $150,000 loss on the sale of securities as an ordinary loss by virtue of §1221(a)(1). In an early case, however, courts held that securities bought and sold by individual investors did not fall within the inventory exclusion from capital asset status because they were not sold to "customers." Van Suetendael v. Commissioner, 3 T.C.M. 987 (1944), aff'd, 152 F.2d 654 (2d Cir. 1945). The reasoning of the court in that case (and other courts in similar cases) is questionable, but the holding is now firmly established: For all but a handful of taxpayers, securities are capital assets. Securities are a noncapital asset by virtue of §1221(a)(1) only for registered brokers (such as Morgan Stanley or Merrill Lynch) that have regular clientele. Brokers can avoid noncapital asset treatment on some or

all securities by so electing at the time of purchase and maintaining such securities in a segregated account. §1236.

4. The issue here is whether the land constitutes "property held . . . primarily for sale to customers in the ordinary course of his trade or business" and is therefore a noncapital asset by virtue of §1221(a)(1). Carl will argue that he acquired the land for use in his beef and dairy operations and that he held the land for that purpose for many years until shortly before the ultimate sale. Carl will point out that, apart from the land in question, he is clearly not in the real estate business, that over the years he has earned most of his income from his beef and dairy operations, and that neither he nor any of his employees improved the land or engaged in any sales efforts. Carl would then treat the property as section 1231 property (real property held in a trade or business). As discussed in the next part of this chapter, net gain on section 1231 property is capital gain.

The Service may argue that the sheer number of sales, the absolute amount of gain recognized on the sales, and the relative importance of that profit during the years in question to Carl's total income put Carl in the trade or business of selling real estate.

One obvious source of contention is the correct characterization of the deal with Sproutsville. The Service will support its arguments above by stating that Carl applied for and received permission to subdivide the land. The Service will also attribute the improvements to the land (in the form of roads, and perhaps parks and schools) to Carl. While the improvements were nominally constructed by the city, the construction clearly benefited Carl and was in some sense "paid for" by his contribution of land to the city. Carl will argue that the deal was forced upon him by the threat of even less favorable zoning action.

Which party is more likely to succeed? That depends a great deal on the jurisdiction and the trier(s) of fact. For a sense of how the issue plays out in one jurisdiction, compare Houston Endowment, Inc. v. United States, 606 F.2d 77 (5th Cir. 1979) (holding that property was a noncapital asset, under §1221(a)(1), where the taxpayer, a lender, obtained property through foreclosure, did not subdivide the property, but did install utilities, and sold over 200 parcels over 27 years), with Byram v. United States, 705 F.2d 1418 (5th Cir. 1983) (holding that property was a capital asset where (i) the taxpayer made seven sales in a single year but made no improvements and (ii) there were no sales efforts by the taxpayer or brokers but the taxpayer had sold 15 other parcels in a three-year period).

Note that it is possible, though unlikely, that the bulk sale of land to the developer would generate capital gain but the sales to individual purchasers would generate ordinary income.

5. Andy and his partner will argue that the units were either capital assets or §1221(a)(2) property, in which case the units would also be §1231

property (discussed below); in either case, they would generate capital gain. Andy and his partner may be expected to argue that they did not purchase the building with an eye to selling off the individual units, but instead bought the building either as a long-term investment or in the hope of producing a steady stream of rental income. They are likely to emphasize their lack of other real estate investments, their lack of direct involvement in the sales, and the relatively small cost of improvements made as part of the conversion process.

The Service is likely to argue that, whatever the original motive or other sources of income, the sale of 64 units necessarily puts one in the business of selling units. The Service is likely to see the $150,000 in improvements as significant. It is also likely to impute the efforts of the broker to the taxpayers to buttress its claim of business activity.

There is no obvious "right" way to characterize this transaction. About all one can say is that, in the past, courts have been surprisingly lenient in giving capital asset treatment to gain recognized on condominium conversions. See, e.g., Gangi v. Commissioner, 54 T.C.M. (CCH) 1048 (1987) (gain from the sale of condominiums was capital where the taxpayers constructed an apartment building for rental use, operated it as such for eight years, then converted the apartments to condominiums and advertised the sale of the condominiums, in order to maximize their profit on the liquidation of the investment when the taxpayers decided to part company).

6. Gloria's prime concern should be the limited deductibility of capital losses. Under §1211, individuals may deduct capital loss against capital gain. Capital loss in excess of capital gain is deductible only to the extent of $3,000 a year; any remaining capital loss is carried over to the following year, where the same rules apply. Assume the building is sold immediately for its appraised value of $750,000, leaving Gloria with a loss of $250,000. If the building is considered a capital asset and Gloria recognizes no capital gain in this or future years, at $3,000 a year it will take 83 1/3 years to deduct her entire $250,000 loss.

In the event of an immediate sale, would the building be treated as a capital asset? Gloria could argue that she purchased and held the building with an eye to developing a steady stream of rental income and that the property qualifies as *section 1231 property* (real property used in a trade or business). (Net loss on section 1231 property is treated as an ordinary loss.) Gloria's case would be strengthened by factors that indicate a business (as opposed to investment) motive and operation. The presence of rents, the employment of a professional manager or full-time custodian, advertising for tenants, and development of a plan of renovation would all be helpful.

The possibility of ordinary loss increases if the building is renovated. In general, the more time Gloria spends on the project, the greater the

463

extent of renovation, and the more employees directly employed on the project, the more likely that Gloria can claim an ordinary loss on the sale. At some point, the renovation itself becomes a trade or business and the property falls out of the capital asset category through application of §1221(a)(1). If the property is renovated and then rented out, ordinary loss treatment becomes even more likely. Gloria can maximize the possibility of ordinary loss treatment by keeping careful business records of the time she spends on the project and by formally treating the project as a separate enterprise. Maintaining a separate bank account for the building rents, for example, may help to characterize the project as a business.

This question illustrates one of the conundrums of tax planning: the pull between saving taxes and maximizing before-tax income (or minimizing before-tax loss). Obviously, Gloria should not throw good money after bad just to obtain an ordinary loss. On the other hand, if she is uncertain in any event which course to take, it would be foolish not to take the course that offers significant tax savings. There are a host of formalistic actions Gloria might take to make her investment appear more like a business. She might, for example, adopt a business name for the building (such as Downtown Towers) and, in accordance with state law, file a "doing business as" notice in a journal of general circulation. She might then order separate stationery for the building, open and maintain a separate bank account in the name of the business, and so on. She could also join associations of real estate professionals and subscribe to periodicals that she will probably never read. There is an obvious air of sham to these actions. An auditor or court may or may not see through them. How much guidance should the tax practitioner give?

7. As discussed in the text and in the explanation of example 3 above, securities are almost always capital assets in the hands of anyone who is not a securities dealer. Here, however, the securities act as a sort of inventory substitute. Information Inc. purchased the securities as a way of assuring itself a steady supply of raw materials at a reasonable cost. Had Information Inc. used the lumber from Timber Company to produce newsprint, it would have saved itself the cost of purchasing newsprint at the market price and increased its operating income by approximately $3 million. For tax purposes, that increase would have been treated as ordinary income. Should the result be different because Information Inc. instead sold Timber Company stock at a profit of $3 million?

Although the purchase of Timber Company stock by Information Inc. might seem to be a hedge against an increase in the price Information Inc. must pay for newsprint, the purchase of stock is not within the special hedging rule of §1221(a)(7). Regulation §1.1221-2(d)(5)(i) specifically provides that "[e]xcept as otherwise determined in published guidance . . . the purchase or sale of . . . an equity security [i.e. corporate stock] is not a hedging transaction even if the transaction limits or reduces the taxpayer's risk with respect to ordinary property. ..." The gain from Information Inc. selling the Timber Company stock would likely be characterized as capital gain rather than as ordinary income.

Note that Information Inc. may be indifferent to whether the gain is characterized as ordinary income or capital gain. Capital gain recognized by a corporate taxpayer does not qualify for a reduced tax rate. §1201(a). Characterization of the gain as capital gain would be advantageous for Information Inc. only if it had an otherwise unusable capital loss. A corporate capital loss can offset capital gain but not ordinary income. §1211(a). To understand this last point in context, suppose Information Inc. had a $3 million capital loss. If the gain on the Timber Company stock were treated as capital gain, it could be offset by the capital loss. No tax would be due. If the gain were ordinary income, it could not be offset by the capital loss, and approximately one-third of the gain would go to the government in the form of taxes.

The importance of the hedging exception to capital asset treatment is greatest when the hedging transaction results in a loss rather than a profit. In that case, the taxpayer will want the loss to be characterized as an inventory loss, so that it is deductible against ordinary income.

8. If the taxpayer uses its rights under its hedge to take delivery of the commodity in question, gain or loss on the hedge will be incorporated into the gain or loss on its operations. The result will be ordinary income or loss. Here, if Northern Company had taken delivery of the oil, the result would have been an operating profit of $7 million.

In fact, Northern Company did not take delivery of the oil but instead paid to avoid taking delivery on the contract at a cost of $3 million. If the futures contract were treated under "normal" rules governing securities, the loss would be a capital loss. The result would be ordinary income of $10 million and a capital loss of $3 million. Unless Northern Company had capital gain from other transactions, this result would dramatically increase its tax burden because capital losses cannot offset ordinary income.

The theoretically correct result appears to be one that treats the futures contract as a noncapital asset. This would leave the company with ordinary income of $7 million ($10 million less a $3 million ordinary loss)—the same result that would obtain if the company had taken delivery of the oil under the futures contract. An opposite result would force companies in the taxpayer's position to take delivery of commodities under these sorts of futures contracts even under situations in which it is more efficient to liquidate the contract and purchase the needed commodity from other sources.

The answer under current law is consistent with the theoretically correct result. The oil is a supply that is consumed in the ordinary course of the taxpayer's business and the hedge was entered into to manage a business risk, so the hedging transaction is characterized as noncapital if Northern Company identified the hedging transaction as such before it entered into the transaction. §1221(a)(7), (8).

D. SECTION 1231 AND DEPRECIATION RECAPTURE

Reading: §§1231, 1245, 1250.

As noted above, under §1221(a)(2), real or depreciable property used in a trade or business is excluded from the category of capital assets. Instead, such property is characterized as *section 1231 property*, provided the taxpayer has held it for more than one year. §1231(b)(1). Each year, gain or loss on any item of section 1231 property is netted against gain or loss on other items of section 1231 property. If, in a given year, a taxpayer has a net gain on §1231 sales or exchanges, the §1231 gains and losses are long-term capital gains and losses. §1231(a)(1). (However, the depreciation recapture rules, discussed below, may recharacterize some or all of the §1231 capital gain as ordinary.) On the other hand, if, in the year, a taxpayer has a net loss on §1231 sales or exchanges, the §1231 gains and losses are ordinary. §1231(a)(2). The possibility of recognizing capital gain on favorable outcomes and ordinary loss on unfavorable outcomes gives §1231 a sort of "heads, the taxpayer wins, tails, the government loses" character.

This pro-taxpayer rule was adopted during World War II in part as a response to arguments that owners of appreciated business property requisitioned for the war effort were "forced" to recognize gain — gain that was then treated as ordinary income. Section 1231 did nothing about the recognition issue but ameliorated the hardship by characterizing gain recognized on all sales and exchanges of qualifying business property (including, quite obviously, on purely voluntary sales unrelated to the war effort) as capital. Section 1231 has changed little since that time, testimony to the staying power of a tax preference.

You should note one technical aspect of the calculation of net gain or loss under §1231: If, in a given year, a taxpayer recognizes a net §1231 gain, but has taken an ordinary deduction for a net §1231 loss within the last five years, the prior ordinary loss deduction is "recaptured" by recharacterizing that portion of the net §1231 gain in the current year as ordinary. §1231(c).

To illustrate the operation of §1231, suppose that in year one, Widgets, Inc. recognizes a gain of $10,000 on the sale of a truck used to transport widgets and a loss of $50,000 on a building used to produce widgets. The result is a net $40,000 §1231 loss, so the gain and the loss will both be ordinary.

Now, suppose instead that Widgets, Inc. sells the building at the close of year one and the truck at the start of year two. Can Widgets, Inc. take a $50,000 ordinary loss in year one and a $10,000 capital gain in year two? No. Section 1231(c) prevents taxpayers from timing sales to recognize §1231 (ordinary) loss in one year followed by §1231 (capital) gain in any of the five succeeding years. Here, those rules will characterize the $10,000 of §1231 gain recognized in year two as ordinary so that, over the two years, Widgets, Inc. recognizes a $50,000 ordinary loss and a $10,000 ordinary gain for a net $40,000 ordinary loss — the same result that would have been obtained had the two properties been sold in the same taxable year.

Section 1231 is an important provision for corporations and most other enterprises since it applies to virtually all noninventory property. Section 1231 property includes machinery used to produce goods, cars and trucks used to transport goods, buildings and land owned and used by a taxpayer in its business operations, and proceeds from the involuntary conversion of property used in the business.

Even if the sale of depreciable property generates capital gain under §1231, some of that capital gain may be recharacterized as ordinary income by the *depreciation recapture* rules of §§1245 and 1250. Section 1245 recharacterizes capital gain from the sale of a depreciable asset (other than real property) as ordinary income, to the extent of prior depreciation on the asset sold. Said another way, on the sale of section 1245 property, a taxpayer includes ordinary income equal to the lesser of (i) the gain recognized on the sale of the asset or (ii) prior depreciation taken on the asset sold. §1245(a)(1), (2). *Property is section 1245 property* if (i) depreciation is allowed on the property under §167 and (ii) the property is one of the types of property specified in §1245(a)(3), including personal and tangible property.

Section 1245 may best be illustrated by an example. Suppose Max pays $10,000 for a car that he uses in a trade or business. Under §§167 and 168, described in Chapter 5 of this book, Max may depreciate the car over five years. The depreciation deduction is treated as a noncapital business expense and reduces the tax Max pays on ordinary income. After the car is fully depreciated and Max's basis in the car is reduced to zero, the car is sold for $2,000. As measured against economic income, the depreciation deduction was $2,000 too generous; the car was treated for tax purposes as having declined in value by $10,000 when in fact it declined in value by only $8,000. Were it not for the recapture provisions, Max would recognize §1231 gain of $2,000 on the sale, which would be capital if Max does not sell any other section 1231 property during the same year. However, under the §1245 recapture provisions, gain to the extent of prior depreciation is characterized as ordinary income. Max therefore includes $2,000 of ordinary income, not capital gain. In effect, the $2,000 "excess" depreciation deduction taken against ordinary income is recaptured by forcing Max to include ordinary income, in the amount of the prior excess deduction, in the year of sale.

Now suppose, instead, that Max sold the car for $13,000. Since Max had taken $10,000 of depreciation on the car, his basis in the car is zero and he recognizes $13,000 of capital gain (via §1231) on the sale of the car, assuming that he does not sell any other section 1231 property in the same year. However, $10,000 of that capital gain (the lesser of the $10,000 depreciation taken on the car or the $13,000 gain on the sale) is characterized as ordinary income under §1245. The remaining $3,000 of gain is capital under §1231.

If the asset sold is real property, §1250 imposes a limited (and today, largely illusory) form of recapture. Generally speaking, §1250 requires recapture of gain only to the extent of depreciation in excess of straight line depreciation.[4] Real property placed in service after 1986, however, is depreciable only by the straight line method. §168(b)(3). Thus, there is generally no depreciation in excess of straight line and hence no portion of gain on the sale is subject to §1250 recapture. (However, if the taxpayer holds the real property for more than a year before the sale and the sale produces capital gain, the portion of the gain attributable to unrecaptured depreciation generally is taxed at a 25 percent capital gain rate and the rest of the gain is taxed at a capital gain rate of 20 percent or, in some cases, less. The capital gain rates are discussed at the beginning of this chapter.)

The Code also includes a host of other, more specialized provisions that govern the characterization of gain or loss on certain transactions. These various provisions are beyond the scope of this book, but you should know to check for specific characterization rules in practice.

Examples

9. In year one, Bigco, Inc. sells land on which its computer operations were located for many years at a gain of $300,000. In that same year the company sells some long-held capital assets at a loss of $200,000. Bigco, Inc. has no other sales or exchanges in year one. Discuss the amount, if any, of ordinary income, ordinary loss, capital gain, or capital loss the company recognizes in year one.

10. State whether the following combinations of §1231 gain and loss generate ordinary or capital gain or loss.
    a. Tex recognizes (i) a $10,000 gain on the sale of vacant land used in his trade or business and held for four years and (ii) a $20,000

---

4. Section 1250 also applies to all depreciation deductions for property sold or exchanged after being held a year or less, but as this form of property does not generate long-term capital gain in any event, and as such early dispositions are rare, the impact of this provision is modest.

loss on the sale of tools used in his trade or business and held for five years.

b. Tess recognizes (i) a $30,000 gain on the sale of vacant land used in her trade or business and held for two years and (ii) a $20,000 loss on the sale of tools used in her trade or business and held for four years.

11. State whether the following combinations of §1231 and §1221 gain and loss generate ordinary or capital gain or loss.

a. Carlos recognizes (i) a $10,000 gain on the sale of vacant land used in his trade or business and held for four years, (ii) a $20,000 loss on the sale of tools used in his trade or business and held for four years, and (iii) a $30,000 capital gain on stock held for four years.

b. Carla recognizes (i) a $30,000 gain on the sale of vacant land used in her trade or business and held for two years, (ii) a $20,000 loss on the sale of tools used in her trade or business and held for four years, and (iii) a $40,000 capital gain on stock held for four years.

c. Carmelita recognizes (i) a $30,000 gain on the sale of vacant land used in her trade or business and held for two years, (ii) a $20,000 loss on the sale of tools used in her trade or business and held for four years, (iii) a $30,000 capital gain on stock held for four years, and (iv) a $50,000 capital loss on stock held for three years.

d. Chuck recognizes (i) a $30,000 gain on the sale of vacant land used in his trade or business and held for two years, (ii) a $20,000 loss on the sale of tools used in his trade or business and held for four years, (iii) a $50,000 capital loss on stock held for four years, and (iv) a $60,000 capital gain on stock held for two months.

12. State the amount of ordinary income included on the following sales. (Assume that the taxpayers do not sell any other property during the year of the following sales.)

a. Jan sells the Shady Acres Apartment Building for $320,000. Jan purchased the property in year one for $300,000. Her adjusted basis in the property at the time of the sale is $260,000 ($300,000 basis less $40,000 of depreciation taken on the building).

b. John sells machinery used in his business to build widgets for $150,000. John bought the equipment in year one for $400,000. His adjusted basis in the property at the time of the sale is $100,000 ($400,000 basis less $300,000 of depreciation taken on the machinery).

c. Jen sells equipment used in her auto repair shop business for $60,000. She paid $50,000 for the equipment. Her adjusted basis in the equipment at the time of the sale is zero ($50,000 basis less $50,000 of depreciation taken on the equipment).

d. Jim sells a copyright for $55,000. He bought the copyright from the person (not related to Jim) who created the copyrighted property in exchange for $50,000. Jim's adjusted basis for the property at the time of the sale is $40,000 ($50,000 basis less $10,000 "depreciation" taken on the property).

Explanations

9. The land is real property used in a trade or business. It is excluded from capital asset status by virtue of §1221(a)(2) but, because it is real property used in a trade or business and because it has been held for more than one year, it qualifies as "section 1231 property" by virtue of (surprise!) §1231. If a taxpayer recognizes a net gain on section 1231 property, the taxpayer's §1231 gains and losses are treated as long-term capital gains and losses. §1231(a)(1). If a taxpayer recognizes a net loss on section 1231 property, the taxpayer's §1231 gains and losses are ordinary. §1231(a)(2). Here, Bigco, Inc. has a net gain on section 1231 property, so the $300,000 of gain on the sale of the land is long-term capital gain and the $200,000 of loss on the sale of the capital assets is long-term capital loss. The $100,000 of net long-term capital gain qualifies for the special capital gain rates of §1(h).

10. a. Tex has a net loss on section 1231 property, so the gain and loss are both ordinary. §1231(a)(2).

    b. Tess has a net gain on section 1231 property, so the $30,000 gain is long-term capital gain and the $20,000 loss is long-term capital loss. §1231(a)(1). Tess has net long-term capital gain of $10,000. §1222(7).

11. a. Carlos has a net loss on section 1231 property, so the $10,000 §1231 gain and the $20,000 §1231 loss are both ordinary. §1231(a)(2). Carlos also has $30,000 of long-term capital gain and the same amount of net capital gain (since he has no long-term capital loss).

    b. Carla has a net gain on section 1231 property, so the $30,000 of gain from the sale of the land is long-term capital gain and the $20,000 loss from the sale of the tools is treated as a long-term capital loss. Carla's $70,000 of long-term capital gain ($30,000 from the sale of section 1231 property and $40,000 from the sale of the stock, a capital asset) is netted against the $20,000 of long-term capital loss, so her net capital gain for the year is $50,000.

    c. Carmelita recognizes (i) a $30,000 §1231 gain, (ii) a $20,000 §1231 loss, (iii) a $30,000 long-term capital gain, and (iv) a $50,000 long-term capital loss. Carmelita has a net §1231 gain, so the $30,000 §1231 gain is a long-term capital gain and the $20,000 §1231 loss is a long-term capital loss. Netting the gains and losses, Carmelita is left with a long-term capital loss of $10,000. She can deduct $3,000 of the loss; the remaining $7,000 of loss is carried forward to the next year. §§1211(b), 1212(b)(1).

d. Chuck recognizes (i) a $30,000 §1231 gain, (ii) a $20,000 §1231 loss, (iii) a $50,000 long-term capital loss, and (iv) a $60,000 short-term capital gain. Chuck has a net §1231 gain, so the $30,000 §1231 gain is a long-term capital gain and the $20,000 §1231 loss is a long-term capital loss. Netting the long-term gains and losses, Chuck is left with a long-term capital loss of $40,000. Chuck can deduct the entire $40,000 of long-term capital loss because he recognizes $60,000 of short-term capital gain. §1211(b). The remaining $20,000 of short-term capital gain is taxed at ordinary income rates.

12. a. Jan recognizes $60,000 of gain, which is capital under §1231. None of this gain is subject to depreciation recapture so Jan includes no ordinary income on the sale. Under §1250, capital gain on real property is subject to recapture only to the extent that the depreciation on the property exceeds straight line depreciation. Since 1986 the only available method by which to depreciate real property is the straight line method. §168(b)(3). Thus, no portion of the gain is subject to §1250 recapture.

Of the $60,000 capital gain, $40,000 is attributable to straight line depreciation deductions that Jan has taken on the property, so that $40,000 of gain is subject to the 25 percent capital gain rate. The remaining $20,000 of capital gain is taxed at a capital gain rate of 20 percent or less.

b. John recognizes $50,000 of gain, which is capital under §1231. However, gain on the sale of tangible physical property such as machinery is subject to recapture in the amount of the lesser of (i) the gain recognized on the sale or (ii) the prior depreciation taken on the property sold. §1245. Here, the total gain recognized is $50,000 and the prior depreciation is $300,000. The lesser of these two figures is $50,000. Thus, all $50,000 of the gain is recaptured as ordinary income. (Another, less mechanical, way to think about the recapture rules is that in this instance, the entire gain is due to the reduction in basis caused by accelerated depreciation. The depreciation reduced ordinary income. The taxpayer here must "give back" that reduction in ordinary income by recognizing ordinary income on the sale of the property.)

c. Jen recognizes $60,000 of gain, which is capital under §1231. However, gain is recaptured as ordinary income to the extent of prior depreciation. Here, prior depreciation was $50,000, so $50,000 of gain is ordinary income. The remaining $10,000 of gain is capital gain.

d. Jim recognizes $15,000 of gain, which is capital under §1231. Copyrights do not have an indefinite life but instead are valid for a fixed number of years. The value of a copyright thus declines (to zero) as it reaches its expiration date. Holders of a copyright can deduct this form of decline through "amortization" (the form depreciation takes for intangible property). Section 1245 applies to intangible property that has been amortized as well as tangible property that has been depreciated. Here, $10,000 of the $15,000 gain (the portion of the gain equal to prior amortization) is recaptured as ordinary income.

E. SUBSTITUTES FOR ORDINARY INCOME

Capital gains and losses are recognized only on the "sale or exchange" of "capital assets," and, as noted above, capital assets are defined in part as "*property* held by the taxpayer." §1221(a) (italics added). In most cases, whether a transaction involves a sale or exchange of property will be self-evident. In some cases, however, whether a transaction is best characterized as a sale of property (generating capital gain) or the collection of rents, dividends, or salary (generating ordinary income) will be unclear.

Consider, for example, a bondholder who "sells" her right to the next two interest payments on a bond she owns. The right to collect interest has value, can be legally sold, and may well constitute a property interest under state law. Perhaps the transaction should be treated as a sale of property; if so, because the "property" does not fall within any of the enumerated exceptions to capital asset treatment, any profit will constitute capital gain. On the other hand, had the bondholder simply collected interest in the ordinary course of events, the proceeds would have been taxed as ordinary income. A decision in favor of capital gain in this case would encourage other taxpayers to undertake the same kind of artificial and (once commissions and the like are taken into account) expensive transaction. Interest would then produce (through anticipatory sales) capital gain rather than ordinary income — a step that seems out of character with legislative intent and common understanding.

Consistent with the intuition expressed in the last paragraph, courts have ruled that transactions such as the one described do not involve "sales" of "property" and therefore do not generate capital gain or loss. Although the stated rationale for the holdings in these cases is murky, the rule the courts have fashioned may be best expressed as follows: For tax purposes, the sale of the right to income from property, for a limited period of time, by a taxpayer who holds the rights to the income from the property thereafter (i) does not constitute a sale or exchange of property, (ii) does not generate capital gain or loss, and (iii) does not allow the taxpayer to offset her basis in the property against the amount received. A temporal interest sold by one who owns the reversionary interest is often referred to as a vertical or "carved-out" interest.

The careful student may note that carved-out interests were discussed earlier, in Chapter 7 of this book. There we were concerned with taxpayers' attempts to shift income to low-bracket family members. We noted that income from property could be shifted by transferring ownership of the property. We then posed a similar question: Does a taxpayer who owns an apartment building have a separable property right (for tax purposes) in the right to next month's rental income? If so, the taxpayer could avoid recognizing that income by assigning the right to a low-bracket family member? We concluded that, for purposes of income shifting, such a carved-out interest is not treated as property. Income from a carved-out interest is recognized by the taxpayer who assigns that interest. Here, we are interested in the definition of property for purposes of determining whether the taxpayer has capital gain or ordinary income, rather than for purposes of determining income attribution, but the answer is the same: For tax purposes, a carved-out interest is not treated as a separate property right. Taxpayers cannot avoid an income inclusion by assigning that interest and cannot convert ordinary income into capital gain by selling that interest.

For example, in Hort v. Commissioner, 313 U.S. 28 (1941), a $140,000 payment received by a *lessor* from a lessee to cancel a lease on commercial property that the lessor continued to own was ordinary income, not capital gain. (The lessor was also not allowed to reduce the $140,000 amount received by any of his basis in the property.) The Court viewed the lease cancellation payment as advance rent; since rent would have been ordinary income, the Court concluded that the lease cancellation payment should also be ordinary income. The lease cancellation payment received by the lessor was for a carved-out interest because the lessor continued to own the lease property. However, note that a lease cancellation payment received by a *lessee* (for example, because the lessor can rent the property at a higher rent) is treated as the sale or exchange of a property interest, so the payment may be capital (either by way of §1221 or §1231). Since the payment made to the lessee is for the lessee's entire interest in the leased property, the payment is not received for a carved-out interest. §1241; Commissioner v. McCue Bros. & Drummond, Inc., 210 F.2d 752 (2d Cir. 1954).

In another carved-out interest case, Commissioner v. P.G. Lake, Inc., 356 U.S. 260 (1958), the taxpayer assigned to a creditor around $600,000 of oil payments from a working interest owned by the taxpayer. As the parties anticipated, the $600,000 amount was paid over about a three-year period. The Court held that the assignment of the oil payments was not a sale of a capital asset, but was instead ordinary income.

There is another broad category of potential sales that, by virtue of both §1221 and a uniform set of court decisions, does not generate capital gain (or loss). This category consists of sales of what otherwise would be treated as salary or personal service income. Suppose that a taxpayer sells the right to her entire career earnings. While the sale does not fall within any statutory exclusions from capital asset treatment, there is little doubt that a court would rule that the proceeds are ordinary income, and that such a ruling would be consistent with settled understanding, legislative intent, and case law. See, e.g., Flower v. Commissioner, 61 T.C. 140 (1973) (holding that payment to terminate a personal services contract was ordinary income).

Attempts by taxpayers to recognize capital gain on less ambitious sales of salary income would also run afoul of the rule governing carved-out interests and various provisions of §1221. For example, the sale of a not-yet-received paycheck for work already performed would generate ordinary income due to §1221(a)(4), which excepts accounts receivable from the capital asset definition. The sale of the right to next month's paycheck is a sale of a carved-out interest and would for that reason generate ordinary income. Copyrights and artistic works held by the person who created such property (or a donee given the property by its creator) are denied capital asset treatment due to §1221(a)(3), discussed earlier in this chapter.

The rule against recognizing capital gain from personal services is not altogether complete. A taxpayer who toils for years to build up the value of his solely owned corporation recognizes capital gain when he sells the stock of that corporation; the same treatment is accorded a taxpayer who sells the goodwill inherent in her noncorporate enterprise.

Similarly, an exception to §1221(a)(3) allows a musician to pay tax on the sale of his self-created musical work at capital gain rates. Under §1221(a)(3), artists who sell self-created works pay tax on their gain at ordinary income rates. Section 1221(b)(3) provides that a taxpayer can elect out of §1221(a)(3) with respect to a self-created musical work or copyright in a musical work. Although royalty payments received by musicians continue to be taxed at ordinary income rates, musicians making the §1221(b)(3) election pay lower capital gain rates on gain from the sale of their musical works or copyrights.

Also, §1235 provides that creators of patents (and certain other taxpayers) can generate long-term capital gain (or loss) on the transfer of "all substantial rights" to a patent. To be eligible, a taxpayer must be either (i) the creator of the patent; or (ii) one who is not related to the creator of the patent and is not the creator's employer, but bought the patent from the creator prior to the patented invention's reduction to practice. §1235(b). Long-term capital gain (or loss) is the order of the day even if the payments are made over a period of years and are contingent upon the use or productivity of the assigned patent, and even if the patent was not held for more than a year. §1235(a).

Other provisions that allow capital asset or §1231 treatment on assets that might otherwise generate ordinary income or loss include §631(a) and (b) (§1231 characterization for certain cutting or selling of timber) and §631(c) (same for qualifying sales of coal and iron ore).

In some cases, it may be difficult to tell whether a taxpayer has sold salary income or "property." In Commissioner v. Ferrer, 304 F.2d 125 (2d Cir. 1962), the actor José Ferrer entered into an agreement with Pierre LaMure, who wrote a book and a play about the artist Toulouse-Lautrec. Ferrer's rights under the agreement included (i) the right to produce the play, (ii) the right to block a movie based on the book until the play had run for a certain period of time, and (iii) the right to share in amounts LaMure might receive from a movie based on the book. LaMure nominally retained all rights in the book and play, except the right to produce the play. John Huston then decided that he wanted to make a movie of the book, so he entered into an agreement with both LaMure and Ferrer. Pursuant to the agreement between Huston and Ferrer, (i) Ferrer was to play the starring role in the movie in exchange for a salary, and (ii) Ferrer assigned the rights he acquired in his agreement with LaMure in exchange for a percentage interest in the movie. The issue in the case was whether the percentage amounts received by Ferrer were ordinary income or capital gain. Ferrer argued, and the Tax Court agreed, that such amounts were received in exchange for the assignment of the dramatic production contract between Ferrer and LaMure and thus were capital gain, not ordinary income from personal services.

The Court of Appeals examined each of the contract rights separately. Analogizing to a payment received by a lessee for lease cancellation, the court concluded that the amounts Ferrer received for the assignment of the right to produce the play were capital gain. Similarly, the amounts received for the assignment of the right to block a movie were capital gain because they were like a payment received by a lessee to cancel an agreement between the lessee and lessor that would have prevented the lessor from renting adjacent space to the lessee's competitor. However, in the court's view, the right to share in LaMure's movie earnings was not property (since LaMure retained almost all of the rights to the book and movie), and the amount Ferrer received for the assignment of the right was an ordinary income substitute, so the court held that the amounts received for assignment of this contract right were ordinary income. It is not clear why the court fragmented the rights Ferrer acquired in his contract with LaMure. However, since Huston would probably not have entered into the assignment agreement had Ferrer not starred in the movie, the court may have fragmented the payments because it viewed part of the percentage payments as compensation for Ferrer's personal services.

Examples

13. Discuss the characterization of the gain or loss recognized in the following transactions.
    a. Attorney Amy agrees to represent Don in a tort suit. In return, Don agrees to pay Amy one-third of any proceeds realized from the suit or settlement of the suit. Shortly before the suit is to come to trial, but after she has done considerable work on the case, Amy receives and accepts an offer to work at a law firm in another state. With Don's approval, Amy sells her right to any share of the contingency award to Dale, an attorney who agrees to carry the case to trial, in exchange for $30,000.
    b. Amy also sells to Dale her right to accounts receivable due from other clients for whom she has worked on an hourly, rather than contingency fee, basis.

14. Discuss the characterization of the income or loss recognized in the following sales.
    a. Sam owns four large office buildings, which he leases to various commercial tenants. One such tenant is Bank Inc., which has signed a 15-year lease with Sam. Rents have fallen since the lease was signed, so in retrospect the deal looks good to Sam and bad to Bank Inc. Sam sells his right to collect rent under the lease to an unrelated third party for $500,000.
    b. Assume the same facts as in part (a), above, except that, instead of selling his right to collect rent under the lease, Sam agrees to cancel the lease. In exchange for that agreement, Bank Inc. vacates the premises and pays Sam $100,000. Sam then leases the property at a somewhat lower rent.
    c. Sam enters into a long-term lease with another commercial tenant, Insurance Company, in a different building in a different city. Rents rise dramatically after this lease is signed. In effect, the lease gives Insurance Company the right to premises at below-market rent. The lease is assignable and, two years after signing the lease, Insurance Company assigns its rights and obligations under the lease to an unrelated third party, the law firm of Wagner and Metro. In exchange, the law firm pays Insurance Company $140,000. As part of that assignment, Insurance Company vacates the premises and the law firm moves in and pays the (below-market) monthly rent due under the lease.

15. State whether each of the following sales generates capital gain, §1231 gain, or ordinary income.
    a. Inventor Aaron sells all rights to his patent for $1 million cash. Aaron's basis for the patent was $30,000.

b. Inventor Bonnie transfers all rights to her golf ball patent in exchange for an amount equal to 5 percent of annual sales of the patented golf balls for the next 10 years.

c. Alternative musician Jim White transfers all rights to a musical composition he has created in exchange for $100,000.

d. Author Yxta transfers all rights to a novel she has written to Bacchanal Press, a publishing company, in exchange for $200,000.

e. Bacchanal Press later sells its rights in Yxta's novel to Walden Press in exchange for $320,000.

Explanations

13. a. The $30,000 will be treated as ordinary income. Under state law, the contingency fee may well constitute a property interest. For tax purposes, however, the sale of a right to what otherwise would constitute salary or personal service income, even salary or income that has already been earned, is not treated as a sale of a capital asset. There are a few exceptions to this rule (for example, inventors may receive capital gain on the sale of patent rights), but this is not one of them. Note that since Amy has retained the right to later streams of income generated by her legal career, the right sold could also be characterized as a "carved-out" interest and for that reason produce ordinary income rather than capital gain. Finally, capital asset treatment might be denied under §1221(a)(4), discussed in the text and in part (b), below, under the rationale that the contingent fee interest is a(n) (odd) form of accounts receivable.

b. The proceeds constitute ordinary income by virtue of §1221(a)(4), which excludes accounts receivable from the capital asset definition.

14. a. Sam has sold his right to collect rent for the next 15 years, but retained his rights to relet the property after 15 years and keep the rent. Since he has kept a remainder interest in the building, the rights sold constitute a carved-out interest. Sale of a carved-out interest produces ordinary income, not capital gain. Hort v. Commissioner, 313 U.S. 28 (1941); Commissioner v. P.G. Lake, Inc., 356 U.S. 260 (1958).

b. The result is the same as in part (a). Sam has in effect sold his right to collect above-market rents for the following 15 years. Since he has kept a remainder interest in the building, the property sold is a carved-out interest. The proceeds are ordinary income rather than capital gain.

c. In this example, the taxpayer, Insurance Company, has no remainder interest in the property sold. As a result, the sale is treated as a sale of property and generates capital gain. (The leasehold presumably constitutes "property used in the trade or business" and therefore qualifies as "section 1231 property," net gain on the sale of which constitutes capital gain.) See Rev. Rul. 72-85,1972-1 C.B. 234.

15. a. Section 1235 provides that a sale of all substantial rights to a patent, or an undivided interest therein, shall be treated as a sale of a capital asset. Aaron therefore recognizes $970,000 of capital gain.

   b. Bonnie, too, recognizes capital gain on the sale of her patent. The fact that the sale price is contingent upon the successful marketing of the patented product is immaterial. §1235(a). (Note that under the complex rules governing contingent installment sales, some portion of payments received in later years will be treated as interest income.)

   c. Section 1221(a)(3) provides that a self-created musical composition is not a capital asset, but a taxpayer can elect under §1221(b)(3) to treat a self-created musical work or copyright as a capital asset. If Jim makes a §1221(b)(3) election, the $100,000 is capital gain.

   d. The $200,000 is ordinary income. The novel is a self-created literary work in Yxta's hands. Section 1221(a)(3) precludes capital gain treatment on her sale of the novel.

   e. Gain from the sale of the novel is §1231 gain, which may qualify for capital gain rates. Section 1221(a)(3) does not apply because Bacchanal Press did not create the novel and has a basis in the novel equal to what it paid Yxta for the novel. The copyrighted novel is not a capital asset, however. The property is used in the trade or business of Bacchanal Press and is thus a §1231 asset. §1231(b)(1).

F. THE TAX ON NET INVESTMENT INCOME

Reading: §§1401(b), 1411, 3101(b).

Beginning in 2013, certain "net investment income" ("NII") is subject to an additional tax of 3.8 percent. §1411. Although the new NII tax was justified as a Medicare tax on investment income, comparable to the preexisting Medicare tax on earned income, in effect, the NII tax functions as an income tax rate increase on NII (which is why we are discussing it in this book). Although §1411 and the final and proposed regulations are too complex to cover in detail here (for example requiring multi-step processes to classify and segregate various types of investment income into three separate categories), the following discussion provides an overview of the NII tax.

Drawing a general distinction between unearned and earned income, §1411 provides that investment income includes gain from the disposition of property, interest, dividends, rental and royalty income, annuities, income from businesses that trade financial instruments or commodities, and income from businesses that are treated as "passive" activities of the taxpayer under §469 (discussed in Chapter 5). §1411(c). Financial instruments are defined broadly to include "stocks and other equity interests, evidences of indebtedness, options, forward or futures contracts, notional principal contracts, any other derivatives, or any evidence of an interest in any of the [forgoing]." Treas. Reg. §1.1411-5(c)(1). Distributions from qualified pension plans are not within the definition of investment income, however. §1411(c)(5). Wages, unemployment compensation, self-employment income, and income from an active trade or business also are not treated as investment income. In addition, certain types of income that are excluded from gross income, such as alimony and interest on tax-exempt bonds, are not treated as investment income. IRS FAQs, Questions & Answers on the Net Investment Income Tax, Q&A 9 (updated Nov. 22, 2013).

"Net investment income" is investment income less deductions that are properly allocable to that investment income, such as deductible investment interest expense, investment advisory and brokerage fees, and expenses related to rental and royalty income. §1411(c) (1). In determining net investment income, capital gains are offset by capital losses. §1411(c)(1)(A)(iii).

Each year, the 3.8 percent NII tax applies to the *lesser* of (1) net investment income, or (2) (simplifying a bit) the excess of AGI less the "threshold amount" applicable to the taxpayer. §1411(a)(1), (d). The threshold amount, which is not adjusted for inflation, is $250,000 for married taxpayers filing jointly and $200,000 for single taxpayers and heads of households. §1411(b).

(The §1411 NII tax is separate and distinct from the additional Medicare tax of 0.9 percent that is applicable to wages and self-employment income in excess of threshold amounts, which are $250,000 for married taxpayers filing jointly and $200,000 for single taxpayers and heads of households. §§1401(b)(2), 3101(b)(2). For high income taxpayers, the 0.9 percent Medicare surtax is added to the base 2.9 percent Medicare tax on wages and self-employment income, adding up to a 3.8 percent Medicare tax on such income.)

Examples

In the following examples, assume that current law is in effect in all years.

16. In year one, while he was employed as a high school teacher, Jeff purchased $10,000 of JumpCo. stock. He began law school in year two and graduated in year five. In year six, Jeff works as a junior associate at a Beverly Hills entertainment law firm and is paid $80,000 in salary. In March of year six, Jeff receives $10,000 in dividends from the JumpCo. stock. In June of year six, Jeff sells the JumpCo. stock for $100,000 and uses the sale proceeds to pay down his law school student loans.

     a. How much is Jeff's year six NII tax?

     b. Assume the same facts as in (a), except that, in year six, Jeff is a junior associate at a large New York firm and earns $160,000 per year in salary. How, if at all, does this change Jeff's year six NII tax?

     c. Assume the same facts as in (b), except that, in year six, Jeff is a senior associate and earns $340,000 per year in salary. How, if at all, does this change Jeff's year six NII tax?

17. In year one, married taxpayers Andre and Shirley bought a personal residence for $500,000. In year ten, they sell their residence for $1.1 million.

     a. In year ten, Andre is retired but Shirley still works full-time and earns $60,000 of wages. That year, Andre and Shirley also receive $20,000 of interest on corporate bonds and $15,000 of dividends on stock they have owned for years. How much is Andre and Shirley's year ten NII tax?

     b. Assume the same facts as in (a), except that Shirley is a single taxpayer. How, if at all, would your answer in (a) change?

18. In year one, Annie buys a partnership interest in Fuzzy Focus Films Limited Partnership (FFF LP), which produces independent films. In year three, FFF LP earns a profit on a film, TwiNight, that is well-received at highbrow film festivals. Annie's share of the year three partnership income is $160,000. Annie also earns $140,000 as a self-employed freelance film editor in year three.

     a. Annie's partnership interest in FFF LP is a passive, limited partner interest. How much is Annie's year six NII tax?

     b. Annie's partnership interest in FFF LP is a general partner interest. She serves as the sole general partner of FFF LP and spends 1,000 hours actively managing FFF LP during year three. How much is Annie's year three NII tax?

Explanations

16. a. Jeff's year six AGI is $180,000 which is the sum of his $80,000 salary, the $10,000 of dividends he received, and the $90,000 of long-term capital gain he realized on the sale of the JumpCo. Stock. Although the dividend and capital gain are "investment income," Jeff's year six NII tax is zero because his $180,000 AGI is less than his $200,000 threshold amount.

    b. Jeff's total year six NII is $100,000. His year six AGI is $260,000, which is the sum of $160,000 in salary, $10,000 in dividends, and $90,000 in capital gains. Jeff is taxed only on the lesser of (i) his

$100,000 NII or (ii) $60,000, which is the amount by which his $260,000 AGI exceeds his threshold of $200,000. Jeff's year six NII tax is 3.8 percent of $60,000, which is $2,280.

c. Jeff's year six NII still is $100,000, but his AGI in year six changes to $440,000, which exceeds his $200,000 threshold by $240,000. The 3.8 percent NII tax is imposed on the lesser of (i) his $100,000 year six NII or (ii) the $240,000 of year six AGI in excess of his threshold. Jeff's year six NII tax is $3,800, which is 3.8 percent of all of his NII.

17. a. Although Andre and Shirley realize a gain of $600,000 on the sale of the residence in year ten, they can exclude $500,000 of that gain. Only $100,000 of the gain in included in AGI and NII. §§121(b)(2)(A), 1411(c)(1)(A)(iii). Andre and Shirley's year ten AGI equals $195,000, which is the sum of $100,000 of gain from the sale of the residence, $60,000 of salary, $20,000 of taxable interest, and $15,000 of dividends. Their year ten NII is $135,000, which is the sum of the gain included in income, the taxable interest, and the dividends. Although they have $135,000 of NII in year ten, they owe no NII tax in year ten because their year ten AGI is less than the $250,000 threshold amount.

b. Shirley, a single taxpayer, can exclude only $250,000 of the $600,000 of gain realized on the sale of her residence. The remaining $350,000 is included in her AGI and in her NII. Her year ten NII equals $385,000, which is the sum of $350,000 of gain, $20,000 of taxable interest, and $15,000 of dividends. Her year ten AGI is $445,000, which is the sum of her $60,000 of salary plus the $350,000 gain from the sale of the residence, the $20,000 of taxable interest, and the $15,000 of dividends. Her year ten NII tax equals $9,310, which is 3.8 percent of the lesser of (i) her $385,000 year ten NII or (ii) $245,000, which is her $445,000 year AGI less her $200,000 threshold.

18. a. Annie's $160,000 share of FFF LP year-three income is NII because her partnership interest is a passive, limited partner interest. Her AGI is $300,000, which exceeds her $200,000 threshold amount by $100,000. Her year-three NII tax equals $3,800, which is 3.8 percent of the lesser of (i) the $160,000 of year-three NII or (ii) the $100,000 excess of $300,000 AGI less the $200,000 threshold amount.

b. Annie's $160,000 share of FFF LP year-three income is not NII because her partnership interest is a general partner interest and she materially participates in the business. Her year-three NII tax is zero because her year-three NII is zero. Note, however, that her $160,000 of year-three partnership income and her $140,000 of film editor income are subject to a Medicare self-employment tax at a rate that is comparable to the NII tax. §1401(b).

G. THE SALE OF A BUSINESS

Reading: §1060.

We noted above that stock is a capital asset in the hands of taxpayers other than brokerage houses and other dealers. The sale of the stock of an incorporated business thus generates capital gain or loss; the fact that some portion of the rise (or fall) in the value of the business may be due to the appreciation (or depreciation) of inventory or other noncapital assets is irrelevant. In other words, the sale of the stock is not treated as a sale of the assets owned by the corporation.

Suppose, however, that a taxpayer operates a business as a sole proprietorship and holds the assets of the business in her own name. The taxpayer then sells all of those assets in a sale of the business to an unrelated party. The assets consist of some capital assets (such as goodwill), some section1231 assets (such as the building in which the business is conducted), and some noncapital assets such as inventory. Consistency would seem to require that this sale be treated like the sale of stock of an incorporated business. If so, the gain or loss would be capital.

In fact, the sale of a business that is operated as a sole proprietorship is treated as a separate sale of each of the assets of the business. Williams v. McGowan, 152 F.2d 570 (2d Cir. 1945). The purchase price for the business is allocated among the assets of the business based on the classification of the assets and their fair market values. §1060. The seller then computes the amount and character of the gain or loss on each asset. For example, the seller might recognize long-term capital gain on the sale of capital assets and ordinary loss on the sale of noncapital assets, such as inventory.

This rule applies not only to the sale of a sole proprietorship but also to the sale of an unincorporated business owned by a corporation or some other business. United States Mineral Products Co. v. Commissioner, 52 T.C. 177 (1969). On the other hand, if an unincorporated business is operated by a partnership, the sale of a partner's interest in that partnership produces a hybrid result that combines elements of stock sales and asset sales. As a starting point, the sale of a partnership interest is treated as the sale of a capital asset, producing capital gain or loss. §741. However, if the partnership has certain ordinary income producing assets, such as inventory, complicated partnership tax rules may recharacterize some of the capital gain or loss as ordinary income or loss, in many ways mimicking the result of a sale of a sole proprietorship.

Examples

19. Roger Wagner is a California-based concert promoter who specializes in rock groups appealing to a young audience. Roger rents arenas and other venues in California and the Pacific Northwest, books groups in those arenas, subcontracts out the concessions (beer, soft drinks, and so forth), advertises, and employs security personnel at the concerts. Roger splits ticket sales with the performing artists; his profit is the excess of his share of the sales over the costs involved. Roger has 40 or so full-time employees and hundreds of part-time employees.

    Roger also has two children and is frustrated at the small selection and high prices of most children's clothing stores. Roger decides to sponsor a series of "Kidfests" at exhibition halls in leading cities throughout the nation. The Kidfests will feature hundreds of merchants selling children's clothes and toys—ostensibly at a discount from prices found in stores. The Kidfests will offer live entertainment—saccharine performers who sing about whales, frogs, and ducks. Over the next 14 months, Roger spends hundreds of hours of his and his employees' time planning the Kidfests and spends over $250,000 in advance payments to auditoriums, baseball stadiums, newspapers, and radio stations in order to secure facilities and advertising. A month before the first Kidfest, Roger sells his rights in the events to a promoter of trade shows for $450,000, for a profit (ignoring the value of his and his employees' time) of $200,000.

    Is the $200,000 profit ordinary income? Argue the question from the perspectives of both Roger and the government. State any additional facts that might affect those arguments.

20. Donna is the sole owner of a bicycle shop. The shop is organized for tax purposes as a sole proprietorship rather than a corporation, so Donna owns all of the assets in her own name and all of the income is taxed at Donna's individual rate. Donna sells the shop for $240,000 in year five. The purchase price is allocated as follows:

Land on which shop is located	$50,000
Building in which shop is located	40,000
Inventory	60,000
Equipment	20,000
Goodwill	70,000

    Donna's basis for each of the above-listed assets is as follows:

Land	$10,000
Building	35,000

Inventory	65,000
Equipment	5,000
Goodwill	0

Donna paid $40,000 for the building in year one and has since taken $5,000 of depreciation on the structure. Donna paid $30,000 for the equipment in year four but has depreciated the equipment so that her current basis for it is $5,000. Donna has no other sales or exchanges in the year in which she sells her bicycle shop. Discuss the tax consequences of the sale.

Explanations

19. Roger will argue that he has, in effect, sold all of the assets of a separate business — the business of promoting one or more Kidfests. Under case law and established practice, the sale of a wholly owned, unincorporated business is treated as the sale of the assets of a business, so it makes no difference, as a formal matter, if Roger's argument is framed in terms of a sale of a business or a sale of assets. In either event, if the argument is successful, the treatment of the gain will be determined on an asset-by-asset basis. The hypothetical does not tell us, specifically, what particular assets Roger has sold. Presumably, the major asset sold is simply Roger's right to profit from at least the first Kidfest, a right that stems from Roger's advertising and contractual arrangements with arenas and the like. Roger can argue that none of these rights falls into any statutory or judicially created exception to capital asset treatment, and that the gain is therefore capital gain.

    The Service is likely to characterize the transaction as the sale of the right to ordinary income from Roger's continuing business as a promoter. Since Roger retains a reversionary interest in that business — that is, he retains the rights to income from promoting later events — the right sold is a carved-out interest. For tax purposes, that right is not treated as a property right that generates capital gain. The Service may argue that, if the gain is characterized as capital, Roger would continue to promote events, and then sell out his rights immediately before each event at a profit and claim that any gain is capital. (Of course, at some point a court could rule out capital gain on the grounds that "events" were a form of inventory to Roger.)

    The Service might also argue that the assets sold are noncapital because they are the product of personal services or because a sale so close to the income-generating event is in effect a sale of accounts receivable. These arguments seem weaker than the first argument stated above. (There is also some old authority denying capital gain treatment for the sale of "mere contract rights." The rationale of these cases is fuzzy, however, and at this point we are getting to a level of detail that exceeds what even the most diligent law student should be expected to know.)

Is the Kidfest a separate business? Roger's argument in favor of this proposition is supported by the new location of the Kidfests and by the new nature of this event. His argument would be enhanced even further if he could argue that Kidfest promotion requires a different set of skills and contacts than concert promotion and that his income in past years has been exclusively from concert promotion. The hypothetical does not state the reason for the sale. Roger's argument that the Kidfests were unrelated to his main occupation would be strengthened if he could present evidence that the rights were sold because he and his organization felt they were getting into an unfamiliar area.

20. The sale of a sole proprietorship is treated as the sale of the individual assets. Williams v. McGowan, 152 F.2d 570 (2d Cir. 1945). As a result, some assets may produce capital gain or loss, while other assets may produce ordinary income or loss.

The equipment is a depreciable asset used in a trade or business and might for that reason be expected to produce §1231 gain or loss. However, the $15,000 of gain from the sale of the equipment is subject to the recapture provisions. Under those provisions, capital gain is converted into ordinary income to the extent of prior depreciation taken on the property. §1245. Here, the $15,000 of gain is less than the $25,000 of prior depreciation taken on the equipment, so the recapture amount is $15,000, and Donna must include $15,000 of ordinary income from the sale of the equipment.

The building and land are also section 1231 property (real or depreciable property used in a trade or business). Gain on real property is subject to recapture only to the extent it has been depreciated on an accelerated method rather than a straight line method. Real property placed in service subsequent to 1986 is depreciable only on the straight line method, so recapture will not apply to the sale of the depreciated building. §§1250, 168(b)(3). Land is not depreciable so the issue of recapture does not arise. Thus, the entire $45,000 gain on the sale of the land and building is §1231 gain. Because Donna has no other §1231 gains and losses, the gain is long-term capital gain. (All of Donna's $5,000 gain on the sale of the building is attributable to the straight line depreciation she has taken, so that $5,000 of capital gain is subject to the special 25 percent capital gain rate.)

Inventory is a noncapital asset by virtue of §1221(a)(1). Donna has a $5,000 ordinary loss on the sale of the inventory.

Goodwill (attributable to the shop's reputation) is a capital asset. Donna recognizes $70,000 of capital gain on the sale of the goodwill.

Thus, Donna has (i) a $5,000 ordinary loss (on inventory), (ii) a $15,000 ordinary gain (on the equipment, through recapture), and (iii) long-term capital gain of $115,000 (from the building, land, and goodwill).

H. CONNECTED CURRENT AND PRIOR TRANSACTIONS

The depreciation recapture rules discussed earlier in this chapter enforce a type of characterization symmetry; since the prior depreciation deductions were ordinary deductions, gain on the sale of the depreciable asset should be ordinary to the extent of the prior depreciation taken on the property. In other situations in which no Code section requires characterization symmetry, courts may impose a judicially created symmetry rule. For example, in Arrowsmith v. Commissioner, 344 U.S. 6 (1952), two taxpayers recognized capital gain on stock when they liquidated their corporation. Four years later, the taxpayers were required to pay a liability of the liquidated corporation and took ordinary deductions for the payment. However, the Service argued and the Supreme Court agreed that despite the absence of a sale or exchange in the year in which the payment was made, the payment made by the taxpayers should be characterized as a capital loss because it was connected to the capital gain transaction in the earlier year. The Court was of the view that its holding on the characterization issue was not inconsistent with the annual accounting period.

Sample Examinations

APPENDIX

INTRODUCTORY NOTE

This appendix includes eight sample final examinations given in the basic federal income tax class by tax professors from five different law schools. Model answers supplied by the professor follow each exam. (Don't peek at the answers until you take the exam!)

As you will see from these sample examinations, tax professors vary in their approach to examinations. Some professors emphasize policy issues; other professors emphasize technical tax issues. Some professors expect precise answers to their exam questions; other professors are looking for more general answers. Some professors expect students to support their answers by referring to specific Code sections and cases; other professors do not expect students to cite many sources.

Note that some of the model answers are much more detailed than the answers you could write under the time constraints of an exam. Other model answers are brief and approximate the type of answer you would be able to write. A few of the model answers simply sketch the type of answer expected and are briefer than the answer you might be able to write.

We should warn you that these exams include a few idiosyncratic questions on special topics that are not usually covered in the basic tax course and are not discussed in this book. The model answers also include a few citations to cases that were not discussed in this book. However, you should be able to answer almost all of the questions in these sample exams. We have included the professor's instructions for each exam so you can tell which kinds of materials the professor intended for students to be able to use during the exam. (We have edited these exams and model answers to reflect changes in the law enacted after the exams were given. The answers reflect the law as of March 31, 2014.)

Good luck!

FINAL EXAMINATION NUMBER ONE
PROFESSOR BLATT
UNIVERSITY OF MIAMI SCHOOL OF LAW

Instructions

1. This is a closed book examination. You may bring only pens and a calculator. The proctor will give you an appendix with relevant provisions from the Internal Revenue Code. If a relevant provision is missing, explain how it would affect your answer.
2. The exam consists of three parts. You have three hours to complete the exam. I include my estimate of the time required to complete each question.
3. Explain the reasoning behind your answers fully but concisely. State and assume additional facts if needed to answer a question. If appropriate, discuss alternative positions and results. Organize your answers. Feel free to use abbreviations and incomplete sentences.
4. Unless otherwise stated, assume that (i) parties are unrelated, (ii) taxpayers have adopted the calendar year, (iii) corporations report income on the accrual basis, (iv) debt instruments periodically pay market rate interest, and (v) individuals report income on the cash basis.

Appendix

Part I (60 minutes, allocate as needed over six questions)

Question 1. Jack and Jill have two young children and a taxable income of $50,000. Their marginal tax rate is 25 percent. Jack and Jill pay $4,000 during the year for the care of their children. Jack's employer makes available to them $4,000 through a dependent care assistance program. Should they forgo the exclusion under §129?

Question 2. Evaluate the best arguments for and against the deduction for contributions to charity.

Question 3. In year one, Allen purchased a vacation home on a two-acre lot in Florida for $100,000. In year three, Allen built an addition to the house at a cost of $50,000. In year five, a hurricane destroyed the house, leaving a two-acre lot with a fair market value of $75,000. (Immediately before the hurricane, the house had a fair market value of $250,000.) In year seven, Allen received $100,000 in insurance proceeds for the damage to the house. What are the federal income tax consequences to Allen in year seven?

Question 4. Fred owns land with a basis of $200,000. He discovers oil and sells the land to Oil Company for five annual payments equal to $100,000 plus 10 percent of production. The total payments made in each year are as follows:

Year 1	$150,000
Year 2	$150,000
Year 3	$150,000
Year 4	$100,000
Year 5	$100,000

Assume that this transaction is treated as a sale for tax purposes and ignore special rules governing production rights and depletion. How is gain from the sale taxed under the rules governing open transactions, closed transactions, and installment sales?

Question 5. In years one, two, and three, Hanna worked as an assistant manager for Bank of America. From January to August of year three, she earned $40,000 in her job. In August of year three, she enrolls full-time in the Stanford University MBA program. Hanna does not know what she will do after earning her MBA. She pays $15,000 for tuition and $10,000 for room and board in year three. Hanna's marginal tax rate in year three is 25 percent. How is Hanna taxed in year three under present law? How should she be taxed? How would she be taxed under a consumption tax?

Question 6. Mark is negotiating salaries with two prospective employers: an accrual method for-profit corporation and a tax-exempt charity. Assuming that each is willing to pay the same present value salary, which employer can offer Mark the highest nonqualified deferred compensation? Why?

Part II (60 minutes, 20 minutes per question)

Question 1.   Peter is a solo practitioner in Miami. He purchases the following items: a photograph of Port-au-Prince, which he hangs in his office to make his predominately Haitian clients feel comfortable; a special chair that prevents backaches; a laptop computer, used exclusively for work; and a $50 Christmas gift to his secretary.

How do the expenditures affect Peter's tax liability? Would the items be excluded from Peter's income if Peter works as a lawyer for Miami Legal Services, which reimburses him for expenses?

Question 2.   Richard owns Blackacre, with a fair market value of $4,000, a basis of $1,500, and which is subject to a mortgage of $1,200. Sarah owns Whiteacre, with a fair market value of $2,000 and a basis of $400, and a car with a basis of $400 and a fair market value of $800. Blackacre, Whiteacre, and the car are held for productive use in a trade or business. In a transaction that qualifies under §1031, Richard trades his house (subject to the mortgage) for Sarah's house and car. What are the tax consequences to Richard and Sarah?

Question 3.   Betty and Carl are getting divorced. Betty is a novelist and expects to earn $300,000 per year for the foreseeable future. Carl's expected earnings are $20,000 per year.

Carl will have custody of their nine-year-old child, David. Betty wants to provide for David's college. She is considering transferring to David the following: (i) stock that does not pay dividends and will be sold during David's college years, (ii) the copyright to one of her novels, already entitled to royalties, and (iii) cash that David would invest and later repay her without interest. What are the income tax consequences of each arrangement?

Part III (60 minutes, 30 minutes per question)

Question 1.   Tycoon hates paying taxes. His current income is $200,000, half of which is interest on taxable bonds, the other half of which is from a trade or business in which he does not materially participate. To eliminate his taxes, Tycoon concocts the following scheme. First, he converts half his portfolio from taxable to tax-exempt bonds. Next, he purchases a suburban mall for $10,000 and a $10 million nonrecourse note that requires payment of interest only for the first 20 years. He then leases the mall back to the original owner for a rent roughly equal to his interest payments on the note. The projected interest and depreciation deductions from the mall will offset his remaining $100,000 of income. What problems do you foresee for Tycoon's plan?

Question 2.   How well does the present law definition of capital asset implement the policies behind the special treatment of capital gains and losses? Be specific.

END OF EXAMINATION

Model Answers

Part I

Answer 1. No. The §21 child care credit reduces their taxes by $800, which is 20 percent of $4,000. The value of the exclusion to them is $1,000, which is 25 percent of $4,000.

Answer 2. The income measurement argument for the deduction is that it reflects reduced wealth. An argument contra is that the donation represents consumption.

The subsidy argument for deduction views charities as performing decentralized governmental functions. Critics of the subsidy might prefer greater oversight and challenge its use for religious purposes. In addition, in a progressive system the deduction operates as an upside-down subsidy, giving the greatest benefit to persons in the highest brackets.

Answer 3. Allen's basis in the house is $150,000. In the absence of insurance his loss would be $75,000 ($150,000 − $75,000). After the receipt of the insurance proceeds, Allen has a $25,000 gain ($100,000 − $75,000). Because his entire loss is compensated by insurance, he is not entitled to a §165 casualty loss. The gain is taxed unless converted into similar property. §1033.

Answer 4. Under the open transaction approach, Fred would recover his basis first. He would have no gain in year one, $100,000 of gain in year two, and the remaining payments would all be gain.

Under the closed transaction approach, Fred would be taxed immediately on the present value of the obligation. His basis would be applied against payments made under the contract.

Under the installment sale approach, Fred would have proportional recovery of basis. Since this instrument is contingent as to the amount but fixed as to the five-year time period, his basis would be allocated $40,000 per year. Reg. §15a.453-1(c)(3).

Answer 5. Hanna's room and board are nondeductible personal expenses. Her education expenses are not fully deductible because she is changing professions. However, Hanna qualifies for the §222 higher education expense deduction. If "year three" is 2014, the §222 deduction is capped at $4,000. Hanna also qualifies for the §25A Lifetime Learning Credit. The credit is 20 percent of up to $10,000 of Hanna's "qualified tuition and related expenses." Her qualified tuition and related expenses include the $15,000 cost of tuition but not the $10,000 cost of room and board. Hanna's credit is $2,000. Hanna does not qualify for the Modified Hope Scholarship Credit because that credit does not apply to graduate level education. Hanna cannot take a §222 deduction and a Lifetime Learning Credit in the same year. The §222 deduction would save her $1,000 of taxes. The Lifetime Learning Credit would save her $2,000 of taxes. Hanna should take the Lifetime Learning Credit in year three.

One might argue that (i) she has imputed income for her own work toward the degree, (ii) her imputed and actual costs of obtaining the degree should be deductible, and (iii) these costs should be capitalized because they produce an asset with a useful life exceeding one year.

Under a consumption tax, she would be taxed on her room and board. Amounts spent acquiring the business degree would be deductible if deemed to be investment.

Answer 6. The answer depends on whether the employer will be taxed on the earnings on the deferred payment. Under general principles, the accrual method corporation would not be currently taxed on earnings because it would be able to deduct those earnings when the right to deferred compensation accrued. Section 404(a)(5), however, defers the deduction until the year in which the employee includes the amount in income. The tax-exempt charity can invest the deferred compensation tax free and thus can offer Mark higher deferred compensation.

Part II

Answer 1. Absent other statutory provisions, these expenses are ordinary trade or business deductions under §162(a). The photograph is probably a deductible business expense. Although *Henderson* ruled that a district attorney could not deduct office decorations, Peter has clients, albeit nonpaying ones. The chair may also qualify as a medical deduction (subject to the 10 percent floor), although one may question whether it is incurred for the "cure, mitigation, treatment, or prevention of disease." §213(d)(1)(A). Deduction for the computer is probably disallowed under §280F, since there is no evidence that it is "for the convenience of the employer and required as a condition of employment." §280F(d)(3)(A). The gift is deductible only to the extent of $25. §274(b)(1). As assets with a useful life of more than one year, the photograph and chair would ordinarily have to be depreciated, but might qualify for immediate expensing under §179.

The effect of reimbursement: These items would be excludible as working condition fringe benefits to the extent that they would be deductible under §162. §132(d). The laptop computer would likely still be subject to §280F as it is unlikely to be used "exclusively" at the establishment. §280F(d)(4)(B). In addition, the items may be excludible as de minimis fringes. §132(e).

Answer 2. *Richard:* Richard's amount realized is $4,000 ($2,000 Whiteacre plus $1,200 liability assumed plus $800 car). His basis is $1,500. Thus, his realized gain is $2,500. Richard recognizes gain to the extent of the $2,000 of boot received ($800 car plus $1,200 liability assumed). Richard's basis in the car is $800, its fair market value. His basis in the house is $1,500 ($1,500 original basis plus $2,000 gain recognized less $2,000 boot received).

Sarah: Sarah's amount realized on the car is $800, its fair market value. Her basis is $400. Thus, her realized gain is $400. She recognizes the entire gain because the car is not like-kind property. Sarah's amount realized on Whiteacre is its fair market value, $2,000. Her basis in the land is $400. Thus, she realizes a gain of $1,600. Sarah recognizes the gain to the extent of boot received, which here is none. Her basis in the house is $2,400, which is her $400 original basis plus $1,200 liability assumed plus the $800 amount she paid (the car).

Answer 3. The proceeds from the stock sale will be taxed at Carl's capital gain rate, since David will be a full-time student and will not have reached age 24 by the time of the sale. §1(g). *Heim* suggests that the assignment of the copyright would be respected for tax purposes. Thus, royalties would be taxed to David, but at Carl's top rate. §1(g). Betty will be treated as receiving annual interest on the loan at an imputed interest rate equal to the applicable federal rate. §7872.

Part III

Answer 1. The interest deduction may be disallowed if the debt is used to "purchase or carry" the exempt bonds. §265(a)(2).

The at-risk rules probably do not apply because the note appears to be qualified nonrecourse financing. The passive loss rules do not prevent the offset because both the income and the depreciation are from passive activities.

However, the transaction might be attacked as a sham under *Knetsch.*

The transaction also resembles *Estate of Franklin.* Under the Tax Court's theory in that case, Tycoon would be treated as holding an option. Under the Court of Appeals approach in that case, the debt would be disregarded, eliminating his interest and depreciation deductions.

The alternative minimum tax may be a problem if the bonds are private activity bonds. Although the alternative minimum tax affects ACRS, it does not affect the straight line depreciation for real estate.

Answer 2. The policies for preferential treatment of capital gains include income measurement (alleviation of bunching and inflation) and economic effect (relief from lock-in and creation of business incentives). The policies for disallowing capital losses include the prevention of paper transactions, cherry picking, and straddles. After describing these policies, an answer would then consider whether they applied in particular situations, such as:

    (i) stock in trade (trading in stock versus trading in real estate);

    (ii) transactions related to the taxpayer's regular business (including hedging transactions);

    (iii) bootstrap sales (*Clay Brown*);

    (iv) copyrights and patents (distinction between creators of patents, who are treated as creating a capital asset, and creators of copyrights, who generally are not treated as creating a capital asset);

    (v) substitutes for ordinary income (carved out interests); and

    (vi) property used in a trade or business, governed by §1231.

For example, one might justify the stock in trade exception as excluding assets that are unlikely to raise bunching, inflation, or lock-in problems, and do not represent the long-term investments suitable for business investment. It may also be that the expected turnover of these assets makes them unlikely vehicles for loss transactions. The special treatment afforded stock under this exception reflects the ease with which stock can be used in loss transactions.

FINAL EXAMINATION NUMBER TWO
PROFESSOR CAVANAUGH
PENNSYLVANIA STATE UNIVERSITY,
DICKINSON SCHOOL OF LAW

Instructions

1. Please adhere to the time limitations specified for each question. For each question, address all the issues raised by the facts contained therein. Then cite to and discuss the relevant Code provision and any case law interpretation helpful for understanding how to apply that Code section to the facts at hand. Be specific in your answers. Also attempt to be concise. A brief discussion of the relevant Code provision and case law should be sufficient to show your mastery of the material. Always apply the applicable law to the facts to come to a conclusion. If the facts raise the possibility of multiple interpretations, identify any facts you would need but always state the basis for your conclusion based on the facts stated. You could state what facts would lead you to an alternate conclusion. Incomplete facts do not justify simply stating the rule(s) without conclusion. If a numeric answer is possible, be sure to state it clearly as well.

2. Please read through the entire exam before beginning so that you can identify the issues covered in the exam. If you discuss an issue in one question that you think relevant to a discussion in a subsequent question, you must cross-reference specifically to that question if you want me to consider your answer there as part of the answer to the current question. By reading the exam through completely, you should be able to avoid such duplication and make use of the time provided to answer completely each question.

3. Unless a question states otherwise, disregard the alternative minimum tax.

Question 1 (1 hour). Leonidas (Leo to his friends) was a much-admired law professor who was also much sought after as a visiting professor, even after his retirement from Goldcoast University. His skills were not limited to the classroom, but indeed extended far beyond the ivy covered halls of Goldcoast or any university. Fortunately for Rockyville University, it had many connections to universities far and wide, including Goldcoast. When an opportunity arose, Rockyville took advantage of this connection and offered Leo an opportunity to return to the classroom. Leo was happy to leave retirement and return to Rockyville even knowing that this engagement was likely to require more travel than customary since he had a full schedule of arbitrations back in Goldcoast. There was no likelihood that Leo's work as an arbitrator would interfere with his teaching schedule, since all of the arbitration sessions could be scheduled for periods when Rockyville was on break (e.g., weekends, Thanksgiving, or Christmas break). Leo knew that he was going to have to schedule these trips with care to avoid travel difficulties during such periods. Unlike the students, however, he was not limited to the cheapest fares for these trips.

Leo's friends and family were concerned that the work schedule — a full teaching load plus his arbitration work — would overtax Leo, who had just recovered from no fewer than five major surgeries during the year. Nonetheless, Leo was unstoppable. Indeed, the massive bills associated with these five surgeries were an incentive for Leo to work. These surgeries, their associated, extended hospital stays and long periods of recovery once out of the hospital, cost $52,500. The fact that they had been the result of the first surgeon's incompetence was of little satisfaction. As a lawyer and an arbitrator, Leo wasn't sure that pursuing a legal remedy was likely to give him anything other than indigestion. He knew that he would receive $40,000 from the insurance companies and have to seek assistance from the tax code for the rest. Of course he would seek recovery from the surgeon of the portion (20 percent) denied by the insurance companies, but he realized that he would only see these amounts, if ever, some time in the future.

Glad to be back in the classroom, Leo equitably endured the inconvenience associated with temporarily making Rockyville his base. Lucky, his spouse of 50 years, stayed back in Goldcoast because of her own health problems and so she could be closer to the grandchildren. Certainly her remaining at home had lots of advantages, including making their normal expenses there seem worthwhile. For example, their mortgage meant annual interest payments of $5,000 and state and local taxes totaling $10,000. Leo's office where he conducted his arbitration business cost $10,000 annually for his lease. Since his absence was short, Leo saw no reason to upset these long-term arrangements.

Lucky's decision to stay in Goldcoast meant that Leo needed only a small apartment in Rockyville, which cost a reasonable $2,000 total for the semester. His salary for a semester of teaching was $50,000, not a princely sum, but adequate for the work given its associated benefits. The school provided adequate office space and everything else he needed. Besides, Leo's main source of income from current activities came from his arbitration. Six months of such arbitration activities would bring in $75,000. (Assume this constitutes his entire arbitration income for the year.) Of course, the increased travel between Rockyville and Goldcoast meant increased travel expenses from next to nothing to $10,000 (for the plane trips now scheduled to allow Leo to keep to his arbitration schedule). Although he could — and did — walk to school for his teaching every day, he needed to rent a car (for the ridiculous cost of $5,000 for the semester) just to get to the airport. Short-term leases to the semi-retired seemed to be viewed as a cash cow in the eyes of the rental companies. But Leo needed such flexible transportation to the airport, so he had little choice.

Because his life is a little more complicated than usual (between the events that have occurred and his busy schedule), Leo knows that he will likely incur more costs to prepare his tax return. Normally, he simply prepares his own return, but this year he lacks the time. As a result, this year he expects to incur at least $500 in preparation costs.

Leo wants you to explain the tax consequences of his currently busy life to him as part of preparing his return. He needs an item by item explanation with reference to the applicable legal provisions (he is, after all, a lawyer) and would like an assessment of the dollar consequences of this entire series of events, including a recommendation on whether he should itemize his deductions or take the standard deduction for married filing jointly, which you should assume equals $10,000. For purposes of this question you should ignore the consequences of the personal exemption, section 68, and any additional tax benefits allowed to the elderly or disabled. There is ample material to discuss in the facts provided.

Question 2 (30 minutes).   Natasha Hartung was on track in 2010 for a gold medal in skating at the winter Olympic games when she was attacked by a fan who had been stalking her for months. The frustrated fan had failed to gain Natasha's positive attention and decided that sterner measures were called for, in the form of a tire iron. Poor Natasha ended up on crutches, sidelined from all scheduled performances and missing the winter Olympics. Fortunately, the doctors all agreed that a full recovery was likely, although there would be a long period of recuperation and physical therapy. The frustrated fan, Johnny Izusu, was the son of a wealthy industrialist who was heavily insured against the acts of his occasionally deranged children. Thus, when Natasha filed suit against the Izusu family for $6 million, including $3 million for lost wages (after all, Walt Dizzy's Show on Ice had already scheduled Natasha for its shows after the winter Olympics, counting on her success there), emotional distress ($2 million), and the cost of physical therapy and nursing that was not covered by her insurance ($1 million), the family was only too happy to pay, thereby avoiding a lengthy public trial exposing its various and sundry peculiar business dealings.

Natasha's problems did not end with the settlement with the Izusu family and its agreement to have Johnny seek psychiatric care. McRonalds decided to capitalize on Natasha's bad luck. Having already distributed ads featuring Natasha's endorsement of the positive health consequences of eating the best onion rings in the world (to which she attributed her ability to skate circles around all of her competitors), McRonalds failed to pay Natasha $200,000, the amount agreed, for which Natasha had already performed all of her obligations (including filming 10 different ad sequences and eating 200 packages of onion rings). Now Natasha has been forced to sue for McRonalds' failure to pay. McRonalds decided to pay up, with interest, following the filing of her suit, so that it can avoid bad publicity for reneging on its contractual agreement to a much beloved sports figure.

Advise Natasha on the tax consequences of these events.

Question 3 (45 minutes). Fresh from law school in year one, Thom Wolf was working long hours as a lawyer in an investment banking firm in Atlanta. At the time of his decision to purchase real estate, an investment far safer than Internet stocks in his opinion, land values were not cheap but nevertheless still reasonable. Thus, Thom decided to buy 10 acres of land for $100,000. Following his purchase, Thom made some additional decisions, first to build a house for himself and his family on some portion of the land, while reserving the rest of it for future suitable uses that would become obvious over time.

In year four, Thom built a house for $250,000 on two acres of land that he decided to keep for his personal use. In the course of the lengthy building project, Thom decided to help finance another project with potential for significant return, far better than real estate. In year seven he sold two acres, then valued at $100,000, to his best law school buddy.

In year 10, Thom was prospering in all his ventures. Rather than pay for his child's legal education, Thom settled upon the following course of action because of his desire to instill a strong work ethic in his beloved and only child. Thom made a gift of the two acres adjacent to his daughter, Thomasina. By giving her the land, Thom hoped that his child would recognize that education too is an investment, perhaps an even better one than real estate. Thom assumed that Thomasina would sell the land to pay for her education. Thomasina, however, was even more astute than her father. She understood that the real estate market would only appreciate even more while she was in law school to acquire the skills she needed to run her own real estate firm. Thus she used the land, then valued at $200,000, to take out the loans she needed (approximately $100,000 for her law school education). Only when she finished her education in year 13 did she sell the land, pay off the loan, and reinvest the proceeds in her own law and real estate firm that specialized in the legal practice related to real estate development. The land was valued at $250,000 when Thomasina sold it, paid off her loans in full, and embarked on her own career.

Thom was overjoyed by the success of his daughter, but heartbroken that she had sold the land. (Secretly he hoped she would somehow keep it and build her own house next door.) As a result, he sought solace in increased spiritual activity. As he became more devoted to his church activities, Thom realized that there would be many benefits if he donated the two acres adjacent to his own property (the two acres adjoining the other side of his property from those given to Thomasina). The church was looking for a more pastoral setting in which to expand. By donating the land to his church, Thom advanced the church's mission and protected his own investment in his property. Thus in year 15, he made a gift of two acres to his church. (We know the church is a good §501(c)(3) organization for purposes of charitable contributions.) At the time of the gift, the land was valued at $250,000 and Thom's adjusted gross income was $300,000.

Thom was even more glad of his increased devotion to his church in the face of Thomasina's departure and the fact that his wife had instituted divorce proceedings against him following Thomasina's departure (which she predicted and for which she held him responsible). Thom's wife (soon to be ex-wife) asked for the house and two acres of land in the divorce. She intended to sell it once she had title. Thom is reconciled to her taking the house because he has decided to build a smaller cabin on the remaining two acres that happen to adjoin the church property on that side of the property. By reducing his material possessions, Thom thinks he will be better able to focus on his spiritual needs.

Thom wants to know what tax consequences resulted from these various transfers. Be sure to discuss the tax consequences of both his gift to Thomasina and her subsequent transactions involving the land. Because the transactions occurred in different years, simply explain the consequences of each by giving both a legal explanation (Code, regulations, case law) and numeric answer for each transaction. Assume that the currently applicable law was at all times in effect throughout the transactions described. Assume further, for purposes of answering the question, that any fair market value given for the land represents the total fair market value of the acres described in that transaction alone. You should not try to calculate a total gain or loss on the transactions as a whole.

Question 4 (45 minutes). Mr. McIntosh, Mr. Pippen, Mr. Fuji, and Mr. Gravenstein (known collectively as the Apples) have decided to invest in a pharmaceutical business because of its growth potential. They purchase a pharmaceutical business that really consists primarily of the patent to produce a drug with significant potential to rid the world of hoof and mouth disease. Hoof and mouth is not necessarily fatal but poses such significant debilitating consequences for the beef industry that affected or exposed animals are routinely slaughtered.

The Apples are members of a significant farming community in the Midwest. While hoof and mouth has not been a problem in the United States, it has had flare-ups around the world that make it likely that any quickly effective vaccine would be a blockbuster drug. Its preliminary trials, which occurred prior to the Apples' purchase of this start-up pharmaceutical company, look promising indeed. The community and its leaders show strong support for the Apples' new enterprise because the Apples have promised to reinvest part of the proceeds from this vaccine, once it is successfully being produced and marketed around the world, in the local community, which has otherwise seen a dearth of development dollars.

One measure of community support is the willingness of the community bankers to finance the Apples' purchase with nonrecourse debt. This seems fitting since the community and its economic leaders see themselves as stakeholders in this enterprise that should help bring capital, and thus new jobs and vitality, back to the community. Thus it is with great excitement that the bank loans the Apples on a nonrecourse basis all of the $1.5 million required to purchase a business whose chief asset is the patent for the hoof and mouth vaccine.

At the end of the third year following the Apples' purchase, the entire town waits expectantly for word that this new fast-acting vaccine is being used successfully in the United Kingdom to help conquer the outbreak of hoof and mouth that has so devastated the country, causing the slaughter of large numbers of animals and reducing its tourism because of the tight travel restrictions. Unfortunately, actual trials under circumstances such as those in the United Kingdom show that significant work remains to be done on the vaccine before it will truly be the blockbuster that it still has potential to become. Clearly it is not worthless. But devastated by their failure to achieve immediate success, the Apples decide that their heart isn't in animals and meat production (and, understandably, they start thinking about the benefits of apples, and other fruits and vegetables). They decide to turn over to the bank all rights to the pharmaceutical business and patent when its value has declined to $1 million. Unfortunately, after only three full years, the Apples are no longer the darlings of the beef-loving Midwest.

First discuss the depreciation to which the Apples are entitled and from which they would have benefited during their first years of business. For purposes of this question you may assume that the pharmaceutical company being purchased constitutes a trade or business despite the fact that this patent is not yet being marketed worldwide. Although you might want to discuss generally all of the elements necessary for depreciation, calculate any results using only whole years of deductions.

Then discuss the tax consequences to the Apples when they turn over all the rights to the pharmaceutical company and its primary asset (the patent) to the bank.

END OF EXAMINATION

Model Answers

Answer 1.   This question asks for a determination of Leo's income (including an assessment of his deductions — what is deductible by the express provisions of the Code and whether these deductions are above or below the line) and whether he would prefer to itemize or take the standard deduction.

Leo's Income: Leo receives a salary of $50,000 as an employee of Rockyville University. He also earns fees of $75,000 in his capacity as an independent arbitrator. His total gross income is $125,000. §61. Although Leo does receive some benefits through his employment with Rockyville, there are no facts that indicate these would be other than tax-free under §132 (de minimis or working condition fringe benefits).

Leo's Deductions: Expenses that are ordinary and necessary business expenses (including travel away from home, office rental) are deductible. §162. As a threshold matter, because Leo's gross income is earned as both an independent businessman and an employee, his expenses must not only be assessed to determine whether they are deductible but must also be categorized as either "above-the-line" or "below-the-line." §62(a). The expenses necessitated by Leo's continuing arbitration work, even while he is an employee at Rockyville, will be deductible as ordinary and necessary expenses and deductible from gross income. §62(a)(1). "Above-the-line" expenses are those allowed to all taxpayers, whether they take the standard deduction or elect to itemize their deductions. Compare §62 with §63. For a taxpayer in a trade or business (not an employee), an above-the-line deduction is necessary in order to tax only net, not gross, income. See Reg. §1.62-1T. Leo's expenses of $25,000 related to his arbitration work, including the lease for his office and his travel expenses (air travel and the car rental described as unrelated to his daily commute but necessary for his travel to Goldcoast), will reduce his gross income to $100,000 of adjusted gross income (AGI). §62.

The preceding analysis assumes a determination of Goldcoast as Leo's "tax home." See *Rosenspan* and *Andrews* (considering factors such as income and length of time). Expenses related to his temporary employment as a visiting professor might at first glance appear to be nondeductible personal expenses under §262. Because these are temporary (expected to last less than one year), these expenses will be deductible (see §162 and *Peurifoy*), but they will be allowed only as a "below-the-line" itemized deduction, subject to the 2 percent floor, and only if Leo chooses to itemize. §62(a); Reg. §1.62-1T; §63; §67(a). See below.

The determination of what expenses Leo may take in determining his adjusted gross income is the necessary first step to determining what itemized deductions are available to Leo and determining whether he should itemize or take the standard deduction. Having determined his AGI ($100,000), Leo can now determine the availability and utility of deductions allowed to individuals who itemize. Leo's unreimbursed medical expenses are $10,000. (Because he will be reimbursed for 80 percent of the $50,000 incurred, $40,000 will not be available as a deduction.) His deduction for medical expenses will be limited to those in excess of 10 percent of his AGI, or $2,500 (amount in excess of $10,000 (10 percent of $100,000)). See §213(a). The limited facts suggest that all of the medical expenses satisfy the §213 requirements, but this should be confirmed. See §213(d). If Leo later recovers any of the costs associated with his medical expenses, under the tax benefit rule (codified in §111), he will have to adjust accordingly (either filing an amended return or adding these amounts back into income).

Deductions that are not limited to any percentage of AGI but are only limited by the express terms of the applicable statutory provisions include Leo's mortgage deduction of $5,000. Section 163(h) contains all of the necessary requirements ("qualified residence interest" defined) — which are satisfied according to the facts given. Leo's property taxes would similarly be deductible. §164. These deductions (medical, qualified interest, taxes) are all expressly identified in §67(b) as not "miscellaneous itemized deductions" and therefore are not subject to the 2 percent floor imposed by §67(a). Aggregate miscellaneous expenses subject to the 2 percent floor include Leo's unreimbursed living expenses and his tax preparation fees. See §162 (temporary living expenses, see flush language); §212(3) (tax preparation fees); §67(a). The resulting total for miscellaneous expenses is $2,500, $500 of which exceeds the 2 percent floor ($2,000) and will therefore be deductible. It should be added that his tax preparation fees are being treated as personal, rather than related to his arbitration business, and so deductible under §212(3).

Itemize or Standard Deduction: Given a choice between itemized deductions of $18,000 and a standard deduction of $10,000, Leo would prefer to itemize.

Answer 2. The $6 million in damages received by Natasha were all received on account of personal physical injury at the hands of her deranged fan and are thus completely excludable from income under §104(a)(2). Generally, in assessing the taxability of any damage award, we would need to know "in lieu of what" they were awarded. However, where damages are awarded "on account of personal physical injury" we can assess their taxability solely by the terms of §104(a)(2). Whether achieved by judgment or through settlement, however allocated, §104(a)(2) is clear that amounts received on account of *personal physical* injury, except amounts allocated to punitive damages (see §104(a)(2) (first parenthetical)) or reimbursed by insurance, are excluded from income. See §104(a)(2).

In contrast, the $200,000 received from McRonalds was received for services rendered, despite the need for legal action. See *Raytheon* ("in lieu of what" were the amounts received). As a result, those amounts are includible in income. §61.

Answer 3.　　Thom's transactions began with his initial purchase of 10 acres of land for $100,000. His "basis" in his land purchase is important for determining all subsequent events. His cost basis in the land was $100,000 or $10,000 per acre. §1012 (no facts indicate other than ratable allocation).

When Thom built his house on the first two-acre parcel, his basis in the land ($20,000) and the house ($250,000) totaled $270,000. §1016. When he sold the first two-acre parcel to his law school buddy, his amount realized was $100,000. He realized and recognized an $80,000 gain, the amount realized less his basis in the two-acre parcel ($20,000). §1001. The purchaser's new cost basis was $100,000. §1012.

When Thom gave his daughter Thomasina another two-acre parcel, the land was valued at $200,000. Because this is an *inter vivos* gift, Thomasina stepped into Thom's basis ($20,000 for the parcel). §1015. Thomasina's use of the land as security for the loans necessary for her law school education had no effect. See *Woodsam Associates*. Because she did not use the proceeds to improve the land, no adjustment to basis was necessary. Because she had an equal and offsetting obligation to repay the loans, she did not realize income upon receipt of the loan proceeds. When Thomasina sold the land for $250,000, she calculated her gain ($230,000) as the amount realized ($250,000) less her basis ($20,000). §1001. Her repayment of the loan proceeds from the amount realized upon sale of the land received as a gift similarly had no tax consequences.

Thom's donation to the church of appreciated property that he held as an investment allowed him a significant tax benefit. To arrive at the appropriate total and current charitable deduction, we need to identify the donee (public or private); the gift (appreciated property); and the donor's contribution base ($300,000). Thom made a gift of appreciated property the sale of which would have produced long-term capital gain to a qualified public charity, a contribution that allowed him to take the full fair market value of the land ($250,000) as his contribution. See §170(e). In donating such appreciated property, Thom's charitable deduction was restricted to 30 percent of his contribution base (essentially his AGI) for this year. See §170(b)(1)(F) (contribution base); §170(b)(1)(C) (contribution of appreciated property). With a contribution basis of $300,000, Thom was entitled to take a $90,000 deduction that year, carrying over the excess ($160,000) to be used in the subsequent five years. See §170(b)(1)(C). Thom could have elected to reduce the amount of his contribution by the gain and thus be subject to the higher 50 percent contribution limitation. See §170(b)(1)(C)(iii). Because of the significant difference between the property's basis and fair market value, he would not have made such an election. No other charitable donations are discussed in the facts so no consideration need be given to the total charitable deductions allowed when there are donations to both public and private charities. See §170(b)(1) (A) — (B).

Finally, the property settlement between Thom and his soon-to-be ex-wife was governed by §1041. See §1041(c). As a result, there were no current tax consequences to either party. See §1041(a) — (b). Thom's ex-wife took the house and land with a transferred basis of $270,000 ($20,000 for the land and $250,000 for the house). §1041(b)(2). Generally, upon the sale of property received in a transaction governed by §1041, a taxpayer will realize and recognize gain based on any amount realized less her adjusted basis. See §1001. However, §121 now allows for an exclusion of $250,000 (assuming she sells the house following her divorce, not when she is still filing jointly with Thom). §121(b).

Thom continued to hold the final two-acre parcel with a basis of $20,000, his original cost basis. §1012. It should be noted that the land can be characterized throughout these transactions as a capital asset. See §1221. As such any gain recognized on the land will be taxed at the preferential rates applicable to capital assets (assuming the holding period in all cases exceeds one year). See §§1222 — 1223; §1(h).

Answer 4.   The Apples purchase a pharmaceutical company whose assets, for all intents and purposes, consist of a patent, a single intangible asset, the value of which is stated at $1.5 million. They are able to obtain nonrecourse financing in the entire amount, and they will include that amount in the basis of the asset. See *Crane* and *Tufts.*

In the absence of other facts, we will assume that the entire $1.5 million cost is allocable to the patent. §1012. But see §1060 (providing allocation rules for applicable asset acquisitions). This will allow easy calculation of the amortization deduction available under §197 (amortization of intangibles acquired as part of a trade or business). A patent is a §197 asset. See §197(d)(1)(C)(iii). Assets used in a trade or business having a determinable useful life are allowed annually a recovery of their bases through a deduction for the use or obsolescence of the asset as a cost of doing business. See generally §§167 — 168. Section 197 permits amortization of the cost of intangible assets ratably (i.e., straight line) over the 15-year period specified in that section (if applicable, §197 is the only applicable Code section governing assets defined as §197 assets). See §197(a) — (c). In other words, the Apples will be allowed $100,000 amortization as a deduction each year. As they recover basis through the amortization taken, each year they will reduce the asset's basis by that amount. See §1016. Only whole years of depreciation/amortization are required for calculation purposes (as stated in the question).

Despite high hopes and best efforts, the Apples turn back to the bank the pharmaceutical business/patent the value of which has now declined to

$1 million. Because the facts do not state otherwise, we will assume that the nonrecourse loan still is $1.5 million. After three full years of amortization, the adjusted basis of the patent is $1.2 million (assuming three full years only of amortization deductions). Based on the analysis provided in *Tufts*, we know that the full amount of the nonrecourse mortgage is the amount realized ($1.5 million) despite the decline in its fair market value. See also §7701(g). By disposing of the property, gain must be calculated as the amount realized less the adjusted basis. In short, the Apples will realize and recognize $300,000 of gain. §1001.

FINAL EXAMINATION NUMBER THREE
PROFESSOR FRIED
STANFORD UNIVERSITY LAW SCHOOL

Instructions

1. Except where otherwise stated, you should assume that all taxpayers are on the cash method of accounting and that all taxpayers report on a calendar year. Any expenses for depreciation of real property should be handled using straight line depreciation over a 10-year life. Any expenses for depreciation of tangible personal property should be handled using straight line depreciation over a five-year life. With respect to tangible personal property, you should assume that the recapture rules of §1245 apply. For all depreciable property, depreciation for the first year of service should be prorated on a daily basis from the date the property is placed in service. Ignore the alternative minimum tax.

2. This examination consists of six (6) questions. You have three and a half hours to spend on the examination. The suggested time allotted to each of the parts reflects the proportional weight that will be given to your answers.

3. Please write legibly. Any words that I cannot decipher with moderate heroics I will (by necessity) have to disregard.

4. This examination is open book. You may refer to any written material you wish.

5. In answering each question, please be as concise and precise as possible. If you provide numerical answers to any question, make sure you show how the relevant numbers were derived.

6. Although many of the problems posed have clear answers under current law, some do not. If some of the facts necessary to resolve the question are omitted or uncertain, state what those facts are, and what different results will obtain depending on which factual assumptions turn out to be correct.

Question 1 (20 minutes). Wendy is a resident dorm adviser at a Stanford undergraduate dorm. As part of her job, she is required to live in the dorm and eat at least one meal a day with the students in the dorm. At no charge to Wendy, Stanford provides Wendy and her registered domestic partner, Ann, with a four-room apartment in the dorm and gives both of them the right to eat up to three meals a day in the dorm. In addition, Stanford provides Wendy and Ann with free use of the university's athletic facilities and library and the right to buy tickets to University events at a 30 percent discount. In addition, Stanford pays one-half of Wendy's and Ann's medical insurance, at a cost to Stanford of $100 a month for each of them. Which, if any, of these benefits are taxable to Wendy or Ann?

Question 2 (20 minutes). On January 1, year one, Martha bought an office building in downtown Palo Alto for $150,000 in cash to use as a commercial rental property. At the time of purchase, the building was assessed at $100,000 and the land at $50,000. For the next five years, Martha rented out the building, taking all allowable depreciation deductions on the property. On January 1, year six, when the property was worth $200,000, Martha exchanged it for a vacant lot outside of Fresno worth $150,000, plus $50,000 in cash. The vacant lot was near a site where the state planned to build a new campus for the University of California. Martha planned to develop the land once the campus was built. In year seven, Martha took out a nonrecourse mortgage, secured by the vacant lot, for $50,000. In year eight, California announced it had abandoned its plan for the Fresno campus, and the land became virtually worthless. In year nine, Martha defaulted on the mortgage payments on the loan, and the bank repossessed the land. At the time of repossession, the land was valued at $10,000. What are the tax consequences to Martha in years six through nine of the foregoing events?

Question 3 (30 minutes). Mimi owned 3,000 shares of Corpco stock, which she had purchased at $2 a share in year one. In year 10, when the stock was worth $1 a share, she gave the 3,000 shares to her son, Sam, as a present for his graduation from dental school. In year 12, when the stock was worth $3 a share, Sam gave 1,000 shares to his friend Libby in exchange for Libby's stereo system, which she had bought two years earlier for $4,000; he gave 1,000 shares as a donation to his undergraduate college; and he gave the last 1,000 shares to his dental school classmate Roberto in gratitude for Roberto's having referred a number of patients to Sam to help Sam start up a practice. What are the tax consequences to Mimi, Sam, Libby, and Roberto from the foregoing events?

Question 4 (30 minutes). In year one, Ben purchased a vineyard in Sonoma for $100,000. In year eight, Ben's upstream neighbor, John, discharged runoff water from his fertilizer processing plant into a stream that ran through Ben's property. The runoff water contained some chemicals that leached into the soil, leaving one-half of Ben's land permanently unfit for cultivation of any sort. Ben filed a tort suit against John for pollution. John's attorney advised John that the chemical discharge did not violate relevant EPA guidelines, and he could probably win the lawsuit. The local agricultural community, however, was among John's biggest clients. In order to avoid any bad publicity within that community, John therefore agreed early in year nine to pay Ben $500,000 in exchange for Ben's dropping all claims against him. Shortly thereafter, John's business hit a downturn, and he never paid Ben anything. Early in year 10, Ben filed a new suit to enforce the settlement agreement. After some negotiations, Ben agreed to accept a $200,000 payment from John in full settlement of John's obligations, which John paid in late year 10. What are the tax consequences to Ben and John of the foregoing events in years eight through 10?

Question 5 (50 minutes). Linda purchased 100 raffle tickets at $1 a ticket for a drawing to benefit the Legal Aid Society. The back of the ticket said that the winner of the raffle would receive a three-day cruise to the Bahamas, with a fair market value of $1,000, and that the Legal Aid Society reserved the right to sell up to 10,000 tickets. By the day of the drawing, the Legal Aid Society had sold only 1,000 tickets.

A week before the drawing, Linda gave all 100 tickets to her full-time child care person, Jana. One of the tickets ultimately proved to be the winning ticket. Jana went on the cruise. What are the tax consequences to Linda and Jana from the foregoing events?

Question 6 (1 hour). Juan is a lawyer in solo, general practice in San Jose. His clients are mostly small local businesses and individuals of modest means. Juan has a sliding fee scale for his clients, depending upon their financial situation, ranging from $35 an hour to $100 an hour, and generally requires that bills be paid within 30 days of receipt. For clients who cannot afford even the lowest charges, Juan often defers or forgoes payment entirely, or makes other arrangements to accommodate clients' need.

(a) In year one, Alicia's Market, an accrual method taxpayer, retained Juan to defend it in a slip-and-fall case filed by a customer. In early October, year one, Juan negotiated a satisfactory settlement on behalf of Alicia's Market and presented Alicia with a bill for $2,000 for work done on the case, payable within 30 days. In late October, Alicia called up Juan and said, "I've got your bill here. I could pay it now if you really want me to, but things are very tight right now, and I'd be grateful if you'd let it ride until early next year." Juan said that was fine, and in February, year two, Alicia sent him a check for $2,000. Early in year three, when Juan's accountants were auditing his books for the previous year, they discovered that Juan's secretary had mistakenly mistranscribed the hours Juan had worked for Alicia's Market, and that Alicia should have been billed $1,500 rather than $2,000. Juan immediately wrote Alicia an apologetic note, explaining what had happened, and enclosed a check for the $500 difference. What are the tax consequences to Juan and Alicia's Market from the foregoing events?

(b) In year one, Juan did about 200 hours of legal work for Betty, in connection with her efforts to buy a restaurant. In lieu of any cash payment, Betty and Juan agreed that Juan would receive a 10 percent interest in the profits of the restaurant for as long as Betty owned it. The restaurant opened in year one, and by year three it became clear to Betty that the restaurant was unlikely to show a profit for a very long time, if ever. Feeling it was unfair not to compensate Juan for his work, in mid-year three, Betty offered to amend their agreement to provide that she would pay Juan $1,000 a year for 10 years, beginning in year four. Juan agreed. What are the tax consequences to Juan of the foregoing events?

END OF EXAMINATION

Model Answers

Answer 1.   *Wendy*: As to Wendy, the value of the apartment (at least her allocable share of it—see below) is clearly excluded from income under §119. The apartment meets all of the requirements of §119. The dorm room is on the premises of the employer. It is clearly furnished for the convenience (read necessity) of the employer, as a chief function of a resident dorm adviser is to be in *residence*, and hence available to students at all hours. Although the facts do not explicitly state that Wendy is required to accept the dorm housing as a condition of employment, that seems reasonably implied by the fact that her job is as "*resident* dorm adviser." As to the meals, they also are furnished on the premises of the employer. Unlike lodging, to have meals excluded under §119 employees need not be required to accept meals as a condition of employment. Like lodging, however, the employer must provide meals for its own business necessity. Reg. §1.119-1 (a)(2) interprets that requirement to mean that the employer must provide the meals for "a substantial noncompensatory reason." The regulation goes on to state that if "the employee is required to occupy living quarters on the business premises of his employer as a condition of his employment, . . . the exclusion applies to the value of any meal furnished without charge to the employee on premises." That would appear to cover Wendy. Even in the absence of an express provision covering this situation, however, it seems apparent that Stanford has substantial noncompensatory reasons for wishing Wendy to eat in the dorm, so she can fraternize with students. That seems irrefutable as to the one meal a day Stanford *requires* Wendy to eat in the dorm, but almost certainly is the case with respect to the other two as well.

    As to free use of the athletic facilities and library: The athletic facilities do not seem to fall within the express exclusion in §132(j)(4). The facilities are on the premises of the employer and are operated by the employer. However, the employees, their spouses and their children do not account for substantially all of the use of the facility, given the heavy utilization by students. The provision is probably intended to distinguish between employers that are in the business of selling athletic facilities (for example, private athletic clubs) and those that are not. Technically, Stanford falls in the former category since it "sells" the use of athletic facilities to students as part of the bundled rights they get for their tuition. But clearly it is not Stanford's primary business, and it is doubtful whether the requirement was really intended to apply here. Nevertheless, on its face it does seem to knock out §132(j)(4) here. Happily, this may not matter, as use of the athletic facilities, like the library, is probably excludable under §132(b) (no-additional-cost service). As just noted, Stanford is in the business of providing use of the athletic facilities and libraries for sale to customers (for example, to students and others who purchase day passes) in the ordinary course of business. The requirement that Wendy be in the "line of business" in which the services are provided probably does not present a problem as to either athletic facilities or libraries. In a unitary operation like a university, all services routinely provided to students would probably be considered part of one line of business. (Contrast the case if, for example, Stanford as landlord provided discounts to employees at the Stanford Shopping Center.) Assuming that Wendy is simply using excess capacity in the athletic facilities and libraries (which given the nature of the operations would almost certainly be deemed to be the case), that would meet the requirement that her use impose no additional cost on the university. In the unlikely event that Wendy lost the foregoing argument, she could also seek to exclude these as de minimis fringes. Unfortunately, the benefits are neither small in amount (Stanford charges outsiders a hefty fee, for example, to use the libraries and athletic facilities) nor are they hard to value, given that Stanford has already priced the services for outsiders, and there is (at least in the case of athletic facilities) a well-established market price for private athletic clubs with facilities akin to Stanford's.

As to the right to buy tickets at a 30 percent discount, the value of the discount is excludable, if at all, under the "qualified employee discount" exception in §132(c). The discount seems to be for services, not property. (While the tickets themselves are in some sense property, they are merely evidencing the right to acquire services, for example, in the form of concerts.) As such, the allowable discount is limited to 20 percent of the normal ticket price. Thus, Wendy will be taxed on 10 of the 30 percent discount provided on any tickets she actually purchases. Does this discount otherwise qualify under §132(c)? Section 132(c)(4) requires that the services be offered for sale in the ordinary course of the line of business of the employer in which the employee is performing services. Although Stanford is not principally in the business of putting on concerts, or athletic events, it clearly seems to satisfy the requirement that it offer tickets to such events for sale in the ordinary course of business. For reasons stated above, it is unlikely the "line of business" requirement will be construed narrowly here to limit it to employees (for example) working in the concert or athletic offices that organize events for which the discount is made available.

Finally, Stanford's contribution to Wendy's medical insurance is clearly excludable under §106.

Ann: First, it should be noted that any benefits provided to Ann that cannot be excluded from income will be treated as additonal wages for Wendy. As Stanford is providing such benefits to Ann because of its employment relationship with Wendy, and as a form of compensation to Wendy, they are part of Wendy's wages. As California registered domestic partners, Wendy and Ann will file a joint state income tax return but must file separate federal income tax returns. For purposes of their separate federal returns, they must split their income because California community property law applies to registered domestic partners. Half of Wendy's wages (potentially including taxable Stanford fringe benefits provided to Ann) will be reported by Ann on her separate federal income tax return.

Which of Ann's benefits will be treated as part of Wendy's wages? The use of athletic facilities, libraries, and employee discounts will almost certainly be taxable. The exclusions in §132 for no-additional-cost fringes, qualified employee discounts, and on-premises athletic facilities are limited to employees, their spouses, and their dependent children. For purposes of the Code, "spouse" means anyone to whom a taxpayer is legally married under state law. The federal government now recognizes same-sex marriages (applying a "state of celebration" rule), but does not treat non-marital civil unions, such as registered domestic partnerships, as marriages. For federal tax purposes, Ann is not treated as Wendy's "spouse." Ann obviously does not qualify as a "dependent child." Thus, unless Wendy can argue that the portion of the benefits transferred to Ann should be treated as a de minimis fringe to Wendy (a doubtful argument, for reasons suggested above), Wendy is in theory taxable on the value of such benefits to Ann. (For valuation, see below.)

As to the lodging, meals, and medical insurance payments: Sections 119 and 106 both extend to spouses and dependents of the employee. Again, Ann cannot qualify as a spouse. Here, however, "dependent" is not limited to dependent children. It includes any individual who is a dependent of the taxpayer for tax purposes under §152. For Ann to qualify, she would have to (among other things) be receiving more than half of her support from Wendy. There are not enough facts provided to know whether Ann would qualify here. If she does not, again they are out of luck. Wendy is taxed on the value of lodging, meals, and medical coverage provided to Ann.

How should the taxable benefits be valued? The general rule is that in-kind benefits should be valued at their fair market value. For the ticket discount and Stanford's contribution to medical insurance, the fair market value is the amount of the discount/contribution. For meals, libraries, and athletic facilities, assuming the latter two are sold separately to outsiders and hence have an established price, fair market value would be equal to that price. That rule may be harsh for Wendy, who might not value them at their full fair market value, but she remains free to decline to accept any benefits if she does not value them at least at the cost of the tax on such benefits. In the case of lodging, however, if Stanford would have provided Wendy with a four-room apartment even if she were living alone, then Wendy might well be able to exclude the entire value of the lodging. That is, she would argue that only that portion of incremental housing provided to her because of Ann's presence should be treated as provided to Ann. Section 119 and the regulations do not explicitly deal with this situation, but common sense suggests this approach should prevail.

Answer 2.   The Palo Alto property is real property used in Martha's trade or business (rental). Hence, the $100,000 of the original $150,000 purchase price allocated to the building is depreciable (under the exam assumptions as to depreciation schedules) straight line over 10 years, leaving an adjusted basis of $50,000 on January 1, year six. The land, which is not depreciable, retains its original cost basis of $50,000. Thus, on January 1, year six, the Palo Alto property has a total adjusted basis of $100,000 in Martha's hands.

Year six: The exchange is a qualified §1031 like-kind exchange. Both the property given up and the property received are real property. Although unlike in many respects, the generous interpretation of "like-kind" for purposes of §1031 would seem to cover even this exchange of a building for undeveloped land. In addition, Martha does not appear to be a dealer in either the property given up or the property received. The one given up was used in a trade or business, and the one received was held for investment. Thus, while the change in Martha's economic interests is clearly substantial enough to constitute a realization event under *Macomber* or *Cottage Savings*, she is eligible to defer recognition of a portion of the gain on the exchange under §1031.

Where, as here, like-kind properties of unequal values are exchanged with boot provided to equalize the exchange, §1031 provides that the party receiving boot must recognize any gain (appreciation) in the relinquished property, but only to the extent of boot received. Martha's realized gain on the exchange of the Palo Alto property is $100,000 (fair market value of $200,000 minus an adjusted basis of $100,000). She receives $50,000 of boot (cash). Thus, in year six Martha must recognize $50,000 of gain. Since the Palo Alto property is section 1231 property in Martha's hands (held for use in a trade or business), the $50,000 gain would be capital gain.

Under §1031(d), Martha takes a carryover basis in the new property ($100,000 from the old), adjusted downward by the amount of boot received (here, $50,000) and upward by the amount of gain recognized ($50,000). The result: She takes a basis of $100,000 in the land, which has a fair market value of $150,000. This has the effect of preserving for future recognition the $50,000 of the total $100,000 of gain in the Palo Alto property that was realized but not recognized in the exchange pursuant to §1031.

Year seven: Taking out the nonrecourse mortgage has no tax effect for Martha. Loan proceeds are not included in income, since the proceeds are offset by the obligation to repay the loan. The loan also does not increase the basis of the land securing it unless the proceeds of the loan are invested in capital improvements on the land. I will assume for the balance of the question that it was not invested in the land.

Year eight: The only question implicated here is whether Martha can recognize a loss in year eight for the decline in value of the property. The answer is no. To be recognized under §1001, a loss must be "realized" by a closed and completed transaction. In the case of tangible assets, that generally requires a sale or other disposition (including abandonment). A mere decline in value of the property as a result of market forces, where the taxpayer continues to hold such property, would not constitute such a realization event.

Year nine: This scenario poses a Tufts problem. Under the non-bifurcated approach adopted by the Court in Tufts for property subject to nonrecourse loans, Martha is treated as selling the land to the bank for the outstanding principal amount of the loan. Assuming that Martha has not paid down the principal, that would be the original loan amount, or $50,000. Martha's basis in the land remains $100,000, as land is not depreciable. Result: She recognizes a loss of $50,000 on the repossession. Is it a capital loss or an ordinary income loss? That depends on how we view Martha's investment in the land. The Palo Alto building that she exchanged for the land was a §1231 asset in her hands since she was using it in an active trade or business. As she had not developed the land yet, however, she cannot treat it as a §1231 asset. The only other way to get the loss characterized as ordinary would be if Martha can claim dealer status in land. Since the land was disposed of in one unitary transaction, under the facts and circumstances test for separating investor from dealer status Martha almost certainly cannot claim dealer status on the basis of this one investment. If, however, this was only one of many short-term investments in land in which Martha was engaged, she may well be able to claim dealer status on the strength of all of her dealings in land put together. There are obviously not enough facts to resolve the question here. If Martha can get dealer status, the $50,000 loss is an ordinary loss that she can use to offset ordinary income. If she cannot get dealer status, the land will be treated as a §1221 capital asset in her hand, and the loss will be a capital loss. She would therefore be able to deduct the loss currently only against current capital gains, plus $3,000 of ordinary income, with the unused balance carried forward to succeeding taxable years.

Answer 3. Year 10: There are no tax consequences in year 10 to Mimi or Sam from the transfer of the Corpco stock. Since the transfer is clearly a gift for tax purposes (the classic case of detached and disinterested generosity), the transfer itself is nondeductible to Mimi and excluded from Sam's income under §102. Mimi does not recognize the depreciation in her stock since the original purchase. Since there is a built-in loss in the stock at the time of transfer, it is subject to the special basis rules in §1015(a), modifying the usual carryover basis rule for inter vivos transfers. Sam's basis in the stock will therefore depend upon the fair market value at the time he disposes of it (see below).

Year 12: First, since the stock has appreciated to $3 a share, above Mimi's cost basis, the special basis rules in §1015(a), which apply only to dispositions where the fair market value is lower than carryover basis, do not apply here. Thus, for purposes of calculating any gain on the year 12 transfers, Sam takes a carryover basis of $2 a share (Mimi's cost basis) under the normal rules of §1015(a).

Transfer to Libby: The 1,000 shares Sam has given Libby are worth $3,000. Although Libby bought the stereo two years earlier for $4,000, a decline in value of $1,000 over two years in this sort of consumer good is not unreasonable. Thus, I will assume for the balance of the question that, notwithstanding the friendship, there is no gift element involved, and this is an arm's-length market exchange of property for property, at a fair market value on both sides of $3,000. (In the event it is not, the same analysis given below would hold, except that Sam, in addition to disposing of the stock for its value ($3,000), would probably be deemed to have received (and Libby would be deemed to have given) a gift of the *excess* value of the stereo above $3,000.)

This exchange of personal property constitutes a realization event for both sides that is not eligible for nonrecognition under §1031 (the stock, as intangible property, does not qualify for §1031, and would in any event not be considered "like" a stereo for purposes of §1031). Thus, Sam will be treated as if he disposed of the stock for its fair market value of $3,000, recognizing a gain of $1,000 ($3,000 minus the carryover basis of $2,000). Since the property exchanged was held by Mimi and Sam for more than a year, the gain is treated as long-term capital gain. Sam takes a cost basis in the stereo of $3,000, its effective purchase price for him.

As for Libby, I will assume that Libby used the stereo for personal purposes. If so, the stereo is not depreciable, since any decline in value is treated as personal consumption. Libby thus retains the original cost basis of $4,000 in the stereo at the time of the exchange, disposing of the stereo at a loss of $1,000. Libby is not entitled to claim that loss for tax purposes, however, for the same reason she could not anticipate it through depreciation deductions. Libby takes a cost basis of $3,000 for the stock (the amount she has paid for it with property worth $3,000).

Donation of 1,000 shares to undergraduate school: Assuming that the school is a qualified, charitable organization for purposes of §170, the donation will be deductible by Sam in year 12 as a charitable contribution. Since the stock is intangible property that would have generated long-term capital gain in Sam's hands (see above), under §170(e)(1), Sam is permitted to deduct against ordinary income the full fair market value of the stock ($3,000) without recognizing the $1,000 in built-in gain in the stock, irrespective of the uses to which the school puts the stock. The $3,000 deduction is subject to the limitation in §170 that it not exceed 30 percent of Sam's contribution base for the year (roughly, AGI), with any excess carried over to the next five years.

Transfer to Roberto: The threshold question is whether this transfer is motivated by detached and disinterested generosity, so as to constitute a gift (with no tax consequences to either side, and a carryover basis to Roberto), or is instead a form of compensation for referral services. This seems very close to the facts in *Duberstein*—Sam has given Roberto something in appreciation for past services rendered to him that were of value, presumably with an eye to encouraging future referrals as well. Thus, notwithstanding the absence of any express quid pro quo, the presence of the word "gratitude," and the possibility that Sam and Roberto may have a genuine friendship, this almost certainly flunks the "detached and disinterested generosity" test, and should be treated by both sides as compensation paid to Roberto.

For Roberto, the stock constitutes property received for services rendered. Under §83 and *Drescher*, Roberto is required to treat the property as current income to him at its fair market value ($3,000), provided that his right to the stock is fully vested and the stock can be valued. Both conditions are clearly met here. Thus, Roberto reports $3,000 of ordinary income in year 12, and takes a stepped-up cost basis in the stock of $3,000.

Sam is treated as having purchased services for appreciated property, which is reconstructed for tax purposes as a two-step transaction: Sam is deemed to have sold his stock for its fair market value of $3,000, recognizing $1,000 of long-term capital gain; and then to have paid $3,000 to Roberto in compensation for referral services. The compensation seems to be an ordinary and necessary expense of building up a practice, and hence should be allowed as an offset against income from the business in some form. The problem for Sam is whether it would be currently deductible, or instead would have to be capitalized in the business, and recovered through amortization deductions or at the back end when the practice is sold or abandoned. Sam is paying Roberto for a number of discrete patient referrals. The question is, is this more like acquiring a patient list (an expense Sam would clearly have to capitalize, subject to possible amortization over the useful life of the referral) or is it more like an advertising and promotion expense, which is currently deductible notwithstanding the fact that it may create goodwill with a useful life considerably longer than one year. As a practical matter, one suspects such expenses are routinely deducted as current expenses. But as an analytical matter, it is unclear which analogy is stronger. On the side of current deduction, courts may conclude that a bunch of discrete referrals, unlike a patient list, lack a "property-like" quality, and hence do not rise to the level of an intangible asset at all. (The distinction seems more metaphysical than real, but one suspects it might be determinative nonetheless.) On the other side, like patient lists and unlike general advertising expenses aimed at the world at large, the goodwill purchased here is embodied in identifiable individuals. If the individuals referred will in most cases become long-term patients of Sam's, courts may well conclude that Sam must capitalize the referral fees but may take amortization deductions with respect to the fees.

Assuming that courts opted for the advertising analogy here, there is a further hurdle for Sam to deduct the $3,000 currently. The facts suggest that the referrals were provided prior to the time that Sam had a going practice. If so, under §195 the expense must be capitalized and written off over five years, notwithstanding the fact that it would otherwise (if incurred in an ongoing practice) be currently deductible. Bottom line: Sam probably must capitalize the $3,000, deducting $600 a year for each of the first five years he is in practice.

Answer 4. Ben: The first question for Ben is whether the pollution of the land itself constituted a realization event for Ben in year eight, permitting him to recognize a loss in that year in the value of his property. The answer is unclear. Under the revenue ruling dealing with airline deregulation and other precedents, this would clearly not qualify as a sale or other disposition of a portion of the property for purposes of §1001. That would probably require that Ben show that the damaged portion was severable from the rest (and hence should be treated as a separate asset), and then either abandon the damaged portion or at a minimum show that it was entirely worthless. He has done neither here. Although the land was rendered permanently unfit for cultivation, it may well have other profitable uses (for example, putting up a fermenting or storage facility, or selling the property to someone else for nonagricultural development). Ben may, however, be able to claim a loss under §165(a). It is unclear what sorts of losses would be covered by §165(a) *other* than casualty losses. This may, however, qualify as a casualty loss, provided that the pollution was sudden and unexpected enough to seem like the sort of "force majeur" contemplated by the IRS and courts. The facts of the case are much like *Midland Empire*. Unfortunately, the decision in *Midland Empire* is little help here, as the court, deciding to treat the expenses of reversing the damage as currently deductible expenses, did not reach the taxpayer's alternative argument that the loss from the oil seepage itself was a currently deductible loss under §165(a). Since Ben is not repairing the property in year eight, the court's theory won't help him.

If Ben were permitted to claim a casualty loss in year eight, he would recognize a loss, equal to the lesser of (i) the decline in the fair market value of the damaged portion of the property as a result of the pollution or (ii) his basis in the damaged portion of the property. (Because the loss is to business property and not personal property, it is not subject to the $100 deductible and 10 percent of AGI floor in §165.) It is unclear what either figure is here. (For a discussion of how to allocate basis, see below.) Given what appears to be the substantial appreciation in the property from its original purchase price, indicated by John's generous settlement offer the following year, it is likely that the basis will be the lower figure here, even if (as is likely) the fair market value of the damaged portion of the property has not declined to zero. Whatever the total amount of the deductible loss is, for purposes of characterizing the loss Ben would be treated as if he had sold off the portion of the damaged property. Where, as here, the property is section 1231 property, that loss would therefore be an ordinary loss and not a capital loss.

For the balance of the answer, however, I will assume that Ben is not eligible for a casualty loss deduction in year eight.

In year nine, John agreed to pay Ben $500,000 in settlement of the suit. Since Ben is a cash method taxpayer (the default assumption in the instructions), that promise itself does not constitute current income to Ben, unless it is fully funded and secured on behalf of Ben. As subsequent events indicate, that is not the case here. Thus, there are no tax consequences to Ben in year nine from the settlement agreement.

In year 10, John actually paid Ben $200,000. The difference between the $500,000 promised and the $200,000 paid is irrelevant for tax purposes for Ben. As he never took the $500,000 into income, he cannot treat John's failure to pay it as a loss for tax purposes. It is at worst a mere expectancy that never came to pass.

The actual $200,000 payment will, however, have tax consequences. The payment is in settlement of a tort suit arising from physical damage to Ben's property. The treatment of the $200,000 for tax purposes will depend upon what it is compensating Ben for. See *Glenshaw Glass*. The facts here are reminiscent of *Inaja*, suggesting the payment could be characterized in one of two ways: as the purchase price for an estate in land (a perpetual easement to pollute); or as rental payments for a perpetual license to pollute. In the former case (the characterization the court ultimately opted for in *Inaja*) Ben will be treated as having sold a portion of his land for $200,000, giving rise to capital gain to the extent that the proceeds of the sale ($200,000) exceed the allocable share of the original $100,000 basis. In the latter case (the one the IRS argued for in *Inaja*) the entire $200,000 would be ordinary income to Ben, without a basis offset, since it is treated as just prepayment of ordinary rental income. Obviously, Ben would prefer the former characterization. On the strength of *Inaja*, he appears to have a good shot at it.

Assuming this is treated as a sale of an easement, the remaining problem is how much basis should be allocated to it. This is the second problem in *Inaja*. The answer in theory is that he should allocate a fraction of the $100,000, equal to the fraction of the total fair market value of the property represented by the loss in value from the pollution. The taxpayer in *Inaja*, persuading the court that the fraction was uncertain, was able to get the entire basis of the property frontloaded on the recovery. Ben is unlikely to be treated so generously. Assuming that the whole property is fairly uniform in quality and that the pollution damaged only one-half of it, he could allocate at most $50,000 of the basis to the recovery. If the polluted half retained some value for other purposes, the $50,000 would have to be reduced further.

John: Since John also is a cash method taxpayer, there are no tax consequences to him until year 10, when he actually pays the claim or otherwise sets money aside irrevocably for Ben.

John obviously would like to deduct the amount paid currently as a business expense. There are a number of problems for him. First, it could be argued, pointing to *Welch*, that because John's lawyer advised him he would probably win the suit, any payments he made to settle it were extraordinary and/or unnecessary, and hence are not legitimate business expenses under §162. This argument should lose. It is doubtful that Cardozo's opinion in *Welch* is sound even on the facts of the case. These facts are much stronger for the taxpayer. Taxpayers routinely make payments to settle nonmeritorious suits against their businesses for a variety of sound, business reasons. Maintaining the goodwill of the plaintiff and others who will hear of the suit is a prime reason. John should be able to claim this as a business expense under §162.

Second, is it a currently deductible expense or must it be capitalized? The answer turns on what John has acquired for his money. If he were paying damages in a slip-and-fall case on his property, he would clearly be entitled to a current deduction: The payment is to erase a liability that generates no asset of lasting value for him. Here, however, one could argue he has purchased an asset of lasting value, on one of two theories. If (as in *Inaja*) the settlement gives him a continuing right to pollute, it creates a valuable business asset with a life as long as his continued use of a fertilizer manufacturing process that throws off pollutants. Alternatively (and more plausibly), he has purchased goodwill in the community of a long and indefinite duration. However, that is often a side benefit of legal settlements that in the first instance are merely removing a liability, and are currently deductible. Should the mere fact that generating goodwill is John's predominant motive change the result? If so, how would we police/establish motives? And doesn't the fact that the payment is made to generate goodwill in the community at large make it more like an advertising or promotion expense that should be currently deductible even if it creates an asset of long life? (See discussion in question 3.) On balance, it seems like this should be a currently deductible expense to John.

Finally, there is the question of whether John recognizes $300,000 in income from discharge of indebtedness under §108, as a result of having settled a legal liability to pay $500,000 for $200,000. The answer is almost certainly no. The agreement to pay $500,000, assuming it was a binding contract, created a legal liability for John. Hence, on the face of it, the partial discharge from that liability falls within §108 (see §108(d)(1)(A)). However, §108(e)(2) provides that no income shall be realized from the discharge of indebtedness to the extent that payment of the liability would have given rise to a deduction. Assuming that whatever payment John does make to Ben is deductible (see above), that fits this case. The logic of the rule is clear. If a deduction is permitted, and if income must be recognized from discharge of indebtedness, the taxpayer should be permitted an offsetting deduction for that amount as if he had constructively paid it (that is, John gets to take a deduction for the full $500,000, but then recognizes income to the extent a portion ($300,000) is not paid). The same result is achieved more directly under §108(e)(2) by not including or deducting the $300,000. Second, even if §108(e)(2) does not cover this case, this seems like the sort of retroactive adjustment of purchase price that is routinely treated as outside the scope of §108 (although there is no express statutory authorization for it, since it does not qualify as a purchase money debt reduction). Third, John could try to argue that the year 10 agreement was merely the settlement of a disputed claim, and hence under *Zarin* does not give rise to §108 income. The problem here is that, unlike the situation in *Zarin*, Ben and John had agreed in year nine to liquidate the debt at $500,000, and hence the amount of the liability (under the logic of the *Zarin* court) was no longer in dispute as of year 10. That difference, however, might not be fatal with other courts. Finally, if John's financial troubles rise to the level of insolvency (no evidence of that on the facts), he could get relief under §108(a)(1)(B). All in all, it seems extremely unlikely that John will recognize income under §108, although if §108(e)(2) were not available, the precise theory would be uncertain.

Answer 5.   *Purchase of raffle ticket by Linda:* The first question is, assuming that Legal Aid is a qualified §170 charitable organization, can Linda claim a charitable deduction for any portion of the tickets purchased? Linda has gotten something of value in return: a chance to win a cruise worth $1,000. It is quite plausible that Linda disregarded the possibility of winning entirely when she bought the tickets, and was motivated solely by a desire to make a contribution to Legal Aid. However, unless she renounced any right to win ex ante, it seems likely that the IRS would assume at least a partial self-interested motive. Under *Ottawa Silica*, if this were an implicit quid pro quo, the fact that Linda anticipated getting something of substantial monetary value in return might disqualify the entire purchase from a charitable deduction. But because it is an explicit quid pro quo, as in the case of a mug given to donors to public radio, Linda may be permitted to deduct the price of the tickets ($100), to the extent it exceeds the value of what she is getting in return. If Linda is permitted to do that here, how would we value what Linda has gotten in return? It seems clear that, even if Linda had retained the winning ticket herself, she didn't bargain for the *cruise* in return for the tickets. She bargained for a *chance to win* the cruise. Thus, the value of what she got in return at first cut should be equal to the *expected* return on the tickets. But as of when? When she purchased the tickets, it was still plausible that Legal Aid would sell all 10,000 tickets it reserved a right to sell. If it did sell them, then Linda's 100 tickets would give her only a 100/10,000 (or one in a hundred) chance of winning a $1,000 cruise. At those odds, the $100 investment had an expected return of only $10. By the time of the drawing, when Legal Aid sold only 1,000 tickets, Linda's odds had increased to one out of 10, for an expected yield of $100. If we go with the former odds, Linda could argue that only $90 of the $100 ought to be deductible; if we go with the latter, none of it is deductible, since Linda is by then engaged in a fair gamble, with an expected return equal to investment. Which is more appropriate? If, as *Ottawa Silica* suggests, what we are after in judging the deductibility of contributions is charitable intent, the former seems fairer to Linda. When she made the decision to purchase the tickets, if she had checked the back of the tickets she had every reason to think that, ex ante, 90 percent of the ticket price was a contribution to Legal Aid.

But is it clear that the quid pro quo to Linda ex ante was limited to the expected financial return on the tickets? Most commercial gambles do not have an expected return equal to investment, although few are at odds as bad as this one (10 percent return). People nonetheless gamble because they irrationally believe they will beat the odds, and for the pure pleasure (consumption value) of gambling. We deny a deduction for gambling losses under §165(d) in part because we believe (given the personal consumption element in gambling itself) that such losses are not real losses. Should that logic carry over to this situation, leading us to conclude that the entire $100 was personal consumption in the form of gambling at very bad odds? Hard to say. These are very bad odds; that fact, combined with the fact that the proceeds are going to a worthy organization, make it likely that most purchasers of charitable raffle tickets in situations like these really are motivated in substantial part by charitable intent.

For the balance of the question, I will assume that Linda is entitled to deduct $90 of the $100 spent on the tickets.[1]

Transfer to Jana: The first question is whether this transfer should be treated as a gift, or as compensation to Jana. As a full-time child care person, Jana is Linda's employee, not an independent contractor. Section 102(c) creates a categorical rule that *any* transfers from employers to employees cannot be excluded from gross income as gifts. (There is a minor exception in §74(c) for employee achievement awards, an exception that is inapplicable here.) Although the rule is categorical, it seems unlikely it would be enforced where an employer and employee also had an independent friendship, and (purely in a role of friend) the employer gave, for

---

1. In fact (although I did not expect you to know this), courts have consistently held that the cost of raffle and lottery tickets sold by governmental and other charitable organizations is nondeductible. The cases rest on the assumption that the purchaser's intent is to win, not to donate money. That seems plausible as to state lotteries, bingo games run by churches, etc., but less likely with raffle tickets in situations like this. But given the administrative nightmare of trying to distinguish among different sorts of gambles, the utility of a bright-line rule is obvious.

example, a birthday present to the employee. Perhaps excepting such cases could be reconciled with the language of §102(c) by saying the amount is not being transferred by the employer in the capacity of employer at all. Be that as it may, there is no indication here that Linda and Jana have a friendship wholly independent of their work relationship. If they do not, then the tickets should be treated as compensation to Jana. Thus, they are included by Jana as salary income. Since child care is a personal expense to Linda, the cost is not deductible by Linda, except to the extent it could qualify for a tax credit under §21, or is reimbursable out of Linda's pre-tax earnings through Linda's employer's dependent care assistance program under §129.

How much should be included by Jana/deducted or credited by Linda under §21 or §129? For Jana, this would be treated as property received for services. Under §83, Jana, who has gotten the unrestricted right to these tickets, is treated as receiving compensation in the amount of the tickets' fair market value at the time of transfer. Normally, fair market value would be the cost to Jana of acquiring the same property in an arm's-length exchange — here, $100. But that seems like a harsh rule here, since (due to the charitable element built into the tickets) the property rights Jana acquires on receipt of the tickets, measured solely by the mathematical chance of winning the cruise, are worth considerably less than the cost of the tickets. Under the analysis above, at the time of transfer, when Legal Aid might still have sold all 10,000 tickets, those rights are worth only $10. Moreover, even as to the $10, the tickets are a form of quasi-forced consumption for Jana: If she were given $10 in cash, she might well not choose to spend it on 100 raffle tickets for a cruise to the Bahamas. The normal rejoinder — that she is free to refuse the tickets if she does not value them at least at the tax cost to her — may give somewhat less comfort here, where the personal nature of the relationship between Linda and Jana may make it hard to turn them down. That's probably too bad for Jana — we can't make these sorts of distinctions administratively. But it's still not clear how we ought to value them. Fortunately, it does not matter, since anything not included as income under §83 will be included by Jana as winnings (see below).

As to Linda, the same analysis suggests that what she has given Jana as compensation is really closer to $10 than to $100, with the balance reflecting her own consumption choice to support Legal Aid. In any event, if she has deducted $90 of the $100 previously as a charitable contribution, she may not deduct it again as an expense of child care.

Cruise: Under *Glenshaw Glass*, all windfall earnings like this are fully taxed to the recipient. Jana is the owner of the winning ticket at the time of the drawing. Thus, the cruise is taxable to her, not to Linda. (One can analogize this to a transfer of stock that appreciates in value after the transfer. Whether the transfer is a gift or compensation, any appreciation in value of the stock post-transfer belongs to the transferee.) There are only two questions: The first is whether Jana can offset the winnings by the cost of the tickets to her, measured by the amount she was taxed on as salary at the transfer. The answer should clearly be yes. Raffle tickets (setting aside the charitable wrinkle) are a form of gambling. Under §165(d), taxpayers may offset gambling gains by gambling losses. The "gain" on the winning raffle ticket would be the proceeds (the cruise) minus the cost of the ticket. All the losing tickets would be gambling losses. Thus, Jana should be able to subtract whatever portion of the ticket price was taxed to her as compensation from the amount taxable as winnings.

What amount is taxable as winnings here? The usual rule under §61 for all in-kind income is that it should be valued at its fair market value. As noted above, that is normally the price at which the recipient could acquire the property in an arm's-length transaction. If Jana can find a better price than $1,000 for the cruise, she can probably use the lower price in valuing it. But if not, she is stuck with the $1,000 value, even if she herself would not pay that much to obtain it.

Answer 6.   (a) *Year one:* Juan is a cash method taxpayer (default assumption). Thus, he is normally taxed on income only as received in cash or cash equivalent, subject to two exceptions: the constructive receipt and economic benefit doctrines. The latter does not apply here: There is no indication that Alicia has set the $2,000 aside in a fully funded account secured on Juan's behalf. The problem is constructive receipt. The heart of the doctrine of constructive receipt is that if a cash method taxpayer has it within her volition to obtain cash currently but simply chooses not to exercise that right, she will be treated as if she had received the cash. Notwithstanding some confusing language in *Amend* suggesting that a contract right to current payment creates constructive receipt, it seems clear that Juan did not have constructive receipt of the $2,000 in November year one merely because he sent Alicia a bill in October saying that the bill was payable in 30 days. Even if he and Alicia had agreed in advance that she would pay within 30 days (a reasonable inference from the statement that he "generally requires that bills be paid within 30 days of receipt"), constructive receipt requires more than a legal right to payment currently; it requires also that the payee have the unilateral power to obtain it. The conversation with Alicia in late October, however, raises a more difficult question. Alicia indicated her willingness to pay immediately if Juan insisted. Does that give Juan constructive receipt of the money? Probably not, but it seems a closer question. On the one hand, her offer to pay could be construed to create the unfettered opportunity for Juan to be paid currently if he so chose. On the other hand, an offer to pay is quite different from actually tendering the cash or making it available in a location where Juan could get it without her cooperation — the classic case of constructive receipt. Maybe Alicia didn't have the cash, or would have reneged on her offer if he had accepted. On balance, no constructive receipt seems like the better answer.

As to Alicia, who is an accrual method taxpayer, the expense (which is deductible as an ordinary and necessary business expense) should be deducted in year one. An accrual method taxpayer may deduct expenses at the *later* of when the "all events" test has been met and there is "economic performance" within the meaning of §461(h). The "all events" test is met as of early October, when Juan completed the work and presented her with a bill, as her liability to pay is fixed at that point, in an amount determinable with reasonable accuracy. As to "economic performance," §461(h)(2)(A)(i) provides that if the liability of the taxpayer arises out of the providing of services to the taxpayer by another person, "economic performance occurs as such person provides such services." Thus, in this case economic performance coincides with meeting the "all events" test.

Year two: Juan takes the $2,000 into income, as the cash is actually paid. There are no tax consequences for Alicia, who has already accrued the deduction in year one.

Year three: Juan's accountants discover the mistake, and Juan returns $500 of the $2,000 to Alicia. Clearly, both sides should account for the return in some fashion for tax purposes. The question is, how? In general, our regime of annual accounting requires that the taxpayer take each year as he or she finds it, irrespective of whether payments made or received may relate back to a transaction reported for other purposes in an earlier year. A taxpayer's right to go back and reopen old returns to recompute tax liability in light of subsequently discovered facts is severely limited generally to arithmetical or other errors that were knowable at the time the original return was filed. As to Alicia, that standard is clearly not met. Like the taxpayer in *Lewis*, she had no way of knowing in year one that the other side had misbilled her. As to Juan (who could have known of the error) it seems a closer question, but on balance it seems like he should not be allowed to amend. He did not merely miscalculate his tax liability; he actually got paid the $2,000, having use of the money for a year, and taking it under a claim of right.

Assuming that neither side may reopen earlier returns to recompute tax liability (with interest owed to or received from the government on the difference), they must take the $500 into account for tax purposes in year three. As to Alicia, the treatment is clear. Under the "inclusionary" wing of the tax benefit doctrine, as limited by §111, she is required to report the $500 as income, taxable at year three rates, to the extent she gained any tax benefit from the deduction in an earlier year (here, year one). Assuming that she had sufficient income to use the full $2,000 deduction in year one, that means she must include the $500 as income in year three. Juan is clearly entitled to deduct the $500 from income in year three. The only question is whether he can avail himself of the special rule in §1341. That section applies only where the taxpayer took an item into income in any early year because it appeared from all facts available that he was entitled to it, and subsequent events establish that he is not. §1341(a)(1), (2); Reg. §1.1341-1(a). It is unclear this would qualify, as Juan could have known in year one, from facts then available to him, that he was not entitled to the $500. But it is not necessary to resolve this question, as the $500 is below the minimum $3,000 necessary to invoke §1341. Thus, Juan claims a deduction in year three for $500, at year three rates.

(b) This fact situation resembles that in *Olmstead*, and raises many of the same problems.

Year one: The 10 percent profits interest in the restaurant that Betty gave Juan is noncash compensation for services. Thus, whether and when it is taxable to Juan is governed by §83 and the deferred compensation rules. Section 83 provides that *property* transferred to someone in compensation for the performance of services is taxable in the first year in which the rights of the transferee to the property are transferable or not subject to a substantial risk of forfeiture. The 10 percent profits interest meets the latter requirement in year one (Juan has an absolute, unconditional right to it, notwithstanding the chance Betty may never pay) and may meet the former as well. The deeper question, however, is whether this interest rises to the level of "property" at all, or is simply an unfunded and unsecured promise for future compensation. This seems arguable, but on balance the latter seems the better answer. The profits interest is an equity interest in the restaurant, and in that sense one could view this like Betty paying Juan with stock in her own company. If Betty's restaurant were IBM, the stock would clearly be taxable to Juan upon receipt at its fair market value. But in the absence of any well-functioning market for such an interest to provide both valuation and liquidity, it is doubtful it rises to the level of "property" for purposes of §83. If not, it is — like the promise in *Minor* — simply an unsecured promise to pay deferred compensation, the amount to be measured by the profitability of the restaurant. On that assumption, Juan, as a cash method taxpayer, will not be taxed until actual receipt of money under the agreement. Since he never receives anything under the original agreement, there are no tax consequences from it.

In the unlikely chance that Juan was taxed in year one on receipt of the 10 percent profits interest, he would be taxed on its fair market value, presumably equal to the present value of the expected future payment stream to Juan. Here, it may be hard to fix that value by reference to either side of the transaction. The future profits of a business like this seem quite uncertain. Consistent with the general presumption that values exchanged in a market transaction are equal, the IRS could seek to value it by looking at the market value of Juan's services. But given that Juan has a sliding scale from $35 to $100, and may make even more generous arrangements than $35 for clients who need it, that value is uncertain as well.

Year three: The new agreement to pay $1,000 a year for 10 years seems unambiguously an unsecured promise to make future payments for services. Assuming that the original agreement is construed to be that as well, we have the *Olmstead* situation: a promise of deferred compensation is exchanged for a somewhat different promise of deferred compensation. Either promise taken alone would not be currently taxable to the recipient. Does the mere fact that one promise is exchanged for the other change that result? The IRS in *Olmstead* argued yes, on the ground that the taxpayer was selling one intangible property right for another, which amounted to a disposition of property under §1001. Since an unsecured promise to pay may well amount to property received for purposes of §1001 (even though it does not rise to the level of property under §83), the IRS argued that the taxpayer was taxable on gain at the moment of the exchange. As applied to Juan, that argument would mean that he is taxed on the present value of the promise to pay $1,000 a year over 10 years. (Since we are assuming he was never taxed on the original promise, he has no basis in that "intangible property" to offset the value received under the new promise.) The IRS's position in *Olmstead* clearly seems wrong. One could argue, as the court did in *Olmstead*, that the exchange of rights is not a sale at all, but merely a novation of a contract. But that argument seemed doubtful in *Olmstead*, and even more doubtful here, where the rights given up are substantially different from those received. A more promising argument would be to say that the original promise of a 10 percent profits interest is not property at all for purposes of §1001, for reasons discussed above, and hence its exchange for a new unsecured promise to pay is not a disposition of property under §1001, but merely a change in the terms of the deferred compensation arrangement. The net result: Juan is not taxed until actual receipt of the $1,000 each year beginning in year four.

In the event we did treat the original 10 percent profits interest as property for purposes of §83, and hence its exchange in year three as a disposition of property under §1001, the exchange would clearly be of materially different enough rights to constitute a realization event under *Cottage Savings*. In the absence of any express nonrecognition provision (§1031 does not apply), Juan would be taxed in year three on the gain or loss on that disposition, equal to the difference between the present value of the $1,000 over 10 years' income stream, and his basis in the 10 percent profits interest (whatever amount he was taxed on in year one based on its then assessed fair market value). (Query whether he could elect installment sale treatment under §453.)

Last point: Given that Juan's 10 percent profits interest may have been worthless in year three, was Betty's offer to give him $1,000 a year over 10 years instead simply a gift? Probably not — although she may have been motivated by fellow-feeling rather than self-interest in preserving her business relations with Juan, the fact that the offer relates back to work done in an unambiguous business relationship would likely require that this be treated as compensation on both sides.

FINAL EXAMINATION NUMBER FOUR
PROFESSOR GRIFFITH
UNIVERSITY OF SOUTHERN CALIFORNIA
GOULD SCHOOL OF LAW

Instructions

1. You have three hours to complete this examination. This is a closed book examination. The only written material you may consult is the statutory package distributed with this examination. In addition, you may use a hand calculator.

2. There are 12 questions on this exam, many with more than one part. I have listed the *approximate* value next to the question. The lowest score you can receive on any question (or subpart) is zero. Incorrect analysis of a question may lower your score on that question, but it will not lower your score on other questions.

3. Be sure to explain briefly how you reached your answers. If you believe that a question is ambiguous or that relevant information is missing, state the ambiguity or missing information and how the answer would be affected. Some questions may be deliberately "ambiguous" in the sense that the appropriate tax treatment is uncertain because the law is unsettled or because the facts are incomplete. One of the skills being tested is your ability to recognize these situations.

Question 1. State whether each of the following statements is true or false. Briefly explain. (3 points each)

    a. Donations to United States political parties generally are deductible. Donations to foreign political parties are nondeductible.

    b. Although enforcement is generally lax, under the law, employees are taxed on the value of free coffee and donuts provided by the employer if the refreshments are not connected to any business meeting.

    c. Repairs and advertising expenditures can be deducted in the year in which they are incurred.

    d. Gabriel owns an annuity that will pay him $5,000 per year for the next 10 years. He signs a contract giving his sister Ann the right to receive $2,000 per year from the annuity for the 10 years. Gabriel will be taxed on the $5,000 payment and will be treated as making an annual $2,000 gift to Ann.

    e. Eliminating the personal exemption for all taxpayers would make the income tax less progressive.

    f. An excise tax on clothing is likely to be regressive.

Question 2. Mary earns $80,000 a year as the manager of the Mountain View Hotel and Resort. Mary is required to live at the hotel because she must be available 24 hours per day to handle emergencies.

Mary receives free meals and lodging at the hotel for herself, her spouse, and her children, and use of an automobile with "Mountain View Hotel" painted on the side. The hotel also reimburses Mary for the purchase of three formal gowns each year, up to a maximum of $1,000 per gown. She is required to wear a formal evening gown at the hotel's monthly balls. Mary never wears the gowns at other times.

A guest staying a year at the hotel would pay $150,000 for such lodging and $50,000 for such food. It would cost Mary $40,000 per year to purchase lodging outside the hotel and $20,000 to purchase food outside the hotel. (4 — 5 points each)

    a. How is Mary taxed on the free lodging? How is Mary taxed on the free food?

    b. How is Mary taxed on the use of the car?

    c. How is Mary taxed on the reimbursement for the cost of the gowns?

Question 3. Ned works at McClown's Bunburgers from 6:00 P.M. to 12:00 midnight. Ned comes to work each day at 5:45 P.M. and consumes a sandwich, drink, and fries. McClown's does not charge its employees for such meals. What are the tax consequences to Ned of the receipt of the free meals? (4 points)

Question 4. Which is more likely to produce inefficient behavior: high marginal rates or high average rates? Explain. (4 points)

Question 5. Jack, who has an AGI of $100,000 per year, purchases an antique vase for $30,000 and places it on a pedestal in his living room. Jack was pleased because the fair market value of the vase was $50,000. One month later, his dog Fido is startled by a bolt of lightning and knocks the vase off the pedestal, shattering it. Is Jack entitled to a deduction for the loss of the vase and, if so, for how much? (5 points)

Question 6. Tim is highly allergic to grass and most other greenery. At the recommendation of his doctor, he replaces all of the grass in his lawn with Astroturf (an artificial grass used in sports stadiums) at a cost of $25,000. What are the tax consequences to Tim of the Astroturf purchase? (5 points)

Question 7. Avery is a dentist. Neighborhood children frequently cut across the lawn in front of his office. Avery hates the unsightly bare patches caused by this traffic so he replaces all of the grass in front of the dentist office with Astroturf. What are the tax consequences to Avery of the Astroturf purchase? (4 points)

Question 8. Duncan is a wealthy alumnus of Granite University and a fan of Granite football. After several meetings with the President of Granite, Duncan agrees to donate $2 million to Granite to be used for the purchase and maintenance of Astroturf for their football stadium. In return, the playing surface will be called DuncanTurf and his gift will be announced at a gala party to which 50 of his friends and relatives will be invited. In addition (although there is no specific promise), Duncan knows that the children of major donors are given very favorable treatment in the admissions process. Duncan has a 17-year-old daughter who wishes to attend Granite after high school, but who has high school grades and test scores that are somewhat below the normal standards for admission. Duncan will meet the $2 million pledge by transferring stock to Granite with a basis of $500,000 and a current market value of $2 million. What are the tax consequences to Duncan of the donation to Granite? (6 points)

Question 9. Mahogany is a high school English teacher who would like to quit her job and earn a living as a writer. During the past five years, she has written several short articles related to teaching. Although some were not accepted, she published two "how to" articles in a magazine for English teachers and three humorous articles on life in the public schools in more general magazines (e.g., *Good Housekeeping*). She also published two op-ed pieces in the newspaper *USA TODAY*. In year one, she earned $900 from her writing, while in year two, she earned $800. The fees were almost entirely profit because she had few writing expenses.

In year three, Mahogany took a semester-long sabbatical leave from her high school. She decided to write a humorous book about life on cruise ships. To gather material she took cruises to Mexico, Greece, Alaska, and Scandinavia at a total cost of $12,000. In addition, she purchased a high-quality camera and lens for $2,000. During the cruises, she kept a detailed daily diary, and took photos. After her return home, she was able to sell the story and photos of her adventures in Scandinavia to an automobile club magazine for $500. Now that she is back in school, she works on the cruise ship book a few hours per week and expects to finish writing it in year five.

Discuss the likely tax treatment of the expenses and income associated with her cruise ship project. (6 points)

Question 10. Four years ago, Fred and Ginger were divorced. Under the divorce agreement, Fred was required to pay Ginger $200 per month in child support. He has made no payments and currently owes Ginger $9,600 in back child support payments. Despite her best efforts in court, Ginger has been unable to collect any payments from Fred and it is now clear that she will not be able to do so.

What is the best tax argument that Ginger should be permitted to deduct the $9,600 she is owed by Fred as a bad debt? Is this argument likely to succeed? Explain. (5 points)

Question 11. Mike, a plumbing contractor, purchased a home for $450,000, putting $50,000 down and borrowing $400,000. The outstanding mortgage is currently $300,000. The home is now worth $600,000. Mike refinances his home by borrowing $500,000, secured by the home. Of the $500,000, $300,000 was used to repay the previous mortgage. Of the remaining $200,000, Mike spends $80,000 adding an additional bedroom and bath to the home, $90,000 on new furniture, and $30,000 to purchase a new sports car for his own personal use. What part, if any, of the interest that he pays on the new loan is deductible? Explain. (6 points)

Question 12. What is the best argument that the current tax treatment of alimony is favorable to the spouses who receive it? (5 points)

END OF EXAMINATION

Model Answers

Answer 1.

    a. False. Deductions to domestic political parties are not deductible under §170.

    b. False. These items are tax-free under §132(e) as de minimis fringe benefits.

    c. True, even though advertising expenditures have a value that extends beyond the taxable year in which they were made.

    d. False. This is not a carved-out interest because Gabriel retains no remainder interest.

    e. True. A taxpayer with a low taxable income has her average tax burden dramatically reduced by the personal exemption, whereas a high-income taxpayer only sees a slight reduction in her average tax burden. Eliminating the personal exemption thus would cause a larger increase in the average tax burden of low-income taxpayers.

    f. True. Although high-income taxpayers purchase more clothing, low-income taxpayers spend a higher percentage of their income to purchase clothing, making a tax on clothing regressive.

Answer 2.

    a. The free food and lodging are required as a condition of Mary's employment and there is a good business reason for Mary to be available for emergencies. Thus, the free food and lodging is tax-free under §119. This is similar to *Benaglia*, where the manager of a hotel was not taxed on free room and board because it was given to him for the convenience of his employer.

    b. Mary probably is taxed on the value of her use of the car for personal purposes. The mere fact that the car has "Mountain View Hotel" painted on the side does not make its use tax-free. Mary will not be taxed on the use of the car for hotel business.

    c. Mary probably is taxed on the value of the gowns because formal gowns are usable for personal purposes even though Mary never uses them as such. Mary might argue that in modern society, gown use is so unusual that it should be treated as a uniform. This argument would probably fail.

Answer 3.   Tax-free. Section 119 permits restaurants to serve tax-free meals to their employees immediately before and after work.

Answer 4.   High marginal rates. A taxpayer's marginal rate determines the after-tax income she will receive from working an extra hour. If the rate is high, she may choose not to work even if, in the absence of a tax, she would be willing to do so.

Answer 5. Jack gets no deduction because it is not a casualty loss (like a fire, etc.). This is governed by *Dyer*, in which the deduction was denied for damage caused by a cat that had a surprise fit. The fact that Fido was startled by lightning probably makes no difference since the lightning didn't directly cause the damage.

Jack might argue that the vase was purchased as an investment and thus should be deductible like any other investment loss. If the vase is considered an investment, Jack has a capital loss of $30,000, his basis in the vase.

Answer 6. The cost is probably deductible since the measure is needed to alleviate a medical condition. This differs from the person who hires a gardener to avoid mowing the lawn because replacing the lawn with Astroturf is a drastic step seldom taken by homeowners in the absence of medical need. Tim's deduction will be reduced by the value, if any, added to his home by the Astroturf. In addition, the deduction is subject to a 10 percent of AGI floor.

Answer 7. The Astroturf purchase is probably deductible as an ordinary and necessary business expense even though it has an element of personal pleasure. Since the Astroturf is an asset with a useful life beyond one year, Avery would have to recover the cost through depreciation.

Answer 8. Duncan gets a charitable contribution deduction of $2 million. Neither the naming of the playing surface, nor the party (assuming it is not too extravagant) are large enough benefits to negate the charitable nature of the contribution. Nor is the likely admission of his daughter, unless there was a specific agreement to admit her in exchange for the donation. The donation amount is the fair market value of the property because Duncan would have received long-term capital gain treatment on the property if he sold it and it was not personal property.

Answer 9. The issue is whether or not Mahogany had a profit motive in taking the cruises. Mahogany doesn't get a presumption that her writing is for profit because she only made a profit in two of the past five years. But there is no presumption to the contrary. Some of the factors that weigh in favor of treating this as a for-profit activity include: (1) she has earned a profit previously through her writing; (2) she has already sold an article based on the trip; and (3) she appears to be serious about publishing the book (kept a diary, took photos, is currently working on the book). Factors that weigh against treating the activity as for-profit: (1) taking cruises has a very high level of personal enjoyment; and (2) none of Mahogany's prior success involves fees over a few hundred dollars, so it may be unreasonable to expect to make back a $12,000 expense.

Note also: (1) she would have to depreciate the camera because it has a useful life of more than one year; and (2) I have not discussed issues relating to the capitalization of her research expenses because this was not covered in class.

Answer 10.   For: The general rule is that you are allowed to deduct your basis in a debt when the value of the debt is zero. Because she is owed $9,600 by Fred, Ginger was forced to pay the expenses of her child without his help. Her basis in the debt should be the amount spent to cover the expenses in the absence of Fred's payment. Because she has spent her available income on the child, Ginger has less ability to pay taxes on the amount owed. Thus, the amount owed should be deductible as bad debt.

    Against: In *Diez-Arguelles*, the court denied a deduction of this type because the woman had no basis in the debt, as she did not actually loan the father the money. The court concluded that there are so many outstanding child support obligations that Congress should decide whether to open the floodgates on this type of deduction. In addition, allowing the deduction would provide an incentive for parents to inflate child support payments so that one parent would be able to write off a large amount of income once the other parent defaulted.

Answer 11.   The initial loan of $400,000 is acquisition indebtedness and the interest is entirely deductible since the amount of the loan does not exceed the $1 million statutory limit. The $300,000 Mike borrowed to repay his previous mortgage is also acquisition indebtedness and the interest is deductible. Of the remaining $200,000, the $80,000 Mike spent on home renovations is acquisition indebtedness so the interest is deductible and the $80,000 is a capital expense so it is added to his basis in his home and recovered upon sale of the home. The remaining $120,000 that Mike spent on new furniture and a sports car is home equity indebtedness. However, home equity indebtedness is subject to a $100,000 statutory limit, so the interest on $100,000 of the loan is deductible while the interest on the remaining $20,000 is not deductible.

Answer 12.   Under current law, alimony is deductible to the payor and taxable to the recipient. At first glance, this would seem to be bad for the recipient. However, since the recipient is generally in a lower tax bracket than the payor, the total tax burden is less. The tax savings can be split between the spouses. That is, the higher-earning spouse can increase his or her payment so that, after taxes, both the payor and the ex-spouse have more money than they would if a smaller nondeductible child support or property settlement were paid.

FINAL EXAMINATION NUMBER FIVE
PROFESSOR GRIFFITH
UNIVERSITY OF SOUTHERN CALIFORNIA
GOULD SCHOOL OF LAW

Instructions

1. You have three hours to complete this examination. This is a closed book examination. The only written material you may consult is the statutory package distributed with this examination. In addition, you may use a hand calculator.

2. There are 8 questions on this exam, many with more than one part. I have listed the *approximate* value next to the question. The lowest score you can receive on any question (or subpart) is zero. Incorrect analysis of a question may lower your score on that question, but it will not lower your score on other questions.

3. Be sure to explain briefly how you reached your answers. If you believe that a question is ambiguous or that relevant information is missing, state the ambiguity or missing information and how the answer would be affected. Some questions may be deliberately "ambiguous" in the sense that the appropriate tax treatment is uncertain because the law is unsettled or because the facts are incomplete. One of the skills being tested is your ability to recognize these situations.

Question 1. State whether each of the following statements is true or false. Briefly explain. (3 points each)

    a. Debby is blind. Debby's parents send her to a special school for the blind. The tuition qualifies as a medical expense under §213, but only to the extent it exceeds the cost of an ordinary private school.

    b. Jack's grandfather dies and leaves him $100,000. Jack is not taxed on any portion of the $100,000.

    c. An individual cannot deduct mortgage payments on a vacation home unless that vacation home is declared her principal residence.

    d. It is easier to avoid paying taxes on income from investments than to avoid paying taxes on earned income.

    e. In times of rising inventory prices, FIFO will produce a lower tax liability than LIFO.

    f. The top marginal tax rate is lower today than it was in the 1950s.

Question 2. Greta, a young lawyer with an income of $60,000 per year, is a fan of the heavy metal group Steel Carriage. When she learns that their tenth anniversary concert will be televised on pay-per-view, she invites all her friends to her house to watch the concert on her big screen TV. For the final song, Greta turns off all the lights in the room and she and her friends light cigarette lighters and hold them overhead to honor the band. Unfortunately, Greta drops her lighter, the drapes catch on fire, and the house burns down. Although Greta has insurance, $50,000 of her $200,000 loss is not covered. What portion, if any, of the $50,000 loss can Greta deduct? (4 points)

Question 3. Lewis is an 18-year-old who is about to enter his freshman year of college at an expensive private school. His wealthy Aunt Mabel says, "I'll loan you $10,000 per year to attend college. To encourage you to do well, I promise that if you graduate with a 3.5 average or better, you won't have to repay the loan. Otherwise, you will be required to repay $1,000 plus interest each year until the loan is repaid." Lewis graduates four years later with a 3.6 average. Aunt Mabel forgives the loan. What are the tax consequences of these transactions? (Disregard §7872.) (5 points)

Question 4. Ruby is employed as manager of Hippo Records, a 10-store chain of music stores that sells compact discs, tapes, and related items. Hippo also produces a small number of CDs itself, mostly of up-and-coming artists. Discuss the likely tax consequences of the following transactions to Ruby and Hippo.

    a. Ruby purchases a deluxe set of headphones for $2,000. She uses these headphones late at night to evaluate CDs that Hippo is considering ordering. Ruby is reimbursed by Hippo. Hippo is the legal owner of the headphones, but Ruby keeps the headphones at her home. (5 points)

b. Ruby attends Miseryfest, a two-day festival of alternative music in Seattle, Washington. Ruby is less interested in headliner Bush than in lesser-known groups that Hippo might wish to sign to contracts. During the trip, Ruby spends $2,500 for first-class airfare, $400 for meals (some alone, some with bands), $100 for a ticket to Miseryfest and $400 for an overcoat (when the weather at the outdoor concert turns unseasonably cold). All of these expenses are reimbursed by Hippo. (8 points)

c. Ruby subscribes to the music magazines *Rolling Stone* and *Vibe* at a cost of $40 per year. She is not reimbursed by Hippo. (3 points)

d. Ruby occasionally uses a bicycle and weight machine purchased by Hippo. The equipment is located in a spare room at the company's main headquarters where Ruby works. All employees are entitled to use the equipment. (5 points)

e. Ruby parks for free in Hippo's underground parking lot. Hippo charges nonemployees $100 per month for a space in the lot. (4 points)

Question 5. Anita purchases a used car for $1,000 in year one. While cleaning the car's interior two weeks later, she finds a diamond ring worth $2,500 under one of the seats. In year three, Anita sells the ring for $2,800. What are the tax consequences of selling the diamond ring? (4 points)

Question 6. Under what circumstances, if any, can an individual deduct the cost of attending graduate school? (4 points)

Question 7. Liz is a senior guide for Adventure Tours, a tour company, earning a salary of $80,000. The company specializes in luxury tours of wilderness areas in Alaska in specially designed campers. While on tour duty Liz and her longtime female companion, Mindy, are provided with free food and lodging in a luxury camper.

Liz is on duty eight months of the year. During the four winter months when Liz is not on duty, she and Mindy rent a beachfront apartment in Florida. They are reimbursed by Adventure Tours up to a maximum payment of $5,000 per year for their rent in Florida.

During their off hours, Liz and Mindy are permitted free use of all of the tour recreation facilities. These include nighttime outdoor movies, concerts by local Alaskan performers, use of exercise bikes, and hunting lessons. Liz's employment contract also provides that she and Mindy will be provided with free medical services (under a plan that is tax-free to the extent authorized by law). Mindy does not perform any duties for Adventure Tours.

What are the tax consequences to Liz and Mindy of the rent reimbursement and of the free goods and services they receive? (12 points)

Question 8. What are the arguments for and against excluding pain and suffering damages from taxation? (6 points)

END OF EXAMINATION

Model Answers

Answer 1.

    a. False. The costs of special schools required because of blindness or any other medical reason are fully deductible, unlike the costs of Braille books, which are deductible only to the extent that the cost exceeds the cost of ordinary books.

    b. True. Bequests are received tax-free. Jack's grandfather's estate might be subject to an estate tax if the estate was large enough.

    c. False. An individual is entitled to deduct interest on two personal residences as long as the total amount of the mortgages is less than the statutory limit.

    d. True. Income from investment can be shielded in many ways. Perhaps the most important is the realization requirement. This permits an individual to avoid taxation on the increase in value of investment property until it is sold. Qualified pension plans are another important method of tax-free investment. Moreover, investment gains can be offset by investment losses. In many cases, these losses do not reflect a real economic loss, but are due to accelerated depreciation and other write-offs. It is difficult to shield earned income because of the passive loss limitation rules.

    e. False. Under FIFO, it is assumed that the first goods purchased are the first goods sold. In times of rising inventory prices, these goods will be the cheapest. Thus, the cost of goods sold will be smaller and the taxable income of the business will be larger under FIFO.

    f. True. The top marginal rate in the 1950s was at least 70 percent and sometimes higher. Substantial cuts in the top marginal rate were made during the Kennedy, Reagan, and George W. Bush administrations. Many special deductions and exclusions, including a large capital gains preference, offset the high marginal rates in the 1950s.

Answer 2. Greta gets no deduction for the $150,000 of loss that was covered by insurance. She can deduct the remaining loss as a casualty loss if the fire was caused by her own negligence, but not if the fire was caused intentionally or by gross negligence. Greta's actions are ordinary negligence. It isn't a great idea to hold up a lighter in the house, but the chances of causing a fire are small. Greta's actions are much less culpable than the husband in *Blackman*, who intentionally burned his wife's clothing. If the casualty loss deduction is permitted, Greta can deduct the portion of the loss that was not covered by insurance, less $100, less 10 percent of her AGI. Thus, Greta can deduct $43,900, which is $50,000 less $100 less $6,000 (10 percent of $60,000).

Answer 3. The original loans of $10,000 per year appear to be legitimate loans, so Lewis would not be taxed on the receipt of the money and Aunt Mabel would not get a deduction. Aunt Mabel would be taxed on the interest earned. Lewis would not get a deduction for the interest because these were personal loans.

The treatment of the loan forgiveness depends on whether it was a gift. If it was a gift, then Lewis will not be taxed on the relief of indebtedness. Aunt Mabel's gift may subject her to gift tax on the gift. If, instead, Lewis earned the discharge of indebtedness by doing well in school, he would be taxed on the discharge of indebtedness. Aunt Mabel would not get a deduction (nor pay any gift tax). Rather, she would be treated as having made a nondeductible personal purchase. Is this a gift? Probably. Aunt Mabel appears to be discharging the debt out of a detached and disinterested generosity. It is true that she wants Lewis to do well and that she is getting what she wants. Lewis's academic achievement probably would be valid consideration for purposes of contract law. Nevertheless, Aunt Mabel's motivation probably was to get Lewis to study for his own good. This is a very different case from *Duberstein*, where the businessman gave a car to a person who recommended potential customers.

Answer 4.

a. The headphones probably are an ordinary and necessary business expense for Ruby, given her job of deciding which CDs to order. It doesn't matter that the headphones may be more expensive than required. (Business travelers can deduct, for example, first-class seats.) Moreover, there might be a business reason to have high-quality headphones. If, however, Ruby also uses the headphones for personal listening, she might be taxed on the value of her use. Ruby might argue that all listening is business-related because it improves her knowledge of music. Hippo would be required to capitalize the expense of the headphones if they have a useful life greater than one year.

b. This seems to be a valid business trip given Hippo's involvement in music production. The $2,500 airfare would be deductible by Hippo and tax-free to Ruby. First-class business travel is okay. The meals for Ruby are tax-free to Ruby as travel expenses. The cost of buying meals for bands is tax-free as a business expense if a bona fide business discussion took place. Even if the meals qualify as business expenses, they are only 50 percent deductible by Hippo. The ticket is tax-free to Ruby and 100 percent deductible by Hippo because it is directly related to Hippo's business. (It is not business-related entertainment, which is only 50 percent deductible to Hippo.) The overcoat doesn't qualify as a uniform because it is suitable for ordinary use. Assuming that Ruby gets to keep the overcoat, it is probably treated as compensation that is taxable to Ruby and deductible by Hippo. If Hippo keeps the coat and loans it to other employees (unlikely), it might be treated as an ordinary and necessary business expense and be tax-free to the employees and deductible (or perhaps capitalized) by Hippo.

c. The cost of *Rolling Stone* and *Vibe* would be deductible employee business expenses since Ruby is in the music business and needs to stay informed about the industry. These can be taken by Ruby as a personal deduction subject to the 2 percent floor on miscellaneous personal deductions.

d. The equipment would be tax-free to Ruby as an on-premises athletic facility (albeit a modest one). Hippo could deduct the cost of running the facility (e.g., the cost of the lights, etc.). The cost of the bike and weight machine could be capitalized and depreciated by Hippo. If the bike and weight machine are the only items in the facility, use of it might also qualify for tax-free treatment as a de minimis fringe.

e. This is a tax-free transportation fringe to Ruby. The value of the parking is below the statutory maximum amount. Hippo can deduct the cost of running the parking lot and can depreciate the cost of the parking structure itself.

Answer 5.   The diamond ring is a treasure trove and will be taxable income to Anita in the year in which she finds the ring. Anita will thus be required to report $2,500 of ordinary income in year one. This will give her a basis of $2,500 in the ring. When Anita sells the ring for $2,800, she will have a taxable capital gain of $300.

Answer 6.   The cost of graduate school is fully deductible only if the school will improve the taxpayer's performance in her existing career and will not prepare her for a new career. On the other hand, graduate students may take a limited deduction, under §222, for their higher education costs. In the alternative, graduate students may claim the §25A Lifetime Learning Credit.

Answer 7.   Liz is taxed on the rent reimbursement because she is providing the services to Adventure Tours. Thus, Liz is taxed on the full $5,000 even though Mindy is sharing the beachfront apartment with her. Mindy's use of the apartment is a gift from Liz to Mindy. Liz cannot avoid taxation under §119 because the housing is not on the business premises of the employer.

Similarly, Liz is taxed on the full value of all of the other services provided by the company to Mindy. Services provided to Mindy cannot qualify for no-additional-cost fringe treatment under §132 because she is not an employee, a spouse, or a dependent child of an employee. Even if Liz and Mindy function as a married couple, tax law doesn't treat such relationships as favorably as married couples.

Liz may be able to exclude the movies and concerts as no-additional-cost fringes under §132(b) if she isn't taking any space away from paying customers. Her use of the exercise bikes and weight machines might also be excluded under the same rationale. Liz might also argue that under §132(j)(4) the exercise bikes and weight machines are an employer-provided athletic facility. However, the argument may fail because this section requires that substantially all of the use of the facility be by employees, and the exercise bikes and weight machines may be primarily used by customers.

The hunting lessons do not qualify as a no-additional-cost fringe because of the substantial service element. Reg. §1.132-3. However, they might be excluded as a working-condition fringe if hunting skills would improve Liz's ability as an adventure tour guide. She might also argue that the use of the exercise equipment could be deducted on the same grounds.

Liz would not be taxed on the medical care, since employers are allowed to provide tax-free medical care to employees. §106. She probably also would be able to exclude the housing and meals provided to her while on duty. §119.

Liz would not be able to exclude the medical care and on-duty housing and meals provided to Mindy unless Mindy is treated as Liz's "dependent." Sections 106 and 119 allow exclusion of employee fringe benefits provided to an employee's dependent. The term *dependent* is defined to include the taxpayer's "qualifying relative." §152(a). A partner is the taxpayer's qualifying relative if: (i) the partner's gross income for the year is less than the dependent exemption amount (e.g., $3,950 in 2014); (ii) the taxpayer provides more than half of the partner's support for the year; and (iii) the partner has the same principal place of abode as the taxpayer and is a member of the taxpayer's household during the year. §152(d)(1), (2)(H). If these requirements were met for Mindy, Liz would be able to exclude the medical care and on-duty meals and lodging that Adventure Tours provided to Mindy. Liz would not be able to exclude the §132 fringe benefits provided to Mindy, even if Mindy were her "dependent," because, for purposes of the §132, a dependent is treated as an employee only if the dependent is a dependent child.

Answer 8.   Some of the arguments are:

- *For taxation:* Tax liability should be based on an individual's financial status. Pain and suffering damages compensate an individual for a nonmonetary loss. Thus, the individual is better off financially because of the injury and the resulting recovery. Since the individual has a greater ability to pay, she should pay more. Noting that individuals generally do not insure against nonmonetary losses reinforces this idea. Another argument is that injured individuals who do not receive pain and suffering damages (perhaps because there was no tort liability) are not permitted a deduction, so individuals who do receive a recovery should be taxed.

- *Against taxation:* Pain and suffering damages simply compensate an individual for a loss. They do not make the individual better off. Indeed, they just replace untaxed imputed income from good health that has been involuntarily lost. Moreover, victims are often undercompensated for losses, especially when legal costs are considered. Tax-free treatment is needed to make the injured individual whole. Finally, it could be argued that it is unseemly to tax an injured individual on a tort recovery.

FINAL EXAMINATION NUMBER SIX
PROFESSOR GRIFFITH
UNIVERSITY OF SOUTHERN CALIFORNIA
GOULD SCHOOL OF LAW

Instructions

1. You have three hours to complete this examination. This is a closed book examination. The only written material you may consult is the statutory package distributed with this examination. In addition, you may use a hand calculator.

2. There are 15 questions on this exam, many with more than one part. I have listed the *approximate* value of each question next to the question. The lowest score you can receive on any question (or subpart) is zero. Incorrect analysis of a question may lower your score on that question, but it will not lower your score on other questions.

3. Pace yourself to be sure to finish the examination.

4. Be sure to explain briefly how you reached your answers. If you believe that a question is ambiguous or that relevant information is missing, state the ambiguity or missing information and how the answer would be affected. Some questions may be deliberately "ambiguous" in the sense that the appropriate tax treatment is uncertain because the law is unsettled or because the facts are incomplete. One of the skills being tested is your ability to recognize these situations.

Question 1. State whether each of the following statements is true or false. Briefly explain. (3 points each)

    a. Under current law an individual's average tax rate generally is higher than his marginal rate.

    b. It is possible for an employee to receive a 30 percent discount on goods and services provided by his employer without being taxed on any portion of the discount.

    c. No gain is recognized on property transferred incident to a divorce.

    d. Under the accrual method of accounting, an attorney is required to report income for legal services she rendered and for which she billed the client, even if she has not yet received payment.

    e. Annual net losses associated with stamp collecting generally are not deductible.

Question 2. What are the most important policy arguments for not taxing unrealized gains on property? (4 points)

Question 3. Which of the following items (if any) generally are included in taxable income? No need to explain your answers. (2 points each)

    a. Death benefits received from insurance on the life of your spouse.

    b. A full tuition scholarship to U.S.C. law school.

    c. Damages received for lost wages resulting from a personal physical injury.

    d. Money received for winning the jackpot in the state lottery.

    e. Barter exchanges where the items exchanged have a fair market value less than $100.

    f. Embezzled funds.

    g. Money withdrawn from a savings account.

Question 4. Janet is a violinist employed by the Cleveland Symphony earning a salary of $40,000 per year. State the likely tax consequences to Janet of the following transactions. If additional facts are needed, state them and indicate how they would affect your answer. (3–5 points each)

    a. Janet uses one room in her apartment as a practice and listening room. She practices two to four hours per day and usually spends an additional hour listening to music, mostly classical pieces.

    b. While on tour, the symphony pays for Janet's hotel room and reimburses her for all meal expenses up to $35 per day.

    c. During the two months prior to the new season, rehearsals are held during both mornings and afternoons. During this period, the symphony provides a box lunch to all of the musicians at the rehearsal hall. Janet and about two-thirds of the other musicians typically eat the box lunch. The rest either bring their own lunch or eat at a nearby pizza shop.

d. Janet purchases new violin strings at a cost of $40 per month.

e. During the off-season, Janet travels to Europe. On her trip she attends a classical music concert at least three times a week. The trip costs her $5,000 plus $1,000 for the tickets.

f. Janet purchases a violin for $30,000.

g. The symphony director believes that physically fit musicians generally are better able to endure long rehearsals and will miss fewer days of work. Thus, the symphony reimburses its musicians up to $1,000 per year for a health club membership. Janet joins a health club and is reimbursed for its $800 annual fee.

h. Janet is required to wear a floor-length formal black evening dress at her performances. Most musicians spend about $400 on their dresses. Janet purchases a custom-made dress for $2,200. She says the expensive dress looks better and is much more comfortable than cheaper dresses. She only wears the dress during performances.

Question 5. Which one of the following two fringe benefits is subject to the non-discrimination rules?

a. Working condition fringes
b. Employee discounts

Does the different treatment of these two items with respect to the non-discrimination rules make any sense? Explain. (4 points)

Question 6. Mary and Ned each have $200,000 to invest. Mary purchases a condominium for $200,000 and lives in it. Ned puts the $200,000 in the bank, earns $20,000 in interest and uses that interest to rent an apartment. Ned's taxable income will be $20,000 more than Mary's taxable income. Make the best case for the position that this result is not unfair. (4 points)

Question 7. What are the policy arguments for and against making employer-provided parking tax-free? How do you think employer-provided parking should be taxed? (6–8 points)

Question 8. Alice is a high school English teacher earning a salary of $30,000 per year. For each of the following items, state how Alice would be treated (i) under current law (CL), (ii) under a Haig-Simons (comprehensive) income tax (HS), and (iii) under a comprehensive consumption tax (CT). Explain very briefly. (3–5 points each)

a. During the summer, Alice tutors the child of her plumber. In return, the plumber installs a new sink at the home of Nellie, Alice's mother.

b. Alice's friend Mike repays $4,000 he borrowed from her the previous year.

c. Alice uses $2,000 of her income to purchase two years of karate lessons.

d. Alice enrolls in a night law school and spends $5,000 of her salary on tuition.

Question 9. Polly purchases an asset that can be depreciated over a five-year period. The asset costs Polly $8,000.

a. What is the depreciation under the double declining balance method during each of the first two years? (Disregard the half-year convention and "bonus" depreciation.) (4 points)

b. Which depreciation method is closer to the consumption tax ideal, the 200 percent declining balance method or the straight line method? Why? (3 points)

Question 10. What is the utilitarian argument in favor of a progressive rate structure? Would a utilitarian favor complete equality of income? (5 points)

Question 11. Robert owns Blackacre with a fair market value of $4,000 and a basis of $1,500, which is subject to a mortgage of $1,200. Sally owns Whiteacre with a fair market value of $2,000 and a basis of $500, plus a rare stamp with a basis of $400 and a fair market value of $800. In a qualifying like-kind exchange, Robert transfers Blackacre (subject to the mortgage) to Sally for Whiteacre and the stamp.

What are the tax consequences to Robert and Sally? (8 points)

Question 12. Jed discovers oil on his land, which has a $120,000 basis. He sells the land to a drilling company for $100,000 immediately plus additional payments based on the value of any oil produced. Adequate interest will be paid on any additional payments. It is estimated that the additional payments will be $50,000 per year for the next four years, after which the well will be dry. Thus Jed's expected payments will be as follows:

Year 1: $100,000
Year 2: $ 50,000 (estimate)
Year 3: $ 50,000 (estimate)
Year 4: $ 50,000 (estimate)
Year 5: $ 50,000 (estimate)

a. If the estimated amounts are accurate, what are the tax consequences to Jed if he is taxed on the installment method? (3 points)

b. How would Jed be taxed if this were taxed as an open transaction? (3 points)

c. How would Jed be taxed if this were taxed as a closed transaction? (For this part c, do not attempt to calculate the precise numbers.) (3 points)

Question 13.   Bill owns a small jewelry shop. He brings his dog Max to work with him. One day a cat follows a customer into the store. Max leaps at the cat and destroys the store's plate glass window. Bill replaces the window with shatterproof glass at a cost of $3,000, double the cost of ordinary glass. How will Bill's $3,000 expense be treated? (4 points)

Question 14.   Ed gives Fred a rare coin as a gift. Ed purchased the coin for $5,000; at the time of the gift, the fair market value of the coin was $3,000. Two years later Fred sells the coin for $4,000. (5 points)

    a. What are the tax consequences to Fred on the receipt of the coin?
    b. What are the tax consequences to Fred on the sale of the coin?

Question 15.   Jack's store was destroyed in a flood. It had a basis of $400,000 and an estimated fair market value of $600,000.

    Jack received $550,000 from insurance. He purchased a new store for $500,000 and used the remaining money to buy two delivery trucks for $25,000 each.

    What are the tax consequences to Jack of these transactions? (4 points)

END OF EXAMINATION

Model Answers

Answer 1.

a. False, since marginal rates rise throughout most of the income range.
b. True for goods, but not for services, where the tax-free discount is limited to 20 percent.
c. True.
d. True.
e. True. Stamp collecting is a hobby, so net losses will not be deductible.

Answer 2.

- The taxpayer does not have the money to pay the tax.
- It is hard to determine the amount of gain until the property is sold.

Answer 3.

a. Not included.
b. Not included.
c. Not included.
d. Included.
e. Included.
f. Included.
g. Not included.

Answer 4.

a. This is unlikely to qualify as a home office. A deduction is allowed only where a portion of the home is exclusively used (i) as the principal place of business (not true here) or (ii) as a place of business used by patients, clients, or customers (not true here).
b. The reimbursement is tax-free to Janet.
c. Almost certainly taxable. The box lunch is not for the convenience of the employer because the availability and use of the nearby pizza shop suggests there is no business reason to eat lunch at the rehearsal hall.
d. Deductible as an employee business expense, subject to the 2 percent of AGI floor.
e. This is unlikely to qualify as a business trip. Travel as a form of education is not deductible.
f. This is a business expense, subject to the 2 percent of AGI floor, but Janet must capitalize the cost of the violin and take depreciation deductions.
g. The reimbursement is taxable to Janet. Under §132, a health club provided by the employer on the premises of the employer is not taxable to the employee. Nothing in the tax code, however, excludes reimbursement for health club memberships. The connection between the club and Janet's job is tenuous.

h. This is a fairly close call. Uniforms are deductible, but clothing that can be worn in ordinary life is not. The best argument for Janet is that a floor-length formal black evening dress is not usable except at her job and thus should be considered a uniform. If this is correct, it does not matter that she purchased an expensive dress. However, the dress is suitable to wear to very formal events like opening night at the opera, so the cost may not be deductible.

Answer 5. Only employee discounts are subject to the nondiscrimination rules. Nondiscrimination rules do not make sense for working condition fringes because such fringes will vary according to the nature of the job. An office with a view, for example, might serve a business purpose for an attorney, but not for a plumber.

Answer 6. Some of the arguments are:

- Because the tax benefits of the condo would be capitalized into the price, the condo may not be as nice as the apartment.
- Mary is taking a higher risk owning the condo.
- Ned could have purchased the condo if he had wanted to.

Answer 7. *For*: Parking can be viewed as a business expense. In general, it is desirable to permit a deduction for business expenses.

Against: Parking can be viewed as a personal expense because the individual chooses not to live near work. If parking is provided tax-free, an individual will have less incentive to car pool, thereby increasing pollution. If parking is tax-free, an individual may choose parking rather than cash even if, in a no-tax world, the individual would prefer cash.

Answer 8.

a. *Current law*: Alice is taxed on the fair market value of the sink. Barter exchanges are taxable.

Haig-Simons: Either Alice or Nellie is taxed on the fair market value of the sink, since it represents an increase in wealth (and/or consumption). Arguably, both are taxed if the gift is viewed as consumption to Alice and to Nellie. The taxation of gifts under a Haig-Simons income tax is unclear.

Consumption tax: Strictly speaking, the use of the sink is consumption so Nellie would be taxed on the rental value each year. The sink (or the rental value) seems to be consumption to Nellie. You could also argue that Alice received consumption from making the gift.

b. *Current law*: Not taxable. Repayments of loans are not taxable.

Haig-Simons: Not taxable. The increase in consumption is offset by a reduction in wealth.

Consumption tax: Taxable (assuming that Alice spends the $4,000 on consumption rather than reinvesting it). Dissaving is taxed under a consumption tax.

c. *Current law:* Alice gets no tax deduction for the purchase of the karate lessons.

Haig-Simons: Alice gets no tax deduction for the purchase of the karate lessons. Lessons taken this year are consumption. The right to lessons next year is a form of wealth.

Consumption tax: The purchase of the karate lessons should be viewed as the purchase of an asset and Alice should get a $2,000 deduction. Alice should take the value of the lessons into income as she uses them.

d. *Current law:* The educational expenses are not fully deductible because the education prepares Alice for a new profession. However, Alice would qualify for: (i) a §222 higher education expense deduction (limited to $4,000); or (ii) a Lifetime Learning Credit of $1,000 (20 percent of the $5,000 of tuition expense).

Haig-Simons: Alice gets no tax deduction because the reduction in consumption is offset by an increase in wealth from the education. Arguably, under a Haig-Simons income tax Alice should be taxed on the value of the education that is derived from the imputed income from her studying.

Consumption tax: Alice gets a deduction for the tuition unless the law school cost is viewed as a form of personal consumption. Since night law school is not much fun, the cost is likely to be viewed as an investment in human capital rather than consumption.

Answer 9.

a. Year one: $3,200, leaving a basis of $4,800.
   Year two: $1,920.
b. The double declining balance method provides faster depreciation than the straight line method. Since under a consumption tax the entire amount would be deducted in the first year, the double declining balance method is more like a consumption tax approach.

Answer 10.
The utilitarian argument in favor of a progressive tax is that money is more valuable to the poor than to the rich. A utilitarian would not favor complete equality of income because it would eliminate most work incentives and thus lower total wealth greatly. A utilitarian would balance the utility gain from redistribution against the utility loss from decreasing total wealth.

Answer 11.
Robert: He received like-kind property worth $2,000 and boot of $2,000 ($1,200 assumption of liability plus $800 stamp). He has a realized gain of $2,500. He recognizes gain to the extent of the boot, so he recognizes $2,000 of gain. He has a carryover basis of $1,500 in Whiteacre and a fair market value basis in the stamp.

Sally: She received like-kind property worth $4,000. She received no boot, so she recognizes no gain on the receipt of the property from Robert. She recognizes $400 of gain on the transfer of the stamp, which is not like-kind property, and thus has an adjusted basis of $800 in the stamp. Sally's basis in Blackacre is her basis in Whiteacre of $500, plus her $800 basis in the stamp, plus $1,200 of basis from assuming the loan, for a total basis of $2,500.

Answer 12.

    a. Jed's basis is $120,000. The total payments received will be $300,000. Thus, the gain is $180,000. $180,000/$300,000 = .60. Thus 60 percent of each payment will be gain. So Jed will recognize capital gain of $60,000 in year one and $30,000 in each of years two through five. Jed will also recognize ordinary income on the interest payments received.

    b. Jed would not recognize any gain until he recovered his basis. Thus, there would be no gain in year one (basis reduced to $20,000). He would include: (i) interest received (as ordinary income); (ii) $30,000 of capital gain in year two; and (iii) $50,000 of capital gain per year in years three through five.

    c. First, the present value of the future payments would be calculated. Then Jed would recognize gain in year one equal to the difference between that present value and his basis. Suppose the present value was $200,000. Then Jed would recognize $80,000 of capital gain in year one. All additional amounts received by Jed would be ordinary income. These amounts would be reduced by amortizing the present value of the future payments.

Answer 13. The issue here is whether this is a capital expense or a repair. If the replacement of the broken window is a "repair," Bill can deduct the cost of the new window. If the new shatterproof window "improves" the property, however, Bill must capitalize the cost of the new window. Although the new glass improves the window, the unit of property is the entire shop building and its structural components. Comparing the condition of the entire shop building before the window broke and after the $3,000 replacement of the window, the new window probably does not result in a "betterment" of the property.

Answer 14.

    a. Donees are not taxed on gifts received. Fred takes a carryover basis of $5,000.

    b. Fred realizes no gain or loss. A donee takes a carryover basis for purposes of recognition of gain and the lower of carryover basis or fair market value basis at the time of the transfer for recognition of loss.

Answer 15. Jack realizes $150,000 of gain on the involuntary conversion. He recognizes capital gain on the $50,000 spent on the trucks because they are not similar use property. Jack will have a basis of $400,000 in the new store and a basis of $25,000 in each of the new trucks.

FINAL EXAMINATION NUMBER SEVEN
PROFESSOR GRIFFITH
UNIVERSITY OF SOUTHERN CALIFORNIA
GOULD SCHOOL OF LAW

Instructions

1. You have three hours to complete this examination. This is a closed book examination. The only written material you may consult is the statutory package distributed with this examination. In addition, you may use a hand calculator.

2. There are 11 questions on this exam, many with more than one part. I have listed the *approximate* value of each question next to the question. The lowest score you can receive on any question (or subpart of a question) is zero. Thus, incorrect analysis of a question may lower your score on that question, but it will not lower your score on other questions. Pace yourself to be sure to finish the examination.

3. Except where otherwise indicated, explain briefly how you reached your answers. If you believe that a question is ambiguous or that relevant information is missing, state the ambiguity or missing information and how your answer would be affected. A few questions may be deliberately "ambiguous" in the sense that the appropriate tax treatment is uncertain because the law is unsettled or because the facts are incomplete.

Question 1. Each of the following four problems can be answered in a few sentences or less. (3 points each)

> a. List the following taxes from most regressive to most progressive. (No need to explain.)
>> i. Federal "Social Security" tax
>> ii. Federal excise tax on cigarettes
>> iii. Federal income tax
>
> b. List the following items produced by the Treasury in order of the "strength" of their authority in a federal tax case from *weakest* to *strongest*. (No need to explain.)
>> i. Regulations
>> ii. Private Letter Rulings
>> iii. Revenue Rulings
>
> c. If all individuals, regardless of income, were required to pay a tax of $5,000 per year, the tax structure would be: (Choose one and explain briefly.)
>> i. Progressive
>> ii. Regressive
>> iii. Flat rate
>
> d. Alice purchases Blackacre, which has a fair market value of $1,000. She finances the property as follows: $200 cash, $500 recourse loan, $300 nonrecourse loan. What is her basis in Blackacre?

Question 2. Each of the following four problems can be answered in a few sentences or less. (3 points each except as stated)

> a. Betty is a medical doctor. She spends one day each month working without pay at a free clinic for the poor. If she had worked for pay that day instead, she would have earned $500. Is Betty entitled to a $500 charitable deduction for the donation of her time? Does this rule make sense?
>
> b. Which of the following exchanges (if any) can qualify for a like-kind exchange? (2 points each) (No need to explain.)
>> i. Ford stock for General Motors stock
>> ii. Male cattle for female cattle
>> iii. Developed real estate for undeveloped real estate
>
> c. What word or words should be placed in the blank in the following sentence:
>> "If there is adequate _____ it will not be necessary to calculate OID." (No need to explain.)
>
> d. Carol is driving home from her law school tax class. Deep in thought about whether a consumption tax is better than an income tax, she runs into the rear end of a taxi that unexpectedly comes to a full stop at a stop sign. Carol's car is destroyed. She has no collision insurance.

Assume the 10 percent of AGI floor is met. Can Carol deduct the loss of her car as a casualty loss?

Question 3. Each of the following two problems can be answered in two or three paragraphs. (5 points each)

a. It is a longstanding tradition at Johnson Law School for first-year students to purchase a class gift for each of their professors. Most students contribute $5 for each first-year class, so that professors generally receive gifts worth between $400 and $600 (depending on their popularity and the size of their class). Are the gifts taxable income to the professors under current law?

b. Albert's factory was destroyed in a flood. It had a basis of $500,000 and an estimated fair market value of $900,000. He receives $800,000 from insurance, borrows an additional $200,000 and purchases a new factory for $950,000 and a new steamroller for $50,000. What are the tax consequences to Albert of the transaction?

Question 4. The following questions relate to the proper taxation of our canine friends.

a. Mighty Mutt Dog Food corporation pays a $15,000 fee for the use of the popular beagle "Foam Francis" in dog food commercials. Is Foam required to file a federal income tax return? (2 points)

b. Debbie owns the Six Star Circus. She purchases a piano-playing dog, Rex, for $20,000. Food and veterinary expenses for Rex are $1,000 per year. During the season Rex travels with the circus, but during the off-season, Rex lives with Debbie. Discuss the tax treatment of the costs associated with Rex. (5 points)

Question 5. Maria sells her oil rights in Blackacre to the Xenon Drilling Corporation. Her basis in the oil rights is $100,000. Xenon agrees to pay her $50,000 immediately, plus an additional amount, plus interest, depending on how much oil is taken from the well. The parties estimate that payments are likely to vary in amount from $15,000 to $30,000 per year (plus the interest), and that drilling is likely to continue for six to eight years so that she expects to receive six to eight additional payments. In year two, Maria receives a payment of $20,000 plus $1,400 interest.

a. Under the open transaction approach adopted in *Burnett v. Logan*, how much taxable income would Maria report from the payments received in years one and two? (4 points)

b. How much taxable income would Maria report from the payments received in years one and two if the installment method of reporting were adopted? (6 points)

Question 6. Each of the following two problems can be answered in two or three sentences. (5 points each)

> a. Kirk, Bones & Sulu is a law firm specializing in space law. The firm provides attorneys with free donuts, bagels, cream cheese, and Milky Ways in the morning and free Mars bars in the afternoon. Free coffee and soda also are provided. These items are available at the attorneys' lunch room. Secretaries and support staff are provided only with free coffee and must purchase other foods and beverages at vending machines in the building lobby. Discuss the tax treatment of the food and beverages provided to the attorneys.
>
> b. Carlos, who is 65 years old, purchases a deferred annuity that pays nothing for 10 years (until Carlos is 75 years old) and then pays $2,000 a year for life. The annuity costs $3,000. At the time he purchases the annuity, Carlos has a life expectancy of 15 years. Since during the first 10 of those years Carlos will receive nothing under the contract, the annuity is expected to pay out $2,000 a year for five years.
>
> In fact, Carlos lives until the age of 81 and thus receives six payments of $2,000. Discuss the tax treatment of these payments.

Question 7. Bob is assistant manager at the Imperial Bowling Alley and Pool Hall. Like all full-time Imperial employees, Bob is permitted to bowl and play pool at no cost whenever there are open alleys or pool tables. If, however, a paying customer wants to use the facility, Bob is required to leave after finishing his current game (typically about 10 minutes). Under a reciprocal agreement between Imperial Bowling Alley and King's Pool and Pinball World, Bob is permitted to use the pool tables and pinball machines at King's (under similar restrictions) at no charge.

In addition to playing for free themselves, Imperial employees are permitted to bring their spouses or "significant others" and their children with them at no charge. Pursuant to the "significant other" provision, Bob often brings his longtime companion Carl with him. During the year, Bob plays pool at Imperial Bowling Alley about three hours per week and plays pool and pinball at King's Pool and Pinball World about four hours per week. Carl accompanies Bob about half the time. Neither Bob nor Carl pay any fee for using the facilities.

What are the tax consequences to Bob and Carl of the free use of these recreational facilities? (10 points)

Question 8. For each of the following four problems, state how Zeke would be treated (i) under current law (CL), (ii) under a Haig-Simons (comprehensive) income tax (HS), and (iii) under a comprehensive consumption tax (CT). Explain very briefly. (3–4 points each)

a. Zeke owns a miniature golf course. The old windmill at hole six of the golf course is in bad shape from years of use. Zeke tears it down (except for the foundation) and constructs a new windmill in its place. The new windmill is of the same appearance and construction as the old one.

b. During January, when the golf course is closed, Zeke remodels the basement in his home. The cost for materials is $2,000. Zeke saves $3,000 by doing the work himself.

c. Zeke is hit by an automobile while crossing the street and suffers a permanent scar on his forehead. He files a claim against the driver of the car and later accepts a settlement of $10,000.

d. Zeke owes $1,000 to Valerie. She agrees to discharge the debt in exchange for Zeke's baseball card collection. Zeke purchased the baseball cards 15 years ago for $50.

Question 9. The Middletown Savings and Loan Company learns that maintaining a flower garden in front of the bank and decorating the interior of the bank building with plants and fresh flowers would cost $1,200 per month. It is estimated that the new decorations would increase the number of bank customers by an amount that would generate $800 of profit per month (not considering the cost of the decoration). Under what circumstances, if any, is it efficient for the bank to redecorate? (4 points)

The last two questions on the examination are policy questions. A fairly good answer to each question can be made in one to four short paragraphs (or in a list) and the points indicated would be awarded for such an answer. If, however, you have extra time and wish to write a more comprehensive essay, you may receive a few additional points. You should do this, however, only if you have completed the rest of the examination.

Question 10. Under current law, taxpayers receive a personal exemption of $3,950 for each dependent. What are the best arguments for and *against* replacing the exemption with a tax credit? (9 points)

Question 11. State the best arguments *against* the current deduction for charitable contributions. Please present arguments in favor of entirely eliminating the deduction and sensible suggestions for limiting the deduction. (11 points)

END OF EXAMINATION

Model Answers

Answer 1.

    a. The order is (ii), (i), (iii).

    b. The order is (ii), (iii), (i) (but if a PLR was issued to the taxpayer herself, it is the strongest authority).

    c. Regressive. Although each taxpayer would pay the same absolute amount, the poor would pay a higher percentage of their income in taxes.

    d. $1,000. The debt is included in basis.

Answer 2.

    a. Betty is not entitled to the deduction. The rule makes sense because Betty is not taxed on the imputed income she would have earned from practicing medicine. Betty is in the same position as if she had worked for pay and donated the money.

    b. i. No.

        ii. No.

        iii. Yes.

    c. Stated interest.

    d. Carol can deduct the loss. Ordinary negligence will not prohibit a casualty deduction, but gross negligence or willfulness will disallow a deduction. Here, Carol's negligence appears ordinary.

Answer 3.

    a. The answer is uncertain.

       Arguments in favor of taxation:

- For most students the gift is not from love and affection.
- The gift arises out of an employment relationship, like "tokes" and tips.
- Tradition may lead professors to expect gifts.

       Arguments against taxation:

- Apparently, professors who are not first-year professors do not get a gift. They probably are paid the same.
- Gifts are not mandatory. The size of the gift depends in part on the popularity of the professor.
- There is no indication that such gifts are a normal part of the compensation for professors.

    b. No gain is recognized on the involuntary conversion because all of the insurance proceeds were reinvested in similar use property. Albert will have a basis of $650,000 in the new factory and $50,000 in the steamroller.

Answer 4.

    a. No. Foam Francis's owner will pay the tax. Dogs cannot own property and do not pay taxes. Animals are not persons under the Internal Revenue Code.

    b. Rex would be a business asset. Debbie could deduct the cost of the food and vet expenses. The cost of Rex would be capitalized since Rex is an asset with a useful life greater than one year. Debbie would be able to "depreciate" Rex over his useful life as a performer. Since it probably is less costly to keep Rex in her home during the off-season than anywhere else, it would be reasonable for Debbie to deduct the cost of keeping Rex at her home even though he might have a "pet" value.

Answer 5.

    a. Maria reports zero in year one. In year two Maria includes only the $1,400 of interest. Under the open transaction doctrine, basis is recovered first.

    b. Maximum total receipts are: $50,000 + (8 × $30,000) = $290,000. Basis is $100,000. ($290,000 − $100,000) / $290,000 = $190,000 / $290,000 = .655. Thus, 65.5 percent of each payment is taxable and Maria has taxable income as follows: Year one, $32,750; year two, $13,100 plus $1,400 of interest. (Here, the regulations require that the computation use maximum total receipts because both the exact amount of the payments and the period over which the payments will be made are uncertain. Reg. §15a.453-1(c)(2).)

Answer 6.

    a. This probably is excluded as a de minimis fringe benefit. Nondiscrimination rules do not apply to de minimis fringe benefits.

    b. Carlos paid $3,000 for the annuity and is expected to receive $10,000 if he lives the expected 15 years. $3,000 / $10,000 = .30. Thus, 30 percent of each of the first five payments is recovery of basis; 70 percent is income. After five years Carlos has recovered all his basis so the entire payment in year six is taxable income.

Answer 7. This is a no-additional-cost fringe. Probably the 10-minute wait will not disqualify the use of the alleys, unless it appears likely that business is lost because of the delay. The reciprocal agreement (if in writing) is okay if the businesses are the same. Probably the availability of pinball would not disqualify the agreement. Significant others (same sex or different sex) are not allowed to receive no-additional-cost fringes tax-free. Bob (not Carl) would be taxed on the value of Carl's play because Bob is performing the services to the bowling alley. Carl's use would be a gift from Bob to Carl.

Answer 8.

    a. *Current law:* It is not clear whether this would be characterized as a repair or capital expenditure. If capital, depreciate. If repair, deduct.

Haig-Simons: Capitalize and depreciate. The decline in value of the old windmill was already deducted in prior years under a Haig-Simons tax.

Consumption tax: Deduct immediately as a form of investment.

b. Current law: No taxation of imputed income, no deduction for cost of materials. Add the cost of materials to the basis of the home.

Haig-Simons: Taxed on the amount by which the value of the home increased, less the cost of materials. Presumably this is $3,000 ($5,000 increase in value less $2,000 cost of materials).

Consumption tax: Deduct the cost of materials. There is no tax on the value of labor. However, Zeke will be taxed annually on the consumption value of the remodeled room.

c. Current law: Not taxed on the personal injury recovery.

Haig-Simons: Unclear. Under Haig-Simons, Zeke would be taxed on the receipt of the recovery, but it is unclear if the permanent scar would constitute an offsetting change in wealth. Henry Simons probably would not have permitted the deduction for the scar.

Consumption tax: Taxed on the cash received, unless it is saved. Unclear if the scar would reduce his consumption (of good looks) each year.

d. Current law: Zeke is taxed on the $950 of unrealized gain in the cards.

Haig-Simons: No tax. Zeke would have been taxed in earlier years on the growth in value of the cards.

Consumption tax: No taxation. Zeke has neither increased nor decreased his consumption.

Answer 9.   When the total value of the plants and flowers is greater than $1,200 per month. Thus, when the value to the employees, customers, and passersby is greater than $400 per month.

Answer 10.   The basic argument for a credit is that a credit is more progressive than a deduction. For example, a $3,000 deduction is worth $1,050 to a 35 percent bracket taxpayer, but only $450 to a 15 percent taxpayer. A $300 credit is worth $300 to a 35 percent bracket taxpayer or a 15 percent taxpayer. On the other hand, the personal exemption phase-out (PEP) applies to high-income taxpayers, potentially reducing their exemption amounts to zero. In addition, personal exemptions are not allowed under the Alternative Minimum Tax. (Section 24 provides a limited credit to taxpayers for each qualifying child, but that child tax credit does not replace the personal exemption for dependents.)

The argument for a deduction is that the personal exemption is designed to make the tax base more accurately reflect a family's true economic circumstances. A family with children is likely to be less well-off financially than a family with an identical income without children. In addition, the cost of raising a child arguably increases as a family's income increases.

Answer 11.

    a. Some of the main arguments against the deduction are listed below.

       i. The charitable deduction often supports causes like fine arts rather than the truly needy.

      ii. The deduction is an upside-down subsidy. It costs the rich 60 cents or less to give a dollar to charity while it costs the poor a dollar to give a dollar since the poor do not itemize deductions.

     iii. Donors often get benefits for their gifts such as prestige, invitations to meet stars, buildings named for them, and so on. Spending money on charitable contributions can be viewed as just another form of consumption and should thus be taxed.

     iv. Fundraising for charities is very expensive — taxation is a much cheaper way of raising money for worthy causes.

      v. The deduction is an indirect support for religion and therefore violates the principle of separation of church and state.

     vi. The government should fund worthwhile activities directly, rather than indirectly through the tax system. Direct expenditures are subject to better oversight.

    vii. There is a lot of fraud associated with the charitable deduction. Individuals often lie on their tax returns about the size of their charitable donations. In addition, individuals often overvalue gifts of property, particularly art or other items that are difficult to value.

    b. Here are some ways the charitable deduction might be limited.

       i. Limit the tax deduction for property donations to the basis of the property donated.

      ii. Permit a charitable deduction only for donations to institutions that help the poor, such as the Salvation Army or college scholarship funds for the needy.

     iii. The charitable deduction might be replaced by a tax credit. This would eliminate the so-called upside-down subsidy.

     iv. Deductions for charitable contributions might also be made subject to a floor.

FINAL EXAMINATION NUMBER EIGHT
PROFESSOR KAUFMAN
SAINT LOUIS UNIVERSITY SCHOOL OF LAW

Instructions

1. Materials permitted: any materials other than another person. Calculators are expressly permitted.
2. This examination consists of two questions.
3. You have three hours to complete the exam.
4. Identification and analysis of issues are the substance of this exam. If the facts relating to a particular issue are ambiguous (which is sometimes intentional), it would be wise to answer in the alternative. Purely computational errors are of little consequence unless a failure to address or appropriately analyze one or more issues results. Please thoroughly label any numerical computations so that the grader will be able to distinguish a computational error from a substantive one.
5. Please think before writing. The premium is on the quality of your response, not the quantity.
6. Thank you and good luck.

Question 1 (2 hours).   Thelma is 33 years old. She has one son, Jerome, who is in the fourth grade. Jerome is a good boy and does well in school. Thelma works as a dry cleaner for True Blue Cleaners, Inc. (hereinafter "True Blue"). True Blue operates a local laundry and dry cleaning establishment.

Thelma owns the house in which she and Jerome reside. Jerome has his own room. Thelma's ex-husband, Abe, purchased the house for $55,000 prior to his marriage to Thelma. He financed the purchase with $5,500 in cash and the proceeds of a $49,500 loan secured by a mortgage on the house. While Abe and Thelma were married, Abe remained the sole owner of the house. When they divorced on January 1, year one, Abe transferred the house to Thelma pursuant to the divorce decree. The house was then worth $63,000. Thelma assumed the then outstanding balance of $41,500 on the mortgage loan. Thelma paid interest of $4,000 on the mortgage in year one.

The divorce decree ending Thelma's marriage to Abe also requires Abe to pay Thelma $150 per month until Jerome is 18. To fulfill this obligation, Abe paid Thelma a total of $1,800 in year one.

Thelma owns an automobile, a Ford, which she purchased shortly after she and Abe divorced. The Ford gets pretty good gas mileage but seems to eat oil. Thelma drives the Ford to and from work and to run personal errands.

True Blue, Thelma's employer, pays Thelma an hourly wage. In addition, Thelma and her son participate in True Blue's group accident and health insurance plan. True Blue pays the health insurance premium.

Since Thelma is on good terms with her coworkers who run the washroom and presses, she usually gets her laundry and dry cleaning done for nothing. True Blue has a written policy against using company facilities and time for this purpose. However, the management has found it impossible to stop the practice entirely. In year one, the free laundry and dry cleaning services Thelma took advantage of would have cost a customer $950.

The people in the dry cleaning trade in St. Louis know Thelma to be just about the best dry cleaner in the metropolitan area. The stain has not yet been found that Thelma cannot remove. Thelma maintains her expertise by subscribing to a journal for the dry cleaning industry. The journal regularly has articles describing the latest techniques for efficient dry cleaning and the pros and cons of the chemicals currently available on the market for removing spots. Thelma's subscription to the journal cost her $35 in year one.

Thelma is a calendar year, cash method taxpayer. Please discuss the federal income tax consequences of the foregoing to Thelma.

Question 2 (1 hour).   Collectible Inc. is a corporation formed under the laws of one of the 50 United States. Collectible Inc. is engaged in the business of buying and selling baseball cards and other collectible baseball paraphernalia. Collectible Inc. rents store space in which it operates a small shop.

Collectible Inc. has been in business for many years, and the shop has come to look a little dingy. In October year one, Collectible Inc. obtained a commercial loan for $6,000 from Friendly Bank to finance a complete redecoration of the shop. The loan required repayment with interest at market rates on May 31, year two. Among other things, Collectible Inc. purchased three new display counters. It also hired a painter to do a very fancy paint job in red, white, and blue, the colors worn by the local professional baseball team. All of the work was completed by the end of year one. However, Collectible Inc. did not get around to paying the painter until January of year two.

Business was not as good as anticipated. By the end of April, year two, Collectible Inc. had serious cash flow problems. The value of its assets still exceeded its liabilities but Collectible Inc. simply did not have the cash to pay back the $6,000 borrowed from Friendly Bank in year one. Fortunately, all of the Bank's customers were avid baseball fans and loyal patrons of Collectible Inc.'s shop. Besides, Collectible Inc. had been a customer of Friendly Bank for years. Upon learning of Collectible Inc.'s cash flow problems, Friendly Bank agreed to accept $4,000 in full satisfaction of the loan. Collectible Inc. paid the $4,000, plus all accrued but unpaid interest, on May 31, year two.

Collectible Inc. maintains its books and records using the accrual method of accounting and uses the calendar year as its taxable year. Please discuss the federal income tax consequences of the foregoing to Collectible Inc.

END OF EXAMINATION

Model Answers

Answer 1.   Transfer of the house from Abe to Thelma: The transfer is covered by §1041 since it is to a spouse or former spouse incident to their divorce (related to the cessation of the marriage). §1041(a), (c). Thelma is treated as if she received a gift. §1041(b)(1). The receipt of the house is excluded from Thelma's gross income. §102(a). Thelma takes a transferred basis in the house. §1041(b)(2). Assuming no capital expenditures, Abe's basis in the house at the time of the transfer is $55,000. §1012. His cost was:

(a)   the $5,500 cash he paid for it, plus

(b)   the $49,500 loan proceeds he used to pay for it. *Crane.*

The interest on the mortgage: Interest is generally a deductible expense. §163(a). However, it may not be deducted if it is personal interest. §163(h)(1). It is not personal interest if it is "qualified residence interest." §163(h)(2). The interest paid by Thelma is qualified residence interest because it is paid with respect to "acquisition indebtedness":

(a)   it is paid with respect to debt used to acquire the residence;

(b)   the amount of the debt does not exceed $1 million; and

(c)   the debt is secured by a mortgage on the house. §163(h)(3).

Although it is an itemized deduction, it is not subject to the 2 percent floor. §§62(a), 67(b)(1).

The imputed income from the house: Imputed income is the value of goods and services one provides to oneself and one's family. The imputed income equals the fair rental value of the house. Imputed income has been excluded from gross income as a matter of practice.

The $1,800 she received from Abe: The payment is for child support so Thelma excludes it from income. §71(c). It is not an alimony or separate maintenance payment subject to §71(a). The child support payment is not an accretion to Thelma's wealth but the fulfillment of Abe's obligation to support Jerome.

The cost of maintaining and operating Thelma's car: These costs are nondeductible personal expenses. §262. Commuting expenses are also nondeductible personal expenses. *Flowers.*

Wages: Thelma's wages are includible in her gross income. §61(a)(1).

The accident and health insurance plan: As a general rule, the fair market value of the plan would be includible in gross income. §61(a). However, it is excluded under §106.

The value of Thelma's free dry cleaning and laundry service: This might be a gift because the dry cleaning and laundry service were provided by Thelma's coworkers out of benign and disinterested generosity, having been motivated by their affection for Thelma. *Duberstein.* However, Thelma's coworkers did not own the services they transferred to her so they could hardly give them away.

The value of the services would normally be included in Thelma's gross income as compensation for services. §61(a)(1). However, they might be excluded under §132(a)(1) as a no-additional-cost service because:

a. True Blue provides dry cleaning services to customers in the ordinary course of its business (§132(b)(1));
b. True Blue incurred no substantial additional cost (including forgone revenue) in providing the service to Thelma (§132(b)(2)) (this might also be the case since the fact that True Blue cannot keep track of the practice might indicate that the employees are using excess capacity); and
c. the services were "provided by" True Blue to Thelma (§132(b)) (although this may be a tough one since True Blue has a written policy against the practice).

In the alternative, the value of the services might be excluded under §132(a)(2) (qualified employee discount), but only to the extent the employee discount (100 percent) does not exceed 20 percent of the retail price. §132(c)(1). This exclusion is available only if the service (dry cleaning) is offered for sale to customers (which it is) in the ordinary course of the line of business of the employer in which the employee works. §132(c)(4). However, were the services "provided by" True Blue? If not, §132(c) may not apply. §132(c)(3).

The value of the services might also be excluded under §132(a)(4) as a de minimis fringe benefit since True Blue finds it impossible (administratively impracticable?) to keep track of the exchange of services among employees. §132(e)(1). On the other hand, $950 during the year might be too large for "de minimis."

Since True Blue may not intend to transfer the value of the services to Thelma, the value of the services might be included in Thelma's gross income as a windfall (an accretion to wealth, clearly realized, and over which Thelma has complete dominion and control). *Glenshaw Glass.*

Reasons for deciding one way or another: It may violate public policy to exclude from gross income free services obtained dishonestly (*Blackman* in the exclusion context?). However, one of the purposes of §132 was to legitimize the exclusion from gross income of amounts employees exclude from their gross incomes as a matter of practice.

The cost of Thelma's subscription to the trade journal: The cost is an ordinary expense because one could reasonably expect someone in her trade or business to purchase such a publication. *Gilliam.* Also, it is a recurring expense that will not give rise to income substantially beyond the current taxable year. §§162(a), 262(a); cf. *Encyclopaedia Britannica.*

It is a necessary expense because it is helpful to Thelma's trade or business of being an employee engaged in dry cleaning.

Thelma's §162 deduction for the subscription cost is an itemized deduction because True Blue does not appear to reimburse her for that expense and the performance of services as an employee is not a "trade or business" for purposes of §62. §62(a)(1), (2).

Unreimbursed employee business expenses are not on the list of itemized deductions exempt from the 2 percent floor; hence this cost is deductible only to the extent it and Thelma's other itemized deductions subject to the floor exceed 2 percent of her adjusted gross income. §67.

Thelma should try to get her employer to reimburse her for the cost of the journal. Then the cost would be excluded from her gross income under Reg. §1.62-2, or as a working condition fringe benefit. §132(a)(3), (d).

Answer 2. Entity tax: As a corporation, Collectible Inc. is a separate taxable entity. See §11.

Rent paid: The rent Collectible Inc. pays is currently deductible. §162(a).

The loan proceeds: The loan proceeds are excluded from Collectible Inc.'s gross income on the premise that loan proceeds are offset by a corresponding obligation to repay. Loan proceeds are not an accretion to wealth. *Glenshaw Glass.*

Interest on the loan: The interest is deductible under §163(a).

The cost of the three new display counters: The cost is a capital expenditure because the counters are equipment with a useful life that extends significantly beyond the taxable year. Reg. §1.263(a)-2(a); see *Encyclopaedia Britannica*. The cost is thus not currently deductible. §263. The cost will instead be recovered through depreciation deductions because the display counters are (i) property used in a trade or business and (ii) subject to wear and tear. §167(a). Section 168 will permit Collectible Inc. to use an accelerated depreciation method to compute its depreciation deductions. The basis of the display counters will be reduced by the amount of the depreciation deductions. §1016(a)(2).

The cost of the paint job: The cost of a paint job is generally deductible as an ordinary and necessary business expense because it is more like a repair not significantly adding to the useful life of the shop or increasing its value. §162(a).

When does Collectible Inc. deduct the cost of the painting? Accrual method taxpayers deduct an expense when (i) the fact of the liability for expense has been established, (ii) the amount of the expense can be determined with reasonable accuracy, and (iii) the "economic performance" requirement of §461(h) is met. Here, the first two requirements are met in year one. The third requirement is also met in year one; the expense relates to services provided to the taxpayer, so the economic performance requirement is met in the year in which the services are provided to Collectible Inc., year one. §461(h)(2)(A).

However, the deduction in year one might not be allowed because the expense arguably is a capital expenditure. The fancy paint job here may go beyond the maintenance type of paint job contemplated by the regulations.

The paint job will increase the value of the shop, in terms of the amount of business it does, and may also significantly increase the life of the store space as a shop.

The debt discharge: Collectible Inc. settled its $6,000 debt for $4,000. The discharge results in cancellation of indebtedness ("COD") income in the amount of $2,000, which is the $6,000 amount owed less the $4,000 Collectible Inc. paid to discharge the debt.

Under the tax benefit theory of COD income, the discharge for less than the amount owed is an event that is fundamentally inconsistent with the exclusion of the $6,000 loan proceeds in the first instance. See the dissent in *Zarin.*

Under the *Kirby Lumber* theory of COD income, the discharge creates COD income because the discharge freed $2,000 of Collectible Inc.'s assets from debt. The $2,000 of COD income is includible in gross income. §61(a)(12).

The COD income could not be excluded under §108(a). Collectible Inc.'s liabilities did not exceed the value of its assets so it was not insolvent at the time of the discharge. §108(a), (d). There is nothing in the problem indicating that Collectible Inc. had filed a bankruptcy petition prior to the discharge.

The bank's discharge of Collectible Inc.'s debt was probably not a gift. Whether the discharge could be considered a gift is a question of fact to be decided based on all of the relevant facts and circumstances indicating that the bank was or was not acting with detached and disinterested generosity, out of affection, charity, or like impulse. The discharge might have resulted from detached and disinterested generosity since the bank's shareholders and customers were regular customers of Collectible Inc. On the other hand, they may not have been motivated by detached and disinterested generosity. They may have forgiven the debt so (i) they could have easy access to baseball paraphernalia, (ii) the bank would have profitable patronage from Collectible Inc. in the future, or (iii) the bank would not alienate its other customers by playing hardball (no pun intended!) with Collectible Inc. Any of these motivations would cut against gift treatment.

Table of Cases

Table of Cases

Table of Internal Revenue Code Sections

584

Table of Treasury Regulations

Table of Other Administrative Pronouncements

Topical Index